P9-BIR-886

OUR CAPITAL ON THE POTOMAC

INTERIOR OF THE LINCOLN MEMORIAL

OUR CAPITAL ON THE POTOMAC

BY

HELEN NICOLAY

AUTHOR OF "OUR NATION IN THE BUILDING," "PERSONAL TRAITS OF ABRAHAM LINCOLN," ETC., ETC.

ILLUSTRATED

THE CENTURY CO.

New York & London

PRINTED IN U. S. A.

PREFACE

A town is made up of people, buildings, and ideals, the first being the most numerous, the last the most important. Washington began with ideals and gradually acquired the other two—a manner of growth in which she has differed from most cities.

The chapters in this book aim to give a hint of how it came into being and how it grew, and to tell of certain very human men and women who lived in its houses and walked its streets.

It is the result of much browsing among volumes old and new—a study which might easily be doubled did time permit. To all the authors of these books and to the good friends who have generously contributed family letters and personal reminiscences, I take this opportunity of expressing sincere, if inadequate, thanks.

I also wish to express my indebtedness to Mr. Charles Moore, Chairman of the Fine Arts Commission, and to the courtesy of the War Department, the Columbia Historical Society, and the others who have assisted in finding suitable illustrations for the volume.

The truism that organisms grow more complex as they advance, applies to towns as it does to other forms of life. This explains why greater stress is laid upon individuals in the earlier chapters. A man counts for more in a town of two or four thousand than he possibly can in a city of a hundred times as many people.

The same basic reason explains why the greater part of the volume is devoted to the years during which Washington was being planned and was undergoing the vicissitudes of childhood, watched over, as the sequel proved, by an ever kind though apparently absent-minded Providence.

CONTENTS

		PAGE
I	Rolling Roads	3
II	That Figure of Famine	25
III	A Lodge in the Wilderness	44
IV	Diplomats and a Democrat	71
V	Fire and Sword	94
VI	The Phœnix	115
VII	The Last Cocked Hat	131
VIII	The Man with Two Countries	146
IX	The People's Palace	155
X	Inventors and Other Plagues	174
XI	King Andrew the First	189
XII	Pompe Funèbre	216
XIII	Two Uninspired Presidents	237
XIV	A Brave Lady	253
XV	Growth	269
XVI	"Mess" Life	288
XVII	Songs and Science	307
XVIII	A Republican Court	326
XIX	Pawns in the Game	338
XX	Washington in War Times	356
XXI	The Plumber in Politics	381
XXII	The Age of Eastlake	400
XXIII	Czars of Congress	415
XXIV	Columbia's Queen	437
XXV	Unimportant Folk	452
XXVI	"The Father of All the Children"	465
XXVII	Peripatetic Monuments	481
XXVIII	The High Point	501
	Index	525

LIST OF ILLUSTRATIONS

Interior of the Lincoln Memorial . . . . *Frontispiece*

FACING PAGE

Mount Vernon—the home of General Washington 8

One of the jurisdiction stones 16

Jefferson's sketch map 33

L'Enfant's plan of Washington 40

Washington in 1801 56

The Octagon House 81

The Capitol after the fire 96

St. John's Church and the President's House in 1816 129

The house occupied by President Monroe 144

Arlington and L'Enfant's tomb as they are to-day 152

The Capitol and its environs 161

The Patent Office 176

Statue of Andrew Jackson 209

The President's House as it was in Van Buren's time 224

The clock in the old Hall of Representatives 248

The Treasury Building 273

Greenough's "Washington" 288

The Smithsonian Institution 312

"Armed Liberty" 353

The Capitol dome 368

Pennsylvania Avenue, about 1870 385

FACING PAGE

Looking up Seventeenth Street from the Pan American Building . 400

The main stairway, Library of Congress 432

One of Washington's leafy avenues 449

The Connecticut Avenue Bridge over Rock Creek 456

The intimate side of the White House 472

The Adams Memorial by St. Gaudens 484

The Washington Monument and the cherry blossoms . . . 493

Along the river front in Potomac Park 497

The Tripoli Naval Monument 504

An air picture of Washington 512

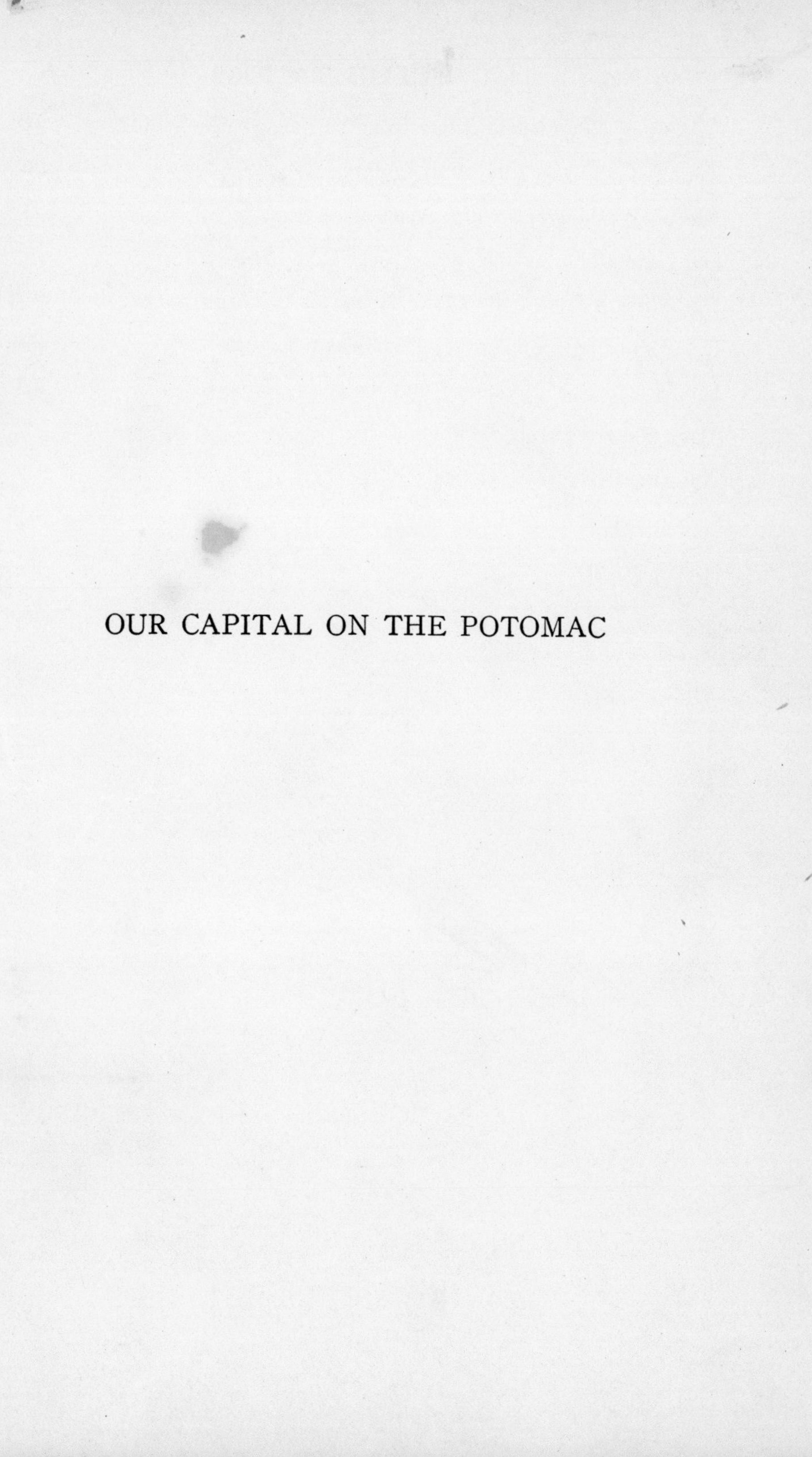

OUR CAPITAL ON THE POTOMAC

OUR CAPITAL ON THE POTOMAC

I

ROLLING ROADS

WE are apt to assume that history began in America with the coming of the white race. Let us be a little less arrogant. Taking a hint from that young man who pondered a moment when told about some recently discovered caves, and then remarked that he supposed they had been there "for some time," let us try to imagine the District of Columbia as it must have looked under the stewardship of the Indians, who had been there "for some time" before Columbus set sail from Palos.

Title-deeds in the District go back to the grant made in 1632 by King Charles to Lord Baltimore, with its picturesque stipulation that in return one arrow-head of the locality must be delivered "at our castle of Windsor on the Tuesday of Easter week." The missiles manufactured in Virginia flew far, and many of them were made at the spot where our national capital now stands. The common belief that that particular site became of importance for the first time when L'Enfant was called upon to lay out the Federal City is natural, if incorrect. Evidence seems at hand to prove that it was a place of consequence long before white men plowed their arrogant way across the Atlantic; indeed, that relatively speaking it can never hope to regain a commercial supremacy it then enjoyed. Obviously such evidence is not to be found in title-papers, however musty. It lies hidden in those stone records which few are wise enough to read, but which, once read, fewer still can refute. To assert that our present city is paved with the art remains of a vanished people, states the matter crudely; yet that is what it amounts to in the end.

Lying midway between the Alleghanies and the Atlantic, the spot was ideal for savage industry, offering an abundance of raw material, a great river for transportation, and, in two directions, a waiting public. The raw material lay in every clay bank of the neighborhood, filled with rounded pebbles and small boulders that had been chipped off mountain ledges in jagged fragments by frost and weather, and then worn smooth by floods as they rolled their playthings toward the sea.

All of these stones are water-worn, but some have in addition been strangely chipped, evidently by human agency. When this was first noticed it gave rise to tantalizing conjectures about a prehistoric race, much higher than the brutes, since its members could bend stone to their will, yet far below Powhatan's Indians in the scale of civilization, as shown by the finish of the tools they used. When at last the riddle was solved, in the decade between 1880 and 1890, the unexpected answer turned a flood of light upon the manners and customs of former dwellers in what is now the District of Columbia.

One of the most eager investigators, Dr. W. H. Holmes, who had a theory of his own about the chipped stones, took two unchipped stones in his naked hands to prove it and taught himself, as the man of the stone age had done long before, how to reduce one of them to something sharp and keen-edged enough to serve as a knife. Incidentally he learned many other things, one being how large a proportion of stones was spoiled in the process; another that, from the first stroke to the last, the stones with which he worked took on the exact character of those lying about him on the ground; a third, that of all the chipped stones to be picked up in the gullies and watercourses of the District, scarcely one is whole, which would not be the case had they been finished tools, used and lost in the ordinary business of life.

The theory of a prehistoric race receded and vanished, leaving in its place one more intriguing still—that here was one spot on the earth's surface where environment had been stronger than heredity; where matter had triumphed over mind, and had made the Indians, who cared little for such pursuits, manufacturers almost against their will. In other words, that these many chipped fragments were the "discards" of a great industrial plant.

Nature had been prodigal in her gift of raw material. To quote Dr. Holmes:

> The floods, with more than human intelligence and power, had selected the choice bits of rock, the tough quartzite, the flinty jasper, the tough and brittle lavas, the indurated slates . . . had reduced them to convenient size and shape and laid them down . . . at the door of the tidewater lodge, ready, or almost ready, for immediate use in the arts.

It was easy to pick up such treasures from on top of the ground, or partly embedded in it: almost as easy to burrow under a bank until the weight of overhanging earth caused it to crumble and reveal its treasures. This was a sort of rude mining, and the miners had neighbors who were eager for what they found. The dwellers on the coast who had few stones suited to savage weapons could pay for them in shells; and in the mountains where there was stone enough, but in masses that defied handling, men had copper which the tide-water Indians coveted. The part which the river played in the exchange is to be learned from the last faint echo of the language once spoken on its banks. The name by which the Potomac Indians were known is said to have signified, "To bring again they come and go,"—succinctly, "The Peddlers."

But stones are heavy, even for a great river to carry. To get rid of faulty pieces and reduce the amount transported, the first stages of manufacture went on beside the quarrying. Stones of approximately the same degree of finish are found close together. Near the gullies where they were taken from the earth, "turtle-backed boulders" abound, stones chipped only on one side, giving them a fancied resemblance to the shell of a tortoise. Farther on, the work appears to have been carried through the next stage; and when sufficiently reduced in bulk the stones were transported to more comfortable quarters than were to be found in the narrow steep ravines where the mines were located. In places that give evidence of having been village sites, "pockets" of fine flakes reveal where workmen sat engaged in the finishing processes. Thus, says Dr. Holmes again, "workshops became factories, one man or group of men giving exclusive attention to a certain process."

The goal of endeavor was the "leaf-shaped blade," a noncommittal form of great usefulness, pointed at one end, broadly rounded at the other, from two to six inches long, and scarcely more than half an inch thick. Many things might be made of it; it was therefore calculated to fire the imagination and desires of a multitude of buyers. Yet we imagine "semi-ready-to-wear" articles a recent invention of commerce!

That the industry was wide-spread, the many quarries and village sites throughout the District prove. "The greatest aboriginal boulder quarry known, and the most important shops yet observed on the Atlantic slope are located on Fourteenth Street two and a half miles from the President's house," we are told. We are also told that the largest village of the whole tide-water province was on the Anacostia River little more than a mile from Capitol Hill. There was another settlement a short distance southeast of the Capitol, in what is now the reservation in front of Providence Hospital.

Similar remains have been found scattered along the Anacostia River as far as Bladensburg: along the Potomac to Little Falls; on Dumbarton Heights in the Tenallytown region; in Zoölogical Park; near the Naval Observatory, which tradition makes the residence of the chief; and at the intersection of Connecticut Avenue and Pierce Mill Road. Nor were boulders the only stones mined. On Connecticut Avenue extended is one of those soapstone ledges that crop out at intervals from Massachusetts to Georgia, which offered a material much prized by the Indians. Here the method of work was entirely different. A stratum of soft rock was cut out in rude circles, much as a housewife cuts biscuits from a sheet of dough, each separate piece being finished afterward into bowl or pipe.

What member of the white race first set foot among these primitive workshops, we do not know. There is no authentic record of a white man's visit before the year 1631, when Henry Fleete, who had been held a prisoner previously by the Anacostian Indians, returned as a trader. Captain John Smith is believed to have failed to reach the site of our nation's capital by a paltry ten miles or so. Ten miles make little difference in climate, and it is to him that we are indebted for the first authentic weather report of the region, which rings convincingly true.

The Sommer is hot as in *Spaine,* the Winter colde as in *Fraunce* or *England*. The heat of Sommer is in Iune Iulie and August, but commonly the coole Breeses asswage the vehemencie of the heat. . . . The colde is extreame sharpe, but here the proverbe is true that no extreame long continueth. . . . The windes here are variable, but the like thunder and lightning to purifie the ayre I haue seldom either seene or heard in *Europe*. From the Southwest come the greatest gustes with thunder and heat. The Northwest winde is commonly coole, and bringeth fayre weather with it. From the North is the greatest cold, and from the East and Southeast as from the *Barmades,* fogs and raines.

Since the inhabitants were of the same stock as those nearer the coast, so often described by early explorers, it is possible, from such descriptions, supplemented by the evidence of the turtle-backed boulders and the spirited old water-color drawings made by John White, who sailed with Raleigh's expedition in 1584, to reconstruct in imagination the kind of life the Indians must have enjoyed here when they were monarchs of all they surveyed.

In spite of the rôle of manufacturers which had been thrust upon them, it was leisurely and in some respects luxurious. River and forest and earth teemed with food, and the aboriginees were philosophers in the matter of work. "An Indian is not lazy," said a white man who knew his Indian brothers well. "He simply has a different point of view. A white man toils like a slave in order that he may have leisure in his old age. An Indian realizes that he may not live to enjoy it then, and takes his vacations as he goes along." So these people labored with commendable restraint, and were never too busy to enjoy the pleasures of the seasons as they rolled around.

As at present, the women and children outnumbered the males; and as is the case now, when Washington is the meeting-place of Congress, the population was semi-nomadic. People lived in houses that were stately for Indian dwellings, and planted and reaped; but such duties sat lightly upon them, and it took little to incite them to the action which was their equivalent for cranking the motor-car. In spring their interest centered upon the river, alive with fish. These they angled for, or harpooned, or took in weirs, or even lassoed by the tail.

Autumn was their real playtime, however. When the leaves turned red the Indians barricaded the doors of their dwellings, as notice to prowling beasts and humans that they were not at home, and went off, *en masse,* toward the hills, warriors, squaws, and little papooses, to enjoy the season of fat game, of brilliant foliage and delightful weather. If an individual, debauched by industry, carried a few leaf-shaped blades in his luggage, meaning to do business "on the side," that was a matter for him to settle with his own conscience. It was the time for hunting, and games of agility and skill. Out of these the red men extracted a variety of thrills. "By excelling in these qualities they get their wives," an old writer explains.

In summer life was more prosaic. They lived in their mat-thatched houses, and women tilled the fields wherein grew half a dozen kinds of vegetables, sometimes planted in plats by themselves, "but for the most part in one ground, mixtly." Maize was their chief crop, and this they stored for winter use: but they liked it best green "lapped in rowles of the leaves and boyled for a daintie." White's village drawings show fields near the houses with crops of varying heights, which he labeled "their rype corn," "their greene corn," and "corn newly sprung"—showing that, like present-day market-gardeners, they prolonged the season of roasting-ears.

In winter they lived on game and such dried or smoked food as it had seemed worth while to prepare in the season of plenty. When winds were "cruel sharpe," the well-to-do huddled in their sumptuous robes of fur or feathers, while the less fortunate sought such warmth as might be found in mats of leaves, and were thankful "that no extreame long continueth."

Politically and socially they lived under conditions more Utopian

MT. VERNON—THE HOME OF GENERAL WASHINGTON

than our own race has been able to produce. They seem to have come near solving the problem of eating their cake and having it too. While individuals owned property,—clutched it, indeed, with a grip firm enough to drag it into the grave after them,—all enjoyed the benefits of land in common, and they had devised a system which rendered profiteering in food-stuffs and fuel impossible, such necessities being distributed throughout the community in times of scarcity, with due regard to the claims of kinship and justice.

Each village or group of villages was governed by a chief whose power, so far as it extended, was autocratic, though he was aided by a council of local wisdom. He was himself subject to the great Powhatan, whose sway at the time the English arrived was newly but firmly established. Villages varied in size, from a few houses to towns covering many acres. If small, they were entirely surrounded by stockades of small upright tree trunks, stout enough to stop an arrow; if large, the stockade encircled only part of the dwellings, limiting the area to be defended while providing shelter for all the inhabitants.

When crops were growing, the houses were sometimes more scattered, extending along both sides of an avenue between tilled fields. But always a space was set aside for a community camp fire, the center of village life. White wrote around the camp fire in one of his drawings the words, "The place of solemn prayer." Larger towns had their temples, which held a sacred image and sometimes the honored bodies of dead chiefs. Having temples, they also had priests, distinguishable by the peculiar cut of their hair and shape of their garments, as upon our own streets.

For both sexes a maximum of jewelry and a minimum of clothing were good form. John White's drawings show the women in short draped skirts of deerskin, with beads and chains around their necks, and much tattooing; their legs, hands, breasts and faces being "cunningly embroidered with diverse workes as beastes and serpents artificially wrought into their flesh with black spots." As in our own case, their most valued possessions were imported. They had chains made of links of soft copper, and, from the seashore, strings of pearls "approaching the bigness of great pease," besides shells of those different varieties which passed among Powhatan's subjects both as currency and adornment. These they wore as women of the East have worn their dowries of coin from time immemorial.

As for their husbands, a little paint, ornaments in plenty, and a distinctive hair-cut sufficed to make a well-dressed man. They were not yet able to express themselves by written symbols, but we are assured that they were so near this stage of culture that their acts and clothing had already become highly symbolic. They had one way of painting the face and body when going to war, another for organizing the hunt, a third for mourning the dead. We substitute uniforms and golf-togs and crape for a neat inexpensive coat of paint. The men had organized a feather-trust with monopoly of the output for their own use, but upon tattooing they were willing to divide fifty-fifty, possibly with the idea that to the victors belong the spoils. Undoubtedly the process of acquiring such decorations was long and painful.

Captain Smith, who was sentimental when it did not cost too much, was inclined to commiserate the lot of the Indian women in contrast with the leisure of their husbands. But since they were members of "an ingenious cunning and witty race," and moreover held in their capable brown hands most of the arts and industries necessary to the comfort of their simple living, it seems likely that they might and probably did bring domestic pressure to bear when they deemed it wise; and that the braves, for all their lordly airs, may have been distinctly henpecked.

The status of the women was advanced, compared with that of the white women who followed them, for Algonquian custom gave house and dogs into the custody of the wife. There are hints, also, that women had a voice in council, either by direct vote, or by representation. It is an open question whether or not, after all, the division of labor between the sexes in Powhatan's kingdom differed materially from that accepted as seemly on both sides of the Atlantic prior to the upheaval of 1914. Indian men went out from their homes to seek food and make weapons or destroy their enemies. When in the lodge they appeared idle and in the way—"underfoot" as New England housewives would say. Women, on the contrary, were forever busy near their dwellings. It all seems quite homelike.

There is no account of women munition workers; that was a development of civilized life. When polishing arrow-heads is mentioned, or the fashioning of leaf-shaped blades, it is always the man who is the laborer. Considering the great number of such articles required by their mode of life, and the patience necessary to make a single one of them, the men appear to have had their full share of work cut out for them.

All in all, life upon the banks of the Potomac seems to have been one of few laws but many binding and time-honored customs; chief among which was the custom of good manners as worked out through savage generations. Underlying motives and impulses were very like our own. Parents loved their children and were intent on rearing them according to the most scientific principles known to them. The English were scandalized to see Indian mothers take their babies to the river bank on cold winter mornings and wash them to make them hardy. Sweat-houses and medicinal herbs, poisons and incantations, rude surgery performed with stone knives: and for adults a course of heroic treatment in the spring of the year, that began with purging drafts warranted to make the patient very sick before he could be well again, indicate that these early residents took the same interest in symptoms, and had the same keen desire to speed up the processes of nature, which pack our sanatoriums to the doors.

If a patient failed to recover, certain conventions had to be observed, no matter what the state of mind of the bereaved relatives might be. We read of a worldly young widow "hastening to finish her grief" and causing her tears to flow in great abundance by artificial means "in order that she might grieve much in a short time" and be married before nightfall to another suitor. There appears to have been much that was cruel, not a little that was laughable, and a great deal to recommend it, in life in oldest Washington.

The men who replaced this savage society were said to have founded their colony "upon smoke," meaning that their prosperity was due to tobacco. This was the plant the Indians cherished next to their maize. They made sacrifices of it to the Great Spirit, smoked it ceremonially as well as for every-day comfort: and counted it as a measure of time—the minute-hand on their great clock of sleeps and moons and seasons. "It took one pipe of tobacco" to do such a thing, they would say.

Though the first explorers had found a dozen native plants from whose culture they predicted great gain, this was the only one in which the settlers or the public at home would take an interest. In the matter of tobacco it was more than an interest, it was an obsession. The settlers could scarcely be induced to plant anything else,—even food enough for their own use,—and in London people flocked to inns frequented by returned sailors, to see them sitting at their ease sucking at pipes or twists of brown leaves, and blowing smoke from their nostrils, like dragons. Seeing is believing. More than one doubting Briton found in this sight conviction that the world was indeed round, with a topsy-turvy continent on its farther side.

Those who had been in America had much to say about the healthfulness of the practice, which they called upon "learned physitions" to confirm. These and others began experimenting on their own account, and even the unlearned found that they could "drink tobacco" as well as men who sailed the seas. In vain the authorities counseled experiments with other products; in vain the king set the weight of his great influence against smoking. The craze grew until mothers sent their offspring to school with "the makin's" of a smoke in their satchels, and conscientious masters flogged the pupils who seemed inclined to shirk this new branch of study. Poets and near-poets broke into rhyme. One celebrated tobacco's health-giving properties thus:

> Ye hot, ye cold, ye rheumatic, draw nigh
> In this rich leaf a sovereign dose doth lie.
> We 'll cure you all; physic ye need not want;
> Here 't is, i' the gummy entrails of a plant.

Another, content to rest his argument on the safer ground of economy, packed it rather neatly into two lines:

Much victual serves for gluttony, to fatten men like swine;
But he 's a frugal man indeed that with a leaf can dine.

The leaf was really no new discovery, being of a family of plants widely distributed over the earth's surface: but, like other large families, it produced only a few members of importance, and the two most important happened to be natives of Virginia. Captain Newport, whose name lingers like a ghost around Newport News, described Virginia soil as "altogether aromatical, Nature's nurst to all vegetables," and as a "nurst" to tobacco it ran true to form, being prodigal rather than wise. Two crops sufficed to drain a field of its richness, after which a few plantings in uninteresting food-stuffs completed the ruin. But with a whole continent to exploit, this seemed no matter, and land was cleared, exhausted, and left to its fate, the banks of the Potomac and other Virginia rivers being dotted with "old fields" before they were adequately supplied with new inhabitants.

The Indians still believed the land to be theirs, and Virginia also claimed it, regarding Lord Baltimore and his Marylanders as Papist interlopers. In point of fact, the bits of territory on both banks of the river which were united in the District of Columbia remained virtually without white inhabitants for thirty years after the granting of Lord Baltimore's charter. Henry Fleete had lived there before it was granted, but only as an involuntary guest. Though his fame looms large, as the earliest white inhabitant, it is entirely posthumous. Neither well known nor entirely respectable during his lifetime, he sailed out of obscurity into history in the autumn of 1621, on the *Tiger* or the *Warwick* when these ships left England together, carrying a miscellaneous cargo to the colonies, including thirty-eight young women destined to be wives of Virginia planters.

It was an exciting voyage. The *Tiger* was captured by the Turks and rescued again before making port in safety: and it was after all this that Fleete's personal adventures culminated. The *Tiger* sailed peacefully up the Potomac on an expedition to buy beaver skins and landed twenty-six of her men at a favorite trading-point of the Indians, a little below the falls of the river, where Georgetown was afterward located. Here the Indians fell upon them and murdered all but five. Though Fleete was held captive for a considerable time, he does not appear to have been ill treated. At any rate, he told engaging tales after returning to England, and came back in the guise of trader, accompanied by two or three brothers, whose names appear from time to time thereafter in the records of the Maryland Assembly. As for Henry himself, he vibrated between the colonies as the exigencies of a rather slippery career dictated, and made a disappointingly respectable exit from life as an innkeeper at a place still known as Fleete's Point on the lower Potomac.

Whether or not his rosy narratives hastened settlement is doubtful. That came about in the regular course of events as plantations pushed their way up the rivers. Though most of the new-comers arrived from the south, a few made their way down from Pennsylvania; but the land when it came under cultivation was given up to tobacco. As if foreign demand and native soil were not enough to insure this, psychology added its spell. No matter whence they came, few of the colonists were of a type to find plain farming congenial, but the hazards of tobacco-culture removed it from humdrum toil to the plane of a highly specialized form of gambling. One pinkish blossom produced seed to the number of thirty thousand or more, each of which might yield its hundreds per cent., but whose growth was beset with peril from the instant it entered the earth until the dried leaves were safely tucked away in a consumer's pipe. Even the first planting had to be done with tricky deftness calculated to win admiration from a sharper at cards. Then came transplanting, and the apparently wasteful tearing off of good leaves to force the juices of the mutilated plant into those that remained. Drought might wither the crop in three days, or hail cut it to pieces in an hour. Fungus and insects menaced it at all times: and if it survived these perils, a totally new set awaited its curing and transportation.

Yet so great was the profit and so exciting the hazard, that long before Robert Beverley wrote in his History of Virginia that "The planters make a heavy bustle with it and can't please the market, neither," it had become the vegetable currency of the South, in which every need of this life and every attempt to provide for the life to come was measured and paid for. Hogs and slaves, gambling debts, gewgaws to please a lady, funeral sermons, and fines for neglecting to have the children baptized, were all paid for in tobacco. But it would have been as convenient to carry a coffin around in one's pocket as enough tobacco for a morning's shopping, so "crop-notes" had been devised, which passed from hand to hand with treacherous ease.

Tobacco having attained the dignity of money, its excellence had to be maintained—a task neither easy nor pleasant. If by a miracle the planters of one colony agreed among themselves to limit the acreage in the interest of good prices, their neighbors across the border rushed in and carried off the reward, leaving behind a fine crop of hard feelings. And the local inspectors, whose sworn duty it was to burn all leaves offered for sale that fell below standard, were not likely to increase their popularity, either with neighbors or buyers.

There were virtually no towns in the region and no good roads, so the inspection took place at the point of shipment, usually a warehouse on some navigable stream. Toward this, rough trails called Rolling Roads were cut through the forest from all the plantations in the neighborhood. Down these narrow green tunnels, scarcely wider than the hogsheads in which the leaves were packed, the hogsheads were rolled, fitted with tongue and axle and propelled by ox- or mule-power, or by the brawn of slaves.

Poor settlers brought their few pounds, rich proprietors sent huge crops; and, since no man who emigrated lost his aptitudes or his previous character in mid-ocean, there was also another class—men who kept aloof from fields and warehouses, to grow rich fingering crop-notes. The majority of settlers earned their living more easily and quite as honestly as they could have done in the Old World, but some unfortunates floundered ever more hopelessly in debt, while speculators who foreclosed mortgages died in the homes the debtors had established for themselves.

A generous soil which made it possible even when in debt to enjoy a rude luxury of warmth and food, combined with the institution of African slavery to work havoc with the theory that there is dignity in personal toil. To command the labor of slaves, to practise open-handed hospitality toward friends and strangers, to enjoy all the good things of this life, and not to appear over-anxious about God or the devil, was the ideal of the planters. There were more sportsmen among them than students, and few good business men among those who were held in highest esteem. It was rather in spite of their traits than because of them that they prospered and that the country gained in wealth. Jefferson, in his day, calculated that the value of Virginia's land and slaves had doubled every twenty years. Robert Beverley thought his fellow-colonists shiftless and ungrateful. "They sponge upon the blessings of a warm and fruitful soil," he wrote, "and almost grudge the pains of gathering in the bounties of the earth."

It was in 1662, about the time Milton was writing "Paradise Lost," that Lord Baltimore granted a goodly number of acres to one George Thompson, an absentee landlord like himself, who, however, sent people to make actual settlement. Every head of a family was allowed fifty acres on his own account, with fifty more for each individual he brought out at his own expense, and the holdings taken up were large.

The tract thus deeded included Duddington Pasture, where the Capitol now stands, St. Elizabeth, the site of the government hospital for the insane, across the Anacostia River, and much land since covered by city buildings. It fell almost at once into the hands of speculators, and within ten years the fourteen hundred acres of Duddington Pasture, which had cost Thompson one pound sixteen shillings "or their equivalent in commodities," were sold to Notley Young, attorney and land-agent, and one of Maryland's deputy governors, for forty thousand pounds of tobacco. The tobacco had very likely not been planted, and Thompson may never have received a shilling on the transaction. This seems to have been the earliest of a long series of real-estate "operations" in east Washington, in which the end rather than the means was the chief concern of both buyer and seller.

Before long the region became known as New Scotland Hundred, a name indicating the character of its inhabitants quite as accurately as their numbers, "Hundreds" being an elastic and con-

Courtesy Columbia Historical Society

ONE OF THE JURISDICTION STONES

venient old English term for purposes of taxation and census taking. Its people lived according to the lavish, hospitable code of the region, in as good houses as they could afford to build. Though these seemed roomy, and solid as the hills compared with Indian dwellings, the expression "Barons of the Potomac," so often met, conveys an impression of magnificence far from truthful. The earliest manor-houses did not show the stately architecture of a century later. "Clean Drinking," for example, in the neighborhood of Washington, was only a modest story-and-half cottage, sturdily built.

Each settler gave his tract the name fancy dictated, and whatever the mental and moral shortcomings, narrowness of horizon cannot be charged to them. "Argyle," "Allinson's Forest," "Cowell," "Lorne," "Rock of Dumbarton," and "Fife Large" show why the place was called New Scotland: but "Mexico" and "Jamaica" and "New Troy" indicate thoughts far afield. Only a few chose names familiar to Indian ears. More were satisfied with those that were merely commonplace and descriptive, like "Green Hill" and "Turkey-Buzzard Point." Some, like "Widow's Mite," "Plain Dealing," "Girl's Portion," "Little Chance," and "Poor Tom's Last Shift," are tantalizing in their half-revelations. What "Scotland Yard" may have stood for, in the mind of its proprietor, is hard to imagine. Probably it had nothing to do with "Knave's Disappointment." Humor was rarely manifested, though there is at least one instance of it. As early as 1663 a tract of four hundred low-lying acres in the present heart of the city was surveyed for a Thomas Pope, and in time descended to his son. Their neighbors called the place "Rome," after which, of necessity, the small picturesque stream known as Goose Creek that wandered through it was re-christened "Tiber," and by this grandiloquent name it flowed into literature through Tom Moore's caustic pen.

Intermarriage and inheritance, bankruptcy and speculation played their several parts in shifting these holdings, through a century. Their respective owners were decorous and law-abiding, according to their lights, if neither so pious nor so learned as some of the more Northern colonists conceived themselves to be. On the Virginia side of the Potomac most of them belonged to the Church of England. In Maryland the greater number were Catholics, with an occasional miracle to attest the quality of their faith.

The river was still the great highway, there being few trails on land better than the Rolling Roads, along which "spontaneous flowers of unknown variety," as Beverley described them, bloomed from the beginning of March to the first fall of snow. If the music of bird songs heard in the same green tunnels were sometimes marred by the sharp tones of an overseer, or the sharper sound of his lash, the discord was soon forgotten. Slavery was lawful throughout all the colonies, and regarded as sanctioned by Scripture, even in New England.

Near the river, the vista at the end of a Rolling Road would be closed by a glimpse of water or the gable end of the tobacco-scented warehouse, swallows twittering under its eaves. Beyond might be seen the prow of a ship waiting to take the crop on the next stage of its long journey. The same ship carried orders from planters to their London factors for merchandise of many kinds. A few good books, rich apparel and furniture in moderation, and an abundance of excellent wine. These were all legitimate things to import, since it was impossible to get them nearer home. But the planters also sent orders for coarse cloth for garments for their slaves, and goods like brooms and wooden bowls which might easily have been made on their own plantations, had not indolence and the policy of the home Government encouraged the easier way. This was also fostered by the merchants, who realized that it was better for their pockets and quite as well for their ships to send them on the western voyage full instead of empty. Important houses kept junior partners in the colonies to look out for their varied interests, one being to discourage manufacture. For fear these young men might develop too great sympathy with the colonists, they were forbidden to marry American wives.

Thus matters went on while English kings were crowned and beheaded, and Cromwell's great enterprise gained headway and came to an end. For a time, in the excitement of home politics, Virginia was left to shift for herself without a governor; but the eastward flow of tobacco kept on, and no matter how much successive governments might differ in other matters, they all opposed measures tending to lessen the dependence of the colonies on the mother-country.

After a time, however, business and trade, which planters were inclined to despise individually, became for them collectively a vivifying influence. Leaders of public opinion dwelt more and more upon the fact that a system which condemned each separate plantation to dependence on an island three thousand miles away, left something to be desired. Proprietors still sent their tobacco and their orders to London, but accompanied by petitions to the king. Later they sent more of these, relating to taxation and other matters, couched in respectful yet decided language, and the habit culminated in the Declaration of Independence.

One stage of this sequence was marked by the impulse toward town-building to foster public spirit and aid in establishing manufactures. This town epidemic struck the Potomac region with such force about the middle of the century that no less than five "places of cohabitation" as they were elegantly called, were laid out within or on the edge of the ten-mile square destined to become the seat of government. An already established settlement known as Bell Haven, on the Virginia side of the Potomac, took on added dignity in 1742, with the new name of Alexandria, and made such men as Lord Fairfax and Lawrence Washington its trustees. The same year saw the birth of Bladensburg on the Anacostia River, just beyond the District line. In 1761 the Maryland legislature authorized a town site of sixty acres "adjacent to George Gordon's Rolling House," where Rock Creek enters the Potomac, close to the spot where Henry Fleete was taken captive. This place flourished from the beginning, but two others, Carrollsburg and Hamburg or Funkstown, laid out later on the shores of the Potomac in the frank hope of diverting its trade, kept only a precarious hold upon life until they were swallowed up in the project for a capital city.

George Gordon, owner of the Rolling House, was one of those merchants born to prosperity. He had built his wooden warehouse on the west bank of Rock Creek as early as 1743, and it had monopolized the fame if not the profits of his immediate business neighbors. He wanted a town, but George Beall, an even earlier settler, a man of little education and no imagination, with enough Scotch combativeness in his blood to put up a stiff fight, strenuously objected. The project seemed to him as mad as the notion that the world was round, or that good ever came of studying Greek or Latin. But the neighbors all sided with Gordon, and forced Beall to submit to a jury the value of his holdings. The law allowed him the first choice of lots, a privilege he thriftily exercised, though with the stipulation that this should not debar him from seeking redress later on. "I have the right of a British subject, I ask no more, God save the king!" he declaimed, as he pocketed his lots and his defeat.

With two belligerent Georges contending over its birth, and a monarch of the same name on the throne, it was inevitable that the place should be called Georgetown, though which of the three was most in mind nobody knows. The one thing certain is that it was not named for that stripling of nineteen, George Washington, who had just received his commission as adjutant of the Virginia forces.

The founding of this town marks not only a solid milestone in local history but the line of cleavage between old colonial habits of thought and the new unrest that culminated in the Revolution. It was only three years later that Franklin made his first suggestion for a federal union of the colonies.

Tobacco kept trundling toward George Gordon's wooden warehouse, which in time he replaced with one of red brick; gardens were planted and houses were built: and out of the holds of ships from many lands came furniture and luxuries that would not have seemed out of place in London itself. The little town's gay and worldly attitude toward life was reflected even in its bills of lading. A merchant advertised these for sale "with or without the Grace of God." This meant that they were printed in two forms, one beginning piously, "Shipped by the Grace of God," and ending, "and so, God send the Good Ship to her desired port of safety, Amen," while the other pointedly ignored the Deity.

When, less than five years after the town was laid out, General Braddock arrived, he was not at all prepared for the sophisticated little community he found at the head of tide-water and virtually at the point beyond which there were no wagon roads. Though he was prejudiced against the colonies, he had expected a certain amount of civilization at Annapolis; but "Never have I attended a more complete banquet or met better dressed or better mannered people than I met on my arrival in George Town," he wrote to a friend in England. He described the men as large and gallant, the women as beautiful, and the homes in their gardens as stately. "In fact, my dear Madam, I might sum up by declaring George Town is indescribably lovely: and I am loath to leave it and its hospitable people." Had he been willing to accept the advice of its hospitable people about the tactics of Indian fighting, his own history might have ended less tragically.

The bold rock called the Quay of Quays, upon which his red-coated soldiers landed when they scrambled out of the *Sea Horse* and the *Nightingale,* has disappeared almost as completely as the men of that ill-fated expedition. Part of it was destroyed to build the Chesapeake and Ohio Canal, the second link in the line of communication between the Ohio Valley and the Atlantic, the road Braddock himself built being the first. Still more of the ledge was used in foundations for the Capitol and the President's House, and to-day only a small fragment remains, which has to be diligently searched for, since it is far from the present course of the river and below the surface of the made ground surrounding it in Potomac Park. But an inscription marks it as the spot where these friendly British soldiers landed.

It was on April 12th that they came, at the moment when the river banks were breaking into vivid green. A fortnight later they marched away toward Fredericksburg, never to return, accompanied by the Georgetown men and residents of the neighborhood who had joined them. Young Colonel Washington rode with Braddock as a member of his staff; and one of the party was Dr. Craik, who was destined, like Washington, to pass unscathed through the rain of bullets on Braddock's day of doom, and was to stand, years later, beside Washington's own death-bed.

The French and Indian War, in which Braddock's expedition perished, was one small portion of the great Seven Years' War embroiling Europe, out of which England emerged with greatly increased prestige and territory, and woefully in need of money. It was to meet the expense of her new position that those taxes were devised to which the American colonies made such strenuous objection. The South was fully as voluble in complaints as New England, and while the ingenuity her orators displayed in inventing arguments against them had no effect whatever upon England's policy, they had a great effect in uniting sentiment on this side of the Atlantic.

Patrick Henry's denunciation of the Stamp Act was so convincing to the agent of the Crown that when he reached Virginia with the stamps, he deemed it the part of wisdom to forget his errand. No Boston Tea Party took place in Southern waters, but the *Peggy Stuart* and all her cargo went up in smoke at Annapolis. The merchants of Georgetown and Bladensburg showed their spirit by agreeing not to receive the consignments they expected; or if the chests should be delivered in spite of them, to turn them over unopened to a responsible committee.

In all the preliminaries that led up to hostilities, the locality bore its full share. Virginia was the first colony to put into operation the plan of intercolonial committees of correspondence on which so much depended, and Georgetown was represented on these committees by no less than seven men, one of them being a red-headed descendant of Notley Young, the second purchaser of Duddington Pasture. The news that the port of Boston had been closed was met with a very practical expression of sympathy in a shipment of supplies and a subscription of ready money; best of all, by Washington's indignant declaration:

"If need be, I will raise a thousand men, subsist them at my expense, and march myself to the relief of Boston!"

Local forges and smithies went vigorously to work improvising munitions of war. The Foxhall foundry, near Georgetown, became one of the most important sources of supply, and two companies recruited just north of the city were among the first to start for Massachusetts after the battle of Bunker Hill. The total number of soldiers from the neighborhood who took part in the

Revolution has never been ascertained, but is believed to have been large in proportion to the population.

Armies passed the region by, the usual line of travel between North and South being by way of the Eastern Shore of the Chesapeake to a ferry near Annapolis, while another ferry took them across the Potomac south of Alexandria. But occasionally a detachment of marching men or a slow-moving wagon train strayed far enough from the beaten path to gladden the eyes of small boys in Bladensburg or Georgetown, and the sound of fife and drum in local musters became as much a part of the natural order of things as the song of the "mock birds" on the Rolling Roads.

Ladies who had sipped tea and danced the minuet with Braddock and his officers, flaunted their homespun and wrote down in ink their firm resolve to "eat mush and milk, drink water, and live frugally" until husbands and brothers returned victorious. Victory was long enough in coming to give all who stayed at home ample opportunity for those minor deeds of courage which swelled the great tide of American patriotism. As reports of suffering in the Continental armies grew frequent and circumstantial, it became a point of honor to put up a good bluff of cheerfulness. Men and women who had wealth gave generously. Few women could match in this the "apronfull of gold pieces" donated by a patriotic lady of Georgetown: but many were called on to make a richer sacrifice, and lived thereafter stricken in heart though sustained by patriotic pride.

Soldiers who came back brought with them scars and a wealth of experience which they were anxious to share with neighbors or to hide, according to their natures. A certain Lieutenant Dorsey, who owned land stretching from Braddock's Rock to Widow's Mite, never willingly spoke of the tortures he had endured on the foul prison-ship *Jersey,* in company with corpses and men who would gladly have been dead. Those confined upon her had graphically rechristened her *Hell.* Wounds were pleasant things to dwell on in comparison, and it was his fancy after his return to name his several tracts for the battles in which he had been injured. One he called "Harlem," another "Middlebrook." And when the project for a national capital began to be discussed, no man was more enthusiastic than he in favor of the site on the Potomac.

II

THAT FIGURE OF FAMINE

THE Continental Congress, always homeless, spent its entire life as the guest of local authorities in one town after another. Even before the war for independence was over, the embarrassments of this guest system became manifest.

In June, 1783, when it was meeting in Philadelphia, mutinous Pennsylvania soldiers appeared before its doors, clamoring for pay long overdue, a reasonable request which could not be granted, for the very best of reasons. Congress called upon the city authorities of Philadelphia for protection, but this was denied on the ground that the local militia might object to serving before an actual outrage had been committed. The mutineers finally went away, after doing nothing more outrageous than point guns and use vile language, but Congress also took its departure, refusing to stay longer in a city where the treatment it received was seemingly a matter of indifference.

Then the authorities woke up to the fact that, in transgressing the laws of hospitality, they had been rude to a guest whose presence netted the city a good hundred thousand dollars a year. They begged the offended legislators to return, but Congress set forth, instead, upon that pilgrimage which took it from Princeton to Annapolis, from Annapolis to Trenton, from Trenton to New York, and ended only when the old Continental Congress unofficially went upon the scrap-heap, its sessions being merged for all practical purposes into those of the first Constitutional Convention, to which so many of its members had been elected.

In planning for the future, the convention recognized that a wandering capital would be looked upon by the world as a sign of weakness, and decreed that the first Congress to be elected under the new Constitution should choose a permanent abiding-place. This proved to be difficult. A central location was indispensable, and commercially it was desirable to be on navigable water, yet a capital must be far enough inland to be safe from foreign invasion. Moreover, men who were vocal for states-rights and jealous of federal authority, denounced national ownership of land, even of the small amount needed for erecting government buildings. Experts placed the minimum required for this purpose at three miles square, the maximum at six; a mere bagatelle, but, like that insignificant little tax on tea, one that involved tremendous principles.

New York, having hastily remodeled its city hall for the use of Congress, saw no reason whatever for a change. Why go in search of trouble by acquiring federal territory, when there was a comfortable ready-made town waiting, on the old terms? It was safe to wager that New York would not repeat Philadelphia's blunder.

Offers of territory poured in from other quarters. New York State, whose interests, then as now, were quite distinct from those of New York City, was willing to let states-rights take its chance, and offered a tract ten miles square anywhere within its borders. Maryland and Virginia matched this with a joint offer of land upon the Potomac River, each contributing a share. Virginia, in addition to this, offered Williamsburg, which was rejected as too remote. Robert Morris, who held large property interests near Trenton, favored a location on the Delaware River. Pennsylvania was sure Wright's Ferry, upon the Susquehanna, filled every condition. And there was a party which sought to gain the blessing promised to peacemakers by upholding the wisdom of having two capitals, one in the North and one in the South, with Congress oscillating like a pendulum between them.

The choice finally narrowed down to sites upon the Susquehanna and the Potomac, with the Susquehanna decidedly in the lead. In fact, the House of Representatives voted definitely in favor of the latter, in September, 1789. But the Senate was partial to Germantown; and James Madison's deft parliamentary skill in taking advantage of this difference, saved the Potomac project from defeat and sent the matter over to the second session of the First Congress, when a man of foreign birth, who had no seat in Congress and no right to cast a vote, brought it to success.

It happened that the only other measure of importance before that session of Congress was the Funding Bill, Alexander Hamilton's wizard scheme for turning state liabilities into national assets, his proposal being that the Federal Government assume the war debts of the states, in return for which the states should give up to the general Government their unoccupied Western lands, to be held as a national domain and used as a basis for a national currency. This extended the principle of federal control from a paltry ten miles square to dimensions quite beyond calculation. The lines of cleavage for and against the two bills were different. The states with the heaviest war debts were enchanted with Hamilton's proposal, while those upon which debts sat lightly saw little to recommend it. Virginia desperately wanted the national capital, but was not troubled about its war debt.

Both bills seemed likely to fail, when Hamilton intervened. He cared less about the location of the Government than about placing the country upon a sound financial basis, and saw the possibility of offsetting one measure with the other. He believed that if they were shaken up together, the number of votes clinging to each might be found slightly altered when they were again separated. Only a small change was needed, a matter of one vote in the Senate and four or five in the House.

Congress was at the time sitting in New York, and Hamilton invited Senator Morris to meet him in the quiet, secluded park known as the Battery, where they paced up and down under the trees near the water's edge until Morris agreed to give up his preference for a Northern capital. Then Hamilton staged another outdoor meeting, to take place apparently by accident. The scene this time was a city street in front of President Washington's New York residence; the man waylaid was Thomas Jefferson, recently returned from France to be Secretary of State. Jefferson and Hamilton seldom agreed on matters of policy, but after Hamilton had walked back and forth with him before the President's door for a long half-hour, Jefferson found it in his heart to end the interview by inviting the Secretary of the Treasury to dinner on the following afternoon "to meet a friend or two."

Thus, with the connivance of his excellent cook, Jefferson assumed the rôle of go-between in this political marriage of convenience. Two Virginia members of Congress, whose votes were needed, listened to Hamilton's siren voice: the Funding Bill was passed and the capital was located upon the Potomac, while, as a sort of consolation prize, Philadelphia was made the seat of government until the new capital should be ready for occupancy.

President Washington favored the Potomac site, a preference that critics ascribed to its nearness to his own estates and to the active part he had long taken in efforts to make the Potomac River a direct line of communication with the Ohio country. In this matter of selecting a home for the Government, he seemed inclined to exercise all his official authority and a little which might have been left to others under strict interpretation of the law; but, whatever his motive, posterity has small cause to complain.

Three commissioners were appointed to locate and survey a district not exceeding ten miles square, upon the Potomac between the Eastern Branch (the Anacostia River of early maps) and the Conococheague, a stream approximately sixty miles up the river.

It was the middle of October, the same enchanted season of the year which the Indians chose for their hunting festival, when the President himself appeared in Georgetown to view with the principal citizens "the country adjacent to the river Potowmack in order to fix on a proper selection for the Grand Columbian Federal City."

One day was devoted to exploring the neighborhood of the Eastern Branch, and next morning, at the painfully early hour this good man always chose by preference, he turned his horse's head toward Great Falls and "that Indian place," as Conococheague was spitefully called by people who refused to pronounce its name. As the President rode away, betting was lively and hopeful on the streets of Georgetown; but, with his gift for serene silence, he left the inhabitants guessing and returned home by another route.

It was not until January 24, 1791, that an official proclamation settled the matter. Meantime, Maryland and Virginia had made concessions in the way of granting money and agreeing to condemnation of property for government use. But as this did not provide enough ground, the commissioners were given authority to "purchase or accept land." It was their duty to see that suitable buildings be ready for the Government on the first Monday in December, 1800.

Washington had confessed his "limited acquaintance with convenient characters who were free enough from local prejudices to qualify them for the task," and, as the best way of securing men he could trust, chose the three commissioners from among personal friends. Only one resided in the neighborhood. This was Daniel Carroll, an aristocrat in feeling and an autocrat in bearing. The second was Thomas Johnson, a highly respected lawyer of Maryland, with a kindly heart and marked executive ability, though brusque and "given to strange oaths." The third was Dr. David Stuart, a practising physician who lived near Fairfax Court House, Virginia. He is described as "an elderly benevolent gentleman, fond of quoting the classics." In view of this personnel it does not seem strange that the President was called upon to intervene occasionally as a peacemaker between owners and commissioners.

Their earliest care was to secure the services of Andrew Ellicott of Pennsylvania for the work of surveying boundaries. He appeared in February, 1791, and began clearing timber from a line forty feet wide around the entire tract. In this space were planted, at mile intervals, square-sawn posts of native freestone, with beveled edges, standing two feet high and bearing on one side the initials of the state and on the other the pregnant words: JURISDICTION OF THE UNITED STATES. After one hundred and thirty years a few are still standing as he placed them, many are overgrown, and some have vanished utterly.

The first stone was set up with masonic ceremonies on March 15, 1791, on a spot now covered by the foundations of the lighthouse on Jones's Point, Alexandria. Owing to "neglect or accident," as was darkly hinted, notices of this first District ceremony were not spread abroad in time to secure a worthy audience, but the commissioners of the federal district were on hand to meet the mayor and city officers and the local masonic lodge of Alexandria, at Mr. Wise's tavern at three o'clock in the afternoon, and drink a toast before marching to the appointed spot in as good an imitation of a procession as their limited numbers allowed.

Then they came back to the tavern for a dinner and real toasts, one of which was: "May jealousy, the green-eyed monster, be buried deep under the work which we have this day completed, never to rise again within the Federal District,"—a pious wish that, fulfilled, would have shorn local history of much interest.

As a matter of fact, the green-eyed one did not stay buried long enough even for the stone to settle firmly in its hole, but wriggled out and left it so unsteady that it had to be replaced by a new one in a very few years. The new stone bore the legend: THE CITY OF WASHINGTON IN THE TERRITORY OF COLUMBIA, this having meanwhile been agreed upon as the official name.

The square of ground thus set apart was covered partly with forest trees, partly with country houses and half-exhausted old fields, the legacy of a hundred years of spendthrift tobacco-culture, over which Nature had spread a mantle of useless flowering weeds and relays of sturdy young saplings. Also there were "two hundred and thirty-six varieties of birds," near half a hundred kinds of reptiles, and "fish in great numbers," none of which could aid much in the development of the project. Of greater moment, as helps or hindrances, were the five small towns inside or just beyond the line of freestone posts: Alexandria, to the south, decorous and staid; Georgetown, growing daily more elegant; Bladensburg with its chalybeate spring and its blossoming peach-trees just across the line to the northeast; and the two anæmic settlements upon the river bank, Carrollsburg and Hamburg.

Andrew Ellicott, the surveyor, was not favorably impressed and wrote in confidence to his "Dear Sally": "This country intended for the Permanent Residence of Congress bears no more proportion to the country about Philadelphia and German-Town for either wealth or fertility than a crane does to a stall-fed ox!" But he added, "As the President is so much attracted to this country I would not be willing that he should know my real sentiments about it." Ellicott was only the surveyor: his not to reason why; his but his work to ply, to show where streets should lie, where boundaries rise.

Fortunately, President Washington's ideas were liberal. Desiring a capital worthy of a great nation, he saw the danger of incorporating in it the village standards of Hamburg and Carrollsburg. Landowners near Georgetown and near Carrollsburg, one on Rock Creek and the other on the Eastern Branch, already showed an inclination to make excessive demands. He really desired both sites, and had in mind a city covering the entire area, but did not deem it necessary to take the neighborhood into his confidence. Dealing with the problem as a business man and a military strategist, he instructed two gentlemen, upon whom he could rely, to do their best to purchase tracts near Georgetown without letting it be known that they were acting "on behalf of the public"; and in his character of general he made a feint to mislead the enemy. Acting on the principle so successful in the surprise of Stony Point, that a feint is most likely to succeed when the forces engaged in it believe it to be a real attack, he told the engineer who had been selected to make preliminary city plans, to begin his work as far as possible from the Georgetown region.

To the two friends who were in his confidence, Washington wrote:

> GENTLEMEN,
>
> Major L'Enfant comes on to make such a survey of the grounds in your vicinity as may aid in fixing the site of the Federal Town and buildings. His present instructions express those alone which are within the Eastern Branch, the Potomac, the Tiber, and the road leading from George Town to the Ferry on the Eastern Branch. He is directed to begin at the lower end, and work upwards, and nothing further is communicated to him. The purpose of this letter is to desire you will not yourselves be misled by this appearance.

The green-eyed monster and the city's guardian angel must have been equally pleased when Pierre Charles L'Enfant was chosen to make the plans. It would have been hard to find a man better qualified artistically and less fitted by temperament, had a search been made the world over. Son of a French "painter in ordinary to the King in his manufacture of Gobelins," the young man had reached this country a few weeks in advance of his compatriot Lafayette, and, like him, had entered the Continental Army as a volunteer. Aside from rendering valuable service as a major of Engineers, he had achieved a unique unofficial position, becoming an Adviser in Æsthetics to the new government, because of his taste and training in a field of which Americans of that day were for the most part completely ignorant. "Whenever," says Ambassador Jusserand, "during the war or after, something in any way connected with art was wanted, L'Enfant was as a matter of course appealed to."

His quick pencil had enlivened the dreary monotony of Valley Forge. Even Washington sat for his likeness to "Monsieur Langfang." He designed the insignia for the Society of the Cincinnati. At a time when something spectacular was needed to rouse enthusiasm in favor of adopting the Constitution, he devised a wonderful pageant in New York City, in which floats and trumpeters; Christopher Columbus on horseback; the good ship *Hamilton* firing salutes as it trundled along on wheels; Indians in native costume; brewers, butchers, tanners, and confectioners, all contributed their part to the picturesqueness and success of the occasion.

It was L'Enfant, also, who rebuilt and redecorated New York's City Hall for the use of the Continental Congress, making it a sort of gay martin-box to attract that desirable bird of passage.

Possessed of more than a touch of genius and cursed with a most difficult disposition, he was always rendering valuable service, overestimating his own importance, and getting into serious trouble in consequence. He appears to have conceived a dog-like affection for General Washington, in spite of the murderous way in which the general pronounced his name, and Washington, who had remarkable patience with men of temperament provided their motives were pure, returned L'Enfant's regard in an austere way.

New York's City Hall, the young man's most important commission, had been brilliantly completed, and not enough time had elapsed to show the hasty workmanship which dragged it so speedily to decay. He had reveled in inventing ornaments for it of purely New-World symbolism. The use of American marbles, the weaving of stars and rays and the initials "U. S." into capitals, had seemed pleasingly original, while the eagle clasping thirteen arrows in its energetic claws, which formed the chief decoration of its

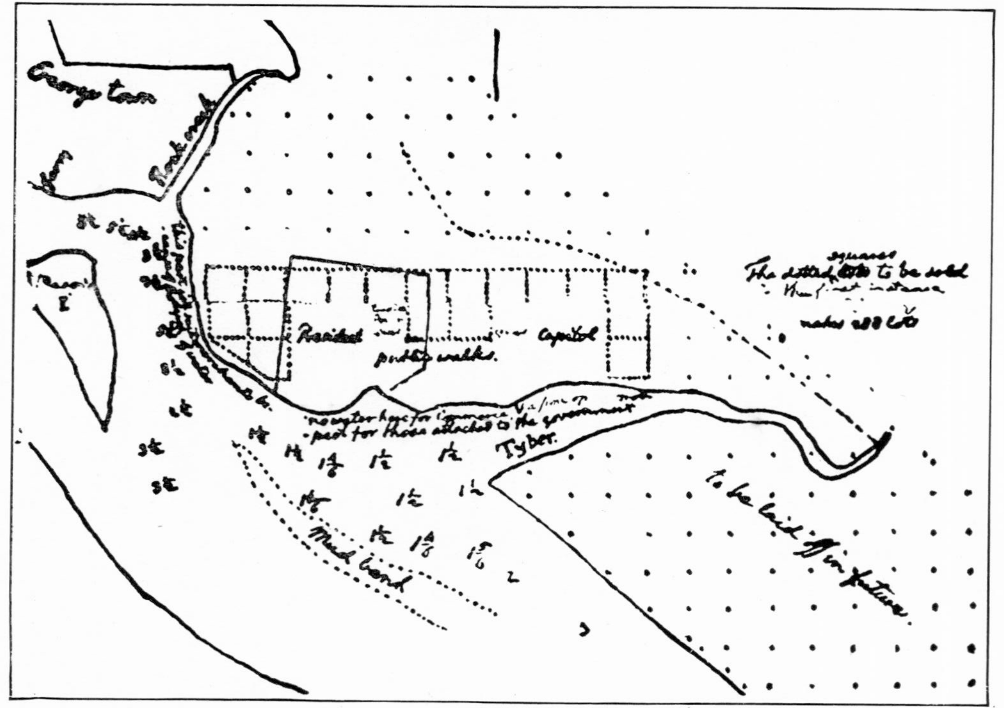

JEFFERSON'S SKETCH MAP

pediment, rather dazzled the imagination of the lawmakers. Pursuit of such fancies had caused the cost to soar to twice the sum agreed upon, but the business men of New York decided it was worth the price, and paid the bill without a murmur, adding as a "testimonial" an offer of ten acres of land near Provost Lane, which the architect imprudently declined.

A friendly biographer, who willingly admits L'Enfant's lack of system and his inability to see any connection between an object on which he had set his heart and mere money, says that he always saw things *en grande*. The idea of a brand-new capital built from the ground up, was sufficiently *grande* to appeal to his innermost longing. Two years before the Residence Bill became a law, he wrote to General Washington, applying for the chance to plan the new city and outlining his conception of the opportunity. He got his chance and, heedless of pitfalls which wait for those who gaze only toward the clouds, became the *Don Quixote* of the city's history, a figure at once laughable and tragic and inspiring.

The eagerness with which he hurried to his task is betrayed in the letter he wrote to Jefferson on his arrival in Georgetown, telling how he had "traveled part of the way on foot and part on horseback, leaving the broken stage behind." It was raining, but even in the first fog-shrouded glimpse he saw enough to give wings to his imagination, and from that moment until his eyes closed in the mists of death, thirty-four years later, the city of his vision was ever before him, bright at first with hope, later shadowed with bitter disappointment, but always loved and always fair. He wrote in his imperfect French-English:

> I passed on many spots which appear to me really beautiful and which seem to dispute with each other who command. In the most extensive prospect on the water the gradual rising of the ground from Carrollsburg toward the Ferry Road, the level and extensive ground from there to the bank of the Potomack far as Goose Creek present a situation most advantageous.

Already he saw the ground covered with streets prolonged to distant vistas, while the springs and creeks, augmented by recent rains, set his mind to planning aqueducts and ponds and cascades.

The town has indeed a wonderful natural setting, in the circle of hills dropping into a plain through which the Potomac flows with its two kinds of river beauty—a rock-girt stream between high wooded banks above Georgetown, and below that point wide-spreading reaches of shining silver. The late Ambassador James Bryce, beloved of Americans, who was an enthusiastic pedestrian, and during his residence in Washington grew to know it and its environs as not one in five hundred of its own people knows it, thought that none of the great capitals of Europe, "except of course Constantinople with its wonderful Bosphorus," could compare to it in natural advantages. And not even Constantinople has, near at hand, a cataract like the beautiful Great Falls of the Potomac.

Acquaintance with the locality only increased L'Enfant's enthusiasm. He wrote to Hamilton:

> I feel a sort of embarrassment how to speak to you as advantageously as I really think of the situation determined upon. I become apprehensive of being charged with partiality when I assure you that no position in America can be more susceptible of grand improvement.

The great river, so important commercially at a period antedating railroads, interested him mainly from its artistic aspect. Jefferson, on the other hand, kept the idea of trade constantly in mind. He had no official connection with the undertaking, but gave it much thought, and, even before the official proclamation had been issued, presented a sketch map of his own for a town at the junction of the Potomac and Eastern Branch, extending along the lesser as well as the greater river. "The former will be for persons in commerce; the latter for those connected with the government," he wrote. Jefferson thought an area of fifteen hundred acres ample for the city of the future, while Washington desired four times as much; an interesting comparison of the breadth of view of the Virginia planter who had never been abroad, and that of the much-traveled Jefferson.

Washington, who possessed instinctive feeling for dignity in architecture, wished to proceed "only according to the rules of acknowledged masters." One of his first efforts had been to collect maps of the noted cities of Europe, so that those in charge might benefit by their mistakes as well as their successes. Jefferson, lately returned from abroad, was able to supply a dozen from his private store and sent for others. In the letter accompanying his own plan, he remarked that not one of them was "comparable to the old Babylon revived in Philadelphia." It is known that L'Enfant had under his eye maps of London, Paris, Versailles, Venice, Madrid, Amsterdam, Naples, Florence, Frankfort, Carlsruhe, Strasburg, Orleans, Bordeaux, Lyons, Montpellier, Marseilles, Turin, and Milan, besides the American Babylonian-Philadelphia combination, the sketch-plan of Jefferson's devising, and plans of Williamsburg, Virginia, and Annapolis, Maryland, the last of which owed its inspiration to the unused plan of Sir Christopher Wren for rebuilding London after the Great Fire.

One of these modest American towns possessed a mall, the other, streets radiating from focal points—both features that L'Enfant incorporated in his design. He appears to have derived only isolated hints from any of the plans; and it seems fitting that the capital of our composite nation should have been made by welding together many bits into a new and beautiful whole. While the city's broad radiating avenues invite the hasty conclusion that Paris, with its open spaces and its Place de l'Etoile, may have been L'Enfant's inspiration, it must be remembered that Paris was at that date still a medieval city of narrow, crooked streets, a veritable rabbit-warren of a place, whose transformation only occurred at the end of the French Revolution under Napoleon Bonaparte, who was an unknown second lieutenant at the time the Washington plan was drawn. L'Enfant did, however, have knowledge of the wonderful park at Versailles, and his imagination may have conceived the idea of turning its leafy avenues into brick and stone.

For once he literally obeyed orders and confined his attention to the region near the Eastern Branch, wherein it seemed to him that Jenkins's Heights stood "like a pedestal awaiting its monument," the predestined site for a capitol building. This was no other than the wooded ground in Duddington Pasture, conveyed by deed from Lord Baltimore to George Thompson in the year 1662. Who Jenkins was or how he became connected with the hill is a mystery. Nobody of that name appears to have owned a foot of it. He may have been some tenant who imposed his personality deep upon the spot and upon his neighbors. In view of the rumors that fly and buzz about that hilltop, it is an amusing coincidence which links that particular name with the site of the Capitol.

While L'Enfant was surveying and seeing visions in one part of the field, negotiations for the entire tract were proceeding with delay and exhibitions of selfishness that exhausted even George Washington's abnormal store of patience.

In the latter part of March, 1791, he came in person to settle matters. Bands of gentlemen on horseback rode out to meet him and to tender addresses and public dinners. Less ceremony and more public spirit would have pleased him better. The rival desires of Georgetown and Carrollsburg were still so keen and the demands of four large landowners and several small ones so far from reasonable, that he called their leading representatives together and lectured them, quite as if he were the father of a quarrelsome family instead of the Father of his Country. His diary records:

I requested them to meet me at six o'clock this afternoon at my lodgings. To this meeting I represented that the contention in which they seemed engaged, did not in my opinion comport either with the public interest or that of their own—that while each party was aiming to obtain the public buildings, they might by placing the matter on a contracted scale, defeat the measure altogether; not only by procrastination, but for want of the means necessary to effect the work. That neither the offer of George-Town nor Carrollsburg, separately, was adequate to the end of insuring the object. That both together did not comprehend more ground nor would afford greater means than was required for the Federal City; and that, instead of contending which of the two should have it, they had better, by combining more offers, make a common cause of it and thereby secure it to the district.

One of the landowners, referred to in Washington's letters as "the obstinate Mr. Burnes," owned Beall's Levels, a tract of two hundred and twenty-five acres near the mouth of Tiber Creek, which was absolutely necessary to the larger plan. He was one of the longest to hold out, and of him the tale is told, with embellishments in Scotch dialect, to the effect that Washington, laboring to get him to sell at a reasonable figure, reminded him at last that he owed something to the city, since he would have died a poor planter with no chance to sell at any price, had the capital not been located there. To which the Scotchman replied with emphasis:

"Aye, mon. An' had ye no' married the Widow Custis wi' her naygurs, you'd a' been a surveyor the day—an' a michty poor ane!"

It seems a pity to cast a slur upon such a neighborhood classic.

Mr. Burnes did hold out long enough to annoy the commissioners seriously. It is doubtful whether he attended the meeting at which Washington lectured the assembled landowners, but the general's logic appealed to his canny Scotch mind and when it came to signing the agreement, his was the second name put down. By these terms, dated the morning after Washington's little talk, the owners of land in the space between Rock Creek, the Potomac, and the Eastern Branch, a tract about three miles long and half that width, agreed to let the Government have so much of their holdings as it might need, at the rate of twenty-five pounds per acre.

The portion used for streets was not to be paid for. All other land required for public use was to be bought at the rate specified; lots were to be divided equally between the Government and the individuals making the sales, but proprietors would be entitled to the wood growing upon the lots they sold and might continue to use the lots deeded to the Government, until the latter found purchasers for them. Such buildings and graveyards as did not interfere with street plans might remain standing.

"This business being thus happily finished, . . . I left George-Town, dined in Alexandria and reached Mount Vernon in the evening," Washington recorded with satisfaction. It had been a wearisome experience. Even Nature had been on her bad behavior. His engagement to ride over the ground with Major L'Enfant had been kept in a thick mist. "From the unfavorableness of the day I derived no great satisfaction." But L'Enfant must have been in a seventh heaven, knowing now that he was to have the whole fair sweep of land upon which to erect the city of his dreams.

It is hard to imagine a man more variously and actively employed than he was during the succeeding months; going over the territory in detail, mapping out districts, writing reports, making sketches for public buildings, for gardens, for bridges and market-houses and canals; details not strictly within his province, perhaps, but which his fancy could not let alone.

In June, Washington came again—in better weather, let us hope—and rode over the ground with L'Enfant to choose locations for the "Legislative Halls" and the "President's Palace," the two buildings that must be erected, no matter what was left undone. Jenkins's Hill seemed to dominate the larger area, as it had the smaller one, and they determined upon it as the site for the Capitol. A tentative choice was also made for the President's House and for the executive offices. Washington wrote later that it was a mere "matter of moonshine" to him where these might be built; but, with his experience in New York and Philadelphia in mind, he took care to commend a site well removed from Jenkins's Hill.

Complications and misunderstandings having again arisen, the President was obliged on this occasion also to call landowners and commissioners together for explanations and admonitions. As usual, he was able to get deeds cheerfully signed and the signers were rewarded by a sight of the city plan, exhibited with the warning that "certain deviations might take place—particularly in the diagonal streets and avenues."

If L'Enfant's military eye saw in the radiating avenues a means of protecting the city in case of revolution from within, just as the chain of encircling hills would protect it against attacks from without, he loved them still more for the vistas they offered. That checkerboard plan of Old Babylon, dear to Jefferson, displeased his artist's soul. He called it "a mean contrivance of some cool imagination wanting a sense of the grand and truly beautiful." Yet it seems to have been from Jefferson's rough sketch that he drew the inspiration for what both of them called the "mall or public walk," a great stretch of park extending from the Capitol to the President's House, upon which the lesser public buildings were to face.

Water was to flow in abundance. Five large fountains spouting perpetual streams were to tumble in a great cascade to the foot of the Capitol Hill, and from there lagoons and canals, crossed by stately bridges, were to carry it to the Potomac. There were to be monuments and two towering columns; one, the starting-point from which to calculate distances to all places in the United States, the other, erected in view of the widening reaches of the river, to be a naval itinerary column, not only for measuring nautical miles to the ends of the earth but to commemorate the rise in the world of a new sea power. A park was to be allotted to each state, in which these states might erect monuments recording the good deeds of their own citizens. There was to be an impressive temple, dedicated to no creed but used for semi-religious public celebrations such as thanksgiving and funeral orations, a spot which in time might appropriately become the burial-place for the country's illustrious dead.

The whole plan was designed to "leave to posterity a grand idea of the patriotic interest which promoted it." It was a wonderful conception—a city the like of which had never been seen on earth; at once a golden New Jerusalem and a perpetual education in patriotism for the youths who were to walk its streets in centuries to come. No wonder it "received general approbation," as Washington wrote in his diary.

It was in turning such a glowing vision into fact that the pinch came. L'Enfant was invariably an optimist, at the beginning of an undertaking, and there was surely need for optimism. As he pointed out in his letter to General Washington when applying for the position, few capitals in the world's history have been deliberately built to order. The best-known instance of modern times, St. Petersburg on its flat morass, had little in the way of inspiration to offer, and it had been under construction for seventy years. Probably not even Tel-el-Amarna, built by Egyptian absolutism, had been made ready in a decade. It remained for Congress to decree this impossible thing, in a country where men worked or not as they chose, and where skilled workmen, willing or unwilling, were rare. L'Enfant did the best he could and poured out his genius and enthusiasm lavishly; but the commissioners developed ideas of their own, based on sordid trial balances and mathematical sums —mainly in subtraction.

L'Enfant, ridden by an idealism which was deaf and blind to mathematics, refused to recognize the authority of the commissioners or to take orders from any man except Washington.

Gently and considerately, at first, the President tried to reason with him. He might as well have reasoned with the wind. From small matters, the dissension spread to great ones. L'Enfant's refusal to hurry work on the preparation of plans which might be useful in selling lots; his quarrels with individuals, and an unaccountable repugnance to giving his plan, after it was made, into the hands of the engraver, all served as an undertone to his more spectacular altercation with the commissioners.

He ordered the foundations of the Capitol dug; the commissioners stopped the work because they had not been properly and officially consulted. The President tried more sternly to bring the major to a sense of his real position. L'Enfant continued to carry things with a high hand. Finally he ordered the demolition of "Duddington," a fine new house belonging to Daniel Carroll, a relative of the commissioner, because it happened to stand in the way of one of the projected avenues. The commissioners interfered and had Roberdeau, L'Enfant's assistant in charge of the work of demolition, arrested. L'Enfant finished the job himself and came near being jailed. Washington wrote to the commissioners and to L'Enfant, suggesting a compromise, since similar circumstances could scarcely be expected to arise again. The tone of his two letters was very different. To the commissioners he counseled patience, pointing out that the loss of Major L'Enfant would be a great misfortune; "I know not where another is to be found who could take his place," he wrote. But to the major he was peremptory: "In future I must strictly enjoin you to touch no man's property without his consent, or the previous order of the commissioners. . . . Having the beauty and regularity of your plan only in view, you pursue it as if every person and thing were obliged to yield to it."

That was exactly L'Enfant's belief. To him the beauty of the town was paramount, all else mere detail. Jefferson, a firm believer in the efficacy of little dinners, took occasion to invite L'Enfant to discuss the Federal City over a meal with him tête-à-tête, and between them a truce was patched up and compensation was made to Mr. Carroll. But the peace was temporary. The discovery that Notley Young was building a house in the middle of another projected street did nothing to make L'Enfant more amiable. The commissioners threatened to resign unless something were done to keep the major in his place, and charged him with gross extravagance. "If L'Enfant is made independent of the Commissioners, then the Treasury of the Union will not be adequate to the expense incurred," Dr. Stuart wrote.

In the last days of February, 1792, L'Enfant demanded that the commissioners be dismissed or that he be allowed to act independently; whereupon he was notified that his services were no longer needed. All the landowners of importance, with the two exceptions of Daniel Carroll and Notley Young, signed a testimonial expressing regret at his departure, and he left the District feeling ill-treated—a state of mind that lasted the rest of his life.

From this time his fortunes steadily declined. Whether or not personal habits aided his descent, is not clear. Vague hints in private letters and in the memorials which he addressed to Congress from time time indicate that this was so. His first claim upon Congress was for $95,000, calculated as follows: Services for one year, $6,000; profit that he had a right to expect from the sale of maps, $37,000; and $50,000 "for perquisites of right in particular negotiations and enterprises." Congress reckoned that it owed him $2500 or $3000, with a city lot thrown in for good measure. The claimant was rendered speechless by the discrepancy between the two sets of figures, and remained so for nearly eight years. He did, however, manage to refuse the money and lot offered him. In 1804, pressing needs made him ready to accept the smaller sum, and Congress passed a bill to pay him at the rate decided on by the commissioners, but he got none of the money himself, a creditor having obtained judgment. Two years later he applied to Congress for $300 or $400, which he still believed due him and which would enable him to pay a board bill and have about $100 to his credit. In 1810, another Congress voted to pay him $666.66 with accrued interest, amounting in all to a little less than $1400. Congress appears to have had, all the while, an uneasy feeling that it was treating shabbily this man who had rendered great services, whatever his personal faults.

He was occupied for a time with plans for a purely commercial city at Paterson, New Jersey, the first industrial town projected in the United States. Then he was retained by Robert Morris as architect of a magnificent private dwelling in Philadelphia, whose cost multiplied as its master's wealth decreased and which remained unfinished when Morris took up his residence in a debtor's prison.

In 1812, Madison urged L'Enfant to accept an appointment as military instructor at West Point, which he declined. Like an uneasy spirit, condemned to haunt the scene of its greatest achievement, he drifted back to Washington. After the British attack, he helped care for the wounded, and a month later he was directing a force of fifty laborers with spades and axes in work at Fort Washington. Even this pitiful commission was taken from him before completion, because of his inability to carry it on with reasonable economy.

For eleven years he wandered about the city, growing, with increasing poverty, daily more like *Don Quixote*. Children pointed at him or stood, finger on lip, arrested by the pathos of his queer old figure, with a faithful dog following at his heels. Congressmen had a way of miraculously vanishing at his approach. Sometimes he stopped for a "friendly glass of wine" with some acquaintance of old days with whom he yet felt at liberty to consort; and then his courtly ways and elaborate politeness belied the unhappiness gnawing at his heart.

At last, when his fortunes had reached their lowest ebb, Dudley Diggs, one of those good souls who exist in the world to keep alive a fading faith in Providence, wrote him this charming letter.

> I have to inform you that it will give me pleasure if you will come up and take your residence here. I have furnished George with what articles you may stand in need of at present; you will also be able to visit the city house at your ease and as often as you may please in order to attend to your business before Congress. . . . You may rest assured my Dear Sir, that I have considered your situation and know it has been an unpleasant one; if a hearty welcome to Green Hill will make it more pleasant, I can assure you you have it from all my family.

Here, in the vicinity of Silver Spring, not far from the old manor of "Clean Drinking," Major L'Enfant passed the last years of his life and laid out a wonderful garden, patterned after his beloved plan of the city, traces of which may yet be followed in fragmentary patches of box and hedge. And here, under the trees, he was buried when death claimed him at last.

He was in actual command of the work of laying out the capital only one short year,—the critical first year,—and in it he did a tremendous amount of constructive work, as we can see now, though to his exasperated fellow-workers he appeared to be muddling everything he touched. His great achievement was to conceive the plan, which he did so brilliantly that his genius has dominated all his successors, bad and good, in the century and a quarter since he reluctantly gave up his task. Even the most indifferent of them, in the worst periods of sloth and civic carelessness, never quite dared to spoil his plan, however much they marred it.

He was by no means a hero. Something unpleasantly like a whine crept into his appeals to Congress, and most of his unhappiness and misfortune undoubtedly came from his own faults. Far from heroic, he is nevertheless a striking and picturesque figure in Washington's early history, a figure half grand, even at his worst; tall and elegant in his prosperity, appealing and pathetic in the bitter days when his old bell-crowned hat and surtout had become painfully shabby and the dog at his heels was the one creature in the whole wide world who believed in him whole-heartedly and without reservation.

Looking back at L'Enfant in the cold light of history, without considering justice or even moral worth, thinking only of the city's good, it seems a benign interposition of Providence that lent us this mind from Cloudland long enough to make the wonderful plan, and then removed him before disorder and impractical extravagance ruined it and us beyond repair.

III

A LODGE IN THE WILDERNESS

IT was Andrew Ellicott who stepped into L'Enfant's shoes. Having been on the ground longer than L'Enfant himself, he was not unfamiliar with the difficulties he assumed; nor were they unknown to his assistant, Roberdeau, who had been arrested for helping to pull down the Carroll mansion. Ellicott was fortunate in having three other helpers of his own choosing—his two brothers, Benjamin and Joseph, and the negro prodigy Benjamin Banneker, a self-taught astronomer, who looked, in his beaver hat and suit of Quaker gray, like a dark-skinned Benjamin Franklin, though he was really the grandson of an African prince and a characterful English wench, transported to the colonies for the theft of a pail of milk.

Even with a whole regiment of able and congenial assistants, Ellicott's task must have been difficult, owing to lack of time, funds, and laborers, striving to make up for which he worked harder than any mortal should. "I eat alone in the office to which I confine myself as closely as a bear to his den in winter," he wrote his wife. "I have scarcely time to shave or comb my head. . . . I have spoken but to one female, and to her but once for a week past." His day did in truth begin by candle-light, and lasted well into the night. Washington once described him as a man of "more placid temper" than L'Enfant and of "uncommon talents"; but even his placidity gave way when he saw that, in spite of his efforts, the commissioners feared that the year 1800 would not see the task completed. Urging haste, they complained in a breath of all he did and all he did not do. Having a more logical mind than L'Enfant, he sometimes came off victor in arguments with them; but this did not increase their love for him nor his for them. Before the year was over he sent in his resignation, to take effect on the first of May, 1793. The commissioners responded that he need not wait that long, but might consider himself discharged and take his staff with him. Washington assumed his periodic rôle of peacemaker, but the State of Pennsylvania offering Ellicott an important commission of roadbuilding about this time, he soon departed, though one of his brothers remained.

Ellicott's chief work had been to redraw L'Enfant's plan of the city, the Frenchman having refused to allow the use of his plans after his quarrel with the commissioners. Ellicott did the best he could from memory, aided by personal knowledge of the ground; so the final plan of the city is virtually all L'Enfant's in conception, and all Ellicott's in detail. This explains the mysterious dropping out of striking features of the original scheme, like the arcaded shops on East Capitol Street, the naval column, a great national church, and the cascades that were to tumble from the base of the Capitol into the Potomac.

After Ellicott's departure, the commissioners preferred to trust the execution of the plan to subordinates who would report directly to them, rather than risk the appointment of another superintendent who might develop troublesome views of his own. Washington did not think this wise, his military training leading him to believe that some one man "of skill and judgment, of industry and integrity" should not only be in charge, but be required to live in the District, the commissioners at that time being at liberty to reside where they would. He pointed out that they could not possibly obtain at their quarterly meetings the detailed information which a resident would acquire as a matter of course. The commissioners had their way, however, and for a time work was carried on, a bit here and a bit there, according to individual capacity and the momentary state of finances. Little resembling a town was to be seen, and as the months and years rolled along toward the date of removal, the chief change seemed to be that chaos spread over an ever-increasing area. L'Enfant's plan was too excellent to be given up; but it took a century to prove conclusively how good it was, and the city grew in haphazard fashion, as might have been expected upon ground that had belonged originally to a colony founded "on smoke."

Looked at with practical, unimaginative common sense, the enterprise was fantastic in the extreme. In the first place building capital cities from the ground up is "not done." Granted that it can be done, a decade is a ridiculously short time to allow for extensive building projects anywhere, even where money and materials and skilled labor may be had in abundance, let alone in the woods and abandoned tobacco fields of Virginia. The choice of a site had been thrust upon the country unfairly, as many thought, by Hamilton, a brilliant interloper who was a foreigner by birth and had no right to meddle in the matter anyway. The man who designed the city was a foreigner also and so impractical that he had never been able to bring one of his plans to completion. Upon this foundation of smoke and moonshine, the methods of work were casual at best. Not one of the first three commissioners had experience of a helpful kind. What could Dr. Stuart, a country practitioner "of Hope Park and Ossian Hall"; Daniel Carroll, a despotic Southern planter (albeit a benevolent despot); and Thomas Johnson, a lawyer with a hot temper and a plentiful command of invective, know about building cities? During the first two years of actual building, the cash the commissioners had at their disposal as the result of selling lots was about sixteen thousand dollars, though the payment of Maryland's grant, and the partial payment of money voted by Virginia raised the sum to one less pitifully inadequate.

The first sale of government lots took place about the middle of October, 1791, and in advertising it the "Maryland Journal" extolled the plan of the town as "an inconceivable improvement upon all other cities in the world, combining not only convenience, regularity, elegance of prospect and a free circulation of air, but everything grand and beautiful that can possibly be introduced into a city," adding the prediction that it would "not only produce amazement in Europe, but meet the admiration of all future ages."

These were ambitious words. But when the seventeenth of October arrived there was little to prove them, except a hand-drawn plan for exhibition in the dark and crowded public room of Suter's tavern in Georgetown. Even the ground itself could not be seen, for Nature seemed to hold a grudge against the city project and sent such a deluge of rain that it was impossible to hold the sale out of doors, or to give those who attended it a sight of the lots for which they were invited to pay their good money. The innkeeper furnished plenty of wine and firewood to dispel the gloom indoors (for which later he sent his bill to the commissioners), and Washington and Jefferson and Madison all made a point of being present on the first day of the sale. But the purchasers were not impressive, either in numbers or in importance. Dr. Stuart said disparagingly that they came mostly "from the Westward," a place for which he had little respect, since the classics did not flourish there. Next day he was cheered by the sight of gentlemen from Norfolk and the Carolinas; but by the end of the third day purchasers from all points of the compass had faded away, and the sale came to an end with a total of thirty-five lots sold at prices aggregating $8756; of which only about $2000 was available in cash.

This could not rouse enthusiasm, but the advocates of the site upon the Potomac had pledged themselves to carry on the work if possible without asking Congressional aid. Juggling with words and with hope in the way real-estate dealers have done since landowning became a matter of fees and parchments, the commissioners made a fine show of contentment, basing their calculations on the average price paid and conveniently ignoring the number of lots sold. Washington indulged in the same kind of mathematics when he assured Congress that "there is a prospect favored by the rate of sales which have already taken place, of ample funds for carrying on the necessary public buildings"; but persons less deeply involved expressed the frank opinion that the prices paid were too high and that only President Washington's interest in the Federal City kept it alive. In the event of his death, they said, it would instantly collapse.

The great need of the moment was to nurse enthusiasm and get enough building done, or at least begun, to convince a doubting public that the project would go through. Washington was well aware of this and urged that work upon the public buildings be pushed forward, pointing out the danger which might threaten the whole scheme if this were neglected. Thereafter it became a sort of race between the new town, heavily handicapped, to prepare shelter for the Government within the specified time, and Philadelphia, which lost no chance, by caustic phrase or innuendo, to accent the value of the fleshpots Congress was then enjoying as its guest and might continue to enjoy so long as it chose to remain.

Washington's desire was that the public buildings in the new city should be ample and dignified; and not even his keen appreciation of the need for haste swerved him from the belief that both in size and elegance they "should look beyond the present day." He hastened to explain:

> I would not have it understood from hence that I lean to extravagance. A chaste plan sufficiently capacious and convenient for a period not too remote . . . would be my idea for the Capitol. For the President's House I would design a building which could also look forward, but execute no more of it at present than might suit the circumstances of this country when it shall be first wanted.

L'Enfant in his first enthusiasm had made sketches for a President's House and a capitol, and other important buildings, in hours which should have been spent in developing the city plan. While they were not far enough advanced for actual use, or had been rendered useless through his quarrel and dismissal, it is very possible that these mirage sketches of his set a standard which served the country well. His wish for the President's House had been to combine "the sumptuousness of a palace and the agreeableness of a country seat," and a union of these very qualities was found in the plan drawn by James Hoban, an Irish-American resident of South Carolina. He modeled it partly on the Vice-Regal Lodge of his native Dublin, and partly on the lines of a luxurious plantation home to be set, like all the luxurious plantation homes of its period, in a broad park facing the river. This plan came into possession of the commissioners so early and so easily that actual work upon the mansion was begun late in 1792, a second sale of lots being arranged in December, to take advantage of whatever enthusiasm might develop during the laying of its corner-stone.

Finding a suitable plan for the Capitol proved much more difficult. Funds were at the moment so low that the commissioners were forced to borrow the five hundred dollars offered as a prize in the competition; and it seemed quite in keeping with the casual nature of the whole affair that the winning contestant should be not a trained architect but only a wealthy amateur, and, like Hamilton, a native of the West Indies. The capital of our country is therefore indebted to that little spattering of islands in the Caribbean Sea, not only for its location, but for the outlines of its most important building. The many-sided man who carried off the prize was William Thornton, possessor of a degree of M.D. from the University of Edinburgh, though doctoring was the one thing in life in which he took no interest. He was a traveler, a patron of inventors, an essayist on literary subjects, an illustrator of books upon natural history, advocate of teaching oral speech to deaf-mutes; altogether, as an old notice tells us, "a scholar and a gentleman full of talent and eccentricity," whose "company was a complete antidote to dullness."

This was not his first incursion into architecture, for while in Philadelphia, engaged in courting an American wife, he had chanced upon a newspaper advertisement of a forthcoming competition for plans for the public library. Though ignorant of practical construction, and not particularly interested in buildings during his travels abroad, he got together a few books, labored a few days, and won the contest—a success that did little to curb his self-esteem. We learn from a stray bit of autobiography, however, that in preparation for this more serious trial, he "studied some months, and worked almost day and night." The design he submitted was so far superior to the others in beauty that there was no question of its acceptance, but, true to the casual manner in which things were being done, his plan for the Capitol must have been chosen entirely "on its looks," since it was unaccompanied by estimates.

It became the thankless task of the man who just missed success, Stephen Hallet, whose plan was adjudged second best, to take the design of the versatile doctor and reduce it to a working basis. As a professional architect he soon became convinced that it was impractical at any cost; and the scene was set and the curtain rung up on a second quarrel, a deal more involved and quite as protracted as the dispute between L'Enfant and the commissioners and Ellicott about the real authorship of the city plan.

In September, 1793, the corner-stone of the Capitol was laid with all possible pomp, as befitted the important occasion. Two bands of music marched in the procession which moved from the President's Square to the spot where the exercises took place. Masonic lodges from three towns participated; volleys of Virginia artillery punctuated the orations and prayers; and Washington himself was present in three separate capacities—as world-famous general, as member of the ancient fraternity of masons, and as President of the United States. The silver plate deposited in the cavity under the stone had engraved upon it the fact that the ceremony took place in the thirteenth year of American independence, in the first year of the second term of the presidency of George Washington, and in the year of masonry 5793—a comprehensive linking together of ancient and modern history. After the stone was declared truly and fittingly laid, festivities were continued under an "extensive" booth near by, a barbecued ox weighing five hundred pounds being the central feature, surrounded with "every abundance of other refreshment."

This sounds lavish and stately and sophisticated; but when we learn that the procession with its two bands of music and masonic lodges from three towns was unable to move along Pennsylvania Avenue for the excellent reason that the street had not yet been cut through swamps and standing timber, and that as it descended from the new post-road on the F Street ridge toward the Tiber, which wound through Thomas Pope's old farm at the base of Capitol Hill, the trombones and Worshipful Grand Masters and government officials and members of the Virginia artillery had to break ranks and cross the water in their individual capacity, on horseback or by means of the foot-bridge made of a single log, we gain a truer idea of conditions after two years of actual labor.

"The Potomac Almanac or the Washington Ephemeris for 1793," a publication that hastened to secure the distinction of a Washington date line, though its printing was perforce done elsewhere, described the town as being in "a great variety of detached pieces." The two principal pieces were the President's House, which had now been under construction about a year, and the jumble of stones and workmen's huts so lately assembled on Jenkins's Hill. A third imposing "piece" was a large brick building with stone trimmings in process of erection not far from the road on the F Street ridge at the point where it dipped toward the Tiber. This, though important enough to be regarded as semi-official, was really the property of a private individual, one of that group of enterprising, blundering well-wishers who at the outset made large investments in the District and reaped larger losses for themselves and others. Samuel Blodgett, Jr., of New Hampshire, owner of the stone and brick building, was an early American writer upon economics, and the first American, it is said, to form a joint stock company. It was he who lent the commissioners the five hundred dollars offered as a prize in the competition for a capitol plan.

He had purchased in January, 1792, for 39,520 Mexican dollars, the tract called Jamaica, which stretched northeast across the city-to-be from the point we now know as Dupont Circle, and, having become a landowner, immediately began to take a prominent part in local affairs. His first venture was the unlucky bridge across Rock Creek at K Street, which toppled into the creek instead of playing its expected part as connecting link between the unbuilt wilds of Washington and the already compact and comfortable little city of Georgetown. But since another had designed its faulty arches, this disaster could not be laid to his charge and it was regarded purely as a misfortune. In January, 1793, Blodgett was appointed Supervisor of Buildings, for the period of one year, the commissioners having meantime come around to the opinion expressed by Washington that some person resident in the District should be in authority.

Blodgett was an agreeable companion, the master of good hunting-dogs and a keen sportsman, and clever at making sketches besides. He may have been an excellent theorizer upon economics, but his practice developed in a manner most unfortunate. On the very first day of his official connection with the commissioners, he proposed to them the scheme for aiding city finances by means of a lottery, of which his fifty-thousand-dollar brick and stone building, a hotel designed by the architect of the President's palace, should serve as the grand prize. Lotteries being considered at the time perfectly legitimate business ventures, his proposal was accepted, and even General Washington participated to the extent of buying at least one ticket, which he passed on to the little son of his friend and former secretary, Tobias Lear, with a note expressing the hope that it might draw the big prize.

Although the hotel's corner-stone had been laid with every festal observance on the national holiday in 1793, and work had been pushed in order to make an impressive showing on the great day when the Capitol's corner-stone was laid, neither the hotel nor the lottery prospered. The building was never finished as a hotel, though it had a varied career of after uses, and the lottery proved Blodgett's undoing. His effort to retrieve the losses of this first one, by a "Federal Lottery No. 2," impressed the commissioners and General Washington as grasping and misleading both in name and fact, "Federal" giving it an official sound which was wholly unwarranted. His service as superintendent had not measured up to expectations, and at the end of the year he found himself not only relieved from further duty but under suspicion of dealings not quite honorable.

As the president of a bank, Blodgett made another effort to reëstablish himself, but constantly falling fortunes landed him, by 1802, in a debtor's prison, from which only the kindness of Dr. Thornton enabled him to walk abroad (within limits) "for the benefit of his health." When, one day, he overstepped these limits and failed to return, it cost his benefactor ten thousand dollars. But he came back to the District at the first opportunity to practise those uneasy and picturesque subterfuges common to men of his hopeful, improvident, visionary kind, who talk in large figures and advocate measures of ornate civic usefulness. His pet project in these later years was a monument to the Father of his Country; and it is said that even while in prison he solicited five-dollar subscriptions toward the founding of a great national university.

Other gentlemen who came to the city for the purpose of investing greater or larger sums fared scarcely better, and the account of the town's early decades is largely a record of fallen fortunes and often of smirched reputations.

The Government confined its operations to erecting the White House and the Capitol, and an office building of brick trimmed with stone, destined for the exclusive use of the Treasury, but which temporarily had to shelter the Department of State as well. It was thrown together hurriedly by contract for the bargain-counter figure of $39,511, just before the Government took possession, and stood not far from the southeast corner of the President's House, being the first of four similar buildings planned and in time erected at the four corners of the White-House grounds.

Rivers were still the natural highways of trade, and the promoters of the city believed the junction of the Eastern Branch with the Potomac a foreordained site of commerce, since at that point there was what the "Potomac Almanac" claimed "might justly be considered one of the safest harbors in the United States." It will be remembered that Jefferson's sketch plan emphasized the commercial aspect of the town and that L'Enfant had embellished his plan for this part of it with arcaded shops and other elegances for business *de luxe*. To prove that Washington shared the belief in its commercial future, we have his letter telling how "to prevent jealousy," and while President he bought lots at each end of the town, "valuable in my estimation for different purposes; those on the Eastern Branch on account of commerce, which I always did and still do think will centre there, the other as a site for a private gentleman to live at."

Perhaps the commissioners thought the natural advantages of the city so attractive that it needed no attention from them. In any case, they had no money to spend upon it, and this section lay undisturbed until two gentlemen of wealth, who came frankly to speculate, chose it as the scene of their enterprises. One was a young man of twenty-seven, James Greenleaf, of the Massachusetts family which gave us the poet Whittier. He arrived a few months after Blodgett, just in time to witness the laying of the corner-stone of the Capitol, and within a week had laid large plans of his own and made larger purchases, by reason of which Turkey-Buzzard Point became Greenleaf's Point, and rows of buildings, out of keeping with their country surroundings, soon began to rise on the level land between the Capitol and the Potomac. But these had a history more dismal even than Blodgett's hotel; financial disaster overtook their owner before they were finished, and they stood rotting until their roofs fell in, useful only as the objects of endless lawsuits.

Greenleaf had brought with him a letter of introduction from President Washington, stating not only the young man's purpose to build houses if conditions seemed to justify it, but that he had recently been appointed United States Consul at Amsterdam, where, during a former residence as vice-consul, he had persuaded Dutch bankers to make a loan on American security. An angel from heaven could not have been more welcome to the commissioners at that moment, harassed as they were for funds; and on his offer personally to furnish them with $2200 a month at 6 per cent. until the public buildings were finished, provided he could show his friends the Dutch bankers a title to Washington real estate, they made it very easy for him to purchase three thousand lots upon terms better than they had heretofore been willing to grant.

But he never went back to Holland. The disturbed condition of Europe had something to do with this, as did forebodings of what would befall him personally should he chance to meet the titled Dutch lady he had ardently wooed and married, but had left behind on sailing for America. After he had taken to wife a virtuous daughter of Pennsylvania, these last considerations assumed even more weight.

Although he did not come to reside in the District until 1826, he plunged at once into speculation, associating with him Robert Morris and John Nicholson, the Comptroller General of Pennsylvania, whose great fortunes were then on the point of vanishing like fairy gold. The magnitude of Greenleaf's transactions and the association of the affluent-sounding names of the other two men with his own, gave a decided impetus to real-estate transactions in the eastern end of the city in 1794.

A man whose name is usually pronounced in the same breath with that of Greenleaf was Thomas Law, who came to Washington two years later and "put up in Georgetown because there was only one little tavern in the city." He had made a fortune in the East Indies, but on returning to his native England had found himself out of sympathy with conditions there. Having met Mr. Greenleaf and secured an option on some property from him, he came to inspect it and was sufficiently pleased to take up his residence in the District at once. Although still under forty, he had lived through a varied gamut of experience in the Orient, and brought from there three well-grown sons to remind him of it; but he began all over again in Washington, with the ardor of youth, let his imagination catch fire at the possibilities of the city's future, looked deep into the eyes of Mrs. Washington's granddaughter, Elizabeth Parke Custis, married her, and settled down to spend the remainder of his life. This proved to be long and somewhat bitter, yet egotism and brilliant eccentricity enabled him to get more satisfaction out of it than falls to the lot of average mortals.

While these gentlemen and a few others, not so picturesque nor so prominent, were working for their own ends, progress upon the government buildings continued in hit-or-miss fashion. The number of workmen varied according to the season and the supply of funds, which was always far below the needs of the undertaking. A letter written by a young stone-mason to his parents in London on July 4, 1795, reported that:

> Excepting the Capitol and President's house all the other buildings are begun by a parcel of adventurers and speculators. . . . There are ten stone-masons employed at the Capitol and seventeen at the President's Palace, with five more at different places, and that is the whole amount of our profession in Virginia and Maryland, as the people have no taste for stone work, it being so very expensive.

Only the north wing of the oldest part of the Capitol was being built. Whether the workmen were few or many, the matter of first securing them and afterward keeping them was a serious problem, of a kind which had already been faced by the builders of the canal locks in the vicinity of Great Falls. Very likely it was his knowledge of the difficulties they encountered which prompted Washington to urge securing artisans from abroad; particularly "redemptioners" from Germany, who were said to be steady and industrious, and might be secured at reasonable rates. He also thought Scotland a good field. He wrote:

The more I consider this subject, the more I am convinced of the expediency of importing a number of workmen. . . . The measure has not only economy to recommend it, but it is important by placing the quantity of labor which may be performed by such persons upon a certainty for the term for which they shall be engaged.

The trouble canal officials had experienced with runaways, in spite of cropping polls and shaving eyebrows to make dashes for home unpopular, caused the good President to long for wide stretches of water between the workmen and their native land.

But the scheme for importing laborers came to nothing, wars in Europe having claimed virtually every able-bodied man for their own. The bells which rang at the Capitol and the White House at sunrise, to call workmen to their tasks, and at sunset to release them, sounded mainly for American ears; and another of the anomalies and contrasts which abound in the town's early history, is that the home prepared for the Government in this Land of the Free, was built largely by slave labor, for which the commissioners offered wages of twenty-one pounds a year, the masters of "good laboring negroes" being required to see that each had sufficient clothes and a blanket, while the commissioners undertook to provide them with suitable food.

Native or foreign, bond or free, all had healthy appetites; and those contractors who undertook to turn an honest penny by furnishing "an equal number of fore and hind quarters" from which to carve their daily ration of a pound and a quarter of beef, and to see that each man quarrying stone down on the Quay of Quays in August and September had his sustaining daily half-pint of whisky, had troubles of their own. The nature of these is easy to surmise from announcements like this, printed in the local papers: "Mr. Brent has had no profit on the May ration. He is therefore to be allowed thirteen pence Virginia currency per ration for the June, July and August rations."

From the Beginnings of Washington by P. L. Philipps.

WASHINGTON IN 1801

By the time half the years allotted for preparation had rolled by, there were in the District of Columbia half a dozen well-defined scenes of building activity, some federal and some due to private speculation. Between them were long-undisturbed stretches of field and swamp and woodland, over which old lanes and bridle-paths wandered from country house to country house, regardless of the new city plan. One by one, however, changes occurred which marked decisive steps in the coming of urban conditions, a permit to sell liquor within the city limits being among the earliest.

As time went by, more and more gashes of felled trees marked where streets that already had names were going to be, though no houses might be built upon them for years to come. The avenues in the northern section were called after Northern states, those in the southern part of town after the states of the South. One by one, privileges hitherto enjoyed by the original owners of the ground were curtailed. An order signed by the commissioners went forth forbidding the cultivation of corn upon land whose title had passed to the Government; the reason given being that its growth obscured the view of possible purchasers. Oats, not being open to the same objection, might still be planted.

The Bank of Columbia, organized in Georgetown for the convenience of commissioners and lot-buyers, started on a long career, its first president being the discredited Mr. Blodgett. A printing-press was imported from Norfolk and set up on Greenleaf's Point to issue the first number of the "Impartial Observer and Washington Advertiser," earliest in that long line of impartial journals which have sought vainly to sustain life upon Washington soil. A post-office was opened to obviate the delay and annoyance of having letters held in Alexandria until somebody remembered to send the seven miles for them.

After he had convinced the authorities that the road running past his home on F Street was sufficiently good to warrant it, a man named Johnson was made postmaster. From his house mails started north and south three times a week at an inordinately early hour in the morning. Possibly that was the reason the position was so singularly fatal. Mr. Johnson and his successor were in their graves before a year had rolled by, and life looked dark to Lund Washington, another incumbent. The Postmaster General wrote him from Philadelphia late in 1796:

> I am much obliged to you for your information as to the condition in which the mails have arrived at your office. . . . The mail is of too much importance to be carried any longer under the driver's feet, and I shall endeavor to prevent it in future.

And six weeks later:

> You will be allowed to charge 30 per cent commissions on the two winter quarters in which you are engaged with the mails three times a week at five o'clock in the morning, which is a very unseasonable hour to be obliged to rise at.

Early rising made Lund Washington neither healthy, nor wealthy, nor wise. An unfortunate partiality to drink caused his dismissal as a defaulter, and, like Robert Morris, Greenleaf, Nicholson, and others, he spent some time in a debtors' prison. Prison society was really excellent in those days.

About this period a toll-bridge was built across the Potomac, which La Rochefoucauld criticized as disgusting in the quantity of timber and iron wasted upon it. But at least it was finished and in use, thanks to the public spirit of John Templeton, "who gratuitously engaged in the superintendence of the work." Mr. Templeton was a born benefactor; fifteen years before, he had appeared out of the void to dazzle Bladensburg boys with his deeds of prowess upon a tight-rope; and here he was again, at middle age, in the character of a benevolent merchant and engineer.

By the end of the year of 1795 the walls of the north wing of the Capitol—the only part even begun—had reached the height of the first story, while the White House was almost ready to receive its roof. But the cash-box was empty, and an appeal to Congress could no longer be delayed. In view of this it was unfortunate that the relative progress on the two buildings was not reversed, for to a certain type of well-meaning congressman the fact that the President's House was the farther advanced was in itself an affront. Washington, who had a serviceable share of worldly wisdom in his make-up, had warned the commissioners of just this danger and urged them to make all possible speed upon Jenkins's Hill.

He transmitted the memorial of the commissioners to Congress in a message that was tactful in the extreme but served only to open up again the whole question of the location of the seat of government. A broad inquiry was ordered, including the wisdom of having a Federal City at all, and running through charges of mismanagement and misdemeanor, to the question whether the plans of the public buildings might not be altered to make the White House serve the uses of Congress, since that structure was indecently gorgeous for the home of a republican president.

The commissioners were now an entirely different set of men, Dr. Stuart having returned to his private practice and study of the classics and his confreres withdrawn because of ill health, or ill temper due to the friction of the position. Dr. Thornton was one of the present group; another was Alexander White, whose vote had been won for the District by Hamilton, at Jefferson's dinner party. Being experienced in congressional ways, he hastened to Philadelphia to explain that up to that moment not a penny of government money had been used, and that even yet no appropriation was asked, all that was desired being permission to make government real estate the basis of a loan. He found the rôle of lobbyist difficult, however, his former colleagues melting away mysteriously at his approach; but after a delay of several months Congress unenthusiastically granted the desired permission and agreed that on the whole it would not be wise to try to remodel the White House.

After this, renewed building activity set in, inspired partly by the victory just gained and partly by the nearness of the new century. Perhaps it was because of this Congressional investigation—at any rate, it was about the time it occurred—that the commissioners decided to open Pennsylvania Avenue from the President's House to the Capitol; a showy bit of work repeatedly urged upon them, but which they had delayed, as they gave the "obstinate Mr. Burnes" to understand, because of their unwillingness to incommode him and his growing crops. The opening of this broad street made a sort of causeway through the central swamp, and did much to bind the two principal "detached pieces" of the city together, but even yet the connection was, to quote a distinguished visitor, "quite loose."

Visitors, distinguished and otherwise, were coming to gaze upon the experiment in city-building. Volney, Niemcewicz, Kosciusko, Louis Philippe and his brothers, Richard Parkinson, La Rochefoucauld, and Von Humboldt, all visited it and delivered their opinions. Whether the verdict was favorable or not depended upon the observer's cast of mind. Parkinson, whose practical aim was money-making, was disappointed, but Francis Baily, a future English astronomer and F. R. S., saw the city's tenantless radiating avenues in 1796 and pronounced them admirable, his mind being used to bridging interstellar spaces. He wrote:

> The truth is that not much more than half the city is cleared. The rest is in woods, and most of the streets which are laid out are cut through these woods, and have a much more pleasing effect now than I think they will have when they shall be built. . . . Now they appear like broad avenues in a park, bounded on each side by thick woods, and there being so many of them, and proceeding in so many directions, they have a certain wild yet uniform and regular appearance which they will lose when confined on each side by brick walls.

At a period considerably later, a French lady described Washington as "a city of streets without houses," while Georgetown, whose handsome homes were set in gardens, she called a town made up of houses without streets.

Travelers who lacked imagination and to whom a city meant something finished, were either puzzled or scandalized to find that this odd place was scarcely begun. Mr. Parkinson had dreamed of adding a brewery to its civilizing influences, but concluded that it was "too young" for such a luxury. If the traveler had his mind prepared beforehand by the orderly map hanging over the fireplace at the inn in Bladensburg, he was even more mystified. One gentleman who diligently studied the streets and buildings portrayed on this, continued his journey next day in the rain and rode for hours, in a coach with its curtains drawn, without being conscious of passing so much as a blacksmith shop; yet was told on reaching

Georgetown that he had driven through the nation's capital from end to end. Next day he rode back to find and call upon his friend Mr. Law; blundered into the building activity upon Jenkins's Hill; was directed to Greenleaf's Point, where Mr. Law had by this time built a house upon the river front; lost his way in a morass; managed to attract the notice of a gentleman in a distant coach and on coming up to it, found Mr. Law himself, who forthwith took possession of him. As his guest he was made so comfortable that he fell completely under the spell of Washington and its ways, and in his journal wrote sentimental accounts of the visit, including a moonlight evening when he was becalmed upon the Potomac in company with another house guest of the Laws—a lady who wrote "elegant" poetry.

His was a common experience. A traveler might come to wonder or to criticize, but if he lingered to partake of the city's bread and salt, he forgot all except the beauty of its setting and the hospitality of his friends. For a place of its size it already had an unusually large circle of well-to-do, cultured people who kept up old customs—a circle made up not only of new-comers like the Thorntons and the Laws, but old residents like the Carrolls, born and bred in the neighborhood and in the best English traditions.

Already a population of from three thousand to five thousand was hidden away in this apparent solitude. One third of it was black, slave and free, the rest contained representatives of many nations. Scotch and English had come up long before from the sea, by way of Chesapeake Bay and the Potomac; Dutch and Germans arrived a little later from Pennsylvania; and there were in addition French refugees lately escaped from the Terror, besides laborers of assorted nationalities, chiefly Irish, who had drifted in since the building of the town began. The well-to-do were always willing to stop and play to honor a visiting stranger, hence the water excursions and dinner companies and tea-drinkings which crowd every record of a visit to the city.

When there was no visitor to entertain, the inhabitants were equally ready to assemble for the purpose of laying a new cornerstone. What was to happen to the building afterward lay upon the knees of the gods. Their business was to give it a good send-off. So, down the wooded alleys would come fifty or more gentlemen wearing masonic regalia, six or a dozen musicians blowing and pounding upon their instruments in more or less harmony, a reverend individual in bands to make a prayer or deliver an oration, and a suitable number of prosperous-looking landowners in shorts and satin waistcoats to form an audience and join afterward in toasts and felicitations at the barbecue. If ladies chanced to be present, they were invariably well dressed and usually good-looking.

After the Congressional investigation of 1796 had settled all doubts about the Government's taking possession of its new home, there was a rush to enter the hotel business. The house vacated by the Laws, on the brow of Capitol Hill, was occupied as an inn; Mr. Tunnicliff, who operated a well-established hostelry, the Eastern Branch Hotel on Pennsylvania Avenue, S. E., near Ninth Street,—an excellent location on the road leading into town from the ferry,—put up a much more elegant building near the Capitol, where President Adams lodged during his first visit to the city in June 1800; and the Little Hotel, on F Street ridge not far from Fifteenth, next door to the late Thomas Johnson's post-office, was already a favorite, proximity to the White House being deemed almost as desirable as nearness to the Capitol.

The Little Hotel soon had a rival in Lovell's, and about this time advertisements of the Franklin House appeared, signed by William O'Neil, a name destined to long familiarity, even to notoriety, in Washington—not because he was keeper of a perfectly satisfactory tavern, but because he happened to be the father of a not entirely satisfactory daughter, a lively young person named Peggy, who set the whole town by the ears in Jackson's day and almost disrupted the cabinet. Her father's hotel began thus early, in a small way, in a three-story brick dwelling near the spot where Twentieth Street runs into Pennsylvania Avenue. But it met all the requirements of the Maryland and Virginia statutes, which demanded that the keeper of a public house at a county seat be able to supply "six good feather beds with sufficient covering for the same, and stabling for ten horses." These modest figures explain why, when the transfer of the Government from Philadelphia actually occurred, so few persons could be comfortably taken care of in the new city.

Albert Gallatin, who called Washington "a hateful place," wrote his wife exactly what was to be seen there by unimaginative eyes:

> . . . Around the Capitol are seven or eight boarding houses, one tailor, one shoemaker, one printer, a washing-woman, a grocery shop, a pamphlets and stationary shop, a small dry-goods shop and an oyster house. This makes the whole of the Federal City as connected with the Capitol.

We can take our choice as to which of these shops carried the stock praised by Mrs. Thornton, who stopped as she passed while making a round of calls and found it "a better hardware store than any in Georgetown."

> At the distance of three-fourths of a mile, on or near the Eastern Branch, lie scattered the habitations of Mr. Law and of Mr. Carroll, the principal proprietaries of the ground, half a dozen houses, a very large but perfectly empty warehouse, and a wharf graced by not a single vessel. And this makes the whole intended commercial part of the city, unless we include in it what is called the Twenty Buildings, being so many unfinished houses commenced by Morris and Nicholson, and perhaps as many undertaken by Greenleaf, both which groups lie, at a distance of a half-mile from each other near the mouth of the Eastern Branch and the Potowmack, and are divided by a large swamp from the Capitol Hill and the little village connected with it. Taking a contrary direction from the Capitol towards the President's House the same swamp intervenes, and a straight causeway, which measures one mile and a half and seventeen perches, forms the communication between the two buildings. A small stream, about the size of the largest of the two runs between Claire's and our house and decorated with the pompous appellation of "Tyber" feeds without draining the swamps, and along that causeway (called the Pennsylvania Avenue) between the Capitol and the President's House not a single house intervenes, or can intervene without devoting its wretched tenant to perpetual fevers. From the President's House to Georgetown the distance is not quite a mile and a half, the ground is high and level the public offices and from 50 to 100 good houses are finished; the President's House is a very elegant building and this part of the city, on account of its natural

situation, of its vicinity to Georgetown, with which it communicates over Rock Creek by two bridges, and by the concourse of people drawn by having business with the public offices, will improve considerably, and may within a short time form a town equal in size and population to Lancaster or Annapolis.

The most elastic imagination, working overtime, could count only 370 houses that ought to be called habitable, though it was hoped 750 might be made ready during the next eighteen months. Two thirds of the available buildings were made of wood, a material which had been prohibited in the earliest building regulations, but it had speedily been found necessary to modify that rule if the city was to be built at all.

Georgetown meanwhile had profited not only by the proximity of the new city but in other ways. Its tobacco trade might not be so great as formerly, but it had become, during the decade of capital-building, an important place of transhipment for goods arriving by sea, and destined for sale in the "Back Country," that was now to be reached over Braddock's old trail. Six-horse teams, brave in brass-studded harness jangling with bells, carried this merchandise westward in high-swung Conestoga wagons, bringing on the return trip such rich loads of furs that the Indian trade headquarters, near Gordon's old warehouse, was piled high with thousands of otter skins. Out of the profits, spacious new homes had been built in box-bordered gardens on the heights overlooking the river, and it was to this prosperous community so near at hand and to older, staid Alexandria seven miles down the river, that the hopes of perturbed and homesick officials turned when the move was finally made from Philadelphia to this Federal City, already too ambitious for a village but very far from being even a reasonable apology for a town.

The fairy tale that all the goods and chattels and records of the Government were brought in a single sloop that sailed by way of Delaware and Chesapeake bays up to the Potomac River, must be relegated to the limbo of discarded myths, since about sixty-four thousand dollars were paid out of the Treasury for the expenses of transferring government property from Philadelphia, while a bill for approximately half that sum, for the traveling expenses of officials and their families, was disallowed by a committee of the House of Representatives, though apparently settled later by a more obliging Congress.

The date of the meeting of Congress was the third Monday in November, but President Adams directed that the various bureaus be ready for business in their new quarters by the fifteenth of June. As a matter of fact, archives, equipment, and personnel trickled in, little by little, during the summer, thereby lessening the strain, which would have been tremendous had the whole federal force of one hundred and thirty-one clerks, with a corresponding proportion of higher officials, appeared at one time. As it was, the strain was bad enough, but they found lodging where they could, adapting themselves to temporary inconvenience with the good grace Americans always show if they can see a prospect of betterment ahead. The fortunate ones went to the homes of friends in Georgetown. Dr. and Mrs. Thornton invited John Marshall, Secretary of State, to be their guest. President Adams, who left Philadelphia on May 27th and traveled by way of Frederick and Lancaster for the sake of the "opportunities of entertainment on the way," reached Georgetown on June 3d. True to their idea of the ceremony due a chief magistrate, the residents of the District turned out *en masse* to meet him at the jurisdiction stones and escort him to his lodgings, the official nature of the welcome being emphasized by discharges of artillery, one for each state in the Union. His formal reception by the commissioners took place two days later in the Capitol, being the first event of a public nature celebrated there.

What Mr. Adams really thought of his reception or of the place itself, we shall never know, for he did not even tell his diary. This is what he wrote his wife:

> I like the seat of government very well, and shall sleep or lie awake next winter in the President's house. . . . An abundance of company and many tokens of respect have attended my journey, and my visit here is well received. Mr. Marshall and Mr. Dexter [the Secretary of War] lodge with me at Tunnicliff's City Hotel very near the Capitol.

The City Hotel was the "one good tavern" mentioned by Oliver Wolcott in a dismal letter to his wife, written a month later, in which he intimated that Washingtonians had gone mad:

> There appears to be a confident expectation that this place will soon exceed any in the world. Mr. Thornton, one of the Commissioners, spoke of a population of 160,000 people as a matter of course in a few years. No stranger can be here a day and converse with the proprietors, without conceiving himself in the company of crazy people. Their ignorance of the rest of the world, and their delusions with respect to their own prospects are without parallel.

Several other hotels had been built or were in process of construction, but he did not see how the members of Congress could find accommodation unless they would "consent to live like scholars in a college or monks in a monastery, crowded ten or twenty in one house, and utterly secluded from society."

President Adams, though less depressed than Mr. Wolcott, wisely refused to describe the White House to his wife, writing: "You will form the best idea of it from inspection." This was both cruel and kind—kind in sparing her as long as possible knowledge that could not fail to distress her orderly soul, cruel in whetting curiosity. This much could be said for it: It was the most beautiful building in town, and habitable, according to masculine ideas, when in the autumn they took up their residence there. But it was still far from complete. During the months they lived there, entrance was gained by temporary wooden steps and a rough board platform. Inside, the main staircase was totally lacking, wooden shelves served as makeshifts until the marble mantelpieces should arrive, and "the great audience chamber," now known as the East Room, was a windowless shell, suitable only for drying the Presidential linen. Mrs. Adams wrote to her daughter that the house required a force of twenty servants to keep it in order and that there was not a single bell in the place. Nor were bells installed until after she ceased to have a personal interest in ringing them.

This was not due to indifference on the part of those in charge of the work, and certainly it was not because of negligence on the part of the Secretary of the Navy, Benjamin Stoddert, who as an old resident of Bladensburg and Georgetown felt the responsibilities of a host in looking out for the comfort of the President and his wife. He had begun prodding the commissioners with questions and suggestions a year before, and the story of those bells, written out in full, would make a novel well supplied with harrowing incidents, not omitting sudden death. Secretary Stoddert was equally anxious to clear away the huts of the laborers who had been working upon the mansion, in order that some care might be bestowed upon the grounds. He wrote:

That large naked ugly looking building will be a very inconvenient residence for a Family without something of this kind is done at once. The ground should not be levelled but trees should be planted at once, so as to make it an agreeable place to walk in, even this summer.

I do not think the Commissioners have sufficiently attended to the accommodation of the President—a private gentleman preparing a residence for his Friend, would have done more. . . . Would you not be ashamed to conduct the President to the House without there being an enclosure of any kind about it?

This was addressed to Dr. Thornton as commissioner, and Mrs. Thornton made record in her diary ten days later that her husband was answering it, evidently making excuses on the score of expense. It was not lack of funds, however, but the will of the Great American Workman that put the final veto upon the plan. The men laboring there rose in wrath, when they learned that it was proposed to clear away the huts in which they lived, and wrote:

GENTLEMEN COMMISSIONERS:

You cannot be ignorant of the utter Impossibility of Procuring houses for the Married or Lodgings for the Unmarried Carpenters employed at the President's House. Should your intention of removing the Buildings they at present Occupy be carried into effect. At this advance season such Men as are able to build must use every Exertion to prepare for the day when they are to remove. Consequently, the men will be all employed either for themselves or their friends and the President's House remain unfinished . . . but if you persevere in taking the houses down we shall every man leave the employ on the return of this bearer by whom we expect your answer in writing. Signed by the

Carpenters of the White House.

So the shacks remained cheek by jowl with the White House until the natural course of employment took their occupants elsewhere, and President and Mrs. Adams remained fence-less, stair-less, bell-less, and at times almost fire-less in the chilly new dwelling until the end of their term.

Trees stood thick over half the city lots, but firewood was one of the things hardest to purchase in Washington. Mrs. Adams wrote her daughter:

If we can by any means get wood we shall not let our fires go out. But it is at a price indeed. From four dollars it has risen to nine. Some say it will fall, but there must be more industry than is to be found here to bring half enough to the market for the consumption of the inhabitants.

The reason for this antipathy to providing fuel is not explained. It was neither new nor directed particularly against new-comers. Nicholas Young, son of that Notley Young who had been active on committees of safety during the Revolution, was heard to complain bitterly of the "heavy tax imposed upon him" in keeping his step-mother warm. He resented having a four-horse team busy all the time at such work.

Perhaps a little of the chill felt by visitors to the White House during the short sojourn of John and Abigail Adams was due to this purely physical cause, but part of it was psychic. Not being the people to shirk duty as they saw it, they held their levees and gave ceremonious dinners conscientiously, sometimes with aching hearts. A short entry in Mrs. Thornton's diary for December 9, 1800, throws a flood of light upon the Spartan pair in the White House, and on the customs of the times. It reads: "Sent Joe to town to get some groceries and a crape band for Dr. Thornton to wear to the Levee, Mr. Adams's son in New York being dead." Standing side by side, they gained strength for the ordeal from the near presence of each other; discouraging words of sympathy, but noting the crape bands or the absence of them as their guests advanced. Dr. Thornton weakly took the line of least resistance and shunned the levee that night, accompanying his wife instead to the Assembly, where there were thirty-nine ladies and a great many gentlemen, and all passed a very pleasant evening.

It is doubtful whether a very pleasant evening could have been passed at the President's House under less abnormal conditions, for, though perfectly courteous to his guests, Adams, when he donned his black velvet coat of ceremony, put on a manner which implied that there was no possible connection between official civility and personal interest; and Mrs. Adams, albeit a short lady with "a sensible look," seemed a very grand personage indeed in her sober rich silk and handsome lace.

So Washington's first winter of official life dragged along with the tacit assumption that everything was comfortable and satisfactory, when everybody knew quite well that it was not. The Adamses held frigid state in the White House, legislators made their way daily to the unfinished north wing of the Capitol and returned at the end of business to their lodgings, to remain until next day or to venture forth after nightfall, as their courage dictated. Few of them had brought their womenkind with them—which was a mercy, since accommodations were so limited that honorable senators and judges were forced to "double up" and sleep sometimes four in a room.

Lack of normal family life induced loneliness which made the hearth-fires and lavish tables of Mrs. Law and Mrs. Thornton, and young Mrs. Samuel Harrison Smith, a bride from Philadelphia, attractive enough to warrant stumbling through ruts and pitfalls and darkness to their hospitable doors. The code of the neighborhood began and ended with hospitality, and calling threatened to become an all-day affair, for gentlemen sometimes appeared before breakfast to discuss business. This was not, however, for press of time; there seemed always to be time to sit down and discuss politics or farming or music or the latest corner-stone laying. It was just the leisurely Southern way. Georgetown, whose luxury had astonished Braddock forty years earlier, was very near, and though roads might be bad, saddle-horses were good and abundant, and when merrymakings were planned, the few family coaches creaked and swayed on their leathern straps to do service not only for their owners but for coachless neighbors. When spring opened and excursions on the Potomac became alluring there was opportunity for sport by day and sentiment by moonlight. Horses escaping from pasture frequently delayed the day's proceedings, but never entirely blocked them, even when the objective was the Capitol, to hear a speech in Congress. When at last the ladies arrived, they were gallantly welcomed to seats upon the floor of the House or Senate, their hosts standing beside their chairs.

Life in the new capital in the woods was most hard upon the representatives of foreign governments, who were less adaptable than their American hosts had become after two centuries of pioneering, and who lacked, moreover, all personal interest in the new town. They frankly cursed their luck as they settled down to a season of diplomacy in the wilderness.

"My God!" was the cry of one French diplomat. "What have I done, to be condemned to reside in such a city!"

IV

DIPLOMATS AND A DEMOCRAT

THE discomforts of life in Washington, during that first winter, were partly political. Like the rest of the country, the capital fell a prey to growing anxiety, as the situation developed. Adams, candidate of the Federalists, had been defeated for reëlection by an apparently safe majority of eight electoral votes, but it turned out that Jefferson, his principal rival, had likewise failed of election and that Aaron Burr, always difficult to reckon with, had once again achieved the unexpected. Running far ahead of his estimated strength, Burr received exactly the same number of electoral votes as Jefferson, which threw the choice of President into the House of Representatives. The vote there would be very close, and no election could be held until after the official count, in February, of the ballots cast by the electoral college.

Instead, therefore, of safely landing Burr in the honorable isolation of the Vice-Presidency, as was doubtless the intention of many who voted for him, there was an active chance that this disquieting man might slip into the Presidential chair; and once he was there, nobody could predict what he might do next.

For three months anxiety increased, as the full possibilities of this situation sank into the public mind. The Federalists saw in Jefferson's possible triumph nothing less than anarchy—a letting down of the bars to all sorts of altruistic theorizing. The followers of Jefferson read in the brilliant and shifty selfishness of Burr a portent of disaster.

Jefferson, the Vice-President in Adams's administration, arrived late in November and took up his residence at Conrad and McMunn's, a public house lately opened in the elegant mansion that Mr. Law had built for his own use, but deserted for a newer home near the river. Because of his office, Jefferson enjoyed the unusual privilege of a private sitting-room as well as a whole bedroom to himself, and to this sitting-room came emissaries from the Federalist leaders, it was said even from that conscientious God-fearing patriot President Adams, himself, to whisper that the Democratic candidate had only to say one word to render his election sure. If he would let it be known that he did not intend to do any of the radical things threatened by his party during the campaign, such as abolishing the Navy and turning all the Federalists out of office, he would be chosen on the first ballot.

Jefferson refused to make promises, allowing his friends and his opponents to go on guessing what he meant to do, while the session dragged on through the alternate slush and ice and sunshine of a Virginia winter to the rainy week in February when the House and Senate met together to see the electoral votes counted. The tie being announced, the Senate withdrew and the House began its task of electing a President, which speedily developed into a deadlock that lasted six days and was broken only after a final struggle continuing thirty hours.

During that time every representative was present, even sick Mr. Nicholson of Maryland, who had been brought from his lodgings two miles away and lay on a cot in an anteroom, where his wife kept watch beside him and roused him every hour to trace his name upon the successive ballots. Dawn of the last day showed the legislators with haggard, sullen faces, weary but unwilling yet to give in, and the end was brought about only by a diplomatic bit of juggling, one man's vote being withheld and one blank ballot cast, in order that a majority for Jefferson might be counted without any member having to confess that he had changed his vote. The name of the member who thus "gave up his party for his country" was well known, however, and nerves were so completely on edge after the long fight that the managers of the subterfuge hurried away to their lodgings, half fearing bodily harm. A small crowd waiting outside for news was almost as weary as the representatives themselves, and having greeted the announcement of Jefferson's choice with a few perfunctory cheers, melted away to sleep and to recover from the strain.

Adams being one of those who sincerely believed that Jefferson in the White House unhampered by promises, might prove almost as dangerous as Burr unhampered by conscience, put his own conscience above good manners and during the short remainder of his term set himself to the ungracious task of doing everything in his power to thwart Jefferson's supposed plans. His last days in the White House were neither personally agreeable nor politically happy. Mrs. Adams had already returned to Massachusetts, so he was deprived of the comfort of her companionship. He wrote her letters giving a humdrum account of his doings, in which the only colorful note is mentioned of a White House dinner described in one short sentence: "I gave a feast today to Indian kings and aristocrats."

Until nine o'clock at night of the third of March he was busy over the appointment of judges, which as a matter of courtesy should have been left to the incoming President, but whose positions he felt he must secure to the Federalist party. Early on the morning of the fourth, he stepped into his traveling carriage and drove away, too perturbed and censorious to remain and take a formal part in the ceremonies of the day.

His departure in itself robbed the simple ritual of inauguration of half its impressiveness, and Jefferson still further curtailed pomp and ceremony by strolling over from his near-by lodgings with a group of friends to take the oath and read his inaugural in the Senate chamber. A vigilant artillery company did its best by firing a salute as he entered the Capitol, but pageantry was at loose ends and the real thrill of the day, for those in the secret, lay in the mutual antipathy of the three men who stood so close together at the moment Jefferson became President. Chief Justice Marshall, who administered the oath, was a man whose ability Jefferson acknowledged, but whose mind he considered "viciously malignant," while Burr, the new heir apparent, he thoroughly distrusted. It was one of those moments which might have been awkward had not dignity and good breeding carried it off.

Not one person in a hundred in the crowded Senate chamber knew that anything was amiss; and to one person, at least, the really questionable member of the trio seemed wholly admirable. This was Burr's brilliant daughter, who had stopped on her wedding journey to her new home in South Carolina, to see her father made Vice-President of the United States.

After his inauguration Jefferson returned to his tavern as unostentatiously as he left it, and public recognition of the day ended with "a general illumination," whose little candles must have thrown their beams very far indeed to make any impression on the long stretches of empty road between the houses near the Capitol, or near the deserted President's House, and the few scattered dwellings and inns which constituted the city of Washington.

The new President remained at Conrad and McMunn's a fortnight before taking possession of the Executive Mansion, refusing meanwhile the seat at the head of the table or any of the honors his hosts pressed upon him.

Once he was installed in his official home, it began speedily to reflect the character of its new master. A corps of his plantation servants upset Mrs. Adams's careful arrangements in the kitchen, while in the room he called his "cabinet" he accumulated everything dear to his heart, from violins to vegetables, in a confusion that must have affected that lady's slumbers five hundred miles away. Carpenters' tools, illustrated books on art, scientific treatises, dirty little flower pots in which "experiments" were being tried, manuscripts, musical instruments, and miscellaneous books jostled one another over the room. His wife had died years before, his two daughters were occupied with their own growing families and could do no more than pay him occasional visits, so he made himself comfortable alone, after his own fashion. One winter indeed, his eldest daughter, Mrs. Randolph, lived in the White House with her entire family and allowed herself the luxury of having a baby born under its roof; but as a rule he kept bachelor's hall, relying on the gay and gracious Mrs. Madison, wife of his Secretary of State, to act as official hostess of the mansion. This lady considered herself privileged to go over it from garret to cellar, and did not hesitate to lead intimate friends up to the President's own dressing-room, at discreet hours, to exclaim over the odd contrivances he had installed, notably "the machine like a turnstile" for holding his coats and breeches. But she knew her own business—and her husband's—too well to attempt innovations.

Jefferson still believed in the politic effects of little dinners, and having a cook whose talents it would have been a pity to hide, substituted frequent, indeed, almost daily companies of ten or twelve people for the dreary state banquets of the former administration, bringing his guests together by means of billets "sent into the Hall" if they chanced to be members of Congress, or by that day's equivalent of an informal telephone call, if they were to be found elsewhere. After the meal he led them into his cabinet to continue a conversation which had already lasted from mid-afternoon until long past candle-light and had wandered through realms of time and space and matter.

"The dinners are neat and plentiful," wrote one of the participants. "No healths are drunk at table, nor are any toasts or sentiments given after dinner. You drink as you please, and converse at your ease. In this way every guest feels inclined to drink to the digestive or the social point, and no further." It was undoubtedly a gain, both in comfort and sobriety, over the usual custom of the time, but the new President's easy flow of language and frank interest in a great number of things, such as music and natural history, for the fun he could get out of them, seemed to some of his guests little short of immoral. They felt this was no way for a statesman to conduct himself. "His genius is of the old French school, it conceives better than it executes," wrote John Quincy Adams, the son of the Ex-President, who was then serving as a senator from Massachusetts. "You never can be an hour in this man's company without hearing something of the marvellous," which was his way of saying that Jefferson stretched truth beyond the limits of probability.

The former President had insisted upon ceremony in every detail of his official life, not because ceremony was agreeable to him personally, but because it was due to the great position he held. The fact that the Government had taken up its abode in the woods, seemed to him no reason for curtailing one bit of etiquette. Therefore, through the uncomfortable months he spent in the White House, he and Mrs. Adams had reproduced as far as possible the rules and formal observances practised in New York and Philadelphia.

Jefferson could be formal enough when he chose, but his sense of humor was developed to a point where he saw the absurdity of trying to keep up formal state in a city that consisted mainly of open fields, or of requiring etiquette in a house lacking even a proper doorstep. He had, moreover, a strong personal preference for old coats over new ones—with all that implied. He proposed to retain for himself a certain amount of liberty even though President, and, when business permitted, continued to ride about the country unattended, on his favorite Wildairs, returning with a flower in his buttonhole, the richer for the memory of some chance encounter with a person who very likely failed to recognize an august official in the unconventional gentleman stopping to chat or to offer a gift of imported vegetable seeds. Sometimes the President of the United States was seen, down one of those long green vistas which were to become city streets, standing in his saddle the better to reach a bough high overhead.

He had done the same things as Vice-President, but the light that beats upon that step to the throne is never very bright, and even to his friends his actions appeared more eccentric after he assumed the higher office. To the diplomats he was quite incomprehensible. A new envoy going to present his credentials might be met unceremoniously in the hall by a tall man with neglected hair and friendly manner but rather satirical expression. This strange being might wear every hue of the rainbow—a blue coat, a gray hairy waistcoat, showing a line of red underwaistcoat, green velveteen breeches trimmed with pearl buttons, stockings frankly made of yarn instead of silk, and slippers undeniably down at the heel. Small wonder that when he turned out to be the President of the United States, a gold-encrusted foreign minister, very conscious of his regalia and of his own importance as well as that of his sovereign, was astonished and even shocked.

Jefferson believed it a President's duty to be accessible to party friends, and decreed that his official doors remain always open. But since there are only twenty-four hours in a day, it was necessary to make up for this in some way and he proposed to restore the balance by closing his doors to purely formal intercourse. He therefore made it known that the fortnightly levees of his predecessor were to be discontinued and that the general public would be received at the White House only twice a year, on the first day of January and the Fourth of July.

The ladies of Washington, loath to lose the social glory shed over the budding capital by official entertaining, determined to override this edict and appeared *en masse* at the Executive Mansion at the usual time. Told that the President was out riding, they said that made no difference and, invading the drawing-room, settled themselves to wait. When the President returned, he received them cordially enough but without a word of apology for his absence nor for his dusty coat, and they retreated laughing, acknowledging themselves beaten.

It seems possible that Jefferson was astute enough to see the value of keeping up an interest in his personal doings, and that he deliberately turned it to account during his first weeks in the Presidency. Viewed down the vista of years, there appears to have been method in the way in which popular attention was focussed on little things while he got his bearings and decided larger questions, without regard to the threats and assertions made by his party during the campaign. He did not dismiss Federalist office-holders in great numbers, as had been predicted; they were allowed to complete the terms for which they had been appointed and then were gently dropped. The chief exception to this rule was made in the case of the "midnight" judges named by Adams in the last hours of his term. These nominations Jefferson ignored altogether. Far from disbanding the navy, which his partizans had denounced as an immoral war-breeder and used as a bugaboo in the campaign, Jefferson made aggressive use of it before he had been in office three months, sending it half around the world to teach a lesson to the pirates of Tunis and Algiers. Nor did he make objection to developing the Washington Navy Yard on a tract of forty acres near the junction of the Potomac with the Eastern Branch, which had been purchased for that purpose before he became President. Indeed, his ready acquiescence was looked upon by his enemies as proof positive that he had purchased in this manner the help of Federalist leaders in his contest with Burr.

Several notable changes took place in the appearance of the city during his years of office. The neighborhood of the White House was rendered sightly by the removal of the workmen's huts and the erection of a post-and-rail fence around the grounds. The old race-track, whose course crossed the line of Pennsylvania Avenue near Seventeenth and again near Twentieth Street, was done away with and a new one laid out, under the patronage of the Jockey Club, upon the high ridge of land now known as Columbia Road, between Fourteenth and Sixteenth streets. As a final tribute to the dignity and elegance of the neighborhood, a market heretofore held in the "President's Square" opposite the White House, was transplanted to buildings erected by public subscription midway on Pennsylvania Avenue, not because the location was convenient to any one group of customers but because it was within reach of several. This fully entitled it to the name of Center Market by which it is still known, though it was long called the Marsh Market, on account of the nature of the ground on which it stood. The name conjures up visions of ague-stricken hucksters and unsanitary stalls, but the swamp had advantages in the matter of transportation, since a very little poling and persuasion enabled flat-bottomed boats, laden with terrapin or fruits and vegetables from down-the-river plantations, to be brought directly to the market's back doors.

The greatest change of all took place in the aspect of Pennsylvania Avenue, which under Jefferson's direction was planted from the White House to the Capitol with four rows of sturdy young Lombardy poplars, trees desirable under the circumstances because of their quick growth and formal habit. Two rows in the middle flanked a main driveway, while two rows near the building line shaded paths for pedestrians, transforming the ragged thoroughfare into a street of stately, half-military appearance.

Feeble attempts at street-lighting were also made when in 1801 an order of the commissioners went forth that lamps must be placed on the bridges at M Street and New Jersey Avenue "and on a tree near the turn from the Capitol into Pennsylvania Avenue."

Extensive changes occurred at the Capitol, where the south wing was begun. Work at the Navy Yard resulted in the establishment of a little community of employees near its gates, and within the charmed circle of the old race-track west of the Presidental mansion several handsome dwellings were built, notably the beautiful Octagon House designed by Dr. Thornton for his friend John Tayloe, who was probably the richest planter, as he was undoubtedly the most enthusiastic horse-breeder, of the region.

The local government took two forward steps, being incorporated in 1802 and granted an enlarged city charter in 1804. But it is for social and political excitement rather than for material changes that Jefferson's eight years are notable in local annals. He had scarcely entered the White House when he exploded a social bomb by attempting to put into practice his personally devised "Canons of Etiquette," which swept away all known rules of precedence and substituted within its walls what he called the "rule of *pêle mêle*," reducing all guests to a state of absolute equality.

This was highly displeasing to Mr. Merry, who represented Great Britain and had already been offended by the informality of his first interview. It was even less to the taste of that masterful lady Mrs. Merry, a grenadier in character as well as bearing, to whom the minister was distinctly secondary when they appeared together. One memorable evening, when the President offered his arm to Mrs. Madison as dinner was announced, instead of to herself, as custom ordained, it was well for Mr. Jefferson that glances could only stab—not kill. Quick to respond to signals, Mr. Merry loyally played up to the part so suddenly thrust upon him, offered his arm to his outraged spouse, conducted her to the table, and, while seating her, cast a possessive eye upon an empty chair next to a charming lady, the American wife of the Spanish minister. But before he could take possession, it was snatched from under his very hand by a mere congressman, and his cup of humiliation was complete.

Mr. Merry wrote, complaining, to his Government, but did not go so far as to ask to be recalled. Indeed, he seemed distinctly surprised two years later when he received a dispatch announcing that his "request had been granted" and that he was to come home. After that uncomfortable evening he and his wife had retired to the stronghold of their hired house, which she described as a mere shell, "bare walls, without fixtures of any kind, even a well," and from there carried on a kind of social warfare against the Administration. Taking advantage of Jefferson's ban on levees, Mrs. Merry held drawing-rooms every week, with dancing and cards for the frivolous, and the honor of her conversation for those who could appreciate it. Being the only official parties given at the time, they scored a distinct triumph. The President and his daughters made good-natured advances from time to time, which were answered by inquiries whether the invitations were to be regarded as official or merely personal, nagging objections being raised in either case. To these the Jeffersons replied with spirit, as did Mrs. Madison when the English lady's criticism fell on her for choosing to set a bountiful rather than a fashionable table. It was a harmless quarrel, which added zest to life in the new capital; but it is significant that Jefferson dropped his effort to reform etiquette at the White House, just as Jackson was forced to do when he attempted a similar feat thirty years later. It is also significant that for some years after the Merrys were recalled only unmarried ministers were sent to represent England on the banks of the Potomac.

One of the excitements of Jefferson's first administration was the departure of Meriwether Lewis and William Clark upon their trip of exploration across the continent. Both were well known in Washington, Lewis having served as Jefferson's private secretary, while Clark was the younger brother of that famous Indian fighter George Rogers Clark. Mrs. Madison and other kind ladies saw to it that the young men left in a blaze of glory, the recipients of dinners and farewell parties and every kind of portable creature comfort that could be devised—gifts which, perforce, they had to leave behind. Then after years of silence, during which friends began to think of them as dead, members of a strange tribe of Indians appeared suddenly in Washington, with the explanation that these young travelers had told them to come. Those who cared for them took hope again, but a silence even more profound settled down again after this and continued until they returned triumphant in Jefferson's second term, and raised the first monument to their expedition—an uncommonly stout bit of fence put up in the White-House grounds for the mutual protection of the public and the bear they brought back as a gift for the President.

Politically, the greatest excitement of Jefferson's term was the news that reached the city at dusk on July 3, 1803, barely in time to add gusto to the next day's celebration. It was that Louisiana had become, overnight, so to speak, a part of the United States, almost doubling the young republic's extent of territory. Great was the rejoicing and great the misgiving. Great, also, was the celebration which began with a sunrise salute of eighteen guns, followed by a procession, an oration, a midday reception at the White House attended by all the gentlemen of consequence and, so large had society become by this time, by fully fifty ladies in their best finery. Then, following the reading of the Declaration, came a purely masculine dinner at Jefferson's old boarding-place, Conrad and McMunn's, which lasted, with toasts and convivial songs, from four o'clock until nine—and indeed, for some of the participants, until the next day.

The inhabitants of Washington took seriously the fact of living in a capital. They appeared to care little about empty warehouses and rotting wharves, so long as the chambers of Congress echoed to debate. Daily the galleries of Senate and House were filled with listeners who met afterward to talk over the things they heard, not only in executive offices but before sitting-room fires in all the sparse dwellings scattered from Funkstown to the Jockey Club, and from Mr. Law's mansion on Greenleaf's Point to Tudor Place, Mrs. Peter's stately home in Georgetown. One social rule of almost world-wide application seemed to be reversed in Washington. In civilized regions—indeed, in the haunts of savagery also—men are prone to leave their homes and womenkind and congregate in clubs and coffee-houses to discuss matters of interest. In Washington just the opposite occurred. Picked men from all parts of the Union had been sent to the capital, where, because of the shortage of houses, they were condemned to a tavern existence to which most of them were unaccustomed and unreconciled. Hence alone, or in couples, or by dozens, they went a-visiting, searching out the homes that were open to them, where "a seat by the ladies was always much coveted."

Sir Augustus Foster, the bachelor left in charge of the British legation after the Merrys departed, thought it would be hard to find prettier women anywhere in the world, though he hinted that their conversation was not always brilliant. Mrs. Smith, young wife of the editor of the "National Intelligencer," wrote to her sister that in the evenings "some one or more of the gentlemen of Congress are always here." Since visitors seemed to be inevitable, wise matrons accepted their presence gracefully and cultivated the art of entertaining. In addition to firelight conversations, there were many dinners and supper parties "which necessitated constant recourse to the pages of Mrs. Glasse," with results so pleasant that even John Quincy Adams occasionally had a thoroughly good time, for which he reproached himself afterward in his diary, writing that he had been "too sociable" and had talked too much. Not the least interested nor the least sociable at these affairs were men from new Western states; frank and genuine gentlemen of the backwoods, who were not afraid to show their curiosity or to ask questions about something that was novel to them, whether it happened to be the gold embroidery on the coat of the French minister, or the internal workings of Susan Smith's new piano. They fingered both, asking naïve, searching questions, but did it with a self-respecting dignity that disarmed criticism.

A steady if slender stream of visitors from out of town brought into the circle enough new faces and accomplishments to add zest to party-giving. Mr. Adams mentions a lady from Philadelphia "who entertained the company at Mr. Erskine's one night by her performance on the tambourine." Men as a rule were not so ready to oblige, but occasionally one came for the express purpose of showing off. One lion of the hour was the erratic Scotchman James Ogilvie, an ex-schoolmaster who had graduated from teaching into opium-eating and from that into public entertaining, and is credited or blamed with originating the whole system of American lecture courses. General Scott, a pupil of his in boyhood, described him as "rich in physical and intellectual gifts." Undoubtedly he lacked the gift of humor, since a single grain of that, either Scotch or American, would have restrained him from donning a toga and mounting a carefully built rostrum to declaim orations of his own composition, with the "organ swell and dying fall" of Cicero's voice as well as he could reproduce it, handicapped by flown centuries and a strong Scotch burr. But Americans of that period were reverent where oratory was concerned. "He is quite the *ton* here," wrote a feminine admirer. "How much more rational these amusements are than our balls and parties." If his hearers expected to be gently shocked by his atheistic opinions, they were disappointed. His public utterances "could not offend the most pious," and he gave his auditors their money's worth, beginning with the toga and ending with recitations of Scotch poetry.

The town had a few literary and artistic lions of its own to exhibit to strangers. Gilbert Stuart spent the winter of 1804 in Washington, working hard at his portrait-painting, playing hard socially, and, rumor had it, drinking hard likewise. He became a landowner to the extent of buying a lot near the market on Pennsylvania Avenue, "to build a temple upon"—Washington's first projected art gallery.

Dr. Bruff, the city's earliest practising dentist, being something of an inventor as well, built on Observatory Hill a lofty wooden tower from whose top he demonstrated his favorite "horizontal windmill."

Joel Barlow, shrewd Connecticut Yankee, Revolutionary chaplain, business man, statesman, philanthropist, and poet, who aspired to fame as the American Homer, having returned from diplomatic service in France, made his home on a beautiful estate of thirty or forty acres north of the city that Jefferson picked out for him and which he named Kalorama because of its wonderful view. Just what inspired him to choose Washington as his residence, is not clear. It was not speculation, for he took no part in enterprises to promote the city's growth and bought no other real estate. He appears to have been the first man of wealth and literary taste to choose it deliberately as a congenial home. His wife and her sister Mrs. Bomfort were liked better than he, and the attention of visitors was called to the trio, with some pride, it being explained in tones of more or less awe that the grave gentleman was the author of the "Columbiad" and, less importantly, that he had also written that amusing and merry piece "Hasty Pudding." His library was the best in town and his guest-rooms were rarely empty. Tom Paine, rugged and red of face, and much more outspoken regarding religion than Mr. Ogilvie, helped him to plan improvements at Kalorama, as did Latrobe; while Robert Fulton, ten years his junior, occupied almost the place of a son in his household.

Mr. Gales and Mr. Seaton, joint owners of the "National Intelligencer," after Mr. Smith deserted it for farming and government office, were prominent figures. The former, small and compact, with a precise vocablulary and a lively taste in waistcoats, "seemed to have dwelt all his life among the graces." Mr. Seaton, taller and a little younger, had recently acquired a household Grace of his own, a most attractive wife who could with equal ease play a waltz at Mrs. Madison's bidding or help her husband take down a congressional speech in shorthand—an unusual accomplishment in those days.

Mrs. Smith, wife of the former editor of the "Intelligencer," was regarded by her friends, and by herself, as a novelist of merit, though her voluminous family letters describing Washington society were destined to longer life than her stilted romances.

The omnipresent Dr. Thornton might be trusted to appear in any assemblage, with something to say which an impediment in his speech forced him to say with impressive slowness. He too had an unpublished novel in his desk, and, what is more to his credit, strength of character to keep it there, this being the one field in which he did not rush in as an amateur and try to win professional honors.

Mr. Law wrote execrable verses and considered himself a literary light; John Threlkeld (Danish, by the way of Yorkshire), who lived opposite the Catholic College in Georgetown, could quote a Latin epigram and ride a horse at the same time. Encountered on a leafy road, he was apt to rein up his handsome chestnut, let fly the barb of some long-dead poet, and, wheeling, be off with a clatter of hoofs. "He was also well-read in Boccaccio," says a biographer, "but in spite of that left highly respectable descendants."

The town was full of odd contrasts and given to metropolitan airs which sat queerly upon the framework of accomplished fact. Tom Moore, prejudiced by his hosts the Merrys, actually saw all the absurdities he set down in his satiric rhymes about Goose Creek and Tiber, Democrats and frogs in

This embryo capital where fancy sees
Squares in morasses, obelisks in trees,
Which second-sighted seers ev'n now adorn
With shrines unbuilt and heroes yet unborn.

The gilded wheels of the Spanish minister's coach seemed decidedly out of keeping, spinning and bumping over ill-made clay roads; but it could not be denied that the capitol to which they bore him was a great and beautiful building, if as yet only in the making, and the standards of fashion and gossip were distinctly those of the gay world.

Even before Jefferson became President, Mrs. Smith described old General Van Cortland in his powdered wig, posing and attitudinizing through a quadrille "as though he had taken lessons from some dancing gentlemen of the year One"; and mentioned seeing at the same party a lady who was called "Madame Eve," by whispering matrons, because of her scanty dress. Three years later she wrote again:

I am half tempted to enter into details of our city affairs and personages; but really, I shall have to be so scandalous that I am afraid of amusing you at such a risk. . . . Certainly there is no place in the United States where one hears and sees such strange things, or where so many odd characters are to be met with.

A Madame Eve about whom gossip fluttered at that later date was the beautiful Elizabeth Patterson of Baltimore, just married to Napoleon's younger brother, and in Washington as a bride, unaware of the long losing fight she must wage for her name and position against the most domineering man in history. Partly because royalty exercises glamour in a republic and partly because of her own fair shoulders generously displayed, boys followed her carriage and crowds gathered to peep through the blinds of houses where she was being entertained.

Once a year, oratory and music and literature and even gossip went into the discard, and for six days the Horse reigned supreme. Race week was an event almost as important as the meeting of Congress, and locally of far greater antiquity, for races had been held in the neighborhood of Georgetown since five years before the battle of Bunker Hill.

Congress was too dignified to adjourn for the sake of attending mere races, but both houses found that week in November an excellent time for making minor repairs in their respective halls; and it would have been a poor board of trustees that could not discover equally good reasons for dismissing schools whose benches would have been empty in any event.

So senators and Supreme-Court justices, school-children, ambassadors, visiting strangers, sharpers, and fine ladies, followed by as many servants, black and white, as could manage to crowd upon the heels of their masters and mistresses, made their way out to the Jockey Club, whose track lay on the hills north of town, almost directly in line with the Presidential mansion. The District jail was about the only institution whose personnel—indoors—remained undiminished.

One who saw the gathering in 1803, estimated it at between three and four thousand people, white, black, brown, and yellow, and of all social grades from the President of the United States to the beggar in rags, adding that about one third of the crowd was made up of "females."

Another stranger averred that these were "decorated as for a ball," though the day was raw and threatened rain or snow. He was in a censorious mood, having been obliged to saddle his own horse at the inn if he meant to go to the races at all, and finding on arrival that he had to pay twenty-five cents admission to the grounds. "Rather than turn back, though no sportsman, I submitted." Neither was he mollified by learning that the "most miserable" chaise had to pay fifty cents, and that four-wheelers were charged a whole dollar.

Mrs. Madison in her chariot; Mrs. Tayloe in her coach-and-four; "Madame Jerome, wife of the King of Westphalia," in a modest but exquisite turnout, and all the other folk who came in carriages, took up their position "on the western side without the circus," where the afternoon sun would not shine in their faces. Sir Augustus Foster's curricle was one of the very best equipages there. The French minister came on foot, followed by a single servant.

Inside the race-track was a succession of booths whose tops served as platforms to accommodate spectators, while below, drinks and food were dispensed "and lavishly paid for," though perfectly good dinners went to waste meanwhile on boarding-house tables in the city. Between these booths and the oval track congregated the riders or drivers whose position did not entitle them to a place among the elect, or whose eagerness forbade taking advantage of it. Here they were at liberty to follow the race as closely as was physically possible, and they sped madly from one part of the field to another as the horses flew around the track. Everybody was keyed to the highest pitch of excitement. This week was for the denizens of the capital what the annual migration to the mountains had been for their Indian predecessors—the grand autumn holiday of the region.

The presence of foreign representatives added at all seasons of the year to the picturesqueness of life and to the possibilities of gossip. The Portuguese minister was suspected of dark duplicity. Turreau de Garambonville, who represented France, came with too much gold lace on his coat to please Jefferson and too luxuriant a growth of whiskers to please society. It was whispered that he had married the jailer's daughter after she saved him from the guillotine, and that he repaid her in blows, her cries being drowned by the cello-playing of an obliging secretary of legation. At last their disagreements became so vocal that, the cello notwithstanding, a mob gathered outside the legation. The gallant Dr. Thornton burst in upon them, gave the husband a piece of his mind effectively, in spite of the impediment in his speech, and helped the lady to escape to Georgetown, where she dwelt for a number of years in peace and comparative poverty.

During Jefferson's first administration, the sinister figure of Burr seemed ever present, even when not visible—always elegant, never without its suggestion of evil. In another kind of society he might have passed for a sardonic wit. In Washington, which for all its assumption of metropolitan ways, was earnest and honest and provincial at heart, his ironic jesting was disquieting. When he answered a hostess who asked why he appeared so seldom in society that he "had no wish to be a killjoy and knew his presence overpowered the company," it was taken literally and resented. Is it not barely possible that his whispers to Merry about getting a British foothold in Mexico and his impudently audacious suggestion to the Spanish minister that Spain lend him money with which to foment revolution within her own colony, had their origin in this same perverse humor? People thanked the gods that the country had been spared his Presidency. More than one of the many duels of the period seemed traceable to his door. Then, as if to justify the instinctive repulsion, came his own duel with Hamilton and his disappearance from the haunts of men. Yet on the reassembling of Congress he came back and took the chair as presiding officer of the Senate as if nothing had happened.

Early in February the bizarre spectacle of a fugitive from justice, under indictment in two states of the Union for murder, presiding over the deliberation of the United States Senate, was raised to still greater heights of improbability when the Senate resolved itself into a court of impeachment to try Justice Chase of the Supreme Court of the United States on a charge of malfeasance. It became Burr's duty as the Senate's presiding officer to conduct this trial also. He had the Senate chamber fitted up as a court of justice, with full regard for scenic effect: boxes reserved for the ladies, extra galleries hung in green for spectators, chairs upholstered in red for diplomats and in blue for managers and opposing counsel. John Randolph of Roanoke, eloquent if eccentric, conducted the prosecution; Luther Martin, invariably audacious and witty, always slovenly and never quite sober, maintained the defense; and Burr himself held the balance, deciding between them "with the impartiality of an angel and the vigor of a devil." His gravity and skill caused his own shortcomings to be forgotten, for the time being, in respectful admiration.

The trial began early in February, almost upon the fourth anniversary of Jefferson's contest with Burr for the Presidency, and dragged on until nearly the date of Jefferson's second inauguration before it resulted in Judge Chase's acquittal. So once more

Burr managed to sap Jefferson's inauguration day of personal glory. The public was physically weary from the long trial, in which Burr had been the outstanding figure, and on the second of March he had stepped to the front again in most dramatic fashion. A senator from New York wrote in a letter to his wife:

Senate Chamber, March 2, 1805 . . . this day I have witnessed one of the most affecting scenes of my life. Colonel Burr, whose situation and misfortunes you well know, after having presided in the Senate during almost the whole session, came in as is customary, and took the chair today. He went on with the public business as usual until about two o'clock. Then, the Senate Chamber happening to be cleared for the purpose of considering some matters of an executive nature, he rose from the chair, and very unexpectedly pronounced to the Senate his farewell address. He did not speak to them perhaps, longer than twenty minutes or half an hour, but he did it with so much tenderness, knowledge, and concern, that it wrought upon the sympathy of the Senators in a very uncommon manner. Every gentleman was silent, not a whisper was heard, and the deepest concern was manifested. When Mr. Burr had concluded, he descended from the chair, and in a dignified manner walked to the door, which resounded as he with some force shut it after him. On this the firmness and resolution of many of the Senators gave way, and they burst into tears. There was a solemn and silent weeping for perhaps five minutes. . . . My colleague, General Smith, stout and manly as he is, wept as profusely as I did. He laid his head upon his table and did not recover from his emotion for a quarter of an hour or more. As for myself, though it is more than three hours since Burr went away, I have scarcely recovered my habitual calmness. Several gentlemen came up to me to talk about this extraordinary scene, but I was obliged to turn away and decline all conversation.

It is said that Burr was present upon the fourth of March to see Jefferson take the oath a second time. But emotion had been drained dry. We are indebted to a British Secretary of Legation for the information that the President "proceeded on horseback from the palace," attended by his secretary and his groom; that he wore a black suit and silk stockings, and that on his way back to the White House he had an escort of congressmen and persons of distinction. The "National Intelligencer" tells us that part of his escort was made up of employees of the Navy Yard, who marched with military music and displayed "with considerable taste" the insignia of their profession.

Small wonder that these men escorted him with banners and enthusiasm, considering all he had done for the Navy Yard. A ship of seventy-four guns was then in process of construction, with the *Wasp* and the *Viper* and other fighters whose names ring in history soon to follow. The President's critics asked why it was that the capacity of the yard had been increased just in time to influence the Presidential election, and why the architect of the Capitol, Latrobe, had been instructed to make plans for a fine new imposing gateway at the Navy Yard.

Politically and socially, the years of Jefferson's last administration were less exciting than those of his first, but they were by no means dull. Lewis and Clark returned in triumph from the West; Thomas Law and his spirited young wife decided marriage to be a failure and separated, to the scandal of their friends, this being the first and only divorce in genteel society for many years. The arrest of Burr in the Southwest and his trial for treason in Richmond had many echoes in Washington. The growing tendency of both French and English to prey upon American commerce caused deepening anxiety and ever-increasing satisfaction with the output of the Navy Yard, where Commodore Tingey, who had seen its small beginnings, watched over each detail with eagle-eyed devotion.

The most pictorial and spectacular social event of Jefferson's whole administration occurred during the winter after his second inauguration, and was itself a tribute to the prowess of the navy. It was nothing less than the arrival of an embassy from Tunis to arrange details of the treaty which was the result of the deeds of those American ships Jefferson had sent out at the beginning of his Presidency. The city was practised in entertaining distinguished visitors without undue emotion, having been trained by ambassadors' wives in proper ceremonial behavior. But nothing like the gorgeousness of this ambassador and his suite had been seen upon Pennsylvania Avenue. They outstayed their welcome and cost the Government a pretty penny before they left, but as a show they were supremely satisfactory and, while the novelty lasted, the town was in a flutter of entertaining and feverish comparing of notes.

Sedi Cellanelli's imposing person and splendid flowing garments were discussed and inventoried from the crown of his plaster-of-Paris turban to the curved-up toes of the slippers he dropped upon the floor, in Eastern fashion, when he settled himself on the Chippendale davenports, which were the best substitutes he could find for the divans of his native land. Society came to know a great deal about his wardrobe, for when the heat of crowded rooms grew excessive, one garment after another fell from his ambassadorial shoulders, revealing new wonders of color and embroidery, but causing shivers of apprehension as to what might happen next.

His Ambassadorship's reaction to the unveiled ladies who passed before him nobody ever knew. The Italian in which he conversed with Mr. Jefferson and other learned gentlemen was always polite, and what the Greek interpreter saw with his quickly darting brown eyes was never fully told. Only once did Sedi show emotion at the sight of a female. That was in a private house where, just as the ambassador entered the front door, he caught a glimpse of a fat negress waddling toward the kitchen. Springing forward, he clutched her in a mighty embrace; explaining afterward (the only time, of course, when explanations were possible) that she reminded him of his fattest and costliest wife, who, like this houri, was "verily a load for a camel."

We are indebted to John Quincy Adams for the description of a White-House dinner given to these elegant barbarians, at which President Jefferson's daughter Mrs. Randolph and a little girl, the eldest Miss Randolph, were the only females present. It must have been a harrowing affair, for the usual dinner hour had been postponed from half-past three to "precisely sunset" for the convenience of the guests who were keeping Ramadan. Yet with Oriental disregard of time, they kept the company waiting.

The Americans were very frankly hungry when the ambassador arrived, half an hour late, yet he signified that he must retire and smoke before eating. Jefferson, determined that his famished guests should enjoy the spectacle if they could not partake of food, requested him to do his smoking on the spot, "which he did, taking at the same time snuff deeply scented with otto of roses." "We then," says Mr. Adams, "went to dinner, where he freely partook of the dishes on the table without enquiring into the cookery." When Mrs. Randolph retired, he quickly followed her into the drawing-room "to again smoke his pipe," but his wild-looking secretaries lingered to drink the wine they had not dared to taste in his presence.

On the day when Sedi Cellanelli made his first visit to the Capitol, the Senate of the United States adjourned to receive him, "though not without some debate." Marching straight to the Vice Presidential chair, the ambassador appropriated it to his own use and, addressing the gentleman who usually occupied it, said severely that he had "found a man talking in the other room," referring to the House of Representatives. When it was explained that the man was in no way overstepping his rights, being one of the members of Congress, the ambassador asked increduously if "all the men he had seen there had a right to speak," objecting that under such conditions it would take two or three years to finish the most trivial piece of business. It was like Italy, he said, where a case might be argued for twenty years without a decision being reached. In his own country, any piece of business could be concluded in half an hour. In vain did the American who was substituting that day for the Greek interpreter try to explain the difference between a parliamentary body and a court of law. The ambassador, frankly bored, waved him aside, announced that he had seen enough, and took his departure.

On New Year's Day Sedi and his suite, in their most brilliant best, went again to the White House, to attend President Jefferson's levee. From across the room they were eyed by a band of Osage chiefs, as dark of skin and as haughty in bearing as themselves. As gaudy, also, with their painted faces, their feather head-dresses, nose ornaments, blankets, embroidered buckskins, and little jingling bells. The two groups measured look for look, while Americans of European descent, in the few feet of space that separated them, commented upon the fact that this capital in its chrysalis stage had already become the meeting-place of people literally from the ends of the earth. After a time the ambassador, who was a friendly barbarian, removed his wonderful plaster-of-Paris turban, which looked like sheerest muslin, and pointed out to the Osages by signs that his own hair was cut in the exact manner affected by them. They solemnly grunted, but showed no wonder. Their dignity permitted no such unseemly behavior in public.

V

FIRE AND SWORD

EARLY in March, 1809, when Jefferson's second term came to an end, a Washingtonian wrote:

> The city is thronged with strangers. Yesterday we saw four or five carriages-and-four come in, and already two have passed this morning. The Miss Carrolls, Miss Chases, Miss Cooks, and I don't know how many more Misses have come from Baltimore. There are parties every night, and the galleries [of Congress] are crowded in the morning.

All these visitors had come to witness Madison's inauguration, which took place in the Hall of Representatives in the south wing of the Capitol, lately completed under the direction of Benjamin Latrobe. It was literally packed with a throng made up almost equally of women and men, thanks to the visitors from out of town; and as all the ladies were in what the newspapers called "full" dress, the scene presented, it was said, "rather a gay than a solemn appearance."

Solemnity centered in the new President, who never appeared to advantage in public and on this day seemed particularly ill at ease. The saying of Francis Jeffreys that Madison "looked like a schoolmaster dressed for a funeral" may have been a libel, but he looked distinctly unhappy as he rose to begin his inaugural address and "trembled excessively"; and his opening words could scarcely be heard. He gained confidence as he proceeded, however, and excitement even brought a tinge of color to his sallow cheeks. Jefferson, who was close by, beamed encouragement upon him and seemed to feel all the pleasure of an elder brother in his success. If he experienced any chagrin at leaving office amid more bustle and festivity than had attended either of his own inaugurations, he successfully concealed it. The likelihood is that he was really glad to have responsibility slip from his shoulders upon those of a younger man, in whom he believed and whose mind he had helped to form. His own Presidency had been both brilliant and successful, but, of late, dark clouds had gathered upon the horizon and war seemed probable, either with England or with France.

Attacks upon our commerce by both these nations had roused so much resentment that Mr. Madison's admirers had presented him with a suit of clothes of strictly home manufacture to be worn on this day of days. It was made of wool which had been grown on the backs of thoroughly American sheep, spun by patriotic American women, and woven in American looms.

Fortunately for the elegance of the occasion, Mrs. Madison did not feel it necessary to show the same devotion to home industry. Neither the marvelous purple bonnet with white plumes, in which she appeared at the Capitol, nor the regal buff velvet, pearls, and turban with paradise feather of her ball costume could have had their origin on American soil, but she was so popular and so wholeheartedly American that nobody criticized this.

The Madison inaugural ball, the first in the city's history, was a wonderful success, measured by usual standards of crowding and discomfort. It was held at Long's Hotel, a new place containing the incredible number of fifty rooms, that had been built not long before on the site of the present Library of Congress. The four hundred people who attended filled the parlors so literally to suffocation that it was necessary to break the nailed-in upper sashes of the windows to admit air.

It was Mrs. Madison's hour. While her short, inconspicuous husband was quite lost in the crowd, the paradise feather in her turban could be seen easily from any part of the hall, as she nodded and bowed her happy, cordial greetings. He, poor man, looked woebegone and was anxious to leave early, but, in view of her elation and the urging of the managers, consented to remain for supper, "though I would much rather be in bed," he assured a friend.

Jefferson, who came early and stayed late, and mingled with the crowd, seemed as care-free as a boy, and appeared to enjoy the occasion as much as Mrs. Madison. Those two and an elderly dandy "perfumed like a milliner," who strutted about with great knots of black ribbon on his shoes, were the outstanding figures of the ball.

Almost immediately after the inauguration, Jefferson departed in his phaëton for Monticello, attended by a servant leading his favorite saddle horse, and the roads in the neighborhood of Washington, where he had so often been seen doing un-Presidential things, knew him no more.

The Madisons slipped with little or no friction into the place vacated for them. Mrs. Madison had already been official hostess of the White House for eight years, and on taking the Presidential oath, Mr. Madison merely stepped from his office in the State Department to another in the mansion across the way. Even in the matter of transferring their household goods, they were only repeating on a larger scale a pleasant experience of a few years before, when they had left their first residence in the District, a small house in Georgetown "on Bridge Street beyond High," for more spacious quarters next door to Dr. Thornton.

The White House was a more convenient place than it had been in Mrs. Adams's day. The ardently desired bells had been installed early in Jefferson's term, the main staircase had been built, and Mrs. Madison, who had a way with carpenters as well as with cabinet ministers, had managed other improvements since.

But what a house-cleaning the mansion must have undergone when the last of Jefferson's miscellaneous treasures had been trundled away "in wagons drawn by six mules and four horses," his eleven black servants sitting on top of the loads! And how eagerly its new mistress must have consulted with Benjamin Latrobe about spending the eleven thousand dollars appropriated by Congress for its refurnishing. A piano, a guitar, mirrors, and much yellow satin for upholstery and curtains completely transformed the drawing-room, while a goodly sum went to replenish the linen and cutlery worn out by Jefferson's many dinners.

Jefferson, though by no means an Adonis, never let his lack of good looks interfere with his prominence in any company, but his successor had none of his showy social qualities, though his knowledge may well have been as deep and his range of interests as broad. His short, insignificant figure with its springing gait, his wrinkled

From A History of the United States Capitol by Glenn Brown. Used by permission

THE CAPITOL AFTER THE FIRE

face, his pitiful little pipe-stem of a queue, and the cast in his eye, all seemed to debar him from leadership, even in his own drawing-room. In a small circle of intimate friends he could talk long and wittily on almost any subject, and listeners forgot that his eyes did not focus, in noting their merry, mischievous twinkling and their clear hazel color; but the presence of one stranger rendered him dumb. Since the Presidential office cannot be exercised in solitude, and an executive must know what people are saying and thinking, he relied upon Mr. Cutts, brother-in-law of Mrs. Madison, to bring him a daily budget of gossip, which the two discussed over a quiet glass of sherry.

The President was most abstemious, barely touching the glass to his lips in the elaborate wine ceremonies then in vogue, and very possibly it was for health's sake as well as from inclination that, whenever possible, he took the place of inconspicuous guest rather than of host at his own board. Young Mrs. Seaton has left a description of a White-House dinner at which the guest of honor, who happened to be an aged lady, was not seated beside the President but next to Mrs. Madison, while the private secretary took the foot of the table and served the guests, Madison himself shirking all duties and finding a place on one side.

Mrs. Madison was amiable rather than strong-minded, but on certain points she was adamant. One of these was her preference for a "groaning" American table, over foreign fashions in dinner-serving. The White-House wagon fared forth in the early morning for the day's supplies and returned with a load which cost sometimes as much as fifty dollars at the prevalent low prices.

The Presidential dinner hour was advanced from Jefferson's half-past three to four o'clock, and the majordomo of the White House was a Frenchman named Jean Pierre Sioussat, who as a lad had experienced the tragic vicissitudes of the Terror, and, drifting to America, entered the service of Mrs. Madison, to whom he remained devoted to the hour of her death. She returned his regard, but it is evident that his Gallic taste had no effect upon her dinner menus. An unknown congressman who pronounced the White House table "excellent" wrote that the chief dishes the day he dined there were "bouilli . . . the round of beef of which the soup is made," cooked with spices and sweet herbs and served with rich gravy (quite like beef à la mode), a lordly ham surrounded with much-boiled cabbage "cut in long strings and somewhat mashed," and a "good" dessert, "much as usual, except two dishes which appeared like apple-pie in the form of half of a mushmellon, the flat side down, top creased deep, and the color dark brown." This was manifestly not one of the fifty-dollar days.

Mrs. Madison's conception of the duties of a President's wife was simple, but wearisome to fulfil. She let politics alone, announcing that her province "began at the drawing-room door," but within that limited field she exercised enough genius to counteract her husband's unsocial behavior. It was no longer the easy matter to return visits in person that it had been eight years before, when she began the practice as wife of the Secretary of State. At that time the purchase of a second-hand coach and silver-mounted harness had marked the migration from the Georgetown home to the larger one in Washington, and in it she had driven from Georgetown to the Navy Yard until she and her turnout were as familiar a sight on country roads as President Jefferson himself, mounted upon Wildairs.

But at that time boarding-houses and taverns were few and strangers were quickly located. Since then Washington had passed beyond its early park-like phase of avenues cut through standing timber. Streets were still liable to be closed by fences and cultivated as fields, but the number of possible abiding-places had greatly increased, and the ladies who called upon Mrs. Madison, while punctilious in following the new fashion of leaving visiting-cards, were not always thoughtful enough to put their addresses upon them. She deplored the amount of time wasted in looking them up in order to invite them and their husbands to the White House. But she hunted them out with unfailing patience, and in so doing had need of the two stout new White-House coaches and the fleetness of the four grays that drew them.

Pennsylvania Avenue, redeemed from bareness by Jefferson's four lines of poplar trees, had begun to show patches of real sidewalk here and there, replacing the row of stepping-stones between White House and Capitol which it was said an early Secretary of the Navy, Benjamin Stoddert, laid at his own expense, out of gratitude that his favorite "Cool Spring" had been stricken from the list of government property.

People were beginning to pipe water from the numerous springs on the hills north of town, for their own use and that of their immediate neighbors. One enterprising person turned this to business account by opening a bathing-establishment at which three warm and four cold baths could be bought for one hundred cents.

A few more shops were struggling into existence and two rope-walks were in operation down on Greenleaf's Point. A theater had been the scene of spasmodic activity for some time. People were talking of starting an evening paper. The original government office building had been duplicated in all its ugliness on a lot west of the Executive Mansion, and the city had achieved its first monument—a column with ships' prows sprouting from its sides and surmounted by an eagle whose back was bored full of holes to represent feathers. Surrounded by emblematic figures of an angel, a warrior, and the Muse of History, it stood in the Navy Yard to commemorate the officers and sailors who fell in the war with Tripoli. Not far away was the new entrance gate designed by Latrobe and built about the time of Jefferson's second inauguration. These two works of art afforded the eastern part of the city the satisfaction of knowing that it was not without architectural splendor.

Two public schools, one east of the Capitol, the other west of the White House, had been opened in 1806, though free schools were at that time unusual outside of New England. Power to establish them had been granted in the enlarged city charter of 1804, in spite of strenuous opposition, the idea of paying fifteen hundred dollars a year for school furniture and pens and ink and tuition for indigent children being denounced as fantastically absurd, when a like sum expended on roads and bridges could be made to benefit all ages and every degree of intelligence. Early in Madison's administration the sum available for such use was arbitrarily cut down to eight hundred dollars by the city authorities, because the schools "seemed to have plenty of money" and the expense was "much complained of."

These "poor schools," as they were unfortunately called, were by no means the only institutions of learning in the District. Besides private schools of varying degrees of usefulness, there was Georgetown University, which had opened its doors the year the corner-stone of the White House was laid, with very modest entrance requirements and a senior class of seven studying logic and metaphysics and ethics. The sight of the cheerful red waistcoats, which were part of the student uniform, had carried respect ever since, when encountered in highway or leafy lane, and every year Presidents and those in authority had taken part in the university's strenuous graduating exercises. People were forgetting, if they ever knew, how nearly this Jesuit college had come to crowning Jenkins's Hill instead of the Capitol. The Duddington Pasture tract had been offered as a site for the college, shortly before the District project took shape, and had been declined by good Bishop John Carroll because it seemed too "remote."

Even with a college and a monument, a Capitol with two solid wings, though as yet no middle, a White House almost finished, public baths, stores, pieces of sidewalks, and more hotels and boarding-houses than Mrs. Madison's coach could easily visit in an afternoon, Washington appeared strange and unfinished compared with older capitals. Like all infant prodigies, it had been over-stimulated along certain lines and under-nourished in others. It reminded Felix de Beaujour, who saw it shortly before the War of 1812, of "those Russian towns traced in the deserts of Tartary, in whose enclosures we behold nothing but naked fields and a few glimpses of houses." To another visitor it suggested that fantastic creature whose spread of limb is out of all proportion to its body-displacement or to its consequence in the animal world, a gigantic daddy-long-legs.

Benjamin Latrobe, who had followed its growth to its present size, waxed darkly pessimistic when he considered the future. According to him, speculation had reduced men like Mr. Law and Mr. Greenleaf to straits from which the grave alone offered honorable exit. Master artisans, having invested the savings of a lifetime in homes that had neither present nor prospective value, were almost as poor and ragged as the day laborers who knew not where they were to turn for their next meal. Congress had demoralized the labor market by its capricious manner of making appropriations, long seasons of idleness being followed by periods of hectic work at excessive wages. The swampy ground near the river caused a great amount of sickness, and this was increased by unhealthful and un-American standards of living brought in by foreign laborers who had come seeking employment and stayed on from sheer inability to get away.

Though Latrobe's pessimism over-emphasized these evils, everything he said was true, and every ill he described might be found by one who knew where to look for it, within fifteen minutes' walk of the White House.

L'Enfant's plan contemplated waterfalls and cascades and canals. Neither he nor Washington had been discouraged by the swamp in the center of the town, knowing that in time engineering skill could take care of that accidental blemish, but the city had developed thus far totally without so unpoetic a thing as a system of sewerage. The commissioners recognized its desirability but also their own limitations. "Without funds, what can we do?" they asked, and left the situation trustingly to Providence, as the one authority powerful enough to cope with it. Providence seemed inclined to overlook the matter entirely, for with the exception of a smallpox scare in 1800 there had been nothing in the nature of an epidemic, though agues and intermittent fevers were considered part of the annual program, to be deplored but not fussed over. That story of an invitation to dinner—"Will you dine with me on Friday?" "Let me see, Monday, Wednesday—no, I cannot come Friday, Friday is my chill day,"—may be a flight of the imagination, but one of the matrons of Washington actually wrote to a correspondent:

> I have unexpectedly been a good deal in company and have seen much more [of society] than I designed. . . . I have often gone out with the ague, sometimes with fever on me, so much has habit done in reconciling me to this enemy. I know that nothing will keep off the fit, and

may as well have it in one place as another. I very seldom now go to bed, but sit up, or lie down on the sopha, have a bowl of tea and a basin by me, and give no one further trouble.

Old Dr. May, the first competent physician to establish himself in town, and the son who followed in his footsteps and eclipsed him in skill, were experimenting with preventive measures. Jefferson also had found time while President to interest himself very much "in propagating cow-pox and had even inoculated many persons with his own hand." The only public hospital was the infirmary of twelve beds, with its rudimentary equipment of porringers and blankets and sick-diet, and medical services at fifty cents a head, that the commissioners had been forced to squeeze from their limited funds at the outset of building operations, to care for sick laborers. During the yellow-fever menace of 1800 it had been distressingly inadequate, and at that time Mrs. Thornton's diary gave a pathetic picture of a man lying desperately ill under a tree, nobody being willing to take him in for fear he was a victim of the dreaded scourge. Her husband had discovered him, and stopping Dr. May as he rode by, took him to see the sufferer. Between them they "got him into the new stable built for the President," where he died the next day.

That was at a time of extreme need. In ordinary seasons people of all classes shunned the infirmary. The well-to-do could have better care at home; the poor regarded a hospital as a vestibule to the charnel-house.

One cause of much illness, the canal begun under L'Enfant's orders to bring in building materials and then abandoned for lack of funds, lay as it had been left, an open grave of too much preparedness, slowly turning the Tiber into an evil-smelling lagoon.

Business men interested in the lagging commercial development of the city cast hungry eyes upon it, and argued that its completion was the one thing needed to bring in the millennium. Mr. Law wrote:

No sooner is a canal formed through a town or city, than stores, &c are erected on its banks. Unless this canal is formed, Pennsylvania Avenue and the other central streets will only promote the extremities of the city by having all their supplies from thence; but as soon as it is effected, the boarding houses, the houses of the public officers, the houses of ambassadors, the stores &c all will have their articles from the banks of the canal, and all will combine to create business and population. *Then* will cease the complaint that the houses are too scattered, *then* will the streets leading from the canal shew the excellency of the plan; . . . *then,* in short will the city become independent, and constantly increasing.

Incidentally it might benefit the health of the community; but that was a minor consideration. By the time Madison became President, enough money had been accumulated to warrant engaging Mr. Latrobe to survey the route of this wonder-worker, and on July 2, 1810, the enterprise was inaugurated with a great barbecue and so much enthusiasm that a six-horse plow actually got to work before the last toast had been drunk and the little pickaninnies had rushed in to finish the crumbs of the feast.

But the money soon gave out, war came on, and it was 1815 before the first loaded ship passed through the canal. Even then prosperity refused to follow, and the only ships that ever willingly found anchorage below Georgetown were those whose business took them to the Navy Yard. To-day we recognize this outcome as providential, but to the men who counted so confidently upon the canal to retrieve their fallen fortunes, the Potomac lapping against idle wharves must have had a cruel sound.

One cause of Washington's failure to develop as a business center was doubtless political. Our system of representative government was founded on the theory that "where your treasure is, there will your heart be also," with the corollary that men sent to Washington should be commissioned for short periods only and remain there merely as sojourners. If they entered into business in the capital city, they would cease to represent adequately their constituents. Another reason was geographic. The Potomac flowed within the charmed region dominated by the planter's idea that attention to business details was sordid. A gentlemanly vagueness as to the condition of one's own books, and great courtesy in lending to one's friends, created a delightful atmosphere to live in, but was not calculated to make two wharves hum with trade where only one had mildly hummed before. Georgetown could and did take care of all the natural commercial energy of the neighborhood.

At the time Madison was inaugurated, war with England seemed almost certain. Then the cloud lifted a little, but experience proved that Britain had no intention of mending her ways. The war party clamored louder than ever and was led in Congress by two exceptionally able young men, Henry Clay and John C. Calhoun, the former acting as spokesman for the West and the latter for the South.

Monroe, who was Madison's Secretary of State, also favored war, but the new President held back. Having made a study of the matter while Secretary of State under Jefferson, he knew better than any one else the nature and extent of British aggressions; but on the other hand, few realized as he did how ill equipped our country was for a struggle with a nation whose army was wonderfully effective, and whose navy was called the best in the world. Our navy at that time consisted of just five available ships. Our army, which had won the Revolution a quarter of a century before, had been reduced to a mere skeleton and virtually all the successful officers of that war had gone to their graves or were incapacitated for active service. Moreover, Madison's type of mind (he had been a chess-player in his youth) was less prone to take chances than Clay, who was born with the gambler's instinct.

"Free Trade and Sailors' Rights" made a taking slogan, however, while cold figures and mathematics were neither picturesque nor inspiring. Members of the war party had ready answers to objections. To those who said the navy was too small they replied that the navy would have little to do. This was going to be a land war. As for the army, only give our people a chance and they would rise in their righteous indignation, invade Canada, and dictate a successful peace before the English Army had embarked on its transports. Washington Irving made a visit to Washington in the interest of family business at this time, and found himself in the thick of the discussion. He wrote:

One day I am dining with a knot of honest furious Federalists, who are damning all their opponents as a set of consummate scoundrels, panderers of Bonaparte, etc. The next day I dine, perhaps, with some of the very best men I have heard thus anathematized, and find them equally honest, warm and indignant; and if I take their word for it I had been dining the day before with some of the greatest knaves in the nation; men absolutely paid and suborned by the British government.

War was declared in June, 1812, Madison's hand being forced, his critics said, by the threat to nominate somebody else for President at the next election.

While the opening of hostilities made changes in the life of the town, they were not of a kind to emphasize the horrors or even the discomforts of war. An increase in the size of the army brought a large number of new people to Washington who were, for the time being at least, immensely earnest and impressed with their own importance. For some unknown reason, which nobody cared to connect with the unsatisfactory news that came slowly from the front, there were more resignations from the cabinet than ever before, especially from the office of Secretary of War. When the latest incumbent gave out and an interregnum occurred, James Monroe performed the duties of that officer in addition to his own, acting as an intermittent *Pooh Bah* for the Administration. It required some mental agility to remember who was in and who was not in official life, and this in itself was stimulating. In time all the young men, even those of foreign birth, like Mr. Law's "Asiatic sons," joined the regular army or some local military company.

There was no Red-Cross work, or its equivalent, but the young women of various neighborhoods instituted "fringe parties," coming together between breakfast and dinner to make the cotton trimming which served as epaulets on the uniforms of their brothers and lovers. Society breakfasted at nine, made morning calls when not making fringe, attended congressional debates, dined bountifully at four o'clock, and drank tea rather frugally at eight.

Americans were by nature patriotic, and for the same good reason were impatient and puzzled by the slow progress of our arms toward victory; but, all in all, the war seemed very far away and impersonal—not half so exciting as local happenings. News of a victory was made the occasion of social festivity: news of defeat, if it was very bad, sent them to church on a fast-day. When there was no recent war news to discuss, Scott's latest romance formed a polite topic of conversation and young ladies who sang were asked to oblige with "Lochinvar" or "Hail to the Chief," which had just been received at Cooper's Book Store on Pennsylvania Avenue.

In spite of assertions that this was to be exclusively a land war, the navy afforded the greatest number of occasions for rejoicing, beginning with a grand ball in November, 1812, to celebrate the capture of the *Guerriere,* which did so much to convince Europe that America was after all, a real antagonist. All the distinguished people in town, native and foreign, and some who claimed homes in both hemispheres came together to rejoice, and there was a deal of elegant dressing. If the celebration took the form of a banquet at one of the hotels, two hundred and fifty gentlemen might sit down to it and drink patriotic toasts.

There was a flicker of fear in the spring of 1813, when a British fleet appeared in Chesapeake Bay to pillage Havre de Grace, but that blew over and was speedily forgotten, and the social pageant never seemed more impressive or more lively than during the early months of 1814, just before the Battle of Waterloo. After that victory the troops that England held for home defense, so long as Napoleon roamed the earth, were released for other duty, and Admiral Cockburn hurried to Chesapeake Bay, accompanied by several thousand of the men who had humbled the Corsican. This news, received only six weeks before Washington was actually in flames, changed the war from a matter of fast-days and public rejoicing to one of vital personal concern.

An empty treasury was not reassuring, and in addition there was a well-founded suspicion that the available troops—few enough, in all conscience!—were poorly officered. General Washington had believed the city well situated for defense, and L'Enfant regarded its encircling hills as potential fortresses; but nothing had been done to improve such natural advantages, beyond beginning Fort Washington, on the Potomac just below Alexandria. This, however, was not completed or even kept in repair.

When Havre de Grace was attacked in 1813, a few earthworks

had been hastily thrown up on Greenleaf's Point and a committee of citizens had been appointed to coöperate with the Government in reorganizing the District militia; but even these trifling preparations had lapsed. A feeling of astonished, helpless rage vented itself in abuse of Madison, who two years before had been denounced for delaying war so long. Now criticism of the President for exactly the opposite reason penetrated the White House itself, one woman driving there in her carriage to shake down her beautiful hair and say she wished it might be made into a rope wherewith to hang him.

The Citizens' Committee was hurriedly revived; the mayor called upon all able-bodied men, including free negroes, to assemble at the Capitol and march from there to raise earthworks to defend the bridge across the Eastern Branch. The open square opposite the White House on Pennsylvania Avenue became the scene of almost continuous drilling, and a crop of tents rose overnight upon Meridian Hill—a welcome sight to Mrs. Madison's eyes.

News came that the British had landed and that there was nothing to prevent their marching straight upon Washington; but some phlegmatic people, the momentary Secretary of War among them, believed even yet that there was no reason for anxiety, and that the enemy would pass Washington by for the richer spoil offered by Baltimore. There seems, indeed, to have been some discussion between the British commanders whether to pursue gold by attacking a commercial city, or glory by capturing their enemy's capital. They prudently concluded to do both.

Washington placed its greatest reliance upon Captain Joshua Barney, who commanded a fleet of gunboats in Chesapeake Bay. The navy had done such remarkable things in this war, and the admiral's career had been so full of bravery and of luck, that it seemed natural to expect greater marvels. A man who had been in full command of a vessel before he reached the age of fifteen must surely prove a match for Cockburn's fleet and General Ross's veterans. It was a sad blow to learn that the old sea hero harbored no such illusions, but had landed his men and burned his boats and was marching to join whatever forces the Administration might be able to get together. These amounted to about one thousand regulars under General Widner and an uncertain number of militia, varying from three to six thousand, according to the historian who tells the story.

People began to leave the city, and streamed away until it was estimated that nine tenths of the population had departed, taking with them as many of their household treasures as possible. Clerks in government offices worked frantically to get records into portable shape and sent some here, some there. Papers from the State Department were packed in linen bags and dispatched toward Leesburg. The working outfit of the city post-office, confided to the custody of a boy in his teens, was carried to a farm-house near Clean Drinking and unceremoniously stored in its cellar, after which the lad, feeling he had discharged his full duty, returned to town to see what was going on.

Mrs. Smith, the lady who so stoically fulfilled her social engagements while shaking with ague, was as resolute in this emergency, and, having sent her valuables and linen to a place of safety, continued to sleep in her own bed at Sidney, her country house near Georgetown University, trusting, for protection, to a loaded pistol under her pillow. Her sister Ann, who objected to explosive weapons, contented herself with "a pen-knife in her bosom." Their house being on a main road from town, these ladies were kept busy listening to rumors and news of actual happenings, unable to distinguish one from the other, and here they remained until a neighbor roused them in the dead of night with loud knocking and the agonized entreaty: "Go! for God's sake go!" before he sped on to warn others of the British approach.

Six days before the British attack, General Widner's force had gone into camp a dozen miles southeast of the city on hearing that the enemy was steadily advancing. On Monday, August 22d, President Madison, Mr. Armstrong, Secretary of War, and a few others rode out to join the general, then encamped at Old Fields. Here the next day's sun rose on the unwonted spectacle of a cabinet council in a spot redolent of pre-Revolutionary tobacco culture.

That night General Widner withdrew into the city, posting his forces to defend the bridge across the Eastern Branch, not knowing by which of two roads converging upon that point the enemy was approaching. It was an unfortunate move for the morale of the army and also of the town itself, for it brought undisciplined men too near home to resist the temptation of visiting their families, while the sight of soldiers on the streets added to the general alarm.

When Widner learned that the British were nearing Bladensburg over the Marlboro Road, he strove to reassemble his small band, but his men were scattered and Bladensburg was a weary march distant. He recovered only a part of his troops, and these, in the language of a contemporary diary, having been "marched off their legs," were in no condition to meet an enemy "who tho' likewise fatigued by a long & forced march, had a regular plan, had discipline & a desperate attempt to make to succeed in a plan both bold & hazardous."

Madison had left one hundred men on guard at the White House when he rode away to join General Widner, but these soon melted away. Mrs. Madison stayed on, busying herself in packing government belongings into the stoutest and most useful of the White House coaches. Her private property "must be sacrificed," as she wrote to her sister. Her chief helper was French John, who breathed slaughter and defiance and wanted to spike the one cannon left behind at the gate by the faithless hundred, and to lay a train of powder to blow up the British when they crossed the threshold. "To this," Mrs. Madison wrote, "I positively object, without being able to make him understand why all advantages in war may not be taken." French John was a product of the Terror.

Even with the British at the door, his mistress lingered to direct removal, from its place on the wall, of the Executive Mansion's one art treasure, Gilbert Stuart's official (but not truthful) portrait of General Washington. After she had seen this done, she drove away. John locked the door, took the key to the house of the Russian minister, carried Mrs. Madison's pet macaw to another friend, and himself retired to Philadelphia.

General Widner's management of the short campaign has been a matter of national chagrin for more than a century, though blame for that day's misfortunes should in justice be extended over the long previous period of neglect. Once again the best work was done by the navy, represented by Captain Barney and the sailors he turned into land troops by the simple expedient of burning their boats. Planting his force and his guns just beyond the District line, he put up a spirited defense, but his six hundred, like another famous force of similar number, stood no chance, and their badly wounded commander was taken prisoner. Widner's regulars, augmented by as many of the District militia as had returned to duty, with a few from surrounding states too footweary and exhausted to be useful, had been stationed nearer the city. Under the best circumstances they would have been no match for General Ross's four thousand British regulars. They made virtually no resistance, but turned and fled through the city and out again, some into Virginia and others toward Montgomery Court House, Maryland.

"God only knows when the Executive Government will again be organized," Mrs. Smith wrote from Brookville, Maryland, where she had gone when her neighbors bade her flee. The woods were filled with flying soldiers and women and children and old men. Her good Quaker hostess set her table time and again to feed the wanderers.

Though the battle, if such it may be called, took place in the early afternoon and Bladensburg is only six miles from the capital, it was nightfall before the British entered the town. Admiral Cockburn's report stated that "the victors were too weary and the vanquished too swift" for more energetic pursuit. As happened more than once during our Revolution, the sultry summer heat well nigh sapped the vitality of the British, burdened with heavy uniforms, arms, rations for three days and sixty rounds of ammunition. By eight o'clock, however, the Capitol was in flames and before midnight the White House shared its fate, both fires being kindled, according to scandalized patriots, with accompaniment of rude jests and horse-play, though how the natives were in a position to hear these British jests is unexplained. Meanwhile, Commodore Tingey, the officer in command at the Washington Navy Yard since its beginning, carried out the orders of the Secretary of the Navy and set fire to the plant he had so lovingly helped to create

Two bridges also were in flames, and at least one private house was fired in retaliation for a volley that issued from it as General Ross and Admiral Cockburn rode past. Then weariness and a soaking shower put an end to destruction for the remainder of the night. The twenty-fifth of August dawned as hot as though no rain had fallen, and during the morning the temperature mounted steadily toward a brazen climax of heat and tempest.

The visitors, going about their work of ruin, seem really to have tried to distinguish between public and private property and to have shown more than common courtesy to the few inhabitants who had courage to remain. The "National Intelligencer," which is unlikely to have been partial to the English, since they wrecked its establishment, stated that "greater respect was certainly paid to private property than has commonly been exhibited by the enemy in his marauding parties"; and some years later a journalist not noted for writing good things about people, if anything bad could be said, reported that the memory of General Ross "was much respected in the city, because of his gentlemanly conduct toward the females." He was quoted as saying that he would have spared the White House had Mrs. Madison remained there. During the occupation he was less conspicuous than Admiral Cockburn, whose fantastic appearance on Pennsylvania Avenue astride a white mare with a black colt frisking at her heels, was commented on by more than one eye-witness.

Next to Mrs. Madison's serene conduct, the best-known and most satisfying incident of the occupation is the rescue of the Patent Office by the omnipresent Dr. Thornton, who dashed up on horseback at the critical moment and besought the officer in charge of the work of demolition not to burn it, arguing that, since patents were the private property of their inventors, there was nothing in the building worth burning; and in the same breath that the hundreds of models represented arts so useful to mankind that their destruction would be vandalism comparable only to the burning of the great library at Alexandria, a crime which has rung through the ages. The double-barreled nature of the attack, reinforced by the eager doctor's array of legal and historical assertions, was too much for honest Major Waters, who passed on the responsibility to his colonel and was ordered to take his squad elsewhere.

This is Dr. Thornton's own version of the affair. Another represents the impetuous doctor reining in his horse and declaiming: "Are you Englishmen or vandals? This is the Patent Office of the United States, depository of the inventive genius of America, in which the whole civilized world is concerned. Would you destroy it? If so, fire away; but let the charge pass through my body!"

Less familiar and less pleasing to American pride is the story of the way in which John Law, one of the "Asiatic" sons of the eccentric Thomas, after serving faithfully all day, as sergeant in the District militia, doffed his uniform and paid his respects to General Ross, in his character of nephew of the latter's friend, Lord Ellenborough, and invited the invaders to dinner at his father's house. Perhaps the city fared better on account of it.

The stay of the victors was short. An accidental explosion at the Arsenal on Greenleaf's Point, on the morning of August 25th, resulted in the death of about one hundred British soldiers and this, with the excessive heat, evidently shook their morale. Some of them may actually have believed they saw a "powerful army of Americans," which figures in one British account, coming to the rescue, though our own War Department knew nothing about it.

But it was weather, not valor, that speeded the departure of our unwelcome guests. On that day the elements did enough to redeem all their previous caprices in the treatment of the city on the Potomac. An English subaltern wrote concerning the mythical American reinforcements:

Whether or not it was their intention to attack I cannot pretend to say, because it was noon before they showed themselves, and soon after when something like a movement could be discerned in their ranks, it grew suddenly dark, and the most tremendous hurricane ever remembered by the oldest inhabitant in the place, came on. Of the prodigious force of the wind it is impossible for you to form any conception. Roofs of houses were torn off and whisked into the air like sheets of paper; while the rain which accompanied it resembled the rushing of a mighty cataract rather than the dropping of a shower. The darkness was as great as if the sun had long set . . . together with the noise of the wind and the thunder, the crash of falling buildings and the tearing of roofs as they were stripped from the walls, produced the most appalling effect. . . . This lasted for nearly two hours without intermission. . . . Our column was as completely dispersed as if it had received a total defeat; some of the men flying for shelter behind walls and buildings, and others falling flat upon the ground to prevent themselves being carried away by the tempest; nay, such was the violence of the wind, that two pieces of cannon which stood upon the eminence [Capitol Hill?] were fairly lifted from the ground and borne several yards to the rear.

The demoralized Britons got themselves out of the city as best they could, and made their way toward Baltimore, not stopping even to take all of their wounded with them. In an age of religious faith, such interposition would have counted as a holy miracle. Even in the age that produced Tom Paine and in the city which gave him shelter, a church was built as a thank-offering; not by a Catholic but by a devout Methodist, whose munition-works on the edge of Georgetown, already important in Revolutionary times, was saved from destruction by the opportune bursting of the storm.

Neither British nor Americans felt proud of their record in this attack. Members of Parliament denounced the burning of Washington as senseless and stupid; and Americans, on their part, were angrily critical of soldiers who abandoned the national capital and fled after a loss of only eight killed and eleven wounded. They called it, bitterly, not the battle of Bladensburg but the "Bladensburg Races." Widner's name ingloriously faded from history. What was thought of him was scratched in accusing doggerel on a mile-post near the site of the disaster.

Poor Captain Barney, the only commander whose actions showed spirit, finally died of injuries received in his useless resistance. The one man whose reputation was made by the occasion was Francis Scott Key of Georgetown. He hurried after the British as they moved upon Baltimore, to intercede for Dr. Beaver, a physician of Upper Marlboro, who had been taken prisoner as they passed through, on the pretext that he had shown discourtesy to the invaders. Though Admiral Cockburn appeared to harbor particular rancor against the doctor, Mr. Key succeeded in obtaining his release, but only after a night of confinement on a British ship had forced him to witness the bombardment of Fort McHenry, and had given him the inspiration and leisure to write "The Star-Spangled Banner."

Days of grave anxiety remained for Washington, so long as Cockburn's ships lay only seven miles away, loading themselves richly from the warehouses of Alexandria. They might easily sail up-stream to repeat the visit of the British soldiers. In addition there was that ever-present haunting fear of a slave insurrection in the South, to torment the white people, who saw how such an uprising might be fostered and used by the enemy. But the slaves remained loyal. Many kept persistently in hiding while the British were in the city. Afterward, ranging the fields, they brought in trophies of arms and haversacks and ghastly finds of dead and wounded. The weapons they cheerfully turned over to the authorities, and they did all they could in their ignorance for the human flotsam and jetsam of battle. About two hundred British dead were buried by a committee of citizens, while more than one hundred wounded were taken care of in a hastily improvised hospital opposite the Capitol grounds.

VI

THE PHŒNIX

IN those days a city ordinance imposed a fine of eighty-three cents for "profane, swearing." The returning fugitives who looked upon the black and sodden ruins left by the British and the storm must have felt that the luxury was well worth the price. Even the Patent Office was injured, the storm having been less lenient than the enemy. Several semi-public buildings, like the office of the "National Intelligencer," had been burned and also a few private dwellings, in reprisal it was claimed, for shots fired as the British passed. The house Washington had built on North Capitol Street was one of these. About two million dollars' worth of property had been destroyed, but it was not alone the material loss that rankled. The people felt that the place had been defiled, and partly through their own cowardice. When they found the base of the monument to the heroes of Tripoli hacked by British saber cuts, they took some comfort in adding a grim line to the inscription telling by whom the damage had been done.

The burning of the city opened up anew the question of a site for the nation's capital. "It is not to be expected that Washington will ever again be the seat of government," wrote one of its residents, mournfully. Its defenselessness from a military point of view was dwelt upon. Philadelphia invited the Government to return to its old quarters. Lancaster said it would be welcome there; Georgetown tendered Congress the use of its college buildings in case it should not care to go further away, adding with barbed friendliness an offer to board members of Congress for ten dollars and a half a week instead of the Shylock charge of sixteen dollars recently made by Washington hotel-keepers. But when Congress came together in special session, the House of Representatives decided within three weeks to suffer inconvenience in its own home rather than seek shelter elsewhere. One member declared he would rather sleep under canvas in the Federal City than inhabit a palace in any other place. The Senate, more deliberate, reached the same conclusion within three months.

A public subscription was opened by the residents of Washington and Alexandria to complete Fort Washington, and the work was put in charge of Major L'Enfant, who had emerged from his seclusion to care for the wounded. Interest in this project soon died, however, and the money raised was not enough to pay (at the rate of a dollar a day and a pint of whisky) for the work actually done. Christian Hines, a local worthy who lived to extreme old age, used to dwell on this episode of his youth and tell how he drank "a friendly glass of wine" with L'Enfant, but that, having engaged the workmen, he was forced to pay them out of his own pocket. Later he was reimbursed.

Local banks came to the rescue, with the loan of half a million, to enable the Government to rebuild at once. The different departments settled down as best they could, mainly in private residences. Congress, on coming together for the special session, found its refuge in the Patent Office, which had already passed through three phases of failure—as Blodgett's prize for a grand lottery, as a hotel, and as an unprofitable theater. In 1810 it had been bought by the Government, and at the time of the fire housed not only the Patent Office but the Federal Post Office Department and the city post-office as well. To make room for Congress, the patent models, which Dr. Thornton had neatly arranged for display, were swept aside and chairs and desks installed in the limited space. The Supreme Court found inadequate accommodations but a hearty welcome in the home of the Clerk of the Court, Elias B. Caldwell, on Capitol Hill, who had suffered greater loss than most residents, his fine private library of law books, generously placed in the Capitol for the use of the court, having gone up in smoke.

The Department of State leased a dwelling on G Street between Seventeenth and Eighteenth streets. Fortunately, the personnel of the department was still small, though it had expanded beyond the nine individuals headed by the Secretary of State and ending with a colored messenger, which constituted its entire force at the time Madison entered Jefferson's administration.

The War Department found a home on F Street, near Fifteenth. The Navy Department betook itself to the useful Seven Buildings on Pennsylvania Avenue near Nineteenth Street, which had been put up while Morris and Nicholson still had money for such enterprises.

The Register of the Treasury set up his office on I Street, between Twentieth and Twenty-first streets, next to the residence of James Monroe, Secretary of State, whose handsome old doorway now opens to the members and guests of the Arts Club. The Treasury temporarily occupied William O'Neil's Franklin House.

President and Mrs. Madison, who had spent the hours of storm, following the battle, in a miserable hut in the Virginia woods, returned over a half-burned bridge across the Potomac and sought shelter with Mr. and Mrs. Cutts in the dwelling they had themselves occupied during President Jefferson's administration. Soon after, the French minister obligingly gave up for their use Colonel Tayloe's beautiful Octagon House, which he had leased, and this served as the Presidential residence until the Executive Mansion was again ready for occupancy.

The city hummed with tales of harrowing experiences, and, as is always the case after fire, painful efforts were made to locate and recover lost possessions. One gentleman had taken such active part in the "Bladensburg Races" that he preferred to remain nameless, yet wanted his property back and advertised for it in this fashion:

A Sword was left the evening of the battle of Bladensburg at some house in Washington. The person into whose possession the sword was left will please send it to this office to be forwarded to the owner. The sword is brass mounted with a broad belt attached to it.

3 or 4 times. Pd 1 Doll. R. C. C.

The manuscript copy for a "Lost" advertisement, printed in the "National Intelligencer" four months after the fire, reads:

On Thursday Evening the 22nd day of December 1814 between Capitol Hill and the presidents old House as I was walking between the

2 places to look at the Burnt Buildings, a small Red morocko pocket Book faced with a small Picture Covered with Glass Containing a twenty dollar bank note on the union bank of Maryland wraped up in a piece of brown paper a reward of Five Dollars will be given to the finder of the Pocket Book and money by returning the Pocket Book With the $20 in it to the Editors of the National Inteligencer, my name is rote In the Said Pocket Book.

William Riley
of Washington County
Maryland

December the 23rd
1814

Messrs. Gales and Seaton smoothed out a good many of the human kinks in this notice before it appeared in their exemplary journal, but even in its expurgated state it bears testimony that the "Burnt Buildings" were the dismal goal of sight-seers long after the fire.

The winter was spent in making plans and gathering supplies. In February matters became lively. Not only did the opening spring permit active building operations but war news was decidedly inspiriting. On February 6th the "National Intelligencer," startled out of its conservatism, announced in type of astonishing size—quite three quarters of an inch high—the "Almost Incredible Victory" won by General Jackson at New Orleans, four weeks and a day earlier.

This delay, long even for that era of slow mails, had been caused by freshets in the Mississippi Valley. The Mayor of Washington suggested a city-wide illumination as a proper way of celebrating the event, and on Saturday night, the eleventh, between the hours of seven and ten, the windows of houses small and great, public and private, shone as brilliantly as candles and astral lamps permitted.

About noon on Monday, February 13th, still more exciting rumors began to fly about, to the effect that peace had been signed and the war was over. Peace had indeed been signed, in Ghent late in January, but Mr. Henry Carroll, bringing with him a copy of the treaty, had landed in New York only two days before. An enterprising merchant took advantage of his leisurely preparations to continue his journey, and sent off in advance a secret and private courier to warn his own Southern correspondents.

Thirty hours before Mr. Carroll reached Washington, a Connecticut congressman who had friends in the South got the news, which he seems to have been more desirous to pass on than to impart to the Government. He asked the city postmaster to delay the departure of Southern mails for thirty minutes or so, a courtesy often granted in those easy-going days. This time the postmaster was inconveniently curious to know why, and on being sworn to secrecy and told, insisted that the President be informed. Mr. Madison, shaken into something like animation, declared that no such secret messages should be sent with his sanction. Every one felt bound, however, by the pledge previously given to the member of Congress. The President's private secretary was therefore sent over to the War Department, to repeat the story as an interesting rumor. An officer drew his own conclusions and offered to mount his horse and spread the news as far as the animal would carry him. The congressman meanwhile deemed it prudent to dispatch a messenger of his own, and these two galloped off in an exciting race toward Fredericksburg. All of which was energy wasted, for the British fleet off Amelia Island had notified Savannah, and the South had known of the treaty before Mr. Carroll left New York, the Washington public, half-way between the two centers of information, being almost the last to learn the news.

It was after dark on February 14th that the wooden bridge across the Tiber thundered its confirmation as Mr. Carroll's four coach horses pounded across it, bearing him and his treaty toward the office of the Secretary of State. People rushed out into Pennsylvania Avenue and cheered as the coach disappeared in the shadows. Washington being fond of party-going, its people spontaneously came together that evening at the Octagon House, where judges in their robes and foreign ministers in their gold lace, officers in uniform, senators, members of Congress, pretty girls, and "old ladies of fifty," with bare bosoms and wreaths of roses and gold leaves in their false hair, rejoiced in Mrs. Madison's drawing-room, while the murmur of their happy voices ascended the curved stairway to the room over the front door where the President and his cabinet sat in grave conclave.

In that home nobody had been forgotten in the general rejoicing, for Sally Coles, a cousin of Mrs. Madison's, rushed to the head of the basement stairs and called, "Peace! Peace!" to which each of the servants responded after his own fashion. Paul Jennings, the President's body-servant, seized his fiddle to play the President's March; the butler, obeying orders, served out wine liberally; and French John drank enough of it to impair his usefulness for several days.

It was after this that attention turned whole-heartedly to the work of rebuilding. Advertisements appeared in Baltimore and Philadelphia, announcing that the commissioners were ready to give instant employment to large numbers of stone-cutters, bricklayers and joiners, at wages of $2.00 a day to first-rate workmen in stone and brick and $1.75 to joiners; those who were "not first-rate workmen to receive pay in proportion to the service they can render."

In May the President was informed that contracts had been let and that the two executive offices would be rebuilt and ready for use by the beginning of the New Year. It was evident, however, that repairs upon the Capitol would consume much more time,—years, in all probability,—and that meanwhile Congress could not stay in Blodgett's old hotel, which was less suited to its newest rôle than to any that preceded it.

Daniel Carroll of Duddington, Thomas Law and Frederick D. May united in a letter asking for a congressional appropriation of $10,000 to put up a temporary building on Capitol Hill for the use of Congress, since this would give "time to reëstablish the conflagrated edifices" and relieve the boarding-houses near the Capitol from the hardship of being deserted, as they had been during the previous session. Congress refused to vote any sum whatever for the purpose, but mitigated the refusal by hints, if not actual assurances, that if the gentlemen chose to put up such a building as a private enterprise, Congress might be counted upon as a tenant.

A stock company was formed which tore down that pride of the city, Tunnicliff's Grand Hotel near the Capitol, increased the devastated area by plowing up gardens north and south of it, and covered the whole space with a three-story brick edifice capped by a high-pitched roof, in which large halls were provided on the first and second floors. The work went on with such vigor that the building was ready for occupancy ahead of time and was opened in December, 1815, with feasting and toasts, in true Southern style. The occasion was further distinguished by the reading of an original "poem" by Mr. Law, in which he told how "A peal of victory rung And the new edifice in splendor sprung, Like a Phœnix from its ashes, While a sound of triumph and rejoicing rose around."

The construction of the "Brick Capitol" was fortunately superior to that of the poem. It still stands and much history has been made within its walls.

The work of restoration on the real Capitol proceeded as rapidly as possible in view of the thorough destruction it had undergone. Benjamin Latrobe, who had built the south wing and put in strengthening walls and arches in the north wing during his ten years of service between 1803 and 1813, was recalled to superintend the work. Judging from a diary he kept during his first term of service, he must have been secretly of the opinion that the British had done Congress a rare good turn.

Work upon the executive offices and at the White House was in charge of James Hoban. Repairs were in progress at the Navy Yard and the Arsenal, and, like begetting like, the contagion of building extended to private owners, who planned and erected handsome residences. In consequence of all this activity the years of business depression following the war were less felt in Washington than elsewhere. In other parts of the country they were spoken of as "Anno Domini eighteen hundred and starve to death," but the Government, even when hard pressed, managed to pay its laborers in cash and its local creditors in kind if not in real money.

The Old Testament picture of swords being turned into plowshares found its literal paraphrase in Georgetown, where a thrifty merchant named Reuben Dow accepted in payment of a government debt the barrels of flint-lock muskets and, giving them fancy tops and a rock base, converted them into an iron fence which is still doing duty and is not odd enough in appearance to attract a second glance. Search, however, reveals an occasional gun-sight to prove its strange origin.

To this same decade of active building belongs the City Hall, for which ground was broken in 1820. Planned by George Hadfield, one of the group of men in charge at the Capitol in early years, it was by far the most ambitious white-columned building undertaken since the Capitol was begun. Enthusiasm for his really noble design cooled perceptibly when it was discovered that it would cost at least seven times the hundred thousand dollars to which competitors had been asked to restrict their imagination. But Hadfield was willing to redraw his plans on a more modest scale and work was begun, not on a lot upon Pennsylvania Avenue as had been hoped, but near Blodgett's old hotel and the infirmary and District jail, at the head of a dismal common stretching up from the low parts of Pennsylvania Avenue. President Monroe had refused to sign the bill for the erection of a City Hall on Pennsylvania Avenue, because it was for the use of municipal officers and District courts only, and not a federal building. The necessary money was to be raised by a "Grand National Lottery," a title misleading in that it was national in name only. This one was expected to furnish means for the City Hall, for a penitentiary, and for new public schools.

Unfortunately for this enterprise and the odd trinity it was designed to benefit, it was launched so late that it suffered shipwreck in the wave of anti-gambling sentiment which swept the country about this time, causing near-by states to prohibit the sale of wicked lottery tickets within their borders. Yet locally the need for courts and penitentiaries never seemed greater than when the manager of the lottery absconded and left a deficit behind. Before this climax was reached, the mayor had opened his office in a suite of rooms in the unfinished building, and for years thereafter, as new municipal and federal offices were required, other groups of rooms were finished and occupied, though the outside continued to present an almost indecently naked surface of unstuccoed brick.

The most important private house erected in the decade was built within pistol-shot of old David Burnes's story-and-a-half farm cottage in its grove of trees near the Tiber. This stood just as it had when Washington argued with its crusty owner, though the surrounding grounds had shrunk to the dimensions of a city square. Here his son-in-law, General John P. Van Ness, a former representative from New York who had wooed and won the Scotchman's pretty daughter, was building, with the heiress's money and his own, a home which was believed to be the most elegant residence in the United States, now that Robert Morris's wonderful house in Philadelphia had come to grief.

The Van Ness mansion had a porte-cochère, an elegance the Executive Mansion still lacked, and hot and cold water might be had in any bedroom by merely turning a tap. No other house in the country was thus equipped, and drawing-rooms and kitchens and wine-cellars were on a correspondingly lavish scale. People wondered how old David felt about the extravagance, if such news found its way across the Styx. Latrobe was the architect. Rumor whispered that L'Enfant had offered his professional services, which were politely but firmly declined.

Latrobe found time amid his official duties to make several building plans for his friends. One was a country house north of the city known as Brentwood, for Mr. Brent, a potential mayor. The most important of all was St. John's Episcopal Church, the first edifice to rise opposite the White House, across the common then known as President's Square. This church was begun in 1816 and has counted more Presidents among its regular attendants, opened the door of matrimony to more society girls, and closed the tomb over more distinguished men than any other in Washington.

Latrobe also drew plans for the first dwelling erected upon this square, the massive, stately house of Commodore Decatur, whose gentle drawing-room manners were oddly out of keeping with his deeds upon the sea. It was he who, as a mere lieutenant in command of a single tiny overladen vessel, had audaciously carried war into the harbor of Tripoli and recaptured the *Philadelphia* under the muzzles of pirate guns. And during the recent conflict with England he had exhibited the same spirit, tempered but slightly with the prudence of middle age. He and his slender, dark-eyed wife were notable additions to the Washington circle and added distinction to any drawing-room they entered. In building his own drawing-room, the admiral manifested the initiative he showed at sea, choosing his lot on the west side of what is now Lafayette Square, before the park had been divided from the building lots abutting upon it. The town authorities kindly allowed a roadway to be made in front of his dwelling, the commodore advancing fifty dollars to pay for the labor, on the understanding that it should be refunded some time when the city's treasury was less nearly empty. Two years later Mr. Madison's brother-in-law, Mr. Cutts, put up his much more modest dwelling on the opposite side of the same square, near the little graveyard which was then its chief ornament.

There is a tradition that Washington himself wrote Lafayette's name upon this square in L'Enfant's original map, though it was not so called until after the French general's famous visit in 1824. With the Executive Mansion facing it on the south, a fashionable church on its northern edge, and these two homes marking its eastern and western limits, the square became instantly the social center of the town, a supremacy it held for a century, which old residents with regret now see slipping away to regions that were forests and stubble fields even after the Spanish War.

Outside the Navy-Yard gate the employees had what was to all intents and purposes a community of their own, neither fashionable nor elegant but full of rural charm, with its little houses and its church facing a well-shaded village green.

The unfinished City Hall, ugly duckling though it was, standing in pin-feather nudity on a reservation scarcely touched by scythe or pruning-hook, gave promise of the beauty that it would one day attain as a building of Doric columns set in a green and lovely park. People who had imagination to see beyond the present were soon to build around it substantial homes with curved front steps and fanlights over their doors, the advance-guard of another nucleus of fashion.

Standing amid the clutter of materials on the west front of the Capitol, one could see the whole low-lying portion of the city known as the Island, bounded by the Potomac, the Tiber, and the canal. It was now dotted with well-to-do homes and with some not so prosperous. The town was still as primitive in regard to a system of sewerage as it had been in the days when the makers of stone knives sat fashioning their wares. Indeed, it was worse off in that respect, for every new building increased the menace of the Tiber, a sluggish stream "two thirds of a street wide" with a soft muddy bottom and many little gullies and watercourses flowing into it.

Even the Van Ness mansion in its grandeur was not exempt from the plague of miasma. There were diverse theories as to the best way of meeting these unhealthful conditions. The English Mr. Faux, in 1819, going to call upon "Elliott of the City Gazette," compiler of the earliest Congressional Directory, found that gentleman's house almost hidden in sunflowers and was told that "sunflowers breathe each as much in one day as twelve men. I consider them as highly propitious to health, particularly in low or marshy situations. I therefore surround my hermitage with them." On the river front were the wharves and the landing-place of the Alexandria ferry, most prosperous of all the un-prosperous attempts to build up business south of Pennsylvania Avenue. As the eye swept toward Georgetown, it noted the paper factory and a "glass house" before coming to rest on the college buildings.

The stretch of Pennsylvania Avenue from Capitol to White House also was in full view, with Jefferson's four rows of poplars growing rapidly. Shops were fewer and boarding-places more plentiful toward the two ends, each of the principal taverns being surrounded by a flock of boarding-houses, to which they stood in the relation of a hen to its brood of chickens. Before 1825, the whole length of the avenue was dotted with groups of houses, within friendly reach of one another, though by no means continuous. Midway between the Capitol and the White House, on the south side of the avenue, stood the collection of sheds and stalls called Center Market.

Among other urban assets, at this time, were three city banks and a branch Bank of the United States, an insurance office, and a bath-house where even in winter a hot bath might be secured for fifty cents "every Saturday and on Sunday morning until ten o'clock," and at any other time on an hour's notice and the payment of one dollar. There were seven printing-offices and four newspapers, two of which were dailies, while the other two resembled the jam in "Alice in Wonderland" by appearing only every other day.

Two or three exhibition halls stood waiting for visiting attractions, and when not thus engaged were available for balls and assemblies. There was also a theater managed by a woman; but this was not profitable, Washingtonians preferring, for steady amusement, the debates in Congress. On higher ground, F Street, formerly known as the Ridge Road, duplicated Pennsylvania Avenue with a scattering line of buildings from the executive offices to the new court-house, though the street was narrower and a larger proportion of its houses were private dwellings. John Quincy Adams lived there, not far from the Treasury. On the same street, a few blocks farther east, was St. Patrick's Catholic Church, with its rectory and gardens and fine spring. Later, when real city buildings were put up, the subterranean stream which had its outlet here played havoc with foundations until it was securely sealed under cement and stone, in the Washington Loan and Trust Building.

Though sewer-pipes were so conspicuously absent, water-pipes were no novelty. This simply meant that a few natural springs, like the one in St. Patrick's garden, had been put to work. Therefore, in spite of agues and possible typhoid, it was an advantage to live on ground not too high to be reached by the natural flow of water. One of the city improvements made at this time was the addition of a new "fountain," which had its source in what is now Franklin Square and yielded "sixty gallons a minute." Another was the gathering and storing of water in brick-lined underground tanks at suitable points for use in case of fire.

Where drinking-water could not be obtained from natural springs, wells had been dug and "the pump-mender was a municipal officer of importance," who contracted for his job by the year and went from spot to spot making needed repairs. Advertisements of houses for sale or rent enlarged upon the purity and convenience of the nearest supply in this manner:

For Rent—On Greenleaf's Point, next door to the residence of Com. Rodgers, a 3 story brick house, with excellent carriage house and stables. The house is, in all respects, suitable for the accommodation of a genteel family, and is near to a pump, the water from which is not excelled by any in the city. For terms apply to Mr. R. Goldsborough living near to Major Davidson's wharf—or to Com. Rodgers.

The corner pump was only an upright cedar-wood post with a short spout and a creaking handle. It had not one atom of the charm and grace of Old-World fountains with their backgrounds of stone and mellow brick, but drew about it characteristic groups, particularly in the less fashionable parts of town. Negro laundresses, whose skins shone like ebony in the morning sunlight, pumped brimming pails and, swinging them to their heads, paced off with a majesty queens might envy; and on warm summer evenings householders strolling up with pitchers, to get the bedtime supply of water, lingered to gossip. Mothers, blissfully unconscious of germs, held to the mouths of their babies the long-handled iron dippers that were chained to the post as securely as Bibles were ever chained to reading-stands, while their elder children splashed one another joyously from puddles left behind by previous visitors, who thought they had fulfilled every canon of cleanliness and good manners by tossing to the ground the water left in the dipper after their thirst was satisfied.

At all hours of the day wayfarers stopped at the pump, for copious drafts, to the amazement and horror of foreign visitors. "Two or three of the English have this day and recently fallen dead at the city fountains in consequence of drinking excessively of cold water while they were in a high perspiration under a heat of 98 or 100 in the shade," wrote Mr. Faux. But it was easy enough to avoid this danger if one knew how. "It is only necessary to drink a wineglass half full of brandy first, and a pint of water immediately after. Thirst is thus quenched with much less water than would be necessary without the spirits."

America was a strange place: but, after all, life was not devoid of charm to the initiated!

Little streams from springs that had not been put to work wandered over the face of the earth, creating miniature swamps, particularly in the depressions of the city streets. This emphasized one curious uncomfortable result of the local form of government. Dual ownership alone had made possible a grandiose city plan, but the same divided authority constantly hampered its execution. No matter how vigorously the edicts of the mayor and his associates might be worded, they could be executed only against individuals: against the Federal Government they were as powerless as thistledown, and for some inscrutable reason the Federal Government refused to do its part toward caring for and improving city thoroughfares.

Few private owners of lots aspired to the elegance of real brick sidewalks as yet, but they usually had enough pride, if not enough consideration for their neighbors, to furnish some sort of footway in front of their property. Only the Government remained oblivious; and on Pennsylvania Avenue, near the Capitol grounds, where the federal authority held reservations on one side for a distance of six blocks and on the other for three or four blocks, conditions were worse than anywhere else. Most congressmen and senators had to pass twice daily over this section of the avenue in attending to their duties at the Capitol, and every one of them knew how bad it was. They alone had the power to make it better, yet is was in vain that they declaimed passionately upon the subject, in Congress, or, assuming a plaintive tone, asked if this was as it should be. Equally in vain did they indulge, outside the chamber, in language both sulphurous and unparliamentary, declaring that the avenue was impassable after dark, on foot or on horseback, and that they were kept prisoners in their rooms, unable to walk abroad without danger to life and limb.

For years nothing came of it beyond an occasional appropriation, granted as largess, not as a right. Undoubtedly this was the main reason why congressional boarding-houses crowded around the larger hotels. Their nearness afforded some chance for meeting strangers and constituents comfortably outside of business hours.

If the sidewalks were bad, the streets themselves were worse. John Quincy Adams, who, though a realist, was conscientious and

From the Beginnings of Washington by P. L. Philipps.

ST. JOHN'S CHURCH AND THE PRESIDENT'S HOUSE IN 1816

not given to exaggeration, wrote in April, 1818, this tale of the difficulties of going out to dine at Mr. Middleton's in Georgetown:

> The weather having been foul the roads were bad. Our carriage in coming for us in the evening was overset, the harness broken, and the boy Philip took a sprain in the side, so that we were obliged to take him home in the carriage. We got home with difficulty, being twice on the point of oversetting; and at the Treasury Office corner we were both obliged to get out of the carriage in the mud. I called out the guard of the Treasury Office and borrowed a lantern with which we came home. We immediately sent for the surgeon nearest at hand who came and bled Philip. It was a mercy we all got home with whole bones.

The only people thoroughly satisfied with the streets were the hackmen—black, brown, coffee-colored, cream, and albino—in all styles of decrepit vehicles, who hovered about the worst mud-holes, soliciting patronage.

With its limited funds and divided responsibility, Washington became an even stranger mixture after its rebuilding than before. It stretched sprawling over an immense amount of ground, with long waste spaces between houses. The white-columned public buildings and an occasional glimpse of a stately home in its brick-walled garden, with slave quarters and solid out-houses, furnished the architectural high lights, for each of which the darkest shadows were easily found. The citizens dwelt as little as possible upon the shadows when speaking with strangers; and never forgot to mention the high lights. Visitors were frequently tempted to believe that they had strayed into a community of lunatics, for to their incorrigibly ardent hosts the vision of Washington of the future glowed so brightly that they acted as though it were verily before their eyes.

Strangers saw costly elegance and slovenly commonness close together at every turn. If they were discerning, and looked a second time, they realized that what was good was very good, though for the most part unfinished, while that which was bad was not tawdry but frankly a makeshift for the moment's need, to be removed and replaced by something better at the first opportunity. If they were unused to seeing cabins jostling Greek columns, they were puzzled. Cabins and columns were commendable and easy to understand separately. Together they produced an odd bewilderment which was apt to curdle into indignation, as though the beholders had been asked to look upon something not quite moral.

Then mysteriously would steal in upon them from somewhere an understanding that the columns had been planted to endure, while the cabins were only a symbol—a rough shorthand of columns yet to come. And after that, if the visitor's heart was not iron hard, it would fill with real affection for the city and its optimistic, hospitable inhabitants. "In spite of its inconvenience and its desolate aspect," wrote Sir Augustus Foster, "it was, I think, the most agreeable town to reside in"; and fastidious Henry Adams expressed much the same idea some thirty years later, remembering his own youthful reactions to the place. The town was absurd, impossible; but its very absurdities endeared it to those who once came under its curious spell.

VII

THE LAST COCKED HAT

WHEN Monroe became President, in 1817, Congress was still holding its sessions in the Brick Capitol. Had the custom of four successive inaugurations been followed, the ceremonies would have taken place indoors, probably in the Senate chamber, in the presence of as many people as could crowd into that narrow space. But an untactful Senate committee having the ceremonies in charge, applied to the Speaker of the House, Henry Clay, for permission to use the larger room, and not only asked exclusive control of it, but in a burst of unnecessary frankness confided its plan to bring the "fine red chairs" from the Senate Chamber, to add comfort and splendor to the scene.

Clay took umbrage at being asked to give to any power on earth "exclusive" control of the room in which the representatives of the sovereign people met, and in addition waxed indignant at the idea that the stout democratic wooden seats he and his colleagues habitually used were not good enough for anybody. The absurd incident caused so much feeling that neither room was used, a still earlier precedent being followed, whereby, on a temporary platform built against the east front of the real Capitol, Monroe took his oath out of doors, in sight of the people, as Washington had taken his on the balcony of the City Hall in New York. Thus originated the custom which, in the course of a century, has possibly hastened the death of one President and undoubtedly killed many lesser folk.

Monroe owed his almost unopposed election in the campaign of 1824 largely to chronology, since by stern decree of the calendar he was the last man it was humanly possible to make President who had taken part in the affairs of the nation from its beginning. He had been a Revolutionary soldier at the early age of seventeen, and had served the country faithfully ever since. This election came as the crowning and well-earned recognition of his personal worth, and was also the final tribute of American voters to the group of great men who brought the nation into being. They spoke of Monroe as "The Last Cocked Hat," and of the campaign as the "Era of Good Feeling," but there was no overflowing of good-will in Washington when, with the passing of Madison's administration, a cold and chilly fog seemed to settle down over the genial social landscape. Those who went to pay their respects to the new President and his wife were met with a frigid "not at home," and stood with unbelieving eyes, watching the door of the house on I Street where the Monroes continued to live until the Executive Mansion should be finished, slowly close, leaving them on the step outside.

Mrs. Madison, who had set the social fashions for sixteen years, had such a fund of good humor, and was so spontaneously willing to meet advances more than half-way, that this new attitude seemed incredible. Any woman coming after her was doomed to suffer criticism; but Mrs. Monroe was unwise enough to let it be seen that she considered the duties of her new position a burden instead of an opportunity. She had neither the strength nor the desire to follow in Mrs. Madison's footsteps. She never forgot that she had been a New York beauty in Revolutionary days, nor that in Paris she had been known as *la belle Américaine,* while her husband served as minister there. She gave the wreck of her former good looks every advantage of cosmetics and discreet lighting, and cultivated a manner that was passive and elegant but not cordial. To make matters worse, her married daughter Mrs. Hay, upon whom part of the social burden must fall, had a fatal gift of arousing antagonisms, seeming aggressively afraid that too much might be demanded of her. A younger unmarried daughter had grown up in Washington while her father was occupying one, and sometimes two or three positions simultaneously in Madison's cabinet. She had been a lovable, lively child, but had lost some of her high spirits with advancing years, and, though beloved by her intimates, had not the power to counteract the prejudices roused by her elders.

The President was totally without social aggressiveness. Indeed, he had a genius for losing himself in his own drawing-room; but he had also a well-defined notion of the dignity of his office and had lived enough among diplomats abroad to know that the informality of Jefferson's manner of receiving envoys, and even Mrs. Madison's gracious friendliness, might be misunderstood. The diplomatic corps had fallen into lax habits of dropping in to call at the White House in a way that Monroe was sure would not be tolerated one instant if practised by our ministers toward the sovereigns of the countries to which they were accredited. If he and Mrs. Monroe consulted together and agreed that the least obnoxious way of enforcing an embargo against diplomats would be to deny themselves to every one, obviously that was not a decision to be shouted from the housetops. So callers stood on the Presidential doorstep and fumed.

It is immaterial whether the discussion began among dissatisfied ladies and spread to their husbands, or among husbands and spread to their wives; official Washington soon found itself engaged in a battle of etiquette such as had not raged since Jefferson exploded his rule of *pêle mêle,* the point at issue being whether senators or cabinet members held the higher office and were therefore entitled to the courtesy of a first call. One side argued that the cabinet should receive the first visit, being members of the President's official family. The other maintained that this was all wrong, because a vote of the Senate was necessary to confirm any cabinet minister. The Secretary of State, John Quincy Adams, with real worry but with a flash of unusual humor recorded in his diary the progress of the quarrel, and reduced the contention of the senatorial party to absurdity by applying the same rule to their own cases, picturing all the senators rushing about to make first calls upon all the members of the state legislatures that had elected them.

Semi-official invitations, difficult to accept gracefully or to decline without giving offense, added embarrassments amusing enough in retrospect but bothersome at the moment; and an innocent baby became almost an international complication when the British minister and his wife sent out invitations to the christening of their latest born and the Secretary of State accepted, as was proper if he chose to do so. The rumor got abroad that Mr. Adams was to act as proxy for the prince regent and this was denounced by hot-headed one-hundred-per-cent Americans as "too damn friendly to England."

A little later much was made of the absence or presence of the White-House family at a grand ball given by the French minister, Hyde de Neuville, to celebrate the evacuation of French territory by the allied troops. Mr. Monroe was entirely willing to attend the ball if a precedent could be found for the appearance of an American President under the roof of a foreign minister. Search failed to yield such a precedent. A man who had once served as private secretary to General Washington solemnly asserted that his honored chief "never did so," and Monroe concluded to stay at home, but left Mrs. Monroe to make her own decision. She promptly announced that a place where her husband ought not to be seen was no fit place for her.

Then the French minister, who coveted the presence of a Monroe at his party for the glory this would lend his report to the home office, turned his persuasion upon Mrs. Hay, although she was at daggers drawn with the foreign ladies, having flatly refused to return their calls. She promised to appear as a personal favor to the minister, but hedged her acceptance about with so many conditions as to make it seem almost an insult instead of a gracious act. It was small wonder that, with a spirit of such prickly arrogance, she was not liked! Adams, who was rather prickly himself, regarded her as the trouble-breeder of the Administration. Yet she was kind after her fashion, and when the Calhoun baby lay ill and friends offered their help in nursing, as was the custom before trained service could be hired, she came three nights in succession at a time most inconvenient to herself, and begged with tears in her eyes to be allowed to stay.

Simple as Monroe's personal tastes were, even he may have remembered the minor slights and annoyances that had fallen to his lot while he was representing the United States abroad. At any rate, one day he confided to the unimaginative Secretary of State his wish that a uniform dress might be devised and adopted for the heads of departments and officers of the Government. It would be interesting to know whether this was a reminiscence of his own uniformless days in Paris, or a sally of humor, or a bit of prompting from his womenkind. The innovation was never tried, but Mrs. Monroe speedily put the servants of the "President's Palace" into discreet livery, which made the oft-repeated formula "not at home" seem still more frigid—quite as if the door had been slammed in one's face.

A certain amount of official entertaining was obligatory, little as hosts or guests enjoyed it. Under the new dispensation, a Presidential dinner-party became a real ordeal, if we may credit a new congressman's account of his first adventures in the White House. Promptly at five o'clock, the hour named, the representative and his party were ushered single file into the drawing-room, where they found the guests in two mute segments of a circle, the women seated near Mrs. Monroe, the men in a group by themselves. The new-comers advanced toward the President's wife, who rose and greeted them pleasantly enough, but made no effort to prolong the conversation or to indicate what they were to do next. After a few agonized moments, they retreated guiltily and found seats for themselves; then they discovered the whereabouts of the President, this being one of the days when he sought the shelter of protective coloring and lost himself among his guests. Horrified and embarrassed at having seated themselves without paying their respects to their host, they advanced, bowing. He rose and shook hands with them, but again conversation languished and all was still. Once more the guests retreated and, this time attaching themselves firmly to their gold chairs, "joined the silence," from which they looked out as more victims were ushered in, and the ghastly ceremony was repeated over and over for an interminable half-hour until dinner was announced.

The torture suffered at a Presidential levee was not so acute, there being more people to dilute it, but neither was the glory of being invited so great. In time resentment wore away and the innovations were highly approved, as lending tone and distinction to society. It was the familiar sequence of disapproval, which first endured, then pitied, then embraced.

Without question, curiosity to see the inside of the restored mansion played its part in patching up the truce. New furnishings had to be provided; everything having been burned by the British, from the yellow-satin hangings in the drawing-room to kitchen pots and pans. On the day before Monroe's inauguration, Congress appropriated a sparing twenty thousand dollars for this purpose, adding thirty thousand a year later. Such articles as could be found in America were bought at once, but furniture for the oval drawing-room had to be ordered from abroad. Mrs. Monroe, who liked French things, had brought home with her a goodly supply of mahogany, so it seemed natural to order things of a similar character.

Just at the moment when the social quarrel was losing zest, mysterious packing-cases, shipped from Havre, were landed on the wharf at Alexandria. Opened at the White House, they disclosed gilt sofas and chairs and elegant smaller luxuries in the way of table ornaments and clocks. A long letter of explanation admitted they were not what had been ordered and cost a deal more, but that, the letter said, "must be ascribed to the gilt wood and crimson silk trimmings, fringes, etc., which are fifty per cent dearer than other colors." The agents continued: "We should also add that mahogany is not generally admitted in the furniture of a saloon, even at private gentlemen's houses." *Noblesse oblige.* Evidently they felt that they had discharged a difficult task very creditably, for they went on to tell how hard it had been to find French ornaments suited to the pure atmosphere of a Republican capital: "We had great difficulty in getting *pendules* without nudities; and were in fact forced to take the two models we have bought on that account." Once more *noblesse oblige!* Whispers of these marvels got abroad, so when people received invitations to the trying White-House dinners, they argued with alacrity that they "had" to accept; and, once in the oval drawing-room, as the long minutes ticked themselves off on the dials of the prim pendules they looked with veiled and rather hostile curiosity at the gold-and-pinkish-crimson French furniture set out on the wonderful green Aubusson carpet woven in a single piece with the arms of the United States in the center.

This hostility blazed up openly after the sudden death of the Commissioner of Public Buildings, whose books, revealing a discrepancy of about twenty thousand dollars, disclosed the fact that the President had accepted from the dead official an advance of several thousand dollars for the temporary use of his own furniture in the White House, with the understanding that the money was to be returned on the arrival of the shipments from France. It was a private transaction between gentlemen, which became public only by reason of Colonel Lane's untimely death. No one who knew the President dreamed for a moment that anything wrong had been intended on either side. But the "Era of Good Feeling" completely passed away during the eight years of his incumbency, and this provided too juicy a morsel of political gossip to be overlooked.

Quite aside from graver questions, it is a pity for the glory of Washington's history that the years Monroe was in the White House could not have passed under more magnetic leadership. The opening of the restored White House; the return of the two houses of Congress to their rightful chambers; the laying of the corner-stone of the central portion of the Capitol; the ovation to Andrew Jackson, fresh from his campaign which added the Territory of Florida to the Union; and the nation's enthusiastic welcome to Lafayette, were occasions whose skilful handling should have caused his Presidency to be remembered as the Golden Age of Washington society. Instead, it was a time of social discomfort.

It would be hard to find a period when more individuals whose names have stood the test of time, walked the city streets. The last of the old Virginia dynasty of Presidents was finishing his term. Marshall, the great Chief Justice, was in his vigorous old age, Adams, Jackson, Van Buren, Clay, Calhoun, and Webster, all held high office. Congressmen of the old era, like John Randolph, sat side by side in the House of Representatives with men emphatically of a new day, who represented states that had been unopened wilderness in 1800.

Dr. Thornton and Mr. Law and John Quincy Adams's cousin Mr. Greenleaf each in his way represented elements contributing to the development of the town. Mr. Greenleaf, who had not before lived in Washington, much as he had speculated there, was about to build the home of his old age in the eastern section, next door (though a good eighth of a mile away) to that of his brother-in-law Judge Cranch, perhaps the city's best-loved resident, who served for half a century as Chief Justice of the Supreme Court of the District. General and Mrs. Van Ness generously dispensed hospitality in their splendid new home near the mouth of the Tiber. The Custis family at Arlington, and Mrs. Peter at Tudor Place, in Georgetown, a stately residence finished by means of the legacy left her in Washington's will, kept up the traditions of pre-Revolutionary aristocracy, while saucy Peggy O'Neil, daughter of the man who kept the Franklin House, was growing up with good looks and audacity and high spirits, to work mischief in the next political generation.

There was already a group that considered itself literary; and at intervals the diplomatic corps blossomed in court dress as vivid as that of the Indian delegations who walked Washington streets every month in the year. The War of 1812 was not yet so far away that the naval officers who served in it brilliantly had ceased to be heroes, or that the few army officers who managed to gather laurels upon land were not marked men. One of the best of these, old General Jacob Brown, the Quaker farmer, was now commander of the entire army, while young General Winfield Scott, tall and showy and efficient, appeared and reappeared as his duties called him to the capital. The slaves and free negroes who made up a large proportion of the District's inhabitants were picturesque if humble, and the artisans of assorted nationalities at work upon the public buildings formed a varied human background.

Unfortunately, the Monroes had no skill in combining such elements to their own or their party's advantage. Even the opportunity for graciousness afforded by a White-House wedding was allowed to go to waste when "little Maria Monroe" was married to her cousin Mr. Gouverneur. Instead of opening the doors of the mansion wide in Southern fashion for several days of festivity, they adopted what was known as the "New-York style," and chose to treat the occasion as a very private affair. True, it was announced that the great unfinished "ball-room" would be lighted and opened the following evening to accommodate the crowds expected at the regular drawing-room. But that was not at all the same thing as being invited to the wedding.

The little bride was too much loved, however, to be allowed to change her name without some demonstration by her friends, and in spite of the chilling effects of the "New-York style" enough entertainments had been planned to make the week of March 20, 1820, the most brilliant of the season. The Decaturs gave a grand ball, and invitations were out for a wonderful evening at the Van Ness mansion. But all this festivity was brought to a sudden close by the pistol-shots which rang out in the early morning of March 22d, when Admiral Decatur and Commodore Barron met for their duel, upon the very farm on which the Battle of Bladensburg had been fought.

It was one of those unnecessary tragedies that might have been averted had friends been willing to interpose, but in the strange code of personal honor then prevalent nobody felt himself at liberty to interfere. And, in the early morning, brilliant Admiral Decatur opened the little low side door in the brick wall of his dwelling, closed it softly, not to wake his sleeping household, and rode away toward the rising sun to keep tryst with his fellow-officer in that secluded amphitheater among the trees, just across the District line, which was perhaps the best-known dueling-ground in America. Both men fell at the first fire, Barron badly wounded, to be nursed slowly back to health at Beall's Tavern and to find his way back more slowly still into the good graces of his fellow-men; Decatur mortally hurt, to die at his home late that night, in the arms of his wife.

Instead of festivity, the week ended in a succession of funerals. An imposing cortege accompanied Decatur to his tomb at Kalorama. On the day before his funeral, a long line of carriages, grotesquely out of proportion to the tiny coffin, followed Mrs. Calhoun's baby out to the cemetery near the Navy Yard; and on the morning of the day Decatur was laid to rest, a solemn requiem mass, as rich as the Catholic clergy of the District could make it, was sung at St. Patrick's Church in memory of the French Duke de Berri, news of whose assassination had just reached America.

The city was long in recovering its normal tone. A summer intervened. The year 1821 saw serious discussion of temperance and other moral problems. During the late summer and early autumn of 1822 much sickness developed in the District, which took the form of a baffling and often mortal bilious fever. Letters from the city were filled with names of acquaintances and friends who had been in excellent health one week and were dead the next. Mr. Law lost one of his sons. Mrs. Madison's sister, Mrs. Cutts, passed away. In one Georgetown family, six were smitten and three died in an interval of two days. The dreaded word "cholera" was whispered. Doctors went without proper food, snatching sleep where and how they could; and the melons and fruit they forbade their patients to eat had never looked so enticing. Piles of such fruit rotted upon the ground, but some was sold surreptitiously at back doors in spite of city edicts and physicians' orders.

As Monroe's term drew to an end, the "Era of Good Feeling" dissolved in bickerings which were more an expression of the unrest of youth than of disagreement on principles of government. The older statesmen and their political generation had been honored in Monroe's two virtually unopposed elections. The country was young; voters had been docile a long time. The field was open: devil take the hindmost! Candidates sprang up all over the country, most of them speedily to disappear again.

Never before had Washington been so personally interested in an election, for the five strongest candidates were government officials resident in the city for a part at least of each year. One was the Secretary of State, John Quincy Adams. The regular nominee chosen by congressional caucus, after a custom followed ever since Burr had come so near being made President, was the urbane and popular William H. Crawford, Monroe's Secretary of the Treasury. John C. Calhoun, Secretary of War, was a third candidate. The fourth was Henry Clay. Last, but by no means least disquieting to the others, was Andrew Jackson, who was momentarily taking a vacation from military life to fill out an unexpired term in the Senate. To use a political phrase of recent coinage, the "front porch" was located in Washington that summer.

Speeches and dinners and political meetings followed one another in quick succession while scurrilous printed attacks fluttered from every press. In Washington these added to their offense by being directed against people personally well known. "It seems," wrote Adams, "as if every liar and calumniator in the country was at work day and night to destroy my character. It is impossible to be wholly insensible to this process." The office he held had come by long usage to be looked upon as a stepping-stone to the Presidency; but Adams was not popular. So thoroughly did his detractors do their work that the accident of Mrs. Adams's English birth was dragged into the discussion and used as an argument against him.

Crawford was well liked, but precedent-breakers regarded him with distrust, as being the "regular" nominee, and whispered that a man so uniformly lucky through a long political life could not be blameless. Moreover, he had scarcely been seen for months. It was believed that he had suffered a stroke and that his name should never have been allowed to stand. Calhoun's lack of active enemies lost him the race. All factions being willing to unite upon him for Vice-President, he was considered only for that uninteresting office. Clay's well-known weakness for gambling was not overlooked, and Jackson's tempestuous way of riding roughshod to a desired end was made the text of much warning and denunciation.

Women were as interested as men, and the District of Columbia was the one place in the Union where their opinion had equal weight, neither sex enjoying the franchise. In nine cases out of ten they could give as logical reasons for their preferences, and in resourcefulness and initiative they were fully as clever. Crawford's sick-room was invaded by women partizans, who insisted that, since he was better again and able to admit visitors, he must give up his great invalid chair in the shadow of dark green curtains, for a fashionable "sopha" in a becoming light filtered through crimson silk. Amused, and too weak to resist, he consented, though protesting at electioneering with dry goods. There he sat, with the stamp of fatal disease upon him, hopeful and pathetic, awaiting the outcome, while Clay, always a drawing-room favorite, half reclined on other "sophas" in other drawing-rooms,—not because of illness, but because his long and graceful limbs disposed themselves naturally in this fashion,—while he discoursed in golden tones to admiring circles of ladies.

Political theater parties became the rage, and in these the wives of the candidates took very active part. Mrs. Adams appeared one night and Mrs. Calhoun another, surrounded by friends of their own sex and as many masculine satellites (congressmen and senators preferred) as could be lured to the theater. After these ladies had displayed their willing captives, Mrs. Crawford emerged from months of retirement spent in nursing her husband, and sat in "the front box" supported on one side by well-dressed, gentlemanly Senator Van Buren of New York, and on the other by Howell Cobb of Georgia and Senator Lowrie of Pennsylvania, "with a phalanx behind," the magnet of all eyes in an audience composed almost exclusively of Crawfordites. The partizan ladies who arranged these affairs drove about gaining recruits, and did not scruple to invade the sanctity of an executive session, sending in their visiting-cards and requesting the gentlemen they wished to interview to meet them in front of the wood fire in the Library of Congress.

The wife of one candidate, however, took no part in all this politico-social campaigning. To Mrs. Andrew Jackson's straightforward, pious mind Washington seemed a place whose iniquity might have given points to Sodom and Gomorrah. Angry epithets flying about streets and hotel corridors were bad enough; denunciatory political speeches had to be endured. More deplorable than either seemed to her this spectacle of female Adamsites and Clayites, Crawfordites and Calhounites smiling and disporting themselves in the wanton atmosphere of a playhouse, or meeting with their menfolk in apparent good nature at social functions. Dwellers in official Washington had long since learned to keep their political and social lines of talk in separate compartments, but to this good lady the ability to do so added hypocrisy and lightness to their other sins.

Distressed, she unburdened her heart to her friend Mrs. Kingsley of Nashville:

To tell you of this city, I would not do justice to the subject. The extravagance is in dressing and running to parties: but I must say they regard the Sabbath, and attend preaching. Oh my dear friend, how shall I get through this bustle? There are not less than from 50 to 100 persons calling in a day. . . . Don't be afraid of my giving way to these vain things. The Apostle says 'I can do all things in Christ, who strengthenest me.' The play actors sent me a letter requesting my countenance to them. No. A ticket to balls and parties. No; not one. Two dinings: several times to drink tea. Indeed, Mr. Jackson encourages me in my course.

As there was no single election day at that time, the final choice could not be the matter of concentrated excitement it has since become. The polls were open on different dates in the different states, and news of the results in each, traveling slowly toward Washington, kept the fortunes of the several candidates in what might be called a fluid state for weeks. The whole autumn was one continued interrogation-point, with a growing certainty that there had been no election and that the choice was once more to be thrown into the House of Representatives. Thus the emotional strain of the campaign was prolonged through the winter, into the early spring of 1825, with Washington the scene of final efforts, by all factions, to influence Congress.

The partizans of each candidate talked confidently up to the last moment. Jackson's followers believed he would win because he had received the largest number of electoral votes; the Crawfordites relied on their candidate's great personal popularity; those who favored Adams maintained he would be chosen because, dispassionately, he seemed the man best fitted for the task. The new law provided that the House must choose among the three candidates receiving the highest number of electoral votes, and this eliminated Clay, who had run true to form and polled fewer votes than any of the others. It was a standing pleasantry that he always drew larger audiences and got less result from them than any man in the Union. But as Speaker of the House of Representatives, presiding over the final choice, he would be in a position of great power—virtually that of President-maker.

Colonel Lavasseur, who accompanied Lafayette as scribe and secretary on his voyage to America in 1824, was impressed by the "calm" that prevailed in the American capital on the eve of a change in administration. He was accustomed to the melodramatic French way of doing things. The weather, on the day that the House met in joint session with the Senate to count the electoral votes, may have been responsible for some of the "calm," for a heavy snowstorm was weaving a veil about the Capitol, thick and soundless, and white as a winding-sheet. Carriages and groups of people plowed their way along Pennsylvania Avenue, however, and at ten o'clock the Frenchman found the galleries and antechambers of the House well filled.

At eleven Mr. Clay called the House to order, and at noon, when the Senators arrived in a body, the members rose and uncovered, for the old custom of wearing hats at ordinary sessions still prevailed. The counting of votes continued, Lavasseur noted, for three hours "without the slightest sign of impatience on the part of the audience." But the result being well known in advance, the announcement that there had been no election caused only a "*très-légère* sensation." It was after the Senate withdrew that the real business of the day began. Nobody, however, expected an election on the first ballot, and when Webster and John Randolph, who acted as tellers, had finished their count and Webster, in his clear impressive voice announced a majority for Adams, astonishment was so great that absolute silence reigned for a few startled seconds. Then a low murmur from the floor was answered by applause in the galleries. The Speaker promptly ordered the galleries cleared, but again Lavasseur failed to find the melodrama he seemed to long for. The ejected left "without the least opposition" and carried the news into the snowy streets, where a feeble cheer raised by black people was all the rejoicing heard.

But there was plenty of talk later. Crawford's parlor was filled for three days with friends explaining how it happened and atoning for previous gentleness of speech by the free use of words like "treachery" and "cowardice" and "damned falsehood," directed usually against Representative Van Rensselaer of New York, for taking Clay's advice and voting for Adams, thus ending the contest. When it was learned that Adams had asked Clay to become his Secretary of State and that Clay had accepted, Van Rensselaer was forgotten in denunciation of Adams, who was accused of buying success, and of Clay for taking a bribe. Had the weather not been so bad, Adams would have been burned in effigy. After all possible epithets had been expended upon the President-elect

Photograph by W. F. Roberts Co., Washington, D. C. Courtesy Columbia Historical Society

THE HOUSE OCCUPIED BY PRESIDENT MONROE

and the Secretary of State to be, more were lavished upon the unsuccessful candidates, especially upon Jackson, who was called a hypocrite for displaying ordinary good manners and congratulating Adams when they met at the President's reception on the night the vote was taken.

VIII

THE MAN WITH TWO COUNTRIES

IT is hard to determine whether Lafayette's visit was a godsend to the country or a calamity, so far as the Presidential campaign of 1824 was concerned. It may be that the voters used up their kindliness in acclaiming him, and had only bitterness left to scatter among themselves, or, on the other hand, perhaps it was his calming influence alone that saved them from flying at one another's throats. He saw the Federal City for the first time about the middle of October, when he became its guest for one short week. After this visit, he went to Yorktown, to attend the celebration there. Returning, he rested twenty-four hours and went off to the Maryland State Fair. He came back for the opening of Congress, which received him officially on the ninth and tenth of December. It was at this time that Clay reminded him that he "stood in the midst of posterity" and Lafayette answered with the delightful rebuke that Clay was mistaken—he stood in the midst of his friends.

On the eleventh he departed on a round of visits, returning in a few days to attend the first commencement exercises of Columbia College, held in the old Presbyterian Church on F Street, which some of us remember in its fallen estate as Willard Hall. On the sixteenth he gracefully absented himself, that Congress might not be embarrassed by his presence while it discussed Monroe's recommendation that a sum of money and a grant of land be voted to him in recognition of past services.

On New Year's Day, 1825, Lafayette was guest of honor at a grand dinner tendered by Congress. There being no room in town big enough to make a banquet-hall worthy of the occasion, all the people living in the front tier of rooms at Williamson's Hotel were turned out of their quarters.

On February 9th he made his way through snowy streets to the

Capitol, to witness the counting of the electoral vote. On February 23d he set out on a long, roundabout journey south and west, finally reaching New England in time to lay the corner-stone of Bunker Hill Monument, the ceremony for which he had crossed the Atlantic. After this, traveling slowly southward, he reached Washington early in August, and remained, with only short absences, until September 7th, when he took his leave to go aboard the new United-States frigate *Brandywine* that was to carry him back to France.

For almost a year, therefore, he went in and out, accepted by Washingtonians as a pleasant matter of course. Between reporting the first official honors and the burst of publicity attending his final departure, the city newspapers contained only casual and ever-dwindling references to him; short paragraphs, saying that he had returned or was about to set forth and would be accompanied on the first stage of his journey by the local troop of horse which constituted itself his guard of honor; or, on one occasion, that he was to have the escort of a company of visiting Indians. By this very lack of publicity the town testified to the thoroughness with which it adopted him, and to its serene belief that, famous and charming as he was, he was not the only man of consequence in Washington in the years of grace 1824–25. An inscription worked prominently into the decorations of the theater, for the night of December 5, 1824, when a gala performance was given in his honor, summed up the case with lawyer-like precision, "The Nation's Guest; France gave him birth, America gave him Immortality." When so much might be claimed by both sides, it was well to keep nations and individuals strictly in their place.

No community was more eager in its welcome, and no other city had a national as well as a local reputation to sustain. The city authorities cheerfully appropriated twenty-seven hundred dollars for his entertainment, by far the largest item in the year's budget, exceeding the sum for public schools by almost a thousand dollars. A committee of arrangements made magnificent plans. One was to throw a rainbow of colored lights clear over the dome of the Capitol. It was explained that this would require thousands of lanterns "in primary colors," but that recent inventions made it possible to obtain them "at a mere marivedi" of former cost. The project was too audacious, however, and the rainbow went glimmering in favor of a triumphal arch.

In the midst of the preparations Mayor Smallwood died, and for fear that this might dim the luster of the festivities, his successor, Roger C. Wightman, was chosen with almost unflattering haste.

The October sun shone cloudlessly when at last the committee of arrangements, accompanied by Commodore Tingey of the Navy Yard, Major-General Brown, and a little knot of patriarchs who had served in the Continental Army, met Lafayette at the District line, and he made his entry in an open calash drawn by four gray horses, along "the avenue of Maryland," to the booming of big guns at the Navy Yard and the cheers of crowds wearing the black and white cockade of early revolutionary days. From a third-story window of the Brick Capitol the street along which he came could be seen for a long distance, while in the other direction there was an equally good view of the triumphal arch at the east entrance to the Capitol grounds, and beyond that of double lines of school-children making a lane through which Lafayette was to pass. But the general himself was scarcely visible. A cloud of dust showed where he was when afar off, but as he approached, only the necks of his four gray horses rose out of the crowd.

Lafayette had passed under a similar triumphal arch, built of muslin and scantling, in every town he visited; and every mayor, in every speech of welcome, had called his attention to twenty-four young ladies dressed in white, telling him they represented the states of the Union. This arch differed from the others only in the mystery of its origin. It had risen overnight and had been trimmed in secret by half a dozen young women whose imagination rioted in symbolism. The structure was topped by an American eagle, genuine if not alive, "obligingly lent for the occasion by Mr. Griffin of the Museum."

The decorators of the East Capitol Street market near by, even more enterprising, had secured as the crowning glory of their effort, an unfortunate live bird. Lafayette walked through this building, and came out opposite the arch and the damsels in white. They carried flags and wore scarfs of blue, and wreaths of eglantine in their hair. This time the number was twenty-five, an increase small in every sense—a nice child of eleven, who represented the District of Columbia and stepped forward to recite the inevitable ode. Lafayette listened attentively, shook her hand, and passed on toward the Capitol, through the lines of children who showered flowers and, if we may believe one eye-witness, "jewels" upon him. Near by stood "students from the seminary" and "a company of adolescents in military uniform," very slim and erect and important, the sight of whom brought tears to the eyes of proud mothers and caused the hearts of the states of the Union to beat tumultuously under their blue scarfs.

The eastern portico was already in place, but the great flight of marble steps leading up to it had not been built, so that he was taken inside and "up the grand staircase" to the rotunda. This must have been the graceful circular stairway near the Supreme Court room, used at that time as the Senate chamber. The rotunda and the north wing had been reserved for ladies and "such gentlemen as may attend them." The generous ladies brought so many escorts that the rotunda was packed on this first occasion of its public use.

After a season of speechmaking and hand-shaking Lafayette continued up Pennsylvania Avenue while cannon boomed and spectators cheered. The little leaves on Jefferson's poplar trees clapped joyously together and people in the windows of the houses along the way followed the progress of the guest of honor by the ripple of white handkerchiefs that broke out, like foam on a cresting wave. At the White House the visitors were met on the "elegant peristyle" by the "Scherif du district de Columbie," Mr. Tench Ringgold, a fat and prosaic American gentleman, into whose title the intrusion of a single unaccustomed letter brings all the color of the Orient. Next moment, with the effective suddenness possible only in a democracy or in the Arabian Nights, they found themselves in the presence of the President and all his cabinet, who awaited Lafayette in the drawing-room, which has become, by reason of the many ceremonies enacted within it, the nation's "best parlor." Lavasseur described it as "in form elliptic," "sufficiently vast" and "carpeted and decorated with a sombre richness truly remarkable." Evidently the green Aubusson carpet and the gold-and-crimson chairs had by this time lost their garish freshness.

Monroe and Lafayette were by no means strangers, for they had been wounded on the same battle-field and while Lafayette languished in an unknown Austrian prison, Monroe, as Minister to France, had done his best to find and aid him. The President himself introduced the general and his son and secretary to every person present, and at the end of what was probably the least ceremonious visit of ceremony within those walls, the "Scherif" escorted them to the door and they went to the hotel selected for their entertainment.

Between the rapidly succeeding functions of that hurried first week, Lafayette found time to spend a whole morning with Secretary Crawford, who, paralytic though he was and threatened with blindness, had made a supreme effort and was present at the official welcome in the White House. The visitor remained for hours, sitting so close beside the invalid that his attitude seemed an embrace.

He was no stickler for first calls. Learning that General Jackson also was staying at the Franklin House, he promptly left his room to find him; and Jackson, bent on the same errand, met him upon the stair landing. Mrs. Jackson, writing to her friend Mrs. Kingsley, told all about it and added this homely description of the French hero: "He wears a wig, and is a little inclined to corpulency. He is very healthy, eats hearty, goes to every party—and that is every night." He was surely a hearty eater; it was said that he could dispose of half a dozen fine Chesapeake perch as a mere preliminary to a meal of canvas-back duck with hominy; and his party-going capacity appears to have been equally generous.

In addition to all the official entertaining, there was much polishing of silver and moving of furniture to make ready for company at private houses, whose floor space always seemed to diminish when Lafayette was expected.

Mrs. Adams's "first alternate Tuesday" after the meeting of Congress was attended by "General Lafayette and his family, 8 Senators, 60 Members of the House of Representatives, and about 120 others," including the Misses Wright, English maiden ladies who mildly shocked society by their very evident desire to bask in the general's presence. They had come to America to join some community like that of "Mr. Owen of Lanark," but found it much more thrilling to follow the nation's guest.

Lafayette's secret opinion of the town which the newspapers of the period delighted to call the Metropolis of the Union, we shall probably never know. At the time of his previous visit it had not existed even in dreams, and it was still rural enough for "the Bull belonging to the Second and Third Wards" to figure prominently in advertising columns of the daily papers, under the heading "Lost." Colonel Lavasseur, who looked upon it and our American ways with lively appreciation not untempered with amusement, thought its vacant lots doomed to remain vacant for half a century to come. But the general was plentifully dowered with imagination, else he would never have come over in his youth to help our struggling cause. In proposing a toast, he called the city "the centre star of the constellation of states."

The difficult rôle of the visit fell to George Washington Lafayette, who could neither join in the ovation to his father nor acknowledge greetings not meant for himself. American ways had no novelty for him. They had been seared deep into his troubled boy-mind during the years he spent under Washington's care, waiting to learn what fate had befallen his father at the hands of the Austrians. Washington had been kindness itself, but the boy had felt miserable and misunderstood, and as a man he gave the same impression of aloofness and gloom. He was slighter and darker than his father, and already bald. When noticed at all, he was sure to be compared unfavorably with the older man.

The general was broader of shoulder and distinctly heavier than he had been forty years before. His once fair complexion had burned brown, and his once reddish hair had turned gray; but that was a secret hidden by the chestnut wig, pulled low enough to conceal some of the wrinkles etched by Time upon his forehead. He carried a cane and walked with slight limp, in which Americans felt a proprietary interest, remembering the wound he received at Brandywine. Knowing how much this added to their friendliness and their satisfaction, he did not deem it necessary to mention a comparatively recent fall upon an icy pavement. In matters like this Lafayette was a gay opportunist.

One of the least important incidents of Lafayette's stay in Washington, retrieved from a short newspaper paragraph and hints elsewhere, is worth setting down because it typifies a phase of the admiration that followed him over the country. After the morning spent with Mr. Crawford, he and many others were guests of Commodore Tingey at the Navy Yard. While waiting for the commodore to finish showing the visitor all the wonders of his beloved machinery, officers in uniform and civilians in ruffled shirts chatted together or with ceremonious bows offered their left arms—etiquette was strict—to ladies in concealing pelisses and poke-bonnets.

Commodore Rodgers brought up a countryman, "a plain man of genteel appearance," and introduced him as Amos Lawrence, a soldier at Yorktown. Lafayette shook hands and began his serviceable joke, kept for soldiers of the Revolution. "How do you do? I am glad to meet you. Are you marri—?" Then he stopped, for the expression on the old man's face, a look very like adoration, cut short the well-worn pleasantry. "I am happy to see you, sir," the countryman said. "I was at Yorktown. I heard you were here, and came on to shake your hand. I am a poor man, sir, but I am not insensible to the occasion. I would not take a thousand dollars for this chance to shake your hand." Genuinely moved, Lafayette began to speak, but a new arrival claimed his attention; somebody pressed in between and all the veteran could do was to gaze hungrily across the widening space.

To-day we go to Mount Vernon in an hour, linger ten minutes under the trees planted by Washington, and rush back to town to keep our next engagement. Lafayette traveled at a decorous pace when he went to lay a wreath on the tomb of his old friend. He spent the night at Alexandria on the way, and that staid town saw to it that his slumbers should not be disturbed. "Crowds were kept at a respectful distance, grog shops were closed, . . . a sentinel was placed at his door . . . and total silence was enjoined throughout the city."

Next morning the tomb had been opened, and "Mr. Custis had caused to be made a plain gold ring containing a lock of the Gen-

ARLINGTON AND L'ENFANT'S TOMB AS THEY ARE TO-DAY

eral's hair and bearing the device *Pater Patriæ,"* which was presented with a speech in which Lafayette was addressed as "Venerable Man." The ribbon of the Order of the Cincinnati, on which the ring had been carried, was cut into smallest shreds and distributed among the young men present.

George Lafayette, returning to this scene of the mingled hope and wretchedness of his boyhood, was almost as much moved as his father, for he noted with a pang that the beautiful place already showed the loss of its master and had taken the down-at-heel air of so many Southern plantations.

Lafayette spent his last weeks in Washington as a guest at the White House, where John Quincy Adams was now the host. Early in his visit a hall decorated for his reception had exhibited this motto: Où peut-on être mieux qu'au sein de sa famille?" and on the eve of his departure it was no mere compliment, for he had grown to seem like one of themselves.

On the Friday before he left, a large public reception in his honor was tinged with the personal sadness of leave-taking. On the sixth of September, his birthday, a farewell dinner was given at the White House, and on the seventh, when he set sail, stores and public buildings were closed and the streets were as full as on the day of his arrival.

The hour named was early afternoon, but the mayors of the three towns within the District came to the White House soon after eleven. At noon Mr. Adams and a group of officials passed out into the vestibule and took seats where the ceremonies of farewell might be seen by as many spectators as possible when the doors of the mansion were thrown open. The cavalry company which for a year had escorted the general here and there, ranged itself on the driveway outside. After an interval Lafayette, accompanied by the President's son and Marshal Ringgold, the "Scherif" of the French accounts, joined the circle in the vestibule. Mr. Adams made a brief address and Lafayette began his reply, but was so overcome with feeling that he was forced to stop. Regaining composure, he went on again, only to bring his little speech to an abrupt close by opening his arms wide to include the whole company and ejaculating a fervent "God bless you!"

Friends in the vestibule and the crowd outside pressed forward and surrounded him until he retired to Mrs. Adams's private sitting-room for the leave-taking with the family. Then he and the President reappeared upon the north portico. Lafayette stepped into a waiting carriage, Mr. Adams waved farewell, flags dipped in salute, the cavalry fell into place, and carriage and escort took up a line of march down Pennsylvania Avenue to Seventh Street and down Seventh Street to Cana's Wharf, where a little steamer waited to take him to the *Brandywine,* that lay at the mouth of the Potomac.

Before entering the small boat, Lafayette stood beside relatives of his old friend Washington and reviewed for the last time the local militia. Then he stepped aboard, guns boomed, the paddle-wheels began to turn, a sound like a wail went up from the crowd, the boat drew away from the wharf, and the spectators went sadly back to their homes. The tiny steamer bore him down-stream past Alexandria and, just as the sun was setting, past M. Vernon; and so away from Washington and the country, forever.

IX

THE PEOPLE'S PALACE

THE history of the Capitol resembles the nursery classic known as the House that Jack Built. Beginning with a simple statement, it soon becomes so involved in interesting but not always relevant detail, that it is hard to follow the main thread of the story.

Planned to be the most imposing edifice in the new city, for the use of the most showy and impressive of the three coördinate branches of government, the Capitol was built in that casual manner typical of the way things were done in early Washington. The plans, designed by an amateur gifted with more imagination than practical skill, were a source of constant irritation to the professionals upon whom the task of construction fell, and the spirit of indignant criticism in which they worked did nothing to render easy their hard task of making pennies do the work of pounds.

In 1800, when the Government moved to Washington, only the north wing had risen above-ground, and even that was erected sketchily, with temporary props in place of stone arches, and wooden partitions where the plans called for solid walls of masonry. Into this unfinished building the House, the Senate, the Supreme Court, and the Congressional Library all crowded, and here they strove to live peaceably, making the best of circumstances it was impossible to alter at once.

At the end of the first session, however, the House of Representatives gave up the attempt and moved bodily into the "Oven," a queer one-story circular brick affair which it had caused to be built on foundations already laid for the south wing. Its name indicates at once its appearance and its discomfort. Here the members remained until 1804, when it was pulled down to make way for the next stage in capitol-building, the erection of the south wing. It was in the "Oven" that Jefferson's contest with Burr, for the Presidency, took place. After it was torn down, the members returned amicably enough to the crowded discomfort of the north wing.

Benjamin Latrobe, the architect in charge at this time, could not resist making changes in Dr. Thornton's plan, though he felt constrained to adhere to its general outlines, much as it irked him to work from the plans of a mere amateur. He altered the shape of the Hall of Representatives from an oval to a room with straight sides and rounded ends. Dr. Thornton's idea for a glass roof above it, he retained with many misgivings. "What shall I do when the condensed vapor of the hall showers down upon the Members from one hundred sky-lights?" he asked in a letter to Jefferson. It turned out that artificial rain did not fall upon legislators, just or unjust, but there was much unfavorable comment when the members assembled in their new hall for the first time at the beginning of the extra session in October, 1807, on account of the acoustics, which were bad, and because Latrobe had installed one of those devilish new inventions called a hot-air furnace.

The Senate Chamber in the north wing was heated by Christian fireplaces; but in the new room columns of hot air rushed up from unsightly registers, to mingle with the odors of fresh paint and scarcely dried plaster in a way offensive to the nostrils and prejudices of all right-thinking men. It was true that on cold days the Senate's fireplaces drew men from their seats as surely as magnet draws iron. But, even so, there was cheer in the light from hickory logs, as it flickered over the groups gathered within the radius of their warmth, lingering on strong faces, accenting the white of shirt frills and twinkling back from silver shoe-buckles. Those who criticized the Hall of Representatives had to admit that it was stately and beautiful, with its colonnade back of the Speaker's chair; and it was hoped that something could be done to better the acoustics, by hanging curtains between the columns.

After finishing the south wing, Latrobe turned his attention to the older sections of the building, replacing wooden partitions with materials more enduring, and employing the Italians he had imported, to carve the capitals of the columns in the House of Representatives, in making decorations of purely American forms. Among these were the slender columns, with capitals inspired by the stalks and leaves and fruit of the maize, that survived the British fire and are still to be seen in the little hallway from which a circular stair ascends to the room now occupied by the Supreme Court. This is the stairway by which Lafayette reached the rotunda.

In 1810, Latrobe's work on both wings was finished. His nerves were rasped to a sharp edge, and as money was not at hand to erect the connecting central portion of the building, he resigned and went elsewhere. For several years nothing was done at the Capitol except to keep up minor repairs. Then came the British, who burned out very nearly everything in the interior, leaving only blackened walls. Called back to undertake the task of rebuilding, Latrobe had, therefore, an opportunity not vouchsafed one man in a million—that of working out an important problem a second time virtually unhindered.

In some mysterious way, the second war with England had netted the United States several hundred per cent. in national prestige, and despite the lean years of "eighteen hundred and starve to death," started the country on a grand career of expansion and assertiveness. Every sturdy patriot swelled with pride at being an American, and every member of Congress, aware that he represented thousands of such complacent citizens, felt it his duty, and their due, to exact from the world at large all possible respect and glory. The restorers of the Capitol were instructed to make a handsome job of it. While it is not a matter of record that the tiff over the Senate's fine red chairs, at the time of Monroe's inauguration, had anything to do with the scheme of decoration, it is safe to infer that it was not without influence in the elaborate finish bestowed upon the restored Hall of Representatives.

It was indeed a hall of splendor when finished—ninety feet in length, semicircular in form, with a gallery for spectators sweeping entirely around its great curve. Back of the Speaker's chair, on the straight side of the chamber, a slightly raised lobby screened by finely proportioned columns provided a place in which congressmen might receive their visitors. The capitals of the columns were of white carved marble, but the columns themselves were of "pudding-stone from the banks of the Potomac," words that had a homely, thrifty sound to democratic ears, while their Italian equivalent, *breccia,* rang as pleasantly in the ears of the learned. The beauty of the stone's varied coloring commended it to all, but owing to difficulty in working the local product, each of the twenty-four columns cost before it was finished about eight thousand dollars, rather more than a congressman's full pay for the space of three years, and a deal more than imported marble columns would have amounted to. Congress was startled, but decided it must be getting something very fine indeed.

A really beautiful marble clock, representing the Muse of History in the winged chariot of Time, had been installed over the main doorway, directly opposite the Speaker's chair. This was the crowning and combined effort of the talented Franzoni family of sculptors, who had come to Washington at the time the south wing was built. A graceful daughter of the house posed for the figure in the chariot, who stands writing upon her tablets as the minutes are ticked off on the round face of the clock which serves as chariot wheel. The elder Franzoni had made the design, and a nephew completed the work left unfinished when the designer died.

All over the hall were small bits of ornament adapted from American plants, particularly the cotton-boll in various stages of its development. The painted ceiling was believed to reproduce that of the Pantheon at Rome—with improvements made necessary by our more trying climate, light being admitted through a glass cupola instead of a mere hole in the roof. "The massy bronze-gilt chandelier" hung, with its weight of candles, from the center of this cupola to within a few feet of the floor.

When the members gathered in their wonderful room for the opening of the fifteenth session of Congress, it was a shock to find the acoustics worse than in the old chamber. Sounds rumbled upward and outward by strange aërial routes, to explode near the ceiling in provoking echoes. A whisper breathed in one part of the room could be heard with the utmost distinctness in a far-off corner, while, close by, a man might call from a well of silence and scarcely make himself heard ten feet away. This was serious, alike for the orators who had so much to say and those who came long distances to listen to congressional wisdom. The effort to correct the trouble, as had been done in the older chamber, by hanging woolen curtains between pillars and from the gallery rail, met with small success. But the draperies added fine color to the apartment, supplementing the crimson silk about the Speaker's chair, which was a sort of canopied throne with curtains that would have hidden its occupant as completely as the mysterious veil hid the Prophet of Khorassan, had they not been caught back in low, hanging folds. As it was, people in the gallery could see little more than Mr. Clay's slim, long black legs.

A writer who signed himself "Calamachus" attempted a thorough description of the rebuilt Capitol, but, beginning with this room, seems to have got no farther. Perhaps he died of his emotions. He said it contained architectural "barbarities never equaled," denounced the screen of columns as appropriate only to the ruins of Palmyra and, coming down to practical details, pointed out that the doorways were most ingeniously contrived to block passage in times of crowds, and asserted that not all the woolen cloth in the Union could give the human voice its full effect in such a room. On the other hand, there were optimists who regarded the defect in acoustics as providential—"a happy circumstance for the worthy fellowship of fault-finders, who would otherwise have to hang themselves from the galleries in despair."

The general belief was that the new Hall of Representatives was the most beautiful legislative chamber in the world and the one least suited to its purpose. Basil Hall, a young lieutenant in the English Navy, who liked almost everything he saw in Washington when he visited it in 1829, was of opinion that the room was being used wrong end around, like a coat put on hind side before. Its plan resembled half a spider's web, with aisles radiating from the Speaker's chair, and he thought the acoustics might be excellent for a theater, with a stage in place of the Speaker's dais. He, at least, had no difficulty in hearing every word spoken by Mr. Clay from inside his red-curtained lair; but it must be remembered that Mr. Clay had a wonderfully clear, penetrating voice.

To foreign visitors it seemed odd that the members should be provided with so much household gear, and they saw a distinct connection between the comfortable arm-chairs and private desks, each with its locked drawer, and the lack of critical interest that members seemed to take in what was said in the chamber. The representatives busied themselves writing, or walked about, conversing with fellow-members, at every step pushing aside scraps of paper with which the floor was strewn. It looked more like a large shabby club than a legislative assembly. Englishmen were sure that their members of Parliament, who were forced to sit on uncomfortable wooden benches, would never tolerate such prolix speeches.

The Senate Chamber was a room of sober dignity, smaller and less ornate than the Hall of Representatives, semicircular like the other, but longer for its width. The fireplaces were at the two ends of the lobby, back of the presiding officer's chair. The speeches heard here were sometimes no better than those in the House, but the senators gave the impression of listening to what was said.

There was another room of great interest in the Capitol, a shadowy, spacious chamber under the Senate where the work of the least showy of the three branches of government was carried on. This was the meeting-place of the Supreme Court, the small group of men without whose steadying influence the oratory in the other chambers would have been only sound and increasing fury, for it was their duty to interpret and define the laws passed by Congress and executed by the President. During the first years of the republic, when there were few laws and not many people to engage in litigation, its labors had been counted of small value. John Jay, its first Chief Justice, resigned to accept what he considered a greater office, that of Governor of New York State, and often enough, in those days, the monotonous record of the court's proceedings began and ended with the statement that it met and adjourned, there being no business to come before it.

But during the third of a century that John Marshall was Chief Justice it became of immense importance. Since 1800 he had been one of the familiar honored figures of the city, a man as unjudicial in appearance when off the bench as Jefferson was un-Presidential. His rise to prominence had been of meteoric suddenness; he

Courtesy of the United States Army Air Service

THE CAPITOL AND ITS ENVIRONS

had been only an unassuming middle-aged congressman, with small apparent likelihood of higher honors, when a single speech, wrung from him by the injustice of giving up Jonathan Robbins (a seaman who claimed he was an American citizen) to be hanged from a British yard-arm, had changed his own, and very possibly also his country's, history. Within nine months he had discharged unsuccessively the duties of Secretary of War, Minister to France, Secretary of State, and Chief Justice, his proper office, which he held for thirty-three years, to the lasting benefit of his countrymen and to his own increasing fame.

On the street, the Chief Justice might have been mistaken for a small tradesman, so simple was his manner in an era of rather high-flown elaboration, and so lacking in judicial girth was his long, slouching, never well-groomed figure, with its small gray head and kindly eyes. On the bench, however, his coat and linen, not always immaculate, were covered by the all-enveloping judicial robe and his friendliness was wrapped in dignity as with a mantle.

One of his first associates had been Bushrod Washington, cold, small, pale, and nervous, "with only one eye, and a profusion of snuff distributed over his face," a nephew of the general's, little as he resembled his great kinsman, who held his appointment from the preceding century and was so indefatigable that he had been known, when on circuit, to hold court for sixteen hours at a stretch. Then the bold-minded Brockholst Livingston had been appointed, and Madison had outraged the feelings of the Federalists by naming as judge, Joseph Story, only thirty-two years of age, who added to the offense of his scandalous lack of years a handsome person and a talent for brilliant conversation; a man who seemed "in love with himself, his station, and all mankind" and when in company let his tongue run upon every possible subject not connected with his judicial labors. Of those, he could not be coerced to speak.

The court had been increased in number, but, with all the changes in personality and mental equipment brought by time, Judge Story's mind, gaily humorous as he seemed, was the one that fitted best with that of the Chief Justice, both in their hours of ease and in their very serious task of "interpreting Constitutional law by the light of Commonsense." Both these great men kept their vigor and energy long. Only a year before Marshall's death a spectator in the court-room described the Chief Justice as looking not more than sixty-five, though he was nearly eighty; and Story, after a quarter-century's labor upon the bench, still kept his bubbling flow of good spirits and kindly outlook upon life.

In the court-room neither Marshall's simplicity nor Story's social gifts obtruded themselves. Very impressive, statuesque figures the judges appeared, and far removed from every-day life, as they sat in a row on the straight dais raised a foot or two above the rest of the floor, the light from deep windows behind them falling upon the shoulders of their black silken robes and on the tops of their heads, leaving their faces in shadow. It was as if they had withdrawn into a sanctuary of justice. The Chief Justice sat in the center, with his colleagues to the right and left in the order of their appointment—the oldest judge on his right hand—the next on his left, and so on. Before them, at tables within the semicircle of the bar, a few lawyers were seated, intent and quiet. Outside the bar a small number of benches along the curving walls usually afforded more than ample seating capacity for spectators who strolled in.

The place, in its orderly stillness, was the antithesis of the House of Representatives. "The transition from the Town Meeting in our House to the quiet of the Court Room has a great effect upon one's feelings," wrote a Connecticut representative. Everybody who came to Washington visited the court-room, though some of the ladies who fluttered in (properly escorted, as when they entered the Senate) felt qualms at appearing in "a place in which women had no business." The arguments to which they listened were the best that the foremost lawyers of the country could make, but few of the spectators stayed long. The "town meeting" in the House offered more to interest the general public, while here there was something a little awe-inspiring. Gentlemen and ladies on the benches near the wall might have been dining, on terms of intimacy, with judges or learned counsel the night before, but in the hushed quiet of this basement room the judges, in their black, appeared infinitely official and remote. The learned counsel were more like voices of opinion than human beings, and even their rotund little friend Tench Ringgold, Marshal of the Court, assumed a solemnity which nature had denied him.

With the exception of the court-room and the supplementary rooms assigned to the Supreme Court, Congress dominated the entire Capitol, from nethermost basement to the lantern which topped the low dome over the rotunda. The rotunda had been the next addition made after the two wings were finished. On the fourth anniversary of the British visit, August 24, 1818, President Monroe had laid its corner-stone, and six years later it had been opened on the occasion of the city's welcome to Lafayette. It had not been finished at that time, however, and work upon it continued, with fluctuating energy, for years thereafter. In 1826, two hundred men were laboring amid a wilderness of stone blocks, which seemed numerous enough to reproduce the entire building.

According to a plan to have Washington's body lie in the crypt under the center of the Capitol, the rotunda had been built with a circular opening in its floor, through which the reverent might look down upon the tomb of the Father of his Country. This plan was abandoned out of deference to the wishes of Washington's family, and in time the floor was extended over the entire space, the crypt beneath, with its massive supporting pillars, becoming a place of dark mystery, not free from the breath of scandal. Fenimore Cooper heard it alluded to as the "caucus," because its dim recesses seemed fit to be the hatching-places of political plots, and Ann Royal expressed even wider possibilities of iniquity when she called it, in plain English, a place "where no honest person ought to be seen." It was lighted only by the fitful gleam of hand lanterns, and the feat of seeing anybody, of any degree of morals, was beset with difficulties. Below it were still darker cellars, filled with oak and hickory wood for the official fireplaces.

An effort made by certain progressive Washingtonians, in 1816, to inaugurate a gas-plant in the city, in emulation of London, had met with failure, there being so much else to do about that time, and it was not until 1847 that sparse gas-lights were installed in these lower corridors, to burn as mere tiny points in the blackness until the advent of electricity, well toward the twentieth century.

Describing the rotunda in 1842, an enthusiastic American used words that were more literally eloquent than he realized. He wrote:

> The Rotunda is an attractive place being a perfect circle 90 feet in diameter having a splendid dome which rises 100 feet above the floor with large skylights on the top—and is adorned by means of the Painter's and Sculptor's Art. The voice when elevated in a small degree sounds loud and mournful. Some of the things one sees here create an awful feeling.

In the whitish-gray stone walls of this circular chamber, four doors opened, north, south, east, and west, and over the doorways foreign sculptors, brought over by Latrobe, were at work chiseling bits of American history. Over the east door a Frenchman named Grevelot was busy on a bas-relief representing William Penn making his treaty with the Indians, under the famous oak, the group being confined within a space that made it resemble a successful book-plate rather than a piece of heroic sculpture.

On the walls between the doorways three or four historic canvases had been placed. Congress had ordered these pictures of John Trumbull, in 1816, in its first ardor of rebuilding. Desiring scenes from the Revolution, it had decided that Trumbull was undoubtedly the man for the task; first, because he had served on Washington's staff; secondly, because he was one of the few Americans who at that time had studied art abroad. Like many another incident in the blundering building of the nation's home, the result showed the active interest of a hard-working Providence. These great pictures ("each one about twenty feet square—only think how large!" wrote the enthusiastic American), were not half so bad, either in color or composition, as they might have been, though, owing to the innumerable stockinged legs and low-cut shoes that filled their lower sections, scoffers did speak of them as "shinbone" canvases. One represented the "Signing of the Declaration of Independence," another, the "Surrender of Burgoyne," a third, "Washington Resigning his Commission," and the fourth, the "Surrender of Cornwallis," all subjects requiring the portrayal of crowds of people.

In 1828, just outside the door of the rotunda, Persico, one of the Italian sculptors, was engaged upon the pediment of the east portico, a work dear to the heart of President John Quincy Adams, to choose a suitable design for which he had called together one of the first, if not the very earliest art commission in the city's history. The models submitted had been set up in the scarcely habitable East Room of the White House, and had been inspected and passed upon by the architect Bulfinch and "several distinguished gentlemen of science and taste" named by Adams. Though the newspapers described the models as "most elegant," not one of them proved entirely satisfactory, so the determined little President, who was no artist but never shirked a duty, had stepped into the breach and told Persico just what to do. The subject must be "The Genius of America, listening to the inspiration of Hope and indicating her reliance upon Justice." The result of their collaboration is still perched up aloft, to be seen of all who take the trouble to look.

America, the central figure, stands with a very domesticated eagle tucked comfortably among the folds of her skirt. On her arm is a sun-rayed shield, which she appears to be using as a protection against Justice, while she listens to the siren voice of Hope. Justice is not blindfolded; she has her eyes wide open, a bit of symbolism upon which Adams prided himself. In addition to her shield, America carries a copy of the Constitution, and, her hands being full, the scroll shows a tendency to trail upon the ground; but that is a bit of malicious twentieth-century criticism, unworthy of Adams's serious spirit. The President followed the progress of the work with deepest interest, climbing out on the scaffolding occasionally to view it at close range, and writing in his diary what he thought about the figure of Hope and that of the eagle, and how Persico had appealed to Commodore Tingey for the model of "a true anchor of a ship of war."

Some of the sights to be seen in the rotunda might indeed induce "an awful feeling," but in the main they were pleasant. It was a place of noble proportions, and the groups of townspeople and sight-seers walking through it in haste, to reach House or Senate, or loitering on the way to examine its details, had an air of earnestness which spoke well for the interest all took in the affairs of the nation. At almost any hour public characters were to be seen there. Chief Justice Marshall, strolling through with his invariable air of leisure toward the robing-room of the Supreme Court, and stopping for a word with a passing senator, was better worth attention, had the sight-seers known it, than all the pictures on the walls. And after John Quincy Adams graduated from the White House into his career of militant congressman, it was pleasant to see him wandering across the great round space with his arm laid caressingly over the shoulders of his little friend, Henry Watterson, son of the youngest representative in Congress, as Adams was the oldest. Despite a difference of sixty years in their ages, there was real friendship between the two.

Usually they were on their way to the Library of Congress, another of the show places of the rebuilt Capitol. It was a long parallelogram of a room directly west of the rotunda, from which one could step out upon a colonnaded portico and enjoy the view up and down the Potomac, from the broad silver reaches of water toward Mount Vernon to the steep and rocky banks above Georgetown, where the river narrows suddenly to become a mountain stream. The view was one which Miss Bremer thought "could not fail to have an ennobling effect upon Congressmen."

The books of the original Library of Congress had all perished in the British fire, but the library itself was as old as the century, having been begun with an appropriation of five thousand dollars made just before the Government removed to Washington. Its first catalogue, printed two years later, showed a total of nine maps and more than 960 books, which were classified not according to subject but according to size, like oranges or prize chrysanthemums.

In spite of the small amount of this original appropriation and annual additions that were microscopic, the library grew in public favor, not alone with the bookishly inclined but with those who wondered at books instead of reading them. Congressmen took visiting constituents there to gaze reverently upon Literature and Art; Art being represented, before the fire, by full-length likenesses of Louis XVI and Marie Antoinette in their royal robes, portraits that had been presented to our Government by the unfortunate monarchs themselves.

After the fire, Jefferson, toward whom poverty was descending on his Virginia hilltop, offered Congress his private collection with which to start afresh. Agitated discussion followed, objections being made to buying the books of such an infidel. Daniel Webster and Cyrus King of New Hampshire were prominent in the opposition, but Congress decided to accept his offer and let the nation's morals take their chance. Jefferson suggested that the collection be valued after the manner in which the old library had been classified, strictly according to size, and a committee appointed to do this allowed ten dollars for folios, six for quartos, three for octavos, and a dollar apiece for duodecimos, Jefferson himself standing by to see that the total did not exceed the twenty-five thousand dollars authorized by Congress, though probably the books had cost him twice that sum.

When the Capitol was rebuilt it was agreed that the room destined for the collection should be large enough to provide ample space for its growth in generations to come and splendid enough in decoration to rival the Hall of Representatives. Stoves cunningly concealed in the pilasters were made to look like part of the original construction. "Wreaths and flowers of the finest stucco" festooned the walls and an open fireplace shed its glow upon comfortable settees and over a carpet that cost a cool thousand dollars. There were quiet alcoves where students might work undisturbed, with books rising back of them, tier upon tier, "like the Alps." But near the fire the murmur of voices was apt to rise in pleasant conversation.

A tactful librarian, George Watterson, who was a local literary celebrity, having written books himself, added the duties of host to those more technically of his office, and made visitors so welcome that the new library became, as the old one had been, a reception room exceedingly useful to congressmen for discharging the social part of their obligations. Here they met their friends, especially the ladies, and called on Mr. Watterson to exhibit everything of interest in his collection. When congressmen wished to bring an unprofitable conversation to a close and at the same time to appear gracious, they extended the book-borrowing privilege to their visitors by means of blanks which they signed in quantity and gave to friends for future use, very much as the infamous lettres-de-cachet had been distributed before the French Revolution.

"It is a most glorious place to lounge," wrote a visitor in 1834, adding that almost every book one could think of was to be found among its twenty-two thousand volumes and that if he "were worth a fortune" he would take up his residence in Washington "for no other purpose than to read the books in the Congressional Library."

Just below the balcony outside the windows of the library, the hill fell steeply away to the west, covered with trees and shrubbery planted by Nature herself. Where the trees were sturdy and tall, sunlight slanted between them. Again there were deep caverns of shade, above which grape-vines and trumpet-creepers threw themselves from branch to branch, and in more open spots a procession of native flowers marched the summer through, beginning with the hepaticas and dogwood and Judas-trees of early spring and ending only with the late asters that fell victims to Washington's lagging winter. Charles Bulfinch, on succeeding Latrobe, arranged flights of steps and gravel walks leading down from the white building to the iron fence below. This was the last work he did before the office of Architect of the Capitol was abolished in June, 1829, as being no longer necessary, since the building was fully and, it was supposed, finally completed.

After that came an era of minor embellishments. In 1832, pipes were laid down North Capitol Street to bring water from the hills north of the city, the only previous source of supply having been two pumps outside. This new improvement led the water into a large pool east of the Capitol before it vanished inside to perform various useful errands and reappeared in another pool on Bulfinch's terrace on the west front, where goldfish blunted their noses against the base of the column to the heroes of Tripoli that meanwhile had been moved from its original place at the Navy Yard. What became of the useful stream after leaving this pool, is not known. Probably it went to fill one of the underground reservoirs where water was stored for use in case of fire. At any rate, this was all that ever materialized of L'Enfant's grand plan for cascades and pools and waterfalls tumbling into the Potomac.

The park to the east and west of the building grew gradually in beauty until the writer of a letter of 1840, describing "quite a display of dragoons and fire engines this afternoon in the grounds of the Capitol," added: "You have no idea how beautifully these grounds are laid out. It is a most charming place to walk in on a fine afternoon—almost equal to the Battery."

Persico's colossal figures of War and Peace were modeled to embellish the east portico, and a seated statue of Washington was ordered from Horatio Greenough by patriots who had become convinced that the larger project of a national monument, so long discussed, would never be carried out.

Experience soon demonstrated that the Capitol was not finished. The Mexican War brought much new territory into the Union, and plans were soon made to double the capacity of the building and to provide new halls for the House and Senate in wings so large that the former wings would serve merely as connecting links with the old rotunda. The plans for these changes were made by Thomas U. Walter, a man as wise in reading human nature as he was skilful in his profession.

He saw at once that new wings extending the building to such size must make the old dome appear ridiculously small, so he contrived a new dome which kept the old proportions within the rotunda yet added dignity without. But knowing that his marvel of curves and columns, designed not only to satisfy the eye but to conform to nature's laws of thrust and stress and expansion and a score of requirements about which laymen do not dream, would cost a far greater sum than Congress would consent to spend, if confronted with the whole scheme, he cannily presented his plans piecemeal—first the wings with their spacious meeting-halls; and after these had been enthusiastically approved, his drawings for the dome, exhibited during the closing hours of a session in order to dazzle the eyes of Congress by their beauty and not allow time for dwelling unnecessarily on the price. Fortunately, since the end justified the means, the ruse succeeded and in course of time the country had both—the new wings, built of Massachusetts marble, and the great dome of iron plates fastened one upon another by huge bolts that allow it to contract and expand hourly with the changes of temperature, "like the folding and unfolding of a lily, all moving together."

All this growth had come about in half a century from the time that Dr. Thornton drew his original design. It was on July 4, 1851, before a crowd in which were still a few people who had seen Washington lay the original corner-stone on September 18, 1793, that the great work of enlargement was begun. This time as before, a President of the United States performed the ceremony, Mr. Fillmore laying the stone, which was cut by a future mayor of the city, Matthew Gault Emery, while Webster, who was Fillmore's Secretary of State, spoke the florid words of dedication that are preserved in bronze on the memorial tablet which lies under the stone:

If therefore it shall be hereafter the will of God that this structure shall fall from its base, that its foundations be upturned, and this deposit brought to the eyes of men, be it known that on this day the Union of the United States of America stands firm; that their Constitution still exists unimpaired, and with all its original usefulness and glory, growing every day stronger and stronger in the affections of the great body of the American people and attracting more and more the admiration of the world. And all here assembled, whether belonging to public life or to private life, with hearts devoutly thankful to Almighty God for the preservation of the liberty and happiness of the country, unite in sincere and fervent prayers that this deposit and the walls and arches, the domes and towers, the columns and entablatures, now to be erected over it, may endure forever. GOD SAVE THE UNITED STATES OF AMERICA.

Fillmore's Secretary of War, Jefferson Davis, took a great interest in the details of the project, particularly in the huge bronze statue of Liberty which was to surmount the dome and in the style of her head-dress—whether she should wear the Phrygian cap or the feathers of the American Indian. A dozen years later, however, when the statue was lifted into place the country was racked with civil war and Davis was President of the Confederacy.

The House met in its new quarters for the first time, in 1857, the Senate occupied its hall in 1859, and it was from these new wings that Davis and his Southern co-workers departed to their homes in the months preceding Lincoln's inauguration.

More than once during the four years of civil war it seemed possible that hostile cannon might cause the destruction which Webster prayed might never come. But it is a bit of allegory in which Americans can take pride and comfort that through all this time of internal conflict, work upon the dome never ceased. The derricks and blocks of marble and great metal plates that had littered the eastern plaza when Lincoln took his oath of office in 1861, were all cleared away four years later and the statue of Liberty, armed and vigilant, looked down upon him as he read his second inaugural. It had been put in place early in December, 1863, less than two weeks after Gettysburg was dedicated as a great national cemetery.

Again in 1892, the growing needs of government forced changes upon the Capitol. A wide area—a sort of dry moat—separated the basement of the building and the uppermost of the grassy terraces on its western front. The terraces had already been burrowed into to make a series of underground rooms, some of which served as bakeries for soldiers' bread during the Civil War. It was determined to add to the stateliness of the building, and to its usefulness, by facing the terraces with marble and turning these underground apartments into committee rooms; all of which was done to the usual obbligato of criticism and commendation.

So the great building grew through a century, added to by a multitude of people from a multitude of designs, good, bad, and indifferent, out of materials good, indifferent, and best—none really bad, though some were not what connoisseurs would have chosen for the purpose. Yet the building as a whole, like the composite nation for whose use it was made, is astonishingly firm and good. To quote again an English opinion, that of Charles Augustus Murray who saw it about 1835:

> It certainly cannot claim the merit of simplicity or uniformity of character, neither are its proportions or decorations in strict accordance with the rules of Grecian architecture; but the effect is altogether grand

and imposing; and well will it be for America if the moral materials composing its congressional assembly prove as well-proportioned and durable as the building in which they hold their sittings.

After it became evident that the needs of Congress could never be satisfied within the limits of the old building, however much enlarged, it was wisely determined to leave it as it was, using it only as a meeting-place for the Senate and House, while necessary committee rooms and offices were provided in new and modern structures close by.

The Library of Congress had long since overflowed the single room provided for it when the rotunda was built. Alcoves and galleries had become choked with books, which also lay in great heaps in the crypt. Only a librarian like Mr. Spofford, who entered on his duties by Lincoln's appointment in 1861 and died in harness more than forty years later, could have made the library of any use whatever under such conditions. He held in his head the clue to the labyrinth, and by some wonderful process of intuition knew just where and how to put his finger on any given paragraph in any book of the great disorderly mass. But he liked the disorder no better than any one else, and dreamed of a beautiful and adequate building in which to house the priceless and rapidly growing collection.

It was one of the few dreams of the kind whose realization was vouchsafed in the lifetime of the dreamer. In 1886 the members of Congress, moved by the eloquence of his appeals, reinforced by the argument of their own eyes, authorized the erection of the present library, east of the Capitol, a wonderful palace of books, which Mr. Spofford happily lived to enjoy in use.

The necessary ground, condemned by the Government and bought from private individuals, was covered by about seventy small dwellings, many of which in years past had sheltered famous statesmen. One of these was the modest boarding-house in which Lincoln lodged during his single term in Congress. Near it was the stone-yard, where in the early decades of the century monuments to deceased congressmen were fashioned according to a prescribed and particularly hideous pattern.

A high board fence around the entire tract hid from public gaze the intimate and sometimes pathetic secrets that dwelling-houses reveal as they are torn down—the routes smoke and soot have followed up dusky chimneys, the pattern of bedroom wall-paper, and details of pantry shelves. Soon the confusion of demolition changed to one of new building materials: derricks, and blocks of New Hampshire granite, steel girders, masses of brick, terra cotta, lead, copper, and a hundred other substances found their way within the fence and in the course of ten years were made part of the library that has faced the Capitol since 1897, across greensward dappled by the shadows of old trees which were young when the Capitol was new.

Since the completion of the library a huge white marble office building for the use of members of the House of Representatives has risen south of this park and a similar building to the north of it for members of the Senate. Though the rooms in each are numbered by hundreds, there is, mercifully, nothing to suggest the commercial office building about either of them. Low and broad, they are built in a style in keeping with the dignity of the Capitol and the library. All three of the new buildings are connected with the old Capitol by underground passages, so that in reality the wide Capitol plaza where inauguration crowds gather—the park where Whigs and Democrats feasted in their respective barbecue groves, where congressional babies trotted about, gathering clover and dandelions in the grass, and congressional ladies in balmoral striped skirts wielded their mallets and played croquet—is now but the central courtyard of the People's Palace that has grown from Dr. Thornton's first amateurish but beautiful sketch.

X

INVENTORS AND OTHER PLAGUES

HARRIET MARTINEAU was not far wrong when she wrote that the American people impressed her as "a great embryo poet, now moody, now wild, but bringing out results of absolute good sense." They treated Pegasus as a draft-horse, but Pegasus was undoubtedly the motive power that made them a nation of inventors, as other nations had reached eminence in poetry or architecture or law.

Individually they brought their inventions to Washington and searched out their congressmen, expecting sympathy and, still more, practical help in getting their patents.

Even with the advantage of big new wings, the Capitol was not a convenient place for every-day use. Much of the work of Congress had to be done in committee rooms, which were tucked into all sorts of odd corners to conform to the outline of the building: some were down in the "caucus," some wedged into queer-shaped spaces between more important apartments, others literally up under the roof; and each developed drawbacks of its own in lighting or heating.

When the members of the Committee on Manufactures came together for their first meeting of the session of 1831, they found themselves shivering in an unheated room on a December day. With one accord they invaded the premises next door, assigned to the Committee on Foreign Relations, but at the moment unoccupied save by a fire on the hearth.

The rotunda, in spite of its noble proportions, became for a time a very extraordinary place; not through any fault of builders or decorators, but because of uncertainty as to who controlled it. Officers of the Senate managed affairs in all the Senate wing of the Capitol; officers of the House had charge of the House end, but how far into this central space their authority extended, and where, if at all, authority overlapped, was a subject of protracted argument. Until the matter should be settled, the rotunda was a No Man's Land to be used by the people as they would. Fakers flocked into it and spread out their wares to charm money from the pockets of sight-seers, until it looked like a county fair; and inventors, hungry for grants of government money, took up their stand under the painted eyes of the figures in Trumbull's pictures, looking placidly down from their canvases upon mouse-traps and tombstones and patent cook-stoves, displayed in the spot which was to have been the nation's most sacred shrine. It was like a dream-come-true of the theorists of the French Revolution.

At the moment, the contriving of new things or new ways of doing old ones seemed almost an obsession, for invention was work at which Americans were wonderfully adept. Two hundred and fifty years of frontier life had given every pioneer household practical training along those lines, while the creative power which lay back of the inventive faculty was a national birthright.

Not only had a tremendous flight of imagination brought the first settlers overseas, but a later outburst had ushered the new nation into being. And scarcely was the Government in blundering working order before daring spirits roamed the invisible again—this time in buccaneering mood to capture untested forces of nature and enslave them to daily tasks.

It is possible that under slightly different conditions the pent-up floods of imagination might have found outlet through old channels. It is at least a coincidence that Fulton and Morse were both artists before they became inventors. But early Americans had imbibed distrust of painting and sculpture, along with reverence for the Hebrew prophets; and in poetry they were tongue-tied. Close at hand however, lay a wilderness continent-wide, out of which to contrive a new civilization, and joyously and audaciously imagination accepted the challenge.

Looked at in this light, the exhibit spread out on the floor of the rotunda and in the Patent Office makes one of the most impressive chapters in our national story—a chapter starred with well-loved names; for Franklin and Jefferson were inveterate inventors; Washington generously aided those dowered with a gift denied to him; and young Abraham Lincoln's big kindly hands whittled out a model of a steamboat which was to be lifted over troublesome shoals by a method of his own devising.

The first patent issued under a national law was dated 1790, the very year in which work began in earnest upon the capital city. It had to do with bean-pots and pearlashes, humble and unpoetical things compared with England's first patent to "two friars and an alderman" in the reign of Edward III, for discovering the philosopher's stone; but on American soil pearlashes and beans developed such potent magic that America was soon issuing three patents to one in the mother country.

It throws interesting light on the leisure of official life in our good old days, to discover that, for three years after the national law went into effect, applications for patents were examined by a committee consisting of the Secretary of State, the Secretary of War, and the Attorney-General. If they were deemed of sufficient importance, they were then discussed with the President in cabinet, and the patent bore the signature of Washington himself. We can imagine the kindly, if not always technical, interest he showed, and how Jefferson looked upon this as the pleasantest duty of his office; but the other two may not have been so well pleased. When the law was amended in 1793, they were excused and the power of life and death over inventors' hopes was lodged in the Secretary of State alone. In 1802, after Jefferson had become President and Madison Secretary of State, the law was again changed and a Superintendent of Patents was appointed as an officer of the Department of State. Dr. Thornton, who filled so many small important chinks in the capital's early history, became the first incumbent at a salary of $1400 a year, his staff consisting of one messenger and one clerk. His salary was slightly in excess of the whole revenue of the office at that time. By way of contrast it is interesting to learn that the fees alone for the fiscal year ending June 30, 1923, amounted to $3,026,486.36, that the year closed with 74,286 applications awaiting action, and that American patents are popularly believed to issue at the rate of one every seven minutes.

Dr. Thornton retained the office until his death, twenty-six years

THE PATENT OFFICE

later, lavishing on it the enthusiasm he had previously scattered over a dozen hobbies. Almost the first thing he did was to take possession of a hall in Blodgett's Hotel, and to install there an exhibit of patent models that speedily became one of the sights to which visitors, native and foreign, were led as soon as possible after their arrival. They were sure to write home about it, usually in wondering admiration, and thus it bore its part in making Washington, even before the city plan had emerged from woods and fields, a clearing-house for practical ideas as well as an experiment station in new theories of government.

Some foreigners thought the practical nature of this exhibit a flaw instead of a merit. The Duke of Saxe-Weimar, who visited it about 1825, marveled that clever people should be willing to waste their genius upon trifles like apple-corers and the ninety-eight models of nail-making machines he found on exhibition. Peter the Great's axiom, that "Nothing seems small to a great man," and Franklin's maxim that human happiness depends upon taking advantage of little things that happen every day, were alike absent from the genial duke's philosophy.

It was in Blodgett's Hotel that he saw the collection, for though the models had been unceremoniously dispossessed that Congress might use the hall after the fire, the exhibit was reinstalled as soon as possible, and continued to swell with all the things invented, in succeeding years, to make life at once easier and more complex.

Then came a spectacular fire on the night of December 15, 1836, which swept through Blodgett's old hotel and sent most of its contents heavenward in one gorgeous sheet of flame. Even before that happened it had become evident that the Patent Office must leave the shelter of the State Department to enter upon an existence of its own, like those forms of cellular life that break away from a parent to pursue their individual destiny. Indeed, a new building had already been begun, and, by an odd coincidence, was located on the square of ground that had been set apart in L'Enfant's map for a great national temple to Patriotism and Religion—not to creed. That idea was lost completely when Ellicott redrew the plan of the city. The white marble building that did arise on the spot was dedicated instead to invention and the wonders of applied science; as typical, perhaps, of our nation as L'Enfant's temple would have been of the Genius of France in 1790.

Like the Capitol, the new Patent Office grew in sections. The first, with store-rooms and offices on the lower floor and a great exhibition hall extending over the entire space above, was ready for occupancy by 1840. This hall contained not only glass cases full of patent models, but portraits of Indian chiefs and bits of concrete American history, like Franklin's hand printing-press, and the coat that Washington once wore, which lies in the National Museum to-day, with a pin still acting as substitute for a missing button.

In two years the hall was so full of exhibits and so popular with strangers that a custodian had to be on hand to explain things, and time and again the building was enlarged and every inch of added space filled full. To Washington children the exhibition hall was a place of enchantment, as much more enchanting than a mere toy-shop as "true" stories are of greater appeal than fairy tales. It was like a toy-shop, being full of doll-sized models of real things—every conceivable thing—some of them with dolls to represent people operating them. But over it all was the haunting sadness of decay, for the clothing on these manikins was dusty and the machinery was already falling to pieces. Small rebellious brains used to wonder what possible good they could do to anybody, rotting in glass cases, and to wish that if children were not allowed to play with them, they might at least be given the privilege of tidying and mending them. The lifeless manikins aged much more rapidly than the children, and before they were grown, the place resembled a toy-shop far less than a charnel-house.

Many who had hung over its glass cases were actually glad when another fire broke out and the models, save for the few treasures rescued, became a mass of charred and twisted debris. After that the edict went forth that no more models would be received. Owing to lack of space, inventors would be required to file only descriptions and working drawings.

To children and adults alike the crowning interest of the old collection lay in hunting out and locating the family patent; for it was a poor family indeed that had not a father or an uncle or at least one distant cousin the work of whose brain reposed somewhere in that wilderness. To find it and gaze upon it and know that among precious things at home there was a large official document signed and flamboyantly sealed to prove it his very own, seemed to link one's house visibly with the great entity called Our National Government.

Not one in a hundred of the enterprising inventors had money to develop his ideas, but almost any of them could get together the few dollars to take him to Washington; and Congress, it was well known, sometimes made grants of government funds for such purposes. Many therefore joined the army of constituents that annually advanced upon the city.

After arriving, the first thing every mother's son of them did was to hunt up his congressman, confide in him, and ask his help—a neighborly custom with which representatives had to appear enchanted, if they dreamed of reëlection, but which palled with incessant repetition.

Which of the two great divisions of the visiting army was harder to deal with, only a congressman knew: the practical folk—politicians, wire-pullers, and well-meaning neighbors, who made up the larger wing—tested a man's skill in diplomacy, but their minds were commonplace and they might take "No," for an answer, while the smaller group—inventors and artists and such erratic creatures—had too much persistence to be reasonable, and never knew when they were beaten.

The attitude of Congress toward these men was complicated and contradictory. Probably each member felt some tug of sympathy, being of the same breed, and nine out of ten of them were confident in their secret hearts that they could astonish the world in that very field if they gave time to it; but as a body congressmen stood shoulder to shoulder to resist what was, in the last analysis, an assault upon government funds. The best way to treat inventors of trifles was to smooth their path so that they might get their patents and depart quickly. The troublesome cases were men of ambition. The lucky ones of this class got permission to display their contrivances in some committee room; others, despairing of a better chance, took up positions under Trumbull's pictures and spread out their wares on the stone floor, hoping to attract the passing attention of the men whose votes they needed.

It was embarrassing for congressmen to live up to that cardinal tenet of our republican faith that officials must always be easy of access, and at the same time to keep clear of entanglements. Members might be seen hurrying across the rotunda with averted eyes, fearing that if they stopped to examine they would be lost. Representatives were as omniscient as mortals are ever allowed to be in this vale of tears, and senators walked about wrapped in dignity, but it was not always easy to distinguish between fakers and genius. Had not Fulton made boats sail up-stream by the simple expedient of boiling a little of the river water? The perturbed congressmen of the period between the War of 1812 and 1850 might well have added another petition to the litany:

From Artists, Reformers, and Inventors—Good Lord, deliver us!

The very appearance of these folk was disquieting. The expression on the faces of those who had grown shabby and hungry while waiting, haunted one like an accusation of murder, and there were others whose very jauntiness was irritating.

That slim, well-favored Robert Fulton, with his deep-set dark eyes and beautiful mouth, had walked through Washington drawing-rooms, in years gone by, as though he owned them, and congressmen set him down as having "consummate impudence," and "very slender abilities." He was sort of inventor *de luxe,* with not a penny to himself, but with exceptional social backing. The childless Joel Barlow and his wife, having "aided" him in Paris at a time when he sorely needed help, took him into their hearts as a son. Barlow had dedicated his "Columbiad" to him, a courtesy Fulton repaid by drawing illustrations for it; and on pleasant mornings host and guest might be seen trying out the model of the *Clermont* on some quiet stretch of Rock Creek, as it flowed at the foot of the Kalorama estate.

Fulton's invention thus takes on an intimate local character in Washington; but his name is by no means the only one famous in steamboat annals which is familiar in the locality. It was Rumsey, according to common report, who convinced Washington that steam navigation was practicable, and for years a stretch of Potomac shore near Great Falls, where the inventor was employed in construction of the canal, was called Rumsey's Walk and pointed out as the spot where he paced and dreamed, after the day's business was over.

The long-bearded S. F. B. Morse was another of the great inventors who haunted Congress. He gained permission in 1838 to set up his contrivance in a basement room of the Capitol, and promptly festooned the place with ten miles of wire, in the center of which he stood like a watchful spider, ready to pounce upon any one who came in and explain his theories, talking his visitors almost to death. The fanatical look in his eye made it easy to believe stories going the rounds to the effect that his family had applied, or was about to apply, to the Baltimore courts to have him put under restraint. It seemed a pity that such a well-meaning, well-educated Yale graduate should run completely to seed. He had been a successful portrait-painter, a professor of the Literature of the Arts of Design, and president of the newly created New York Academy of Design, before he was smitten with this unholy desire to apply abstract science to the affairs of every-day life.

Morse's congressional critics did not pretend to follow his reasoning. They only knew that his special hobby was the use of "electro-magnetism" for signaling from one distant point of the earth's surface to another—a conception almost impious in its possibilities of annihilating time and space. At times his festooned committee room was very full of people who lingered and asked remarkable questions. Scientists stayed longest and kept on asking questions. On a February day in 1839, President Van Buren drifted in, small and dapper and smiling, surrounded by a cabinet of assorted heights and sizes. They listened to Morse and to his little clicking instruments, clucked their polite astonishment, and drifted out again, and nothing came of their visit nor of the whole long exhibition, save that Mr. Smith, Chairman of the House Committee on Commerce, was smitten with Mr. Morse's own disease and gave up a perfectly good political career to devote himself to the crazy invention. He took Morse abroad and for a few seasons the Capitol had a welcome vacation from this particular line of crazy imagination. Then they came back and in another wire-hung room Morse could be heard arguing as before, with apparently no more likelihood of success. But just one week before the adjournment of Congress in March, 1843, a bill came before the House appropriating $30,000 "to test the practicability of establishing a System of Electro-Magnetic Telegraphs by the United States."

The meager report of the debate is full enough to show how contemptuous members were of the man who annoyed them. Mr. Cave Johnson of Tennessee moved that half the appropriation be diverted to carry on experiments in mesmerism, a popular fad of the day. Some one else suggested a railroad to the moon. Mr. Houston wanted to know why Millerism had been overlooked. Mr. Staley of North Carolina said he would have no objection to experiments in mesmerism provided the gentleman from Tennessee was the subject. The gentleman from Tennessee retorted that he had not the least objection to being the subject, provided the gentleman from North Carolina acted as operator; and the House laughed immoderately and acted like a club of elderly school-boys.

An Indiana member loudly asserted that magnetic telegraphs were all foolishness, since nobody but a born Pottawattomi could understand the ridiculous dot-and-dash alphabet. When Mr. Mason protested that such doings were unworthy the dignity of the House, the presiding officer refused to rule the amendment out of order, being too much in sympathy with the farce-makers. The amendment was lost, and two days later the bill actually passed the House by the narrow majority of six votes. It had still to run the gantlet of the Senate, on the night that the session came to an end, with one hundred and forty bills ahead of it on the calendar. Morse sat in the Senate gallery, a prey to mounting anxiety. At last compassionate friends went to him and told him it was useless to wait longer, and he dragged himself off to bed, bereft of his last hope and his last dollar.

While he was making a pretense of eating breakfast next morning, his little friend Annie Ellsworth, daughter of the Commissioner of Patents, fluttered in with smiles and words of congratulation. He stared at her with tragic eyes, unable to comprehend that she was a messenger from her father, bringing news that the bill had passed after all. Literally in the closing hour of the session, the commissioner had stood over President Tyler and seen him affix his signature. Annie said she came just as early as she dared, and joyfully asked, "Am I really the first?" After Morse had gained self-control to speak, he promised that she should choose the first words to be sent over the line he meant to build between Baltimore and Washington. She responded to his emotion and departed between laughter and tears; then he turned to the cold boarding-house fare, suddenly become of miraculous savor.

During the next two years the jealous earth seemed literally to open and devour the meager sum Congress had granted him. The story of those anxious months and of the "accident" his loyal overseer of constructions staged at a moment when delay was imperative, scarcely belong here, but they will figure largely in the picturesque cinema history of the national capital whose writing is only a question of time.

On the May morning in 1844 when Annie Ellsworth's message flashed over the wires, the Democratic National Convention was in session at Baltimore. James K. Polk having just been nominated for President, there was a bit of important news to wire in return. A few hours later the convention's choice of Senator Silas Wright for Vice-President also was telegraphed to Washington and declined so promptly that the convention refused to be hoodwinked by "a palpable political trick," and adjourned to allow time for a messenger to verify the matter—all of which brought the new invention extensively and effectively before the public.

But there were still hard days ahead for Morse. The new President made Cave Johnson Postmaster-General, and another of his tormentors in Congress succeeded his friend Ellsworth as Commissioner of Patents. When it became Mr. Johnson's duty to report on the offer of Morse's company to sell his patent outright to the government for one hundred thousand dollars, he proclaimed his belief that it never would be worth that sum. When events began to prove his error, lawsuits were instituted to deprive Morse of honor and profit in his invention. Legal fights for ten weary years ended in a day of triumph, when Chief-Justice Taney of the United States Supreme Court read his decision awarding to Morse, and no other, all the credit. Once after this the walls of the Capitol echoed to Morse's name, and the great new Hall of Representatives was too small to hold the throng that came to do him honor; but that was in Grant's term, on the occasion of a memorial meeting, after death had sealed Morse's ears to praise and blame alike.

So far as we know, there is no adequate memorial to this man whose invention changed the ways of the civilized world. Thanks to the activity of historical and patriotic societies, Washington is well dotted with inscriptions to show that famous statesmen lived in this house and that, and sometimes what they did there. There is one modest bronze tablet on the east wall of the Post Office Department on Seventh Street, seen by few of the hurrying thousands who pass it daily. It recalls the fact that on that spot, in the room of a dwelling made over for business purposes, was opened the first office for public transmission of telegrams.

Should erecting tablets to inventors and inventions become common, the number of additional places in the city to be marked might prove surprising, for the steamboat and the telegraph are not the only great inventions of the nineteenth century whose development was worked out, at least in part, in Washington. Some still remember how Alexander Graham Bell looked when he first set foot in the city—a tall, slender, rather threadbare professor of elocution and teacher of the deaf, with a pale face and a mane of very black hair. As years passed, he grew in presence as in well-earned prosperity, and became in later life an impressive figure of stately bulk and king-like bearing; with eyes as piercing as they ever had been in his youth, though his tossed-back hair was as white as snow. On Wednesday evenings his friends were privileged to take their friends to his library—a huge room where in utmost informality he led talk over wide fields, every man present being expected to contribute his bit to the wisdom or enjoyment of the evening. Casual tourists rarely saw him, unless they were fortunate enough to catch a glimpse of him entering or leaving his door, when the sight-seeing wagon rolled by his big brick house on Connecticut Avenue, in which, by the way, he never allowed a pestiferous telephone to be installed.

Professor S. P. Langley, who was director of the Smithsonian

Institution from 1887 to 1906, was another of the pioneers. Gentle in manner, persistent in spite of ridicule, though by no means insensible to it, he spent his days and nights working over the possibility of aërial flight. Some of the young men who flew in the Great War speak of him yet, with a catch in the voice, and say he was killed by the jests of scoffers as surely as man was ever murdered by bullets. He died when his invention was just on the eve of actual success, saying with pathetic resignation, "I have demonstrated the principle; it is for others to carry it on."

Like the steamboat, the telegraph, and the airship, that other modern monster the automobile has its bit of Washington history. In the decade before the Civil War, Charles Page, an examiner in the Patent Office, later connected with the Smithsonian Institution, loaded a wagon-bed, which was a mere platform on wheels, with coils of wire and horseshoe magnets, and ran the strange thing three or four miles out on the road toward Bladensburg. It was brought back by horse-power and lay abandoned and forgotten near the tracks of the Baltimore and Ohio Railroad, but now it is in the National Museum, preserved as an early ancestor of all the shining high-powered motors that go snorting up and down the land.

Less spectacular than these larger affairs, but equally revolutionary, was the typewriter, whose development was much helped in Washington by James Ogilvie Clephane, not by his own inventions, but by testing out model after model as it was presented to him.

More terrifying than the army of inventors was the swarm of artists. Before an artist the average congressman of early decades felt helpless and ignorant, though he might not hesitate to criticize any machine in the Patent Office. Art was something mysterious and exotic, and to be distrusted, just because it was beautiful. Like the company china, it was a luxury to be brought out only on occasions. Had Mark Twain's oft-quoted *mot* about truth—"It is the most precious thing you have, use it sparingly"—been invented, it would have fitted the case to perfection. But, again like company china, art was something civilization could not do without. Classical scholars realized that great nations of the past had made it useful in teaching lessons of patriotism; therefore they favored giving it an honored place in our public buildings, but with the understanding that it renounce evil and sensuous ways and be henceforth strictly allegorical and educational.

Quite early a "picture room" was established in the old north wing of the Capitol, where one or more works were usually to be found, brought by artists who hoped Congress might be moved to buy them. Here, as critics and possible purchasers, trooped the members of Congress, of every type and kind; those with much classical lore and those who had perhaps never in their lives seen a painter's palette. But the ignorant reached virtually the same conclusions as the scholarly, by opposite methods of reasoning. They were persuaded that the capital of the Most Glorious Country on God's Earth ought to show the rest of the world superior examples of everything that had made other nations great, and if Art was one of these, why, Art Washington ought to have. Being conscientious men under oath to do their duty, part of which was spending the nation's money wisely, they visited the picture room and, even on this unfamiliar ground, they could cling to a few time-honored principles. One was that in a multitude of counsel there is safety, and another that those who hold the purse-strings have a right to say what shall be bought. Both classes seem to have been naïvely sure that Art in requisite quality and quantity would be forthcoming on demand. After performing the miracle of evolving a new government and creating a new capital city for the Government to live in, it was certainly a simple matter to provide a few pictures and statues to adorn its public buildings.

The picture room was so small that when as many as three works happened to be on exhibition at the same time, one had to be crowded to the wall. Artists who were content to show their pictures in silence and hope for the best were apt to share the fate of their canvases. The more aggressive acted on the belief that the Lord helps those who help themselves, and supplemented their appeal to the eye with lobbying more or less artistically conducted. Sometimes it succeeded and sometimes it failed, for the members had strange ways of reaching their decisions.

When sex complicated the problem and a lobbyist happened also to be a woman, official life became a burden. Congressmen had to listen; had to be polite to a lady; and had to remember their oath;

and the treacherous quaking morass of artistic merit had to be negotiated somehow.

Possibly the worst plague of this character who ever descended upon Washington was a determined lady named Madame Planton, who claimed both New Orleans and Philadelphia as home and therefore had two sets of congressmen especially at her mercy. She had made up her mind, at the end of the War of 1812, that historical painting should not be allowed to die with Trumbull, and produced a large, highly colored canvas which she said represented the Treaty of Ghent in allegory. America might be seen advancing haughtily in a triumphal car, while Minerva and Hercules in the background made menacing gestures with spear and club at poor Britannia, who, humbled to her knees, was laying in the path of the juggernaut chariot her flag, her laurels, and a rudder supposed to symbolize her sea power.

Some said that the composition was stolen bodily from Regnault's "Triumph of Napoleon," and the most ignorant had misgivings that the picture could not be in good taste. As if the canvas itself were not enough, the terrifying lady caused prints of it to be made, with which she invaded the offices of peaceful gentlemen and laid them "under contribution," to quote John Quincy Adams. "O the voracious maw and the bloated visage of national vanity!" he wrote in his diary, after relieving his feelings by calling the picture "both foolish and bombastic." "But," he concluded helplessly, "Mme. Planton gives herself out to be a native of Philadelphia, and is a painter." Such was gallantry in our country in the year 1817, that, even to a man of John Quincy Adams's caliber, those facts appeared to give her a valid claim upon the United States treasury.

George Watterson, the Librarian of Congress, criticized the picture as severely, and ended on the same note of hopelessness: "It is, however, a national painting, executed by an American female, and should be purchased by Congress, not only to decorate the interior of the Capitol, but to commemorate the event and encourage the arts." Madame Planton returned to the attack two or three times, but Congress as a body refused to be coerced, which tends to prove that there is safety in numbers, after all!

Madame Planton was alarming, but she was only a bird of passage. Ann Royal, that pioneer female journalist who appeared in Washington about 1826, settled down and stayed and grew old and crabbed and shrewish. At first she seemed the less trying of the two, but from the naïve, rather attractive reformer of early middle life, whose mental processes amused the officials she called upon, even while her persistence annoyed them, she became the terror of all she approached, tramping the streets, ragged and slovenly, wearing a man's hat and carrying a huge umbrella, and so abusive in print and in speech, that patience gave out at last and an old colonial law was invoked to have her arrested and tried as a common scold.

It was a farcical trial, and people felt about it much as British and Americans felt about the burning of Washington,—that it did little credit to any one involved,—for she was that most pathetic of all figures, an old woman who had lost in her battle with life. Her paper, whose name she changed speedily from "Paul Pry" to "The Huntress," since even her not over-sensitive perceptions saw that the former was offensive, dwindled to nothing and suspended publication; then began again as a tiny sheet a few inches square, for, poor and repellent as she had become, her pluck remained unabated. It was hardly the part of American men to harry her.

She had, indeed, joined the ranks of that ever-present but fortunately small number of people whose minds dwell close to the border line of sanity, sometimes on its farther edge, and who persistently dog the footsteps of officials. Most of them are harmless. But since there is ever the chance that some of them may harbor murderous designs, their presence adds a very real if not very alarming hazard to congressional life.

XI

KING ANDREW THE FIRST

IF a chronological list were to be made of the various excitements, political, meteoric, hygienic, and social, that swept Washington during the eight years of Jackson's Presidency, one would be left breathless with their number and convinced that, celestial and mundane alike, all were dominated by the tall, spare old man whose inward fires burned so fiercely. For thirty years before he crossed the threshold of the White House he had been in the political firmament, a meteor rather than a fixed star, erratic, brilliant, and effective; and for fourteen years of that time he had been looked upon as a Presidential possibility, Aaron Burr having suggested as early as 1815 the wisdom of bringing him forward to oppose Monroe.

Carl Schurz once explained the difference between him and the President he succeeded, by saying that Adams interpreted law, but Jackson made it. In spite of this difference in temperament, the personal relations of the two men were amicable for many years.

In 1824 the Adams home on F Street had been adorned with evergreens and lamps and paper roses on the eighth of January, and the floor of its ball-room chalked with spread eagles and "Welcome to the Hero of New Orleans," for a grand reception in Jackson's honor, a function long remembered in Washington, about which Mr. Agg, a local newspaper worthy, did a bit of locally famous reporting in rhyme that began:

Wend you with the world tonight?
 Brown and fair and wise and witty,
Eyes that float in seas of light,
 Laughing mouths and dimples pretty—
Belles and Matrons, Maids and Madams,
 All are gone to Mrs. Adams'.

Adams may or may not have liked Jackson, but he was by no means indifferent to the value of Jackson's great popularity, and sought to attach it to his own colorless ticket, in 1824, by suggesting the Vice-Presidency as a pleasant office for Jackson's old age. The general was in truth only four months his senior, but Jackson had brought this upon himself, by urging age and ill health as reasons for not entering the Senate in 1823. If there was a touch of ironic humor in the invitation, it defeated its own end by acting as a strong tonic. Nothing more was heard from Jackson about ill health or advanced years. Instead he entered aggressively into the Presidential race for first place. When Congress chose Adams in preference to himself, like a good loser, he shook hands with his rival and congratulated him heartily, and it was only when he learned that Clay, against whom he nourished bitter prejudices, was to become Adams's Secretary of State that he came to believe Adams corrupt. After that there was no more handshaking, and though the next Presidential election was three years away, he withdrew from the Senate to prepare for it.

He characterized Adams's officials as "these enemies of Liberty" and coined a phrase which did telling work in the campaign, asking dramatically, "Shall the government or the people rule?" The answer given at the polls was emphatic, but how much liberty the people gained thereby may be questioned.

Adams's administration took the shock of its defeat well, and entered on its last winter with spirit and a great show of gaiety. There were new frocks from Paris, and the Marine Band, which had played hymn tunes at the Capitol in the time of the elder Adams, was called upon to furnish music for dancing in the great East Room, an unheard-of frivolity at the White House.

Carriages dashed about at night with their lamps shining like rapidly moving stars, while the roll of their wheels echoed from the frozen earth like thunder, and home-keeping citizens, going to their doors to perform the last rites of locking up, called their wives to look and listen, commenting on the growing elegance of the town.

But this spirited beginning did not last. Bad weather brought in its train so much sickness, that on a single day, toward the end of January, 1829, every member of the cabinet save one, was confined to his bed. Among the poor there was great misery, and charitably inclined matrons like Mrs. Van Ness, and kindly energetic Mrs. Porter, wife of the recently appointed Secretary of War, a lady who aspired to fill Mrs. Madison's vacant place in the social world, extended their large visiting lists to include many who never entered their houses through the front door. Plainly dressed, Mrs. Porter might be seen carrying cheer into the shacks of Swampoodle and Foggy Bottom, almost up to the moment when she appeared at some ball, gorgeous in costume and seemingly without a care beyond the enjoyment of the moment.

Worse than illness was the uncertainty that grew upon the town as the fourth of March approached. Cabinet officers and others whose terms of office expired automatically with the Administration had at least the advantage of knowing their fate, but up to that time it had not been customary to dismiss those who held subordinate government positions, provided they did their work well and kept civil tongues in their heads. Although there had been threats of wholesale changes when Jefferson came into power, the fact was that during all the fifty-odd years of the country's history only seventy-nine officials had been forcibly removed from office. Now Jackson's followers were clamoring that to the victors belonged the spoils, and Jackson said nothing to show he was displeased.

Many of the clerks had seen administrations come and go until they were far beyond the age when it is easy to change occupations or start on a new career. In the War Department, especially, employees were so crusted with years of service that it was referred to facetiously as the Octogenarian Department. Government salaries, though never munificent, had come once every month with a regularity that did not encourage habits of thrift. In the present horrible uncertainty, starvation seemed to stare these good men and their families in the face. As for day laborers who depended upon government work, their state was almost as bad, and the few merchants of Washington were sufferers also, sudden frantic efforts at economy, begun too late, leaving their shops empty of customers.

People of small means who owned homes desired nothing so much as to sell them; those whose homes were mortgaged found nobody willing to arrange new loans, while the larger number who had the misfortune to rent houses were confronted with monthly bills which seemed magnified beyond recognition. The prevailing illness made it harder to throw off mental depression, and, to add the final touch of gloom, Jackson's partizans gloated and boasted.

The first local campaign committee in the town's history had functioned vigorously during the preceding summer, under the leadership of the mayor, John P. Van Ness, who lived in the wonderful house down near the mouth of the Tiber and had no cause for anxiety as to where his next meal was to come from. He and others equally interested, including General Duff Green, who had made the "Telegraph" the Jackson organ, kept the organization intact and saw to it that enthusiasm did not die down. Much to-do was made over an eighth-of-January banquet at Gadsby's and more still over the formal welcome to the President-elect, who reached Washington on the day the electoral votes were counted.

His friend General Eaton rode out to Rockville to meet him, while the whole committee lined up at Twentieth Street and Pennsylvania Avenue to escort him to Gadsby's and arranged an artillery salute to complete the formal announcement by Congress that he had been duly elected.

Professing that he could not bring himself to touch the hand of a man who had reached high office by corrupt means, Jackson ignored etiquette and avoided the White House instead of paying the customary visit to the President. Since such behavior might well have exasperated a man less exacting than Adams, it may be surmised that the outgoing administration took no pains to be polite in return.

Jackson's hotel parlors were thronged by an ever-increasing crowd, but the White House was virtually without visitors. It was the only house in Washington thus deserted, for strangers flocked into the city until beds were at a premium and the privilege of sleeping in queer uncomfortable places like bar-rooms, upon billiard tables, was eagerly sought and paid for. Very busy and important, the campaign committee drew up elaborate rules for the fourth of March, governing the inaugural parade and the approach of carriages to the inaugural ball. These looked most impressive when printed in the "Telegraph," but the committee went too far and called down wrath upon itself when it designated Paymaster-General Towson for Marshal of the Day and ignored our old friend Tench Ringgold, who had acted as master of ceremonies for Lafayette's visit and served at so many inaugurations that Washington considered the honor his by vested right.

Jackson developed ideas of his own on the subject, and as usual these prevailed. Pleading his deep mourning as a reason for avoiding display (Mrs. Jackson had died since the election), he refused all military escort and solved the problem of too many marshals by walking from his hotel to the Capitol with Mr. Ringgold on one side of him and Colonel Towson on the other. Fortunately the day was mild, though the last bit of snow had disappeared only a week before.

From a point of vantage on Capitol Hill, people seemed to fill the avenue from curb to curb, some in carts, some in carriages, more still on foot, all of them striving to keep abreast of the very small procession. This was headed by the committee, preceding a little knot of Revolutionary soldiers, who were followed by a group of men who had taken part in the Battle of New Orleans. Last of all came Jackson between the two marshals, a lean, erect figure dressed in black, walking with his silver head uncovered.

Wherever the sidewalk was good, they kept to that, but in the lower reaches of the avenue, where the Government owned land on both sides and had neglected its duty, the footway dwindled to almost nothing and they were forced into the crowd. Congestion threatened, but the President-elect and his bodyguard reached the historic iron fence in safety, and, passing through its gate, went on up the gravel walk and flights of steps that climbed the grassy terraces.

The police of Washington and Georgetown, called to duty by Marshall Ringgold by notices published in the newspapers, must have been stationed elsewhere, for the main western door of the Capitol was so obstructed that Jackson refused even to attempt to use it, and with characteristic unconvention swung his long legs over the area wall and entered the basement, making his way up to the Senate Chamber to see Calhoun take his oath as Vice-

President. For himself the stage was set in the open air, he being the first President to take the oath and deliver his inaugural from the newly finished east portico, upon whose pediment Adams's figure of open-eyed Justice kept guard.

Adams was not present. Like father, like son. John Adams had believed himself unable to turn over the office to Jefferson with good wishes and social courtesies, and his son found it even more impossible to be courteous to Jackson. Some days before, Mrs. Adams had become the guest of General and Mrs. Porter on Meridian Hill, and there her husband followed her—a lonely little figure on horseback passing along the heights back of the city at the moment when the booming of guns announced the end of his power.

The crowd that filled the open spaces east of the Capitol pushed its way up the new marble steps to the point where a ship's cable had been stretched across, two thirds of the distance from the bottom. It was neither a ragged nor uproarious crowd, only a mass of well-dressed, well-intentioned, respectable people, whose small lapses from good manners were due solely to enthusiasm. The ship's cable, though a very frail protection, kept them effectively from the space reserved for officials, where stood the little mahogany table, covered with a red cloth, that has figured in every public Presidential inauguration since Washington took the oath of office. This table was the sole occupant of the space until at twelve o'clock the doors at the back of the portico opened and Jackson appeared with all the notables—except Adams. Judges in their robes, foreign ministers wearing their orders, ladies gay in scarlet, purple, and yellow, senators, congressmen, and all the officials who had witnessed the ceremony in the Senate Chamber, streamed forth and took their places. Chief-Justice Marshall, grown old in the discharge of his great functions, administered the oath, Jackson read his inaugural and then made his way again through the western grounds to mount a horse and ride, surrounded by cheering crowds, to the Executive Mansion.

The rush of people to greet him there, the broken furniture and china and trampled bits of food, the hogsheads of punch brought out on the front lawn in the hope of diverting admirers bent upon entering, the plight of those who were caught inside and finally escaped through the windows, the story of how Jackson himself, who had never retreated in battle, was forced at last to seek sanctuary in his rooms at the tavern, is an oft-told tale.

"Ladies and gentlemen only had been expected at this levee, not the people *en masse*," wrote Mrs. Smith, disdainfully. But this was the people's day, and enthusiastically they made the most of it.

Jackson began his removals even before he took his oath. Van Buren was to be his Secretary of State, but he was detained for a time by his duties as governor of New York, and Colonel John H. Hamilton, son of Alexander Hamilton, was given a temporary appointment. So keen was Jackson to get the hated Clay out of the State Department that he would not even allow Hamilton to witness the ceremonies at the Capitol.

"You don't care to see me inaugurated," he had announced, turning his steel-blue eyes upon Hamilton, when the latter entered his room at the hotel just before the little procession started.

"Indeed, General, I do; I came here for that purpose."

"No," Jackson insisted, pressing a paper into his hand, "go to the State House, and as soon as you hear the gun fired, I am President and you are Secretary. Go, and take charge of the department." And Hamilton went.

It would be interesting to know exactly what took place within the walls of the Secretary's room at the State Department and to whom Hamilton presented the note which was addressed to himself and read:

Sir: You are appointed to take charge of the Department of State, and perform the duties of that office until Governor Van Buren arrives in the city. Your Obedient servant,

ANDREW JACKSON.

No waiting for confirmation by the Senate; no thought of Hamilton's refusing. Very likely nobody was at hand except a startled messenger; but the inanimate chairs and table must have shivered at the calm audacity of it.

Perhaps not even Jackson himself knew, in the beginning, exactly how far the policy of turning out officials could be carried;

and if he did not, nobody else did. Apprehension had already driven several timid and distracted souls to suicide; but cooler heads, searching Jackson's past record for hints by which to read the future, found some comfort. Only recently he had advocated a Constitutional amendment limiting the Presidency to one term; and at the time Monroe was a candidate for President, Jackson had written him a letter earnestly urging him to "exterminate that monster called party spirit" and to appoint only the best men to office, regardless of political affiliations. If he lived up to these indications, all would be well. They took even more comfort from the fact that the portly and astute Major Lewis, who was Jackson's most trusted unofficial adviser, absolutely opposed a policy of wholesale removals, which he said would be enough to wreck the country.

What actually occurred, according to the testimony of Amos Kendall, another member of the far-famed kitchen cabinet of which Lewis was premier, was the dismissal of about one seventh of the federal office-holders during Jackson's term, most of them for alleged "bad conduct and character," though the charges of corruption in high office, having played a prominent part in the campaign, died a natural death once Jackson was installed. Only a single official of any importance, a Fourth Auditor of the Treasury, whose peculations were not large, was brought to trial and convicted. To emphasize the heinousness of his offense in the eyes of a new and pure administration, the words "Criminal Department" were painted over the door of his cell, an act that was denounced as a "cruel and unusual punishment" by those who called Jackson a Tennessee barbarian. His friends on the other hand, found difficulty in expressing their admiration in an equal number of syllables.

Mr. Cutts, brother-in-law of Mrs. Madison, was among the unfortunates who lost their official heads.

The Senate, hypnotized into acquiescence, confirmed all Jackson's nominations, though some of them were very odd. Daniel Webster was of the opinion that it would have rejected many had it not been cowed by Jackson's great popularity "out of doors."

Some credited him with long-sighted Machiavellian astuteness; others even among his closest advisers, believed that he made his selections solely on impulse. Colonel Hamilton, who remained in Washington several months, asserted that, often as he held conversations with Jackson about appointments, he never heard a man's fitness for a particular office discussed. While it may be far-fetched to attribute feminine qualities to the most masculine of Presidents, the way in which he chose his advisers and decided for and against measures, seems to have been much more akin to what is called feminine intuition than to logic and reasoning.

Absolutely sincere in his likes and dislikes and equally single-minded in his desire for the right, he was not an egoist. The possibility of being in the wrong simply never entered his long, narrow head. It has been said that, having the genius of command, he regarded his party as his army and those opposed to him as the enemy. His military experience had not been of a kind to make him friendly to routine. He had been obliged to fight famine and pestilence and mutiny single-handed, and to wrest success from impossible situations, which cannot be done by primly following fixed regulations. He had, therefore, no objections to taking short cuts to desirable ends. Wherever he was, things had a way of happening; and of happening in dramatic, explosive fashion from the very amount of energy he put into them. How much of the zealot and how much of the actor there was in his make-up, no mortal ever found out, for he had thoroughly learned the military principle that it is well to keep opponents guessing.

Henry A. Wise, who knew him well, made the assertion in his "Seven Decades" that Jackson was a consummate actor, and that, instead of being impulsive and swayed by hot temper, he "was an abundantly cautious man," who imposed upon the world by "the policy of rashness"; that he took advantage of the belief that his tempers were violent, and deliberately simulated rage which sent many a visitor trembling from the room, only to resume his pipe as soon as the door had closed upon his victim and to say with a chuckle, "He thought I was mad!"

It was part of his self-advertising. The public was never allowed to forget that he had wiped out a victorious army in twenty-five minutes and fought an indefinite number of duels, or that he would ride roughshod after anything he chose to obtain. He even made people half believe in the literal fulfilment of his favorite threat to "cut off the ears" of any one who angered him. It must be confessed that there is a certain amount of evidence to bear out this reading of his character.

Perhaps Miss Martineau was right, when she wrote, toward the end of Jackson's second term:

> He is a man made to impress a very distinct idea of himself on all minds. . . . He has acquired a knowledge of people which has served him instead of much other knowledge in which he is deficient. . . . No physician in the world ever [better] understood feeling the pulse and ordering his practise accordingly.

He never took the members of his cabinet very seriously,—even when they disagreed with him,—regarding them as mere pawns in the political game, who had to be given office to satisfy claims of locality or to pay political debts. For actual help he relied on the group of men known as the kitchen cabinet, who were as unconventional and in the main as patriotic as himself, though they were tactful enough to humor all his foibles. Unhampered in his choice here, either by geography or political prominence, he was wise or fortunate enough to select men who could and did supplement his own shortcomings.

Major Lewis was a born politician and successful in the manipulation of men. Duff Green and Frank P. Blair, who in turn managed the administration organ, each knew the inside of a printing-office "like a book," and personally knew how to do everything needful to influence public opinion, from writing leaders to striking off broadsides.

Amos Kendall, a spare Yankee who reached Washington by way of Kentucky, was a far better scribe than his chief, and admirably fitted to put that chief's vigorous ideas into orderly form. Mr. Kendall appeared on the official rolls for a time as successor to that Fourth Auditor of the Treasury who was imprisoned in the "Criminal Department," and later he was made Postmaster-General; but he did his real work in the room at the White House where he and Jackson held nightly tryst. Its main pieces of furniture were a lounge and a desk. Jackson would lie on the lounge and smoke with energy,—*puff, puff, puff; whiff, whiff, whiff,*— until the red ashes of his pipe gleamed from the center of a dense blue cloud, out of which he dictated his ideas, not his words. Kendall put them down in the phraseology that occurred to him, reading them aloud. The President rejected or amended and the scribe tried again, until political letters were evolved that concealed most adroit suggestions under apparently frank ingenuousness. When once in a while Jackson did write with his own hand, the thoughts were his own, forcibly expressed and put down with a rapid pen without blotting or alteration. Mere details of spelling were too insignificant to trouble a nature like his.

Among them all they brought party organization to a pitch that left Aaron Burr's crafty manipulation of the old Tammany Society far in the shade. The kitchen cabinet saw to it that a goodly proportion of editors received Jackson's "impulsive" appointments to office; and recognizing the political possibilities of post-offices, which had increased in number from seventy-five during Washington's Presidency to more than seven thousand, they arranged a system by which the offices that printed news and those that disseminated it worked together like cogs in a set of wheels.

When that inquiring lady Mrs. Trollope was in Washington, early in Jackson's administration, she was told that every deputy postmaster was required to state in his official returns the title of every newspaper received at his office for distribution. With a system like that, the Administration could feel the pulse of the country as a doctor feels that of his helpless patient.

Old Davy Crockett, who fell a victim to this system, tells, in the picturesque language of his autobiography, how the editors in his district were furnished with material "from the journals of Congress" to show the number of votes he had missed in the course of four sessions "whether from sickness or not, no matter." They amounted to seventy all told, and were charged against him at the rate of a day's pay, eight dollars each, as the basis for an accusation that he had virtually swindled the Government out of five hundred and sixty dollars. This, being the kind of unreasonable reasoning that appealed to rural prejudices, lost him a reëlection.

But only once. Clever himself, the old frontiersman did some reasoning and figuring on his own account before the next campaign, and was triumphantly returned in the face of all Jackson's opposition.

The legend of Jackson's ferocity of mind and manners extended even to his personal appearance. Albert Gallatin, who knew him during his first term in the Senate, described him at that time as being an uncouth, ill-favored young man, who wore his straggling hair tied in an eelskin and grew so passionate, on rising to speak, that his words literally choked in his throat.

But the years during which he mastered fortune reacted on his own person. He bore himself with the assurance of one accustomed to command. The features of his narrow, clean-shaven face were fine as well as strong, a type that improves with age, and the dark-blue eyes under his shaggy brows seemed to see everything. A whirl of rather long gray locks fell not ungracefully about a high forehead. His dress was plain and black, a seal dangled from his watch-ribbon, and the shirt was slightly ruffled, after the conservative fashion of the day, two starched points of his collar standing up above a snowy stock. If not positively handsome, he had distinction, and his manners, to quote Webster, were "more presidential" than those of any of the other candidates in the year when the magnetic Clay, and Adams with his formal dignity, and the popular Crawford, were all competing for the prize.

Josiah Quincy, a man not without prejudice, had it borne in upon him that the seventh President was "in essence a knightly personage; who might be prejudiced, narrow, and mistaken upon many points, but was vigorously a gentleman." Van Buren wrote in his autobiography that the Duke of Wellington reminded him much of General Jackson. Amos Kendall, referring to the belief that the President swore outrageously, said that he "never saw him in a passion nor heard him utter a profane word," but admitted that his was a volcanic nature.

The sum of the pen pictures of Jackson that we have inherited seems to be that he was very tender with children; very gracious and courtly to women; very enigmatic to those whose motives he suspected; and positively terrifying to all who could be frightened by bluster: in short, that he kept his friends and the public in a constant state of apprehension as to what he might do next, but never behaved quite so badly as they anticipated.

Sixty-two years of gusty passion had left his body weary, and even frail. Those admitted to his more intimate circle usually found him seated very near the fire, smoking a long-stemmed pipe which surrounded him with an aura of violet haze, from which his deep eyes peered forth, burning or stern or expressionless as the case might be. Even when he was directing affairs, literally, from a sick-bed, his fiery old spirit was so militant that the memory carried away by visitors was not of invalidism but of wiry endurance.

The lines of his lean old face would soften at the sight of a child. Senator Benton used to take his little daughter Jessie with him to the White House, when he went to have a confidential chat with his friend the President. She winced when the long, bony, caressing hand clenched suddenly among her curls in the heat of argument, but she loved the angular old man enough to sit silent through such torture, only turning appealing eyes to her father. Once, at Jackson's own invitation, she came early to see the mansion in gala dress for an evening reception—a fairyland of flowers and lights and blazing hearths, with tables in the dining-room loaded with the most wonderful viands. This was a memory she carried with her all her days. Usually, however, the visits were in the President's commonplace office, and the reward for her tweaked curls was dismissal to go in search of her playmates the Donelson children, whose father, an adopted son of the President, acted as his private secretary, while their gentle mother presided as hostess of the mansion.

The President was very fond of this lady and of her flock, though he sent them all packing to Tennessee, in disgrace, during the heat of the Eaton controversy. But the children were so dear to him and he was so dependent upon their mother's devoted care, that they were soon back again. Born dictator that he was, he tried loyally to respect her authority as housekeeper. Justice Augustus B. Hagner's reminiscences of a boyhood in Washington tell of going with his father to the White House, to call on the military hero upon whom he had previously looked with eager boyish eyes from the family pew in St. John's. The detail of the visit that he most vividly remembered was that Jackson offered the elder of his callers a clean clay pipe and himself tried to puff the smoke of his own well-seasoned corncob up the chimney, explaining that "Emily Donelson hates the smell of tobacco."

Thanks to the young Donelson couple, real family life went on in the White House, toward which Jackson stood in the relation of a kindly, if at times exacting, grandfather. Letters and reminiscences give glimpses of him pacing the floor with the current Donelson baby in his arms; of giving another young relative the social glory of a White-House wedding and a year later, in the Blue Room, standing as godfather at the christening of the child of this union, who was named for him. The story goes that when Father Matthews, who officiated at both these ceremonies, addressed the baby, after the ritual of his church, with the searching question, "Andrew Jackson, do you renounce the devil and all his works?" the President answered in a loud voice, "I do, most indubitably," to the ill-concealed mirth of all present.

But the story about Jackson that one likes most of all shows him at his fighting best in the character of foster-father to the whole White-House family, during the crowded summer of 1832, the year of his reëlection, when the issues of nullification and his opposition to the national bank had become for him personal as well as national questions.

It happened that locally there had been unusual energy in the prosecution of public works. Pennsylvania Avenue was being macadamized, an attempt was being made to improve the condition of the canal, which had become little better than an open sewer, and in the northeast section of the town hills were being cut down and dug into, to bring more water to the Capitol. Attracted by these works, at least a thousand new laborers, mostly Irish, had come into the city and sought lodgings where and how they could. When the Asiatic cholera, traveling slowly down from New York, reached Washington, late in August, it found much to feed upon, and, before its visitation was over, took a toll of four hundred and fifty lives. Some attributed the virulence of the disease to the freshly upturned earth, some to the unsanitary conditions in the cabins where it got its first hold. Victims were found in crowded, filthy hovels, lying literally upon the floor, without bedding; others, stricken after going out to the day's work, sank upon piles of stones and sat there in the glaring September sun, with heads sunk on their breasts, too wretched to look up. Even then force had to be used to carry them to hastily improvised hospitals.

After two weeks, the infection suddenly took a new hold, and in three days spread to all parts of the city and attacked all classes. Colored people, who then as now made up a large part of the population, were in a state of terror. They had no need to read the column carried daily in the "National Intelligencer" under the headline "Cholera Intelligence," for news of who was stricken and who had died. Such tidings traveled by their own swift whispers. And for a week or more, early every morning, those who had ears could hear the death-carts rolling up and down the streets, and the grewsome call of their drivers: "Bring out your dead!" Once heard this was a sound never to be forgotten.

In such a crisis courage was more valuable than medicine. It is hard to imagine Andrew Jackson as a nurse in an ordinary sickroom, but it is not hard to picture the determined old figure leaving his fireside corner to set the household standard of valor by personally ministering to his colored coachman and other sufferers in the Presidential establishment.

Jackson's public acts belong to history rather than to a volume like this. Never was the medley of small incidents and large causes, of patriotism and prejudice, that make up daily political situations in Washington, harder to disentangle than while this earnest, passionate man was President.

So far as can be seen in retrospect, there was a time when the self-will of a gay young woman and the revered memory of Jackson's dead wife had as much to do in shaping national issues as lifetime ambitions of strong men or the subtle power of slavery.

The relations of President and Vice-President are apt to be as strained as those between a reigning king and his heir apparent. Calhoun had accepted the office of Vice-President in the belief that Jackson desired only one term, and that he could succeed him. When it became evident that Jackson meant to seek reëlection, a break was inevitable, and the love stories of two elderly men only contributed interesting details to the final rupture. Jackson, used to having his own way, did not learn for some time that social quarrels may not be quelled by the high-handed methods effective in cholera or military mutiny, and the lessons by which this was brought home to him added greatly to the excitement of Washington life.

The social war, already begun before he became President, centered round a tall, self-reliant beauty who was engaged to be married to Jackson's middle-aged friend Senator John Eaton, slated to be his Secretary of War. The lady had grown up in the Franklin House, of which her father was proprietor, with coal and wood and "coaches to the Capitol for Members" as side lines of business. Very distinguished people frequented the place. Vice-President Clinton had lodged there until his death in 1812; Lafayette had been its inmate when he was entertained officially by the city; Jackson himself made it his headquarters during his last short term as senator.

Since childhood, the daughter had received more petting from her father's guests than was good for her. She had attended a fashionable dancing-school and had been crowned by Mrs. Madison herself as the most graceful of its pupils. Pert as well as pretty, she was as nimble in her wits and her tongue as in her slippered feet, and conscious that she was smarter and better-looking than the wives and daughters of many high in station, she held herself proudly and was apt to answer back when they attempted to snub her. Most of them pronounced Peggy a minx, but good Mrs. Jackson, whose instinct was to mother every young thing in sight, had been kind to the girl.

Eager to taste the experiences of life, Peggy had married a dissipated young man in the navy, named Timberlake, who tired of life and deserted wife and offspring by the suicide route. The news that he had cut his throat while on a cruise in the Orient did not appear to sadden Mrs. Timberlake unduly, which made feminine opinion still more suspicious of her, since it was the fashion to assume grief for such a loss even when it could not be sincere. As a widow she developed more sparkling allurement than as maid or wife, and when it began to be noised abroad that she was to marry

General Jackson's "bosom friend and almost brother," tongues stabbed and pens scratched at the little reputation left her. Much was made of business transactions by which General Eaton held mortgages on a goodly portion of Mr. O'Neil's property. It was not that she was the daughter of an innkeeper, for marriages from boarding-house homes into official circles were fairly common. The point of irritation was the nature of the young woman herself, who had too little discretion and far too much good looks for one in her position. As Peggy O'Neil and as Mrs. Timberlake she had been gently ignored by the exclusive, but the wife of General Jackson's Secretary of War could not be so treated. The situation had caused much uneasiness, and, even before Mrs. Jackson's death in December, a Washingtonian wrote:

> The General's personal and political friends are very much disturbed about it; his enemies laugh and divert themselves with the idea of what a suitable lady-in-waiting Mrs. Eaton will make to Mrs. Jackson.

This harked back to ugly gossip of the campaign, in which incidents of good Mrs. Jackson's early years had been the subject of maliciously unjust criticism. Her husband, who revered her memory, believed these innuendos hastened her death. He was, therefore, the more ready to champion the cause of his friend and his friend's bride, to whom his wife had been kind and against whom the charges were somewhat similar, different as the two women were in character.

It is easy to believe that the campaign did actually hasten the elder woman's death, not alone by its slanders but by the dread she felt of the part she must play as President's wife; though, in truth, her kindly sympathy and ability to remember names would have served her well in the White House. Life in Washington seemed to her both futile and ungodly. She remembered the catlike welcome the city gave her after her husband's return from Florida, and how certain society ladies peremptorily told by their husbands to call had done so with ill grace. Some of them, like Mrs. Benton, had been won at first sight by her evident diffidence and sincerity, and had done all they could to make her stay agreeable, but her happiest hour had been that of departure, when she and Major Donelson's little son Andrew stepped into the waiting coach with its four gray horses, General Jackson mounted Sweet Sally, and with Mr. Donelson and Major Reid and their servants all on horseback, an hostler bringing up the rear with spare horses, they had clattered off, leaving the dust of the District behind them. Perhaps she and the women who whispered that she smoked a corncob pipe and did not know how to dress, were alike content to have gentle Mrs. Donelson act as mistress of the White House.

General Eaton married Margaret Timberlake on a January night in 1829, when "the streets were as light and as full as in the morning," according to one who did not attend the wedding; and even on the fourth of March the bride had disputed the center of the stage with General Jackson. It was said that fully as many people attended the inaugural ball to see the new Mrs. Eaton as to see the new President; in which case, they had the advantage in not being disappointed. Jackson, worn out by the fatigues of the day, did not appear at all, but Mrs. Eaton was there, radiant and triumphant in rose color with nodding black plumes.

Discussion continued to rage about the lady, whose defenders and detractors were very partizan indeed. It is said that the poem beginning

> I fill my cup to one made up of loveliness alone,
> A woman of her gentle sex the seeming paragon,

was written of her. On the other hand, her critics referred to her as "Bellona" the stirrer up of strife.

The cabinet divided on strictly feminine lines. Van Buren, being a widower with no family opposition to face, seized the opportunity to gain favor with his chief by being especially polite to Mrs. Eaton. So, for reasons of their own, were Mr. Vaughan and Baron Kindener, the bachelors of the diplomatic corps, who represented England and Russia; but "ladies had a way of floating away at her approach" and "cotillion after cotillion dissolved into its original elements when she was given a place at its head." The wife of the Dutch minister left the room on her husband's arm rather than sit beside her, and this raised the scandal to the dignity of an international complication and was ended by the minister's speedy recall.

Mrs. Calhoun joined the ladies of the cabinet, who drew their virtuous skirts about them and refused to pay the bride even the customary call of ceremony. Old Madam Calhoun, mother-in-law of the Vice-President, preserved a sardonic neutrality, with her eye on Van Buren, remarking that she and President Jackson were the only truly independent people in Washington.

The storm burst in Jackson's official family when the irascible President, declaring that he had come to Washington to make a cabinet for the nation, not for the ladies, deputed his useful friend Richard M. Johnson to call upon the refractory cabinet members and virtually order them to order their wives to be civil to the wife of his Secretary of War. To this, Secretary Berrien replied that Jackson might be President of the United States and even Commander-in-Chief of the Army and Navy, but he was not master of any man's family circle, and that he, Berrien, was ready to resign but not ready to have General Jackson meddle in his private affairs.

Part of the cabinet did, in fact, resign, while "Bellona" held her head high and, it is suspected, thoroughly enjoyed the situation, with its exciting undertone of rumored duels, of disturbed pastors, and of churches almost rent asunder, when the quarrel spread beyond official circles. After some time General Eaton was forced out of the cabinet, but even then his wife remained a thorn in the flesh. Mrs. Smith wrote in midsummer, 1831:

> It was hoped, on her husband's going out of office, she would have left the city, *but she will not*. She hopes for a complete triumph, and is not satisfied with having the cabinet broken up and a virtuous and intelligent minister recalled, and many of our best citizens frowned upon by the President. . . . Yet no one can deny that the President's weakness originates in an amiable cause.

It is an ill wind that blows nobody good. Hotel-keepers profited, for timid folk in official life who had not the courage to take sides, abandoned housekeeping to avoid the necessity of giving parties which would compel them to decide whether or not to invite the Eatons.

Jackson appointed his friend Governor of Florida, where the lively lady was distinctly bored. She enjoyed better a sojourn in Russia, whither her husband was sent as minister. Some of his friends, not partial to the wife, believed that he had become a little tired of her before they returned to America. After his death, which occurred just before the Civil War, Mrs. Eaton, who was still a beauty though over sixty, made a third matrimonial venture, choosing this time a dancing-master many years her junior, who repented of his bargain and eloped with one of her own Timberlake grandchildren. She lived in Washington, almost forgotten, until her death at the age of eighty-three. People rarely saw her except at the Metropolitan Church, where she slipped into a seat in the side aisle and at the end of service quietly disappeared. She dwelt much in the past and cherished to the last an extravagant admiration for General Jackson, who she declared was "not a man—he was a god."

If ability to carry on several engrossing enterprises at one time is a godlike attribute, Jackson possessed it; and he had another: he knew how to keep his plans unrevealed until the moment came to act. This is no place even to outline the serious features of his administration. For our purpose, it resolves itself into a sequence of dramatic pictures in which invariably the spare old man is the center of interest.

Nothing daunted him. He fought, regardless of odds, whatever he thought it well to fight—Clay and his principles; the national bank beloved of the country's financiers; Calhoun and his Nullification doctrine, with its far-reaching slavery poison; a city's pestilence; his own ill health. In some mysterious way he even appears to have been the one upright, stable thing in nature on that marvelous night of 1833, when for the space of three hours meteors fell thick as snowflakes and the heavens seemed about to pass away in a blaze of awesome beauty.

Perhaps this dauntless courage was one reason of his liking for "Bellona." He recognized in her a fighting spirit akin to his own.

STATUE OF ANDREW JACKSON

Once in the Executive Office he was confronted by a man as fearless as himself, though the black eyes that looked into his steel-blue ones, giving back glance for glance, were those of a prisoner. It was the Indian chief Blackhawk who brushed away all differences of race and rank and fortune in the few short words:

"I am a man: you are another."

Jackson was not one of our outdoor presidents. He did not habitually take solitary rides as Jefferson did, or enjoy a swim, or probe into the White-House turf after secrets of sprouting acorns, or, like Lincoln, drive almost daily to hospitals upon errands of mercy and cheer. Hospitals, indeed, were not in evidence in the town before the cholera visitation, and after that passed, we hear little more of the three so hurriedly improvised to meet it.

When Jackson rode or walked abroad, it was as the central figure of some pageant. Bareheaded in the midst of cheering crowds on his first inauguration day. Entering a closed carriage under the shelter of the mansion's newly erected porte-cochère four years later, in "wicked weather" to take his oath a second time, and after the ceremony returning so blue-lipped that Emily Donelson hurried him off to bed. Oddest of all, perhaps, considering his character and that of the man he honored, is the glimpse we have of him, taking part in a procession that marched up Pennsylvania Avenue on October 28, 1830, to celebrate the accession of Louis Philippe to the throne of France.

One of these pictures, less grave and less often called to mind than the others, gathers into small compass much that, worked up with skill, would provide sumptuous material for that film-history of the national capital which is sure to be written. In addition to Jackson's striking figure, the actors include pirates and abandoned babies, American sailors held in slavery in Tunis and Algiers, the Sultan of Morocco in all his gorgeousness and a king of the jungle.

It will be remembered that in Jefferson's day Decatur and his fellow officers put the fear of God and of gunpowder into the hearts of the Barbary pirates, and that Joel Barlow added a new chapter to his varied career by negotiating a treaty which liberated the hundred and more of our sailors they had held in captivity. After that, to make sure the lesson was not forgotten every naval officer who sailed that way took care to make visits of ceremony which were thinly veiled exhibitions of naval strength.

When Captain Reily, after such a call in 1835, turned homeward, he had on board his ship a gift which the sultan had bidden him take "to his sovereign lord." Translated into Yankee speech, that meant, "Take to Andrew Jackson, President of the United States," and the junior officers on that cruise indulged in hilarious bets as to what Andrew Jackson would do with a full-grown lion, it being scarcely suitable for a household pet, and custom forbidding turning it loose for the destruction of his enemies.

The ship reached port, the captain turned over his charge to the civil authorities, and Congress passed the necessary vote authorizing the President to receive the gift—possibly with inward chuckles on the part of members unfriendly to Jackson. The Secretary of State sent off a note of delighted thanks to the donor and the Administration sat down to consider what was to become of the smoldering-eyed beast, there being no national zoo in which to house it.

It was Mrs. Bomfort, sister-in-law of Joel Barlow, who solved the problem. Her son had now inherited Kalorama, and her charitable heart was full of concern for the welfare of the Orphans' Home, whose special patroness, Mrs. Van Ness, had died "of the prevailing malady" in the epidemic of 1832. (It is noticeable that only the poor died of cholera that autumn; the rich invariably succumbed to the prevailing malady.)

Gentle Mrs. Van Ness had done so much for the little waifs who stood in mournful checked gingham rows and strewed the way with willow as her coffin was borne into the tomb, that people wondered what was to become of them. Mrs. Bomfort tried valiantly to stepmother them, but funds ran low and interest in the institution was now only half-hearted, the Catholics having gathered up their own orphans and established a rival Home.

Mrs. Bomfort heard of the lion, and saw in it an opportunity. She resolved to seek a personal interview with the President, though it is evident she approached him with trepidation. The meager report of the call, set down by a friend from Mrs. Bomfort's own words, is painfully lacking in humor. Once more Jackson astonished a caller who feared the worst, by being affable and gracious. He did not, as the young naval officers would surely have been moved to do, ask whether it was her idea to use the lion to feed the babies, or the babies to pacify the lion. He was so glad to get rid of the encumbrance that he assented with enthusiasm, whereat Mrs. Bomfort burst into tears, seized his hand, and kissed it.

It is quite possible to picture Andrew Jackson in courtly mood, bending over a lady's white hand, but not standing up complacently to have his own thus treated by a large and weeping matron. "He immediately drew an order on the Secretary of State, and signing it, gave it to her"; and, to delete from the interview all emotion, reminded her forcibly that he was giving away a purely non-sectarian beast which must be used impartially, half for the Protestant orphans dear to her heart, half for those under the patronage of St. Ann. We can imagine him, after he had brought the interview to a close and the lady was safely out of the room, looking thoughtfully at his hand and then, with a twinkle in his eye, turning to light his long-stemmed pipe again.

It happened shortly afterward that a convenient circus came to town. The animal was sold and presumably went on tour to gladden the eyes and stir the pulses of countless small boys, while the $3350 it brought, divided equally between the two orphanages, suffered a depressing change into aprons and lukewarm porridge.

But the picture of the President which will outlast the rest belongs to the spring of 1830, after a winter-long debate on states-rights in Congress. Hayne had argued for two days in favor of the South's contention that a state might set aside a federal statute if it saw fit. Webster, shaking off the lethargy that had held him in thrall since the death of his wife, roused himself to answer, and speaker after speaker followed, as the weeks rolled on.

The President, on whose action so much depended, if South Carolina really put in practice its threat and refused to obey the new federal tariff laws, alone remained silent. Far from giving explosive expression to his opinions, as was his custom in less serious matters, he seemed to take a malicious pleasure in keeping to himself what he meant to do. Some of his previous acts appeared to favor the theory of states-rights, others emphatically upheld federal authority, and it was most important for the Nullifiers to find out where he stood.

They quoted the Virginia Resolutions of 1798, as the basis of their arguments, and arranged a grand subscription dinner for the anniversary of Jefferson's birth, to which the President and cabinet were invited. When the invitation was accepted, they looked upon it as a hopeful omen and made great efforts to have the banquet noteworthy in every respect. There must be elaborate decorations; music by the Marine Band; a menu in line with the best traditions of Washington feasts and just enough of nullification daring in the twenty-four toasts,—one for each state in the Union,—so that when the moment arrived wine and kindling enthusiasm should fix the doctrine forever in words of burning import.

As the guests gathered in the lobby of the hotel where the feast took place, they found gentlemen who had preceded them talking in earnest groups, and a few, who were known to have subscribed to the dinner, finding their hats and leaving, with troubled faces. These had read the printed list of toasts and refused to countenance such sentiments by their presence. But those who stayed had enthusiasm enough to overcome the depressing effect of empty seats. The President, erect and immaculate, was distinctly taciturn; Van Buren was urbane and smiling as always; the remainder of the cabinet betrayed nothing. The banquet was eaten and the toasts drunk to music, and responded to with differing degrees of eloquence and sobriety and applause. Then came the great moment for which the dinner had been planned, a point in the proceedings where volunteer toasts were in order. Jackson, quiet and watchful, had listened to the speeches as the evening progressed, with scarcely a change of expression. Once he had scribbled a few words on the back of the list of toasts and then had resumed his silent attention. The toastmaster in calling upon him could not keep out of his voice a note of triumph.

The air was electric as he rose to his full height, a striking figure with its shock of unruly silver hair crowning the long, keen face. "Our Federal Union. It must be preserved," he said, and sat down again in a silence full of portent. It was in vain that perfunctory applause was started. In vain that the chairman quickly called upon Calhoun, hoping that his skill might deflect the blow. In vain that Van Buren's oily tongue added to Calhoun's words another sentiment calculated to soothe ruffled feelings, or that these two were followed by about seventy more to whom nobody listened. Andrew Jackson had spoken.

A tale used to be told which ought to be true even if it is not, since it is one of those character-revealing stories that nobody who enjoys the savor of Jackson's personality would willingly let die. It is to the effect that when the Ex-President lay all but dead, his pastor bent over him and asked if there was anything in his life for which he wished to express regret. The parchment-like eyelids fluttered slowly open, the steel-blue eyes looked straight into those of his questioner, as he answered in tones barely audible but still emphatic, "Yes, I am sorry I did not hang Calhoun."

Jackson's attitude had been so thoroughly defined by his toast at the Nullifiers' banquet, that the public looked for speedy and drastic action; but he again lapsed into silence and for more than a year all the important events seemed to take place in the camp of the enemy. Nullifiers elected Hayne Governor of South Carolina, and in December, 1831, Calhoun resigned the office of Vice-President to take his place on the floor of the Senate as Hayne's successor. This not only gave him a vote with which to serve his faction, but it relieved an embarrassing personal situation, since he could remain in Jackson's administration only as the President's antagonistic understudy. But it is not usual for Vice-Presidents to resign, and the situation had its humorous difficulties, there being to all appearances nobody to resign to. Burr had taken his leave in a speech made directly to the Senate, a precedent which could not be followed because the Senate was not in session. For obvious reasons Calhoun did not care to send his resignation to Jackson, and it was impossible to get it before the Electoral College which had elected both Jackson and himself, that body being scattered to the four winds. In the end he addressed it to the Secretary of State, as to a sort of federal super-chore-boy, whose duties comprise all business not otherwise provided for in the Constitution. That official delayed acknowledgment so long that at the very end of March,

Calhoun felt constrained to address another note to him, asking if his resignation had been received.

Jackson meanwhile kept up an astonishing amount of silence. When the time came for the annual meeting of Congress, people awaited with the utmost eagerness the reading of his message; but, to their stupefaction, Jackson hardly touched upon nullification, dismissing it in a short and unimportant paragraph. It was whispered that the old fighter had lost his nerve and was in his dotage. A month later, however, when he believed the time was ripe, he sent Congress a complete message upon the subject that left no doubt of his vigor or earnestness; and Congress responded by passing a force bill that granted him all the power he could possibly need to meet the emergency, though had congressional approval been withheld, his action would probably have been just the same. He had already quietly taken measures to enforce the law, and if it was only a game of bluff that the Nullifiers were playing, he was by nature fully equipped to hold his own.

General Scott's autobiography gives a characteristic glimpse of President Jackson and Ex-President Adams during that season of watchful waiting. Adams in his rôle of congressman kept so strictly aloof from the White House that four years elapsed before he even saw the man who had succeeded him; but it did not follow that he took no interest in Jackson's doings, or that his patriotic old heart did not throb in response to the general's stand upon nullification. Knowing both leaders, he had his own ideas of the probable outcome of a conflict of wills between Jackson and Calhoun.

General Scott, whose great ability was matched only by his robust prejudices, nourished a long-standing grievance against Jackson. Routine duty brought him to Washington about a month before the nullification message went to Congress, and in the absence from town of Lewis Cass, Secretary of War, he deemed it his duty to report directly to the President, though inclination would never have led him to the White House while Jackson ruled there. The President received him so affably that Scott, who was tenacious of his grievance, felt constrained. After business was disposed of, Jackson began to talk of the situation in the South, and, in a manner which his touchy visitor thought "condescending," asked his opinion and advice. Before the interview was over, Scott found himself receiving oral orders to start south at once on a secret mission of watchfulness, disguised as a routine tour of inspection. Written orders were to follow him, and the President assured him he should have everything he wanted in the way of troops, and that vessels already lay conveniently within call. Astonished and a little flattered, the general rose to take his leave, when Jackson completed his amazement by asking him in homely phrase to "stay to supper." This being a social invitation, not a military command, Scott refused, pleading lack of time and adding, with conspicuous absence of tact, that he could not think of leaving town without paying his respects to his old friend Ex-President Adams. At this, Jackson shot him a quick look and growling: "That 's right. Never desert a friend!" watched him depart.

Adams, on learning of Scott's new assignment, jumped to instant conclusions. "You are going south to watch the Nullifiers," he announced with evident satisfaction, brushing aside Scott's reply about a tour of inspection with the scant attention it deserved. Having been President, he knew how such things were managed. "To watch the Nullifiers," he repeated with conviction. "Mr. Calhoun will be the first to give way. He will show the white feather" —a prediction that time verified when, despite all the fiery talk, the matter failed to come to a trial of arms.

Loyalty to friends and principles was Jackson's guiding rule; and a few words from his farewell address to the people of the United States, on leaving the Presidency, express better than all the laudations of his friends and all the distortions of his enemies, the spirit of the brave, upstanding old man:

> My public life has been a long one, and I cannot hope that it has at all times been free from error. But I have the consolation of knowing that if mistakes have been committed they have not seriously injured the country I so anxiously endeavored to serve; and at the moment when I surrender my last public trust, I leave this great people prosperous and happy.

XII

POMPE FUNÈBRE

STRICTLY speaking, Van Buren was the earliest all-American President, since he was the first to hold the office who had not begun life a British subject. He also bears the unflattering distinction of being the first to fill the rôle of understudy at his own inauguration. He and Jackson rode side by side to the Capitol, on a balmy fourth of March that seemed trying to make amends for the cruel weather of Jackson's second inauguration. They sat in a light and elegant phaëton built from timbers of the old ship *Constitution* and painted with a portrait of the historic vessel. This was a gift from the Democrats of New York, not to the son of their own state who was about to become President, but to the gaunt Tennessean from whom no more favors were to be expected.

Small and dapper, his graying auburn hair standing out on each side of his bald head like a tarnished aureole, Van Buren was round where Jackson was angular, short where Jackson was long, a little too suave where Jackson was brusque, and, his detractors averred, crooked where Jackson was straight. Little attention was paid to him on that ride up the avenue, the eyes of the crowd resting almost hungrily on the strong, marked features of Jackson, whose coming eight years earlier had thrown the town almost into panic. Belief in his integrity had grown steadily in the stormy interval, and now that he was departing, the citizens felt bereft. The huzzahs that burst forth after Van Buren had read his inaugural and the oath had been administered, were so evidently for Jackson the private citizen, that as he descended the steps to his waiting carriage, emotion could be seen tugging hard at the muscles of his lean old face.

Van Buren's features were under perfect control. Serene, smiling, entirely at his ease, by not so much as the flicker of an eyelash did he show annoyance at this ovation to another, at the moment which should have been supremely his own. No man without a certain largeness of nature could have borne himself so perfectly.

People called him the Mistletoe Politician, implying that he fed upon the life-sap of Old Hickory. Perhaps he did; but it had been a triumph of self-control, as well as of astuteness, that enabled him to subordinate himself so thoroughly to the President he hoped to succeed. Throughout his term as Secretary of State and during the four years of his Vice-Presidency, he had given discreet dinners, had dressed well and driven behind fast horses to and from the Capitol, had been always in the picture, correct and elegant in every detail, but rarely attracting more than a passing glance or passing mention. Never was growing ambition more circumspect.

One of the new President's critics described him as "a perfect imitation of a gentleman," and another who knew him as a lad was sure that nothing in his manners suggested the home of his boyhood. His early opportunities had in truth been limited, but he had made the most of them, putting on the ways of the world with each successively better coat, and he had, moreover, educated himself, accumulating a library and a fair knowledge of what its books contained. Some asserted that Aaron Burr, the great man of his section when Van Buren began his career, was his model; if so, he improved on the original, for there was nothing sinister or mysterious about him. He was always punctilious, always cheerful, always self-possessed, even if not so completely master of himself as to conceal the fact that he thought his manners excellent.

One would have guessed that this faintest trace of insincerity—this cat-and-canary urbanity—would have alienated Jackson; but his dexterity either blinded the old hero or commanded his respectful admiration. Jackson's will had dominated his party for so long that when he indicated Van Buren as his successor, the New Yorker was elected amid enthusiastic rejoicing, though it died down almost as speedily as the bonfires lighted to celebrate his victory. The truth was that by election-time in 1836, the party organization of the Democrats had become almost too perfect. The rank and file in that mysterious body alluded to as "they" were growing restive.

Having elected Van Buren, they felt not the least obligation to approve his acts.

Some of the criticism heaped upon him was just enough; some supremely unjust, blaming him for happenings that were either the bitter fruit of Jackson's policies, or beyond human control. He might as well have been held accountable for the visitation of red ants that appeared in certain parts of the District of Columbia during his term, gnawed their way impartially through bank vaults and grocery stores and private residences, and vanished, leaving moral as well as material destruction behind, for the city council offered one silver dollar for every pint of slain insects, which proved a temptation so strong that financiers, male and female, young and old, appeared bearing heaps of corpses manifestly added to by coffee grounds. In retrospect this bit of human depravity seems entangled with other charges of extravagance and corruption made against Jackson's successor.

The great financial panic which came upon the country with a crash shortly after he assumed office grew rapidly worse through terrible months, and then recovery proceeded at a snail's pace during the remainder of his term. The fact that he and other officials of the Government received their salaries in gold, after banks had been forced to suspend specie payments, did nothing to endear him to voters who had lost their all and were trudging west on foot, with their wives and babies and perhaps a handcart of salvaged belongings, to begin life anew. Still less did his ways appeal to men less fortunate because less energetic, who remained in their old haunts brooding over their misfortunes.

His style of living furnished endless texts upon the theme of extravagance in spending the people's money—not his own. In vain figures were published to show how economical he had been compared with Jackson. White-House expenditures had indeed loomed large under Jackson, for the north and south porticos had been completed and after that first joyous invasion when democracy overran the mansion, trampling food into its carpets and ignorantly misusing much that it touched, the house required much refurnishing. But Jackson kept Congress and the country so busy with large issues that small matters like appropriations for household renovation slipped through unnoticed, while Van Buren, cut to smaller measure, suffered among his minor tortures this eagle-eyed scrutiny.

Jackson's four grays trot in and out of history unmolested, almost as often as Washington's useful white coach-horses, and was it Monroe or Madison who owned part of a race-horse?—but for Van Buren it was accounted a crime to like to ride at a brisk pace along Pennsylvania Avenue. His detractors said it took him four and a half minutes to cover the distance between the Capitol and White House, and they described him drawing up before St. John's Church on Sundays in regal magnificence, wearing a bright-blue Spanish cloak over his shoulders, to descend from a "most superb" dark olive-green carriage of Russian design, with "ornaments elegantly dispersed, shining as bright as burnished gold."

A few bunches of artificial flowers bought for table decoration, and a gilt dessert service of three dozen spoons, forks, and fruit knives, four dozen coffee spoons, and a few odd pieces, including "two mustard spoons," were a boon to his enemies and proved invaluable for campaign purposes. Mr. Ogle of Pennsylvania thundered forth in the House of Representatives:

I put it to you, sir, and to the free citizens of this country, whose *servant* the President is, to say whether, in addition to the large sum of $100,000 which he is entitled to receive *for a single term of four years,* they are disposed to maintain for his private accommodation a Royal Establishment *at the cost of the nation!* Will they longer feel inclined to support their chief servant in a Palace *as splendid as that of the Cæsars and as richly adorned as the proudest Asiatic mansion?*

How delightful it must be to a real Loco Foco to eat his *paté de foie gras, dinde de-ossé* and *salade à la volaille* from a silver plate with a golden knife and fork. And how exquisite to sip with a golden spoon his *soupe à la Reine* from a silver tureen.

It was vain to point out that the gold spoons, mostly plated, were the property of the tax-payers and that the glass screen Mr. Van Buren caused to be erected across the "spacious front hall" was put there neither for seclusion nor splendor, but to keep out drafts and aid the work of the open fireplaces which as yet bore the entire brunt of heating the house.

Care bestowed upon the White-House grounds excited still greater ire. There was a man on the government pay-roll—some one had actually seen him at work—whose sole duty was to potter about the public reservations and dig up dandelion roots. And the people received nothing in return for all this riotous extravagance. They were even denied entrance to the White House at a reasonable hour in the morning.

> The court fashion of sleeping out the day and waking out the night, results in keeping the palace doors closed save to persons who have the entrée, until ten o'clock A. M.,

shouted an irate member of Congress from Pennsylvania.

When they did get inside, little cheer awaited them. The public was expected to overrun the mansion now only on the first of January, and

> at this annual levee, notwithstanding the pomp and pageantry, no expense whatever is incurred by the president personally. No fruits, cake, wine, coffee, hard cider, or other refreshments of any kind are tendered to his guests. Indeed, it would militate against all the rules of court etiquette now established at the palace to permit vulgar eating and drinking. . . . The only entertainment there served up consists in profound bows, stately promenades, formal civilities, ardent expressions of admiration for the pageant passing before our eyes, with anxious inquiries about the weather. . . . The Marine Band however is always ordered from the Navy Yard, and stationed in the spacious front hall from whence they swell the rich saloons of the palace with "Hail to the Chief," "Who'll be King but Charlie," and a hundred other airs which ravish with delight the ears of warriors who have never smelled powder.

Van Buren's enemies harped upon this assumption of royal customs, in a manner altogether absurd, and spoke with a sneer of his handsome son as "Prince John," after the young man returned from a trip abroad. Whatever of good was still to be enjoyed was looked upon as left over from a former day, and few recognized the ills of the moment, financial and political, as inherited mainly from the past.

Manners had been less polite in Jackson's time, but they had possessed the merit of frankness. When people got angry and published "cards" in the newspapers or scattered broadsides upon the streets, printed in letters an inch long, denouncing some former friend as "a foreigner, a coward, a puppy, a poltroon, a lyar and a scoundrel," they did a thorough job and spoke what was in their minds.

In these latter degenerate days politics had become so dull that Van Buren was able to keep up a show of friendly relations with Clay, whose Presidential ambition was as unflagging as that of our later perennial candidate William Jennings Bryan. Under Jackson it had not always been safe for Whigs and Democrats to try to be patriotic together, even on the nation's birthday. Jacksonites had gone off in one group and Clay's followers in another, to enjoy separate barbecues and drink toasts vilifying the opposition to their hearts' content. One toast, of about seventy proposed at a local Clay celebration in 1831, had compared "The Present Administration" to "The madness of Don Quixote without his dignity; the vulgarities of Sancho without his good sense."

Now, spare old Don Quixote, beloved if incomprehensible, had gone into retirement and plump Sancho reigned in his stead. Sancho's Vice-President was Richard M. Johnson, who was also reaping his reward for services rendered. Andrew Jackson had sent him upon unpleasant errands, like carrying the message from the irate President to members of his cabinet about being civil to Mrs. Eaton. To some, the whole Van Buren administration seemed like that of well-trained servants who had climbed the basement stairs and were sitting in the parlor.

Its social high-water mark was the courting of a pretty Georgetown school-girl by the Russian minister, Bodisco, who was old enough to be her father and homely enough to have been her simian ancestor. He was such an intelligent and kindly semi-barbarian that Washington looked upon him indulgently when he did things that in others would have seemed ridiculous. Display was the breath of life to him. He drove about in a snowy barouche drawn by four long-tailed black horses, not nearly so fine as those attached to less showy turnouts, but which bore him along at a good pace, while he, bareheaded, bowed right and left. He rented a large house in Georgetown that resembled his horses in being showy rather than smart; and here, although there was no Madame Bodisco, he entertained lavishly, even giving children's parties for which two young nephews who lived with him furnished the excuse. It was a Christmas party for these youngsters that opened the international romance.

The feminine guests were recruited mainly from the pupils of Miss English's fashionable school for girls, where good manners and social ease were prized above scholarship, and where the names on the rolls formed part of history—Bentons and Fitzhughs and Calverts, and even a Washington. Other girls with names less well known were quite as lovely in person. One of these, Harriet Beall Williams, had been unintentionally overlooked in the invitations, an oversight which moved the kindly ogre of a minister to write a personal note of apology and to look at her with particular attention when his guests began to arrive.

She was well grown and blonde, and, in twentieth-century idiom, very easy to look at. Soon he was carrying her books home daily after school, like any lovelorn hobbledehoy. The news that he was to marry this sixteen-year-old daughter of a deceased government clerk caused much talk, and, since Bodisco could do nothing without being spectacular, the plans for the wedding caused even more. There must, he decreed, be many bridesmaids, all of an age suited to the bride, while the groomsmen must be men of his own generation and importance. Once again Miss English's school was robbed of pupils, who were divorced from their studies to master the complicated wedding ceremonial and to learn to manage the trains of their first grown-up dresses, designed personally by the bridegroom and made in the establishment of the imposing "Mrs. Abbott, Milliner and Mantua Maker from London."

And much diplomatic caution went into assigning places to the groomsmen. For instance, should James Buchanan, who had represented his country at the court of the czar and was now a United States senator, be given precedence over eccentric Henry Fox, the

British minister, who really cared for nothing except a game of cards, but might wax touchy over questions of etiquette?

The President and as many important folk as could be crowded into the shabby front drawing-room of the Williams home, gathered to witness the ceremony, while outside the number of carriages and onlookers rivaled those at a county fair.

The bridesmaids wound their trains carefully about them and descended the narrow back stairs to an empty rear parlor, where, hidden from the guests by folding doors, the elderly bridegroom, written list in hand, placed his wedding party in position. Mr. Fox, an unusually odd combination of scarlet-and-gold court dress, gray eyebrows, and general disgust, stood close beside Bodisco, with the rosy thirteen-year-old sister of the bride, while opposite, equally near the bride, the silver-haired Buchanan had as partner ex-President Jackson's little friend Jessie Benton, grown to the mature age of fourteen. The minister from the Hague, Chevalier de Martiti, big, placid and amused, was paired with a slim, lovely girl whose hectic flush foretold her early death. The most insignificant of the eight groomsmen were two young men, one of them merely a son of the President of the United States and the other son of the Secretary of the Navy, who "stood up" with cousins of the bride. When all were in place and the light had been arranged to fall just as it should on young faces and embroidered coats and the stiff bunchs of camellias that were the last word in wedding bouquets, the satisfied groom took his place beside the bride in her Russian dress, with its diamond-besprinkled coronet and silver veil, and the folding doors rolled back, revealing a tableau whose final note of contrast was struck by the tall slim figure of Henry Clay in his black coat, waiting to give away the bride.

As soon as possible after the ceremony, the colorful party was hustled off to Bodisco's larger house for the wedding breakfast and the interminable dinner that closed the day. Between the two feasts the groomsmen disappeared for a season of relaxation, while the bridesmaids, taken upstairs and divested of their finery, curled up on beds and sofas for a reviving nap. A few nights later Van Buren gave a White-House dinner in honor of the wedding party, where the bevy of white bridesmaids surrounding a Juno-like bride in velvet of jade green made another lovely picture. It is believed that the many colds caught on this occasion may have determined Van Buren to build that glass screen across the great drafty entrance hall, for which he was so bitterly accused of extravagance.

The unusual part of this story of May and December is that the wedded pair lived in perfect harmony until the minister's death, years later. He lost his most bizarre mannerisms and gallantly fulfilled his self-imposed task of looking after the welfare of the bride's entire family; while she presented him with lusty children and grew in grace and popularity in Russia and her own country. Even after he died, she scrupulously followed the wishes outlined in his will by marrying again, choosing for her second husband Captain Scott, a short and slender Guardsman, who took her away to India, so that Washington knew her no more.

At this second wedding, which occurred in St. John's Church, it was President Buchanan who gave the bride away. As both President and bride were of full figure, they had difficulty in walking up the narrow aisle together. He "led the lady slightly in advance of himself," until the young groom in scarlet stepped forward to claim her. And because the church was crowded, only a few saw that the bridegroom stood upon a hassock during the ceremony, to make the difference in height between himself and his bride less apparent.

When it came to reëlection, Van Buren was doomed, but, Van Burenish to the last, he made himself agreeable to as many factions as possible. The Whig party managers passed over better-known men, to choose William Henry Harrison, who had a good if short war record, and, in addition, had made an excellent governor of Indiana Territory and had served acceptably in a diplomatic post in South America. While these were all good points, his chief asset for campaign purposes lay in his simple mode of life, that could be effectively contrasted with Van Buren's gold-spoon tendencies. An opposition newspaper of Baltimore unwittingly gave the tone to the campaign by making the slurring assertion that Harrison had no ambition, and that if he were given a log cabin and assured an income of two thousand a year, with unlimited cider to drink, he would willingly retire from the fight and settle down to end his days.

THE PRESIDENT'S HOUSE AS IT WAS IN VAN BUREN'S TIME

The Whigs caught this up and played it against Van Buren's love of luxury and, inventing the rallying cry, "The Union of the Whigs for the sake of the Union," called on each faction of the party to do its bit to defeat the man in the White House. Oratory in praise of the simple life spouted on every side. Each town set up its log cabin, with a coonskin tacked to the door, and an adjacent cider-barrel by no means empty. Lucky in the number and catchy quality of their campaign songs (perhaps the cider added zest to the singing), the Whigs were equally fortunate in the audacity of their leaders, who made the campaign one of unparalleled enthusiasm and polled one hundred and seventy-four more electoral votes for their candidate than Van Buren was able to muster.

There was a very active Whig committee in Washington that summer, and from the windows of their log cabin on Market Space, songs rolled forth with great vigor. One whose refrain was, "Van, Van is a used-up man," must have had a mocking sound as it assailed the ears of the Democratic candidate riding by in his green Russian turnout. But he kept his wits and self-control as thoroughly as he had done when the cheers of his inauguration day were given to Jackson instead of to himself. His annual message to Congress after the election was looked upon as the best of his term, and in the realm of manners this "imitation of a gentleman" and Harrison, who had been denounced by Van Buren's followers as a sot and a boor, developed greater mutual courtesy than was shown by Presidents whose claim to the title of gentleman nobody would presume to deny.

The statement that Van Buren entertained Harrison at the White House "several weeks before the inauguration" is true, though capable of wrong interpretation, for Harrison confused the record by making two entries into Washington. The first occurred just before the counting of the electoral vote, when he passed through the city on his way to visit a kinsman in Virginia. At that time he was the guest of political admirers at Gadsby's, but he promptly called upon the occupant of the White House, who as promptly returned his visit and invited him to dinner. On his second arrival, a few days before the inauguration, he became the guest of the mayor, Mr. Seaton.

By that time the city was full of jubilant Whigs, many of them wearing coonskin caps and provided with all sorts of campaign emblems. Gadsby's dining-room, famous in stage-coach days, was turned into a dormitory of "a hundred pallets," and an Englishman who thought he might as well take in the sight of an American change of dynasty, was graciously told he might lie down on Bed Sixteen in parlor Number Four.

It was on a rainy day about the first of March that the President-elect reached Washington, after the visit to his nephew, and was met at the railroad station by the mayor, with whom he walked arm in arm to the City Hall, to begin at once the arduous task of handshaking. There was no carriage nor omnibus in waiting, but the assembled crowd, plentifully supplied with umbrellas ("mostly cotton" an eye-witness tells us), held these over the distinguished arrival "in a manner completely to protect him." Which goes to show how much umbrellas have deteriorated since the year 1841. Imagine the streams of water that would deluge a great man's collar if such a thing were attempted now!

By March 4th, rain had given way to a piercing icy wind, but Harrison did not spare himself on that account. He prided himself upon his vigor, though nearly seventy, and, disdaining a new coach presented by Baltimore friends, joined the inaugural procession on horseback as it passed Mr. Seaton's door. Ex-President Adams, who was looking down upon it from his second-story windows, thought it "showy-shabby" and surveyed with more curiosity than approval its civil section, in which fire-engines and blatant bands, log cabins on wheels and a cotton-mill with a loom in full operation, broke the monotony of ardent Tippecanoe Clubs, marching with pinched faces against the biting blast. Adams had difficulty in locating the President-elect, who was riding "on a mean-looking white horse, in the centre of seven or eight others, in a plain frock coat or surtout, undistinguishable from those before, behind or around him."

The street crowds, less critical, hailed the spectacular parts of the parade with joy as these marched and countermarched to keep themselves from freezing during the proceedings at the Capitol. The Englishman, rescued from Bed Sixteen in Parlor Four, by a friend at the British legation, joined her Majesty's minister and other diplomats who met at the residence of the French minister to ride to the Capitol, their carriages forming a select little procession of their own. They first witnessed the installation of Vice-President John Tyler, in which the outstanding feature was his Virginia pronunciation of the word "chair," repeated many times in his address and sounding to their ears strangely like "cheer."

Then they followed Harrison to the chilly east portico where, defying wind and cold, he delivered an inaugural "seven-eighths of two hours long." This was the address from which Webster, to whom it had been confided for polishing and revision, labored so hard to banish classical allusions. According to his own count, he succeeded in "killing seventeen pro-consuls," but enough survived to enmesh Harrison and his auditors in a web of ancient history for which neither the occasion nor the weather was propitious. He neglected not a single one of the Roman officials Webster left him, but read about them in a loud voice, standing bareheaded while his hearers slowly congealed. Those on the platform, less patient than the crowd below, began at last to move about with chattering teeth, poor emaciated Mr. Fox, in his unbuttoned uniform coat and canary-colored pantaloons shrunken from many washings, looking particularly chilled and uncomfortable.

There were three inaugural balls that night, local campaign enthusiasm having ended in a grand quarrel. The native American faction danced by itself in Masonic Temple. Tickets to the New Assembly rooms on Louisiana Avenue cost ten dollars; and for half that sum it was possible to attend the "Tippecanoe" ball at Carusi's, on E Street near Eleventh. Temporary rooms had been added, and the ball-room itself was decorated with a unique collection of campaign flags "presented by the ladies of Baltimore to the Tippecanoe Clubs of that city." Some of them must have been rather funny. One singled out for solemnly rapturous description in the "National Intelligencer" was a Janus-faced banner displaying on one side a "log cabin beautifully worked by a lady" and on the other a plump cider-barrel with the inscription: "Your cause is just. Our Prayers are with you."

The newspapers said that the ten-dollar ball was "a magnificent affair" to which fashion went early and stayed late, but the New Assembly Rooms were so very new that their whitewashed walls reflected light most garishly, and drippings from spermaceti candles spattered down impartially upon the shoulders of a most motley crowd, in which muscular giants from the frontier jostled planters from the South and Bostonians of the bluest blood. Statesmen old in public life were eyed, not without apprehension, by men newly borne to office on the wave of Harrison's popularity; and fashionable ladies trailed their floating sleeves and generous flounces before wives and daughters of the newly elected, whose cherished finery, made at home, grew momentarily less desirable in their own eyes. But they held their heads high and with grim spirit wore their narrow skirts and bodices of antiquated cut, confident that their head-dresses at least were as elaborate as any to be seen.

The new President fairly radiated good-will, and excitement for the time banished all traces of weariness from his face. "It was so pleasant to see a man of his age and experience give loose rein to his natural feelings that one lost all inclination to criticize his deportment or tone," wrote a foreign visitor. The pleased old man would have been utterly astonished to learn that he was expected to assume aloofness of manner with the title of President.

He settled down to the routine of office as naïvely as he had enjoyed the triumph of its first hours. As if the duties of President were not enough, he kept in his own hands the marketing and household chores he had been doing for years in his white frame home at North Bend, Ohio. Disdaining overcoats, he was up at dawn and off on his famous walks; and midnight found him entertaining visitors. He had told his soldier friends that they would always find his latch-string hanging out and he more than lived up to this promise.

Whoever called to pay him a visit was asked to stay to dinner; whoever asked for a place was sure to get a promise; whoever hinted at a want of money was sure to receive a draft; until it became the common talk that the President was over-drawing his account, over-promising his partizans, and over-feeding his friends.

Instances of his mistaken good nature were apparent even to children. A little boy who saw him gallantly helping ladies into his carriage in front of St. John's Church, on a chilly March Sunday, noticed that, while he wore no overcoat, his hands were encased in strange-looking white silk gloves, on the backs of which a picture of the famous log cabin had been printed in gayest greens and brown. The kind old man was wearing these "to encourage American manufacture" and because he had been asked to do so by the firm that made them.

He took a fatherly interest in the ladies, exacting from young and pretty ones the toll that he considered a perquisite of his years and position. A little bride of sixteen, who called with her husband at the White House, never forgot how he put his fingers under her chin and tilted the flower-like face toward his own as he asked, "How old are you, my child?" Her newly acquired matronly dignity was outraged, but she could not help loving him for his kind eyes.

He was inordinately flattered, and even his family did not know how far he saw through the designs of people who had ends to gain; but false friends and true soon found that his good nature covered a determined will. In spite of all Webster could do, he had kept in his inaugural more pro-consuls than were good for it; and he meant to dominate his own administration. Clay, who had refused to become his Secretary of State, felt at liberty to offer good advice: inside of ten days he was warned that he was overplaying the rôle of unofficial adviser. "Mr. Clay, you forget that I am President," Harrison told him bluntly, adding that "to avoid exciting jealousy in others," it would be well to make suggestions in writing instead of in person. Too angry to remain, Clay left the city and never saw the President again.

General Harrison's kindness, stubbornness, and inexperience might have proved disastrous to the country as well as to himself had he lived; but the campaign had made greater inroads upon his strength than he was willing to admit, and the fatigues of the inauguration, added to long hours and Washington's treacherous spring climate, proved more than he could stand. A severe cold turned to pneumonia and he died after an illness of a week, having been President exactly one month.

His short tenure had no effect upon the spirit or aspect of the city, but it is safe to say that no President has provided it with so much pageantry and excitement in the same length of time. First came the booming, noisy campaign, more spectacular than any preceding it; then the inauguration with its crowds and its procession two miles long, to be followed four weeks later by a funeral as impressive as real sorrow and official pomp could make it. After the dismal fashion of the time, it moved between houses draped in black. The coffin, banked with flowers, was drawn upon an open car, by eight white horses caparisoned in black with plumes and netted harness, a groom in white livery marching at the head of each. There were pall-bearers from every state in the Union, and the military display was all that could be devised to do honor to a President who had also been a successful general. If Adams found the inaugural parade "showy-shabby," this must have been more pleasing to his sense of fitness, unless in looking for fitness he demanded some connection between the simple spirit of the man who lay dead and this theatrical show of grief.

The simplest part of the ceremony took place in the East Room, crowded with officials and blazing with color and jeweled orders in the section where the diplomats sat. But Harrison's favorite aides in his campaign against the Indians had been given seats just as prominent, and, in contrast to the crossed swords upon the flower-strewn pall, a little stand at the foot of the coffin held the dead President's Bible and prayer-book. Pastor Hawley, in the few words he uttered, managed to convey a sense of personal loss when he stated that it had been Mr. Harrison's intention to present himself at St. John's the very next Sunday to unite formally with the church.

Funeral pomp is an important thing in Washington, even to-day, though most of the customs of old times have fallen into disuse. More often, perhaps, than in any other American city, a flag-covered coffin is seen, surrounded by horsemen and crape-shrouded banners, moving to the sound of a slow march, toward Arlington.

When a high federal official dies, Congress adjourns, flags float at half-mast, and the body is taken to lie in the rotunda of the Capitol, guarded by soldiers, who stand immovable, as, hour after hour, the people pass by the catafalque, in slow procession.

At first it was the custom to follow the coffin on foot, to the place of interment. This was done in 1802, at the funeral of the first congressman to die in the city, Nainsworthy Hunter of Mississippi Territory. The members of both houses walked from the Six Buildings on Pennsylvania Avenue, where he had lodged, to the churchyard of Mr. Balch's meeting-house in Georgetown. But two years later, when Representative Heister of Maryland died, the body was taken home to Hagerstown for burial, and his colleagues contented themselves with walking in procession "around the President's Square."

After that they abandoned altogether the practice of walking, to ride in carriages, whose hire from that time forward became one of the funeral expenses borne by the Government. As the public carriages were of many types and all degrees of shabbiness, they were brought into a temporary semblance of uniformity by supplying all the drivers with broad bands of white cloth which they wound about their hats and left floating down between their shoulders.

As many as fifty or sixty carriages were provided, but it sometimes happened that nobody volunteered to go to the cemetery except the committee in charge and a handful of idle spectators; then the unoccupied carriages rumbled over the long, rough road that led out to the Congressional Cemetery in the southeastern portion of town (between E and G streets and Eighteenth and Nineteenth), where after 1807 such interments took place. How far away it seemed even twenty years later, President Adams's diary shows in the entry which tells how Marshal Ringgold came "just after noon" to call him to join the funeral cortège of his old friend General Jacob Brown, but that, the roads being heavy with mud, it was "near three o'clock" before they reached the grave, where Pastor Hawley, that man of excellent sense, conducted the burial service "much abridged." The President lingered to hear the last volley fired over the grave, and then turned homeward; but even at the smarter pace permitted for the return journey, it took a full hour to reach the White House.

Tastes differ. Some extravagantly admired this graveyard with its white stones and its neatly kept grass and flowers, upon which one came with a sense of surprise out in the open country. The *Vade Mecum,* published by the "National Intelligencer" for the guidance of visitors at the time of Harrison's inauguration, asserted that "no place in the metropolis is visited with greater interest"; yet it was to this same plot of ground that John Randolph referred when he said that the possibility of being interred there beside some political enemy added the final terror to death. All congressmen who died in office were supposed to be buried there, or, if they were not, to have a monument raised to their memory by a grateful republic. These monuments, queer pyramidal affairs cut to the same pattern and lettered in very permanent black, were turned out in a stone-yard on Capitol Hill. For years the Congressional Cemetery was the goal of most of the important funeral processions that wound their way out of town, and many imposing monuments were erected there, two of them to Vice-Presidents. Washington mourned conscientiously in those days, and took pride in doing it thoroughly. When Vice-President Clinton died, at the Franklin House in 1812, the newspapers printed not only high-flown obituary notices, but a program of the procession under fourteen heads. A report of this solemn function did not appear until Clinton had been lying in his tomb two days, but when it came it left nothing unsaid:

The mortal remains of the late Vice President of the United States were on Tuesday evening interred at the burial ground near the Navy Yard in this city in the presence of a concourse of people greater than ever has been gathered together in this city on any similar occasion. The shops were shut at an early hour; and a general gloom pervaded all ranks of society. The hearse with its escort reached the Capitol about four o'clock, and the procession moved thence in about half an hour afterward, in the order which was announced in our last. The scene was awful and impressive. The martial parade, the glistening arms and nodding plumes of the military corps which preceded the hearse—the solemn melody of the martial band which attuned all hearts to melancholy—the sable hearse attended by eight veteran pall bearers, who partook of the toils of the Revolution—the well-known carriage of the deceased—the Chief Magistrate of the Nation mourning the loss of one of its noblest sons—the Senate deploring the loss of a revered President—

But why particularly describe the lengthened train? Suffice it to say that this assemblage of mournful and interesting objects inspired feeling suited to the occasion. When a Clinton descends to the tomb of his ancestors it is fit that the whole nation bewail the general loss and history immortalize his name. Hallowed the ashes of the honored dead.

In 1846 an inquiring stranger, bent on finding out how state funerals were managed, was told that it was the custom of Congress to adjourn for two days when a representative or a senator died, and that the sum of two thousand dollars was appropriated for expenses.

But even graveyards are subject to fashion. Mere mathematics demonstrated the impossibility of raising a monument to every worthy official who died in office. The shining stones became discolored, undesirable neighbors like jails and almshouses closed in about it, and long ago this cemetery was abandoned save as a burial-place for forlorn officials who have no friends who desire their interment elsewhere. The town offers no better place in which to hunt for forgotten pomp and pathos. The names on many of the headstones are familiar: Tobias Lear found burial there after seeking death by his own hand in his garden pavilion; and Elbridge Gerry, who died suddenly in his carriage; and among many others less arresting to the eye, there is a crested stone bearing the name of a crabbed and mysterious Count Gurowski who held a minor position in the State Department when he died, virtually penniless, during the Civil War. It was whispered that he was a spy—and also that he was the husband of the Infanta of Spain.

It was a custom followed intermittently, as late as the Mexican War, to assign a prominent place in the funeral cortège to "the physicians of the deceased," who wore long scarfs of white linen over their shoulders as special badges of mourning—surely not to link them with the coach-drivers as instruments in forwarding the deceased on his last journey! At congressional funerals the committee having the obsequies in charge wore similar linen scarfs, which, being of excellent quality, were eagerly treasured by housekeepers to be cut up and stitched into bosoms and wristbands of fine shirts. Thus they became an innocent form of congressional graft, like the biscuits and spirits served at the house of mourning, and paid for from public funds, which were a relic of the funeral baked meats of colonial days, when it was only common humanity to offer relatives and friends refreshment before they started on their long homeward journeys. At Charles Sumner's funeral, held in the Senate Chamber on March 13, 1874, all the senators and members of Congress appeared in badges of mourning, while Mr. Blaine, who as Speaker of the House headed the procession of representatives as they filed into the chamber, wore a broad white silk scarf across his breast.

Fortunately, the custom of draping the public buildings in black, upon the death of a high official, has fallen into disuse. When one such disaster quickly followed another, as sometimes happened, the sable decorations, soaked and wind-swept and twisted untidily around pillars until the days of official mourning passed, were depressing in the extreme. The writer remembers wondering, when a child, whether it would not have been wiser and in the end more economical, to build the entrances of alternate black and white stones and cover the black during the rare intervals when there was nobody to mourn for.

One such depressing interval occurred in Fillmore's administration, which of course began with a state funeral.

But it is a deep gloom that does not carry concealed somewhere about it one gleam of light. Enterprising coffin-manufacturers seized upon this mortality in high places as a heaven-sent opportunity to advertise their wares. At the Exhibit of Industrial Arts, held in the spring of 1853, in "the new and splendid East wing of the Patent Office," their appeals were so eloquent that it really seemed ungracious as well as unfashionable not to die and be buried in one of the "marble slat coffins," or one of "Fisk's patented tight metallic burial cases for sale by M. M. White," which had been used "for the remains of the following persons:

"Mrs. Madison	"O. Fowler	"Daniel Webster
"Hon. D. Kaufman	"J. C. Calhoun	"Comm. Morgan."
"R. Rantoul	"H. Clay	

—a grewsome variation on Who's Who in Society.

Photographers struck this same funereal note:

"Delay not to have your husband, your wife, your children and friends taken before the trying circumstances of a final separation takes place," urged Smallwood's Daguerrean Gallery of Georgetown, with more unction than grammar, while Professor Plumb, who had been established in Washington for some years, extolled his own performances in words exhaling the mingled aroma of flattery, chemicals, and tuberoses.

A death within the diplomatic circle complicated official grief with the customs of two hemispheres. John Quincy Adams, when Secretary of State, wrote:

> The Barons de Tuyll and Stackelberg came and mentioned several of the minute particulars of the funeral arrangements for tomorrow, which they proposed in conformity with usages existing in Europe, but which they wished to accommodate altogether to impressions of propriety prevailing here. One proposal was that Baron Maltitz should carry upon a cushion, preceding the hearse, the ribbon and cross of the Order of the Red Eagle of the third class, of which Mr. Greuhm was a Knight. Another question was, whether the Corps Diplomatique should attend in full-dress embroidered uniforms, or merely in black clothes. . . . I advised them not to carry the cushion with the ribbon and cross; for if they did, there would be a danger that the people would take them for Freemasons; that they should rather go in black clothes than in full-dress uniforms and that the pall-bearers should all be members of the Diplomatic Corps.

In the year 1854, following close upon the other funerals that marked the administrations of Presidents Fillmore and Pierce, came that of kindly, ill-favored old Baron Bodisco, who should have had the best that pageantry could offer when borne to his rest in Georgetown cemetery.

The procession was indeed imposing, all the dead man's household following the hearse, beside which, one on the left and one on the right, strode his two handsome nephews, Boris and Vladimir, in their white Russian uniforms. But there had been an unfortunate quarter of an hour during the service at the house, which nobody resented more deeply than his American friends. Misplaced sentiment had caused the pastor of Madame Bodisco's family to be asked to make an address, and narrow zeal on his part had turned this into a homily on the "errors" of the minister's belief. The speaker trusted, however, that "the influences surrounding the closing years of his life" had altered his views, and that if he could look down upon us now he would say—

"He would say," wrathfully whispered one of Bodisco's old friends to another, imitating the dead man's never-to-be-forgotten accent, " 'What a bad-manage ceremony!' "

Even more foreign than diplomatic funerals was the procession that followed the remains of Archbishop Eccleston of Baltimore, who died in Georgetown during a visit to the Academy of the Visitation. The priestly robes, lighted candles, and swinging censers that accompanied his remains across Rock Creek and through the long streets to the railroad station might have marked a similar procession through a medieval city.

Nor, in recalling picturesque scenes of this character, must the simple funerals of slaves be forgotten, when they carried their dead comrade on an open bier to the grave, singing the African melodies that no white man's throat can quite imitate.

At every white funeral there was sure to be a little group of colored people in the background—servants, free or slave, who mourned as truly as any one present; and following on foot after every notable funeral procession in Washington, for years upon years, might be seen one lame, grizzled negro with whom this was an obsession. He earned a precarious livelihood as a waiter where extra help was needed, but whether he knew the deceased or not, he would leave any job at any hour for what he seemed to consider an imperative duty.

When asked whose funeral it was, or if he knew the deceased, he would shake his head and look reproach at his questioner and trudge silently and respectfully after the last mourner in the last coach.

XIII

TWO UNINSPIRED PRESIDENTS

VAN BUREN'S administration has been likened to a parenthesis, which may be mentioned in a low tone of voice or passed over altogether without breaking the continuity. Harrison's was too short to affect the story one way or the other. That of his successor became a national calamity. But the blame for this should rest less upon Tyler than upon our optimistic habit of taking long chances when choosing understudies to the President. Tyler owed his nomination to an exhibition of weakness; and when he ran true to form, there was little cause to be astonished. He called himself an Independent, but was really a weathercock. In the convention of 1840 he had been such an emotional follower of Clay that he shed tears when that leader's chances dwindled and faded away. Party managers noted this outburst, and, thinking it a shrewd move to give the barren office to one of Clay's Southern followers, nominated him forthwith.

Tyler might have passed as an interesting Vice-President, for he possessed many good qualities, but in the office of President these qualities neutralized one another; and he showed his weathercockness by giving the party to understand that he would do certain things, and then doing exactly the opposite. He veered so often toward the South, that the Whigs felt themselves betrayed, while the Democrats, on their part, saw no reason to trust him. He remained, therefore, a President without a party, indeed without personal followers except the little knot of friends in Congress that Clay reduced to less than insignificance by calling it contemptuously "the Corporal's Guard."

Clay had not been impressed by Tyler's histrionic burst of tears, and refused to regard him as more than "a mere regent" when he assumed the higher office. This was the first time a man had been so promoted, and Tyler roused criticism first of all by assuming that he was as thoroughly President as though elected by the people. From this small beginning, dissatisfaction spread and grew and culminated in a storm of denunciation when he vetoed Clay's bill to establish a national bank. Harrison's cabinet, which had remained in office at his request, registered its protest by resigning in a body, with the single exception of Webster, who remained in office long enough to conclude a treaty with Lord Ashburton defining the boundary between Maine and Canada. In Washington, local indignation expressed itself in noisy mass meetings, which frothed and boiled over in a mob that streamed from the Log Cabin Tavern to the White House in the early morning hours, invaded the grounds, and uttered drunken catcalls under the Presidential windows.

The only gainer from this disgraceful exhibition was the town itself. A committee of Congress, appointed to investigate the matter, brought to light the interesting fact that with the exception of two privates under a sergeant, who had been patrolling the east and west fronts of the Capitol nightly since John Quincy Adams was President, the city of twenty-three thousand inhabitants and much government property was without an organized police force after dark, and that disorders and incendiary fires had become so frequent that private citizens were banding together for their own protection.

Tyler recommended to Congress the creation of an "adequate" force to protect the public buildings, but his unpopularity was so great that endless objections had to be met before Congress consented to an "Auxiliary Watch" of fifteen men under a captain, for night duty only. It was charged that even this pitifully small force might be used by the President to seize arbitrary power and be made into a subservient Imperial Guard.

As time went on, fair-minded people came to believe Tyler weak rather than wicked, and the country settled down to dogged endurance of an evil which could be remedied only at the next Presidential election. Meanwhile Congress labored as best it could, usually in direct opposition to him. Some letters from Thomas B. Osborne, a member of Congress from New Haven, written to a friend at home, reflect the perplexity of those who tried to be just to all concerned. "Certainly," he wrote, "there can be very little glory in carrying on a war against Mr. Tyler. . . . The President is as much entitled to his opinion as is Congress. He is equally elected by the people. . . . The real question is what the good of the country demands."

Again he wrote:

But it is exceedingly difficult to accommodate the action of Congress to the caprices of a weak vacillating President who does not consult his Cabinet on any of the great questions of public policy, and who is endeavoring in his awkward way, to use all the power and patronage of his office to secure a reëlection. Tyler has now neither the support nor the confidence of any party. He is dining and courting the Locoes, who bow and are polite to him and then come away laughing at his folly and despising him for his perfidy. The government is in a strange condition. The President vetoes the bills approved and recommended by the Cabinet and his Secretary of the Treasury. "The Guard," the only men in Congress who profess to defend him, *vote* for bills and then defend his vetoes. If Congress were now, as I know it was at the extra session, sincerely disposed to agree and co-operate with him, there is no responsible quarter to which they can look and on which they can rely for the opinions of the President. In addition to this, there is not the slightest respect felt for his understanding, character or motives. . . . If Tyler shall veto a revenue bill without the land clause as some think he will as Congress would adjust it, there is no remedy left but to impeach him on the ground of *insanity*.

But the Connecticut congressman refused to be excited by the charge that the President aspired to arbitrary power. "I have no fear of the government running into a despotism under Tyler," he wrote. "There is more danger of it falling into contempt." And in another letter he summed up the President's character and dismissed him from serious consideration, in a phrase as short and damaging as Clay's, by calling him "an unlucky accident."

The city is indebted to this unpopular President for the beginning of a real police force, as already noted, and for the pleasant custom of summer concerts on the White House lawn. Tyler having a large family and Southern ideas of hospitality, the Executive Mansion became during his term more like a normal home than it had been for many a day. Young people gathered around the piano, and the President himself took part in the home-made music by playing the violin. From this it was an easy transition to having the Marine Band make music for them once a week under the trees south of the White House.

The fact that Washington got on so well at night for forty years without police, and waited twenty years longer before it had an adequate force, speaks well for its law-abiding instincts and emphasizes wherein it differed from other cities. The census in Tyler's day credited it with twenty-three thousand, but in reality its population waxed and waned like the tides. When Congress adjourned and went home it took half the inhabitants with it, leaving the city to dream through the summer, on the banks of the Potomac, in a sort of somnolent enchantment. Even street fights between rival fire-companies, which furnished excitement at other seasons, lapsed in an atmosphere that forbade more fire or more exertion than was absolutely necessary. Those who have recently spent midsummers in Washington can imagine how the town felt and acted in summers before the Mexican War, when Congress had departed, the mercury had climbed heavenward, and no amusement was to be found on Pennsylvania Avenue more thrilling than a Panorama of Rome or a sight of Apollo the Grecian Dog. With movies and radios and refrigerating plants and rapid transit and soda fountains yet uninvented, stagnation reigned; even crime itself languished and lost energy.

But the city was never too inert to express its opinion about Tyler. Even his personal appearance varied with the prejudices of the beholder. His many critics could see little except his prominent nose, but the fervid Southern rhetoric of his friends brought that also within the limits of perfection. Henry A. Wise described him as

> a man of striking manly beauty, with hair of silky soft chestnut brown, floating in curls imperial as those of Jove when Olympus shook with his nod; a strong gray eye, which glowed as he breathed forth his

inspiration of intellect and heart; a finely chiselled mouth expressing the most delicate taste and sweet benevolence; and a nose and chin of manly fortitude—

words which suggest a wax figure rather than a President.

Tragedy and comedy trod swiftly in each other's wake, toward the close of his administration. On February 28, 1844, Commodore Stockton of the navy gave a party on board the new battleship *Princeton,* taking his guests for a run down the Potomac. The pride of the vessel was a great gun called the Peacemaker, which was fired twice on the outward voyage as part of the entertainment. On the return, while most of the company lingered around the luncheon table, a group gathered on deck and asked that another shot be fired.

At this third discharge, the gun exploded, killing Mr. Upshur, who had become Secretary of State, Mr. Gilmer, Secretary of the Navy, Mr. Virgil Maxey, lately returned from service at the Hague, Captain Beverly Kennon, U. S. N., and the President's friend Mr. Gardiner of New York. Senator Benton and others, including the President's servant and eleven seamen, were injured by flying fragments, two of the seamen mortally. The President himself, with some ladies, had turned back to the cabin only a moment before.

The sadness of that home-coming, the pall that overspread the city, the White-House funeral, with its row of five coffins in the great East Room, were not soon to be forgotten. Mrs. Madison, who had been one of the guests upon the *Princeton,* could never be induced to speak of it.

The first Mrs. Tyler had died, a victim of paralysis, in the autumn of 1842. There was no reason why the President should not marry again after a suitable interval, though to his intimates it seemed unnecessary, since he had several grown daughters to manage his household. He felt otherwise, however, and proceeded to choose a mate from the group of young people who had gathered to sing and gossip around the piano in the family sitting-room.

One of this group was Virginia Timberlake, daughter of Peggy O'Neil and her unfortunate first husband. Another was Julia Gardiner, the daughter of one of the victims of the *Princeton* disaster. She was a handsome, plump, self-possessed girl, who had enjoyed the advantages of European travel; gay and laughing, but knowing her own mind thoroughly. Upon her the President centered his affections. At first she took his middle-aged amorous advances as a joke, and shook her head so violently at his first proposal of marriage that the gold tassel on her crimson Phrygian cap almost flew into the Presidential eye. But his great kindness at the time of her father's death changed her feelings to real affection: and, besides, it is not every girl who has a chance to marry a President of the United States. It was during a drive in the Kalorama hills that Senator Wise learned from Mr. Tyler that he was soon to be a bridegroom. As an intimate friend he was indiscreet enough to protest, on the ground of disparity in years. The President was too fatuously in love even to be offended. "Pooh, pooh!" he chuckled. "I am just full in my prime." It was spring; he felt the warmth of youth once more in his veins, and had even been inspired to write a serenade beginning, "Sweet Lady, awake!"

The wedding took place quietly in New York, the President and his son John having made the journey from Washington with as little publicity as possible. But the matter could not be kept out of the newspapers. The very fact that the unpopular President desired secrecy was enough to stir all the young reporters in New York to greater vigilance and the ferry-boat *Essex*, on which the couple made a honeymoon tour of the harbor, was greeted with a pandemonium of whistles and salutes.

When the pair returned to Washington, society went to the White House to offer congratulations and found the bride and her elderly husband dispensing liberal champagne and cutting a magnificent bride-cake.

There was a little laughter at the fair Julia as she set to work to make the most of her golden hour. The newspapers printed a few malicious paragraphs, of which the following is a sample:

> We understand by private letters from a Washington belle that the lovely Presidentess is attended on reception days by twelve maids of honor, six on either side, all dressed alike, and that her serene loveliness "receives" upon a raised platform, with a headdress of bugles resembling a crown.

She revived a fashion, abandoned years before by her predecessors, of driving in a carriage drawn by four horses. Important matrons were distinctly annoyed when she chose to receive them seated on a raised dais, wearing feathers in her hair and purple velvet with a regally long train. They considered it an affront that she delayed coming into the drawing-room until her guests were assembled, and, after a spectacular entry, seated herself and had them brought up one by one to be introduced, their names being loudly announced as they approached. She frankly enjoyed all the homage her position brought her, and wrote to her mother that Mr. Packenham, the new British minister, and his secretary, and "at least 50 Members of Congress" had been "devoted" at her last reception. Even Calhoun quoted love verses to her at a White-House dinner-party, this being the one time on record that the unromantic man strayed in such strange fields.

But she played her game gallantly, and the time of her triumph was, after all, so short that nobody really grudged her the little peacock turn. The pleasantest memories of her as President's wife, however, center around the closing days of the administration; when she presided at a brilliant dinner in honor of Mr. and Mrs. Polk, and at five o'clock on March 3d entered the Blue Room with her husband, for the last time, to take leave of their friends. She wore upon a chain around her neck the "immortal" gold pen with which he had a few hours before signed the bill admitting Texas as a state of the Union, and though passing from the gaiety she loved to the dullness of life on a James River plantation, she held her head high and seemed as happy as if about to be released from prison.

Next day Tyler rode with his successor to the Capitol and back to the White House, in a sadly water-soaked inaugural parade, then effaced himself, neither he nor his wife taking part in the evening festivities. They had planned to slip away early on March th, by the boat plying between Washington and Acquia Creek, on way to "Sherwood Forest," the new estate Tyler had bought fe. But futility pursued him to the last. The captain of having been informed, sailed without the pair and ced to return to their hotel. They left the city finally, that night, by the glare of a great fire raging at the National Theater.

Twenty-four hours earlier this theater had been the scene of a most crowded five-dollar inaugural ball, the higher-priced affair at Carusi's having lost prestige through a stupid blunder on the part of the managers, who forgot to send special invitations to the diplomatic corps. The sensitive feelings of the foreigners being hurt, they betook themselves to the more democratic gathering, followed by their friends and all who strove to achieve social glory by imitating them. "There surely never was, since the time of the Ark, such a strange mixture," wrote a young journalist whose laughing eyes lost no detail of the bizarre groups upon the floor. He hoped the foreign minister's lady who found herself face to face with her gardener, in a quadrille, had democratic leanings, or a sense of humor.

At Carusi's the music echoed through virtually empty halls, while the crowd at the other place grew to such proportions that, after all expenses were paid, more than a thousand dollars remained to be divided among local charities. But there had been discomfort in proportion to the profit. Not anticipating such a crush, the management had provided neither supper nor adequate protection for wraps and purses. Many of those present left the hall minus all three; and after the last guests had departed, a mountain of miscellaneous dry goods was bundled up and taken to the offices of the "Globe," in order that the theater might be made ready for a performance of *Beauty and the Beast,* billed for the following evening.

The obliging editors of the "Globe" printed a notice inviting owners of missing garments to come and claim their property. Had they been left in the theater, not a single person would have seen his belongings again, for it was during the initial performance of the play that fire broke out and consumed the theater and several other buildings, in spite of the best efforts of local firemen, aided by those from Alexandria, who dragged their little engine to the rescue, over eight miles of clay roads. Fortunately, no fatalities occurred, though some in the audience barely escaped with thei

Perhaps it was due to the sobering influence of M

the National Theater was not rebuilt for five years. She was a marked contrast to lively Mrs. Tyler, and went to work at once to banish all traces of the frivolous Tyler régime. There were to be no more singing groups of young people around the piano; especially no more girls like Virginia Timberlake dimpling at a middle-aged President. Under her rule the mansion sank into austere and immaculate order once more, no small achievement after the hard usage it had received and the insignificant appropriations available for repairs.

She possessed undoubted charm of a sober kind and was credited with excellent taste. In dress she affected "the subdued though elegant costume which characterizes the lady"; a slap at blonde Madame Bodisco, whose Rubens-like display of shoulders and mantua-making at the inaugural ball had totally eclipsed the guest of honor. In deportment Mrs. Polk "never discussed a subject upon which her sex was supposed to be ignorant," though she was believed to be unusually well informed upon politics. This was A. D. 1845, three years before Elizabeth Cady Stanton outraged all the proprieties by holding a women's-rights convention in her own drawing-room.

Mrs. Polk's husband possessed neither magnetism nor power nor presence. He was merely an instrument in the hands of Fate, to bring one step nearer the inevitable final struggle between slavery and freedom. He had been elected to consummate the admission of Texas, which few people believed Mexico would supinely let slip from her grasp solely because our Congress had voted it into the Union. He knew exactly why he was elected, and, looking upon the Presidency as a business contract to be performed in a business way, set out methodically and unemotionally to fulfil his part of the bargain. Efficiency, not over-hampered with conscience and totally unleavened by enthusiasm, was the key-note of his administration. Personally he was unattractive. Some one described him as a sober-looking man of plain habits, including tobacco-chewing. Another said he was so thin that if his clothes had fitted he would have been "the merest tangible fraction of a President." Alexis Gardiner, Mrs. Tyler's brother, who wrote letters full of Washington gossip to enliven the tedium of her life on the plantation, assured her that the new President lacked both tact and manners.

The most important local event of his administration was the retrocession to Virginia of the land she had ceded to the Federal Government when the District of Columbia was set apart. This was returned at the request of taxpayers of Alexandria, who complained that they paid their share for improvements across the river which benefited them not at all, and in addition were deprived of the vote which they would have as residents of Virginia. There was vigorous protest even among Virginians, but the Act of Retrocession when referred to the citizens of Alexandria County, received an affirmative vote of more than three to one, whereupon President Polk issued his proclamation declaring it duly ratified. Congressman Lincoln, who was then serving his one term in the House of Representatives, thought the retrocession a mistake. But the matter attracted little notice because the Mexican situation had become so engrossing.

When the long-expected war came at last, it was reflected upon the streets of Washington almost instantly in the number of tight-waisted, long-skirted military tunics, and shakos like miniature mansard roofs that replaced snowy stocks and high-crowned beaver hats. Young lieutenants galloped importantly on mysterious errands for their superiors all day long, and after nightfall were as busy on errands of their own. Kindly people, entering a drawing-room in the dusk, walked circumspectly, lest they intrude on sentimental farewells.

After the farewells had been said and the youngsters had departed, time dragged on for long intervals without word from the front, for the telegraph which had reported President Polk's inauguration, from the very platform on which it took place, had as yet little to do with forwarding news from distant lands. When dispatches, traveling slowly by land and water, came at last, they brought tidings of victory amid incredibly romantic surroundings. But something was wrong. Even amid the rejoicing there seemed to be a tang of Dead Sea fruit about it, as if everything save the individual worth of the soldiers had suffered a cheapening blight.

Some spoke of it slightingly as the "West Point War." It was, in fact, the first in which graduates of the Military Academy had borne prominent parts; and this recalled the argument used in Jefferson's time, that owning the machinery of destruction begets a desire to use it and leads to moral decay. Others recognized in it the dreaded onward march of the slavery issue. The frankest of the Southern leaders admitted that it was waged in the interests of slavery. Lewis Cass, in a burst of candor, declared the admission of Texas to the Union was not enough—that the sleepy Spanish colony of California must also be added, because the South "needed room"; and Tom Corwin made his famous retort: "If I were a Mexican, I would ask: 'Have you not room in your own country to bury your dead? If you come to mine, I will greet you with bloody hands and welcome you to hospitable graves!'" Such words, even when spoken in righteous anger, do not fall acceptably from a man's lips when his country is at war.

There were, indeed, two fields of battle in this struggle, and the more bitter was not in Mexico. The other was in the halls of Congress, where, day after day and through vote after vote, Whigs resisted the effort of Democrats to make them admit that the war was just and had been begun by act of Mexico. The Whig position was difficult, for while denouncing the war as a wicked political plot, they voted liberal supplies to the soldiers in the field, contenting themselves with fastening upon every army bill the Wilmot Proviso that slavery must never exist in land ceded by Mexico. Abraham Lincoln said he voted for this proviso, in one form or another, forty-seven times. The Whigs claimed that it was not right to make soldiers suffer for the sins of the Administration, when they were only obeying orders and risking their lives in a foreign land. The Democrats answered mockingly that if they thought the war so wicked, they had the power to stop it by withholding supplies.

Recrimination spread from the halls of Congress and infected all the relations of life, even the comfortable easy-going intercourse of hotel and boarding-house, where hitherto senators and representatives had broken bread together in friendliness even after mercilessly scoring one another in debate. Now old acquaintances moved their seats, to escape the strain of perfunctory politeness. Transient visitors, too, felt the tension in hotel dining-rooms. One of them wrote that colored waiters, with their sleeves tucked up, ran about and jostled one another in their eagerness to serve everybody at the same time, but that none of the guests seemed quite happy; even when party spirit did not find expression in actual rudeness there was "a constant state of agitation." Mrs. Sprigg, in her modest little house on Capitol Hill, two doors from the marble-yard where those hideous official tombstones were made, must have blessed her tall lodger Abraham Lincoln as his hearty laugh rang out to clear the air.

To get as much as possible and to give as little in return seemed the one idea of the Administration. President Polk even introduced efficiency into his hand-shaking, instead of regarding it as an expression of friendliness or a valuable political gesture. He worked it out in this way:

> If a man surrender his arm to be shaken by one horizontally, by another perpendicularly, and by another with a strong grip, he cannot fail to suffer severely from it; but if he will shake and not be shaken, grip and not be gripped, taking care always to squeeze the hand of his adversary as hard as his adversary squeezes his, he will suffer no inconvenience from it. Now I can generally anticipate a strong grip from a strong man, and I then take advantage of him by being quicker than he and seizing him by the tip of his fingers.

On gala occasions visitors to the White House found themselves face to face with a little man looking like a Methodist parson, who was engaged in shaking hands methodically and unjoyously as fast as his guests could be herded past him, while across the room fifty or sixty gentlemen stood motionless, looking on at this "national show, admission gratis." The crowd increased; the room grew hot; out in the corridor the Marine Band, dressed like monkeys in scarlet coats, pounded and tooted, and at intervals a sober-minded attendant, with A on his coat collar by way of uniform, appeared at the elbows of the onlookers to repeat in a monotone that made itself heard as an under rhythm to the music, "Gentlemen-who-have-been-presented-will-please-walk-into-the-East-Room-don't-block-up-the-passage."

Courtesy B. S. Reynolds Company, Inc.

THE CLOCK IN THE OLD HALL OF REPRESENTATIVES

It was noticeable that, among the groups in the East Room, interest centered about people who had to do with the war or the West, rather than upon the older statesmen or upon literary celebrities, as had been the case under Tyler and Van Buren.

"Dr. White and his lady," soon to depart for Oregon by the shortest route across the Isthmus, held a little reception of their own, and dashing General Shields was promised enough ribbon slings to keep his wounded arm tied up for the rest of his natural life; while Fremont, the "Pathfinder" of the Rocky Mountains and hero of the recent coup in California, was again an object of interest because of his runaway marriage with Senator Benton's daughter Jessie.

President Polk regarded White-House receptions as part of his business contract, but he cared too much for efficiency to submit gracefully to other time-honored, time-consuming customs. He resented sitting for the Presidential portrait, and disliked still more being called upon by a diplomat in court regalia, come to deliver some futile routine communication: a note from Queen Victoria perhaps, written by some obscure secretary, full of complimentary platitudes about our retiring Minister to England, or, more futile still, a letter announcing the birth of two French princelings, the Count of Paris and the Duke of Chartres, presented by Alphonse Pageot, gorgeous in blue and gold. "I confess the practice of announcing officially the birth of foreign princes to the President of the United States, has always appeared to me supremely ridiculous," Polk wrote testily; and who can blame him?

It is not often that instigators of a war are embarrassed by too much victory, but as General Taylor's successes piled up, Democratic leaders began to be alarmed, forseeing their effect upon the coming Presidential election. General Taylor was a Whig, and they remembered that Americans "like an odor of gunpowder about their candidates for president." It behooved them to keep this foray after new territory as inconspicuous as possible—to push victory far enough to make Mexico give up the coveted land but not so far as to become brilliant. But in this they counted without Taylor's military skill. His victories continued. They could not well remove him for being too successful, and, considering the psychology of both Mexicans and Americans, they saw it would be unwise to order him to halt and merely hold the cities already taken, until Mexico agreed to our terms. Senator Benton pointed out that Spaniards, "past masters at the art of sitting still," had twice won at that game in their mother country, by outsitting the Moors for seven hundred years in southern Spain and the Visigoths in the North for three hundred.

There seemed nothing to do but to send another general to Mexico. Unfortunately for the Democrats, there was no one of fitting rank in their own party, and General Scott was more of a politician and more of a Whig than Taylor. But they sent him, and got what they deserved politically, as well as more spectacular victories. The situation was out of hand for both parties. The Democrats were hopelessly doomed in the next election, but the military success made it equally certain that the Southern element would carry out its plans with a high hand and lead the country exultantly toward the final day of reckoning.

Of the two Whig generals, they preferred Taylor for President, and, since one or the other must be elected, bent their energies to influence the choice of Taylor as the candidate. He was receptive but not enthusiastic, knowing himself to be a military man and ignorant of politics. He said that he would not "cross yon ferry" to become President, but if his fellow citizens chose to elect him he would serve them to the best of his ability. His wife opposed the idea. The general declared that before the nomination she had prayed fervently every night that the honor might fall upon Henry Clay.

General Taylor's coming to take the oath of office was more like the migration of a patriarch than a political triumph. In addition to his family he brought with him his favorite slave and favorite dog, and his faithful war-horse Old Whitey, whose non-military appearance caused the Washington Committee of Arrangements considerable anxiety of fear his master might wish to ride him in the inaugural parade. But he was content to drive to the Capitol behind four matched grays, and the beast that had borne him to success in Mexico was turned out to graze on the White-House lawn, where he grew daily rounder in body and thinner in tail, his white hairs being plucked for souvenirs by enthusiastic sight-seers.

Taylor's career as President, like that of General Harrison, was too short to alter the appearance or the destiny of Washington. Frederika Bremer, who was in the city enjoying the gentle lionizing "literary" ladies received in 1850, has told how on a beautiful summer afternoon one of the senators from New Hampshire took her to the White House "just outside the city," where the military band was playing, and three or four hundred people strolling under the trees presented a scene of republican enjoyment that filled her European soul with rapture. The President's daughter, lately married to Colonel Bliss and still affectionately known as Miss Betty, in spite of her wedding-ring, did the honors so prettily that people liked to linger in the stately, rather bare rooms or in groups on the lawn, even with Old Whitey grazing contentedly close by. The President, "simply, almost negligently dressed," wandered about among his guests, and, like Miss Bremer, shook hands with all who came up, and admired the babies.

It was rumored that he was troubled by the political quarrels that had by no means ceased with the end of the war. He was disarmingly simple, and freely acknowledged the handicap his ignorance of politics had already proved, even in the matter of choosing a cabinet. He was too old to learn easily such a complicated new game. Perhaps it rested him to chat with foreign ladies.

Soon after this Miss Bremer heard that he was ill, and, having sturdy prejudices against certain American articles of food, she was sure he must have been eating oyster patties—which was unlikely in the middle of summer! History ascribes his malady to a Fourth-of-July oration complicated by cherries and iced milk, the President having lunched unwisely and too well upon them after returning almost exhausted from long patriotic exercises held on an oppressive day at the unfinished Washington Monument. By July 7th he was reported to be much better, but on July 9th, as Miss Bremer sat in the Senate gallery, listening to Mr. Butler, who was droning on about slavery, she saw Mr. Webster enter. An electric thrill seemed to pass through the chamber. People came in hurriedly by various doors, as Webster, pausing before his colleague, made a gesture of apology for interrupting. Mr. Butler bowed and was silent. Webster also stood silent for a moment;

then, speaking very slowly and evidently laboring under deep feeling, made his announcement:

"I have a sorrowful message to deliver to the Senate. A great misfortune threatens the nation. The President of the United States, General Taylor, is dying, and probably may not survive the day." In the hush that followed, Miss Bremer imagined she saw faces turn pale. One senator bowed his head upon his hands "as if he heard the thunder of judgment." Somebody moved adjournment, and all quietly left the room.

Webster's own emotions must have been poignant, for once more a lifetime's ambition had passed him by. He wished intensely to become President. He had been offered the place of Vice-President on the ticket with General Taylor, and had indignantly declined, denouncing the general's nomination as "unfit to be made." If instead, he had accepted—!

President Fillmore was sworn in and filled out General Taylor's term. After him, the Democrats elected Franklin Pierce "of New Hampshire and the Mexican War," a New Englander who believed slavery firmly rooted in the Constitution. Then they elected Buchanan, another Northern man equally in sympathy with the South.

Under them all, Washington continued to grow as she had been growing from the first, a Southern town spreading over much territory, unfinished everywhere, shabby in many places, but beautiful in spots and with a charm all her own.

XIV

A BRAVE LADY

WASHINGTON is the town of the politically triumphant. Better be dead than out of office, if you belong to the political set. Presumably the dead are so occupied with their new surroundings that they do not realize how soon they are forgotten. The defeated are allowed to remember nothing else. After a few days of pitying glances they pass as unheeded as ghosts through the scenes of former triumphs, watching new people receive all the bows and lip-service expressed in the cynical phrase "a lively expectation of favors to come."

If, as rarely happens, an old face gains respectful attention from a new political generation, we may be very sure that a remarkable personality dwells behind it.

When Thackeray visited Washington in 1853, he found it "'Wiesbadenish,' with politics and gaiety straggling all over it,"—a bit of word painting that fitted years before he saw it, and can scarcely be bettered to-day. It has persistently maintained a festive attitude, putting forward its best foot with a company smile and ignoring the other in a manner quite maddening to virtuous folk, who never feel so virtuous as when calling a spade a spade. Its interest in politics is gossipy as well as patriotic; it has been only spasmodically interested in philanthropy, and as for business, to this day it does not mind holding up traffic to accommodate the flimsiest kind of street parade.

Mrs. Fremont called it the drawing-room of the nation. A drawing-room "in action" presupposes women, also in action, their presence being the chief factor in making it that kind of room. It was in Washington that the American Matron came into her own, at a time when elsewhere in the Union social gatherings were given over to the very young, who danced their way into matrimony, or sought that desired end by the more staid paths of singing-school or prayer-meeting. Their elders meanwhile remained virtually invisible, the men immersed in business, the women attending to a matron's first duty—to serve nourishing food to husband and offspring.

In Washington, politics was the chief business of the men, and business of a kind impossible to confine to offices. Wives, called upon to provide entertainment for political leaders, found it well to gain a shrewd idea of how far and in what direction they were leading. Hence they flocked to the Capitol in such numbers that the custom of welcoming them to seats upon the floor had to be abandoned. Instead, the front row of the four lines of seats "with backs" in the gallery was cushioned and reserved for their use, and later they were given a gallery to themselves. As for the young, they took secondary place from the start. It was not the custom, however, for wives or daughters to appear at the Capitol unaccompanied. "No lady of fashion or distinction goes to either House without being attended by a gentleman," wrote a visitor in 1830. "But one gentleman frequently attends several ladies." Arriving about one o'clock when noteworthy speeches were expected, they sat on regardless of dinner- and tea-time, as long as congressional eloquence held out to burn. If the session was very prolonged, kind friends on the floor made up parcels of cakes and oranges and passed them up on the tips of their canes, the gallery being low enough to permit such thoughtful attentions.

In addition to visiting Congress, the ladies visited one another and gained further information, some of it purely feminine, the rest masculine, once removed. How much help a woman was able to give her husband, and how much credit she received for it, varied with the personal equation. Usually she gave more than she got credit for, from President's lady down. Mrs. Madison's social gifts added brilliance to her husband's career if they did not actually "make" it. Mrs. Thornton kept her husband's papers and manifold interests well catalogued in her pretty, sharp-featured little head. Mrs. Seaton was a business partner in her husband's newspaper enterprise, in all but title. A nameless colored charwoman in the Treasury sat all night guarding a package of bonds she found outside its iron cage. The main difference between that day and the present lies in the fact that then "nice" women were expected to labor under an assumed name—the one assumed at the altar.

Foreigners added to the mature appearance of Washington drawing-rooms. While ministers brought their wives with them, and perhaps a few unmarried secretaries, they took care as a rule to leave marriageable sons and daughters at home. Occasionally a diplomatic baby chose the city as a place to be born in, but this was regarded as questionable in taste and disturbing to routine.

Though the stellar rôles in society were played by elders, youth did not fare badly. The daughters of officials found great glamour in parties where they met young secretaries of legation as adept in flirtation as they were gaudy in uniform, and few girls were proof against the flattery of admiration bestowed upon them by elderly men of distinction. There were of course occasional young officers in the army and navy, and after the Smithsonian opened its doors, fledglings in science. It was harder for them than for the young women. With every other man in the room a judge or a general or a congressman, what was left for self-respecting youth but to keep silent and hover around attractive nieces and daughters of the great, who were luckily plentiful enough to reduce a little the average age of a roomful of celebrities.

The President was always, in theory, the central star in the galaxy of gray-headed players, even when he was actually overtopped by giants of the Capitol. Presidents' wives held a distinguished place, though candor compels the admission that most of them shone by reflected light.

Toward the end of J. Q. Adams's administration Mrs. Porter, wife of the new Secretary of War, who had something of Mrs. Madison's charm and all of her desire to please, became the cheering light of a depressed social period. Knowing the value of a cabinet lady's nods and smiles, and that at best her reign must be short, she scattered them liberally, and the barometer climbed toward fair weather the moment she entered the room.

"What a pity it is," Calhoun remarked, looking after her, "that all the ladies cannot carry off the defeat of their party so charm-ingly." To which the woman addressed answered with spirit that the men were worse beaten than their wives. "One day last week, with the exception of General Porter, all were confined to their beds."

To single out a few seems invidious, yet one can scarcely omit mention of the charming creole, Mrs. Edward Livingston, whose husband is credited with writing Jackson's Nullification Proclamation. Her social gifts pleased even John Randolph, who urged Livingston to accept the French mission, partly because his wife was so well fitted for the rôle of ambassadress. "It is the very place for her," he wrote. "There she would dazzle and charm, and surely the salons of Paris must have far greater attractions for her than the Yahoos of Washington."

Then there was warm-hearted Mrs. Johnston, wife of a senator from Louisiana, "not only the fashion but the *ton,*" who bought every new book and increased her popularity by lending them recklessly. In 1834 the dashing Mrs. Harrison Gray Otis was a favorite. Besides leading society and reading books, she wrote them. Another writer was Mrs. William Wirt, whose "Flora's Dictionary, a complete botany and floral letter-writer, and a book of quotations" her friends thought quite as remarkable as her husband's "British Spy."

This couple was long in official life, and, at a time when most officials were content with quarters in a hotel, had a real home, a house with a garden, which became by association almost as much an official residence as the White House itself. It was not elegant like the Octagon House or Kalorama, but merely typical; a brick dwelling on the south side of G Street where the immense Department of the Interior now stands; a dignified mansion, which saw the making of much history and some tragedy in its day. Tobias Lear, the friend of Washington, built it and lived in it until he was found in the summer-house at the foot of the garden, one autumn morning, dead by his own hand. The Wirts were its next tenants; after them Edward Everett lived in it while he was Secretary of State under Fillmore, and Jefferson Davis, who occupied it during his term as Secretary of War under Pierce, was followed by Aaron Brown, Postmaster General under Buchanan.

To bring back a picture of a long-vanished Washington let us reconstruct in imagination one of these houses of the decades between 1830 and 1860. A flight of six or eight steps curved up from the sidewalk, in flowing lines to the front door with its fan-light. Although the early building regulations prescribing basement walls of incredible thickness had long been modified, its solid construction showed in the broad sills of this door and of the two drawing-room windows which descended almost to the level of the floor. The three windows of the next story were as wide but not so high, and above these in a steeply pitched roof were dormers whose upper lines frequently echoed the curve of the fan-light over the door. Chimneys, capacious but flat rather than square, rose sharply above the roof, giving an impression of soaring ambition as well as solidity, like a successful member of Congress with his eye on a senatorship.

The vestibule was one step lower than the front hall, which ended at the stairway with its landing and mahogany hand-rail. A door upon the landing gave access to back regions of lower ceilings and less ambitious construction. There were rooms only upon one side of the hall, but their ceilings were so high as to make them almost cubical. The drawing-room in front communicated by wide folding doors with another identical in finish, so that when these doors were opened the two rooms formed one stately apartment. A window at the back afforded a glimpse of garden, and a door in the same wall opened into household offices that made this back parlor available for use as a dining-room. The kitchen was either belowstairs or somewhere in the rear, economy of steps in household service being of little consequence. What were slaves for if not to take steps?

The substantially finished basement was their domain, though it was the custom to have them sleep elsewhere and come into the master's house only for the day's work. Upstairs the bedrooms were spacious and airy, with large closets and chimneys lavish in flues, innocent of any connection with a central heating sytem. Such a house was a comfortable dwelling for the three torrid months of summer and the six months of moderate temperature, but frigid during Washington's three months of winter, which, unfortunately, are the most important of all, politically and socially.

As more and more houses suitable for official residences appeared on Washington streets, an odd thing was noticeable about them—a wasp-waisted effect between front and rear frankly connecting two structures of different styles. These might be termed the Early Enthusiastic and Late Practical periods of local architecture, were it not that sometimes one was built first and sometimes the other. The connecting link, frequently only a porch or a succession of window-sashes crowded cheek by jowl to fill the space, served at first as a passageway and, on the advent of domestic plumbing, evolved into the family bathroom, to the great glory of the house and vast annual profit of the plumber, who reaped a harvest from frozen water-pipes.

Which part of the house happened to be the older depended on its owner. A humble building set well back in the lot, denoted quiet family life. A later structure covering the dooryard, betrayed falling fortunes, or growing ambition. If the lofty front rooms were built first, with only rudimentary provision for running a household, it was a safe guess that the house had been put up as an investment, to lure those who cared more for showy entertainment than for domestic joys.

Yet the front drawing-room of even the most imposing residence was not a darkened place set apart. The reckless use made of front parlors in Washington must have seemed almost criminal to New Englanders. Like the failure to lure trade to wharves on the Potomac, it may be traced beyond the local housing shortage to its lair in the Constitution of the United States. An upheaval scheduled to occur every four years being the one certain fact in our form of government gave Washington its distinctive character, even to fostering the spirit of "after us the deluge," in matters like wearing out rented carpets and sitting on renting chairs. Political Washington looks upon everything it finds as treasure-trove and uses it for all it is worth.

It was the era of the center table. Even when a piano and a harp shared the room with it, those usually overbearing pieces of furniture retired modestly toward the wall, while the table lorded it over all. But, like everything else, it was expected to work. Instead of being sparsely set out with an astral lamp and two or three "souvenir" volumes, it held books that were actually being read, a work-basket with sewing in it and a portfolio of writing materials belonging to the mistress of the house. With these she busied herself in the intervals between callers, for when not listening to the debates in Congress or making visits social or charitable, she was expected to sit enthroned in her parlor, dressed to receive company from ten in the morning until the lights were extinguished and the family "retired" for the night; only unfashionable people went to bed in those days. Supervision of the household was hers, but the actual tasks were left to servants or to the daughters who were learning to be mistresses of homes in their turn.

The young people of the family were either engaged in these duties or busy at Miss English's school, or "taking music," or learning dancing from M. François Labbé, nephew of the late Charlotte Corday,—a strict old gentleman who with his fiddle-bow whacked inattentive pupils,—or being instructed in "Painting in a Superior Manner on Paper, Silk, Velvet, Wood &c . . . in twelve easy lessons of one hour each for the small compensation of ten dollars," by Caspar Limpert (recently from Europe).

In the intervals of this manifold instruction they gathered around the dining-table in the back parlor, making it a colonial offshoot of the mother table, as America had been of England. In the evening the mother, abdicating in favor of her husband, left him in possession of the big table and astral lamp, with his books and mail, while she took her place at a smaller one lighted by tall wax candles near the fire. The daughters remained in the background, or came forward as the age and tastes of visitors dictated. Mrs. Fremont tells us that General Dix and the Prussian minister, von Geroldt, who became by length of service a beloved resident of Washington, "knew music" and always wanted to hear her sister's contralto voice; but that Mr. Buchanan and Mr. Sumner "would have been greatly put out by the interruption."

In spite of admiration for harp-playing and painting in albums, and a deep respect for books, society was not always informed about its visiting celebrities. When Miss Martineau brought her ear-trumpet to Washington, in the winter of 1835, six hundred people, headed by the British minister, hastened to leave their visiting-cards upon her, but few knew exactly why she should be lionized. "I have not met with an individual, except Mrs. Seaton and her mother, who have read any of her works," wrote Mrs. Smith. "Our most fashionable exclusive Mrs. Tayloe, said she intended to call, and asked what were the novels she had written, and if they were pretty." (Mrs. Tayloe was the wife of the local racing magnate.) "The gentlemen laugh at a woman's writing on political economy. Not one of them has the least idea of the nature of her work. I tried to explain them to Mr. Frelinghuysen, Clay, Southard and others."

Miss Martineau, simple soul, never realized what was happening to her. "To my knowledge," she said, speaking of the tendency to make a to-do over celebrities, "I have escaped that. I have never been made a show of, or run after as a lion." It must be confessed that people had difficulty in treating her as a lion, her ways were so embarrassingly friendly. When invited to dinner she thought nothing of appearing hours ahead of time, bringing her evening regalia, slippers, mitts, scarf, and jewelry in a capacious petticoat pocket, taking possession of a spare guest-chamber, and brevetting herself a member of the family.

This had two advantages for her. It enabled her to pursue an intensive study of the American home and it took her out of the boarding-house where after five weeks' experience she summed up Washington as "no place for a person of domestic tastes." Nowhere else in America had she been so uncomfortable, or had such an interesting time.

Evening visits were customary and even when little was going on, groups drifted in and out, coffee was served, or, in summer, cooling drinks "and afterward dried fruits"; and winter or summer there was an abundance of lively talk, bristling with political names.

Gossip was not necessarily about the most famous or the wittiest. Smiles of amusement rippled through a drawing-room when Representative Van Rensselaer passed with his very capable wife upon his arm. His vote had made Adams President, but it was rumored that she ordered him to cast it. She was popularly believed to take entire charge of his brains, because on one wretched occasion when somebody tried to talk literature to him, he had turned to her helplessly and asked, "My dear, *have* I read Humboldt's late work?"

Taken all in all, the matrons who made Washington society the charming, amusing, not altogether consistent thing it was, got a deal out of life on their own account, even if they existed mainly as a background for distinguished husbands.

But better a Van Rensselaer in office than a defeated Clay! The capital has little time to waste on memories. Men come and go, and their wives go with them. Even if they survive their husbands and live in Washington, so far as popular notice is concerned they are as dead as though they had immolated themselves Hindoo-fashion on the funeral pyre. Occasionally, however, the unexpected happens. In old Washington four matrons held their place for years, in a way little short of miraculous.

One was kindly, domineering, sharp-tongued Madam Calhoun. Madam Calhoun specialized in religion, and insisted that those in whom she took an interest be religious after her own formula. Very different from sad-faced Mrs. Pierce,—who Sunday after Sunday besought the White-House staff so pathetically to go to church "as a favor to her," that they went,—Madam Calhoun undertook a soul's salvation distinctly as a favor to the other person. The second of these impressive old ladies was Mrs. Alexander Hamilton, a tiny figure in widow's black, with eyes as bright as they had ever been, though her hair, brushed back over a cushion in the fashion of her youth, was as white as her widow's cap. She spent part of every year in Washington, with her daughter Mrs. Holly, and indulged her passion for visiting schools and exhorting the scholars until within a few months of her death. Her energy was prodigious. She sat out unharmed the torrid heat and the wearying Fourth-of-July exercises that sent General Taylor to his grave, and it was said that after she was ninety, when going to visit her son at his country place on the Hudson, she preferred to leave the train at a way-station and walk across the fields, climbing two fences, instead of being met with a carriage in a manner befitting her years and position.

The third member of this quartette was Mrs. Stephen Decatur, who also never appeared except in widow's black. After the tragedy of her husband's death the great house on Lafayette Square was emptied of furniture and closed, and when opened again it became one of the rented homes occupied by high officials. Some years later the widow returned to live near Georgetown College, in a small home which, like her old one, was a center of social charm. She rarely left it, but when she did, not even the President's wife received greater attention.

The fourth was Mrs. Madison. Sometimes all four of these ladies met under the President's roof, and when that happened younger women found themselves merely ladies in waiting.

Mrs. Madison was the only woman in our history to return to Washington after an absence of nearly a quarter of a century, to find her place waiting for her just as she left it and to fill it adequately despite poverty and creeping age. She had never been witty or beautiful, only clever enough to recognize her limitations and to leave politics and repartee alone, while her good looks were of the sort that the French call "beauty of the heart." Had she been more gifted she would have made more enemies. As it was, she moved through the early years of the city's history, a cheering, unifying influence, at a time when unity and cheer had distinct political value. "What the famous women of France, England, Austria, and other continental countries failed to accomplish by intrigue," wrote Blaine, "Mrs. Madison unwittingly performed by her sincerity, her straightforwardness and earnest desire to please everyone."

When she returned to Washington after the year of rigid seclusion following her husband's death, she and the town had both altered, but less than was to be expected. Time had added a few more wrinkles to her friendly face; the city had acquired new streets instead of new manners. There were more houses and more town pumps, but the people lived the old comfortable, leisurely life at the slightly accelerated pace she herself had set when she bade Mrs. Seaton sit down at the piano and play a waltz while she taught her young dinner guests that startling new dance, in the hour of waiting for the gentlemen to join them after their wine and cigars.

Now she was a little stouter, a little less "Minerva-like" in her movements, but the ringlets showing below her turban were jet-black, and her cheeks wore the same delicate arbitrary flush. Her neck and shoulders were still white and shapely, seen through a softening cloud of tulle, and she by no means clung to widow's weeds. Her acquaintances recognized certain favorite articles of clothing, long ear-rings, a many-hued scarf, and velvet dress of antique cut. These she wore with such grace that people likened her to an old picture. It was only later that they saw in these belongings the livery of courage. No woman ever took a more normal interest in new fashions, but when it came to choosing between old clothes and solitude, she did not propose to let a few yards of velvet erect a barrier between herself and her friends.

Madison had died with his estates involved, partly because of the hospitality he dispensed planter-wise to the admirers who visited him to "pay their respects," ate meals at his table, and fed their horses generously out of his bins before riding away again; partly to the confused business methods of Southern gentlemen, who deemed it unmannerly to keep strict account of loans and borrowings. Even so there would have been enough for her to live and die upon in comfort, had it not been for Payne Todd, her son by her first marriage. Probably she did not realize the inroads he was making on her dwindling fortune, for her greatest gift had always been the faculty for ignoring unpleasant situations.

She had not the slightest talent for economy, but was "a master-hand at doing without," so she settled herself in her new home, filled it with the furnishings she and her husband had enjoyed together through a long married life, carried up into her own bedroom the precious trunk containing his papers, and went on smilingly wearing her old frocks and accepting enough invitations to tax the strength of a younger woman. It is a significant fact that while she was ever hospitable to visitors, none of them mentioned dining at her table, or riding in her carriage, and only once do we learn of her having a new gown.

Her home, now the property of the Cosmos Club, is changed beyond recognition. In 1838 it was a small two-story dwelling, with the usual attic and dormer windows, whose door faced the park, while spacious gardens, now shrunk to one graveled court, stretched toward the center of the block.

It was the second oldest private house on the square, having been built by Mr. Cutts, who served the taciturn Madison as link between him and the outside world. Madison loaned him the money to build it and in time the title came to him in payment of the debt.

Modest as it was, it proved a magnet second only to the White House and took on the sanctity of neutral ground. It is said that Webster and Lord Ashburton met here in friendly informality to discuss their treaty defining the Canadian boundary. While Mrs. Madison lived in it Jackson, Van Buren, the Harrisons, the Tylers, the Polks, and the Taylors occupied the White House in turn. Visitors entered that great portal out of policy or curiosity, but through Mrs. Madison's small door, scarcely a stone's throw away, they passed out of genuine regard, and she received them with the graciousness that had charmed their parents and sometimes their grandparents in days gone by. It became as much a matter of course to visit her on New Year's day as to go to the Executive Mansion. She was a personage in her own right, while the ladies of the President's family, worthy as they all were, remained only political accidents after all.

It is gratifying to remember that every one of the "accidents" loved her. In the reminiscences of those days, we see her in low-necked gown and turban, enthroned in a great chair near stately Mrs. Polk, who received standing. Another pen-picture shows her in antique finery seated opposite her hostess, a five-year-old granddaughter of President Tyler, at a child's birthday party.

Children were instinctively drawn to her. When they asked with naïve directness how old she was, she did not resent it, but she never told; and their parents, amused, remembered how often she had celebrated her seventy-third birthday. She felt young, and meant to remain so as long as the good Lord permitted. Hence the softening tulle and the dash of rouge. If in the activities of snuff-taking a bit of red got transferred from cheek to nose, the onlookers conspired not to see it, which rendered it invisible for practical purposes.

Tulle and rouge and a brave spirit could hide much but not everything, and presently those who knew her best saw unmistakable signs of poverty. It may have been one of her old servants who gave the first hint of how badly things were going. Colored servants have played Good Samaritan in Washington, many times. We can imagine Paul Jennings, Madison's body-servant, who had bought his freedom and entered the service of Daniel Webster, going to his new master with steady purpose in his eye, for all the shufflings and hesitations and deferential bows of his class, and confiding to him the lamentable state of Mrs. Madison's larder, and that for some time past he had been making little purchases for her out of his own pocket.

Webster the statesman can be remembered only as a grandiose figure. Webster the business man should not be remembered at all, since he was scarcely wiser than Mrs. Madison herself, but Webster the gallant gentleman proved a very apt pupil of Paul Jennings. Accepting the hint as to the best way of aiding her without wounding her pride, he instructed the man to use his eyes and see to it that her kitchen lacked for nothing. John Sioussat also, the "French John" who had threatened to lay a train of gunpowder and blow up the British when they crossed the threshold of the White House, began once more to busy himself with her affairs, after his day's work was over (he was now employed in a bank); and there were others who helped with whatever discretion Providence had given them.

It was easier to do this for her than for a woman who was better at figures or more suspicious by nature. When at last she found out, she accepted or declined aid after a strict code of her own. Small sums of money she received from kinsmen with perfect equanimity, knowing how glad she would have been to do as much for them. A brace of ducks from Mr. Webster or a gift of fruit from somebody else were mere neighborly courtesies, to be accepted in the spirit in which they were sent. She wrote Amos Lawrence of Boston, a silk merchant described as the Andrew Carnegie of his generation, a grateful note of thanks for "a beautiful dress from your factory so kindly sent me"; but when another Massachusetts gentleman, Robert C. Winthrop, proposed to purchase an annuity with a fund subscribed by his New England friends, he met with a firm and dignified refusal. As a mere business preliminary, Mr. Winthrop had commissioned Mr. Seaton to find out her exact age, and that, she thought, was a question no gentleman had a right to ask a lady.

Debts, however, cannot be obliterated by refusing to notice them. By 1848 her resources were at such a low ebb that she determined to hold a "raffle," that being regarded in the South as a dignified, ladylike way of raising money. She destined to the sacrifice certain pictures and sculpture and articles of plate, and wrote to Payne Todd, asking his opinion of the value of "the large painting and those of Washington and Jefferson by Stuart" and to "please give some guess and tell what estimate you place upon Columbus, Vespucian, Magellan and the Bard of Ossian." Were it not for the tragedy of the situation there would be irresistible humor in the idea of this spoiled son placing a "value" upon such worthies, for from the first glimpse we have of him as a mischievous child, snatching the wig from the head of old General Van Cortland as he bowed low, we learn nothing to his credit.

She undertook the raffle on the advice of Mr. Richard Smith, but his further advice, that she notify her friends, she could not bring herself to follow. Mr. Buchanan, learning of the plan, was horrified, and expressed himself with such vigor that it was abandoned. Then it was proposed that Congress buy for twenty-five thousand dollars the remaining Madison papers, the Government having long ago purchased his report of the Constitutional Convention. Opposition developed among careful legislators, the most outspoken of them being Andrew Johnson of Tennessee. But another Southerner, Alexander H. Stephens, put all his eloquence into an argument in favor of the purchase, and the bill passed, as it was hoped it would, upon Mrs. Madison's eightieth birthday—means having been taken to find out her exact age after all! It was her little kinsman J. Madison Cutts who started from the Capitol on a dead run to tell her the news, and reached her door sadly out of breath but leading the field.

Twenty thousand dollars were invested for her benefit under the trusteeship of Mr. Buchanan, Mr. Smith, and Senator Mason, the remainder being devoted to paying pressing debts, including a three-thousand-dollar mortgage on her home held by J. J. Astor, and such small and significant sums as seventy dollars to redeem pawned silver and twenty dollars to restore to her use a gold chain. Even this late relief came near being snatched from her, for a fire was discovered in her home one night while the papers were still in her possession. Her trusty servant Ralph carried the old lady downstairs, deposited her in a distant corner of the garden, and rushed back for the precious trunk. The flames were soon extinguished, and Mrs. Madison returned to her smoke-impregnated room, laughing over the spectacle she presented, for she had made her escape in her night-cap, bare feet, and favorite black velvet dress. At eighty she could still laugh and was as full of spirit to meet a crisis as she had been when she rescued Washington's portrait from the oncoming British soldiers, or quietly called the servants to turn a lurking Indian out of her bedroom.

In religion she had remained a nominal Quaker, just as her husband was a nominal Episcopalian, but both had attended St. John's Church in the short interval between its building and their departure from Washington. After her return she resumed the habit of going there, and, as was natural, Pastor Hawley took a deep interest in his most distinguished parishoner. In time he persuaded her that she desired to unite with his flock, and on a July day in 1845 her niece Anne Payne, who lived with her, wrote a few notes like this one:

Dear Aunt Lear:

Aunt and myself intend to be christened this morning in church, and we wish very much that you should be present. It will be at twelve. No one is to be there except Mrs. Adams and her daughter Mary and Louisa Adams.

It was almost exactly four years after this ceremony that Mrs. Madison, stricken with apoplexy, passed into a sleep that was merely more profound than any which preceded it. Hers was by common consent a public funeral, business coming to a standstill and the people, as well as the President and other officials, taking part as they would have done had she been in the eyes of the law, as she was in the affection of their hearts, a beloved queen dowager.

Whether or not Payne Todd was there, we do not know. If he was, it is safe to assume that he was swathed in mourning as black as his heart. It is very certain that he lost no time in attempting to break his mother's will in order to secure all of the trust fund of twenty thousand dollars that she had divided equally between the devoted Anne Payne and himself. He was the one great sorrow of his mother's life, a sorrow borne with a pride and cheerful silence more impressive than that with which she faced impending poverty. Madison had tried to make him his private secretary. The voters repudiated him when the effort was made to start him in politics by an election to Congress and he drifted through life, handsome and graceless, master of a French purer than his English, and with Grandisonian manners that belied the selfishness of his heart.

He survived his mother only two years and came to a rather miserable end, dying of typhoid fever in a second-rate hotel, alone save for the ministration of colored servants. The whole town had taken part in his mother's burial, but only one friend was devoted enough to follow his body out to the Congressional Cemetery.

XV

GROWTH

JOHN SESSFORD, an employee of Gales and Seaton's printing-office, became so interested in the development of Washington that for half a century he published as his private enterprise an annual summary of the changes that took place, ward by ward, in the city. From this we learn that three or four hundred houses went up in an average year. Figures published elsewhere show that the population of the poor-house, known as the Washington Asylum, kept pace oddly with the amount of private building that went on. Three or four hundred new houses put up in a year, three or four hundred admitted to this undesired haven. The long list of names embraced many races, even a few American Indians, and two who may have been Mermen, for their place of birth was given as "Atlantic."

Fire and General Jackson were responsible for the greatest changes that occurred for some time in the aspect of the city. The Government had begun housekeeping, in 1800, with only one small fire-engine, which did excellent service but was totally inadequate for the territory it had to cover. When the city government received its charter, plans were made to purchase three engines, one for each end of town and one for the center, but plans were one thing and the necessary funds quite another. As a compromise five fire-wards had been established, each with its volunteer company, property-owners being expected to coöperate by keeping on their premises a leathern bucket for each story of their dwellings. These fire companies took to themselves high-sounding names like Union and Perseverance and Columbia, and organizing on lines partly social and partly military, became for a time real factors in the life of the town. Their engine-houses served in quiet moments as club-rooms, and at alarms, day or night, the members came tumbling to their posts, donning helmets as they ran, the captain of the first company to reach a blaze having the honor of acting as fire-chief. This plan worked well while the original membership lasted, but after staid citizens dropped out and were succeeded by addle-pated boys strange things happened. Companies were even known to stop on the way to a blaze to settle a dispute with fisticuffs, and could always be depended upon to stage a noisy quarrel when the ashes had cooled enough to allow post-mortem discussion on the spot. In time the engine houses became headquarters for young toughs who were as much of a terror as a protection to the neighborhood.

Fortunately, no very disastrous blazes occurred, thanks to the "openwork" nature of the city, but alarms followed each other so fast that it was hard to believe all of them accidental. Once, during the time that invention raged like a disease, a conflagration was advertised beforehand in the newspapers. The announcement read:

> This is to give notice, that Houses can be preserved from fires without great expense, by painting them with a composition lately discovered which not only hinders them from being burned, but also extinguishes the flames.
>
> To this effect, two small houses will be built of sixteen to twenty feet high, and ten or twelve square, painted with this composition, in the midst of and at the distance of three or four feet from twenty barrels filled with combustible materials, to which fire will be applied, which will become so violent, that it will consume in a few minutes the barrels to ashes, without in the least injuring the house. The doors and windows of one will be open, and the fire will rage within and without; the other will be closed, and within it will be placed a cat or a dog, and a cloth cote; one or two pounds of gunpowder, or more, if desired, will be thrown on the floor when the barrels shall have been consumed, and it will be seen, that the houses will be perfectly uninjured, and also all the articles contained in the one that is closed. The heat shall be so great as to melt several pieces of lead placed on the roof, and to bend a small bar of iron, upon which a small plank, in the shape of a weathercock, will be affixed.
>
> These two buildings will prove, 1st, that a fire however great and near it may be, cannot demolish a house though it may be entirely open, if it be covered with this composition within and without. 2d, by that which is closed containing the articles which have been mentioned,

that hospitals can be preserved with the sick against all fires, if the buildings be so constructed that all the windows and doors in it, can be tightly closed, and have made upon the top of it an aperture to admit the air. 3rd, that fireproof powder magazines, in the form of moveable vehicles, can be constructed. 4th, that merchandise Warehouses so prepared, cannot be injured, and lastly that this composition may serve for forts, &c. This paint can be made of any color, and of high finish; it is exceedingly durable, so that after several months it will be impossible to detach it except by the aid of the chisel, becoming petrified, neither the air, water, nor fire can alter it—the water which flows over it may be drank with much benefit to the health. It will not be more expensive than the common paint which is commonly used for houses. It has moreover the advantage if laid on in several coatings, of preventing leaks in the roof.

The subscription is one dollar, payable on subscribing, to be placed in the hands of Mr. Force, Mayor of the City, who has kindly interested himself in this measure until it be finished with success. The expenses of the experiment will be defrayed from this subscription. It has been tried by the same person at St. Thomas, and at Porto Rico, in presence of all the Authorities and merchants in those places, as proved by Gazette, at St. Thomas, which contains a certificate of the most favourable nature from respectable and numerous eye witnesses. This is also with the Mayor, and likewise the name of the inventor of the composition.

The time and place for the exhibition of the experiment, will be announced by the Mayor in the public prints.

Washington, July 30, 1836.

The date seems never to have been set, presumably because there were only four subscribers—two who paid their dollars, and two others who wrote down their names and let it go at that.

Fires in unfashionable localities were no more exciting than elsewhere, but a blaze in a public building in Washington or in the home of a high official became a real society function, and nowhere else could such smooth-working examples of democratic harmony be found. Everybody, from President to chore-boys, got in line and passed buckets as long as the supply of water held out. Senator Benton's house was destroyed one afternoon while a large reception was in progress at the home of his kinswoman Mrs. Preston. The guests learned of it through the sudden appearance in the drawing-room of her chef, in white cap and apron, waving his arms and gasping excitedly, "The house of Senator Benton BURN!" whereupon they rushed *en masse* to the scene of disaster, meeting on the way all of Congress streaming from the opposite direction, the House and Senate having instantly adjourned. Some visiting Indians also proffered help, but the water gave out and there was nothing to do but to look on and offer condolences.

In Van Buren's day the White-House laundry caught fire, and Henry Clay, in the bucket brigade, called to the President, "We want to get you out of the White House, but not this way!" which was sportsmanlike and characteristic. But that fire, like so many incidents of Van Buren's term, scarcely measured up to the standards set by his predecessor. It was only the White-House laundry that was injured, and small harm was done there. In Jackson's day the blazes were on a more imposing scale.

The Capitol was the only public building that maintained an outside patrol. In the others, inside watchmen made tours of inspection a little after ten o'clock and then lay down to slumber. The watchman at the Treasury was sleeping with an easy conscience when at two o'clock on the morning of March 30, 1833, a passer-by saw flames burst from the building. He wasted no time in calling a fire-company, but hurried to the hotel where the keys of the engine-house were kept, raided a neighboring stable for two trustworthy horses, and got the engine to the scene of trouble. But here again the water gave out, and all that spectators, distinguished or otherwise, could do, as they rushed up in varied stages of undress, was to organize themselves into a band of licensed looters, to carry everything it was possible to save into a row of little dwellings on the south side of Pennsylvania Avenue between Thirteenth and Fourteenth streets. Here the Treasury officials sorted their salvaged property and opened their doors for business within forty-eight hours. And here they remained for the next six years.

Half that time was consumed in discussions, half in rebuilding. There was much talk about the origin of the fire, an employee suspected of making fraudulent pension returns being thought to know

THE TREASURY BUILDING

more about it than he should; but four trials failed to convict him, and the statute of limitations brought his case to a close.

There was much discussion, too, about how to rebuild. The four office structures originally planned to stand close to the four corners of the White House had long since been outgrown, the overflow lodging in rented quarters. The fire in the Treasury brought this situation into strong relief, but the only agreement after three years of talk was that such conditions were undignified and unsafe. One suggestion, fortunately not accepted, was to gather all the government offices under a single giant roof, to be built over Lafayette Square.

That having been definitely rejected, two rival architects made plans for a new Treasury, the winner being Robert Mills, assistant to Latrobe when the latter was in charge of the Capitol. Mills's plan had been drawn without reference to a particular site, and such difference of opinion developed on this point that President Jackson was appealed to as umpire. The old gentleman may never have heard of L'Enfant's plan. Certainly he paid no attention to it; and he appears to have been distinctly bored by the whole discussion, three years seeming more than ample time for the results attained. According to the most cherished of local Jackson traditions, he stalked out of the White House one morning before breakfast, made his way to the ruins of the old Treasury, drove his cane down among them with all the strength in his old arm, and declared that the new building should be placed just there.

The architect and the committee of the House were aghast when it was discovered that the larger dimensions of the new Treasury made it necessary to destroy the vista between the Executive Mansion and the Capitol, even to deflect the course of Pennsylvania Avenue itself; but Jackson had spoken so emphatically that nobody had the courage to reopen the subject. Van Buren, however, inspired no awe, and during the next administration the suggestion was made to take down the walls already built. But hard times were upon the country, and Van Buren had become the target of so much criticism for his extravagance that the proposal found small favor in his sight. So, between Old Hickory, who did not know what he was doing and the Mistletoe President, who knew but did not care to rectify the mistake, a permanent wave was put in the length of Pennsylvania Avenue.

Scarcely had the Treasury been located when Blodgett's Hotel, that housed the Patent Office and the Post Office, burned one night, with such terrifying swiftness that it seemed hardly worth while to man the "hydraulion" after it was brought to the scene. Only in the end of the building where Post-Office records were kept was rescue possible, and here Amos Kendall, who had lately crossed the dividing line between Jackson's kitchen cabinet and his real one, to become Postmaster-General, might be seen, his spare figure silhouetted against the flames as he directed his force of clerks.

The Patent Office had really been begun before the fire, and when the Post Office Department was built on the square directly opposite, that part of F Street gained an official dignity enjoyed before only by Capitol Hill and the neighborhood of the White House. The street between was only an unpaved roadway, with wheel-tracks meandering down the center from the Treasury toward the unfinished, unstuccoed City Hall. Henry Adams, whose childhood memories of Washington clustered around his uncle's home, thought the white marble of these two buildings looked in the distance "like Greek temples in the abandoned gravel pits of a deserted Syrian city." It was President Jackson who chose marble for their construction in preference to freestone—not because of grandeur or artistic merit but on the practical ground of economy, marble not requiring an annual coat of paint. The old President reached conclusions by methods of his own, but they were usually sound.

In 1850 the only part of Washington closely enough covered with buildings to warrant the use of the word "city," save in a most liberal sense, was bounded by Massachusetts Avenue on the north and the Potomac River on the south, the Capitol on the east and the White House on the west. Other areas were developing like sunspots, but the stretches between were connected only by lanes that in former days had run from one country estate to another. Far out on Third Street near I Street N. W., the young and brilliant Senator Douglas of Illinois, one of the few senators to invest in a Washington dwelling, bought two squares of ground and built a home for his bride, a kinswoman of Mrs. Madison's—lovely Adele Cutts of the dark eyes and skin like petals of a water-lily. Surveys being vague, it was found that the position of the house did not conform to the building lines. But it seemed of so little consequence out there in the suburbs, and a senator is a man of such vast importance, that Mr. Douglas confidently asked the city council to rectify the mistake by changing the direction of the street!

The Navy Yard with its surrounding dwellings and shops still formed a self-centered little rural community, with its church and tree-shaded village green over which cows grazed in leisurely content.

Between the Navy Yard and the Capitol were more vacant spaces than buildings, though occasionally a house in its grove of trees rose like an island out of the sea. Duddington, the red brick mansion belonging to Mr. Carroll, over which L'Enfant and the city commissioners had come to blows, was one of these. Another, which was not nearly so fine but attracted more notice, was the frame dwelling with out-buildings that James Greenleaf erected when he came to make his home in the city during the administration of his cousin John Quincy Adams. Here he lived, retired but conspicuous, his library and oil-paintings, his linguistic accomplishments, his red horse and his gray one, his two cows, color not specified, his garden, his "farm" on the low-lying ground of the Island, his duel with one Captain Duncanson,—above all, his newspaper quarrels and interminable lawsuits,—furnishing endless food for gossip. He might well have been, as some believed him to be, the original of Dickens's "Jarndyce and Jarndyce."

Little more enlivening than brick-yards was to be seen in the stretch between the Navy Yard and the Arsenal, though somewhere in that region Washington's oldest dwelling-house might be found. It belonged to a Mrs. Prout, whose father had built it with his own hands, a century earlier. Having descended in the scale of elegance, it was used as a stable for Mrs. Prout's old horse, who looked contentedly out of his window as the sentimental visitor peered past his flanks into the smoke-blackened interior.

The Jockey Club, on the high ground north of the city, was no longer the resort of fashion. Some of the neighboring estates had been subdivided and planted in mulberry groves during the furore for silk culture that spread over the land in the late thirties, when "a Persian farm" was the goal of every optimist's ambition. Washington suffered no more than other places from this obsession, and the trees flourished better, the mulberry being indigenous to Virginia, where it has figured ornamentally in history since 1607. But experiment proved it better as backgrounds for Indian queens, and shelters for General Washington to sleep under, than for serious investment.

Few who bought "Silkworm eggs of the Peanut variety, warranted good," at Charles Stott's drug shop, corner of Pennsylvania Avenue, near Brown's Hotel, harvested anything except debts. Mrs. Madison's scapegrace son, Payne Todd, was one of the losers; and the most fortunate local speculator was an old gentleman who salvaged enough thread from his cocoons to have a silk suit woven, which he wore arrogantly on grand occasions for the rest of a very long life. The trees lived after him; and indeed fell only before encroaching apartment-houses.

According to John Sessford, the City Hall, so long an eyesore because of its unfinished condition, was taking on "a grand appearance" with its final coat of stucco. Though destined to become fashionable, and already boasting two boarding-houses "much frequented by congressmen," the neighborhood still had many rural characteristics. Its resident ducks and geese waddled peacefully down to the Tiber to enjoy their daily swim; and pigs rooted happily in the gutters all summer, oblivious of the fate that awaited them in the fall, when a burly negro and an enthusiastic bulldog rounded them up for destruction. Animals roamed everywhere in spite of orders of the city council. A favorite anecdote among congressmen told of a collision near the Capitol between a fat representative and a fat porker, heavy-weights both, in which the member of Congress got the worst of the encounter.

Out in the river a disquieting change had taken place. In George Gordon's time there had been a bay where Rock Creek entered the larger stream, wide and deep enough for sea-going ships to ride comfortably at anchor, while they unloaded merchandise and awaited cargoes of tobacco, and after the tobacco industry declined, Rock Creek's lively falls had turned mills that ground flour greatly esteemed for its excellence. But an ice-jam dredged a new channel in the Potomac, and the cutting of forests back in the hills brought a steadily diminishing supply of water to Rock Creek, so that flats appeared where deep water used to be.

Dr. Thornton's comprehensive eyes had been the first to see land emerging at low tide, and characteristically he entered his claim to it "by right of discovery." This might have been forgiven as one more manifestation of his eccentricity, had not the willow wands he thriftily planted to encourage the deposit of soil actually taken root and grown. And the flats had grown likewise in extent and noxiousness. While people discussed remedies and instituted law-suits to find out who really owned them, a certain Dr. Kidwell improved on Dr. Thornton's idea and secured a government patent to the water-soaked acres.

At high tide they drew to themselves all sorts of refuse, which festered in the sun when the water receded, and gave out such foul odors that at the time of the Civil War a young secretary of Lincoln's, held at his post of duty during the summer, wrote to a more fortunate comrade: "I am alone in the White pest-house. The ghosts of twenty thousand drowned cats come in at night through the south windows."

These flats became the happy hunting-ground of innumerable crows that flew over the city twice a day. On still evenings the sound of their cawing could be heard above all the street noises, and the slowly flapping cloud of black wings against the sunset sky as they flew to their roosting-place in the hills was an arresting sight. Ignorant folk whispered grewsome stories about these birds. During the Mexican War it was said that they had flown all the way from battle-fields where they had been gorging on dead soldiers.

Within the city proper there were long stretches of vacant lots, lighted after nightfall only by fireflies. Even where buildings were most numerous travel after dark was hampered by the lack of street lamps. Such as there were, called to mind the parable of the wise and foolish virgins, for some had oil and some had not, and many slept. All had slept uninterruptedly between 1830 and 1840 when the "moonlight" system prevailed and darkness reigned if the moon happened to be off duty.

A gas-company had only recently been chartered. Shortly after 1814 there had been talk of installing this new method of street-lighting, already used in London but not yet acclimated in the United States. Nothing came of it, the city being busy with matters it deemed more important and private individuals having no money to invest. Occasionally citizens had been tantalized for a night or two by the spectacle of a building transformed by gas manufactured on the premises, a fact of which neighbors were well aware, but such occurrences were only in the nature of "demonstrations."

Even after the huge bronze chandelier in the center of the Hall of Representatives fell, one day, from its weight of oil-lamps, scattering confusion and broken glass over desks and chairs and presumably valuable papers, Congress hesitated to permit the innovation. Finally, in 1847, an enterprising genius obtained leave to manufacture his own brand of gas in a corner of the Capitol grounds, and, taking a sporting chance, risked his private fortune to lay pipes through the Capitol and show the dazzled legislators their dim halls and committee rooms transformed. Then he led them outside to look up at the old dome where a lantern blazed ninety feet above them in the sky; and they succumbed. The next year the East Room at the White House was lighted in a similar manner, and John Sessford's record for 1850 mentions "very large pipes" being laid from "extensive" new gas-works on Square C to Pennsylvania Avenue, and along that thoroughfare in both directions.

The systematic tapping of water-pipes intended only to carry a supply to public buildings, had reached a point where it could no longer be controlled or safely ignored. The equally vital question of a system of sewerage was left as before to the mercy of Providence; but John Sessford's old scrap-book has pasted in it an invitation to witness near Great Falls, on November 7, 1853, the beginning of work upon the Washington Aqueduct to bring water from the upper Potomac into the city. A canal-boat would leave Georgetown promptly at 8:30 A. M.

Pasted beside this invitation is an extract from a pamphlet dated 1794, showing that the plan about to be inaugurated was nothing new, but had very likely been discussed by Washington and L'Enfant when they made their initial survey. Great Falls, this pamphlet stated, was one hundred and three feet above tide-level, which made it possible to bring the water "if necessary over the tops of the houses," and the way was clearly marked out by a small stream called Watts's Branch, whose course led directly toward the town. Only a short length of canal need be added.

Ten years passed before the town reaped the harvest of work begun that November day. Almost at the moment Lincoln dedicated the war cemetery at Gettysburg, the welcome stream began to flow. It was to carry this conduit over a picturesque valley seven miles above Georgetown that Jefferson Davis, when Secretary of War under Pierce, authorized the building of that perfect stone arch known by the intriguing name of Cabin John Bridge. Before the conduit was in use, Davis had become President of the Confederate States and bitter feeling caused his name to be chiseled from the inscription on the bridge, where the accusing blank remained for more than half a century, until President Roosevelt had the name restored.

Little had been done by 1850 to improve the parks. But houses are, after all, the first essentials in a city, and with so many private lots lying vacant and government reservations on every hand, the development of public grounds must have seemed the least of local needs. In Fillmore's day, Mr. A. J. Downing, a landscape artist of Newburg, New York, was called to Washington to improve the stretch between the Capitol and the river. He laid out the walks and drives near the Smithsonian and designed a park entrance in the form of a triumphal arch. The marvel is that after his untimely death in a steamboat accident on the Hudson, his plan continued to be followed in a desultory fashion until civil war brought such enterprises to a standstill.

But while public spaces were neglected, the center of the town was by no means without delightful private gardens, traces of which still survive. Almost every dwelling, however humble, had its dooryard with rose bushes and honeysuckles. Gentlemen of substance had much more. Several of these had made their homes near Ninth Street just above Pennsylvania Avenue, in what is now the heart of the moving-picture district. Mr. Gales lived here; so did Peter Force, who was mayor during part of Jackson's term, and printer and publisher and leading citizen for years before and after that. His house was only an unpretentious red-brick box, built to hold a roof over the pine shelves groaning under his collection of Americana—books and pamphlets, broadsides and cards, that after his death was bought to enrich the Library of Congress, largely through the efforts of Congressman Rutherford B. Hayes. But his garden had a dignity his dwelling lacked, and was roomy enough to harbor stately old trees around whose roots wild strawberries grew, while in beds circled with box there were plumy white lilacs and whole regiments of tiger-lilies, and larkspur and lady-slippers and marigolds and clove pinks, and all the sweet procession of old-fashioned posies. Here Peter Force came to walk, a handsome figure of a man even in extreme old age, with a stately St. Bernard pacing beside him. Neither man nor dog seemed to notice the cronies of his grandson, who were playing in the garden; and as he entered, the children used to slip silently out, for it was one of the rules of the quiet place that he was not to be disturbed.

In another garden, not far away, mocking-birds sang amid the dark, glossy magnolia leaves, and fig-trees put forth round buttons of fruit that did not always mature. This garden held a pool where the first Victoria Regia brought to the United States burst into bloom. Its owner specialized in foreign plants, even foreign vegetables, and it was to him that Webster addressed his oft-quoted note: "Dear Dr. Hall: Have you a cucumber?"

The location these gentlemen had chosen was very central; on high ground, yet almost within stone's throw of Center Market, near two favorite hotels and within fifteen minutes' brisk walk of the Capitol in one direction and of the White House in the other. It was typical of the neutral ground they were supposed to occupy in a business way, from which they might advance in any direction that interest dictated. Both Mr. Force and Mr. Gales had been conspicuously successful printers in a town noted for its long list of dead and dying newspapers. The cynically minded said that to carry on such a business in Washington a man must have neither politics nor opinions of his own, but be willing to reflect those of the current administration.

Until the Civil War, when Congress set up its own presses, the government printing went "by favor," and yielded a profit of from twenty to thirty-three per cent. to the firm that had the contract. So it was no wonder that these gentlemen had double houses and beautiful roomy gardens. By 1850, however, trade had already pushed its advance-guard in among the magnolia trees in the guise of an innocent-looking bake-shop. Soon Mr. Gales sought a more fashionable home; people who rented offices and lodgings moved in as fashion moved out; trees were felled and flower beds trampled underfoot; and to-day, having run the whole gamut of business, from banking-houses to old-clo' warehouses, the locality has taken on a hectic brilliance of electric signs, by whose light tortured old box-trees and forgotten bits of shrubbery, crushed between ash-cans and bill-boards, may be seen breaking nightly into a travesty of bloom.

On Pennsylvania Avenue the roadway had changed more than the houses that bordered it. Most of the money provided for street improvements during Jackson's two terms—and that was more than had ever been extracted from Congress in a similar period—had been spent in an effort to make this principal thoroughfare "the best piece of macadam in the country," with results not complimentary to the rest. Jefferson's four rows of poplars had been sacrificed, the two middle rows uprooted entirely, while decaying trees in the outer rows were replaced with those of other varieties. The street now stretched in Sahara-like aridity from curb to curb, the least breeze filling the air with dust-particles irritating to eyes and temper and believed to be "very productive of consumption." The vaunted macadam had consisted at first of a strip of broken stone, nine inches deep and forty feet wide, running like a ribbon through the center, the spaces between it and the sidewalks being covered with ordinary gravel.

Whether or not this uprooting and change spelt progress was a matter of personal opinion. Before it was done, surface water from the side streets had made its way across the avenue in what were meant to be broad, shallow drains, but which became gullies that made progress along the street very like riding upon a swelling sea, with periodic descent into the trough of the waves. Underground drainage had been substituted, but even after the original forty-foot strip of macadam was increased to eighty feet, deceitful areas of spongy gravel remained. A story was told about a lady who tried to cross the avenue in front of the National Hotel, one rainy day, and sank in a hole three feet deep. Objectors were well within the truth when they sent a petition to Congress stating that "this is not what the principal street of the metropolis of the nation ought to be."

Before 1850, "pebble pavements" made of rounded stones as big as a man's fist, over which people walked delicately or rode jouncingly, little dreaming that they held secrets of long-vanished Indian predecessors, were put down near the market and in spots where traffic was heavy, and later covered the entire avenue. But durable and soul-shaking as these seemed, they had no adequate foundation, and soon followed the macadam of Jackson's day toward the center of the earth. It is an ill wind that blows nobody good, however. Hack-drivers were happy, and hovered as before on the edges of the worst mud-holes, on the lookout for passengers.

Ladies venturing forth in damp weather looped their skirts high over stout and handsome woolen petticoats of red or blue, and trusted to the providential interposition of crossing-sweepers, who plied their trade in front of those who looked affluent enough to give small coins in exchange for a comparatively clean passage.

"Gum elastic overshoes" were advertised as something highly desirable. Indeed, under the caption, "Look out for Snow Storms and Sloppy streets," the "Intelligencer" waxed almost sensational in extolling the cork soles and "elegant" variety of overshoes, including "Figured Rubbers for Ladies and Gentlemen," that might be bought, at prices ranging from sixty-two cents to two dollars a pair, at the Sign of the Big Black Boot, on Pennsylvania Avenue two doors west of Four and a Half Street. An enterprising boot-black, who aspired to be a Napoleon in his trade, showered the streets with broadsides announcing his willingness to clean boots and shoes daily for a dollar a month and deliver them "by the runner to any location where they may be ordered."

A new spirit was stirring in advertising. Sometimes a questionable medical man like Dr. Kuhl (could a better name be invented?) set up his stock in trade in an empty store and praised flamboyantly his Botanical Remedies, especially Rob Restorer of the Blood, in hand-bills as large as a Presidential message, announcing his intention to keep the place open as long as Congress was in session. In another empty store a merchant who had no qualms about exploiting his own honesty shouted in print:

OLD GOODS, OLD GOODS!

Come and get them at your prices!

Having sold off my stock of good goods, and being about to commence another business, I will open on Saturday the 6th Instant at the store formerly occupied by Walter Harper & Co. between 12th and 13th Streets, on Pennsylvania Avenue decidedly the oldest and most soiled lot of goods ever seen in this country. This lot of trash consists principally of old and soiled Kid Gloves for Ladies and Gentlemen (some of them very good) Laces and Edgings of every description; muslin and cambric Edgings and Insertings (in bad order) Flowers and Bonnet Caps (some very good among them) Cotton and Silk Gloves (in a very bad state) Netts, Gimps, and Fringes, &c. &c. &c., all of which I am determined to sell, give or throw away during the coming week.

There are certainly some good Bargains to be had in this combination of trash. Please remember the place. Between 12th and 13th Streets, Pennsylvania Avenue.

He also had an excellent name for his calling—J. B. Bragdon.

An empty building, usually on the south or "wrong" side of the Avenue, might be occupied for a day or a week by some traveling marvel like the Giraffe or Camelopard, or the Papyrotomia, whatever that may have been, or a picture, say Titian's Venus, thus advertised in the "Intelligencer:"

LAST WEEK

Titian's Venus—The Exhibition of this beautiful painting positively closes this week and goes immediately to Baltimore on its way to New

York. This picture was formerly in the possession of Sir Thomas Lawrence, passing at his death to the Pall Mall Gallery London. It was visited by more than 100,000 persons, including those of the first distinction.

The picture is supposed to have been painted by Titian after his own masterpiece in the Florentine Gallery; is nearly 300 years old, and sold in London for £2000 sterling.

Open from 9 A. M. till 9 P. M. Admission $.25

Ladies Day on Saturday from 11 A. M. to 2 P. M.—exclusively for ladies.

Plumb's Daguerreotype of the picture for sale at the room.

On pleasant days daguerreotype studios advertised their skill by setting out on the sidewalk cases filled with likenesses of their most distinguished patrons. This new process of picture-making had become very popular with congressmen, a class not unduly afflicted with modesty, yet sharing President Polk's impatience at time wasted with portrait-painters. Strangers in town had the diversion of standing near these cases and matching the originals to their counterfeits as the daily after-office parade streamed by. Usually they entered the gallery before leaving town and had their own pictures taken for the sake of the folks back home.

In the business section of the avenue an adequate number of saloons could be found, whose swinging doors moved easily. Hotels had bars as a matter of course. A lesser number of discreetly closed doors opened into gambling-houses. The most famous of these was a house between Four and a Half and Sixth Streets (on the unpopular side of Pennsylvania Avenue, like Dr. Kuhl's office) conducted by a member of a good Virginia family, the Pendletons. Some spoke of it as the "Hall of the Bleeding Heart." Its proprietor preferred to have it called "The Palace of Fortune." Until his death it was entered by no woman, but on pleasant days his wife, who was the daughter of Robert Mills, could be seen exquisitely dressed, with a face composed and almost expressionless, driving on the streets frequented by leaders of fashion, in her perfectly appointed carriage, quite the handsomest carriage in town, followed by two spotted coach-dogs.

Her husband's house was filled with carved furniture and good pictures, in the days when pictures were few in Washington. Gentlemen approached, walking leisurely, then wheeled and vanished quickly within. In the two outer drawing-rooms that had to be crossed before the real center of the place was reached, men of all parties and all walks of life met and fraternized. Its proprietor acquired great power as a lobbyist, for he lent money to his congressional patrons when they chanced to find themselves temporarily out of funds. When he died, James Buchanan and several other Democrats of note were among his pall-bearers.

Public stages, absent from the avenue since the lumbering Royal George made its last trip and fell to pieces, appeared again under the new-fangled name omnibus, which signified that they were hospitable to all classes. Rival lines traversed the weary distance between Georgetown and the Navy Yard, hourly during the day, and strove to outdo one another in size and elegance. On two successive days in the autumn of 1850 new coaches were launched, one by each line. The Union line bore on its interior a frieze of "tasteful oil paintings," while each of its principal panels was adorned with a likeness of Henry Clay, for whom the coach was named. The Citizens line, as might be inferred from its title, preferred local celebrities, and ornamented its newest coach with a portrait of the amiable Joseph Gales. In spite of all this art and elegance, the price of a ride from Capitol to White House was only twelve and a half cents, half the usual cab fare, which liverymen and predatory drivers denounced as tyrannical and arbitrary.

But when walking was possible, the correct thing to do was to walk on this street of so many attractions. Government departments closed their doors at the comfortable hour of three in the afternoon, after which came the daily parade of well-dressed people on Pennsylvania Avenue—people who never hurried, but had time to greet friends and drop in at the book-store to look over the newest invoice from New York, or if they were women, to steal a glance at Godey's Ladies' Book. In the doorway of McClery's drug store, where Fourteenth and E streets join the avenue, old General Gibson would be sitting, his cane firmly planted, his hands resting on top of it, as he had sat on pleasant days, for years, watching this same procession. It was a crowd which formed groups and met and parted in a sort of rhythmic, irregular contra-dance, until, with the approach of the dinner-hour, its members departed for home in new groups, carrying friends with them. If one watched long enough, one was sure to see Judge This and Senator That, and Assistant-Secretary So-and-So, and lesser folk who either took off their hats obsequiously to the great, or stared with American curiosity, eyes on a level, without fear or favor.

It was quite like a Presidential reception turned out of doors, save for the presence of an occasional black-smudged chimney-sweep trudging along with the tools of his trade; or the pump-mender, repairing one of those useful unsanitary machines; or a scissors-grinder passing along with loudly ringing bell.

At train-time society went to the station to welcome its friends or to "see them off," train-time being still a definite hour and something of a novelty. It was only late in Jackson's administration that the railroad had gained access to Washington after a long fight with the stage-coach companies and the Chesapeake and Ohio Canal, a rejuvenated edition of the Potomac Company's old plan for traffic between East and West. Charles Carroll, signer of the Declaration of Independence, had lived to lay a corner-stone for the Baltimore and Ohio Railroad in Baltimore on July 4, 1828; and the very same day, near Great Falls, President Adams had turned the first spadeful of earth for the canal.

The two projects were rivals from that moment, the canal being the favorite in Washington. So energetically was every move of the railroad fought, first with vituperation, then with litigation, and finally by efforts at compromise, that it had required seven years to get the forty miles of track laid between the two cities. Only little by little had conservatives given way, and fortunately they never granted all the privileges the railroad coveted, including a right to lay its tracks along Pennsylvania Avenue. It was allowed to come just to Pennsylvania Avenue and no farther, and its first station was a low wooden shed on a corner not far from the Capitol, into which the trains rumbled, trailing long black plumes of smoke behind them and making a prodigious din of bells and whistles.

Until the beginning of the twentieth century the ugly smudge of railroad track disfigured the public reservation that had been intended to sweep in an uninterrupted stretch of park from the President's home to the home of Congress, though before 1850 the station of the Baltimore and Ohio Railroad was removed from the shed on Pennsylvania Avenue to a new terminal at New Jersey Avenue and C Street N.W., where it remained until the completion of the present monumental Union Station. But that first flimsy wooden shed was more important in the annals of the town than any one or all three of the white marble public buildings which were begun about the same time. The new Patent Office and the Post Office Department, whose white marble columns gave F Street such architectural dignity, and the new Treasury which blocked the vista between Capitol and White House, were more or less inevitable developments, in the old order of things, while the hammers that echoed from the railroad station sounded the knell of one epoch and ushered in another.

XVI

"MESS" LIFE

IN proportion to its size there were more hotels and boarding-houses in Washington than in any other American town. Elsewhere, the inherited British my-house-is-my-castle idea, grafted on our limitless acreage, had made it customary for each family to own its home and work out its domestic problems in decent privacy. Indeed, it was scarcely respectable not to do so, for it was a poor-spirited man who could not under prevailing conditions earn enough to pay for his roof and hearthstone.

Only in the central meeting-place of the nation was gregarious living popular. In early days, shortage of houses had made it necessary and our political system continued it. That biblical text, "Where your treasure is, there will your heart be also," was one which constituents had ever in mind.

In 1850 the town had just acquired its first real hotel. Mr. Willard, a young Vermonter with a talent for hotel management, had remodeled the straggling group of buildings called Fuller's, where Dickens had the misfortune to lodge, and made out of it a house of one hundred and fifty rooms and the beginning of a national reputation; while Fuller, relieved of this heretofore unprofitable plant, erected a new five-story house two blocks away, which he called the Fountain Inn.

Dickens's famous description of "Fuller's" as a group of crazy little houses, some fronting on Pennsylvania Avenue and some on Fourteenth Street, with their yards stretching uphill toward F Street in a tangle of weeds and confusion, went into his "American Note-book," with much else that offended Washingtonians. In the yard was a great metal triangle.

> Whenever a servant is wanted, somebody beats on this triangle from one to seven strokes according to the number of the house in which his

GREENOUGH'S "WASHINGTON"
A manifestation of patriotism and art in the forties

presence is required; and as all of the servants are always being wanted and none of them ever come, this enlivening engine is in full performance the whole day through. Clothes are drying in this same yard, female slaves with their heads tied in cotton handkerchiefs are running to and fro on the hotel business, black waiters cross and re-cross with dishes in their hands, two great dogs are playing upon a mound of loose bricks in the centre of this little square, a pig is turning himself to the sun and grunting. "That 's comfortable", and neither the men nor the women nor the dogs nor the pig nor any created creature, takes the slightest notice of the triangle which is tingling madly all the time.

Mr. Willard, with his inborn desire for economy, sharpened and trained by experience as steward of a Hudson River boat, gave Washington a jolt out of such country-tavern methods. He visited the market at 3 A. M., while his rivals were asleep, and at meal-times presided in the dining-room, carving-knife in hand, to see "that no waste occurred." The office, he put in charge of a brother who had the gift of making a patron feel grateful and charging him a good round sum at the same time. Rotund, obliging, unflurried, the brothers "aimed to please," and how well fitted they were for their task is indicated by the anecdote told by a younger member of the house:

I remember once, when there was a slight fire in one of the upper stories, one of the guests rushed downstairs to my father, who was in the inner office at the time, and said in an excited manner, "Mr. Willard, the hotel is on fire! Where is it? Where is it?" My father, in a very calm way rang for the bell boy and said, "John will you take the gentleman upstairs and show him the fire?"

In the early decades there had been little difference between boarding-houses and hotels: hotels were small, boarding-houses smaller still. The Congressional Directory of 1809, the earliest to print the names of congressmen with their addresses, listed twenty-seven different places of abode, of which only two, Mr. Stelle's and Mr. Long's, were classed as hotels. Of the other twenty-five, fourteen were on Capitol Hill, though even then the trend of fashion was toward the west.

Soon there were three distinct groups, one near the Capitol, another near the White House, and a third, smaller but very popular, in the neighborhood of the Marsh Market, to which ducks and terrapin could be poled from their original haunts almost into the mouths of ultimate consumers.

Officials were The Great; and it was one of the odd features of this town built as a dwelling-place for the Government that the individuals who composed the Government were unblushingly charged more for board and lodging than mere private citizens. Being The Great, they were expected to pay for the glory of their position.

Landlords and landladies were only human, so prices varied. At the time the British burned the city, sixteen dollars a week was the usual charge to congressmen; and it will be remembered that Georgetown thought this extravagant. When General Taylor was inaugurated, the hotels demanded from three to five dollars a day for rooms with meals; but at ordinary times ordinary accommodation for ordinary people was not high. An old bill made out to one of the leading editors of the town for boarding two of his employees for five years and eight months, from October 1, 1844, names the rate of four dollars a week for one of these men and three a week for the other.

When congress adjourned, rooms became empty, and cards like this appeared in the newspapers:

Mrs. Myre will be pleased to accommodate Ladies and Gentlemen visiting Washington with board by the day, week or month, in her spacious house on Pennsylvania Avenue, nearly opposite the National Hotel. Her house having been vacated by the adjournment of Congress, she will be happy to accommodate travelers during the recess.

Washington March 10, 1833.

It was wonderful how comfortable these professional Marthas of Washington made their lodgers, especially lodgers who had grown up in bleak New-England surroundings and found themselves for the first time under the seductive influences of slavery. "Help," as they had known it in New England, "accommodated" grudgingly if at all. In Washington there seemed to be an endless supply of black servants, whose ministrations were slipshod but offered with smiling, almost caressing willingness.

One such new-comer wrote to his wife that he had a neat little room on the fourth story, and a servant to wait on him "whenever I call." He thought there must be a dozen or fifteen slaves in the house, and these were always singing and "apparently as happy a set of beings as ever you saw." One came in the morning to build his fire and stood by while he dressed, ready to brush his clothes or do anything he required. "You have no idea how I am waited on here," he exulted; and to make the picture quite idyllic he sketched as a final touch the establishment's "one little nigger baby."

The negro's native genius for cookery, a talent stimulated by precept and example, had something to do with the comfort of these boarding-houses. Markets were excellent; people from all parts of the country left their favorite recipes behind after a sojourn in Washington; foreign chefs who had come with diplomats sometimes stayed on to set up in business for themselves; and the preparing and offering of food in ceremonial fashion had a distinct value in political life.

Even the humbler boarding-places made a point of "good eating." Food substitutes had not yet been invented; with calories and balanced rations and the tin can, they lurked among unguessed horrors of the future. People bought what pleased the palate, and took it home in generous quantities. In the matter of eggs, alone, one shudders to think of the potential broilers sacrificed to supply the hot breads and Sally Lunn and flapjacks and fried eggs consumed at congressional breakfast tables, not to mention the meals served later in the day. It was the time of honest pound-for-pound cooking, when eight or a dozen eggs went into a cake as a matter of course, and no self-respecting cook would think of preparing dinner without "a quart of cream" into which to dip with lavish hand. Dyspepsia ultimately took its revenge, but the immediate result was satisfactory.

Keeping a boarding-house for congressmen was an enterprise which required no little wisdom. Somebody, scornful of Washington's attempts at commerce, and distrustful of its politics, said with a sneer that the keeping of boarding-houses was the most respectable business carried on there. The man or woman who had the power of making lonely government officials comfortable or miserable, day after day for months on end, was to be treated with respect merely as a matter of diplomacy, and usually deserved it on other grounds. The women who undertook such tasks were often widows of men who had died in office, who chose to stay on rather than to return to their former homes. At that time there were few occupations open to women, and here they could be independent and useful. Often they knew more about the ins and outs of official life than their newly elected guests; and when they had the tact to impart such knowledge, their hospitality was worth far more than they charged, even with the good stiff percentage for official glory added.

When Senator B. took up his residence as Mrs. A.'s star boarder, her house became almost inevitably a stronghold of his party, his friends and would-be friends, C., D., and E., being anxious to secure rooms under the same roof. Thus groups holding similar views gathered in congenial "messes," insuring comradeship at all hours, and spirited but seldom acrimonious talk at meal-times. If the senator or his friends brought their wives with them, so much the better. The ladies exchanged confidences and embroidery patterns, and, after the first fit of homesickness wore off, had a glorious time attending debates at the Capitol and receptions at the White House. Attractions and repulsions were of course inevitable, but they lived in a sisterly fellowship as near the spirit of the millennium as womankind has yet been able to achieve. They hooked up one another's dresses, sat up as a matter of course with one another's sick, and even took a hand in disciplining one another's babies if the youngsters grew obstreperous in a mother's absence. But every one of them stood ready, loyal wife that she was, to defend her husband's interests and reputation against all comers.

Mrs. Henry Clay's one recorded speech comes to mind. Even with the aid of all her husband's reflected glory she never achieved social prominence. Weighed down with the care of her children when they were small and with sorrow for them after they grew older, she simply made no impression. Her friends loved her, but had never a word to say about her intellect or charm or wit. Yet when somebody presumed to offer sympathy because of Mr. Clay's unfortunate passion for cards, her childlike answer let fly a whole quiverful of feminine arrows: "Oh, but you see," she said, "he almost always wins!"

If, as frequently happened in the earlier days, the gentlemen came to Washington without their womenkind, the landlady herself, supplemented by a pretty niece or daughter, gave the needed touch of feminine grace to her establishment. It was pleasant to show such women a bit of attention, and not infrequently the attractive girls entered official life themselves in time. A marriage of this kind was accepted as a matter of congratulation for both parties, unless, as in the case of Peggy O'Neil, the young woman had made herself unpleasantly conspicuous beforehand. Usually it caused less remark than did the wedding, in early years, of Baron Greuhm and a pretty governess in the household of Mr. Middleton, Clerk of the United States Supreme Court.

Life in hotels was merely that of boarding-houses on a larger scale. One political group settled here, its rival there, and each held its peculiar clientele until an adverse election, or a quarrel with the manager, or the attractions of a superior chef dissolved the group and formed new combinations. A cabinet officer usually felt it necessary to take a private house. Webster, in the intervals of holding cabinet positions, made his headquarters in the St. Charles, on the northeast corner of Pennsylvania Avenue and Third Street N. W., which is almost the only old hotel that has survived in its original outlines. Its steep pitched roof with dormer windows, and the typical two-story Southern "gallery" along its Third-Street front give us a last glimpse of Washington as it used to be. The four ugly pilasters near its front door were deemed a notable addition to the city's art treasures when they were put in place.

After Webster's day this hotel became the haunt of the extreme Southern element, which appreciated both its cuisine and its extensive underground accommodations for slaves. Senator Toombs was one of its important patrons, and much lurid secession talk was heard in its lobbies with the approach of Civil War. To-day it is the haunt of Indians who come to Washington on business for their people.

Of the hotels near the center of Pennsylvania Avenue, Coleman's

National held its patrons long after its neighbors lost their first rank. Indeed, it continued to be the Washington home of senators and Justices of the Supreme Court until well into the decade of the eighties. Henry Clay lived there for twenty years, and died in Room 32, whose window, opening upon Sixth Street, is still pointed out to sight-seers. Because of its associations, the room was eagerly sought and was occupied after his death by Alexander H. Stephens.

In its prime it was a typical Washington hostelry. Miss Bremer described it as "a kind of hot oven full of senators and representatives and traveling ladies and gentlemen" where there was much noise and one was oppressed soul and body "by this high-pressure life," but met most interesting people. She found it possible to gain a little privacy either in her own room, or by walking upon the rear gallery, overlooking what she glorified by the name of "courtyard," where there was a plashing fountain fed by springs that had their rise in Judiciary Square.

But solitude was not the end desired in such places. Guests gravitated by common consent to the public parlors after breakfast as well as after dinner. Some letters written home by young Mrs. Hugh White, wife of a representative from New York in 1845 and 1846, and long hidden in family portfolios, draw a better picture of the feminine side of "mess" life than a bookful of second-hand description, and show how short a time it required to become thoroughly acclimated.

The first was written soon after she and her husband reached Washington, a week before the opening of the session. They had not engaged a boarding-place beforehand. That does not seem to have been the custom among the newly elected, if we may trust the lively Mrs. Clement C. Clay of Kentucky, who tells in her book of reminiscences about arriving at two o'clock of a chilly winter morning with her husband, a brand-new senator, disguised as a mere man by a blanket traveling-shawl and a soft hat pulled down over his eyes. The haughty night clerk remarked that the house was "full" and remained stony and impassive until she followed her senator to find out what was the trouble, and by liberal use of his name and title caused the young man to discover, very promptly, that he had plenty of room "for them." "It was by reason of this significant episode that I first realized the potency in Washington of conventional apparel and congressional titles," says Mrs. Clay.

Mrs. Hugh White and her husband had no such unpleasant experience, though this gentleman also seems to have gained in conventional dress and address as the weeks rolled by.

Washington, 24th Nov. 1845.
Gadsby's Hotel.

. . . I expect this will be a long week to us both. I think we made a mistake in coming quite so soon & am inclined to think the Hon. thinks so too, only he does not like to say so. I expected to write as soon as we arrived, but looking up lodgings and fixing something to wear on my head kept me busy Friday and part of Saturday. . . .

We are undecided as to where to go. Mr. White likes it here, & so do I very well. I think I should prefer a little more quiet, or rather to be a little more retired. The house is uncommonly still and quiet—the waiters more attentive than any I ever saw—the table very good—the house new and clean—you know it 's Miss Polk's house rebuilt. The first story is occupied with stores—the next is taken up with parlours dining & reading-rooms & on the next are bed rooms. We have one of the front chambers, & one of the largest, except one, & that is taken by Reverdy Johnson from Baltimore. He is not here yet, but is expected to bring Mrs. Johnson, and the daughters are to be here in the course of the winter—great belles I am told. Mrs. Commodore Stevens and three daughters are here—are disposed to be very sociable & so are we; but I don't fancy them at all. One is about to be married & that one looks cross enough to turn a honeymoon & molasses Candy moon sour in a jiff. I never had stronger evidence that love is blind than this. How a man with his eyes open can take such a sour piece of furniture for better or worse is more than I can tell. The youngest daughter is pretty and knows it—the eldest is not pretty but thinks she is. I think I should rather not stay here for the winter, but there is not any danger unless Gadsby comes down in his price.

Washington, November 27, Thanksgiving.

. . . When I first arrived here for three or four days I was all but homesick, & the thought of staying here all winter was painful. Indeed I would not allow myself to dwell upon it at all. But now that you continue so well, Father, babies and all, I think I shall like it here very much. The *sett* at this house bids fair to be of the first—& we have made some very pleasant acquaintances. I believe we have told you that we have left Gadsby's—and are at Colemans [the National] in the 4th story. I like the room vastly. It is *vast* too, being as large as two of our rooms put together. Very decently furnished—two washstands with their appurtenances, a *good bed,* bureau, dressing table, wardrobe—writing table, and my big trunk. Don't you think, we have had to pay freight on it all the way from New York! Mr. White has borne it like a martyr.

There are three Whig Members from Conn. at this house—Mr. & Mrs. Trueman Smith from Litchfield—Mr. and Mrs. Hubbard from Middletown—Mr. Rockwell from Norwich. Mrs. Rockwell will be here in two or three weeks & then Mr. Rockwell will leave for other quarters. He could not get rooms here. I like him. He is a finished gentleman. They all seem to think the world of their youngest Member's wife—Mrs. Dixon. She has two or three young children & they have taken a house & live by themselves. Mrs. Smith is in delicate health, does not go out at all—speaks in a whisper—but she and her husband are both full of fun. . . . Mr. Hubbard is a good sort of man, but Mrs. Hubbard is the one—She is a character. . . . Some one spoke of her as a "lady of an inquiring mind." But she is excellent company, full of life and conversation, wit and drollery, about 45, and the most *satisfied* face I ever saw. It is right funny. *She knows it all* and on any point of etiquette at which we are at a loss Mrs. Hubbard is referred to at once.

I expected to have a little time to myself, but there is no such thing. Immediately after breakfast which is at eight, the chambermaid comes in, & what with her work, & making fires, the time is mostly consumed until 11 o'clock, when it is time to dress. And dressed I have to be—& well dressed too, or my lord and master is not suited. My muslin-de-lain is too plain for him. He says I must fix it up somehow. Then from 11 in the morning until 10 at night I am liable to have calls at any moment. Mr. White has taken a fancy to see all the gentlemen in his room, and now since dinner we have had Mr. Smith of N. York, Mr. Culum of N. York too, Mr. Rockwell of Conn., & Mr. King of Georgia. They talk gossip with me awhile & then for politics. Mr. White says I am coming on bravely in smalltalk & it may be that even I shall get chalked up to 500. Yesterday several ladies called, but I insisted upon it I had a right to be engaged. I was unpacking & arranging things & by 2 o'clock I was tired enough to go to bed—and to bed I went. Mr. White flew upstairs and down in quite a fuss, but finally concluded I was in the right after all. Why, it 's just like the Springs—with this difference— you dont have to dress for the evening. There is now a good deal of transient company—& will probably be all winter. There are several I have not mentioned whose appearance I like. As yet there are no very great *dashers.*

Have I told you that we have been at church today? Heard as excellent sermon from Mr. Sprawl (so it is pronounced) Churches open and stores closed—Well done, Washingtonians! . . . When is your Thanksgiving—I believe in December.

It is now scarcely remembered that up to the time of the Civil War, Thanksgiving was merely a state holiday, one that New England made much of but to which the South gave little heed. The question of making it national had been discussed and dismissed in John Quincy Adams's time as savoring too much of innovation, and was brought to success only by the active propaganda carried on by Mrs. Sarah Hale, editor of Godey's Ladies' Book, and author of "Mary's Little Lamb."

Washington, Dec. 1st.

. . . Every morning after breakfast we go into the parlour and stay from five minutes to fifty. I generally stay until Mr. White brings in the mail. This morning it proved to be worth having. But such a time as I had to get my letters. I chased him all over the parlours, ladies looking on. At last he gave them up & down we sat to open & see that there was no bad news, then up to my room to read them. . . .

Each letter that I write, no matter who to, is written upon a hand gallop. Why, I have not time to darn a stocking—& for a week I have been trying to make a head-dress & then it is half done. This morning I have been out after gloves & now let me tell you that going to dinner or rather dining in white kid gloves I sha'n't stand any longer. . . .

The "Ladies Ordinary," which occurred at half-past four, had evidently by this time taken on a greater degree of formality. It was the grand meal of the day, with four courses, the third being GAME, featured on the menu in capital letters. The "Gentlemen's Ordinary" opened an hour earlier. Breakfast was at eight, tea at half-past six, and supper at nine. The management evidently did not allow its guests to go hungry.

There was a hop here last evening—They are to be given every two weeks. It was very well got up & passed off exceedingly well, so those say who understand these things. They do not dress much, and only a few dance. It is more like a small private party than anything. It is given by the Ladies of the house. Each lady has permission to give from four to six invitations. It is done for the purpose of returning civilities which can be done in no other way. As soon as the hop was announced I just walked down stairs and told the Ladies I did not wish to have anything to do with it, but would give up my right to invite to anyone who wished it. I then came back and reported myself to Mr. White who told me to walk straight back again & take back all I had said—so I had to mind. All I had to do was to send my card with an invitation on the back to those whom I wished to invite, then to be on the spot when they came & stay in the room until they left. They [the hops] are very select, & they say many beg for invitations but cannot get them. No one is admitted except they present their card of invitation at the door. Coleman *gives* a cold supper & the wine is paid for by the Boarders. I went out to supper. There were two long tables set, each for about 30 persons. There were a dozen that could not get places & some that did not leave the drawing-rooms, so there must have been at least 80 persons here. The gentlemen boarding here are not permitted to enter unless they have an invitation. Gen. Ashby, a Senator & a man of 60 led off the first dance. He is a fine looking man—he danced but once but looked better than any gentleman on the floor. I believe I have told you he is here with his family—we find them very agreeable.

Mark Godwin—(I think that is the name) rooms next to us with his bride. She is the daughter of W. C. Bryant. Godwin edits something. I am not much acquainted. Will stay only a week or two. There is nothing very prepossessing in either of them. [This is Parke Godwin, editor for thirty-odd years of the "New York Evening Post," summarily dismissed.]

To Father I would say that I have not received company or seen anyone in "a state of nudity."

Washington, Dec. 15, 1845. Monday Evening.

. . . I have been up to the Court Room today to hear Webster—dry enough—all I heard was about law & referring to books, pages &c. But I had a fine seat—was within six feet and at his side, & his face was turned our way half the time. He is perfectly self-possessed, calm, quiet and dignified—very imposing in his appearance—spoke slowly, clear and distinct. Had on dark pants, buff vest with metal buttons, snuff col'd coat, metal buttons also. His coat was closely buttoned—But I am writing just as if you never knew or heard of him.

. . . I do not eat as much here as at home, neither does Mr. White. & by the bye he goes the cold water from tip to toe as well as myself every morning—have not omitted it once—I think that is a good deal for the Hon. Shaves too *every* day—the latter he makes a fuss about. He is very neat in his appearance. Only think, he wears nightshirts. And such a brushing his clothes have to take so many times a day! I tell him he will brush all the nap off. . . . Besides the Hon. is exceedingly polite, quite the courtier in his manners. Throws the parlour door open (and with such an air!) for me to walk in, & then springs forward to open it. Take it all together, it is quite a metamorphosis.

Washington, Jan. 3, 1846.

I would like to give you a description of the day yesterday, but my own ideas are too confused to do it well. As Mr. White was not able to go [with me] Mr. Hannegan a Senator from Indiana, kindly offered to escort me. We started from here in a carriage a little before twelve, & all along the streets & sidewalks were filled with people going on the same errand. Men and women, old and young, rich and poor, high and low, all on the move, some hurrying, others taking it quietly, carriages, and horses with their riders dashing along. As we approached the "People's House" the crowd thickened & the carriage way was so full that those who were on foot & whom we had passed with such a dash had decidedly the advantage. At last we arrived at the door & entered the vestibule, which is about 20 feet in width. The crowd was so great, the mass so dense, that we were ½ an hour in going that 30 feet.

This reminds one of the British minister in Jackson's time, who drove to the White House on a similar occasion, took one look at the crowd, and went away saying it was "too democratic" for him.

We advanced by inches, most of the time standing still—at last we arrived at the hall door, and there I thought I should be squeezed to death, for a very large naval officer in full uniform pushed himself in between me & the door. I was completely wedged, and Mr. Hannegan says if the man had not been so fat (something like an India-rubber ball) that that squeezing would have finished me. He could not help me in the least, for his hands and arms happening to be up, and there was not room for him to get them down. I have heard of jams before, but this is the first time I have had a realizing sense of one. . . . We crossed the hall by inches, & entered the reception room in the same way, & were within 4 feet of the President for some minutes before we could get to him. He was standing near the center of the room—received us very graciously, extending his hand. Someone, I have forgotten who, stood with him. We passed directly on and there within 4 or 5 feet of the President stood Mrs. Polk & Ladies. She did the honours well. She is very fine looking & has been handsome—was dressed in purple velvet with a low necked dress—a lace fall about the shoulders and a lace scarf—feathers in her hair. I do not remember the dress of the other Ladies. Immediately behind Mrs. Polk were all the *elite* of the city (except such as had left). We were too late to see all the foreign ministers *together*. They were standing about as thick as they conveniently could, tho' there were some seated, and some seats unoccupied against the wall—though there were not more than half a dozen people seated in the room. We passed through almost as fast as we could, Mr. Hannegan all the while introducing me to all the big folks—the highest in the land. I was very fortunate in that respect in my escort—But no gain without some loss, for had I been with Mr. White I could have looked at my leasure, as I should not have been introduced to so many. As it was, I was kept busy shaking hands &c without giving me a chance to look at them. I can remember only Buchanan & Calhoun. We went into the East Room, where the company was more of a mixed character. We threaded our way through from one end to the other. Many of the Ladies were very handsomely dressed—and the naval officers were in full uniform. Epaulettes and gold trimmings abounded. Old fashioned cocked hats & all kinds and varieties of feathers and plumes were abundant. All the while the band in the vestibule was in full play. It was an exciting scene. We stayed in the East Room but a short time & let ourselves out at a window, as there was no getting out any other way. Mr. Hannegan hurried me very much as he said there would be no getting out of a window soon, & he was right, for some of our mess could not get out for an hour after we left, and one man had his arm broken in the jam.

It was delightful to breathe the fresh air once more. We then proceeded to Mrs. Madison's where we found a long row of carriages before the door & a crowd within. There near the door *stood* Mrs. Madison alone—in full dress—Only think of a low neck dress on a Lady of 80. She had though an under handkerchief on—looked exceedingly well, and was very gracious. We passed through the rooms—only two—as soon as we could, and went to J. Quincy Adams. The crowd here was not so great, but very select & distinguished & here I met & was introduced to the Russian Minister & Lady—for tho' we have exchanged cards, we have never met before. Bodisco was in full dress—a great deal of silver about him & that is the most I can recollect. . . . We met them in the hall—passed on & paid our respects to Mr & Mrs Adams and a Mrs. J. Adams. They were standing & a fine looking couple they were. A feeling of respect would come over one involuntarily. Mrs. Adams had on a black velvet, high to the throat with a very large lace cape. We there had refreshments offered. From there I wished to go to the secretaries, but Mr. H. was under the impression that they did not receive company, so we went to Mr. Benton's who we knew kept open house, as he had sent cards to that effect to all our mess.

There were Mr. & Mrs. Benton & three daughters—one married—a Mrs. Fremont. They were very civil and polite, & there we were offered refreshments. From there we went to Mrs. Alexander Hamilton's—a lady of 80 I presume. There we had the most *home*-like call of any place. No refreshments. Mrs. Hamilton's daughter was there, & Mrs. Duff Green & daughter. Mrs. Hamilton scanned me from top to toe & perhaps I may as well say here that I dressed in my very best—black velvet—new hat and shawl. When we were taking leave Mrs. Hamilton requested my card—urged me to come up of an evening—to come and take *tea with her* & really it seemed right pleasant to be treated so *kindly* here where all is formality. But I attribute my being received so kindly all about to my having a beau that is in favor with the higher powers.

We came home at last in high glee—found Mr. White feeling pretty well, & Mr. Lewis with him. I was tired and went to bed awhile—got up & dressed for dinner. We had more company than usual, some invited & some more strangers. The dinner was better than usual—the table well lighted, the Ladies well dressed & all smiling and in good humor. From the dinner table we all went to the drawing-room (except a few gentlemen who stayed to drink wine) where all were gay and cheerful—music and conversation in abundance.

The time passed quickly until the tea bell rang, or rather gong. We then passed in more as a matter of ceremony than anything, & there we found those gentlemen who stayed for their wine—& sure enough they had had a little too much.

This was a state easy to reach if a man were so minded. A forgotten wine-list of the hotel which has come down to us, when so many more important documents have perished, shows that they had four varieties of hock, nine of claret, four of champagne, eight of sherry, two of port, and nineteen of Madeira from which to choose; and this was after the "Washingtonian" temperance movement, originating in Baltimore in 1840, had made drinking less popular than before.

Washington, 13 January,
Tuesday evening.

. . . Buchanan's invitations are ready for a party at Carusi's Saloon on Friday week, to the extent of nine hundred & Mrs. Plitt who has more to do with it than B. himself, told me today that she promised there would be a thousand invitations given. There is nothing but private parties, balls and assemblies all the time & I am weary of hearing of them, & I presume you are of reading. . . .

Monday night Mr. White attended a grand supper party at Seaton's. Came back perfectly delighted. It was all composed of Whigs & as all our Whig gentlemen were gone the Locos thought they must do something extra so they asked us to go to hear Yankee Bill & like ninnys we went & came home a little ashamed. This is the 4th beautiful day we have had in succession.

Washington, Jan. 26, Monday morning,
11 o'clock.

. . . I wish I had nothing to do but bake a little! I never in my life was in a place where I had so little time to myself. I *must* make 4 calls this day.

I have stopped since I commenced this to fold ever so many papers to send off, & I have now some 2 hundred documents to direct before the mail closes. Muslins are now wet which were put to soak Saturday. I must dry them. We send a good many docs. & papers every day—& some days we work as if for a wager.

You ask about the talk at the dining party at the White House. It was just the same as at any other dinner party—no politics—the subject is avoided—*We* are bearing [ourselves with] discretion. *We* are smoothed down considerable—*We* do not express ourselves so decidedly as formerly unless in our own rooms, & with a Whig & a Whig that we like. Politics are never introduced at the Ladies Ordinary or drawing-room unless for a joke & then the subject is changed very soon.

As to the *weekly* hops you speak of they are weakly in good earnest. There has been and are now, too many strangers in the house—we could not prevent their attendance, that is, the Ladies, & the beauty of these parties is their exclusiveness. . . .

Dont think I 'm crazy, but that levee I fancied—but doubt whether the next will be as pleasant. All the big guns were there—if not all, a goodly portion were. I was told our names would be announced at the door, but it was not so. We went in (as we would elsewhere) & paid our first respects to the President & then to Mrs. Polk who stood a little behind him. Mrs. Madison at her left hand and our Mrs. Maury just back of Mrs. Madison & then the other Ladies. We stayed in the reception room but a few minutes & then passed on into the East Room, which was already beginning to be crowded. (9 o'clock). Of course I did not sit down at all, tho' some did. Gen. Ashby gave me his arm & we promenaded an hour, & then I took Gen. Green's. For a little time it was rather difficult to keep moving. I saw but one person in undress & that was a man in a surtout in the centre of the East Room. There was a good many of the military there in half dress, & the Foreign Ministers—all the Secretaries with them—no refreshments—but that music was enough for me. Mrs. H. W. wore her plaid silk trimmed with black lace across the front, a black lace fall about the neck—low neck, of course—short sleeves—& head dress of black velvet and lace wrought with silver thread, silver flowers & marabo. I put it together after Susan Porter's direction, adding a marabo.

And now for that grand party of the Season—Buchanan's, on Friday last. It was a splendid affair—about 15 hundred present—a regular jam. I moved about but a little, but stood on that raised platform at the head of the room & had a fine view of the whole—it was a sea of heads & so thick were they that while dancing all you could see was some few of the heads were popping up and down. Some were frightened for fear the building would give way—& Mrs. Calhoun who stood with me for a time, left her place with some others & stayed in the dressing room during the evening. Everybody was there—even to Mrs. Alexander Hamilton who is 88 years old—she was dressed in the style of 50 years ago & look'd comical enough—& yet it made one feel rather sad to see her in such a place. A great many went who never go to such places—those who are very strict. It was the greatest party that has ever been given in Washington—so it is said. It cost Buchanan about a dollar a head. The supper was in the room below—& that was a squeeze. But I saw the handsomest part of the table & had all I wished to eat. There was everything on the table that any one ever has & a great quantity, some part hot, & some part cold. It was got up in excellent taste. Mrs. Plitt had a good deal to do with it. There was a high pyramid of confectionary which was illuminated & very beautiful—on the top was a beautiful bouquet which Buchanan gave to Mrs. Madison—she being the one he handed down to supper. Mrs. White had two beaux—Mr. Lewis and Mr. Lowden, & was well taken care of. . . . Flowers and jewellery were scattered about on the floor & not seen until stepped on. A Mrs. Haskins had on the richest dress I ever saw. I have not spelled her name right—& know not now. She is the Granddaughter of Munroe & it was her Grandmother's wedding dress that she had on—it was white wrought with silver—Madame Bodisco had on what is called silver brocade, but it would not compare for richness with Mrs. Haskins. . . .

There was a Miss Polk, a cousin of the President, there promenading with her Brother—of an uncertain age—she might be 40 or 60—you know— . . . & just imagine, dressed in a dirty yellow silk over white—open in front & caught up with roses—short sleeves & low neck—& to cap the climax a whole bird as large (the plumage) as a rooster on top of the head of that tall strange looking woman. Her head & plume could be seen in all parts of the room—it was perfectly ridiculous. . . .

I have been dreading a visit from Mrs. Royal ever since I came, & at last have had it. Friday morning immediately after breakfast & while the girl was making my bed, a loud knock at the door, which was soon thrown wide open by Mrs. Hubbard, who announced "Mrs. Anne Royal and Ladies". She did not enter—I mean Mrs. Hubbard, but shut them in. I gave a look at them & supposed she was playing a joke, & that she had introduced three beggar women. But soon saw by Mr. White's manner that the real Simon-Pure was before me. I asked her to be seated & her attendants also—one of whom had a bundle and looked precisely like a common beggar. Mrs. Royal herself was clad in the most common apparrel and very dirty—if she ever had any mind she has lost it—She kept up a disconnected conversation for a while & then took her leave, Mrs. White going with her and introducing her to Mr. and Mrs. Hunt. I wish you could have seen Mrs. Hunt when I announced Mrs. Royal. Her face was half a yard long & both hands raised. I laughed till I cried. Mrs. Royal called first on Mrs. Ashby who, thinking she would have some fun, sent for Mrs. Hubbard—the latter ran in, thinking a paper or book was wanted & was immediately introduced to Mrs. Royal. She, being quick witted, saw through it at once & greeted Mrs. Royal very kindly, & says: "Why, you have come to spend the day with the Ashbys—Mrs. A. will be delighted—I beg you will stay". The tables were turned at once. Mrs. A. looking blank enough. But Mrs. H. had not had fun enough, so she must introduce me as I have told you. We are all expecting to come out in the next Huntress.

Washington Feb. 10, Tuesday afternoon.

. . . Such a day as it was yesterday in the House! I had to go among the multitude, for tho' I cannot hear, yet I like to be in the hubbub and confusion & witness the excitement. The ladies' gallery was crowded to overflowing. Every gentleman was ordered out, even those that were with Ladies—Side galleries & gents. galleries full likewise—When Mr. Adams spoke all the members crowded around leaving their seats & taking chairs directly in front. I believe *all* the foreign Ministers, the Secretaries, Packenham & Buchanan were present & think the judges of the Supreme Court were behind the *latter* after 3 oclock.

. . . Oh, what a life! I am now preparing to go to Mason's—I supposed I was all ready, but hearing that there are 8 hundred invitations out, & of course a jam, I have changed my plans as to dress—having no desire to spoil a dress—& so am fixing up some little trimmings, which although not much, yet require time. Everybody is at the Senate today—but I had too much to do—besides I do not hear much even there. In the Court Room I hear very well, & if I ever *get time* mean to go often.

I was regretting the party tonight and another at Atlick's on Friday to which we are invited, but Mr. White says no.—"I like them—I like the frolicks well." One comfort, they will be over in less than ? month, at lent, I am told.

. . . The weather has been fine for three days past—clear bright sun—but cold—Went to hear Mr. Sproh on Sunday—preached well—as usual Church very full—rather more than I have ever seen. There is an appearance of solemnity and devotion in the regular church goers there which you do not always see.

. . . This house is now chock full—ever so many *young* Ladies & some quite pretty. I can give you no description now—& dear me unless my husband gets home soon I can not send this today. I requested him to leave me some franks but he forgot it. . . .

XVII

SONGS AND SCIENCE

PRESIDENT FILLMORE did not take up his residence in the White House for some months after he became President, delaying in order that Mrs. Taylor and Mrs. Bliss might not be hurried in their sad leave-taking. He can scarcely be called a self-made man, for the reason that so much of him was made by his wife, at a cost that neither of them regretted. They threw no mystery about their early poverty; nor did the President's father, when that hale old farmer came to visit at the White House. Somebody asked his formula for raising a son, to which he answered promptly, "Cradle him in a sap-trough, sir!"

The sap-trough held most of the luxuries of the elder Fillmore's household; but ambition cost little and yielded an excellent return on the investment. Somehow the son managed to secure by the time he was twenty-two a license to practise law; and after a long, impecunious courtship married the tall, auburn-haired school-teacher who helped lay the foundation of his success. Walking fully abreast, they set out together to make the most of life, and when they entered the White House the wife probably had fewer misgivings than her husband.

They found it singularly devoid of books, and it is to Mrs. Fillmore that her successors are indebted for the library above the oval Blue Parlor. It was a nondescript room with a tobacco-defiled matting on the floor; but, being experienced in stretching small resources to cover much ground, she set about its transformation. The removal of the matting, in the interest of cleanliness, disclosed a Brussels carpet of wonderful design over which baskets too frail for their burden scattered roses of enormous size. Mrs. Fillmore sent to Buffalo for the family harp and piano, shut off, with screens, portions of the room that could not be made presentable, kindled a wood fire upon the hearth, and invited to the cozy place some chosen members of Congress.

They found the President's wife a very genuine, sweet-faced woman in cap and side-curls, who seemed to care about the insides of books, instead of using them as dear Mrs. Madison had done, chiefly as an entering wedge for conversation. At first the one daughter, Mary Abigail, was absent, having pledged herself to teach for a year in the school from which she was recently graduated. After she joined the family, there was music as well as talk about books, and the guests admitted to the intimacy of the upper sitting-room helped try out "In the Desert a Fountain is Springing," and that very latest of Stephen Foster's compositions, "The Old Folks at Home." It seemed only decent to repay such pleasant, unpretentious hospitality by putting through Congress a small appropriation for books to furnish the White-House library.

The apartments below-stairs were dull enough; only the bare knees of a Highlander, or the presence of Elisha Kane the Arctic explorer added chilly excitement to official courtesy; but tradition credits this family with introducing two thrilling novelties into the domestic regions of the White House—its earliest bath-tub and its first kitchen range.

The machinery for a shower had been installed in Jackson's time, but the new marvel was a coffin-like affair of mahogany lined with zinc, such as Adam Thompson of Cincinnati exhibited with pride to the guests at his Christmas party in 1843. Inspired by curiosity and emulation, four of them had taken a plunge and had rashly talked about the experience afterward; and a veritable war of words raged in newspapers and common councils about the moral aspect and the healthfulness of the practice. An ordinance prohibiting bathing between November 1st and March 15th failed of passage in Philadelphia by only two votes; and Boston actually had upon her books for seventeen years an ordinance making bathing unlawful except on medical advice.

President Fillmore was progressive, if he had been cradled in a sap-trough. He succumbed to the charms of the original bath-tub when on a visit to Cincinnati, and at his request the Secretary of War invited bids for the novel contrivance and one was installed in the White House which continued to do excellent service down to Cleveland's administration.

The kitchen range was likewise a subject of bitter controversy, though the area of disturbance was limited. The colored cook, who had seen occupants of the White House come and go for thirty years and had prepared meals for all of them in front of an open fire, would have none of it. After the invention was installed against her wishes she refused to touch it, until the President of the United States resolved himself into a committee of ways and means, visited the Patent Office, mastered the secrets of the stove's drafts and flues, and personally undertook her education.

It is not strange that Fillmore took a lively interest in the schools of the city. Once at least he distributed the annual prizes on that great day of the year when the various schools gathered at the City Hall and marched from there to the Capitol, each with its banner and motto, to the music of the Marine Band. At the Capitol a member of Congress made an oration; Mayor Lenox read out, very loud, the names of the boys and girls to be honored; and as these went forward in turn, blushing and embarrassed, the President placed the medals around their necks, speaking to each "with kindness, affability and encouragement." Could anything be more grand for the children, or more agreeable to the kindly man who owed so much himself to schools and schooling?

It was during the sojourn in the White House of this family, whose members were more attractive in private than in public, that the town received two of its most distinguished guests and experienced two of those whirlwinds of excitement to which Americans are prone. The first was late in 1851, when Kossuth arrived. Crowds stood patiently outside his hotel, waiting for a sight of him, and when he appeared, cheered themselves hoarse. Some inkling of his personal habits must have preceded him, for the hotel where rooms had been engaged was not the new and correct Willard's, but Brown's down near Center Market, a comfortable easy-going place which had been famous years before as the Indian Queen. Here he maintained semi-regal state, keeping a body-guard of armed and oddly clad youngsters always in attendance.

The Government at first shared the popular enthusiasm for the

Hungarian hero and Congress gave him a grand banquet seasoned with much oratory. But when it was discovered that all his utterances, private and public, were to the same effect—that it was the duty of the United States to embroil itself in the affairs of Europe—he became less popular. In fact, he outstayed his welcome and it was with a sense of relief that Washington finally saw him depart. This was not altogether because he presumed to lecture us on our duty and the meaning of our Constitution. There were more personal reasons. Madame Kossuth, unable to overcome her distrust of American food, had sniffed suspiciously at every dish offered her, which hurt the feelings of hosts and cooks; and in addition the members of Kossuth's half-savage body-guard had developed a destructive habit of going to bed in their boots and spurs.

The other guest, though a foreigner, left no such unpleasant memories behind her. Disappointment, if there was any, occurred at the beginning of her visit and speedily vanished. She had been almost over-advertised. "Jenny Lind, the new slave bill, and spirit rappings," Miss Bremer wrote, were the standing topics in the newspapers. Feeling that it would never do to allow Miss Lind to leave the country without singing in Washington, several of the city's business men hastily threw together a Music Hall on the ruins of the National Theater. This was a bit of advertising after Barnum's own heart, and we may be sure the rooms engaged for her were the best Willard had to offer. It may have been Willard's other guests who were at first disappointed, seeing a rather stocky young woman with blue eyes and pale hair, neither so young nor so handsome as her portraits had led them to expect. She had dignity and sweetness of expression, rather than mere beauty of feature, and she acknowledged her twenty-nine years.

The new Music Hall was flimsy and very redolent of fresh plaster and paint when she appeared on the nights of December 15 and 16, 1850, but it was packed to the doors, though tickets sold at the New York prices of five and seven dollars each. Whether or not Washington women, like their New York sisters, stayed frugally at home and her audience was seven eighths male, we are not informed. But we are told it began assembling as early as six o'clock, and was "the largest, most brilliant and most gratified audience which ever assembled at any public entertainment in this city." After this modest beginning the "Globe" exhausted the dictionary's entire supply of adjectives.

Private letters were no whit behind the newspapers in enthusiasm. "Imagine the clearest, sweetest, loveliest notes of the æolean harp, . . . and a compelling power when she chose, that seemed unlimited," wrote one enthusiast. The magic was not all in her voice!

> What will you think if I tell you that her manner of courtesying more than once brought tears to my eyes? . . . It seemed as if she could not get low enough! She bowed her head almost if not quite to her knees: it seemed to my fancy as if a certain feeling of humility and sense of gratitude, and the desire of acknowledgment were laboring to express themselves. . . . Her face is extremely good . . . a very noble fine expression of countenance.

Since she had this wonderful power in addition to an inspired voice, it is not at all strange that the best-remembered incident of her stay in Washington happened as it did. In opening the second part of one of her concerts, she sang "Hail Columbia." The story goes that the Russian minister entertained at dinner that evening, and that his guests, including Webster, reached the National only in time to hear this song. Webster was so carried away that he rose at the end of the first verse and joined in the chorus, though his wife tugged frantically at his coat to make him sit down. At the end of every stanza his voice joined in.

> As the last notes of the song died away Webster, . . . with his hand upon his heart, made a profound bow to the singer. Jenny Lind, blushing at the honor, courtesied to the floor, while the audience applauded to the echo. Webster, not to be outdone in politeness, bowed again; Lind recourtesied; the House again applauded, and this was repeated nine times.

It was indeed fortunate for all concerned that in addition to being a great artist Jenny Lind was a thorough lady; for Webster's musical education had been sadly neglected.

President Fillmore called upon Miss Lind at the Willard, on the morning after her arrival, and, as she was out, left his visiting-card, like an ordinary mortal. She was all in a flutter on her return, and of the opinion that she must rush instantly to the White House; but Barnum persuaded her that a President of the United States did not "command" the movements of foreign singers, though crowned heads might presume to do so, and that it would be in much better taste to return the visit next day. We can imagine her, before she left town, sitting with the music-loving Fillmores for an hour in front of the wood fire in the library, a charming figure in her silver-gray gown and pale-blue hat with its black veil; moving over, perhaps, to touch the old piano, and at last coming away in love with republican institutions and leaving happiness behind her.

The great sopranos of both the first and the last half of the nineteenth century were heard in Washington at almost the same time, for it was also during Fillmore's term that Adelina Patti, then a little girl of twelve, sang at a charity concert to the piano accompaniment of young Henry Watterson.

We are told that Millard Fillmore and Franklin Pierce, the outgoing and incoming Presidents, attended Thackeray's readings in 1853 "arm in arm," to his great satisfaction. We are not informed how either of these gentlemen regarded the theater. Probably like most of the other Presidents, they had no great enthusiasm for it, but deemed it well to appear at performances from time to time for publicity's sake. Even Polk did so, constrained though he must have been against it, both by his own nature and his wife's strong religious convictions. William Henry Harrison's name is the only one missing from the list up to the time of the Civil War, and his short term of office probably accounts for the omission, rather than lack of inclination.

Yet, in spite of continuous official patronage, the theater had a dreary time in Washington for many years after the first unlucky venture in Blodgett's Hotel. On that unhappy night a sudden freshet carried away the newly painted scenery, which had been laid outdoors to dry, and the downpour caused the show to open to such a sparse house that a line in Mr. Law's specially written prologue, "I fear you 've stowed yourselves away too thick," had a most ironic sound.

Our rather censorious national attitude toward player-folk in

Courtesy B. S. Reynolds Company, Inc.

THE SMITHSONIAN INSTITUTION

those years had something to do with the theater's uphill path in Washington. Distances and bad roads, and the chance of finding the theater dark on arrival and the performance "postponed on account of the weather," increased the handicap; but the most potent reason was that townsfolk and strangers were engrossed in the real events that were taking place. They were acting out their own political drama with the whole city as a stage: why go to the theater and look at mummery? It was not until the middle of Jackson's first term that the drama gained sufficient hold to warrant a regular winter season, plays before that time having been given by traveling companies, or in summer by actors who made Philadelphia their winter headquarters.

Then suddenly Washington had an attack of home-grown drama, producing a cycle of plays historic in theme and romantic in treatment, whatever their other merits or demerits may have been. These were acted amid much interest, at the newest theater in town, with the aid of military music and realistic properties loaned by the Government. The first, presented in February, 1836, was called "Pocahontas or the First Settlers of Virginia," and came from the pen of that eccentric gentleman George Washington Parke Custis, who had inherited Arlington and lived there, making life delightful for chance visitors but insupportable for his own family. This incursion into drama was like his other enterprises, notable of its kind though the kind might be questioned. A certain Mr. Baldwin who sat through "Pocahontas" called it the most perfect thing of the sort he had ever seen, and then added that he had never before witnessed such a supremely ridiculous play.

Spurred to emulation by "Pocahontas," General Alexander Macomb offered "Pontiac or the Siege of Detroit," which was presented early in March with lavish use of United States Marines in the martial scenes. In April of the same year, Mr. Custis took a hand again with "Montgomerie or the Orphan of the Wreck." Then, zest for private theatricals having run down, he rested on his laurels until the following season, when, as a sort of farewell to the retiring President, "The Eighth of January or Hurrah for the Boys in Blue," was given, as near the anniversary of the Battle of New Orleans as possible.

Never again has the town had such an orgy of dramatic production.

The great actors who have toured the country for the past century have come for longer or shorter engagements, and fared well or ill according to capricious chance; and those not great but merely popular have done likewise. A list of their names coupled with those of famous men who have sought distraction in Washington theaters would form a curious pattern. Lincoln, snatching an hour's relaxation from the burden of war, and Wilson's unsmiling face looking down on the vaudeville stage, come instantly to mind.

Many of the notable theater folk, from Tom Thumb and his bride to giants physically and artistically, have received courtesies from the White House. Poor Tom Thumb, carried moaning from his coach into a fashionable dentist's office, not only gives a very human touch to one of his visits, but sounds a note in Barnum's progressive advertising.

Though it is invidious to mention names when it is impossible to select even among the great ones, America's best-loved actor must not be passed by. It was in the old and afterward discredited theater on Louisiana Avenue that Joe Jefferson, a toddler of four, began his conscious theatrical life. His father was for a time manager and lived in rooms at the back of the "rickety old frame building with a broad gable facing a wide avenue," a place full of dim shadows, but warm, as the boy remembered it, with family affection. It was in Washington, also, that he made his first venture with "Rip Van Winkle," at Carusi's two years before the Civil War, when the play was the merest sketch groping its way toward the perfection it afterward attained.

Nor must we forget a scene probably never enacted in another theater in the world, a night when a Washington audience saw North American Indians in the odd rôle of patrons of the drama so carried away by a white woman's acting that they rose and threw gifts at her feet with Latin abandon. This was in Van Buren's time. In a box sat a delegation of Sioux and Iowas, Sacs and Foxes, only one of whom had visited the East before; while scattered through the audience were many others who had come to Washington for an important conference. Some were dressed in their native finery, some in coats of military cut and hats with silver bands that the Government had issued to them.

On the stage Miss Nelson, a favorite actress, was making her last appearance as "The Mountain Sylph." Interest quickened as she descended her stage mountain and began to move through the maze of the canvas rocks and trees, appearing and disappearing with mystifying suddenness. The Indians beamed with delight. A young Yankton snatched an eagle feather from his war-bonnet and threw it on the stage. She picked it up and fastened it in her dress, amid applause. A few moments later an aged Sac chief snatched off his whole head-dress and made her a present of it. Another Yankton offered his splendid robe of white wolfskins, and two more presented buffalo robes, the last one bidding his interpreter say that he gave it "to the beauty of Washington."

She made a little speech in return, expressing regret that she could not thank them in their own tongue, promised always to remember them as her friends, and, advancing to the stage box presented each of the men there with a great ostrich plume "which they immediately placed in their head-dresses." Then reascending her mountain for her final exit she lingered for a moment facing them, with the war-bonnet's splendid arch of eagle's feathers over her brow.

Washington's interest in science has been more steady, if not expressed in such spectacular fashion as these bursts of enthusiasm for drama. All of it centers in and radiates from the Smithsonian, whose red towers and pointed arches date from that period locally so drab and nationally so romantic, Polk's administration. To get it in proper perspective, we must turn back once more to the city's quickened life after the British fire. In addition to material activities, like rebuilding, the city felt many needs and tried to meet them all. The women organized the Protestant Orphan Asylum, their first concerted charity. The men formed two associations, the American Colonization Society, for those whose hearts were troubled about slavery, and the Metropolitan Society, whose scope was wider if not so deep. This had its birth at McKeowin's Hotel in June, 1816, when "a few of the citizens of Washington, impressed with the importance of collecting and distributing the various vegetable products of this and other countries," met and organized. It began with a membership of about ninety, made up of men of all professions and none—preachers, bankers, doctors, editors, gentlemen of leisure, army and navy men and assorted government officials—and elected as its first president Dr. Edward Cutbush, an appropriate choice, since its object was primarily agricultural. It did not stop there, however, but planned to have a fine cabinet of minerals, to build a museum, and to collect a library.

Its practical work was begun in a practical way by soliciting from congressmen specimens of grain, fruits, dyestuffs, medicinal plants—anything, in short, indigenous to their districts or grown therein, which might prove of benefit to mankind. The next thing it did was to take a more comprehensive name, the Columbian Institute, and to apply to Congress for permission to use about three hundred acres of the Mall in growing plants from the seeds and specimens received. Congress gave the society a twenty-year charter, the use of a room in the Capitol, and leave to establish its garden on public ground lying between the Capitol park and the Tiber, part of which must have been excellent for aquatic plants. This tract the society improved with seats and paths and hedges, making it one of the few civilized-looking open spaces in the city. And it held weekly meetings during sessions of Congress, at which the members read papers on literary and scientfic subjects and listened to reports from its secretary about his correspondence with pen-and-ink acquaintances, on such diverse topics as the best way to make models of fruit in wax and the discovery of a new kind of hippopotamus in Central Africa.

The treasurer was the only member who got no fun out of it, finding himself beset from the first with the difficulty all treasurers face in this town where many people stay and few reside. While they join societies gladly, they feel the necessity for keeping home ties unsevered, and are apt to regard their Washington obligations in rather stepfatherly fashion. The dues of the Columbian Institute were only five dollars a year, but the treasurer found them hard to collect, and it was embarrassing and often unprofitable to send dunning notes after distinguished men who forgot to pay before leaving. The roll of early members, with intimate addenda by the treasurer, is an interesting document now in the Library of Congress.

This society held in its membership the germ not only of our Smithsonian and great National Museum but of the innumerable specialized groups medical, philosophical, horticultural, anthropological, biological, and every other kind ending in "ic" or "al" that has since flourished here, not forgetting the Phrenological Society, which exchanged skull measurements with Edinburgh in 1827, and, in return for what Adams called "a Golgotha of their great men," sent, as examples of good American heads, the dimensions of those of Chief-Justice Marshall, Calhoun, Clay, Webster, Adams, Barbour, Dr. Rush, and many more.

Shortly before the Columbian Society's twenty-year charter expired in 1838, the Capitol grounds were enlarged in a manner to swallow up the plot of ground it had been cultivating, and Congress flatly refused to refund the fifteen hundred dollars it had spent on improvements, though the society explained that the money would be used to erect a building in which to hold meetings and store its acquisitions of books, minerals, and works fondly believed to be of art. Perhaps it was the report that this collection was to be cast homeless upon the world that inspired an ambitious if not well-educated citizen named John Varden to send out a neat card in the summer of 1836, informing the public generally that he was "in search of curiosities for the purpose of establishing a museum in Washington City," and inviting sympathizers to leave their donations, properly labeled, "at Sarah Shidd's, Fifth Street, City Hall."

Enclosing one of these cards, he wrote a personal letter to the Columbian Institute, wherein he enlarged on his qualifications as curator, particularly of dead animals, and gave assurance that "in the care of birds or beasts that are a grate Deal of trouble to take care of I will do my best to keep them in good order always subject to the orders of your association." The museum, he explained optimistically, was to be built from funds solicited "when Congress is gone, and the citizens are more at leisure." Though the Columbian Institute remained cold, the public response must have been flattering, for a notice of the museum, with the adjectives "entertaining and valuable," stands in the *Vade Mecum,* that list of forty-one places of interest printed by the "Intelligencer" for the guidance of visitors to Harrison's inauguration.

Instead of making John Varden its legatee, the Columbian Institute slept a trance-like sleep for two years, then resurrected itself, changed its name again, and began a new career as the National Institute, getting itself assigned rooms in the Patent Office and entrusted with the custody of government collections that had been accumulating ever since Lewis and Clark returned from the West.

Its secretary, Francis Markoe, junior, became a very busy and important person in his own eyes, a sort of liaison officer between politics and science. Not only did his correspondence with all quarters of the globe reach the total of two hundred letters a month; he acknowledged "munificent donations" from Eastern potentates with a flourish of language suited to the occasion, adding in an aside to the consul who acted as intermediary that he was instructing the Administration how to behave, and had intimated to the Secretary of State the propriety of drawing on the Secret Fund of the State Department for suitable gifts in return.

The most useful of Mr. Markoe's tasks was writing diplomatically worded letters refusing gifts that were not wanted. His usual formula was that the society, being yet in its infancy, was unable to care for so valuable a present. But occasionally when writing to one of his own countrymen he gave tact a vacation and told him exactly what he thought of him. Of what earthly use, he asked, was the skin of a female elk received at an exceptionally busy time, badly rotted, with eyes damaged and both ears missing? The agent must understand that when rats had gnawed a skin the society could do nothing with it. The proper treatment was to immerse a pelt at once in a keg of whisky in which arsenic or corrosive sublimate had been dissolved.

With such a practical and efficient secretary the institute flourished. In the heyday of its prosperity it rejoiced in a membership of sixteen hundred; and in 1845 it had the courage to invite to the city Washington's first congress of men of science. Then, quite suddenly, the National Institute faded out of existence. This was because the Smithsonian came into being in a manner as casual as it was picturesque.

An Englishman, learned and lonely, died in Genoa in 1829, surrounded by the arid wealth his ducal relatives bestowed upon him for keeping out of their way. While, obviously, he was not to blame for the bar sinister that made his presence unwelcome to them, the family ties he forged for himself gave him, apparently, small satisfaction. As a matter of justice he willed his fortune to the "nephew" who was in all probability his natural son; but he cared more for chemistry and mineralogy than for his own kind and added the proviso that if the young man died without issue the whole property was to be devoted to scientific uses.

It is said that a fit of ill temper diverted the bequest to America. His first intention had been to leave it to the Royal Society of London, but when that society refused to publish one of his papers in its "Philosophical Transactions," he altered his will and made the United States the beneficiary instead, though he had never visited the country and, so far as is known, had never been greatly interested in it. His only directions were that the money should be used for founding "at Washington under the name of the Smithsonian Institution an establishment for the increase and diffusion of knowledge among men." Beyond that no plan was laid down, nor was any scrap of paper ever found to shed light upon what was in the donor's mind.

So long as Smithson's heir lived the discussion was, to use a time-honored phrase, "purely academic." But the question of accepting such a bequest roused great interest and strong opposition, both in and out of Congress, on the ground that the increase and diffusion of knowledge was no part of the Government's concern. Conservatives who took this stand deplored the strange new by-paths into which officials were daily being led—a tendency manifest not only in the pressure brought to bear by Professor Morse and his fellow inventors for grants of federal money, but by the establishment in various government departments of bureaus under the direction of men riding scientific hobbies who were paid out of the United States Treasury. The first steps might seem harmless, almost necessary, but there was no telling where they might lead.

As a fine example of this they pointed to the Coast Survey. Nobody could object to running correct boundary lines or to the building of lighthouses, work that began almost with the beginning of the government, but which had developed with the years into bureaus that indulged in all sorts of fancy higher mathematics! There was now a Geological Survey in addition to a Coast Survey; and as if keeping an eye on the waters and the earth and the voters of this continent were not enough, old Professor Hassler of the leonine head and irascible temper, who had been invited from abroad originally to help run boundary lines, was in charge of a Naval Observatory full of telescopes and instruments of which he took inordinate care. Congress had more trouble with men of his type than with all the lunatic inventors and half-crazed artists combined. Once they gained a foothold in some department, they assumed the right to stay there forever, and to hear them argue before a congressional committee one would think the fate of the country depended on nourishing their little specialty.

So the conservatives reasoned. It was hard to predict who would be conservative and who radical on this point. Most of the Presidents had been liberal without regard to personal bent or previous training. Washington, though no scholar in his youth, had dreamed of a great university as part of the equipment of the nation's capital. Jefferson conveniently forgot all his arguments for states-rights the moment they clashed with what his eager mind conceived to be the greater glory of the nation or the dissemination of knowledge among men. John Quincy Adams called attention in his very first message to Congress to what was being done in science abroad, and expressed the opinion that it would be casting away the bounties of Providence if the legislators allowed themselves to be "palsied" by the will of constituents who were narrow-minded. Jackson, though politically inclined to oppose everything Adams favored, welcomed the Smithsonian bequest when Smithson's heir died during his Presidency and the matter changed to the immediate practical question of accepting or declining it.

In spite of a strong undercurrent of conservatism, of which J. C. Calhoun made himself spokesman, Congress voted to receive the legacy—a decision which went a long way toward clarifying the national policy, which up to that time had been to encourage a clandestine affair between Government and Science, rather than an open and honorable alliance.

With gratifying promptness, England notified the United States that 104,960 golden sovereigns awaited its pleasure, and Richard Rush, son of Franklin's old Philadelphia friend, crossed the ocean to get them, bringing them back on an English clipper-ship. Reminted into American eagles, they amounted to about half a million dollars. After that was done the Government seemed inclined to forget all about them.

Had Jefferson been alive he would have busied himself happily devising a plan to use them. A few years earlier Franklin's voice would have had much weight, but with these great men dead there seemed nobody of their stamp to direct the matter, and for six years nothing was done. Mr. Rush, with growing distress, pointed out that suspicion of the Government's honesty was gaining wide credence abroad—a view the more likely to grow because a donation for the education of orphans made to our Government fully twelve years before, by a Frenchman named Girard, had not been put to use. Mr. Rush's advice was that the Smithsonian bequest "be engrafted upon the National Institute."

Almost the opposite of this occurred. Instead of the Smithsonian fund being grafted upon the local organization, the Smithsonian Institution came into being by Act of Congress in 1846 and almost at once absorbed the strong members of the National Institute in its organization. Its governing body of regents, made up of three senators, three members of Congress, and six representative citizens, with the Vice-President of the United States as chairman, soon developed a healthy difference of opinion as to whether the increase or the diffusion of knowledge were the more important. In other words, whether the money was to be spent to encourage original research or for publishing memoirs on scientific subjects.

It was decided that in either case the institution must have a home, and the earliest large outlay was for the erection of that red-stone castle down on the Mall, for which President Polk laid the cornerstone on the first of May, 1847. It seems almost laughable that the builders of a house for Science, youngest handmaid of Government, should have chosen a style of architecture harking back to the time when chemistry and alchemy and medicine and magic were hopelessly entangled. The narrow windows of the "Romanesque as used in Europe during the eleventh and twelfth centuries" were ill adapted to a study whose chief aim is to let in the light; nor were the rooms destined to the private use of the family of the secretary of the Smithsonian, its actual head and director, convenient for nineteenth-century housekeeping, as those were aware who visited the families of Professor Henry and his successor Professor Baird.

What influenced the choice of this style, used in America up to that time only for churches, would be hard to guess, unless it were some obscure suggestion from Smithson's own story. Whatever it was, it had its inspirational value for the youngsters of Washington, who were not inconvenienced by living in it. To those familiar with the time-worn European castles, of which this palace of rosy stone with its turrets and deep-set arched windows was a naïve paraphrase, it was an absurdity. One called it "a fit home for Don Quixote." But, standing aloof in its park-like seclusion of grass and forest trees, it became for many of us embodied romance, investing science with a mysterious charm the years have been powerless to dispel.

It was in Jackson's time that the bequest was accepted; a year after Polk became President the corner-stone was laid. By means of the bulletins of John Sessford, it is possible to follow its growth almost stone by stone. By 1848 enough had been done to show that it was to be "a great improvement to the city." By 1850 only one tower remained to be built. Indeed, it went up so rapidly that the carpenters and stone-masons of the city protested, predicting that the whole thing would be a ruin inside of fifty years.

Like the older portions of the Capitol, it seems to have been deliberately finished in a temporary manner to permit more speedy use. The record for 1853 notes that the center of the building "has been entirely remodelled in solid work." The bulletin for 1855 reports the removal of much woodwork and the completion of the great hall, two hundred feet long by fifty wide, which was to be occupied first of all by the Mechanics' Institute Fair, a sort of temporary Patent Office exhibit with advertising thrown in.

On the different scientific bureaus born in the red-stone castle, there is no space to enlarge. The Agricultural Department was organized in Polk's day; the Weather Bureau, whose reports are so eagerly awaited and universally abused, had its practical beginning here, though its real beginnings may be traced back to 1817, in the observations sent to headquarters by registers of land-offices. It was Professor Henry, the first secretary of the Smithsonian, who used Morse's new telegraph to collect such reports and combine them into a weather-map.

Professor Henry belonged to the party that believed the diffusion of knowledge the important part of the Smithsonian's work. A museum and art-gallery and library, each of which had been established before he took charge, he regarded as things well enough in themselves but of mere local concern. He even resented the money spent on the red-stone palace, contending that the Smithsonian's real work could be performed as well in an unpretentious rented house. And, as the years passed, he quietly but effectively shouldered the art-gallery and the library out of the way. A fire which destroyed the central part of the building in 1865 demolished the Indian portraits which formed its entire art collection. The library was in an end of the building not damaged, but the hall in which scientific lectures were given had been gutted, and this gave him an opportunity. He persuaded the Library of Congress to take the books, both to insure their safety and to give him a new auditorium; and the Corcoran Gallery, established meanwhile, relieved the Smithsonian of further concern with works of art. Simon Newcomb the astronomer was of the opinion that Professor Henry would gladly have dispensed with the National Museum also if he could have found an excuse.

The museum grew rapidly after Professor Henry's death, and has spread out now to include the Zoo, with its hundreds of acres of woodland park watered by Rock Creek, where well-tended live creatures supplement and replace the rat-gnawed skins that so roused Francis Markoe's ire.

The museum collections alone have increased to fill and overflow and submerge two great additional buildings, and it would be rash to say how many smaller ones. Indeed, it is difficult now to locate at first glance the red castle that stood in isolated splendor in its park. Close beside it is a monstrosity of red brick and blue-and-yellow ornamental tiles erected during the doubtful artistic period of the late seventies, to house left-over treasures from the Centennial. This is now known as the Old National Museum, to distinguish it from the huge New Museum, fortunately separated from it by a merciful stretch of trees and lawn, which stands in its white-marble correctness, stately and impersonal, waiting to fit into the plan for a glorified Washington that is some day to make the city all that L'Enfant dreamed it would be—and more.

The exhibits found in these various buildings embrace literally everything from A to Z, with detours for each letter of the alphabet. The annual report "on the progress and condition" of the National Museum, which is, after all, merely the show-room of a few departments of the Smithsonian's activity, makes an imposing, not to say appalling volume. When the eye travels through a list of a single year's additions to its treasures, not classified by subject but entered under the names of donors in alphabetical order, it is hard to decide whether one is reading an excellent jest-book or a homily on worldly pomp and knowledge.

"Thirty-two specimens of rusts." Surely a museum is the one spot on earth where that form of corruption is welcomed!

"Paintings by old masters," valued as almost priceless, yet which would be speedily consigned to the dust-bin if known to be the work of aspiring students.

"Materials and apparatus of the transcontinental telephone line on the occasion of the first telephonic conversation between New York and San Francisco, January 15, 1915"; a "sample of stomach contents taken from the alimentary canal of a basking shark"; autographs of people famous and infamous in history (which, by rights, ought to be in the Manuscript Division of the Library of Congress); miscellaneous Chinese objects including "three wax balls containing pills"; "a piece of stone from the dungeon at Rouen, where Joan of Arc was imprisoned," and a "rhinoceros-hide whip used to keep order among the bearers in Colonel Roosevelt's Safari" are all in a single volume, where they jostle the "incomplete skeleton of a child."

The force of Smithson's bequest gains centripetal power with the years, and matter from every corner of the universe hurls itself toward this haven and resting-place. Correspondents to the number of fifty thousand send letters from the ends of the earth, with a precision of aim that causes Mr. Markoe's little pile of two hundred a month to shrivel to invisibility. One wonders who, if anybody, has fallen heir to that part of his job which consisted in writing polite letters saying "No."

And all this is in addition to departments and bureaus that have an independent or practically independent existence, like the huge Bureau of Standards on the outskirts of the city, covering many times the area of the original sandstone building; the Bureau of Ethnology; the Astrophysical Observatory; the wide-spreading activities of the Agricultural Department, with its field of purely scientific research on the one hand, balanced on the other by its large experimental farm near Arlington; and so on.

It was as far back as 1887 that some mortal with a passion for statistics figured that the District of Columbia held one scientist for every five hundred inhabitants; a percentage which has doubtless immensely increased since. While some are personages whose names are spoken with respect the world over, the majority are unknown to fame—"nice young men without dress suits," as a pretty girl sighed, thinking of the boon their society would confer on the average Washington drawing-room, top-heavy with mothers and daughters.

And every one of these hard-working anonymous youths knows to-day secrets of nature for a knowledge of which Franklin and Jefferson would have imperiled their immortal souls.

XVIII

A REPUBLICAN COURT

BUCHANAN, the last President of the old régime, was a lawyer by profession but an office-holder by inclination—his own and that of his constituents. He had been a private citizen for only four years out of the forty that preceded his term as President. These were the years when Taylor and Fillmore occupied the Presidential chair, and even then his life had not been so private but that the astute Van Buren, learning that Franklin Pierce had sent Buchanan as Minister to England, called the appointment "nothing less than the removal of a rival believed to be dangerous." Perhaps President Pierce was not altogether wise in removing him so far; for in England he was saved the necessity of antagonizing either North or South by taking sides on the Kansas-Nebraska issue, and he returned in time to be comfortably elected in the campaign of 1856.

A New York reporter, who chose to leave praise to others, lamented a growing tendency to make inauguration ceremonies "a raree-show after the manner of an imperial coronation," but the accounts of the inaugural parade are much more suggestive of a circus, Buchanan's carriage being sandwiched between a car drawn by six horses carrying the Goddess of Liberty on a pedestal and a float representing a full-rigged ship manned by sailors from the Navy Yard. A calliope seems to have been the only circus adjunct missing. At the ball which lasted until four o'clock in the morning 15,000 people consumed $3000 worth of wine, a pyramid of cake four feet high, 400 gallons of oysters, 75 hams, 1300 quarts of ice-cream, 500 quarts of jelly, and other things in proportion.

The temptation is strong to look for some connection between this gargantuan feast and the mysterious National Hotel sickness that followed close upon the heels of the inauguration. But that would be treating the malady too lightly. It developed among the guests of the hotel where the President-elect and his party had lodged, and claimed several lives, his nephew being one of the victims. The cause may have been ptomaine poisoning or a contaminated water-supply; party malice strove to distort it into a crime, and to fix it upon the Free-Soilers as a sensational attempt to poison the new President and his advisers.

The truth is that by 1857 Washington had gone beyond the danger point in its civic housekeeping. Work upon the new aqueduct had continued through Pierce's administration, but showed no result as yet. The Potomac flats were increasingly noxious, and nothing was done about it. The town had more than fifty thousand inhabitants but no system of sewerage—and all the drinking water came from wells or small springs in the hills back of the city. The National Hotel where the illness occurred faced a swamp. The real wonder is that after the influx of inauguration crowds the visitation was not more severe.

People began to talk about such matters, however, which was a first step toward understanding them even though the public mind might be hazy as to cause and effect. For example, the building of extensive gas-works in a locality suggestively called Foggy Bottom, where G Street N. W. plunges into the Potomac, failed to "disinfect" the neighborhood as optimists had predicted it would. The medicinal value of the gas may have been neutralized by turning Tobias Lear's old warehouse into a factory for fertilizer. A real achievement was the appointment of a salaried Commissioner of Health to supplement and coöperate with the volunteer boards of health in each ward.

More and better police were much needed, for lawlessness had been on the increase for some years. This was particularly evident at municipal elections, especially in the years when the Know-nothing party was active. At those times a sort of terrorism seemed to pervade whole sections even in broad daylight, and Senators Seward and Douglas stated that after dark streets were so infested with rough characters that law-abiding people kept within doors.

Members of the old fire-companies were largely responsible.

Some of the misdeeds were merely pranks. In 1854 the watchman of the Washington Monument had been locked in his little hut while "persons unknown" possessed themselves of a stone from the Temple of Concord at Rome,—sent as a gift by Pope Pius IX to be built into the memorial,—broke it up, and threw the pieces into the river.

The situation became more serious when the same element tried to change the complexion of the school board and to capture the office of mayor. It made itself a real power, not only in District politics but in Congress, when District affairs were under discussion. In the year of Buchanan's election, though Democrats, Republicans, and Free-Soilers united on a single candidate for mayor, nominating Dr. Magruder, one of the best-loved physicians in town, they won the election only by the narrow margin of thirteen votes out of a total of more than five thousand. Next year the unruly elements called to their aid reinforcements from Baltimore, dragged a small brass cannon from the old engine-house in Anacostia, planted it in front of Northern Liberties Market, where the Carnegie Library now stands, and announced their intention of closing the polls.

Dr. Magruder, who tolerated no nonsense in his patients or his politics, went in person to the scene of disturbance, but, for once in his popular life, power failed him and he found himself quite helpless. The District militia professed to be in the same condition, whereupon he appealed to President Buchanan. The one hundred and ten marines ordered to the scene were greeted with jeers and stones and stray pistol-shots as they advanced upon the cannon, the rioters failing to believe even then that force was to be used against them. But when the first volley killed seven men and wounded three times that number, the rioters suddenly vanished, and, to quote the words of a local historian, "in this and other precinct, the Union or Anti-Know-nothing ticket was successful." A small increase in the number of policemen was made soon after, but as these appointments were used mainly to reward party services, no great improvement resulted.

As often happens at the end of an era, just before disaster overwhelms an established order of things, life flowed on prosperously and happily upon the surface. Officialdom did not frequent those parts of the city where lawlessness prevailed, and Buchanan's administration marked the flowering of a phase of social life that passed away forever with the opening of the civil war.

The prevailing sentiment was pro-slavery, the influential men being those from the South, some of whom spoke with power, while others contented themselves with merely exercising it. The social leaders were also of the Southern type, women as keen-witted as their masculine relatives, and better acquainted with public questions and more interested in them than an equal number of their Northern cousins, though the latter might have excelled in household arts as practised in New England. The Southern women dressed with taste, sang moderately well, danced like sylphs, and when necessity forced a pen into their hands, wrote with grace of diction if somewhat erratic spelling.

President Buchanan had loomed large in the public eye, aided politically by his handsome person and impressive way of pronouncing sentences neither brilliant enough to cause envy nor trite enough to bore his hearers, while his persistence in remaining a bachelor proved no bar to his popularity in private relationships. His high moral character, the breadth of his official experience, and his very solid legal knowledge combined to make it as certain as anything human can be certain that his would be a brilliant and successful administration. "Standing six feet one or two in his bachelor stockings," he was ruddy of face and courtly of manner. If his head was drawn a little toward one shoulder and his eyes did not quite focus, those were minor defects easily overlooked by his well-wishers. Even those who did not like him were forced to admit that he had a "winning way of making himself hateful."

With the advent of the new administration, the White House blossomed into gay life after four morbid years. Mrs. Pierce, poor lady, had seen her young son killed in a railway accident when making the journey to the inauguration, and had never recovered from the shock. She had bravely tried to fulfil the duties of her position, but the White House had seemed like a tomb to all who entered it, and they brought away a never-to-be-forgotten memory of a woe-laden woman in black velvet, with a skin like yellowed ivory and pathetic sunken eyes.

President Buchanan's niece, who was to do the honors for him, was young and gay, a kindly girl who had been under his care almost from babyhood, and upon whose generous impulses he had felt obliged to keep a tight rein while she was growing up. Once, to his secret delight, he had found her trundling a barrow of coal along the streets of Lancaster, in her haste to get it to a needy woman of whom she had heard. Both had reaped the reward of her training in the popularity she enjoyed as head of his household when he was minister in London. Because of that social experience, she came to the White House with a larger fund of knowledge useful to the position than most women had acquired at twice her age.

In person she was blonde and not very tall. People who wished to flatter said she looked like Queen Victoria—those who wished to flatter still more, added hastily "like her, but quite a beauty!" Much was said in praise of her finely shaped hands. "Hands which might have swayed the rod of empire," a diplomat sighed as he bent over them, and her wit was nimble enough to supply the remaining lines: "Or waked to ecstasy the living lyre!"

But it was not alone because of her that the White House took on a more human aspect. Her uncle, with his white hair glistening like spun silk, had a warm place in his heart for children, and by his orders the grounds were opened to them wider than ever before. They were welcomed for the May-Day parade and picnic in which the Sunday schools of the Protestant churches united, and for a festival which has since become an annual event of the Washington Easter season, the rolling of eggs upon the White-House lawns on Easter Monday—a function to which no one is admitted unless accompanied and vouched for by a child.

Styles had changed since the discovery of gold in California. The swollen contours of new walnut furniture, and the Brussels carpets of opulent design, were matched in women's dress by crinoline that distended the human form to amazing proportions, while necklaces of seed-pearls shone above shoulders generously displayed. But fashionable elegance had not yet reached the height of demanding a distinct evening dress for men. The famous Lancaster suit made for Buchanan by a Pennsylvania tailor, to be worn at his inauguration, had thirty-one states symbolically stitched into its black-satin lining, with Pennsylvania's keystone "in the center." So far as one can discover, he wore it alike in the morning and at the ball, and, for all his conventionality, he did not own a "dress" suit. Nor, indeed, did other gentlemen of distinction. A few years later, when Charles Sumner appeared at one of Lincoln's receptions in full regalia of this new style, he created a sensation.

The three weeks of entertaining, with which the administration opened, came to an abrupt end when Miss Lane's brother died of the mysterious National Hotel sickness. But the next season Miss Lane made friends by accepting invitations as well as giving them, and appeared at all smart affairs in "full toilette de demi deuil," whatever that meant in 1858. Society reporters weltered in adjectives and French phrases, showing a taste in the use of words akin to that in crinoline and walnut furniture. Though bad art, it leaves to succeeding generations a colorful if chromo-like picture of richly dressed throngs at the White House, with a few humbler folk, noticeable for the plainness of their clothes, slipping in between, —here a widow in faded brown with a scarf of black lace over her head, a woman whose claim had probably been before Congress for many years, yonder a master and miss "arm in arm, who had but very recently exchanged the jacket for the tail coat and the pantalet for the long skirt," and over there possibly their grandmother, a respectable matron in a mob-cap, her collar fastened with a hair brooch.

Innovations that were made to care for increasing crowds at the White House met with disfavor, as innovations are apt to do. A system of checking wraps caused murmuring, and when it was found on New Year's Day, 1859, that policemen had been stationed from the front door to the place where the President stood, with orders to direct the crowd and see that every visitor presented himself before his host whether he would or not, many angrily refused to enter. The honest had their feelings hurt; thieves did not seem to mind; at least a gentleman wrote that he had enjoyed the privilege of shaking hands with Miss Lane and having his pocket picked, to the tune of the Star-Spangled Banner.

One of the sensations of that season was the appearance at a White-House reception of Piccolomini the opera singer, chaperoned in duplicate—on one side by a sister dressed exactly like herself and on the other by a fat mother in black silk; and guarded in addition by a foreign count whose ignorance of the language was betrayed by a face as expressionless as the back of his bald head. He and the Scandinavian minister and an American judge grouped themselves strategically around the three women, as they sat on a sofa viewing the hand-shaking.

Spectators related by innuendo, rather than direct words, how eager the bachelor host seemed to be to reach Piccolomini and how "precisely at ten," the moment custom permitted him to leave his post, he made his way to her with Mrs. Gwinn, wife of the senator from Pennsylvania, his wonderful head nearer his shoulder than ever, his miraculous eye cocked with unwonted precision of aim. He had first to run the gantlet of the uninteresting sister, and after he reached the diva, conversation was restricted to a confession on his part that he had spent three months in France five years before, but could neither speak nor understand the language—"had no ears nor tongue, now." Buchanan's worst enemies could hardly have been more severe!

He had enemies, for he was proving vacillating and unable to make up his mind. People were beginning to speak of him as the O.P.F.—"Old Public Functionary,"—words he had used in an unguarded moment when alluding rather sentimentally to his long official service. But Piccolomini smiled and used her effective eyes, and the two made a little scene amid a circle of interested spectators. The President might have stayed ogling and bowing until morning, had not Mrs. Gwinn reminded him that it was time to move on.

Mrs. Gwinn was the lady who gave a famous ball, so splendid that memory straightway detached itself from the party given by Mrs. Adams in 1824, about which people had been talking ever since. Mrs. Gwinn's party could scarcely have been given in the atmosphere of 1824, for it was a fancy-dress affair at which staid political lights twinkled in unaccustomed colors and natures not naturally staid made the most of a unique opportunity. Never before had such a gathering of characters from fiction and history been seen in

Washington—knights and ladies, goddesses and peasants, demons and saints. Old Mr. King the portrait-painter wandered through the rooms, ponderous and handsome as Rembrandt come to life again, while the hit of the evening was made by lively Mrs. Clay, who borrowed a friend's son to represent *Ike,* disguising herself as *Mrs. Partington* so completely that her best friends did not know her, and impertinently acted the rôle all the evening. Even the President did not escape her appositely inapropos remarks.

But it was real, not make-believe pageantry that justified Jefferson Davis's claim that Mr. Buchanan's administration presented the nearest approach to an elegant republican court that our country had seen since the days of the first President. In May, 1860, a Japanese ambassador came with a suite sixty strong to return Commodore Perry's visit, this being the first time that people of his nation were seen in the United States. Half the population of Washington went to the barracks to witness the landing of the oddly dressed little yellow men, whose skins had been burned the color of copper by the long sea-voyage. They looked scarcely human as they made their way from the flag-decked ship, through a lane of waiting people. It was almost a shock to see them stop to shake hands, and hear them say, "How do?" in the English learned on the voyage. The gay *Mrs. Partington* was truly shocked when one of them, catching sight of a delicate crape scarf brought her by a member of the Perry expedition, exclaimed, "Me lakee! Me lakee!" and diving among his intimate innermost garments until he got hold of a bit of fabric exactly matching her own, held it toward her smiling, "as if," she said, "in this discovery we had established a kind of preliminary international *entente cordiale.*"

The great moment of their visit was their solemn official reception by the President of the United States, a function which took place at high noon, after the White House had been in the throes of expectation, indeed actually in the hands of the Nipponese, for hours. Several of the lesser members of the party had appeared in the early morning and asked to be allowed to go to the rooms assigned to them. What rites of purification these chambers underwent we shall never know. This scouting party remained in possession until the arrival of the main expediton, escorted by the police, the Marine Band, and everything else wearing a uniform that could be requisitioned in unmilitary Washington.

Divided according to rank, the ambassadors and their personal following were conducted to the Blue Room, their subordinates to the Red Parlor, while fifty Japanese servants ranged themselves along the corridor. At midday the President and his cabinet walked down this lane of Japanese, to the East Room, after which the Secretary of State, Mr. Cass, went back to the Blue Room and returned with the ambassadors, bizarre and stately figures in the court dress of their ancient empire, the prince of highest rank in brilliant purple, those next in rank in green brocade, all wearing the flowing sleeves and trousers, the high, square little caps tied under the chin with strings, and the beautiful swords familiar to us only in pictures of long ago.

At this first presentation they came as the direct representatives of the Tycoon, and, bowing three times while they approached, paused a moment before the President in profoundest silence, then reversed their progress and, repeating the number of their bows, retired to the Blue Room from which they emerged a second time in the character of ambassadors to present their sovereign's autograph letter. When this had been accomplished with much ceremony, the subordinates made reverences on their own account, and finally all retired, the line of servants in the corridor bending, as they went by, as wheat bends under a passing breeze.

In view of their dignity and decorum, it is a little humiliating to have to confess that the Americans present in the East Room so far forgot their manners as to climb upon tables and chairs to get a view of the sceptacle.

A diary of a member of this embassy, which has very lately been released from Japanese archives, gives us the impression made upon his Oriental mind by Miss Lane, at the White-House dinner in their honor. "Had one not known who she was, one would have taken her for the queen of beauty, and her uncle as perhaps her prime minister, so commanding were her manners, and such is the amazing American attitude of respect toward women." "But her questions frequently disconcerted me somewhat," the ambassador confessed, and he had difficulty in following the etiquette of Western table manners. "I had to keep one eye fixed on my neighbor's hands, and then awkwardly follow her example." American food tried the Japanese sorely, there was so much meat and fat in it; and when they tasted their beloved rice desecrated with butter, or worse still, cooked with sugar, it seemed to them a barbarism fit to make strong men weep.

This Japanese diary is the only document extant which commends Washington streets after nightfall. It describes them as "well lighted with gas lamps, so that it is not necessary to carry a lantern."

The first time the ambassador saw them he was on his way to a ball at the residence of Mr. Cass—a most amazing spectacle to Oriental eyes.

Immediately after we were seated the music commenced, and an officer in uniform with one arm round a lady's waist and the other hand holding one of hers, started moving around the room on his toes, many others following his example. Upon inquiring we were told that this was a "dance."

As I watched the various movements of the dancers I could not help smiling at the way in which the very large skirts, called crinoline, which the ladies wore, increased in volume until they became of enormous proportions when the dancers attained their top speed.

This continued until midnight. As for us we had never seen or imagined anything like it before. It was of course with no small wonder that we had witnessed this extraordinary sight of men and bare-shouldered women hopping around the floor arm in arm, and our wonder at the strange performance became so great that we began to doubt whether we were not on another planet. I need not say that we did not remain until midnight.

Congress seemed to them very noisy and ill-tempered; but with the quintessence of manners they refrained from asking questions that might embarrass their hosts. Afterward they found that only the most commonplace matters had been under discussion, and that the Americans felt there was not the least cause for embarrassment.

At the Patent Office they found it very difficult to live up to their conception of good manners and not ask questions, or show impatience at crowding Americans who got between them and the marvels they wished to study. But of all the sights in Washington they were most impressed by the Navy Yard, with its busy maze of steam-driven machines, and by a view of the moon seen through the telescope at the Naval Observatory. "I was filled with envy and a hearty desire to see such works as this established in my own country," the ambassador wrote, and went whole-heartedly about concluding a treaty.

Buchanan was half flattered, half amused. "They never speak without calling me emperor and his Majesty," he told a friend. And he saw that nothing escaped them. "They are always sketching and taking notes of things," and his summing up was: "They are very proud too. They bow very low, but they won't do more than is prescribed for them in their instructions." They had brought with them fifteen packing cases full of rich gifts, some of which still adorn the Executive Mansion. In return Mr. Buchanan presented them with medals.

That was a very princely season. The Prince de Joinville reappeared for a second visit; and a few months later Baron Renfrew arrived from Canada. While not so spectacular as the visit of the Japanese who had emerged from the seclusion of centuries to make their pilgrimage, the presence in Washington of the heir to the British throne was immensely exciting.

In spite of their tact and their manners, the yellow men in flowing trousers had seemed more like figures on grandmother's tea-chest than like human beings, but this rather short, blond young man with a winning smile was not only a flesh-and-blood prince, he was a very near cousin. Through all their fighting, the English and Americans gloried in a common ancestry and had never lost their sense of kinship. At the moment it was of vast political importance to encourage this feeling, since the greater part of the cotton grown on Southern plantations went to feed English looms, and signs pointed to a time not far distant when the friendship of England might mean a great deal to the welfare of the South. Abraham Lincoln had become the candidate of the great new party opposed to slavery. The Presidential campaign was raging, with results still uncertain. Pro-slavery leaders threatened disunion in case he was elected, and if relations with the North should be severed, England's help might make all possible difference in the outcome.

How much of this was openly discussed and how much merely felt, matters little, for courtesy and machiavellian diplomacy dictated the same course. On learning that the Prince of Wales contemplated a visit to Canada, President Buchanan wrote a cordial note to Queen Victoria, expressing the hope that her son might include Washington in his tour; the invitation was graciously accepted and Southern plotters and pretty Washington girls alike were in a flutter.

The White House was neither so large nor so well furnished that it could receive a guest of such importance without going through all the moving of furniture, and cleaning and preliminary to-do that would have beset a small private residence under similar strain. Mr. Buchanan gave up his own bedroom to the Prince, who of course did not know, when he stretched his short limbs in the very long new rosewood bedstead especially built for the occasion, that his tall, silver-haired host was reposing on a makeshift cot in the ante-room to his office.

Miss Lane, being a young hostess, was anxious to give a grand ball in honor of her young guest, but Buchanan, whose own dancing days were over, vetoed this, on the ground that it might offend certain Americans as "profane gaiety in the saloons of the State." The substitution of a very formal dinner, followed by a reception and a musicale, probably thoroughly satisfied nobody except the author of a new song called "Listen to the Mocking-bird," which was dedicated to Miss Lane, and sung in public that night for the first time.

At the reception the President did all the hand-shaking and the prince a large part of the bowing. For exercise, to get in trim for the state dinner, Miss Lane had taken the royal guest, under proper chaperonage, to the gymnasium of a girls' school, to have a game of tenpins. This does not sound thrilling, but nobody can say what happy unrecorded incidents marked the occasion. Nor can we know what features of their visit caused the prince and his suite private merriment. They could not fail to see and appreciate the earnestness with which Washington tried to please them; and in his polite bread-and-butter letter Edward assured the President that rarely, "in a somewhat chequered career," had he experienced so much enjoyment in the space of five days.

XIX

PAWNS IN THE GAME

ONE mile directly east of the Capitol is a little park unfrequented by fashion. In L'Enfant's dream of the city it was here that the Itinerary Column was to rise. Instead, the only ornament of the park is a bronze statue. Not a great statue in any sense, it must yet loom large before that tribunal where motives alone are judged, for it spells gratitude in every line. It represents Lincoln striking the shackles from a kneeling slave, and was paid for out of their poverty by the negroes themselves, the earliest contribution being made by a woman who gave to this use the first money she earned after her emancipation.

Slavery was an evil that smote the consciences of Americans long before the colonies broke away from England. Lord Culpeper, writing about Virginia agriculture early in the seventeenth century, penned the words, "Our thriving is our undoing," and added "the buying of blacks hath extremely contributed thereto." Up to the time of the Revolution nobody seemed to know exactly how to get rid of it, but the best sentiment of the country agreed that slavery ought to be abolished; and it really seemed under control until America's uncanny talent for invention produced the cotton-gin. Sugar-cane and tobacco had been the great crops of the South, cotton being little more than a tantalizing vegetable curiosity, because of the labor required to prepare it for market. When, however, Eli Whitney's devilish little box full of teeth and wheels and rending claws made it possible for a negro man, turning a crank, to separate the seeds from fifty pounds in a single day, in place of the one pound he could have plucked clean by hand, our thriving became again our undoing, and slavery began to cast strange lights and most bizarre shadows upon the white dome of the Capitol.

For a time its golden profits obscured the moral question. But not for long. By 1820 that had become so insistent that only Clay's skill in devising his Missouri Compromise and causing both sides to agree to a line beyond which slavery was never to pass saved the country from serious turmoil. Then covetousness for new territory south of that line, wherein slavery might spread, brought on the Mexican War; and after that the repeal of the Missouri Compromise again strategically opened the subject wide for discussion.

From the first the District of Columbia was important because it was the home of Congress, where laws must be changed if changes were to be made, and because of its position close to the free states, yet at a point where Chesapeake Bay made it a convenient distributing center for much Southern territory. That alone would have made it a slave market. Horace Mann called it "the Congo of America." Week after week and year after year its newspapers printed advertisements of slaves for sale and the wants of dealers who came from a distance to buy. On a single day, toward the close of Jackson's administration, the number of slaves offered for sale was twelve hundred. The purely local market was small but steady, except during race week. One autumn eight hundred Washington slaves changed masters as the result of unfortunate betting.

In matters of domestic service the town was completely under slavery's thrall, for, with the exception of a very few foreign servants brought with them by diplomats, and a few warm-hearted if stony-mannered New Englanders who chose to accompany their employers to the temporary exile of official homes, negroes, slave or free, were the only reliance. The other nationalities, especially the Irish, who figured so constantly in the District's charity problems, furnished a little unskilled labor, but were too erratic to be relied upon for the unexciting endless round of duties upon which a city's welfare depends.

As the proportion of free negroes in the District was unusually large, the colored population may have been mentally above the average. Free and slave alike performed their tasks contentedly enough, but had reduced dawdling to a fine art; they crowded more leisure into a day's work and more physical enjoyment into their leisure than our race could do in half a hundred existences.

Some of the free negroes had been manumitted by grateful masters. More had bought their freedom by long and arduous toil, it being the custom among people who hired out their slaves to credit them with a small proportion of the wages earned. Other free negroes had slipped unobtrusively into the District to earn their living, the many temporary households offering a field not found elsewhere. The authorities did not encourage this, and the first thing a free negro had to do, if he meant to stay in the District, was to find five reputable property-owners willing to give bond for his orderly conduct to the amount of one thousand dollars each. A student of the laws relating to the blacks says that the one privilege accorded a free negro was the priceless right to keep dogs.

Usually his ambition was to keep a horse; for the possession of a sorry nag and even a third-rate carriage exalted him to a job that could be conducted sitting down, and allowed him to enter the competition to lift statesmen over mud-holes and transport sight-seers between public buildings. For those whose minds were incapable of reaching such dizzy heights there were ash-carts and moving-wagons, toward the purchase of which they hoarded "bits" and "levies" and stray pieces of change called by names long since forgotten.

Officials coming from slave states were permitted to bring their household servants with them, which simplified the domestic problem for them; for others the laws were exceedingly complicated. A Maryland slave could be held in bondage in the District only in that part which had once been Maryland soil. A slave brought into that part of the District from any other state automatically became free. And, up to the time of the retrocession, the same held true as to Virginia slaves and Virginia territory. A colored man, therefore, might conceivably pass from servitude to freedom and back again a dozen times a day—a state of things utterly absurd, and capable of very tragic consequences.

To guard against the escape of slaves amid such confusion, drastic laws had been made. Negroes were subject to arrest on the mere suspicion of being fugitives, and the burden of proving their innocence and all the costs of detention fell upon them. If nobody came to claim them within a certain time, they might be sold to satisfy these costs. Furthermore, the criminal law imposed two sets of penalties for the same offense, a slave being punished much more severely than a white person.

Education was absolutely forbidden to slaves; that free negroes were not under the same restriction availed them little, since until after emancipation they had no schools worthy of the name. The best they could do was to pass on to their children such scraps of knowledge as they had managed to pick up. The attendance of negroes at places of amusement and possible instruction was strictly limited. For example, the managers of the Great National Fair held from May 21 to June 3, 1846, to show what had been done and was about to be done in American manufactures, advertised that "a part of Friday afternoon the 29th" would be "appropriated to the admission of people of color." Theaters, where slaves used to be sent in early days to hold good seats for their masters, required them to leave the building before a certain hour or retire to an undesirable gallery. If the piece could be suspected of raising rebellious feelings, they were not permitted to witness it from any point.

The law was not cruel enough to deny these people the comforts of religion; but, to guard against misunderstanding, an act passed by Virginia in 1715 expressly stated that the rite of baptism, making them "free" in the Kingdom of Heaven, worked no such miracle on earth.

Though the Catholics had their proportion of converts, the mysticism and pageantry of that faith did not appeal to the color-loving souls of the negroes as might have been expected. Having been poor and oppressed all their lives, they were left cold by the emphasis that church lays upon seeking godliness through renunciation, while a hierarchy of saints and angels to which few might attain impressed them less favorably than the neighborly democracy of a Methodist or a Baptist heaven. On the whole the Baptist church was the favorite. Passing their meeting-houses, one could hear any Sunday evening "A-mens" and groans and shouts of victory exploding like bombs on the night air, and "a baptizin'" down by the river was a function that drew them from far and near.

Credulous and emotional, they lived close to the marvelous in a world full of signs and wonders. Their religion was very real to them; nobody could accuse them of insincerity; yet in moments of stress the jungle was apt to call, and when it did, silently and secretly they reverted to the ways of savage ancestors. Even to-day mistresses come unexpectedly upon evidences of voodoo rites in the best-regulated Washington kitchens. This being so, it was not remarkable that when that kind magician Signor Blitz set up his paraphernalia in the Presbyterian meeting-house that had fallen in grace and become Willard's dance-hall, he was regarded with terror and veneration, and that such colored folk as nerved themselves to approach him, came with strange and pathetic requests.

Curfew laws drove within doors at nine or ten o'clock all slaves who could not show passes. Only during the holidays were such rules relaxed; and this was a time looked forward to throughout the whole year. On Christmas Eve they went about in groups singing their racial songs and old English carols whose familiar rhythms were strangely transmuted by African throats and temperament. Next day they came again to bob and show their teeth in expectant grins and wish their white friends "Christmas gif' !"—a synonym for "bakshish." Their delight in the cheer and feasting of the season was equaled only by their willingness to do extra work in preparation. That was and remains perhaps their most ingratiating trait as domestics. Other races seem to resent the labor of preparing for company and holidays, but it is the only kind of labor that negroes perform with real joy.

Ordinarily their industry left much to be desired. Colonel Lavasseur, who accompanied Lafayette on his tour in 1824, felt his French blood run cold at sight of the slackness at Arlington. "If instead of the great number of indolent slaves who devour the products of his fields and leave his roads in horrible condition, Mr. Custis employed only a dozen free laborers and paid them well, I am convinced his revenues would speedily increase three-fold," he wrote.

The institution of slavery was wasteful, but there was a baronial grandeur in having many retainers; and why worry about a few extra mouths when food was so plentiful? No one generation was responsible for the evils of the system, and if ever men suffered for the sins of their fathers as well as their own, it was the slave-owners. Madison knew his black people were eating him out of house and home, and said he would willingly free them if they could take care of themselves afterward, but he believed them incapable of fending for themselves. Jefferson, who was a pessimist in regard to negro intelligence, believing them as far inferior to the white race as the mule is inferior to the horse, and created, like the mule, to be the bearer of burdens, said that emancipation would be like turning faithful domestic animals adrift.

Masters who suffered acutely from twinges of conscience, and Northerners with theories but no experience to guide them, organized in Washington, soon after the War of 1812, the African Colonization Society, their plan being to remove the negroes who were fitted for self-government to some spot, half-way around the globe, where they might work out their own salvation under conditions that even the members of this tender-hearted brotherhood were unwilling to grant nearer home.

Henry Clay presided at the preliminary meeting; Madison and Bushrod Washington were early presidents; while Lafayette and Monroe and Francis Scott Key and a hundred others of equal prominence seconded its efforts. Its popularity was so great, indeed, during a long term of years, that the number of men who claimed credit for inventing it grew to be almost an army. But others equally earnest and quite as clear-headed would have none of it. "A sop to philanthropy" and the "handmaiden of slavery" were two of the hard names it was called, because by sending the intelligent negroes out of the country the chains would be riveted irrevocably on those left behind. The people it was designed to serve remained for the most part unmoved. The greater number never even heard of it, or, hearing, were incapable of projecting their imaginations so far through space, while the intelligent minority resented being deported before enjoying rights named as God-given in the Declaration of Independence. A National Convention of free colored men, held in Philadelphia in 1831, made bold to address the Colonization Society in these rococo but forceful words:

[We] Respectfully suggest to that august body of talent, learning and worth, that in our humble opinion strengthened too by the opinions of eminent men in this country as well as in Europe, they are pursuing the direct road to perpetuate slavery with all its unchristian concomitants in this boasted land of freedom; and as citizens and men whose best blood is sapped to gain popularity for that institution, we would in the most feeling manner beg of them to desist; or, if we must be sacrificed to their philanthropy, we would rather die at home.

Slaves were a kind of wealth that deteriorated almost as swiftly as automobiles, and, while the manner in which they were treated depended entirely upon the whim of their owners, it is only fair to remember that, aside from dictates of humanity, the fragile nature of such property tended to restrain cruelty. The inventory of the estate of General Van Ness set down the money value of his retainers in cold unsympathetic ink, and by this we learn that Julius and George, husky men of twenty-five and thirty-two years of age, were appraised at $500 each. Simon and Sally, both about sixty, had life enough in them to be worth $100 and $75 respectively, while after the name of Betty there were no figures, only the words, "Quite old; of no value,"—a tragedy in six syllables.

The evils of the system were great enough in all conscience. In every household group there were the sick and the helpless children and the Bettys to be looked out for, but common sense encourages the belief that a pass written by Dr. Thornton when he sent his man Peter upon an errand to Brentwood gives a truer view of the relations between the two races than a tale current in Washington about a society woman who kept a lash in her bedroom and wielded it unmercifully, while her husband, too fastidious to strike a slave himself, shrugged his shoulders and said it was no affair of his—merely a matter of household discipline.

Here is Dr. Thornton's pass:

TO THE GOOD PEOPLE

Pray let the bearer, Peter pass.
He rides a horse & leads an ass.
This is the *Vicar,* fam'd of *Bray*
He goes, at Mr. Bent's to stay.
Peter returns, without delay.

TO PETER

If any one you chance to meet,
Stay not to talk, but pass & greet,
And neither give nor take a treat.

The chances are that without such a document Peter would have led his charge sedately along the roads north of the city, stopping only to remonstrate, "Git along, mule! What yo' think I feed yo' fo' ?" when he and the Vicar developed differences of opinion. The negroes were like children, proud of executing a commission. But, also like children, they were social creatures and easily diverted. It would be safe to wager that Peter took at least one friendly drink on the way home.

Born mimics, they easily assumed the polish of civilization. It might be only a thin and dark mahogany veneer, but often it struck deep and improved on its original. Nothing could be more elegant than the deportment of the well-trained house servants. From the nature of their calling, body-servants stood at the head of this aristocracy of slavedom. Growing up in some fine old family, accompanying a master to Washington, receiving or purchasing freedom and passing into the service of a noted Northern statesman, they saw the very best of American manners at a time when manners were cultivated. When, as sometimes happened, such a man entered the service of the Government in an humble capacity, that fact in no way detracted from the dignity of his bearing. William L. Marcy who, for all his good qualities, was not "gifted in external graces," looked rather ruefully at a colored messenger of this type, a former servant of Monroe's who came with the rest of the office force to take leave of him when he left the War Department. "Good-by, Datcher," he said, with a wry smile. "If I had your manners, I would be leaving more friends behind me."

But suavity, even subserviency of manner gave no hint of a black man's capacity for individual action. John Randolph's ebony property, "Juba of Roanoke," whose memory is green to this day, was quite as often master as slave. Any day during a session of Congress he might be seen galloping after his master to keep him out of mischief, the dust raised by their two horses eddying in one golden swirl along Pennsylvania Avenue. When the Virginian was sick Juba nursed him like an ailing child, ignoring his vitriolic curses with an indifference born of true affection. But he kept his self-respect by doing or not doing his alleged master's bidding, as seemed to him best. No exertion was too great if it struck him as worth while, but he had an African's love of ease. An illuminating story of master and man recalls a night when a nerve crisis had rendered Randolph little short of insane. He conceived a desire for a cup of water from a particular well in Georgetown a mile and a half from his lodgings, and vowed he would die unless Juba got it for him. Juba left the room obediently, but only to go into hiding and remain until time enough had elapsed for the journey, when he filled his cup from the nearest tap and presented himself, ready to lie artistically, if necessary, about every step of the way. Poor faithful Juba! He followed his master to Russia and died there—like Napoleon's army, a sacrifice to duty.

The feminine counterparts of Juba were not deft-fingered ladies'-maids, who cast possessive eyes on the finery of their mistresses from the moment it entered the house, but broad-breasted Mammies, who "raised" the children of the family from babyhood and tyrannized over them after they were grown. They too could be seen any day in Washington, in gay turbans and big snowy aprons, marshaling their young charges across one of those wide, dangerous empty streets down which Juba and his master might ride like a whirlwind, or a President's wife sway gently by in her carriage. Their methods were not scientific. "Pacifiers" of bacon-rind and tiny inconspicuous "charms" of their own concoction supplemented doctors' prescriptions, but the best medicine of all was the comforting curve of a satin-smooth brown neck upon which to sob out baby woes. How they despised the trained nurse when that cool-looking, unsympathetic person made her appearance some decades later, with nothing to offer in place of bacon-rind and petting except a hospital cot without pillows and meticulously weighed-out infant food! But the trained nurse was the product of a degenerate age. In the golden days "befo' de wah" the mammies had things all their own way, and after attending the daughter of the house from the hour of her birth to her marriage, longed for nothing so much as to begin the cycle all over again with her eldest-born "ef de Good Lawd spare me to see dat blessed lamb."

The family cook was an equal despot in her field; and the most impressive sight of the whole slave retinue was the grizzled butler bearing aloft into the dining-room a great rose-colored ham that had been brought to him from the kitchen by relays of fleet-footed young blacks being trained in the ways of household service. A traffic policeman is humble compared with him.

Such high-class slaves had their own diversions, copied after those of white folk. Masonic lodges and Unions of Friendship were tolerated, though of course in defiance of the letter of the law. Occasionally a colored woman got the mayor's permission to give a supper for the benefit of her church, and then great were the preparations and much was the savory cooking that went on with stores eked out liberally by household supplies. In slavery times food was never in any circumstances stolen—merely "taken." A distinction in moral values that lasted long after slavery days were over.

When the fashion of church weddings came in, a few years before the Civil War, the blacks were quick to adopt it, for besides giving a religious sanction to ties that white masters were apt to regard lightly if they interfered with personal convenience, it offered a combination of pomp and solemnity that appealed strongly to their emotional nature. For those who had not yet "got religion," there were dances, announcements and invitations for which were printed, if the occasion was to be very grand, in the offices of the same newspapers that habitually carried in their columns advertisements of runaway slaves.

COLORED COTILLION PARTY

The pleasure of your company is respectfully solicited at a Cotillion Party to be given at Donevan Hall High Street on Thursday evening November 18, 1852.

Tickets admitting a lady and gentleman one dollar. Single tickets fifty cents.

Managers

Thomas Brown — James Glascoe
James Booth — Arthur Bradley

A permit has been secured.

High Street lay across Rock Creek, in Georgetown.

It requires little imagination to see the pigeon-wings and lordly strutting of the ginger-colored bucks on the dancing-floor, the animated if solid matrons with great golden hoops in their ears, nodding time to the music, and the beauty of the fairest of the girls, with slender limbs and delicately modeled hands, and only the telltale luster of their eyes or the peculiar quality of their dusky hair to betray their birth. If the costumes of some of them were made of carefully hoarded scraps, and those worn by others were "borrowed" outright, without permission, from the white ladies, that was only a minor detail of a race tragedy.

When it came to real joys and sorrows, no blood relations sympathized more whole-heartedly or suffered more keenly with their white families than these people who, taken all in all, lived up to a higher standard of loyalty than anybody had a right to expect. It was usually one of the oppressed race who gave the alarm, if, as rarely happened, danger threatened white folk from within the negro quarters; and when war came, slaves who helped to bury the family silver and did their ignorant best to care for destitute mistresses were so numerous as scarcely to attract notice. The crowning tragedy of the system was that sometimes one or more of these dusky creatures had the blood of the family flowing in their veins.

Occasionally one went to the auction block to recoup the family fortunes, a heartbreaking sacrifice but honorable, toward which the victim might walk upheld by a sense of pride. The selling that hurt was that which came as a punishment, whether merited or otherwise. No matter how intimate or tender the relations between individual masters and slaves, the system as a whole was repulsive, for neither buying nor selling nor hunting of negroes could be an attractive job. That reproach of a slave pen "under the very shadow of the Capitol," was literally true, provided Capitol be spelled with an *a* instead of an *o*. To Washingtonians it seemed a matter of course that a traveling dealer might lodge his chattels in the District jail for safe-keeping. In addition there were several private houses fitted with bolts and bars for this purpose.

One on F Street, in a location no longer easy to verify, was the scene of such a flagrant case of kidnapping that General Van Ness and Francis Scott Key and gentlemen of like prominence rose in indignation to secure justice for the woman deprived of her liberty. What connection, if any, there may have been between the interest this case aroused and the formation of that "sop to conscience" the African Colonization Society, is lost in uncertainty, like the site of the building.

A "Yellow House on Seventh Street" figured frequently for years in advertisements which might read like this:

Two hundred slaves wanted. The subscriber will give higher prices in cash for likely young slaves of both sexes than any other person in the market.

Or, printed in the same column with "A Defense of the Pastoral Letter of the Presbytery of Baltimore,"

FOR SALE. Two likely well grown negro girls about 16 years of age, accustomed to all kinds of housework. They will not be sold out of the State of Maryland.

The Yellow House stood south of the Smithsonian, in full sight of the Capitol, though half a mile away, in a yard well shaded by trees. In the discussion that led to the Compromise of 1850, Clay declared it to be the only house in the city used for such purposes, while another senator called it "a most pleasant-looking place." But after the local slave trade came to an end as the result of that compromise, a purchaser found staples driven into its walls and other mute witnesses of the manner in which human beings had been kept there, chained like wild animals.

Frederika Bremer visited it in company with a lady who wished or pretended to wish to buy a negro boy, and found nothing attractive about it. Only tiny negro children were stirring within the inclosure when the keeper met them at a small side gate. He was a coarse, talkative man, who tried to make himself agreeable to his visitors and soften the disappointment they might feel at not finding what they desired. He told them he had no slaves on hand for sale in the District, though several splendid articles were in his custody "to fatten" before being shipped south. One was a young girl who had been "raised like a lady," and could embroider and play the piano—and dress like a lady too. "Her mind had grown too high for her" and this was her fate. The keeper maintained that "all niggers needed the whip" and laughed at the indignant protest of the visitors as he bowed them out.

A stranger who saw the place only from the outside, on a stifling summer day, received a still more evil impression. It was surrounded with a stockade of wooden palings fourteen or fifteen feet high, set too close to the house to permit a free circulation of air, and at a small window high up toward the roof he saw two or three black heads thrust forward as if seeking a reviving breath. In this place both sexes and all colors, except white, were confined.

But it was not only at places set apart for the special purpose that slaves were sold. A servant might be put up at an ordinary auction and disposed of as a "lot," along with carpets and household gear. Or, to satisfy a debt, he might be auctioned from the Court-House steps. Basil Hall of the Royal Navy chanced upon such a sale, the victim being a yellow boy in his teens named George. Called upon, as he passed, to make a bid, the Englishman indignantly refused and added that he thanked God such things were not done in his country. Whereupon the auctioneer astonished him by replying with evident sincerity, "And I wish with all my heart we did not do such things here!" a sentiment echoed by "Amens!" equally sincere from several bystanders. But the sale went right on. "We cannot help it; we must do our duty," the auctioneer explained between two bids. "One hundred dollars, gentlemen. Do I hear another offer? One—hundred—dollars."

In the best circles such transactions were ignored as much as possible. Nevertheless the tramp of leaden feet crossing Chain Bridge on a journey into bondage might be heard any month in the year; or a slave-driver on horseback, with pistols and whip, might march his captives straight past the Capitol, actually in the shadow of the dome, the men in double files, each fastened by a handcuff and a short chain to a longer chain which passed through the whole group from front to rear. The women walked in the same fashion but unchained, while mothers of infants and the little children brought up the rear, huddled in a cart. This was the coffle-gang, the sight of which inspired Lincoln when a representative in Congress to offer his bill for gradual emancipation in the District of Columbia.

Sometimes the reason of the victims broke under the strain of auctions and of partings, and then court records held the closing scenes of tragedies as moving as ever Greek dramatist wrote.

One was enacted at the District jail in Washington at the Christmas season of 1837, when a woman who believed herself free was torn from her husband and thrust with her four young children into prison, to be held until she and they could be sent south. Resolved that her babies should never grow up to servitude, she set about killing them with her bare hands. Two were already dead when the frightened cries of the others brought the guards. Tried for murder, she was acquitted, on the ground of insanity. Then the sordid, grotesque note which is rarely absent from records of slavery entered into the story. Her purchaser refused to carry out his part of the bargain and charged her former owner with breach of contract in trying to sell him damaged goods!

Occasionally negroes intervened in the sale of one of their own number. Announcement would be made in church that such and such a member of the congregation was to be sold away from wife and children unless enough money could be raised in Washington to satisfy the demands of a master or a master's creditor. Then a contribution plate would be set upon a stool or table near the pulpit, those present filed slowly by, and, as they passed, pieces of silver from scanty hordes rang joyfully against their fellows.

Besides being a distributing center for the slave trade, Washington was an excellent point from which to make a dash for freedom. The city therefore developed in addition to L'Enfant's orderly plan of streets, another that bore the same relation to the first which shadows bear to light. Secret lanes and friendly cellars led toward the water-front, where small vessels poked their noses among the ill-kept wharves to discharge wood or garden-truck. Sometimes they waited until slaves came to them singly or in frightened groups down these secret runways, and departed with hidden cargoes. Obviously, such departures could not be scheduled beforehand nor safely described afterward; but they were of frequent occurrence.

When they did not succeed, the lot of the fugitives was worse than before.

The best known of all these attempts took place on a Saturday night in 1848, when the captain of the *Pearl,* no novice in such enterprises, set sail with about one hundred thousand dollars' worth of human property belonging to Washington citizens,—upward of seventy men, women, and children,—and next morning in forty Washington homes, Mrs. Madison's among them, the Sunday breakfast was not forthcoming as usual. But adverse winds held the *Pearl* at the mouth of the river until a swift steamboat came up in pursuit; and the fugitives were met at the wharf on their return by such a threatening crowd that it was deemed best to lock them in jail to save them from attack, a feat not easily accomplished. Most of them were turned over to Baltimore dealers for sale "south," and the scene on the day when about fifty of them were taken away on the first stage of their journey beggars description. Wives and children and friends who had come to bid them good-by filled the railroad station with their lamentations, and the smoke and the noise of trains and the sad brown faces gave it the setting of an anteroom to Hades. Horace Mann, who had been elected to fill out the unexpired term of Ex-President Adams in Congress, undertook the defense of the *Pearl's* captain; but his client was convicted of grand larceny and languished four years in a District jail.

Feeling upon the question of slavery varied in different parts of the city. The sections inhabited by officials reflected the temper of the Administration, with small hot fires of antislavery zeal burning at boarding-houses and hotels, where representatives and senators from New-England states congregated. In what may be called the native sections around Peter Force's old garden, the Island, the newer unfashionable streets near Northern Liberties Market, and those still less desirable quarters of town where turbulence was liked for its own sake, the residents were proslavery almost to a man, suspicious alike of negroes who presumed to rebel against their lot and of white people who insisted on bringing up moral issues that bank balances and political pride counseled Southerners to forget.

Courtesy B. S. Reynolds Company, Inc.

"ARMED LIBERTY"

There had already been race riots in Washington, when in the summer of 1835 a slave of Mrs. Thornton's who was to become free at her death, according to the terms of her husband's will, suddenly became crazed and attempted to brain her with an ax. The man's own mother stayed his hand and held him until he was taken into custody, but excitement grew for three days and culminated in burning the homes of free negroes, sacking the place of business of one Beverly Snow, a mulatto restaurant-keeper, and breaking the windows of a colored church. It also occasioned the arrest of Dr. Reuben Crandall, a physician of New York State who had come to the city to pursue the study of botany. Somebody found antislavery newspapers at his lodgings, and since he was the brother of Prudence Crandall, who had recently gained unenviable notoriety by opening her school in Connecticut to young women of color, the inference was obvious. He was taken before a justice of the peace, lodged in jail "for safety's sake" because of the threatening attentions of the mob, and left there eight months before his case came to trial.

Exactly the same elements of discord furnished the mob that met the return of the *Pearl;* and like the former mob it showed no tendency to disperse when balked of its original prey. It made a visit to the printing office of the "National Era," the antislavery weekly that had been issued in Washington for about a year. Dr. Bailey, its editor, knew nothing about the sailing of the *Pearl,* but it was natural that he should be suspected, since his business was to advocate abolition, and a previous newspaper venture of his in Cincinnati had ended in wreck at the hands of indignant citizens. Not finding him at his place of business, the crowd reassembled the following night in ugly mood and visited his dwelling, where his fearlessness and disarming words had more to do with rendering his visitors harmless than did the hasty arrival of the famous "Auxiliary Watch." Being inspired by the zeal of a reformer, Dr. Bailey may even have enjoyed the excitement of that evening visit. The emotions of his wife may be surmised. How complete had been the ostracism of this cultured pair in a town famous for hospitality may be gathered from an admission she made in a happier time that during the first six months of their stay in Washington only one woman crossed her threshold to make a friendly call.

Had the enemies of Abolitionism realized the important part the "Era" was destined to play in the national drama, its editor and its press would have been doomed. Dr. Bailey must have had a deft hand in steering his course; he not only managed to avoid making the enemies Garrison's "Liberator" drew upon itself, but made the "Era" too important from a literary point of view to be ignored. People might not agree with its politics, but no one who professed to be well read could afford to pass it by. He devoted to literature all the space not needed for propaganda; induced the young poet Whittier, who imagined that he had abandoned Pegasus for politics, to assist him as corresponding editor; and in addition to the work of men who were on the road to fame or already well known, specialized on women writers. Grace Greenwood, young Gail Hamilton, and that plucky resident of Georgetown, Mrs. E. D. E. N. Southworth, whose stories and articles numbered two thousand before, as she said, she "lost count," all wrote for the "Era."

Its crowning achievement, both as literature and propaganda, was Mrs. Stowe's novel, "Uncle Tom's Cabin," which made its appearance during the summer of 1851 and the following winter in rather haphazard fashion, the first part to see print being the death of *Uncle Tom,* supplemented later by the story that led up to it. Its success was so rapid that only a few days after its appearance between covers, its authoress wrote her husband she was "in a whirl." Her publisher had just returned from a trip to Washington, and was telling her things calculated to turn her head. He had talked with leading senators, and not only had Seward told him "Uncle Tom" was the greatest book of the times, but he and Sumner had gone around with him personally to ask Southern men to read it.

Hastening to fight fire with fire, the slavery party announced "The Black Gauntlet," a romance of plantation life written by a severely majestic lady, Mary Howard Schoolcraft, wife of the ethnologist, historian, and explorer. Mrs. Schoolcraft's friends believed that in elegance and orthodoxy it left nothing to be desired.

They were sure the book would find a "place in the library of every son of the South." But for purposes of propaganda, that was exactly where it was not needed. She reaped neither fame nor fortune from her effort, and before the end of her life was reduced to actual suffering, perhaps to actual starvation. Not all the tragedies of slave times were enacted in the servants' quarters.

Meantime, Mrs. Stowe's novel increased immensely the circulation of the "National Era," but the success of the cause it advocated proved in the end the paper's destruction. Antislavery newspapers multiplied in all parts of the country, and, calling for local support, sapped the subscription list of the "National Era" until it had to suspend publication. Its work was done. The days of ink and oratory were over and the time was at hand when North and South alike were to pay heavily for the prosperity which had been their undoing.

In the last troubled months before the great conflict, when greed and ambition, mistaken statesmanship, loyalty, and personal bias, were hurrying the country on to the climax of war, the least troubled people in the United States were the slaves themselves—which was only poetic justice.

XX

WASHINGTON IN WAR TIMES

THE announcement of Lincoln's election filled the city with mingled emotions, most of them unpleasant. For years Southern statesmen and Southern women had set the tone in politics and society, and this election of 1860 meant greater overturning of personal fortunes than the town had known since Jackson arrived with his hordes. Ladies made pretty gestures of dismay at the thought of barbarians in the White House, and the men swore under their breath, or smiled darkly, well content that they still had four months under Buchanan in which to mature their plans. Buchanan's indecision was a mighty help to them, for even after the crisis of December had put Black and Holt and Stanton in the cabinet, the best the new ministers could do was to keep the President from doing worse.

The South was in the midst of its orgy of state conventions, and after each ordinance of secession there was an ostentatious withdrawal from Congress of the senators and representatives from that state. Southern officers in the army and navy began resigning their commissions. Men occupying subordinate positions in the departments followed their example; and Washington thus became a sort of burning-glass which focussed the many rays of rebellion. Prudence and interest might keep the town loyal in the end, but it was evident that disunion was very popular. Truculent harangues in Congress were applauded from well-filled galleries. The suggestion made from the floor of the Senate that the city remain the capital—of a Southern confederacy—was greeted with appreciative laughter. The most daring of the fire-eaters were feasted and flattered. It began to seem very possible that this feeling might culminate in an uprising to seize government property and prevent the inauguration of the President-elect.

It was known that secession sympathizers had formed rifle-clubs and were drilling at night. How many of these there might be was uncertain; but the Democratic Jackson Association alone was credited with a membership of eight hundred. Its meetings were hinted at, rather than reported, which added to their sinister effect, while sidewalk inscriptions by day, and signal whistles sounding out of the darkness, gave proof that government officials were being systematically watched. This alarmed timid souls and was more than annoying to the stout-hearted, though later events proved the spies to be mischievous rather than deadly. Even ridicule by the "Evening Star," which shortened the association's name to "Dem. Jack. Ass.," and reported in the same contemptuous spirit such of its activities as came to light, failed to change the belief that these men stood ready at a moment's notice to coöperate with Southern forces.

Though minimizing the danger, Buchanan authorized General Scott to take whatever precautions he deemed necessary; and a plan for defending the city was drawn up. Arms were stored at central points, and early in February the officer in charge reported that he had fourteen volunteer companies busy drilling; that these represented nearly a thousand men whose Union sympathies could be relied upon in any emergency, and that he believed the number might be doubled in a week "with proper facilities."

Meanwhile General Scott, who had an army man's distrust of volunteers, however well intentioned, drew toward the capital every possible scrap and detachment of regular troops. But the army at that time was so small and the demands upon it so great that he was able to bring to Washington less than five hundred men. This was five hundred too many in the opinion of the Peace Congress then holding sessions in the city, under the chairmanship of Ex-President Tyler. These worthy gentlemen deprecated all show of military strength. But there is no space to tell the story of the spoiled parade of the twenty-second of February, which was planned and countermanded, and finally allowed to march, hours late, shorn of much glory. Nor is it the place to quote that strange note Mr. Buchanan felt impelled to write to Mr. Tyler—a note from a President of the United States to an Ex-President, apologizing for allowing Federal soldiers to carry the national flag through the streets of the capital on Washington's birthday.

Fortunately the public was not in possession of the facts. It only knew that it waited long upon street corners, and that when the procession came, it was small and not at all "as advertised." Had all been known, however, discussion would have been brief; for next morning the city awoke to a new sensation, the announcement that Lincoln was already in town, ten hours ahead of his schedule, having traveled by night from Harrisburg to avoid a threatened attempt upon his life. Tongues buzzed like angry wasps, and opinion, not too well disposed toward the newcomer, took another turn of dislike; censure being by no means confined by sectional lines. Stanton, who a few months later entered Lincoln's cabinet, spoke in tones of the utmost malignity of the way in which the President-elect had "crept into Washington." Others called it "that smuggling business." The fact remained that he had arrived; that the public had been deprived of the sight of his entry; that he had been met at the station in the early morning by Mr. Seward and driven to Willard's.

A letter from a member of his suite, dated February 24, 1861, read:

> We all arrived here safely last evening at about five o'clock, Mr. Lincoln himself having preceded us the night before. I assure you it was a real pleasure to get to our journey's end, with a prospect of a little rest now and then. During the last week of our trip, in the great whirlpools of New York and Philadelphia, not a moment was our own. . . . For the present we are quartered at Willard's hotel. The original programme was to go to a private house which had been hired for the purpose. This plan having been changed, and no rooms having been reserved, all the party except Mr. and Mrs. Lincoln, have but sorry accommodations. Well, next week we hope to be in the White House, where perhaps it may be better.
>
> You need have no present fears about our entire safety. There is not the least apprehension about trouble at the Inauguration, or any other time. That cloud has blown over. . . .
>
> I have not been here long enough, nor am I yet sufficiently rested to write much or think much . . . or have many impressions of any

kind. I found some 200 or 300 letters here to be attended to, which though (thank the stars!) less than I expected, have been enough to keep me busy.

The next letter to the same correspondent was sent from the Executive Mansion, that stately name being written with a bit of a flourish, as was natural, the very first time, to a most intimate and sympathetic friend:

March 5, 1861. As you see from the heading of my letter, we are fairly installed at the White House. We had a gratifying and glorious inauguration yesterday—a fine day and a fine display, and everything went off as nicely as could possibly have been devised.

And there the writer stopped most disappointingly, when he evidently meant to give a full account of the day. The explanation followed, on the seventh:

I wrote as far as the above on the day after the inauguration, when I had to lay my letter by to do something else, and until now have been unable to find even a moment's time to take it up again. You will hardly excuse me for ten days' silence; but I know you would cheerfully grant me absolution if you could but half appreciate how my time is taken up.

Since I commenced writing I have again been called away to appease visitors who are importuning to see Mr. Lincoln. So, do not be surprised if I break off at any minute and fold my letter up and mail it, for I am going to send you something tonight, if it is only an empty envelope.

The first official act of Mr. Lincoln, after the inauguration, was to sign my appointment as Private Secretary, and I have been busy enough ever since (as in fact I had been before). By and by, in two or three months, when the appointments are all made, I think the labor will be more sufferable. John Hay and I are both staying here in the White House. We have pleasant offices, and a nice large bedroom, though all of them sadly need new furniture and carpets. That too we expect to have remedied after a while.

We all stayed at Willard's the week before the inauguration. There was of course a great crowd there, and so many ladies in the parlors as to make it seem like having a party every night.

Hidden away in reminiscences we find other details of those first days in Washington. A Miss Williams who joined the Presidential train with her father at Harrisburg remembered that it was "Parlor No. 6," really a suite of apartments with a deceitful mirror at the farther end which lured the absent-minded to prolong their stroll, that was set aside for Mr. Lincoln's use, and so thronged as to "seem like having a party every night." Miss Williams sang, and Mr. Lincoln enjoyed her music in moments of rest, and asked for "something sad." She remembered too that Robert Lincoln and John Hay, being less bashful and more carefree than their slightly older comrades, were forever trying to lure Colonel Ellsworth and Mr. Nicolay into the circle of young gaiety at Willard's, with small success. She remembered that Mrs. Lincoln carried her off upstairs, almost at the moment of arrival, to decide upon the dress to wear that night when the peace delegates were received; and in this way she witnessed the reunion of the President-elect and his two small sons, a picture she never forgot—Mr. Lincoln in an armchair, his face beaming; the little boys swarming joyously over him.

From many sources we learn how the President-elect was eyed by visitors who thronged Parlor No. 6, alternately amused and impressed by his apt replies and his utter absence of self-consciousness. As Senator Douglas put it, he "did not seem to realize that he cast a larger shadow than formerly." When the members of the Peace Congress filed in, with Ex-President Tyler at their head, they found, instead of the loud-mouthed boor some of them dreaded, a man as dignified and courteous, if not so well favored, as Mr. Tyler himself; while the short lady at his side, in the "blue and white checked silk, with white footing collarette and cuffs" had manners as self-possessed as their own wives and daughters.

The writer of the letter of March 7th found time, in spite of the pressure of work, to slip in several lines about social doings:

Since my arrival I have been to one party, one wedding, and the Inaugural Ball, which, by the way, was really a very successful and brilliant affair. [It was held, in what the newspapers called "a white muslin Palace of Aladdin" on Judiciary Square.] Today the Corps

Diplomatique made their formal call upon the President, and tomorrow night the first public reception takes place.

On March 10th he wrote:

Do not be surprised if my letters for a while bear the evidence of haste. Although today is Sunday, and I have not been pretending to work, yet to read a letter here, to make a memorandum there, and answer a question somewhere else, has taken up the entire day, so that at nine o'clock at night I for the first time find an opportunity (and not a very good one) to begin a letter to you.

We have had no particular excitement since I wrote you, except the reception on Friday night, which was voted by the oldest inhabitants to have been the most successful ever known here. For over two hours the crowd poured in as rapidly as the door would admit them, and many climbed in at the windows. It was withal more "ton-ish" than such things usually are. Of course in such a crowd crinoline suffered, and at least fifty men have been swearing worse than "our army in Flanders" ever since, over the loss of new hats and valuable overcoats. But for particulars I must refer you to the "Star" I mailed you this morning.

I cannot yet form much of an idea of how I shall like it here. For two or three months the work will of course be pretty arduous. After that I expect to find some time for both recreation and study. As the laws do not provide for an assistant for me, I have had John Hay appointed to a clerkship in the Department of the Interior, and detailed for special service here at the White House, so that he gives me the benefit of his whole time.

Before long he described a gathering typical of Washington society—a party at the home of a lady who had come to the city with Polk's administration, and, being gifted with the genius of hospitality, had continued to draw interesting people about her. Hers was not a grand house. Her sister, Mrs. Gouverneur, is authority for the statement that for some time the rent she paid was less than three hundred dollars a year; but not even at the President's was one apt to meet more celebrities, or hear better talk.

June 30, 1861. . . . On Tuesday night I attended a little party at Mrs. Eames's. Mr. Eames was formerly connected as editor with the

"Washington Union," for many years the organ of the Democratic administrations here, though now, like many other things, passed away. Afterwards he went as Minister to Venezuela. Both he and his wife are very intelligent, amiable, and hospitable, and by reason of their position and long residence here as well as abroad, know almost everybody, and constantly draw around them the most interesting people who visit Washington. Although they have but a small house, and live in very moderate style, their parlor is really a sort of focal point in Washington society, where one meets the best people who come here. By the "best" I do not mean mere fashionable "society people," but rather the brains of society—politicians, diplomats, authors and artists, and occasionally too, persons whose social and political positions merely, and not their brains, entitle them to consideration, such as titled foreigners, pretty women, &c. Politically it is a sort of neutral ground, where men of all shades of opinion—Republicans, Democrats, Fossil Whigs, with even an occasional spice of a Secessionist, come together quietly and socially. Usually we go there on Sunday evenings—say from 8 to 11—without any formality whatever; merely "drop in," coming and going entirely at pleasure, and talking to whom and about what everyone pleases. A variety of people of course bring with them a variety of languages; and so, while the key-note is almost always English, the conversation runs into variations of French, German and Spanish. Mr. and Mrs. Eames speak all of them but the German.

The party on Tuesday evening was given to Lady Georgiana Fane, daughter of the Earl of Westminster, I believe; a very rich, reasonably intelligent, horribly ugly English old maid, who is travelling in the United States. Among the guests were Secretaries Chase and Bates, Mrs. Grimsley, Senator Wilson, N. P. Willis, Leutze the great painter, and other celebrities. It was of course like any other little party, and the guests talked and acted just as the same number of any other well-informed people would do. . . . I find it an agreeable place to visit, and the best place in the city to meet distinguished people.

The next letter, July 3d, reported:

. . . At Mrs. Eames's on Sunday night I had the pleasure of meeting Charlotte Cushman the great actress, and a Miss Stebbins, who is a sculptor, among the other celebrities. Charlotte Cushman is I think the most masculine woman I ever saw; though evidently a woman of very great intellect. She is getting old and ugly.

The hours of leisure for which Lincoln's secretaries longed so hopefully never came. Before the halls and corridors and gardens of the President's House had been cleared of people begging to see Mr. Lincoln, "for just five minutes," about appointments to civil office, that shot in the gray dawn at Sumter changed the character of the crowds and insured their permanence.

The burst of enthusiasm which greeted Lincoln's call to arms, and the anxious days which followed the attack upon Northern troops passing through Baltimore, are both reflected in a letter written on the night of April 19th.

Before this reaches you, if indeed it reaches you at all soon, you will have heard that we are living through rather stirring times. . . . At Baltimore today a collision occurred between a Massachusetts regiment coming to defend the city, and the Secessionists, in which several were killed on both sides. It is I believe the first blood shed in this civil war, and singularly enough, is shed on the anniversary of the first bloodshed of the Revolution. We are expecting more troops here by way of Baltimore, but are also fearful that the Secessionists may at any hour cut the telegraph wires, tear up the railroad track, or burn the bridges, and thus . . . cut off all communication. We have rumors that 1500 men are gathered at Alexandria, seven miles from here, supposed to have hostile intentions against this city, and there is an additional report that a vessel was late this evening seen landing men on the Maryland side of the river. All these things indicate that if we are to be attacked it will be tonight. On the other hand we have some 4000 or 5000 men under arms in the city, and a very vigilant watch out in all the probable directions of approach. The public buildings are strongly guarded; the Secretary of War will remain all night in his office, and General Scott is within convenient reach. I do not think any force could be brought against the city tonight which our men could not easily repulse, and therefore do not feel seriously alarmed, though the apprehension of danger is pretty general. Unless they are obstructed somewhere on the way, we think there will be enough troops here by tomorrow evening to render the city very safe. . . . At this point—it is now half after eleven—Colonel Lamon, just in from the War Department, tells me that all is quiet, but that a "brush" is expected by the Secretary of War before morning. Well, there is nothing to be done but to wait and see what the night brings forth.

The organization of militia and the late arrivals of troops have been making things seem quite warlike for a few days past; but we have been much more impressed with the conditions surrounding us by the arrival this evening of Miss Dix, who comes to offer herself and an army of nurses to the government gratuitously for hospital service.

John Hay also was impressed by the coming of Miss Dix. He wrote: "She makes the most munificent and generous offers."

After communication with the North had indeed been cut off, an apathy settled upon the town which was only one remove from panic. Places of business remained closed. Frightened people locked their houses and departed, or left them with hanging blinds and open, staring windows. Dust settled upon steps and area railings. Deserted household pets endured starvation, dumbly. The streets were empty save when patrolmen, with bunches of hay tied upon their saddles, galloped to the relief of an outpost. Lincoln looked long and fruitlessly from the White-House windows. So controlled was he in the presence of others, that no one guessed the depth of his anxiety until that cry was overheard, wrung from him when he thought himself alone, "Why don't they come! Why don't they come?"

Bits from John Hay's record of that anxious week add color and a touch of youthful recklessness to the picture. On April 18th he wrote:

The White House is turned into barracks. Jim Lane marshalled his Kansas warriors today at Willard's, and placed them at the disposal of Major Hunter, who turned them tonight into the East Room. It is a splendid company, worthy such an armory. Besides the western Jayhawkers it comprises some of the best material of the East. . . . The Major has made me his aide, and I labored under some uncertainty as to whether I should speak to privates or not. . . . All day the notes of preparation have been heard at the public buildings and the armories.

Fear of the President's assassination was already in the air.

Tonight Edward brought me a card from Mrs. —— expressing a wish to see the President on matters concerning his personal safety. As the Ancient was in bed I volunteered to receive the harrowing communication. Edward took me to the little room adjoining the hall and I waited. Mrs. —— who is neither young nor yet fair to any miraculous extent, came in leading a lady who was a little of both, whom she introduced as Mrs. Colonel Lander. I was delighted at this chance interview with the Medea, the Julia and the Mona Lisa of my stage-struck days. After many hesitating and bashful trials, Mrs. Lander told the impulse that brought them. Some young Virginian, a long-haired, swaggering, chivalrous (of course) and indiscreet friend, had come into town in great anxiety for a new saddle, and meeting her, had said that he, and half a dozen others . . . would do a thing within forty-eight hours that would ring through the world. Connecting this central fact with a multiplicity of attendant details, she concluded that the President was either to be assassinated or captured. She ended by renewing her protestations of earnest solicitude, mingled with fears of the impropriety of the step. Lander has made her very womanly since he married her. Imagine Jean M. Davenport a blushing hesitating wife!

They went away, and I went to the bedside of the chief *couché*. I told him the yarn; he quietly grinned. . . .

Friday April 19. . . . About midnight we made the tour of the house. Hunter and the Italian exile V. were quietly asleep on the floor of the East Room, and a young and careless guard loafed around the furnace fires in the basement; good-looking and energetic young fellows, too good to be food for gunpowder, if anything is.

April 20. . . . The streets were full of the talk of Baltimore. . . . I went up with N. and P. and W. to see the Massachusetts troops quartered in the Capitol. The scene was very novel. The contrast was very painful between the gray-haired dignity that filled the Senate Chamber when I saw it last, and the present throng of bright-looking Yankee boys, the most of them bearing the signs of New England rusticity in voice and manner, scattered over the desks, chairs and galleries; some loafing, many writing letters slowly and with plow-hardened hands, or with rapid-glancing clerkly fingers, while G. stood patient by the desk, and franked for everybody. The Hall of Representatives is as yet empty. Lying on a sofa and looking upward, the magnificence of the barracks made me envy the soldiers who should be quartered there. . . . The spirit of our institutions seemed visibly present to inspire and nerve the acolyte sleeping in her temple beside his unfleshed sword. . . . The town is full tonight of feverish rumors about a meditated assault upon the town. . . .

April 21, Sunday. . . . This morning we mounted the battlements of the Executive Mansion, and the Ancient took a long look down the Bay. It was a "water-haul." Any amount of feverish rumors, filled the evening . . . all which tomorrow will sift.

We passed the evening pleasantly at E.'s where were the English legation, and returned to find V. and his borderers guarding the imperial palace, pacing in belted and revolvered dignity up and down the wide portico.

Revolvers and belts were their only insignia of office, for these volunteers were as yet in citizen's dress.

April 22. . . . It was melodramatic to see C. C. come into the President's reception room today. He wore with a sublimely unconscious air three pistols and an Arkansas toothpick, and looked like an admirable vignette of twenty-five cents' worth of yellow-covered romance. Housewives here are beginning to dread famine. Flour has made a sudden spring to $18 a barrel, and cornmeal rejoices in the respectable atmosphere of $2.50 a bushel. Willard's is preparing for war, furling all sails for the storm. The dinner table is shorn of *cartes* and the tea table reduced to the severe simplicity of pound cake. . . .

April 23. At dinner we sat opposite to old Gen. S. who was fierce and jubilant. No frenzied poet ever predicted the ruin of a hostile house with more energy and fervor than he issued the rescript of destiny against Baltimore. . . . He was peculiarly disgusted with the impertinence of Delaware. "The contemptible little neighborhood without population enough for a decent country village gets upon her hind legs and talks about armed neutrality; the only good use for traitors is to hang them. . . .

A gaunt, tattered, uncombed and unshorn figure appeared at the door and marched solemnly up to the table. He wore a rough rusty overcoat, a torn shirt and suspenderless breeches. His thin hair stood fretful-porcupine-wise upon his crown. He sat down and gloomily charged upon his dinner. A couple of young exquisites were eating and chatting opposite him. They were guessing when the road would be open through Baltimore. "Thursday!" growled the grim apparition, "or Baltimore will be laid in ashes." It was Jim Lane.

Tonight there seems to be reliable news at the State Dept. that the Seventh Regiment and the Massachusetts troops would start from Annapolis tonight, and through the favoring moonlight march to the Junction where the Government has possession of the road. . . . A large and disappointed throng gathered at the depot this morning, hoping to get deliverance. But the hope was futile. . . .

April 24. . . . This has been a day of gloom and doubt. Everybody seems to be filled with a vague distrust and recklessness. The idea seemed to be reached by Lincoln when, chatting with the [wounded] volunteers this morning, he said "I don't believe there is any North! The Seventh Regiment is a myth! Rhode Island is not known in our geography any longer. You are the only northern realities." Seward's messengers sent out by the dozen, do not return. The Seventh and Butler's are probably still at Annapolis. . . .

April 25. . . . About noon the Seventh Regiment came. I went to the depot and saw Lefferts, who communicated the intelligence of their peaceful passage, with which I straightway gladdened the heart of the Ancient. . . . Today we got a few letters and papers, and felt not quite so forlorn. . . .

Mr. Nicolay's next letter was dated April 26th.

I have not written since for the reason that I knew the letter would only go as far as the postoffice, or at farthest into the hands of the Baltimore barbarians, and therefore would not in the least relieve your suspense. We too had our burden of suspense. . . . Our intercourse with the outside world was cut off. We heard frequently from Baltimore and different parts of Maryland, but the news had little of encouragement in it. Uniformly the report was that all heretofore Union men had at once turned secessionists. Here we were in this city, in charge of all the public buildings, property and archives, with only about 2000 *reliable* men to defend it. True, we had some 3000 in addition of the District militia under arms; but with the city perfectly demoralized with secession feeling. We were not certain but that at the first moment when fate seemed to preponderate against us, we would have to look down the muzzles of our own guns. . . .

Not that we were at any time in extreme danger. With the reliable force at our disposal we could have held the city against largely superior numbers. But had the rebels suddenly precipitated 5000 or 6000 men upon us, which it seemed possible for them to do, it would have given us an infinite deal of trouble. Then there was another danger. As Sunday, Monday and Tuesday passed by without bringing the expected reinforcements, the suspense and uncertainty among our city population grew to such a pitch that a very small untoward circumstance or accident would have stirred up a riot or a panic. Fortunately everything went on smoothly and quietly until the arrival of the Seventh Regiment from New York, adding a third to our defensive force, and also bringing the certain information that several additional regiments were at and this side of Annapolis. . . . This made the city safe in every contingency, and men went to talking, laughing, trading and working as before; and since yesterday morning at ten oclock you would not discover from anything except the everywhereness of uniforms and muskets, that we are in the midst of revolution and civil war, the end of which will be a serious matter for the side that has to go to the wall.

John Hay's record for April 26th notes that Massachusetts and Rhode Island troops are arriving in large numbers and continues:

Carl Schurz was here today. He spoke with wild enthusiasm of his desire to mingle in this war. . . . He contemplates the career of a great guerilla chief with ardent longing.

April 29. Going to Nicolay's room this morning, Carl Schurz and Jim Lane were sitting. Jim was at the window filling his soul with gall by steady telescopic contemplation of a secession flag impudently flaunting over a roof in Alexandria. "Let me tell you," he said to the elegant Teuton, "we have got to whip these scoundrels like Hell, Carl Schurz. They did a good thing stoning our men at Baltimore and shooting away the flag at Sumter. It has set the great North a-howling for blood, and they 'll have it."

"I heard," said Schurz, "that you preached a sermon to your men yesterday."

"No sir! This is no time for preaching. When I went to Mexico there were four preachers in my regiment. In less than a week I issued orders for them all to stop preaching and go to playing cards. In a month or so, they were the biggest devils and best fighters I had."

An hour afterward Carl Schurz told me he was going home to arm his clansmen for the wars. He has obtained three months' leave of absence from his diplomatic duties, and permission to raise a cavalry regiment. I doubt the propriety of the movement [but] he will make a wonderful land-pirate; bold, quick, brilliant and reckless.

Some of the regiments which poured into the city came equipped, almost ready for service. Others were mere patriotic mobs, lacking everything soldiers should have, except courage and devotion. All

THE CAPITOL DOME

were sent to camps of instruction, and the military machine began to grind, slowly, but with ever-increasing momentum. At first there was a deal of martial show, as well as much suppressed impatience. It seemed so simple a thing to overrun Alexandria and tear down that flaunting flag; yet because of mere military orders no patriot had the right to do so. Ellsworth's Zouaves, in their camp two miles out of town, daredevils culled from the most daring of New York's fire-department, felt hampered by their gaudy uniforms, and fearfully puritanic in obeying the restrictions imposed on them. One May morning news came that Willard's Hotel was on fire, and at a word from their leader they broke joyously into their old calling, started up Pennsylvania Avenue on a run, impressed everything on wheels that came in their way, and, arriving, treated the onlookers to a marvelous exhibiton fire-drill, making human ladders of themselves from the ground to the top story, and disdaining any other means of passing up water-buckets and hose.

Ten days later their colonel lay in the great East Room of the White House with a bullet in his heart, mourned by the entire North as an unnecessary victim of the war; for it was ardor, not duty, which took Ellsworth to the roof of the Alexandria hotel to bring down that taunting Confederate flag.

The President's secretary wrote:

I had known and seen him almost daily for more than six months past, and although our intimacy was never in any wise confidential as to personal matters, I had learned to value him very highly. He was very young, only 24, I think, very talented and ambitious—and very poor—a combination of the qualities upon which sadness and misfortune seem to prey. He had by constant exertion already made himself famous, and that against obstacles which would have been insurmountable to any other. Since my acquaintance with him my position has enabled me to assist him in his plans and aspirations, until I felt an almost direct personal pride in his ability and his determined energy. I knew that he would win a brilliant success if life were spared him. So that to me his death seems almost a fatality; and though I know the whole nation will mourn for him, I am grieved also to feel that they do not half appreciate his worth or their loss.

With so many new regiments at hand, the Fourth of July was made a grand occasion. This is the account of it:

July 8, 1861. The interest of the week just past of course centres around the "Fourth" and the special session of Congress which began on that day, although they were neither of them accompanied by any particularly noteworthy event. On the morning of the "Fourth" there was a rather fine review by the President and others of 23 regiments of New York volunteers, which, as you may imagine formed a procession of considerable length. One very pretty incident varied the monotony of the marching by of the troops. Among the regiments is one called the Garibaldi Guards, made up entirely of foreigners, many of whom have served in European wars. There are, let me say by way of somewhat describing the regiment, men of six or eight different nationalities in it, who speak as many different languages. It is said, I know not with how much truth, that the Colonel gives his commands in French, that being the universal language and understood by all the captains of the companies, who repeat them respectively in German, Spanish, Italian, French, Hungarian, &c., to their men. In preparing for the review, each man had stuck a small bouquet of flowers or a sprig of box or evergreen into his hat, and as the successive ranks passed the platform on which stood the President and other officers they took them out and threw them toward him, so that while the regiment was passing a perfect shower of leaves and flowers was falling on the platform and the street, which latter was almost covered with them. It was unexpected, and therefore strikingly novel and poetical.

This was a great contrast to Fourth of July a year later, of which the President's secretary wrote:

I think that for fourteen years I have not had so dull a "fourth." . . . The day is literally like any other. There has been nothing whatever going on in the city. The little boys have even shot away the bunch of firecrackers they bought this morning, and on account of hard times and prospective taxation, can't afford to buy a second bunch.

By that time war had doffed all its holiday trappings, and there was no longer anything exhilarating in military parade. In earlier days even military routine had been interesting. Everybody wished to visit the camps and to "make the tour of our lines," though these were as yet scarcely lines at all. And when regiments crossed to the Virginia shore over the old wooden Long Bridge, which was so shaky that for safety the companies had to break step, they were still, in Choate's picturesque phrase, "keeping step to the music of the Union." We have one more glimpse of the foreign regiment at such a moment:

Day before yesterday the Garibaldi Guards were sent across the river, and having an idea that there was a fight ahead, they went over the Long Bridge with their loaves of bread stuck on the points of their bayonets, and singing the "Marseillaise."

After April, 1861, the capital was never again cut off from the loyal North, but it saw sights and suffered shocks to which no capital should be subjected. A letter written on the day of the first battle of Bull Run tells how the news of defeat reached the White House:

July 21, 1861 12 M. . . . We still have no news of any decisive battle at Manassas Junction, though it is thought probable that there will be skirmishing all day, and perhaps a small fight. . . . Even while I write this, dispatches come which indicate that a considerable part of the forces is engaged; so that we may know by night whether we are to be successful in this fight or not. . . . We shall have . . . to be impatiently patient until we get reliable news. . . . Of course everybody is in great suspense. General Scott talked confidently this morning of success, and very calmly and quietly went to church at eleven oclock.

1 ½ P. M. Since I wrote the foregoing, during say two hours, the President has been receiving dispatches at intervals of fifteen minutes from Fairfax Station, in which the operator reports the fluctuations of the firing as he hears it at the distance of three or four miles from the scene of action. For half an hour the President has been somewhat uneasy, as these reports seemed to indicate that our forces were retiring. After getting his dinner he went over to see General Scott, whom he found asleep. He woke the General and presented his view of the case . . . but the General told him these reports were worth nothing as indications either way, and the changes in the currents of the wind, the echoes, &c., &c., made it impossible for a distant listener to determine the course of a battle. The General still expressed confidence, and composed himself for another nap when the President left.

From about four to six dispatches continued to come in, saying the battle had extended along nearly the whole line—that there had been considerable loss on both sides, but that the secession lines had been driven back two or three miles. Some of the dispatches said, to the Junction. One of General Scott's aides came in and reported . . . that the General was satisfied of the truth of this report, and that McDowell would immediately attack and capture the Junction, perhaps yet tonight, but certainly by tomorrow noon.

At six o'clock, the President having in the meanwhile gone out to ride, Mr. Seward came into the President's room with a terribly frightened and excited look, and said to John and me, who were sitting there:

"Where is the President?"

"Gone to ride" we replied.

"Have you any late news?" he asked.

I began reading Hanscomb's dispatch to him.

Said he: "Tell no one. That is not so. The battle is lost. The telegraph says that McDowell is in full retreat, and calls on General Scott to save the capital. . . . Find the President and tell him to come immediately to General Scott's."

In about half an hour the President came in. We told him, and he started off immediately. John and I continued to sit at the windows, and could now distinctly hear heavy cannonading on the other side of the river. It is now eight o'clock, but the President has not yet returned, and we have heard nothing further.

Monday morning, July 22. The victory which seemed in our grasp at four oclock yesterday afternoon is changed to an overwhelming defeat—a total and disgraceful rout of our men. The whole army is in retreat, and will come back as far as the lines of fortifications on the other side of the river. These have all the time been kept properly garrisoned, and are strong enough to make the city perfectly secure. . . . At this time (10 ½ A. M.) we have of course few details of yesterday's disaster, though it is pretty evident that there were large losses. . . .

July 23. I send these few lines merely to say . . . that the results of the late battle near here are not any more disastrous than I reported yesterday. Our forces retreated, as I wrote you, but so far we have not heard that they were pursued even an inch by the enemy. I have no doubt that we had fairly won the battle, and that had the stampede not occurred among our troops, the enemy and not we, would have retreated. But the fat is all in the fire now, and we shall have to crow small until we can retrieve the disgrace somehow. The preparations for the war will be continued with increased vigor by the government.

July 28. . . . The city is still very quiet. There were one or two sensation rumors on the street yesterday, but they did not prove to be of any significance whatever. Just at nightfall the city was on the *qui vive* at hearing some cannon firing apparently across the river somewhere, and timid nerves were startled with the impression that the city was being attacked. It turned out that one of our steamers had gone on a pleasure excursion down the river, and was firing salutes on her way up to the landing. Of course there are constantly plenty of incidents on which to found rumors, and plenty of disturbed and lively imaginations to give them shape and utterance. . . .

After the defeat at Bull Run the country settled down to the long struggle, and the months and years rolled by in periods of hope and waiting and dread.

Keeping pace with the unfolding of the drama, the very character of the town altered, the straggling, leisurely village of pre-war days giving place to the ordered disorder of a great military center. Little by little the soft outline of the wooded hills surrounding it changed to a circle of armed forts. Corcoran and Bennett and Haggarty across the river from Georgetown; Runyon and Albany covering the Long Bridge; Ellsworth on Shuter Hill near Alexandria; Craig, Tillinghast, Cass, Woodbury, Richardson, and Strong to protect Arlington Heights. On this side, Fort Reno near Tenallytown, De Russey, whose lines may still be traced in Rock Creek Park; Fort Stevens on the Seventh Street Road; Gaines, Slocum, Totten, Bunker Hill, Saratoga, Slemmer, Thayer, and so on, around to Fort Lincoln near the old dueling-ground—indeed, on the very farm which was the scene of the unfortunate battle of Bladensburg. Others rose thick and fast, until by the spring of 1863 there were no less than thirty-four forts and armed batteries on the south shore of the Potomac alone.

Hospitals sprang up in waste places of the city—a giant fungus growth, bursting with mercy and with pain, battening on human blood. Long before these could be built, there was such need of them that churches were offered for this use. One of the letters written from the White House in July, 1862, says that almost every church in town is thus occupied. Warehouses were taken, and also roomy private residences. Mr. Corcoran's was one of those selected, its owner having chosen to go abroad; but the French minister telegraphed from New York that he had rented it for a legation. Beautiful Kalorama, on the hills north of the town, became a place to be shunned, the hospital for contagious diseases. And all these places of pain filled and emptied again as the tides of battle rolled across Virginia.

From them, two never-ending streams went forth, one back to the army to fight again; the other back to the ground for which life itself had been given. There had been a time in the earlier history of the town when, for health's sake, it was deemed necessary to do away with little burial-places which, after the fashion of colonial days, were scattered about within city limits—one in the corner of Lafayette Square, one on F Street, near Tenth, and so on. These had been carefully removed to tracts so large and so remote that it was supposed provision had been made for generations to come. But the never-ending silent stream from the hospitals soon filled to overflowing the burial-plot at the Soldiers' Home, the only military cemetery in the city. It seemed neither wise nor right to encroach upon other parts of that beautiful park, so, before the war was over, Arlington was set aside for this use. Military authority had taken possession of the estate a few days after it was deserted by its former owners, and for three years it had been a camp and headquarters; but life in and about the old mansion had been permitted, even encouraged, to go on as much as possible in the old way, with the same old slaves pottering about the flower beds.

One of the first rides Lincoln's secretaries found time to take carried them across the river and up to the stately dwelling. One of them wrote:

Washington May 31, 1861. . . . In company with John Hay and Bob Lincoln who is here on a short visit from college, I took yesterday my second horseback ride since I have been here. We went across the Long Bridge over into Virginia, where you know many of our troops are now encamped. They are engaged in throwing up earth breastworks to command the various approaches to the bridge, and judging from their appearance yesterday, the soldiers are beginning fully to appreciate the earnest service of the campaign. . . . We went up to Arlington house, situated on Arlington Heights, about which you have seen so much in the newspapers. Arlington House is the old family mansion of the Custis family, the relations and descendants of Washington, and has one of the most beautiful situations imaginable, just opposite this city on a high sloping hill that rises up from the Potomac. The house looks quite old. I do not know when it was built, but it was evidently in its day a grand affair; and its arrangement, furniture, pictures, &c at once carry one back to the good old "first family" days of Virginia before her social decay . . . had bred political and moral corruption. In those days plantation grandeur atoned somewhat for their assumptions of family pride. The furniture of the house was evidently "stylish," in its time. The chambers are filled up with family portraits—most of them very indifferent as works of art. . . . Deers' antlers, the trophies of the chase in the old days, are nailed up about the halls and passages, and altogether, a historic and traditional atmosphere seemed to pervade the house such as I have not stood in for many a day. In the garden we found an old negro at work who was born at Mt. Vernon before General Washington's death. We asked him many questions—delighted him by introducing "Bob," the President's son, in whom the old darkey expressed a lively interest —and further pleased him with a gift of small change. . . . I do not know when I have passed so satisfactory and pleasant an afternoon.

Lincoln's secretaries came to regard this old negro as their special find, a bit of concrete history, to be enjoyed as one enjoys a first edition and to be exhibited, judiciously, to friends: A later entry in John Hay's diary reads:

E. L. S. son of Lord S. has been here for a week. I took him over to Arlington and showed him the African. He asked more questions than I ever dreamed of in similar circumstances. He applied a drastic suction to every contraband he met with, and came back with brain and notebook crammed with instructive miscellany.

Changes which took place in the city were not all in the line of progress. The thin covering of cobblestones which had been spread over Pennsylvania Avenue, some years before, sank under the weight of war, pounded to prodigious depths by the tramp of marching feet and the endless processions of army wagons. The wide street became a Sahara, above which golden gritty clouds of dust were buffeted by every wind. In rainy seasons the avenue's lower reaches grew speedily liquid, while its higher portions attained a marvelous stickiness. The letters frequently mention such things, coupled invariably with the thought of how the weather will affect the armies in the field. No matter upon what subject one began, one always came back to the war.

Pennsylvania Avenue, in its alternating stages of mud and dust, united the two centers of government activity, the Capitol and the White House, for Washington was still a collection of little centers, rather than one large town. The small business section midway between, particularly that portion below the avenue, became cluttered with undesirable additions—soldiers' eating-houses, variety shows, a horse bazaar, a large wheelwright shop working overtime at mending ambulances; a guard-house, and a series of lofts where embalmers plied their grisly trade, which waxed and waned with the filling of the hospitals. Its momentary state might be inferred from the height of the piles of coffins stacked upon the sidewalk.

Ninth Street between F Street and Pennsylvania Avenue was just passing from residential to business uses. On Tenth Street a Baptist church had been transformed into a theater. Certain fortunate boys who lived on Ninth Street might creep from their beds and watch for glimpses of the actors. The alley back of their home was the one down which, in 1865, Wilkes Booth took his flight.

The arsenal and the Navy Yard were not only busy military centers, but, because society snatched recreation from the very jaws of war, places of official gaiety as well. The letters and diary tell of military musicales where "they sang well, the band played well, and the President listened well," and where, with fine aplomb, a singer interpolated English words in the Marseillaise when his supply of French was not equal to the strain. Again, we read of dancing at the Navy Yard until 2 A. M., in crushes where ball-dresses suffered terribly . . . and it required a quick eye and skilful pilotage to whirl extensively be-crinolined beauty unscathed through the dense crowd at a gallopade.

Near the Capitol the "Duff Green row" erected by Jackson's satellite and later opponent, the house which gave shelter to the Supreme Court after the visit of the British, and the "Old Brick Capitol," now turned to sinister prison uses, were prominent in the landscape. Between them honeysuckle cascaded over fences, apple-trees left from the original farm orchard bore vigorously, and dark-leaved magnolias grew in the dooryards.

Judiciary Square was distinctly fashionable. Secretary Chase and his handsome daughter had taken a house there. Lord Lyons lived at 245 H Street; some of the French secretaries of legation at 199 and 166 Pennsylvania Avenue N. W.; addresses not so startling as they at first appear, since the old system of street numbering was still in vogue. The Italian legation had its headquarters in one of the oldest houses erected in Washington, the "Seven Buildings" at Pennsylvania Avenue and Twenty-first Street. Russia, true to form, had pushed north out into the arid steppes of Connecticut Avenue; but most of the foreign representatives clung as closely as possible to the White House. Surrounding these densely built up localities were sparsely populated regions where might be found the rest of the sixty-odd thousand souls credited by the census-taker to Washington, regions which resembled neither town nor country, but combined the worst features of both. Here might be seen a row of wooden shacks, hurriedly thrown together for war use, there a new hospital, rising out of a wilderness of red clay, and yonder an old mansion with its slave quarters and walled garden, or a new foundation begun and abandoned on the eve of war.

Everywhere, crowding in between the larger houses, were negro huts and cabins. After emancipation the hill which is now Nineteenth Street above Florida Avenue, became covered with their makeshift homes. In whole sections the city plan had not yet emerged from brier-infested fields. Streets had a way of trailing off into country roads or ending abruptly in a clay bank. On the other hand, quite as unexpectedly, they opened up vistas of the white dome, or a row of stately columns, symbolic, like the dome, of the majesty of national government. Washington was a place of contrasts, where anything seemed possible but where only one thing was desired—the end of war.

For this everybody labored, not only high officials and men in uniform but thousands of obscure clerks in the departments, who sat writing endlessly in long-hand or adding up columns of figures whose totals soared to heights undreamed before in American affairs. Some of these laborers were destined to well-earned fame on their own account: John Burroughs, who spent his leisure with the birds out near Fort Lincoln; Clara Barton, one of the women who had made their way into offices where woman's presence was not yet thought seemly; Walt Whitman, pausing, on his way to a hospital after work hours, to see the President drive by; Louisa Alcott doing her bit as volunteer in the hospitals.

With the same will to help, people from all corners of the Union flocked to Washington and moved upon the White House with questions and advice. Dining at Willard's was like taking one's place temporarily on a page of history. Taking one's place in the President's anteroom was to watch the mind of the nation working out its foolish thoughts as well as its brave ones. Lincoln's secretary wrote:

Very queer characters occasionally call upon me. That you may be assured of the prospect of a speedy crushing out of the rebellion, I must inform you of a new leader and agency about to take part in the contest.

The other morning the doorkeeper brought in a plain looking but also very rational looking man, ordinarily dressed, appearing perhaps more than anything else to be a farmer. I asked him to be seated, when he at once, without circumlocution and in a very matter-of-fact and businesslike way, stated the object of his call.

"I am come here" he said, "about the business of this war we are engaged in. I am commissioned from On High to take the matter in hand and end it. I have consulted with the Governor of York State, and he has promised to raise as many men of the militia of that state as I need. But as I did n't want to proceed without authority, I came on here to see General Halleck. I have had an interview with him, and he told me that he could not give me any men or assistance, that nobody but the President had authority to act in the case. I have therefore come to see the President to obtain his consent to begin this work. Although no power is competent to stop or impede my progress, yet I desire to act with approval of the authorities. I shall take only 2000 men, and shall go down South and get Jeff Davis and the other leaders of the rebellion and bring them here to be put in the lunatic asylum—because they are plainly crazy, and it is of no use to be fighting with crazy men."

In reply I assured him that the President was so engaged that it would be impossible for him to gain the desired interview—that the President would give him no men, nor authority of any kind—and that whatever he did in the matter he must do upon his own responsibility. He appeared to be satisfied that I properly represented the President, and went away saying that he should write at once to the Governor of York State to raise and organize his force for him, and proceed with his work.

All this transpired with as much gravity and method as if it had been a little conference about any matter of routine business, and an observer would have thought that I was as crazy as the man himself, from the perfectly serious and natural manner in which both he and I talked the matter over. Lunatics and visionaries are here so frequently that they cease to be strange phenomena, and I find the best way to dispose of them is to discuss and decide their mad projects as deliberately as any other matter of business.

We have no news of special importance.

"We have no news of special importance." That was the recurring burden of the letters. War news was the only news really desired; and much-desired war news comes upon laggard feet, as the world has recently learned all over again. More and more was this note of longing emphasized. At times it seemed to the young man impossible to endure the inaction of his post at Washington. He wrote that he felt he must "get into the most active and thickest part of the fight, wherever that might be."

This being where I can overlook the whole war and never be in it—constantly worked to death and yet accomplishing nothing, grows exceedingly irksome.

Then he would remember the far greater burden borne by his chief, and add, "It is a feeling of duty and not of inclination which keeps me here." Once when the war cloud seemed lifting, he wrote:

Because this prospect is at present so cheering . . . I think I have been more nervous and anxious during this week past than for a year. . . . The President is cheerful and hopeful—not unduly elated, but seeming confident; and now as ever, watching every report and indication with quiet unwavering interest. If my own anxiety is so great, what must be his solicitude.

What indeed must have been the solicitude and the power of painful endurance of this most unmilitary commander-in-chief, the great, gaunt, merciful man whose black-clad figure might be seen anywhere in Washington, at almost any moment; an apparition as unexpected and as welcome as the sight of the shining dome down the long vista of an unfinished street! He would be driving to some hospital, perhaps, or out to the Soldiers' Home for a night's rest; or returning from a flag-raising, or on his way to a review. If afoot, perhaps he stopped under the "Wishing Tree" in Lafayette Square to speak to some poor devil who looked more downhearted than he, himself, felt. Again, long after nightfall, with his gray shawl over his shoulders, he might be seen moving like a deeper shadow across the shadowy square on some errand to the house of Secretary Seward, or over toward the War Department. He once said to General Schenck:

"If to be the head of Hell is as hard as what I have to undergo here, I could find it in my heart to pity Satan himself."

XXI

THE PLUMBER IN POLITICS

THIRTY days after Lincoln's second inauguration, news reached Washington that Richmond had fallen. Instantly the "Fire Alarm Telegraph" set all the bells ringing, and people poured into the streets. Schools were dismissed, courts adjourned, business came to a standstill, department employees suspended their labors. Only the printers kept busy, and they could not supply the demand for "extras," though foremen threw prudence to the winds and shouted to their firemen to "run the engine without the governor!"

A scarlet rash of flags broke out all over town, and in the impromptu festival that staged itself on Pennsylvania Avenue the shrill, sweet voices of school-children could be heard above all other sounds as they walked in procession singing their favorite songs.

The White House was deserted, for everybody knew that President Lincoln was with the army at City Point; but audiences assembled in various parts of the city and listened to speeches. The largest crowd of all gathered outside the War Department, where Secretary Stanton, laboring under strong emotion, made a short address and then called to his side young Willie Kettles, a fourteen-year-old telegraph operator, and introduced him as the one who had taken down the momentous dispatch from Richmond and had therefore been the first to learn the news. The crowd cheered and demanded a speech. Willie, gulping and embarrassed as only a fourteen-year-old boy could be, declared that he "could n't speak," he "felt so"! and, ducking, disappeared into the crowd, which estimated this at its true worth as the most genuine sort of eloquence.

A grand illumination was announced for the following night, when the city expressed its joy in bunting and transparencies. Everywhere the word "Richmond" was seen, surrounded with flags. The

State Department got in a little propaganda, in view of the critical situation in Mexico, by displaying the sentiment: "Peace and Good Will to all Nations, but No Entangling Alliances, and No Foreign Intervention." The Treasury had lights in every one of its hundred and ten front windows, and over its door a transparency representing one of its ten-dollar compound-interest-bearing notes with the legend: "U. S. Greenbacks and U. S. Grant. Grant has given the Greenbacks a Metallic Ring." At the Capitol, in addition to lights in the windows and in the great lantern above the dome, a transparency over the Library pediment proclaimed: "This is the Lord's doing; it is marvellous in our eyes."

Burning gas for mere ornament was still a novelty, and very characteristically the careful manager of Willard's Hotel combined patriotism and economy in five letters by displaying the word "Union" over his door. At Secretary Seward's the decorations ran to paper lanterns; bands serenaded Secretary Stanton; fireworks whizzed in front of General Hunter's residence; and so many private houses were illuminated that it took three columns of the "Star's" finest print to describe them all. The crowds that turned out to view the decorations congested in a great mass meeting near the Patent Office, where men and women stood shoulder to shoulder and boys wriggled up out of the mass to cling like gargoyles against the lighted windows. It was in the last of the speeches made here that Vice-President Johnson struck an unfortunate note when he dwelt on the necessity of inflicting severe punishment upon the leaders of the rebellion. It seemed a pity to cloud that night's rejoicing with even a hint of vengeance.

Two weeks later the streets were again full of people, called from their homes this time by a tale so horrible that they cried out their disbelief as they made their way toward a house on Tenth Street, not far from the center of the former night's rejoicing. Voices in the darkness were asserting and denying that President Lincoln was dead. Another voice added that Mr. Seward had been killed; and rumor, piling horror upon horror, told how not only the President and the Secretary of State, but the Vice-President and most of the cabinet, had been murdered. People pressed on, fearful but unconvinced, until, when they neared their goal, the silent, sorrowful throng told them that part at least of the ghastly tale was true. It was a little dwelling of dingy brick before which the crowd stood hushed and waiting. It had a rather high basement; over that, two small parlors and a little back room, and, above these again, chambers that were let to transient lodgers, usually actors playing in the theater across the way. Up the curving steps of this drab place the President had been carried, and in the small room back of the parlors he lay, while the crowd waited in silence. Night wore on to dawn, and dawn gave way to sunrise that brought no comfort with it. Shortly after seven o'clock Mr. Lincoln's soul took its flight. Stanton came out of the death-chamber, saying: "Now he belongs to the ages." The news was told to the crowd in less dramatic phrase, and slowly and sadly the people melted away.

Within an hour Washington began to drape itself in black. The great public buildings and the houses of the wealthy with their lavish display were not nearly so impressive as the homes of the poor, where even the humblest negro shanty showed its shred of mourning.

But more than sorrow was abroad: the town was in the grip of fear. The Southern feeling so prevalent before the war had by no means been stamped out, though it had been silenced. This plot was so diabolical and seemed so wide-spread that there was no telling where it might break out afresh. As a precaution cannon were planted at commanding points. One was trained upon the old Capitol prison, where certain Confederates were detained. A man who was a very small boy then, has never forgotten how that cannon looked.

Lincoln's secretary, on his way home from Cuba when the tragedy occurred, reached Washington on April 17th. He wrote:

> I cannot describe the air of gloom. As I drove up from the Navy Yard through the city almost every house was draped and men stood idle and listless in groups on the street corners. The Executive Mansion was dark and still almost as the grave itself; the silence and gloom and sorrow depicted on every face are as heavy and ominous of terror as if some great calamity still hung in the air and was about to crush and overwhelm everyone.

In the East Room great crowds are taking their last look at the President's kind face, mild and benignant as becomes the father of a mourning nation, even in death.

Much has been written about the stately pageant of Lincoln's funeral, with its minute guns and tolling bells and the tramp of many feet, civilian as well as military, as his body was escorted from the East Room to the Capitol, and then to the railroad station to begin the sad journey out to Springfield. Amid all the details one fact has been passed over with scanty mention. The train, with its sable hangings, that carried the body of the murdered President back to Illinois, bore also the body of his little son who had died in the White House three years before. Heartbroken over this loss, Lincoln had never allowed his private grief to intrude on public duty. Now he and the child he loved were reunited.

Part of the terror of those first hours after the assassination was because of distrust of Andrew Johnson, who had been nominated Vice-President to please the War Democrats. He had been the one senator from all the seceded states to remain true to the Union in 1861, and this offset in their eyes all his drawbacks, which were many.

He belonged to the class known and despised in the South as "poor white," a description usually completed by the word "trash." He had not learned to read until nearly grown, but good intentions and industry and a fortunate marriage had enabled him to lift himself out of ignorance, and five years in the United States Senate, added to ten in the House of Representatives, had taught him the ways of the world, though they had not made him popular. Many who were merely indifferent at the time of his nomination had become alienated since, owing to evidences of his uncertain temper, and, still more, to his actions on inauguration day, when, as was bluntly charged, he had been drunk when he took the oath of office. That an American of this stamp should be tragically raised to the duties and responsibilities of President, was not only humiliating but serious enough to account for much of that feeling "ominous of terror" that Lincoln's secretary noted.

Those who observed him in the first days of his Presidency felt

PENNSYLVANIA AVENUE, ABOUT 1870

somewhat reassured, though his first short address, delivered while Lincoln's body still lay in the East Room, was conspicuously free from praise of the dead, and contained many allusions to his own career. Senator John P. Hale said dryly that Mr. Johnson seemed willing to share the glory with his Creator, but to forget that Lincoln had anything to do with suppressing the rebellion. He made amends for this in a later speech, but took occasion again to dwell on punishing the Southern leaders for the crime of treason.

But, even so, this was better than had been hoped. Mr. Lincoln's secretary wrote that the new President had "very favorably disappointed" the expectations of almost every one; that he had been "quiet, steady and content to let the government run along under the healthy impetus" it had at the time of Mr. Lincoln's death; and that "all the indications of his personal appearance are very good, except that I think he will not have great physical endurance and is in some danger of wearing himself out."

The members of Lincoln's cabinet, who were asked to continue in office, tried at first to keep a watchful eye upon Mr. Johnson, and to be at hand when he needed a word of advice. But it is hard to keep on advising in friendly spirit a man whose point of view changed as Johnson's did. After being all for stern justice, he underwent such a transformation in his feelings that he seemed to be following in the footsteps of his predecessor Tyler, who on becoming President remembered only his affiliations with Southern Democrats.

It may well be that Johnson's new policy was more in accord with Lincoln's great spirit than his first impulse had been, for Lincoln's waking and sleeping thoughts had been occupied, as victory drew near, with generous plans and kind intentions toward the vanquished. But Lincoln was in his grave; and Johnson had neither his steadiness nor the wisdom of his benevolent moderation. Perhaps also Lincoln himself might have had difficulty in bringing kindness into such anguished resentment as overspread the North after the fifteenth of April.

Washington was the meeting-point and battle-ground of contending emotions. Nowhere else was there the same acute personal interest, as the plot of Lincoln's assassination was uncovered and the conspirators were led out to their execution in the yard of the old penitentiary at the foot of Four and a Half Street. Nowhere else did the prejudices and wrongs and sorrows of both sections come into such sharp contrast and strong relief, for very soon after Appomattox Southerners began to show themselves in Washington, many details in the work of reconstruction making their presence necessary.

They came in poverty but walked proudly, and it was evident that, though conquered, they were unrepentant. Some of the men still wore their gray uniforms, from loyalty to the lost cause or because of necessity. On the whole they accepted the situation with better grace than the women, who returned hollow-cheeked to this scene of former triumphs, to plead for imprisoned husbands and fathers. These saw no reason to conceal their feelings toward the officials with whom they interceded; and it is to be feared that some, in whom egotism and the dramatic instinct were strong, did nothing to make hard situations easier. It must have been difficult for men of the temper of Stanton and Holt, the Judge Advocate General, to name only two, to stifle resentment at the hatred plainly visible under surface manners of good breeding.

Lincoln's office had been the scene of many trying interviews, but the court-martial cases in which he so often interposed to dry a woman's tears, had to do usually with men of minor rank whose breaches of discipline were of no consequence to the world at large, while in this more trying time the problems confronting those in authority involved the pardon or punishment of leaders on whose cases judgment must be just and firm if the nation was to endure.

At first those near the President felt it necessary to invent delays to save the country from the sin of a ferocious blood atonement; later it seemed equally necessary to invent delays to curb Johnson's leniency; and neither of these reasons could be explained to impatient petitioners. It must have been difficult for a man of Johnson's short temper when one of these women told him to his face that he was a mere figurehead, that the autograph letter he gave her to enable her to visit her husband in prison at Fortress Monroe had proved of no more value than so much blank paper, and that he was afraid of Secretary Stanton. She seemed to think that his growing anger was all for the treatment she had received. What he said was:

"Go home, woman, and write what you have to say, and I 'll read it to my cabinet at the next meeting!"

On the whole, allowing for personal idiosyncrasies, he and the others appear to have behaved with commendable restraint.

It was only with the meeting of Congress that Johnson's real troubles began, compared with which interviews with angry women were as nothing. But why dwell on the increasing quarrels which led to his impeachment, or on the long trial that failed of conviction by a single vote? For the city they were a time of sordid turbulence: for Grant, who quarreled with Johnson, the breach was virtually his nomination to the Presidency.

Nor is Grant's administration, which followed Johnson's, a pleasant time to contemplate. The very qualities that made Grant the conqueror of Lee's army proved a handicap in this new office, where he was on unfamiliar ground, pitted against politicians who played the game by rules different from those of a military commander. Even his military genius had nothing in it of the quick thrust and parry which might have enabled another to meet them more nearly on their own terms. He was unsuspicious and unwise in his reading of character; and, once having given his confidence, most reluctant to withdraw it. Perhaps in this way he was blindly trying to pay his debt to Lincoln for long months of trust, when there had seemed little to justify it. As time wore on, the situation seemed to grow worse instead of better. Scandals developed in the cabinet and threatened to besmirch the President's own fame; and Horace Greeley's denunciation of the nation's capital as a place of "high rents, bad food, disgusting dust, deep mud and deplorable morals" seemed scarcely exaggerated.

Washington's growth during the four years of war had been that of a rapidly enlarging military camp, and the curtailment of military forces brought its raggedness into greater prominence. The deserted circle of forts around the city crumbled rapidly to decay. The shed-like corrals for army horses and army wagons became the shelter of dump-carts and their questionable loads, and made a fine meeting-place for gangs of young toughs. The long rows of temporary barrack sheds took on a disquieting air of permanence, for they swarmed with families of negroes who could not be dispossessed, having no other possible homes. Other groups of these helpless, rudderless creatures had formed little communities that offered a fine breeding-place for disease.

The more pretentious dwellings put up since the war had been of increasing ugliness, their sanded tin-and-stucco imitation of stone arguing ill, alike for the good taste and the honesty of the builders. With little money and less time to repair the streets over which regiments and wagon-trains had plowed in endless succession, the condition of Pennsylvania Avenue had become so bad that merchants threatened to move elsewhere. A venturesome mayor had put down as an experiment one block of sticky "coal-tar concrete" on Vermont Avenue. Elsewhere the scanty street paving was of foot-torturing cobblestones. Most of the streets remained frankly unpaved, and when fire-engines answered calls in muddy weather they had to take to the sidewalk or run the risk of being stalled.

At some time during the war, unauthorized save by the law of momentary necessity, a railroad track had been extended across Pennsylvania Avenue, at the foot of Capitol Hill, adding to the difficulties of a journey to the Capitol the perils of a grade crossing. Poultry and live-stock roamed the streets at will. A worthy resident returned from church one Sunday morning to find four hundred pounds of potential bacon fast asleep in his vestibule. People complained that the supply of water brought from beyond Great Falls was already insufficient. It was certainly unattractive in appearance, for as it was not filtered, the least spell of wet weather gave it a hue closely resembling the mud upon the avenue. The canal still acted as a sewer; the Potomac Flats still bred frogs and competing smells. The fog wreaths that floated over the lower part of town were so thick and white, it was inevitable the negroes should tell of ghosts they had seen rolling in phantom coaches up the deserted drive of the Van Ness place to the sagging front door through which bats flitted in the dusk.

It was obviously not because Washington was a finished or beautiful place of residence that people came in larger numbers than ever before and stayed on while Congress was in session, even into the hot summers. The increase in the size of the country and the details of reconstruction, had something to do with it. It was easier to account for the presence of men with the "army look" in their eyes, who were so numerous that army titles were heard quite as often as plain "Mr." than to understand why certain sleek men and their well-dressed womenkind should be so much in evidence, since they seemed to have little to do except display their wealth. People who were critical of Grant believed they had come to work upon his odd combination of credulity and stubbornness, with the object of getting government contracts. They set a standard of luxury that it was hard for the rest of the community to follow.

The town's chief concern, however, was not with Presidential mistakes, or the motives of these plausible civilians, or even with cabinet scandals. It was in the throes of scandals and excitements all its own. While it had never been allowed a voice in federal elections, it had almost from the first enjoyed local suffrage in varying measure. Congress was in the habit of granting the city a charter for a term of twenty years. Its inhabitants elected a council of two houses; sometimes these chose the mayor and sometimes he was appointed by the President. Latterly he had been elected by the people themselves every two years, amid increasing confusion.

Emancipation had greatly complicated the local problem. In 1865 the town expressed itself against extending the franchise to negroes, by a vote of 6591 to 35; but when a federal statute settled the matter the other way, in 1867, politicians were not slow to profit by it, both by influencing the ignorant and by importing outside help on election days. The city's politics were as corrupt as its streets were ill paved.

A word must be said, however, for the negroes themselves, very few of whom had their heads turned by ambition. Only a small number aspired to leadership. Frederick Douglass made his own position and held it by reason of outstanding ability. Some others, like the man who was known to his admirers as the Tall Black Oak Anacostia, had a less enviable reputation and perhaps wielded more influence. Most of them were simple souls, easily led, and therefore open to corruption; but also more easily satisfied than might have been expected. The one who applied to Secretary Seward for the post of Minister to Liberia, but was perfectly content with a place as messenger in the State Department, was typical, and on the whole reassuring.

Early in Grant's administration the shortcomings of the city government gained extra publicity because the last of the city charters had expired in 1868, when Congress was too busy with Johnson's impeachment to do more than hurriedly renew it for one year. Then the Presidential campaign and the inauguration had intervened to postpone action without silencing complaint. The proposal was made to abolish mayor and council and return to the commission form of government tried in 1800. Those who objected to depriving residents in this manner of the last vestige of the franchise, proposed instead that the District be made a territory of the United States and given a delegate in Congress and a governor appointed by the President. St. Louis, feeling the urge of destiny upon her, demanded the removal of the capital to some city in the Mississippi Valley.

To fight this, all factions united in pressing Congress for immediate passage of a bill authorizing the construction of a huge State, War, and Navy building, well knowing that the success of the measure would silence talk of removal. As their second line of defense they indulged in a bit of juggling practised by diplomats in all walks of life, from prime minister to nursery governess. To distract attention from the main issue they substituted another, and proposed to hold a world's fair in Washington during the year 1871. They must have done so with covert amusement and the assurance that if by any possibility the proposal was accepted, its effect upon the run-down town would be like that of giving a party in the average home: it would bring about more or less furbishing and some salutary house-cleaning.

President Grant came from the middle West, but he had no sympathy with the claims of St. Louis, and not only signed the bill authorizing the new State Department but made his private contribution to the fund for a world's fair. The important bill having passed, this proposal was speedily forgotten, most people in and out of Congress agreeing with Senator Stewart of Nevada that the United States should have a capital of which it had a right to be proud before inviting the nations of the earth to come and look at it. As his contribution toward making it such a city, the Senator built in the wilds at Dupont Circle a turreted castle of stucco which stood in lonely grandeur overlooking briers and rabbit-burrows and was called derisively "Stewart's Folly."

Dissatisfaction with local politics had been still further heightened by the action of Mayor Bowen in adding two million to the city's debt for the purpose of paving Pennsylvania Avenue. He was not very popular, anyway, having the interests of the colored race too much at heart to please his pro-Southern townsmen, and when on top of this increase in indebtedness the members of his council brazenly voted to double their own salaries, his defeat at the election of 1870 was overwhelming. His opponent was Matthew Galt Emery, a business man of high standing who, years before, had played an important if little-heralded part in local history by cutting and laying the corner-stone of the Washington Monument. Mr. Emery's election as mayor, however, amounted to little as an official triumph, for Congress, wearied at last by the endless complaining, voted to change the government to the territorial form, beginning on February 21, 1871.

The sentiment in and out of Congress that led up to this result had been skilfully fostered by a group of men who met very quietly at first, and at the proper time enlarged their circle and their activities, and employed such pleasant forms of propaganda as planked-shad feasts and excursions down the river. Their directing spirit was one of Mayor Bowen's own aldermen, Alexander R. Shepherd. Whether, in view of what followed, this constituted disloyalty to his chief or was a case of prophetic vision, each student of local history must decide for himself. He was a Washington product, having been born on the Island while Jackson was President. His father, a "small but intelligent" man, carried on a wood and lumber business according to a strict code of ethics which forbade him to profiteer in fuel during an exceptionally cold winter. The son had inherited his generous disposition, along with the physique of a large and handsome mother, to which nature fitted a correspondingly loud voice and hearty, unrestrained laugh. He had begun his business career with the city's most important plumber, at an age that seriously interfered with his schooling; but if no student, he possessed a mind that resembled Henry Clay's in its instant command of any scrap of knowledge it happened to contain, while in the use of words he had two distinct gifts which flowed on side by side—graceful speech and a wonderful command of profanity. The latter in no way interfered with his piety; his neighbors really enjoyed hearing him begin family prayers with a fervent "O Lord!" and break off suddenly to bid a servant "drive that damn cow out of the rose-bushes!"

Shepherd was one of those men whose vitality make it impossible to do anything on a small scale. In the matter of raising a family he and his wife went beyond the average, successfully bringing up a brood of ten. Nobody was quicker than he to make advances after a quarrel, in which he was a happy contrast to Mayor Bowen. His worst faults were pugnacity while an argument lasted and a magnificent disdain of details at all times. But he was not one to evade responsibility when called upon to make his words good. In his youthful plumbing days, when asked about the strength of a chandelier he had just put in place, his answer had been to jump up, catch hold of it with both hands, and swing from it with his full two hundred and twenty-five pounds' weight.

Having been a very good plumber, and lucky in the real-estate speculations he carried on as a side line, he had saved a comfortable fortune when at the age of thirty-five he came into prominence with the passing of the old city government.

Ironically enough, the bill decreeing this change was signed at the very moment the city was rejoicing over the one important improvement Mayor Bowen had accomplished, the paving of Pennsylvania Avenue with wooden blocks, from First Street to the Treasury. It proved in the end a costly blunder, but temporarily the smooth surface was delightful in contrast to the pitfalls and hollows of half a century and the town gave itself up to two days of merry-making which it called a carnival.

Ash Wednesday and Washington's Birthday came together that year, though Rome might have had difficulty in recognizing it as such, but there was no mistaking the holiday spirit abroad on

Pennsylvania Avenue. The "Star" said its lower end "looked like a picnic" because of the decorations put up by the saloons, and the number of women bringing lunch-baskets and children, who came determined not to miss a single one of the features provided by the Committee on Diverse Deviltries. These included racing of all kinds, from horse to gunny-sack, a civic parade, a "tournament," and the Indian game of la crosse, each being given right of way in turn during daylight, while the nights were gay with fireworks and public balls. Reserved seats were at a premium, out of doors as well as in convenient windows. A tree at the corner of Seventh Street and the avenue bore the legend: "You know how it is yourself. This tree reserved during the carnival."

The Butchers' Union, a float ridiculing the women suffragists by portraying the inauguration of a woman President of the United States, and poor tipsy old Beau Hickman in his exaggeratedly showy clothes, astride a gaunt gray horse and troubled to hold his cane as he felt a gentleman should on horseback, were the outstanding features of the civic parade. The socially elect had their turn when the avenue was cleared for "pleasure-driving," an event described by the "Star" in a manner to combine the glamour of the social column with the political interest of a ward meeting, men's names being substituted for women's and equipages described instead of clothes, in words that have become obsolete since the invention of motor-cars. "Dr. Bodisco Williams in a rockaway with a lady," and "A. R. Shepherd in an open buggy with clipped sorrels," we read. "Clipped" horses were rare enough to cause remark, and the adjective was used in describing the President's fine team of bays, Cincinnati and St. Louis, as they sped down the avenue carrying the ladies of Grant's household to the hotel from whose balcony they viewed the merrymaking.

President Grant was partial to men of Shepherd's showy, loquacious type, perhaps because he was uncommonly taciturn and not at all impressive himself. He also had great respect for large wealth, and he showed both these traits in making appointments to the new territorial offices. For governor he chose Henry D. Cooke, brother and Washington representative of Jay Cooke, whose name called up Aladdin visions of gold, because of the part his banking-house had played in financing the war. And he appointed Alexander R. Shepherd on the Board of Public Works, the group of five men who speedily became the controlling power in District affairs, with Shepherd so thoroughly dominating the five that he did not even trouble to call meetings.

The bill giving the District territorial government had started out in life a very democratic measure with only three Presidential appointees, a governor, a treasurer and a secretary. All the others were to be chosen by ballot; but by processes familiar to legislators it emerged ready for the President's signature totally different, the only officials left to the choice of the people being the delegate in Congress and a lower house of twenty-two members. The President was to name all the higher officials and the House to "provide for" the remainder; a task it found so congenial that it forthwith created two hundred and thirty new positions, for the mere joy of filling them. Under the circumstances the delegate in Congress, General Norman B. Chipman, had little chance to represent anything or anybody; while the only real function of the territorial legislature was to register the will of the Board of Public Works—in the last analysis A. R. Shepherd.

With the one exception of Mr. Mullet, the supervising architect of the Treasury, Shepherd's associates on the board were men who continued under this new name relations they had held with the "Boss" during the past few years, when he had been advocating Washington improvements and working after his energetic fashion to bring them about—erecting whole blocks of dwellings where more cautious investors contented themselves with two or three, and lavishing granite and plate glass on a Shepherd Office Building on the unpopular side of Pennsylvania Avenue.

His methods in office were of exactly the same wholesale slap-dash character, even to the making of debts, which he considered legitimate and necessary in business. He contracted these on a lavish scale, relying on his reputation as "a man who had never been known to cheat or to steal" to bring all right in the end. His prodigality in allotting office quarters from end to end of Pennsylvania Avenue, and the great number of new positions created, worried the taxpayers who were not his business associates, even while they admired his dash and his skill in handling the political aspects of his job, not forgetting the colored vote, which was believed to hold the balance of power. He saw no reason why, on the thrifty principle of making one hand wash the other, these men could not wield the picks and shovels he longed to direct in improving the town and at the same time be made a force to sustain Governor Cooke's administration.

After all, with him politics was only a means, not an end, his sincere desire being to improve the city. As he told an investigating committee of Congress, the Board of Public Works had been created either to do something or to do nothing. Assuming the former, it had been created to "devise and carry out as rapidly as possible" improvements that would bring the capital of the nation abreast of the times.

Shepherd's opponents complained that the newspapers remained his partizans to the end. Conditions as he found them when he took command were summed up in the "Star" in June, 1871, as follows:

> Grades that would n't match; drainage directed up hill; "grading and graveling" done without either grade or gravel; sewers running nowhere; single-brick sewers slumping in on the slightest provocation and engulfing unwary travellers . . . dirt-cutting done "by the d-a-y" at prices that mounted up from 17 cents per yard to $2.50 per yard; street crossings either undergrade or overgrade; sidewalks sloping inward; gutters planned for the accommodation of the hogs. . . .
> The question is, in a nutshell: shall we go on in the old way, or shall we, in entering upon our new territorial career, adopt some general systematic permanent plan of improvements and carry it steadily out?

It was Shepherd's nature to work rapidly, and even such an optimist must have foreseen the enmity he would arouse, and that a rule as drastic as he maintained could not last long. So he did not let official precedent stand in the way of anything he undertook, and work began in all parts of the city at the same time. Men dug and leveled and dumped and laid sewers and planted trees of fast-growing varieties, for he was after quick results. The number of workmen diminished or suddenly grew, as the exigencies of local politics demanded, and he crowded into the thirty-odd months of his dictatorship labors that under normal conditions might have consumed twice that many years. With pardonable hyperbole it was said to be "a daily occurrence" for a man to leave his peaceful home in the morning and return in the afternoon to find it the scene of chaos, sidewalks torn up, curbstones standing on end like the gravestones in a Moslem cemetery, and laborers changing the grade of the street in a way to injure the foundations—which foundations he was ordered to make secure within thirty days, or have his home torn down at his own expense.

It made no difference to Shepherd whether the building undermined was a shack or a stately dwelling. Both kinds were left marooned high on yellow-clay banks, or, worse still, literally "in a hole," with the newly graded road running by at the level of the second-story windows. Senators Edmunds and Bayard, who had built houses side by side on a commanding rise of Massachusetts Avenue, came back at the beginning of a session to find their dwellings poised on the brink of an ochre-colored abyss, while laborers toiled below in a wilderness of sewers and half-laid sidewalks. The new Louise Home, on the same street a block farther west, built by Mr. Corcoran as a memorial to his wife and daughter, shared the same fate.

While these gentlemen were better able to meet the expense than some twelve-hundred-dollar-a-year clerk, their cases were much more talked about, and they were in a better position to fight back. Denouncing such acts as "prodigal," the property-owners set in motion every possible legal device to hinder the Board of Public Works, charging that it was exceeding its authority and that contractors working under it were digging up pavements just laid on one street to re-lay the second-hand materials at full rates—in short, practising every sort of fraud.

Mr. Corcoran, who was one of Shepherd's chief critics, busied himself circulating a petition asking for a congressional investigation, and was able to present it to Congress with a thousand signatures before the territorial government had been in operation a year. The investigating committee made two reports; a majority report admitting that "mistakes" had been made, but exonerating the

Board of Public Works from evil intent, while the minority report sustained the accusations.

Shepherd meanwhile continued his labors and gained audacity as he proceeded. The Northern Liberties Market, on the reservation where the Carnegie Public Library now stands, had long been an eyesore, but was entrenched in public opinion as immovably as the Capitol itself. A decree went forth for its destruction, and tenants of stalls were notified that temporary quarters had been provided on a reservation farther up Seventh Street. Nobody took the notice seriously. It seemed incredible that even "the Boss" could drive them from that stronghold. He gave them no second warning, kept discreetly silent as to his plans, and when the time came to act, guarded against injunction proceedings by inviting all the Judges of the District Court out to his suburban home to supper. While they were enjoying his hospitality a force of workmen appeared at the market and began tearing it down, the remonstrance of the few dealers who were arranging their stock for next day's sales being drowned in the noise of toppling bricks and crashing beams, while the rats and mice, dislodged from the breeding-places of generations, fled in all directions pursued by vociferous small boys and yelping dogs. The work was not accomplished without fatalities, a man and a boy being crushed by falling timbers. This gave a sinister turn to the denunciations heaped upon Shepherd for the night's work; but the market-house was never rebuilt.

Even the property of the nation was not safe from his attack. Keeping his own counsel and watching his opportunity to carry out street grades as he had established them, he took advantage of a Thursday-to-Monday recess of Congress, and massing his workmen near the Capitol, cut down the surrounding streets, leaving the park with jagged yellow edges.

But the crowning audacity was the way in which he dealt with the grade crossing on Pennsylvania Avenue. The railroad, paying no attention to repeated notices to remove the track now that war necessities were over, at last published its defiance by running an engine out on the crossing and leaving it there. Shepherd perfected his plans in silence, and at one o'clock on a Sunday morning assembled his workmen and tore up the track on both sides, leaving the engine stranded and ridiculous. The boldness of the move compelled admiration even from the enemy, and Mr. Garrett, the President of the Baltimore and Ohio System, offered Shepherd a vice-presidency, which he was having too good a time to accept.

The end of his reign was at hand, however. Conditions preceding the panic of 1873 forced Governor Cooke to resign in order to devote all his time to private business. President Grant, who thoroughly believed in Shepherd, appointed him governor to succeed the retiring banker, an office he held from the middle of September, 1873, to the following June; but when panic brought ruin to the banking house of Jay Cooke, which had furnished the millions so lavishly used to tear Washington up by the roots, Shepherd's critics demanded another congressional investigation.

Three senators and five representatives spent three months probing into the methods and motives and hopelessly intricate bookkeeping of those responsible, and failed to connect Shepherd personally with any wrong-doing. Much hasty, wasteful work had been done, and extravagance was proved beyond a doubt, but Shepherd, with every opportunity to make money, had grown poor instead of rich. He always maintained that he never overstepped the strict limits of the law, but his best friends had to admit that at times he skirted very near their edge. Debts had piled up alarmingly. The first estimate for the grand plan named six and a quarter million dollars, in itself a goodly advance over four hundred thousand for street improvements, with which the whole upheaval started. The debts actually incurred during his term of office amounted to about sixteen and a half million.

The result of the entire investigation could be summed up in the traditional "Not guilty: but don't do it again." Congress decided to change the District's form of government once more, and in June, 1874, the territorial officials handed over their authority to three commissioners, as a temporary experiment. Grant, with bulldog loyalty, nominated Shepherd to be one of the commissioners, but the Senate refused to ratify the nomination, by a vote of about six to one, and he departed almost as poor as when he started out in life, to recoup his fortunes by mining ventures in Mexico.

The condition of the city when he left it resembled a bad case of house-cleaning; things were so thoroughly tossed about and uncomfortable that work had to go on in order to make the place habitable, and in the process another million dollars had to be spent in doing over again bad work already done. As time wore on and the good results of his rule became apparent, resentment against his extravagance and his arbitrary acts gave way to a humorous sort of pride in the man's assurance and boundless energy, and also to real gratitude that he had seen the city's possibilities and lifted her out of the mud. He came back to the city twice, and in 1887, the second occasion, received an ovation that must have done a world of good to his weary but militant spirit.

Gradually the streets acquired paving, first of wooden blocks, then of concrete. Honeysuckle and turf masked the high terraces left by Shepherd's excavations, and the parking in front of houses, an innovation made to reduce the amount of necessary paving, began to blossom with forsythia and roses. The shade trees planted by thousands flourished, and little by little the city reservations changed from untidy thickets of weeds to places of decorous paths and flowering shrubs.

XXII

THE AGE OF EASTLAKE

SO much depends on the point of view! Hanging in one of the upper corridors of the Capitol is a painting from which one's impulse is to flee, if it be regarded as a work of art, but which draws like a magnet when approached as an historical document. It shows the Supreme Court room, usually so empty, crowded with men, most of whom wear beards, and with women all wearing the ornate little bonnets in vogue at the time of the Centennial. Even the youngest female, who never saw a bonnet in action in her life, could tell that it was a fashionable crowd. Her grandmother, if she chanced to be an old Washingtonian, could tell much more. Looking over this canvas filled with painstaking little portrait heads about as large as hens' eggs, painted without an atom of feeling for enveloping atmosphere, she could point out, one after another, the celebrities of Grant's second administration—Representative This and Judge That. Mrs. Hamilton Fish, with her white side-curls and determined chin, the social arbiter of the hour. Madame A. and Signora B. of the *corps diplomatique,* lean, smooth-faced Mr. Evarts, standing and delivering a speech to which all the others are listening; and, down in the middle of the foreground, the most conspicuous spot in the picture though he was merely a spectator of the scene portrayed, James G. Blaine—which shows how his political future was read at that time.

The picture represents a sitting of the Electoral Commission, made up of five senators, five representatives, and five members of the Supreme Court, the body Congress created to determine whether Tilden or Hayes should succeed Grant as President. After hearing much testimony and long arguments, it rendered its decision in favor of Hayes, on the second of March, forty-eight hours before Grant's term expired. Tilden had undeniably received the greater number of popular votes, and the new President found himself in

LOOKING UP SEVENTEENTH STREET FROM THE PAN-AMERICAN BUILDING

the strange position of stepping legally into an office to which all the Democrats and many of his own party felt he had no moral right.

It was not an easy situation. People called President Hayes "his Fraudulency." That he got through his term without more friction was due to good luck, and to greater efficiency than either side was willing to give him credit for. On the whole his administration was a time of commonplace prosperity, and of gradual pulling out of the mud, literal and figurative, in which the town had been floundering.

New paving covered old ruts, and new inventions opened the way to living under modern conditions. Gas, which as a means of illumination had seemed brilliant enough, at the outset of Grant's administration, to warrant respectful mention when the evening parties given by Secretary Fish were under discussion, paled before arc-lights that sputtered and flickered and acted like ill-tamed tigers in captivity. Electricity was as yet no domestic pet to be taken into homes, but it had already altered standards, and made a brave show outdoors in high places. It appeared for the first time over the dome of the Capitol to usher in the Centennial New Year, shining forth promptly at midnight, as the chimes in the Metropolitan Methodist steeple began playing "Pleyel's Hymn," fire-bells rang 1-7-7-6, then 1-8-7-6, and shouts, pistol-shots and cheers, sober and otherwise, rose from every part of town.

Alexander Graham Bell's telephone had also just been perfected, and during Hayes's administration these twin agencies of unrest forced their way into private life. Ague assumed elegance and became known as malaria. It still claimed many victims, though not so many as before Mr. Shepherd filled in the canal. The winters were severe and the poor suffered for fuel and food. Possibly they were no colder or more hungry than before, but more notice was taken of it. The formation of an official Board of Charities was favored by the President, and well-to-do women opened soup-kitchens, where they learned, from their successes and failures, first lessons in organized philanthropy. Others worked on older established lines, "Here comes Mrs. Ricketts, with her pocket full of tickets!" used to be chanted in an undertone as that energetic lady bore down upon her friends.

It was for some charitable purpose early in the Hayes administration, if memory serves, that the Octagon House, closed since fashion moved away from the neighborhood, and said to be haunted, was opened to show a loan collection of art objects, not one of which was as fine an exhibit as the house itself, with its carved marble mantelpieces and its elaborate, decaying cornices. The public wandered through it much impressed by the exhibits and also by the names of the people lending them. Owing partly to Mr. Corcoran's gift of an art gallery, partly to men like Senator Sumner, whose lonely home had been filled with paintings and photographs of treasures abroad, partly to the influx of rich people whose intentions may or may not have been praiseworthy, even a little, perhaps, to the carvings and paintings in the late Mr. Pendleton's Palace of Fortune, Washington had for years taken an interest in such matters.

Mr. Corcoran, the donor of the art gallery, had long held the relation to the community that a generous uncle bears to expectant nephews. He represented the rich and conservative element, as Boss Shepherd represented the element that was enterprising and venturesome. In his red-brick home that faced Lafayette Square at the corner of Connecticut Avenue, and had a garden of its own almost as large as a city park, he had begun his collection of pictures long before the Civil War.

Once a year in those days he gave a grand ball "to Congress," to which everybody lucky enough to be invited went dressed in his best and expecting to have the best time generous hospitality could afford. Part of the evening's entertainment consisted in searching out and admiring the art objects acquired by the host since the previous winter. At the party of January, 1851, the guests had no difficulty in finding something new, for it gleamed afar, a life-size white marble figure against a background of dark leaves at the end of the suite of drawing-rooms. This was the "Greek Slave" by Hiram Powers, the statue of a slender girl with head bent and hands shackled. Washington was used to allegorical figures in marble and to portrait busts, but not to things like this. Sedate ladies looked startled; church wardens grew red in the face, and for a short time there was indecision what to do next; but the sheer pathetic beauty of the figure, and the fact that it was under Mr. Corcoran's roof, conquered, and Washington took that night a long step forward in its art education.

John Sessford's bulletin of 1859 mentioned the foundations of "the Art Union building for Mr. Corcoran" being under way, but war postponed the opening of the gallery. The building was taken for government uses, and it was not until 1871 that General Grant, the least artistic of all our Presidents, received the guests with Mr. Corcoran at a grand initial reception. Long ago the gallery outgrew its first home on Pennsylvania Avenue, directly opposite the State, War, and Navy building, whose erection had silenced the clamor of St. Louis to become the nation's capital. In 1897 its treasures were moved to their new home, the white-marble gallery planned by Ernest Flagg, first of those four stately semi-public palaces to be built on Seventeenth Street, in a line stretching down toward the Potomac. The first Corcoran Gallery still stands, having been taken again for government use, but the donor's dwelling and his garden have vanished. Within the past few years his wonderful old box bushes have been replanted at the base of the Lincoln Memorial, and the house has given way to a white-stone building for the United States Chamber of Commerce, a sorrowful change, to the minds of those who felt that its dark-red bricks had gathered into themselves the very essence of the city's old genial, social life. Webster bought the house from its first owner, and after he and Mr. Corcoran were both through with it, it became the winter home of Chauncey M. Depew.

In the time of President Hayes the red-brick art gallery was the Mecca of that part of Washington which was trying conscientiously to profit by the lessons of the Centennial. That inspiring and disturbing exhibition had routed a deep-seated, comfortable belief in the beauty of Berlin-wool work and of knobby chiseled black-walnut apples and pears as decorations for sideboards and wide connubial beds, but had not made it altogether plain what ought to take their place.

There seemed to be two divergent tendencies in art. One was toward conventionalism, as shown by the new square-patterned furniture called "Eastlake" over which incised lines of gilding wandered aimlessly or grouped themselves in sunbursts and pinched triangles. Similar lines also were engraved and gilded on the pink Tennessee-marble bases of lamps and fountains ordered for the plaza east of the Capitol. On the other hand, the new White-House china, painted "by the best talent in America," ran to photographic realism. On dozens and dozens of plates "each one different and all so natural," with special dishes for each course, fruit and fish and poultry were portrayed with an accuracy worthy of a better cause. This was the more popular tendency and seemed to point a way in which art could be brought into the home. The city developed its full quota of instructors in china-decoration, and studios where misguided daughters learned to paint "poppies on a brass plaque," or dogwood in oil on crimson plush.

The new White-House china was generously exhibited to visitors, but there is no record that Mrs. Hayes gave house room to any of these more horrible manifestations. Just what her taste may have been in matters æsthetic, is unknown. She found the White House full of flowers hurriedly sent by Republicans after the decision of the Electoral Commission had been made known. One set piece represented an American eagle, with a head of violets, a breast of camellias, and outspread wings of ferns resting on a bed of roses. This was ordered upstairs to the library, either because it was so greatly admired by the family, or because it was too hideous to remain on view in the public rooms.

Perhaps the new mistress paid no heed to such atrocities, for she was a serious lady and found more important matters for reform. Out of deference to her conscientious scruples, the inaugural ceremonies came to an end with a torch-light parade instead of dancing. The White-House billiard-table was banished to the attic, the wine-glasses were stacked on the highest shelf, and she set her quiet determination against social customs of a century in announcing that no wine was to be served at the President's table, even at state dinners. Praise and blame of this merged into merriment on one side and apprehension on the other, lest foreign representatives, in whose countries wine is a fixed habit and not a moral issue, might take offense. There were undoubtedly awkward situations, which, however, never became serious enough to silence the note of gaiety struck by Secretary Evarts in his remark that at the White House "water flowed like wine." The state banquets were said to be uncommonly dreary, though it was whispered that the resourceful White-House steward did the best he could by smuggling into the menu a course of stiff Roman punch served in orange skins, care being taken that the portions served to host and hostess were flavored more innocuously.

The city's attitude toward the new President and his family is reflected in a story told by one of those Americans who see so few negroes in their home towns that they study them with zest when they visit the capital. Lunching at Harvey's, the famous sea-food restaurant of the period, he encouraged his aged waiter to talk about the changes he had seen. The old man was trying vainly to recall an administration.

"I disremember de President's name, sah. He come after Gineral Grant, an' a right smart while befo' Gineral Garfield was shot."

"Do you mean President Hayes?"

"Yas-sah. Dat it! Gineral Hayes. De gem'man whose wife done run de White House!"

Mrs. Hayes was not only a woman of force; she was dowered with the kind of beauty that triumphed with plain hair in an era of frizzes. Her decorous "square-neck" evening gowns seemed more truly elegant than the most expensive French creations, and she left behind her a memory for sweet austerity that is very badly and baldly reflected in the old darky's statement—which, however, was literally true.

There were plenty of temperance advocates, and all agreed that too much liquid refreshment was served on social occasions throughout the city. Indeed, Mrs. Hayes was only carrying on in an extreme manner a reform launched by the previous Administration. On the first New Year that the Grant cabinet was in office, word had gone forth beforehand and was carried into effect when the day came, that no wines or liquors would be offered at official refreshment tables. Others had followed the example, with the result, favorably commented upon in the papers, that no tipsiness had been visible upon the streets and that receptions had been much more enjoyable "than when made up of a maudlin crowd hiccoughing the stereotyped compliments of the season."

The custom of making New-Year calls was then at its height. The "Star" of December 31st and the morning papers of the day itself printed front pages filled with names of people who would be at home to their friends, followed by a very short list of those who would not, the place of honor being given to the program at the White House, where diplomats were received at eleven o'clock, the Supreme Court at a quarter past eleven, and so on down to "the Public 12–2 P. M."

The regular routine was for the men of a household to pore over these lists after breakfast, jotting down names and addresses, and to start forth at whatever hour their official or unofficial status brought them to the White House, after which the rest of the day was passed in a round of visits. If their position required uniform, wives and daughters solicitously besought them to button newspapers under their tunics to protect their chests, capes being treacherous and overcoats not permitted by the regulations, though Washington's first winter storm had a habit of arriving punctually on this day. Ladies might accompany husbands and fathers to the White House, but nowhere else. From there they hurried home, to spend the afternoon receiving greetings, offering refreshments, and sparkling in repartee to the "ladies' talk" of the men who called.

On other days, throughout the season, the women made calls as assiduously as the men did on the first of January. Distances were so great that a sort of zoning system, partly geographical and partly official, had been devised to save time. Cabinet ladies received on Wednesdays; wives of representatives on Tuesdays; senators' wives and the residents of Georgetown on Thursdays; the ladies of the Supreme Court and other courts and residents of Capitol Hill on Mondays. Visiting hours were from two o'clock until five. The few street-car lines were a help, but their routes were not comprehensive, and the cars themselves, in winter when windows rattled and the floors were covered ankle-deep with straw, were neither comfortable nor clean. Frugal ladies therefore combined to hire a carriage from their favorite liveryman, and wrapped in velvet dolmans or India shawls and furs, went forth together on conscientious rounds.

If there happened to be a vacant seat in the carriage a little daughter might be taken along for the outing and left, with a book, to while away the time that her elders were indoors. Many a child received her first impression of Washington society as a mingling of frosty February air, "best" dresses, dust blowing in clouds along sunlit streets, darky drivers jockeying for positions in front of official residences, fragments of grown-up gossip, and doors opening and closing upon groups of well-dressed people.

Once a fortnight, on Tuesday in Mrs. Grant's day later on Saturday, the mistress of the White House held public afternoon receptions. The little girl was allowed to enter here, if she knew the President's daughter. No girl, whatever her age, who did so in Mrs. Hayes's time, has ever forgotten the graciousness of her manner, or has looked at a camellia since without remembering the loveliness of its waxen petals against her smooth dark hair.

Mrs. Grant, being very near-sighted, needed the help of somebody quicker than herself to place names and faces, and instituted the custom of asking a certain number of ladies to receive with her, mostly wives of members of the cabinet. Mrs. Hayes continued this, but instead of grouping them informally about the room, somebody, perhaps the military aide who made the presentations, had the evil inspiration to marshal them in a stiff line beside the President's wife, in the order of their husbands' official importance. It was a boon to strangers, who, if they knew their cabinet, could guess whose hand they were shaking as they passed down the line; but it was deadly, alike for sociability and for looks. Next to Mrs. Hayes in her square-necked garnet satin stood Mrs. Evarts, wife of the Secretary of State, a Quaker-like figure in a white-lace cap. Towering head and shoulders above her, came Mrs. John Sherman, wife of the Secretary of the Treasury; next, Mrs. Ramsey, wife of the Secretary of War, a lady abundantly gifted for social life; and next to her, large and substantial Mrs. Key, wife of the ex-Confederate whom Mr. Hayes had made Postmaster-General, wishing to give all sections representation in the cabinet.

Mrs. Key had many children, and what seemed to her contemporaries an odd taste in dress. Her rather shapeless red frock with canary-colored sleeves was, however, strictly up to date—one lap ahead of the art taste of Washington—being the forerunner of the "greenery-yallery-Grosvenor-Gallery" cult that was just making its way across the Atlantic; but it looked odd in a society where the hour-glass was still the approved pattern for a woman's figure.

Dress reform (as exemplified by Mrs. Key) was added to the lighter subjects discussed around flower-decked dinner tables. Women's rights was also a standing topic, its pioneers having formed the habit of meeting in Washington for their annual convention. When this subject showed signs of bringing forth too acrid argument,—for it already had vehement supporters,—hosts switched to the latest national or international situation, in the offhand way Washington hosts have, as if it were exactly on a par with neighborhood gossip; or somebody would ask delightedly, "Have you heard 'Pinafore'?" And if this led to mention of the French actress Bernhardt, somebody else was sure to confess rather shamefacedly that she pleased him or her "better than I expected," and stress the purity of her French as an antidote, if not a screen, to her unconventionality.

There was a new German minister in town—a clever man, just at that stage of learning English when he followed the speech of other people with wonderful contortions of his own facial muscles. Because of this he possessed uncanny fascination as a dinner guest. Judge Field, who had been appointed to the Supreme Court by Lincoln, brought an alien and romantic element into any dinner company he joined, for he had been a member of a vigilance committee in California's hectic days, and in Washington he chose to live in one end of the old Capitol prison—a unique combination. Secretary Evarts, who enjoyed his own sallies, whether or not they were appreciated by the rest of the company, was always a favorite; so was Chief-Justice Waite, though some one with a facile pen described him as "mirthful and good natured but with no more wit than a turtle." These and their wives and daughters and many more were constant diners-out, and always there were military men present. In Washington the number of generals was still so great that the fabulous "regiment of brigadiers" might easily have been recruited.

One of the most effective of these was Sheridan, small physically but mighty in his avalanche of words. At one dinner he told Miss Dodge, James G. Blaine's lively cousin, all about his battles, confiding to her that Taylor's poem "Sheridan's Ride" was "not exaggerated." Then he discoursed of the Chicago fire, the freshet in Rome, and his experiences as observer during the Franco-Prussian War, with character sketches of Bismarck, Louis Napoleon, and Emperor William. She admired him as being "modest and simple," and "more like a soldier than any of them," though at first sight his face had seemed hard. Thus *Othello* must have appeared.

Nineteen out of twenty such dinner parties had politics as their underlying motive. "Politics is like Heaven; there is no night there," wrote Miss Dodge. The man around whom ambitions and rivalries seethed at the moment was Blaine. As Speaker of the House from 1869 to 1875, and senator and cabinet minister afterward, Blaine seemed always on the point of reaching the Presidency. It was Garfield, not he, who entered the White House in 1881, but Garfield, his warm friend and admirer, made him Secretary of State. It was an excellent place from which to mount still higher, and under the pleasant surface talk of society, aided and abetted by his own charming manner, ambition continued to work.

His office became doubly a point of interest. General Sherman described it as almost as full as the President's, "with knots of delegations dadoing the four walls." They stayed near the wall while Mr. Blaine, bland and smiling, toured the room, listening to each group in turn, making an occasional memorandum, returning to his desk to sign papers brought him by his clerk, but answering all his visitors in a way to send them off happy.

His mastery of this art was his greatest asset, and he used it on everybody, from ambassadors downward. General Sherman, who had a keen sense of fun, was consumed with admiration and secret mirth when he saw him meet two ladies from an inland Main Street and answer their earnest inquiries about the best lines of steamers to take to avoid seasickness when going abroad. With the utmost urbanity he told them that it was better "to take a very large ship because the larger the ship was the more water she would draw and therefore the less motion of the vessel. . . . It was lovely to hear him explain what he meant."

What he really meant was always difficult to discover. It was disheartening after talking with him twenty minutes to find oneself outside his door, little the wiser about his plans and thoughts than on entering. This close-mouthed seeming frankness was an art he practised even with his own sons and their boy friends. "He would welcome us," says one of the latter, "as if a group of half-grown youngsters was the one thing he desired to see invade his office, chat with us pleasantly, scribbling meanwhile on a scrap of paper, ring his bell, hand a slip to his secretary, and when that young man returned with a small envelope, drop it unostentatiously in a drawer. Then, very soon, as though seized with a brilliant idea, he would open the drawer and say: 'By the way, boys, I have tickets here for a matinée. It is a show I really would like to see, but I haven't the time. Suppose you see it for me!" and send us away charmed, utterly unconscious that we had been ejected." His method with older admirers may have been less crude, but the results were the same.

Having distinct plans for the future, it seemed to him well to secure a more ambitious home; so he arranged to build a big and handsome house on a lot facing Dupont Circle bought with profits from stocks whose ownership embarrassed him politically at a later date. All through that spring and early summer he could be seen on pleasant afternoons, watching the digging of the foundations, comparing blue-prints, and climbing ladders to view the world from the elevation of his second story.

It was on the whole a satisfactory world, from his point of view, with the goal of his ambitions not far away and present duties both interesting and useful. The pleasant relations existing between his family and the Garfields are reflected in a dozen intimate accounts in letters of Mrs. Blaine to her children and in the letters of Miss Dodge. Quiet, gentle Mrs. Garfield, the President's hearty greeting,—"He always was a gusher, though I dare say a short course of the presidency will poke it out of him," and "Grandma Garfield" brimful of pride in her son, are drawn with deft touches. The President said she would have seen him inaugurated even had she been certain she would die of fatigue the next day. A little alert old lady, she had actually split rails in her pioneer youth, and now, in her rich silk and her cap with lavender ribbons, affected an amusing disdain of the White House and society and all it ways. When some one suggested that honors, though gratifying, were tiring, her answer was: "Law, yes! I would rather do a washing!"

On the day of Guiteau's murderous attack, the Secretary of State rose early to accompany his chief to the station. Mrs. Blaine and the family were still at breakfast when her son Tom was called to the door. In that house where no meal passed without interruptions, the family thought nothing of it even when he returned and beckoned his brother Walker from the table. Then one of the servants came running into the room, babbling incoherently the news that had been telephoned from the White House. Wife-like, Mrs. Blaine's first thought was for her husband and what might have happened to him.

The streets were full of people by the time she could reach the White House. Finding that the President had not yet arrived, she and Mrs. Sherman drove down the avenue until they met the police clearing the way for the ambulance and turned to follow in its wake. They stood in the hall as the President was borne into the White House upon a mattress carried high above the heads of a dozen men. "As he saw us and held us with his eye, he kissed his hand to us—I thought I should die!"

Later the President had her summoned to his room and drawing her down toward him whispered, "Whatever happens, I want you to promise to look out for Crete"—the name by which he called his wife. "Don't leave me till Crete comes."

"I took my old bonnet off and stayed," wrote good Mrs. Blaine, whose east-wind manner hid a sympathetic heart. "I never left him a moment, and the day will never pass from my memory. At six or thereabouts Mrs. Garfield came, frail, fatigued, but firm and quiet and full of purpose."

The losing fight against death, the mistake of the physicians at the outset in tracing the course of the bullet, and the weeks of alternate hope and anxiety as Garfield's splendid physique slowly succumbed to poison, form a story sad to read. Fortunately its like could never occur again, thanks to advances in medical science since that day.

More depressing still is the story of the actions of the prisoner and of his trial. He was allowed to revel in publicity and to attract to himself rather more attention than was lavished upon the stricken President. Senator William E. Chandler wrote to Blaine:

> Please stop all these telegrams about the assassin's movements and conversations. As little allusion as possible should be made to him. He has actually been allowed to give his views as to Arthur's cabinet, to name his men and have them printed by leave of the Department of Justice. Cannot you stop this?

The judge who presided at the trial, which began about the middle of November and dragged on for seventy-two days, seemed obsessed by a fear that he might be accused of sharing the popular indignation, and did little to curb the prisoner's desire to interrupt proceedings, or his tendency to grin and rage and conduct himself in a manner both coarse and vulgar. The scenes in the court-room were far removed from the dignity the occasion demanded; and people flocked to the trial as to a melodrama rather than a tragedy. They crowded the corridors of the City Hall in the hope of catching a glimpse of Guiteau as he was hurried to the van after the day's proceedings, since only those who held tickets were allowed within the court-room itself. But when the interminable proceedings came to an end and the case was given to the jury, it took that body only half an hour to return its verdict of "Guilty."

Every day during Garfield's illness, Blaine conscientiously visited Vice-President Arthur, to report on the condition of the invalid and on the political outlook. The two men were by no means in accord, but each deferred to the other, Blaine giving Arthur every opportunity to make suggestions, as he had a constitutional right to do, the President being incapacitated, while Arthur as scrupulously refrained from interfering with the policy of the administration as carried out by the Secretary of State.

After Arthur assumed office, he made, on the whole, a better President than his countrymen had dared hope, for the assertion that he was not chosen Vice-President "with a view to the succession" is well within the bounds of truth. He had been selected after the Blaine and Sherman factions in the Convention of 1880 had united to nominate Garfield, and it was thought necessary to do something to gain the good-will of the Grant men. Possibly no one was more astonished than Arthur to find himself on the ticket with President Hayes's friend Garfield, for Hayes had deprived him of the office of Collector of the Port of New York and he had been working hard in the convention to secure a third term for Grant. Besides, he was a friend of Conkling.

Blaine, being emphatically of the other faction, remained in Arthur's cabinet only until December, when he turned over his office to Frelinghuysen, observing all formal courtesy but with very natural reluctance to see his own work in the State Department undone, as he believed it would be by his successor. He could scarcely meet President Arthur upon the street and stop for a moment's chat, as the President seemed inclined to do, without feeling resentment such as is expressed in the canine world by bristling hair and incipient growls.

The new house in the building of which Mr. Blaine had taken such pleasure had now become a white elephant upon his hands. He could ill afford to keep up such an establishment without an official salary, but he finished and furnished it, and lived in it during the winter of 1882–3. Perhaps he was not so frank with himself or his friends as he believed himself to be when, as the next Presidential campaign drew near, he declared that he "neither desired nor expected" the nomination; though he was most explicitly frank when he added, "But I don't intend that man in the White House shall have it!"

Blaine received it; but it was a Democrat who succeeded Arthur as President, and Blaine, stricken with illness, became little more than a shadow of his former self, one of those living ghosts who haunt Washington from time to time.

"He is so drooped and white and unsuccessful!" wrote Miss Hale in 1889. "Blaine I am convinced will do no more harm, so I can afford to admire and pity him. He was certainly most agreeable."

XXIII

CZARS OF CONGRESS

IT has happened in the see-saw of politics that the influence of Congress and that of the President have alternately been in the ascendant. It may be taken as an allegory that the White House was the first public building to be surrounded by a fence. This was a wooden post-and-rail affair which Mrs. Madison, by the aid of smiles and diplomacy, managed to have adorned with a gate flanked by weeping willows. Ten years elapsed before anything of the kind was attempted at the other end of the avenue; but when a fence was built around the Capitol, it was no mere wooden affair. It was built of brick and iron, and had stout gates which were closed and locked promptly every night at nine o'clock.

Americans revolted against the idea of divine right, but it was one which died hard in rebels of British descent. Washington was called in all seriousness "August Presence," and Jefferson, full of democratic notions as to personal behavior, found it difficult to train his fellow citizens into willingness to see him go about like one of themselves. But when the idea died, it was very dead indeed.

From the congressman's point of view the Capitol building is inhabited by two classes of beings, Legislators and Lobbyists, and the capital city by two classes, Legislators and Others.

With the exception of a single suite of rooms, given up to the Supreme Court, the Capitol and all it contains belongs to Congress; while outside the Capitol, Congress claims almost everything in sight. The two great new office buildings to the right and left were put up exclusively for its use. From the Botanic Gardens packets of seeds have been mailed to constituents and bouquets sent to congressmen's wives for a century. The Congressional Cemetery is open to such as choose to claim its cold hospitality. Hotels and cafés compete to offer members of Congress their best service. (Does not Congress decide the size of the tax the proprietors have to pay?)

The very name of the Library of Congress tells its story. How thoroughly it lives up to its name was revealed when the building was new. A resident wished to show its beauties to a well-known New York artist. It happened to be at that season of the year when appropriation bills are the most important things on earth and congressmen and senators, great as they are at ordinary times, assume about three times their usual stature. Knowing that the House and Senate reading-rooms had been closed to profane eyes, the resident procured a pass signed by a name that was all-powerful. An attendant scowled at the bit of paper when it was presented at the Senate reading-room, but could not refuse to honor it. Grudgingly he opened the door just wide enough to admit the visitors sideways, indicated a spot beyond which they must not advance, and whispered in a troubled voice:

"S-s-sh! Keep very quiet. There 's a Senator READING!"

After all, we must not forget that the town was planned first of all for officials, though it is trying to hear the wife of a newly elected representative say:

"Well, you can move away if you do not like the way Congress treats Washington! *We* have to stay here, so long as my husband is in office."

The worst sinners are the newly elected. After a time members of the national legislature take a kindlier view of the city's needs, though often—alas!—without changing their manner of voting. It is not what they do, so much as what they fail to do, that disturbs the residents. There is truth in the adage, "What is everybody's business is nobody's business"; in looking out for the interests of their home state they are apt to forget that among their other duties they have taken on those of city council and board of aldermen for the capital of the nation. That is what it amounts to, for government by commissioners, adopted as a temporary measure in 1874, was made permanent four years later.

The annoying stumbling-block in a congressman's Selkirkian

sweep of vision over the city is the White House. The man living there is likely to think he has official rights of his own, and to do his best to maintain them. Perhaps rivalries are inevitable between Congress and the Executive, since the man in the White House is elected to look out for the welfare of the country as a whole, while it is equally the duty of the men at the other end of the avenue to look out first for the interests of the sections they represent. It is the President's business to act as a brake on the wheel of legislation, and the application of a brake always causes friction. Personal ambition also intrudes discordant elements, for the Speaker of the House, if a strong man, frequently aspires to be a Presidential candidate, and the Vice-President, who presides over the deliberations of the Senate, is subject to those obscure but potent influences which make an heir apparent prone to disagree with the reigning monarch.

Up to the time of the Civil War only one President lacked congressional experience when he entered the White House. That was Zachary Taylor, who grew up in the army. The next was Grant, another military hero. Since his day, Arthur and Cleveland and Roosevelt and Taft and Wilson and Coolidge show the increasing and differing roads that lead to the White House. They show, too, the sad truth that immunity from congressional opposition is not to be found on any one of them.

John Quincy Adams, our one President to make for himself a notable after career, made it as Representative from Massachusetts; and the difference in his bearing at the two ends of the avenue is enlightening. He occupied the White House at the beginning of that first long period during which Congress dwarfed its one rival. With the exception of Andrew Jackson, the men who dwelt in the Executive Mansion between 1825 and 1861 did their duty as it was given them to see it, without appealing greatly to popular fancy, while Webster and Clay and Calhoun and a dozen others in Congress stirred enthusiasm to concert pitch. Adams was so much more human in his later phase that we lose sight of very lovable human traits he manifested, *sub rosa* so to speak, in the White House. To ordinary visitors he was disconcertingly unresponsive, fixing them with his black eye, "neither sparkling nor dull," and leaving entirely on them the onus of justifying their visit. Yet from his diary we learn that he felt it necessary to steel himself against betraying sympathy with people he had no right to help; and we read an almost pathetic account of the way in which old General Brown, finding himself stricken with a mortal disease, came to him, told his story, and was comforted.

This same cold President was the kind of man who remembered birthday anniversaries, wrote long letters in rhyme to his wife, kept in his dressing-room closet a veritable small boy's collection of cocoons that never developed into butterflies, and hungered for the popular approval that his overworked conscience forbade his doing anything to win. He was often not far removed in spirit from the lad he had been at the age of ten—avid for Shakspere and the "Arabian Nights," deaf to the cadences of "Paradise Lost," and desiring above all things to go swimming.

In younger days he had made for himself a record of a mile and a half without touching bottom, but he cherished no illusion of being able to cheat the years. It was his practice while President to walk down to the Potomac in the early morning, leave his clothes in charge of a devoted Swiss servant, and disport himself in the water twenty minutes or so before returning to earth. After a winter of ill health he was advised by his doctors to discontinue this, but with the first spring days his feet carried him in the old direction. In 1827, before the middle of April, he wrote:

> I have already been tempted by the prevailing warm weather to bathe in the Potomac, but have been deterred by the catarrah still hanging upon me. . . . I took however for this morning's walk the direction to the river, and visited the rock whence I most frequently go into the river. It is yet adapted to the purpose; but all trace of the old sycamore-tree which was near it and blew down the winter before last, is gone. There is yet one standing a little below, but it is undermined with every high tide, and must be soon overthrown. The borders of the river are strewn with dead herring and shad, and the waters are not so high as usual at this season.

An apocryphal story went the rounds that he finally gave up swimming because Ann Royal managed by artifice to detach the

Swiss from his post of duty, mounted guard over the Presidential garments, and attempted to interview the unhappy Adams. It was a story that could never have been told about Washington or even Monroe, had those great men been addicted to a morning plunge. But times had changed. People no longer looked upon a mortal with awe just because he inhabited the White House, and that impish quality of American humor, destined to flower so riotously in the mining-camps of 1849, was already a lusty shoot. The fact that Ann Royal stalked about Washington, and that one morning Adams's canoe capsized with all his clothes aboard, and his servant had to hurry to the White House for another outfit, were quite enough to set the tongues of humorists wagging.

In Congress, instead of being glacial, Adams was fluent, even pugnacious; "a great offhand speaker, . . . who loved a fight better than he loved his friends," which meant that he still loved the right better than peace, and that the same rock-ribbed qualities which made him frigid and non-committal in the Presidency made him just the reverse on the floor of Congress. As the advocate of his little group of constituents, he could let himself go, a luxury conscience had not permitted him during a long, laborous lifetime. One suspects that he thoroughly enjoyed his congressional career. That he valued his success and was a little surprised at it is evident, for he wrote in his diary:

> I bless a merciful creator that hitherto my taking of a seat in the House of Representatives has been successful so far as personally concern myself. I have received there no disrespectful treatment. Many individuals have treated me positively with respect. When I have spoken, I have been listened to with attention, and not without approbation. May I improve the lesson—remember to speak seldom, and above all things, ask from above discernment what to say!

One whose metaphors became a little tangled in the sincerity of his admiration thus described Adams's manner in debate:

> He rises abruptly. His face reddens, and in a moment, throwing himself into the attitude of a veteran gladiator, he prepares for the attack. Then he becomes full of gesticulation—his body sways to and fro—self-command seems lost. His head is bent forward in his earnest-

ness till it almost touches the desk. His voice frequently breaks; but he pursues his subject through all its bearings. Nothing daunts him. The House may ring with the cry of "Order!" he stands amid the tempest, and like an oak that knows its gnarled and knotted strength, stretches forth his hand and defies the blast.

Being no respecter of persons or of parties, there was no telling in what cause he might burst forth. On one dull morning in 1837, he gave his colleagues an electric shock by getting to his feet and launching into a speech sustaining, of all persons in the world, President Van Buren. It was on the slavery issue that he made his most dramatic fight. He held no brief for the negro race. He once told a lady that *Desdemona's* misfortunes were fully deserved; that they were "a judgment upon her for marrying a nigger." Not until late in life did he work with the extreme abolitionists, and then he said grimly it was Calhoun who had converted him. But when the House refused to hear petitions upon slavery and ordered that all such papers be laid upon the table unread, his sense of justice called him to do battle.

To drive the lesson home, he chose a petition of forty-six citizens of Haverhill that Congress take immediate steps for the peaceful dissolution of the Union. This raised such a hubbub that after the session adjourned two excited meetings were held, the Southerners coming together for fiery denunciation, while the antislavery men met in the rooms of Mr. Giddings to tender their aid to Adams. Next day a member arraigned him before the House and stated that his act merited expulsion, but that out of mercy it was proposed only to censure him, leaving the rest of his punishment "to his own conscience and the indignation of all American citizens."

In answer Adams asked that the first paragraph of the Declaration of Independence be read, a request the House could not well deny. This paragraph says it is the duty of a people to abolish or alter their form of government when it has become destructive of the ends for which it was created. Adams maintained that his constituents had a right to ask Congress to do a thing they believed should be done, and that it was "up to" Congress to show why their prayer should not be granted. Henry A. Wise gained the floor and accused Adams of working with British abolitionists to destroy the Union, denounced him for expressing the opinion that the slaves might lawfully be emancipated as a measure of military necessity, and made an impassioned plea for slavery on the ground that if it were destroyed the great democratic principle of equality would be hopelessly gone. At this Adams lost his temper and self-control and descended to personalities he afterward regretted.

The turmoil lasted for days, and whether or not men sympathized with Adams, they could not help admiring the persistence with which he stood his ground. A representative from Connecticut wrote:

> He is still going on with what he calls his *trial,* and having spoken six days, is apparently no nearer finishing than when he began. Whatever may be thought of his conduct, no one can fail to be filled with wonder at the astonishing resources, mental and physical, of this most extraordinary man. He continues to *command* the lively attention of the House and very full Galleries. Nobody goes into the Senate or Supreme Court. . . . What is to be the effect of all this agitation I hardly know, or what the country will think of so great consumption of time—but one thing is certain, that Mr. Adams is a great actor and on this occasion is *performing* as the phrase is, to very crowded houses.

At the end of another week a member from Georgia asked how much time Mr. Adams meant to consume in this manner. Adams replied that he was not responsible for the time consumed, referred to a single speech of Burke's, during the trial of Warren Hastings, that occupied several months; and said he thought he could close "in ninety days." The sheer grit of the old man won friends that his manner and his logic combined might not have gained, and the resolution of censure was lost by thirteen votes.

Even paralysis could not daunt him. A stroke came upon him while he was at his home in Quincy, Massachusetts, and when the next session opened Andrew Johnson made himself comfortable in Adams's seat. But a few months later Adams reappeared, plucky as ever, if sadly shrunken and altered. Johnson hastily vacated his chair, and the House gave him a welcome that made the walls of the chamber ring.

A bronze marker in the floor of the old Hall of Representatives shows where he fell when he was stricken down as he rose in his seat to offer a sheaf of petitions. The room has become the Statuary Hall of the Capitol, to which each state has sent two effigies of its noted sons. Tourists pass through it in droves, looking upon these with more or less horror, but they crowd around the guide who points out the spot where Adams had his seat, and listen absorbed as he tells the story of this intrepid old man's last battle.

Broadly speaking, the dignity of the three bodies that hold meetings in the Capitol is in inverse ratio to their size, and this was true in the days we like best to associate with the Capitol, the golden days of American oratory. Excellent if somewhat stilted arguments before the Supreme Court were delivered to the judges in their robes, the opposing counsel in their space within the bar, and to empty benches. In the Senate there was a ponderous and measured flow of eloquence, while in the "glorified town meeting" of the House, words were uttered with a headlong speed characteristic of the place rather than of the speakers, for as soon as they were translated to the upper chamber their eloquence moved at a more moderate tempo.

Foreigners were sometimes amazed at the assurance with which young members plunged into debate, and the facility with which they coined new words after the old stand-bys of the dictionary had been exhausted. Yet, on the whole, congressional oratory was fairly impressive. "The style of the best speakers is fluent, forcible and perspicacious," wrote a British auditor, "and in cases where it is not possible that their arguments should be sound, they seldom fail to be specious and acute." In general, the men of the South had greater natural eloquence and cultivated it more assiduously than their Northern colleagues.

Though Mr. Poinsett replied, "It is a great misfortune," when, about the middle of the last century, a visitor from abroad praised the American readiness in talking, it was felt that voluble debate had its uses. "If you wish to see with how little wisdom the world is governed, you must come to Washington," the Connecticut congressman wrote in a moment of gloom; but when his correspondent saw fit to criticize the House of which he was a member, he was quick to answer:

> I have no great desire to undertake a defense of the Honorable Body. Indeed, I sometimes wonder how it is that the Government hangs together at all. . . . Our free government is a mixture of good and evil, and sometimes what appears to be evil operates to produce good. There is a great deal of vain, empty and disgusting babbling in the House, which is tiresome to hear—so much so, that I sometimes long to get out of Congress if for no other reason than to escape the everlasting din of congressional speaking. But then, the House of Representatives is a sort of national safety-valve and may keep the boiler of the body-politic from exploding. It also prevents much hasty and impulsive legislation by delaying the action so long that in most cases not only the passions have time to cool, but all interest in the subject matter subsides.

Attending Congress was like taking a chance in a lottery; one hoped for a prize, but had no right to expect it. If one of the born orators spoke, it was time well spent, but on a day when the uninspired held the floor the time consumed by an expedition to Capitol Hill was just as great. A dull session is thus described by Mr. Adams:

> This was a heavily rainy gloomy day. . . . Being Monday the States were successively called for presentation of petitions; a most tedious operation in the practice, though to a reflecting mind a very striking exemplification of the magnificent grandeur of this nation and of the sublime principles upon which our government is founded. The forms and proceedings of the House, this calling over of the States for petitions, the colossal emblem of the Union over the Speaker's chair, the historic muse at the clock, the echoing pillars of the hall, the tripping Mercuries who bear the resolutions and amendments between the members and the Chair, the calls of ayes and noes, with the different intonations of the answers from the different voices, the gobbling manner of the Clerk reading over the names, the tone of the Speaker in announcing the votes and the varied shades of pleasure and pain in the countenances of the members on hearing it, would form a fine subject for a descriptive poem. There was little done in the House after receiving the petitions . . . there was a bill for the relief of

insolvent debtors, partly discussed, and postponed; a question upon printing papers relating to railways and canals, in which Mercer and Ellsworth took part. But the House was thin, the day was dark, and Carson, before three, moved to adjourn, because it was so melancholy. They accordingly adjourned—to the great indignation of Hubbard, of N. H., who has the claimants of the Revolutionary pensions in charge, and burns with zeal to assist them. He asked for the yeas and nays on the adjournment, and to fool him into fury, they were refused. He went out of the House almost sputtering with rage.

But even on a comparatively dull day the House was interesting to unaccustomed eyes. It was thrilling to look down from the gallery and search out famous men, and others whose features might not be so well known but whose careers seemed to exude romance, as a whispered biography accompanied the discreetly pointing forefinger.

In appearance, then as now, some might have been English country gentlemen who had strayed in, thinking it a session of Parliament. A very few belonged to the type familiar to all zones and all ages, born dandies who esteem clothing as a means of adornment, but most of them wore their coats of excellent material with a carelessness to make tailors weep. After the few earnest moments of prayer with which the session opened, they read or conversed in low tones, or lounged in their chairs and spat expert streams of tobacco juice into the nearest cuspidor. Only a few went to the extent of elevating their feet to the tops of their desks, as many of them probably did in the privacy of their own rooms; but the whole chamber looked more like the quarters of a shabby, comfortable club than a legislative assembly. From the vantage-ground of the gallery in either house it was plain that for all their slouching and informality these men had an air of importance. There was nothing casual about being in Congress. It was a career, no mere episode sandwiched in between a business venture and a turn at practising law.

Some busied themselves with correspondence. One could hear the sound of congressional knuckles knocking the sand off freshly written pages and then watch the representatives stroll over to the letter-sealer, who sat at a little table with his wax and scales, ready to answer questions about the time required for a letter to make the journey to far-away points like St. Augustine, Florida, or St. Joseph, Missouri, and the hour at which the mails closed for the South or North or West. At another table sat the professional pen-mender with his knives and bowl of water and bunch of quills. A third public servant to be seen standing mute and dependable in House and Senate and Supreme Court room, was a large urn of excellent snuff. This was the last of the trio to vanish, and they say it may still be found waiting just outside the Senate door. Before a night session began in the House, there was a picturesque moment when attendants came in and lighted the many candles—later the many lamps—on the "massy bronze-gilt chandelier of immense weight" that hung from the center of the cupola to within a few feet of the floor.

If a member clapped his hands, one of a half-dozen boys waiting on the steps leading to the Speaker's dais, ran to receive his orders and vanished, returning with documents or with a tumbler which he placed within easy reach of an outstretched hand.

Suspicious minds questioned the contents of those tumblers, for the fluid was not always colorless; neither, for that matter, was unfiltered Potomac water. The compound in the glasses may have been only "switchel," an innocent beverage composed of molasses, ginger, and Adam's ale, but capable of being made more appetizing by the addition of fluids that figured in the expense account of the House under the non-committal heading "Syrops." When John Randolph addressed the House, he partook freely of something he called "toast-water," which was reported to be one-third whisky.

In the years preceding the Civil War, encounters with fists or firearms took place several times each session, sometimes in the Capitol itself. Like a series of Cruikshank illustrations, they add nothing to the dignity of the great volume of national debate, but immensely increase its vividness. Sometimes two angry men flew at each other and were pulled asunder by their comrades before harm could be done. Sometimes, as in the case of the assault made upon Senator Sumner by Preston Brooks, the harm was far more than at first appeared.

Sometimes an incident which threatened tragedy degenerated to pure farce. When Senator Benton, with his towering physique and ferocious manner, strode up to little Senator Foote of Louisiana with such a menacing air that the latter drew a pistol and pressed it against his adversary's breast, all the materials for tragedy seemed at hand. An Alabama senator intervened and wrenched the pistol from the little man's grasp with the admonition "give me that instrument!" a choice of words which added a touch of the grotesque; and when it was discovered that the pistol was as harmless as a penny whistle, the scene collapsed in total absurdity.

Once, during the slavery debates, men lined up beside their spokesmen and stood facing each other during the better part of a speech, with their hands suggestively near their pistol-pockets.

On Sundays during the first half-century of the city's history the Hall of Representatives became a church, the custom originating when there were few large assembly rooms. Jefferson frequently attended, though sometimes he took his big red prayer-book under his arm and tramped across the fields to worship with the Episcopalians in the tobacco barn on the side of Jenkins's Hill, where they held their first services. The services at the Capitol were non-denominational, having neither settled pastor nor steady congregation, the occupants of pulpit and pew being alike recruited from the material at hand. Visiting ministers of all denominations were given an opportunity to preach; even women, as we learn from an unenthusiastic comment of a member upon the "unpremeditated discourse" of Elizabeth Robbins, which ran through a succession of scripture quotations "like pack-thread through a row of pearls." But sometimes the congregation listened to real eloquence. It was on such an occasion that Edward Everett's voice was heard for the first time in the Hall of Representatives.

When there happened to be no visiting clergymen, the chaplains of the House and Senate took charge of the services on alternate Sundays; and as in the course of years men of many denominations, including one Catholic priest, served in that capacity, these alone provided a diversity of theological food. Curiosity and other irreligious impulses had their part in drawing together the congregation, for the meeting offered a most excellent chance to display new clothes and to be seen in company with the great. All the youth and worldliness within driving distance gravitated to Capitol Hill, while the serious-minded sought their own small places of worship in a distinctly censorious temper.

As the ladies flocked in, members gallantly gave up their seats, and when chairs were exhausted the steps around the Speaker's platform blossomed like a flower garden. Strangers to whom such an experience was new reacted to it in various ways. It reminded Allen Hodgson of the time "when they shall come from the east and from the west, from the north and from the south, and shall sit down in the kingdom of God." Sir Augustus Foster, less earnest, saw only a rather diverting assemblage, though he prefaced his description with the statement that "a church service can certainly never be called an amusement."

The Marine Band in its red coats, which was relied on at first to provide the music, was speedily banished, its performance of psalm-tunes upon brass instruments not being thought churchly. Another worldly interruption occurred each Sunday at noon, when an officer of the House, followed by an attendant carrying a huge bag, stalked through the House to deposit congressional letters in the post.

As for the effectiveness of the sermons, that was a matter depending on the hearers. One frivolous person wrote about a handsome chaplain of Monroe's day:

> I cannot praise the Doctor's eyes,
> I never saw his glance divine,
> For when he prays he shuts his eyes,
> And when he preaches he shuts mine!

Aside from making laws on week-days and acting as church wardens on Sunday, with an occasional assault or duel thrown in to make life interesting, a congressman was kept very busy with his own errands and those his constituents invented for him. The average member, however, was a sturdy animal and had a lot of energy left for play. Golf had not yet come into its own, but if he felt a need for physical exercise, there was the Potomac for swimming and fishing and loafing in canoes, while the hills back of town were wonderful for horseback riding. Few of them, however, indulged in these semi-solitary sports. They were by nature gregarious.

When the columns for the portico outside the windows of the Congressional Library reached the Navy Yard by boat from the quarry, the congressmen turned the occasion into a frolic and dragged the great pieces of stone by hand from the wharf to the Capitol, a distance of a mile, with many jests at the expense of those who took active part and those who did not.

When bells rang out an alarm of fire, a dozen or more members of Congress were sure to join the strangely assorted throng that passed buckets from the nearest bricked-in square reservoir, under the sidewalk, to the scene of the blaze.

Besides being in evidence at "Levees, the parties select and the Jam-parties—balls and theatres and other places of fashionable resort," as an old letter enumerates Washington's social activities—the members had their own peculiar congressional "symposia" held in the private rooms of one or another. Sometimes these were confined to half a dozen choice spirits, sometimes they expanded to take in all the four walls would hold, but in either case they were untrammeled by formality or by the presence of women.

It was impossible to predict what form such entertainments would take. In a tobacco-laden atmosphere, stimulated by liquids that scorned to masquerade as "switchel," discussion of some political problem might wax brilliant and profound; or in an evening given over to nonsense a hush might suddenly fall upon the company as they listened to a visiting actor or to one of their own number reciting verse. Strangers were admittted in just the right quantity to rouse curiosity and interest. The gatherings appear to have been in miniature the forerunners of the Gridiron dinners and the Alibi Club; or, better still of those unique Wednesday evenings in Alexander Graham Bell's big library which linger in memory among the unique experiences of a Washington sojourn, because, as one of Mr. Bell's friends used to say, they produced that most wonderful thing, light without heat.

Sometimes the favored participants made their way over rough and winding roads to an odd house on a bluff upon the farther side of the Eastern Branch, a house whose large, hospitable entrance-hall indicated a great mansion with many servants, but which ended almost before it began in a meager complement of sleeping-rooms and kitchens. It was here that eccentric old Mr. Law had betaken himself when fortune ceased to smile upon him, and here that he welcomed his friends to his dying day.

Sometimes the entertainment resolved itself into a more or less "quiet" game of cards. What these men did in their private capacity was of little moment, save as it reacted on the public through their career. Had Clay been less susceptible to the lure of gambling, Webster a less excellent judge of spirits, and all of them—Calhoun especially—less swayed by ambition, who can tell what turn the fortunes of their country might have taken?

These three, about whom the glamour of congressional life shines brightest, grew old in Congress together. They were all young when they came into prominence. Clay, indeed, had not reached the age required by law when he was appointed to fill a vacant seat in the Senate. And in 1820 he was youthful still, tossing back that raven-black forelock of his as he led the way to the Missouri Compromise. But his body had grown old and his gestures were weary, though still graceful, long before the last speech in 1850 which so cruelly taxed his strength.

Calhoun's upstanding hair became gray and his brow deeply furrowed before he reached middle age. He was a man in his vigorous prime when he resigned the office of Vice-President to take the seat in the Senate vacated by his friend Hayne, the better to aid Nullification. Eighteen years later, when he made his last fight in Congress, the seal of death was visibly upon him. Too ill to speak, he came to the Capitol on the fourth of March, 1850, to hear James M. Mason deliver the argument he had himself prepared. On the seventh, Webster, also a figure worn by age, answered him. Calhoun, suffering evident pain, replied briefly, in a voice broken and hoarse. He had trifled with pneumonia, and he went back across the Capitol Park to Mrs. Hill's boarding-house to die.

He busied himself with his papers. Colleagues visited him and he gave them counsel. A biographer has said that "it was a senator rather than a man who lay dying." Calhoun clung to everything that linked him with public questions. Even after he knew his illness to be mortal, he would not send for his wife or allow her to be told of his condition. The only member of his family with him was his son, a physician. Death came so slowly that people got used to the idea, and for several hours before the end came, he seemed almost deserted by his friends. One who watched beside his bedside through the last night was struck by the absence of feminine touches in the sick-room. On the mantlepiece were a few dried prunes, a lump of cold boiled rice, a tallow candle, and a half-emptied glass of water. Sounds of near-by merrymaking seemed to jangle as they floated into the quiet place. Occasionally a head was thrust in at the door and hastily withdrawn when it was learned that he still breathed.

The interest that surrounds everything belonging to the good old times makes it difficult to estimate at their true worth congressional speeches of the past. Basil Hall, in the twenties, pronounced them "uncommonly juvenile" and thought we had a tendency to rate orators by their volubility. With every desire to accord full measure of praise, not only to the three who were pre-eminent but to others who pressed them closely—Hayne with his flow of elegant phrases; poor old Randolph with his eternal classical quotations and his "lathy pistol-fingered gesticulation"; Pinckney, self-conscious and attitudinizing; Houston, big and showy, laying aside his whittling to draw deft word-pictures of Texan life; Benton and Wise, whose words came like a rushing torrent; Sumner, never so happy as when instructing his fellow beings—the question obtrudes itself, whether, were the same words to be spoken in the same manner before audiences to-day, their magic would be the same.

Life now moves at a swifter pace. We have become impatient of mere oratorical rotundity, impressive words surrounding a vacuum, and, optimists that we are, look for sense as well as sound in every phrase. With the passing of the frock coat and the soft felt hat that Senator Sorghum donned in the closing years of the last century as his panoply to meet the world, has gone also his manner of sawing the air and uttering loud platitudes.

Everybody knows that the spectacular part of Congress, debate in regular sessions, is the smallest part of its activity, a mere blossom on the tree that has roots clamped deep in the soil of constituencies and whose branches gather strength in committee rooms. It is to committee rooms that the public flocks more and more when it has the chance, to attend hearings on this and that measure and listen to the arguments presented for and against by those interested; though the real work of study and investigation and persuasion that goes on to help congressmen make up their minds is not confined within any set of walls.

An intimate history of the Capitol building devoted only to the influences brought to bear upon legislation and legislators, would make strange reading. "Lobbying" is a word of evil association and unpleasant sound; yet, unless congressmen and senators take on superhuman wisdom with their congressional oaths, how are they to fit themselves to vote except by hearing the good and bad points of measures discussed by those interested? Just where legitimate persuasion ends and evil communications corrupt good morals, is a point about which every disappointed memorialist has his own belief.

According to popular tradition, there was no period when lobbying in its evil sense was more practised than immediately after the Civil War. No record of the period is complete without its hint of vast sums of money changing hands and stories of siren women using wiles to gain ends for which they were paid by "interests" of vast power. Such figures are too picturesque to be allowed to sink to the comparatively insignificant place to which they are entitled. Lobbyists there were, and are, of all kinds and grades of rectitude, but for the most part they were and are plain business folk plying their trade openly and unashamed with whatever skill the Lord vouchsafes.

The most famous of his day, which lasted well into the Cleveland régime, was Sam Ward, a round, compact little man, the brother of that estimable lady Julia Ward Howe. He rejoiced in the title "King of the Lobby," but is better remembered for the wonderful dinners he gave and his limitless flow of anecdote than for the reasons which prompted him to use them. Mr. Cannon said that a man could eat Sam Ward's dinners with a clear conscience, for he never asked anything in return. He had prodigious gastronomic knowledge and things to eat seemed to have for him a significance hidden from ordinary mortals. "Gail Hamilton" (Mary Abigail Dodge) wrote that after a pleasant evening at the Capitol during which he and she discussed many topics, he pressed a banana into her hand at parting, as a token of regard, and next morning sent her a box of candied fruits. That was his way of "saying it with flowers."

Sometimes the actions of the most altruistic lobbyists might be open to misinterpretation. Mr. Corcoran and John D. Maury, who was Mayor of Washington at the time when the bill to establish the government hospital for the insane across the Eastern Branch was under discussion, were both deeply interested in its favor. They believed, as Dorothea Dix did, that the time had come to do something more humane than lock up indigent crazy folk with criminals in county jails, as was the custom.

Miss Dix, another type of female lobbyist, had sat in an alcove of the Congressional Library, in her neat black-silk dress, before a table covered with her appallingly convincing array of figures, and "received" congressmen and senators who called upon her (she never demeaned herself to visit any gentleman!), but Congress still seemed inclined to regard the scheme as a fancy philanthropy. At the crucial moment, in the dying hours of a session on a Sunday morning, the mayor came for Mr. Corcoran and the two advanced upon the Capitol. They found the doors of the building locked, perhaps to ward off just such attacks. But they found a watchman who was sympathetic or at least amenable to reason, who helped them in through a window; and having entered like thieves, they advanced upon the committee room like heroes and carried their point.

To one reviewing Congress over a long series of years, the men in both houses fall into groups, mental and physical. There are the orators, the wits, and the mere fun-makers; the band of radicals, and the counterbalancing group of ultra-conservatives, left-overs for the most part from an earlier political generation; and the earnest plodders, numerous but unnoticed, who do the hard drudgery creditably. The proportions of these groups shift, from congress to congress, but, in the long run, remain about the same.

THE MAIN STAIRWAY, LIBRARY OF CONGRESS

The wits and would-be wits run the whole gamut from buffoonery to inspiration. In the decade before the Civil War there was an unspeakable clown named Cobb, who styled himself the "maker of senators" and used his clownishness in sophisticated campaigning to catch the rural vote by eating corn-pone and singing an endless song of his own writing called "The Homestead Bill," whose refrain was "Uncle Sam is rich enough to give us all a farm." Another type was that extravagant talker of the Forty-eighth Congress, "Colonel" Tom Ochiltree of Texas, stocky, red-headed, the source or the butt of most of the tales that flew about the corridors of the Capitol, yet who had a side to his nature as chivalrous as his ordinary behavior was blatant.

"Sunset" Cox of New York, brilliant and witty, who served from the Thirty-fifth to the Fifty-first Congress with but two brief terms as private citizen, and John J. Ingalls, the senator from Kansas from 1873 to 1891, a tall slim man with a ruthless way of pecking at the heart of a matter that won him the sobriquet of the "Bluejay of the Plains," and Thomas B. Reed of Maine, as nimble in wit as he was massive and slow in body, whose sayings had a sub-acid flavor, all had this one trait in common—their ability to make men laugh. Because of it they were lavishly applauded and quoted, but because of it they were not allowed to show what they were capable of doing at the other end of the avenue. Almost the last characteristic Americans retain from their Puritan ancestry is this disinclination to elect to high office men who jest too easily. We may and do revile politics, but regard the business of government as too sacred to be treated with levity. Lincoln, the one exception, used his wit, which was without subacid flavor, to illustrate serious points in the politics that he took seriously.

Occasionally in the halls of Congress, it seems as though a physical reincarnation takes place. Pinckney of the early days—corseted, attitudinizing, vain of his skill, beginning an argument all over again if a notable addition to his audience arrived to warrant it—was apparently back again in the flesh in the person of Roscoe Conkling, with his foppish dress, his curled beard, and his assurance of personal and political importance. Conkling's fight with Garfield, when he resigned his seat in the Senate to prove this importance and emphasize his displeasure that a mere President should appoint a Collector of the Port of New York without consulting him, is one of the most spectacular instances of the difference of view between the two ends of Pennsylvania Avenue. Greatly to Conkling's astonishment, his constituents sided with the President and let him stay resigned, instead of triumphantly reelecting him as he expected.

Physical types stand out as belonging to certain eras. First of all were the men who were physically, as they had been politically, colonial Englishmen. With the opening of the West they took on greater length of limb and more of the pioneer characteristics. The brilliant Southerners who left the legislative halls in 1860–61 could never have been mistaken for New Englanders. Later still the difference in type between East and West was more noticeable than between North and South.

Visitors to the Capitol eagerly point out the marked figures in each political generation. In the after-the-war group, along with men of more prominence, General Burnside's ornamental whiskers, and General Butler, shrewd, unpopular, unhandsome, so small that in spite of his corpulence he was not massive and afflicted with the drooping eyelid which made him a boon to cartoonists, were never overlooked. Later, Lodge and Morton, Bryan and Hanna were conspicuous for widely different reasons.

While the halls of Congress and the committee rooms are the obvious places in which to see such men, there is another part of the Capitol which they frequent daily, the basement restaurants in the House and Senate wings. These are crowded and dingy. Amid a clatter of heavy crockery, black waiters serve in slap-dash fashion food that is not remarkably good. The entire interest of the place is in its patrons. To see Senator Sorghum's successor eating bean soup, or Congressman Fifth-term consuming apple-pie and buttermilk, while conferring with a fellow member or an important constituent, is a sight to make the day memorable for any casual tourist. It is one of those thrilling extras in sight-seeing, like catching sight of a popular actor off his guard, or going hunting in the jungle with a camera.

Of the men who have wielded the gavel as Speaker of the House of Representatives, some have exercised their great power discreetly and some in a way to enhance their own importance. Blaine did it with bland magnetism, nursing his constantly thwarted hopes. Reed, who was intermittently Speaker in the decade between 1889–1899 was called "czar" by indignant congressmen for the emphatic rulings he made, and worse names still by the fakers and venders he drove from the Capitol corridors and the rotunda, where, little by little, they had reëstablished themselves. Champ Clark, the Missourian who was landed in Congress by the tidal wave that brought Cleveland to the White House, and who just missed a nomination that would have landed him in the White House in 1912, was a force to be reckoned with when he was Speaker.

So was "Uncle Joe" Cannon, the able Illinoisan, who entered Congress about the time Boss Shepherd was making life so interesting and uncomfortable for Washingtonians, and who retired from Congress exactly fifty years later, having failed of reëlection in the half-century only twice—the longest term of congressional service on record. He was almost the last man left in public life of the lean type of American, of which Lincoln was the rugged exponent and Sumner the handsome city-bred variant. For good or ill, the physique of these sons of pioneers and grandsons of Puritans has vanished with the entrance into the country of many foreigners. The men in Congress to-day are broader and heavier-jowled.

Mr. Cannon was one of the Speakers called a czar. Champ Clark described him as made up chiefly of spiral springs; and Reed drawled *sotto voce* as Cannon paced back and forth in the aisle one day addressing the House: "Joe, are you making this speech on mileage?" Spare, alert, with chin whiskers trimmed in a style that became obsolete with the passing of the last century, he was still a man of steel springs when he retired at eighty-seven.

Looking at life out of shrewd, kindly eyes, as he puffed the long black cigar tilted at the angle cartoonists have made familiar the country over, he talked one day about past and present congresses; and no man's opinion is entitled to greater weight.

"Yes and no," was his answer when asked whether the body is as strong as it was years ago. Then he went on to say that the individual members were just as able, but that in our complicated modern life Congress as a body holds a relatively smaller place.

Taking it from the beginning, its work has been astonishingly good in the aggregate, far exceeding what could have been expected from its members singly. At times their collective wisdom has gone directly counter to the spirit of the moment, which theoretically they are elected to represent. Such was the case when they chose Adams President at the moment of the country's most inflated self-sufficiency, passing by Crawford, who was plausible and popular, and Jackson, who was peculiarly self-sufficient, to vote for the man whose temper was least like their own, conservative, learned, and burdened with an over-exacting conscience.

Mainly, the difference has been one of externals. The men in small-clothes who met for the first time in the Capitol did not look like those of later congressional generations: Webster's contemporaries in their swallowtail coats and voluminous white neck-cloths; the legislators of the decades between 1870 and 1890, who trod the corridors of the Capitol encased in coffin-like Prince Alberts; or those of the present day, who stroll into the halls of Congress in whatever garments suit their fancy, from golf-hose to the most formal afternoon dress. But scratch a congressman of whatever epoch, and you expose the same bundle of nerves and emotion, prejudice, conscience, stupidity—and inspiration.

XXIV

COLUMBIA'S QUEEN

IN popular estimation Mrs. Cleveland stands next to Mrs. Madison as the woman who has most graciously filled the position of President's wife. Only twenty-two when she was married, in the Blue Room, to a man old enough to be her father, she had two advantages that Mrs. Madison lacked, youth and real beauty. Her youth might have proved a serious handicap, for the rôle of President's wife has become one of greater exactions with every administration, but she filled it marvelously, thanks to the very qualities Mrs. Madison possessed in overflowing measure—self-forgetfulness and a desire to make people happy.

Nobody could resist the healthy, hearty charm of either of them.

It was in Cleveland's administration that the city began to take on its new character as a place of winter residence for people of wealth, unconnected with the Government. Since street-paving had become the rule rather than the exception, its wide avenues could be better appreciated, and the trees planted in such profusion were already large enough to cast grateful shade. They were of many varieties discarded since in favor of the nine that experiment has proved most suitable,—American elm, linden, sycamore, red and pin-oak, sugar-maple and gingko, with which close upon nine hundred miles of our streets are bordered; but at that time a tree was a tree, and the bigger its shadow the more it emphasized the amount of sunshine with which the town was blessed.

Already several handsome houses had been built. The Warders lived in one "by Richardson in the donjon-keep style," and John Hay and Henry Adams had commissioned the same architect to build homes for them side by side, facing Lafayette Square. The Leiters of Chicago leased Blaine's white elephant of a house on

Dupont Circle, and were shortly to build for themselves a palace twice as large.

This addition of a new circle of residents, all of whom had wealth and leisure and most of whom had culture, brought more luxury into daily life. But in truth the town had never wholly lived down the example set by visiting spendthrifts in the "Age of Exploitation"; and President Arthur had led society along the same pleasant road, having a distinct partiality for good living and new coats, and a liking for celebrities. The finest dinner of his administration had been given not to visiting royalty or for reasons of politics or diplomacy but to honor Christine Nilsson, whose voice rose joyously and spontaneously in song when, as she left the dining-room on the President's arm, the Marine Band broke into one of her favorite airs. True, it was at the White House; but it is not often that a prima donna lifts her voice to sing at the close of a hearty meal.

The new tendency to enjoyment and display was further augmented by the presence in Cleveland's cabinet of William C. Whitney, the Secretary of the Navy, who was rich even according to New York standards and willing to use his wealth generously in social ways.

There was an effect of plethora as well as of plenty in entertaining. When hosts gave a party they invited many guests. At dinners or luncheons there were endless courses and elaborate table decorations. Miss Susan Hale, sister of Edward Everett Hale, came in the winter of 1889 to give readings from "Forgotten Novels," for a fashionable charity, and sent home animated pictures of crowded parlors and groaning tables. She wrote of artificial lights at noonday, of jeweled glass and satin embroidered table-cloths on luncheon tables around which there were men as well as women—"a mitigating feature invented by the Warders"—and where the guests

ate and ate and ate and ate. Mrs. Hobson and I used to know what the courses were and how they came, but it 's gone from me now. Anyhow, there was terrapin and saddle of venison and pheasant, and little scalloped things in saucepans with silver handles, and others in shells without handles, shad and cucumbers and asparagus and things in season and out of season, and pain and champaign, and claret and sherry and apollinaris and real water, and all out of beakers that sparkled and shone internally and externally.

We sparkled and shone all that was possible under these circumstances, faint yet pursuing as each new thing came on—and rose from the table a little before four. Then we moved into the picture gallery for coffee and into the drawingroom for tea, and the great huge bank from the middle of the table of Jacqueminot and white roses stuck with hyacinths, was passed round for us each to take a great bunch to carry away. Then the shutters were taken down, and the guests carried off on them. This is figurative, to say we went out into the daylight and made a few K Street calls. Luckily we had no dinner engagement, and were so dead we did n't dream of going to the Bancroft-Davis reception.

That, with variations, was the sort of thing to which fashionable Washington subjected itself and its digestion twice a day during the season. Yet for all its display it was a friendly and in some ways naïve Washington. To fix the period in our minds, it is useful and amusing to recall that at a luncheon given by Mrs. Cleveland, which was very smart and up to date, if less elaborate than the feasts the Warders could give, the great novelty was "sticks of chewing-gum" in fancy papers served with the bonbons that stood within easy reach, one dish for every two guests.

People still knew what was going on in their neighbors' houses, and stopped to chat when they chanced to meet in Dupont Circle or in Lafayette Square, on the way home from market or an "artist's reading." Another acquaintance would stroll up and soon a "curbstone party" would be in full swing—a very pleasant, friendly gathering at which the day's news was well talked over before the group broke up and left the park to the children and the sparrows.

An astonishing proportion of the people who thus met and parted had written books. John Kendrick Bangs once expressed his belief that you could not throw a stone on the streets of Washington without hitting an author. Protesting that the place is given over to politicians and has no literary atmosphere, they came as they still continue to come—historians to study authentic documents, journalists to write up the day's grist of history in the making, travelers to jot down their impressions, and fictionists to get material for that most elusive of masterpieces, the Great American Novel.

Mr. Spofford, who remained Librarian of Congress for nearly half a century after his appointment by Lincoln, wrote a long article in 1902 which is largely made up of names of people connected with the city who had made their contribution to American letters as journalists or scientists or in one of the many intermediate fields of literature. Only the poets fight shy of us; and even these do not keep away altogether. Walt Whitman did hospital work here during the Civil War, and at the time Americans began to recognize Washington as a pleasant place for a winter sojourn, Joaquin Miller put up a little log cabin in the woods near Rock Creek. He was one of the *outré* members of the literary fraternity.

Most of them were content to be conventional in manner and attire and sought out, for places to live in, the best they could afford. Some chose the old-fashioned square-roomed type of house in Georgetown and on Capitol Hill. Grace Greenwood and several of her friends established themselves on New Jersey Avenue, where Mr. Law had built his first home and Jefferson had lodged while Vice-President. Mrs. Frances Hodgson Burnett lived on Farragut Square in one of the houses built in the intermediate period when their general shape resembled a rather thick slice of bread seen "end on," and the drawing-room, known as a saloon parlor, had two mantelpieces, and two more or less ornate chandeliers dangled from the ceiling.

Henry Adams and John Hay built homes as unconventional in their way as Joaquin Miller's cabin, for Richardson and his contemporaries brought to Washington the idea that city houses need not be as monotonous in appearance as boxes in the General Post-Office, and at this period began the diversity in outline and material in its residences which adds so much to the charm of Washington's streets.

George Bancroft lived in one of the handsome, solid double houses on H Street half a block beyond Lafayette Square. He was one of the oldest and most venerated of the fraternity of letters, a familiar figure in the city ever since he had held the position of Secretary of the Navy in Polk's cabinet, though he did not make it his home until the last fifteen years of his life, from 1875 to 1891. He looked immensely old to the younger generation, with his slight figure and snow-white beard. "I came in with the century," he used to say, referring to his age. But he sat his horse erect and rode long after he was eighty. It used to be one of Washington's characteristic sights, watched for and pointed out to strangers, when he and his friend Mr. Spofford, younger but as slight and erect and almost as gray as himself, set off together on their daily rides.

One thing that brought writers to Washington was the fight to secure international copyright, a reform demanded by the guild of letters almost as insistently as civil service reform was being demanded in all government appointments. It was during Cleveland's first term that the writers of the country made their concerted effort before Congress, though victory was not won until the middle of Harrison's administration. So, in addition to resident writers, the town seemed to be filled at times with all the other Americans who had experienced the pains and pleasures of authorship.

It was the kind of reform that might have been expected to appeal to Cleveland's sense of fairness, had not friendship with leaders in the movement also inclined him to that side. The writer remembers as the handsomest party she has ever seen at the White House, a reception given in honor of the visiting authors who came to present their case before Congress. The beautiful rooms were decorated as for a state reception, the beautiful mistress of the White House had a smile and personal word for each guest, and the rooms swarmed with people whose likenesses and books were known the country over.

Mr. Cleveland was, they said, a different man since his marriage. In the short space of two years he had traveled the long road that separates a mayor of Buffalo from the White House, which at first had seemed a rather lonely and ill-fitting habitation. "Sometimes I wake at night and rub my eyes, and wonder if it is a dream," he told a friend. He freely confessed that previous to entering the White

House he had no social experience and knew virtually nobody of prominence. But an American with ability to make such a journey in so short a time could be trusted to take on polish enough to serve.

His remark soon after election, that henceforth, he supposed, he must do without friends, showed a wistfulness that sat oddly on his big frame. Nowhere was his kindly human side more apparent than in his contact with children. Our bachelor Presidents seem to have been especially kind to children.

The pretty custom of egg-rolling on Easter Monday in the White-House grounds, established in Buchanan's day, is not liked by those whose business it is to keep the grounds tidy, the subsequent cleaning up being no light job, and the beginning of Cleveland's presidency seemed an excellent time to stop it. So the edict went forth that it was not to be permitted. But when President Cleveland heard of it his order was to admit the children as usual, and they overran the grounds and the house. When he went into the East Room at one o'clock, as was his custom, to greet chance visitors, he found the place swarming with little people who had come to thank him, and shook hands with them until the fatigue of bending to meet his guests half-way overcame him and he beat a retreat.

His manners pleased children. The beatific expression of one small boy from out of town will never be forgotten.

"I tell you, *these* are never going to be worn again!" he exulted, waving the pair of tan kid gloves that he had donned because of the solemnity of the occasion; "I 'm going to keep 'em always. Grover Cleveland has shaken 'em!"

After Mr. Cleveland married and had children of his own, his interest in young things was in no way diminished. His friend Richard Watson Gilder, writing to his son during a visit at the White House, commented on the real delight the President manifested in watching the babies.

> Some men take no interest, strangely enough, in very little babies, but the President has the sense not to lose the first phenomena of childhood. Now I admire, of course, a boy of your size; but for the life of me I could n't sit and watch you sputter and grab and grin and groan for half an hour.

During Cleveland's bachelor months his valet William laid out the President's best or second-best dress suit as seemed to him proper, acted as his social arbiter, and ordered his master's doings in the way he thought fitting. Usually the President meekly accepted his dictum, but once he rebelled. On a spring evening when he sat down to his lonely dinner a tantalizing odor floated in through the open windows.

"William, what is that smell?" he asked.

"Very sorry sir, but that is the servants' dinner sir—corned beef and cabbage."

"Well, William, take this dinner down to the servants and bring their dinner to me."

"It was the best dinner I had eaten in months, *bœuf corne au cabeau,*" he added as he told the story, dwelling lovingly on his original rendering of the menu in French.

Before his marriage his sister, Miss Rose Elizabeth, acted as hostess. She was a bookish lady, and fond of flowers, but utterly lacking in small talk. Ordinary mortals found conversation with her difficult, and social affairs at the White House were therefore beset with stiffness until the President took to himself a wife.

This happened in June, 1886, the bride being his ward, Frances Folsom, the daughter of his former law partner. She was a beautiful, vigorous girl of twenty-two, with brown curling hair and kind eyes, who instantly won all hearts by her wholesomeness and freedom from affectation. People still made evening calls in those days, even at the White House, and the White House has seen few more charming pictures than its young mistress coming through the door of the red parlor accompanied by her great mastiff, a new possession that she wished to show her visitors. Both were such handsome physical specimens, he as stately in his way as she was beautiful in hers.

Because the official circle had grown so large, a distinction was now made between official and public receptions. One or two of the latter were given in the course of a season, but to officials an invitation was sent for four "state" receptions, all on one card. People went to one or all four as they saw fit, but were not supposed to weary their hosts by asking to be presented more than once during the evening. The mistress of the White House was so popular, however, and her husband was the target of so much praise and blame, that this sometimes happened.

The officer who made the presentations and managed the thousand details of officials etiquette was General John M. Wilson of the Engineer Corps. Never did a man enjoy his billet more, but sometimes it was necessary to think and act quickly, as is illustrated by a story that he used to tell when he was an old man.

Both he and the President had noticed that some of the guests showed a desire to be received several times in succession.

"Can't you stop this repeating?" the President asked. "We have thousands of guests in an evening. Mrs. Cleveland and I get very tired shaking hands, and yet some are not satisfied; they are presented once, then mingle with the crowd, go back, and fall into line and are presented again, two or three times. Can't you stop it?"

"I can try, Mr. President," he said, and called to him a man on the White-House force who had formerly been a member of the New York police; Mr. Lamont had secured him the place.

"Are you anything of a detective?" he asked.

"Sure, that I am, sor."

"Do you think, if you were stationed here in this little passage between the Red and Blue parlors, watching the line as it came through, that you would recognize anybody who had already been presented, and was trying to come through a second time?"

"Sure, I 'd spot them, sor."

"Do you think you could explain, very politely so as not to hurt their feelings, that because the crowd was so great you must ask them to stand aside and let the new-comers pass on?"

"Yes, sor."

"Well, suppose you were detailed for that duty, and such a person came along, what would you say?"

"I 'd say,"—and the doughty Irishman's whole body heaved menacingly toward an imaginary interloper,—"Here, you, git out o' that!' "

"No, no!" and General Wilson drilled him over and over again. At the next reception he was on duty, very shiny and red as to skin, very correct as to clothes, very policemanny as to expression of countenance, scrutinizing each guest who filed past him as though the fate of the nation depended on it. The general tried to keep an eye on him, but there seemed to be no call for his services, and he had almost forgotten him when he heard an explosive, "Here, you, git out o' that!" and wheeled to behold his ex-policeman, truculence expressed in every line of his body, blocking the way of one of society's most regal leaders, a lady of stunning presence if rather recent fortunes. Her imposing manner, her black velvet, even her tiara, were nothing to him. He had caught her in the act.

The stupefaction on her face was beginning to give way to lively anger. The line was blocked; people were craning their necks.

The general stepped forward instantly, offered her his arm, to the amazement of his policeman, and presented her with greatest ceremony to the President and Mrs. Cleveland, whom she had met at least twenty times that winter, engineered her rapidly and safely to a place of honor back of the receiving line, and returned to his post of duty. But to no avail. The more she thought about it the madder she grew. She began to complain that she had been insulted, then volubly that she had been grossly insulted in the house of the President of the United States! What she might have gone on to say, no one knows; he knew she was capable of saying much and that it was a case for quick action unless he wished to labor with a woman in hysterics.

"Madam!" he said sternly, presenting himself before her, "you are mistaken. Far from being insulted, you have received one of the greatest compliments of your life!"

"Wh—wha—what do you mean?"

"That ignorant man saw you when you were here two weeks ago. You made such an impression upon him, your elegance and regal bearing were so overpowering, the image they left upon his mind was so strong, that when he saw you to-night, he was sure you had passed along the line only half an hour before."

"Do you really think that was it?" she purred, quite mollified.

"Oh, Wilson," the President said next morning, "how did you get on with that little affair last night?"

He told him.

"By George!" the President said, "I am going to get you transferred from the army to the diplomatic service." But he never did. Such a man was too useful in the White House.

Washingtonians do not trust themselves to enter upon reminiscences of Mrs. Cleveland unless they have much time or much printer's ink at their disposal, for one pleasant memory leads to another, and it is hard to stop.

Her manifold kindness in little things and the number of friendly acts she performed and of notes she managed to write with her own hand seem little short of marvelous. Reflecting upon them makes one realize how much smaller Washington was in the last century than it is now.

She carried on the custom, inaugurated by Mrs. Grant, of inviting women to assist at her afternoon receptions, but increased the number from the cabinet ladies and a very few others to twenty-five or fifty, seeking out representatives from all circles. What one young woman recorded about her last afternoon reception may well close this chapter:

It rained hard all the morning, but about half-past two the downpour ceased, though the clouds were lowering, and the city looked drenched as I drove, shortly afterward, to the White House. At the southwest gate three policemen and a horse were stationed to take the blue tickets of admission to the lower grounds that had been inclosed with invitations to assist "behind the line." The stalwart fellows were vastly more picturesque in their rainy-day high boots and round rubber capes, than in the ordinary gala-dress of white gloves and broadcloth. After passing them the carriage crawled along the sodden driveway, under leafless branches, past the greenhouses and a mountain of garden benches piled together in winter desolation, to the steps curving up on either side of the southern balcony. Their well-worn flagstones were protected by a dripping yellow awning, and this moist and winding tunnel led to a door opening directly into the Red Room, from which the invited guests passed to the State Dining Room to lay aside their wraps. The long table under its green cover, set at intervals with gilded candelabra and other ornaments, served as temporary repository for cloaks.

After a glance at the top of my head in the mirror, (as much as I could see for the height of the mantels) and a moment's chat with young and pretty Mrs. Faulkner, wife of the West Virginia Senator, who was regarding her top-knot in the same glass, we passed across the Red Parlor again to the Blue Room, where the invited guests were assembling. All told, there were about 40 of us, gathered from varied circles of Washington life—wives and daughters of officials, representatives of the old and new resident sets, of the millionaires, and of the women who work with their hands—frivolous and learned, brides, old maids, young girls and grey haired matrons, besides a few friends of Mrs. Cleveland's from out of town. All were in rich afternoon dress and made a gay picture in the brilliantly lighted room, whose drawn curtains shut out the view of soaked gardens and dreary sky. Palms and wonderful azalias filled the window spaces, the mantels were banked with red and white roses, and a great vase of red roses crowned the round settee in the middle of the room. A line of sofas had been stretched across the room, fencing off about one quarter of its northern portion. These, with the "golden gate" barring the door leading from the Blue Room into the corridor, converted that part of the room into a sort of passage-way, through which people could enter from the Red Room, greet Mrs. Cleveland and the Cabinet ladies receiving with her, and pass on to the Green and East Rooms. They also served as a slight support against which the receiving party might lean, as well as to divide "the line" from those who had been bidden to assist behind it.

A little before three o'clock Mrs. Cleveland entered on the arm of Col. Wilson, and took her place in the improvised passageway, near the northern door leading from the Red into the Blue Room. Col. Wilson stood between her and the door, and another man stood quite in the doorway. A young officer, Lieut. Gilmore, I believe, stood against the wall, directly opposite Mrs. Cleveland. As people were admitted single file, this surrounded each person at the moment of greeting the Mistress of the White House with three able-bodied men, while twice that number were within easy reach—a precaution against possible insane cranks, or against a sudden pressure of the crowd, whose mere weight is at times almost unmanageable. At Mrs. Cleveland's right was Mrs. Stevenson, then Mrs. Olney, Mrs. Carlisle, Mrs. Lamont, and so on down the list in strict order of Cabinet precedence; Mrs. Harmon being the only lady absent.

The few members of the Diplomatic Corps who had gathered in the Red Parlor—Madame Paternotre, Senor and Madame Romero, and one or two others, were first received; then those behind the line were told that Mrs. Cleveland would be glad to greet them. So the forty of us formed a procession, passing out of the Blue Room into the Red Room by the south door, two by two, and in again, single file, by the north door, where we found ourselves directly in front of Mrs. Cleveland. After a word and a handclasp with her, we went on to Mrs. Stevenson, and down the entire line of Cabinet ladies, shaking hands with each in turn, and finally passing again behind the barricade to our old position—a proceeding eminently proper and highly honorable to all concerned, but suggestive of a kitten chasing its own tail.

Then the doors were opened, and the real reception began, when for two hours people of high and low degree, white and black, passed through the room at the rate of twenty-five a minute. Mrs. Cleveland had a smile and hearty handshake for each one, and her quick wit and gracious tact were exercised to the utmost in kindly deeds. The little woman, for instance, who was so absorbed in gazing at her hostess's beautiful face that she missed the outstretched hand, was given another chance, after she had quite passed on; and the children were greeted with special kindness. There were touchingly many children; little ones in arms, toddlers almost as small, who seemed in danger of being trampled underfoot, but who had been brought because it was Mrs. Cleveland's last reception and in after years they would be proud to have seen and touched the hand of this most popular mistress of the White House; and larger children of all sizes, up to the schoolgirl of fourteen with as much finery and more airs than a society belle.

Women of course made up by far the larger part of the crowd, four-fifths perhaps; some shabby, some in brave attire despite the clouds. Many were evidently "flustered" and passed on with set smile and lowered eyelids, hardly seeing the President's wife at all. Others seemed trying to photograph her face in their memory, and many turned after the handshake for a quick glance at her gown. The men were more inclined to stop and make little speeches to the first lady of the land; they cared not one whit what she wore. But the young officer standing opposite laid a warning hand on the arm of each who wished to linger, and urged him on. Sometimes a rather vigorous push was necessary to start the procession again. A few colored people came through, both men and women, more men possibly than women, but not many of either. One regular Topsy of a servant girl, black, undersized, in battered straw sailor, twisted into shapes that only a colored Topsy's hat can assume, with tattered apron and faded clothes, walked down the line, gleams of such exultant daring and satisfied desire il-

ONE OF WASHINGTON'S LEAFY AVENUES

luminating the look she rolled over the daintily clad ladies behind Mrs. Cleveland, that it seemed a whole revelation of character, and a volume of race-history besides. Toward the end of the reception two Indians added their characteristic features to the throng.

From behind the line, the conscientiously donned ceremonious smile on each face as it appeared in the doorway had a curious effect. It was as though, at the moment of entering, faces possessed no other feature than a mouth; after greeting Mrs. Cleveland and while passing down the line, the rest came one by one into view, and on leaving the room each departed with the usual complement of eyes and nose. There were queer characters here and there, but on the whole it was an orderly, sober, decently dressed crowd; paying real homage to the Mistress of the White House, and sincerely sorry that she was so soon to leave it. Many looked pathetically into her eyes, as if they never expected to see her again; and I fancy the answering tears started in her own, more than once. She had a smile for each one— "3000 handshakes in two hours, 3000 smiles," Dorothea Gilder wailed in commiseration, as we counted the people. Occasionally the stream would be held back for a moment or two, that she might rest, and she would turn, a little breathless, to lean on the back of the sofa and survey the group of people behind her, with bright nods to this and that acquaintance. During one of these intervals she showed her shapely ungloved right hand to a lady standing near. It was literally black with the contact, but as she regarded it with an amused smile she asserted that it was not at all tired. Three hours of such exercise might make it so; two hours never did. Then the procession began again, and Col. Wilson's announcement of "Miss Smith, Mr. Jones, Mrs. Robinson," recalled her to her task. The Cabinet ladies stood beside her the entire time, shaking hands or not as they saw fit.

A very few of the 3000 were allowed to pass the barrier and mingle with the people imprisoned behind the sofas. An usher stationed at the narrow opening between the last sofa and the wall regulated that according to his high will and pleasure. He is supposed to know by intuition who is worthy of the honor. Diplomats and the mighty are urged to enter, others are merely suffered to do so, others still are politely requested to move on toward the Green Parlor. In point of fact however, very few of the Great American People claimed the privilege. As a rule they entered, crossing the vestibule and hall to the Red Parlor, went from that to the Blue Room where they whispered their names to Col. Wilson who made the presentations; passed along the line of Cabinet ladies into the Green Room, from there into the East Room and the corridor where they crowded about the "golden gate" for one last look at the President's wife, and made their exit finally by the temporary steps leading from the window of the lobby.

The few who came behind the line mingled with the group there to watch the people pass; or chatting with friends, moved about or sat in the southern part of the room, which was never crowded. Postmaster General Wilson was the only cabinet member who graced the occasion, and the Korean Minister and his wife the only Orientals to add picturesqueness to the scene.

During the previous administration the wives of the newly arrived Koreans, last in the family of nations to set up an establishment in Washington, had astonished society, and perhaps themselves, by extricating themselves from Oriental seclusion. They were meek-looking, undersized little ladies with profiles that resembled those of rag dolls, and manners to match. But when their lords and masters went off to a ball, bidding them stay at home, they ordered another carriage and followed. After that their lords took them with them. There was no telling where they might go if left behind.

At five o'clock Mrs. Cleveland again took Col. Wilson's arm, and followed by the Cabinet ladies two by two a tour was made through the Green Room, East Room and corridor to the private dining room. There the ladies from behind the line, and such as had been personally invited to stay, joined them. A round table was set with tea things, red roses, fancy cakes, and the gold spoons of the State dinner service. Chairs were placed in two or three rows around the sides of the room and Mrs. Cleveland begged us all to be seated. The company broke up into little groups, when tea and ices were served, Mrs. Cleveland being helped first. She then moved about, cup in hand from group to group, sitting and chatting a few moments with each.

It made a picture long to be remembered—the square room with its airy buff-tinted walls, and side-board set with historic china and silver, the dainty table, the groups of attractive women in dresses as many-tinted as a garden of flowers; the gay pinks, greens, cherry, blues and whites subdued to just the right proportion by those of grey and black and rich dull colors; and moving about among them, Mrs. Cleveland in her lavender gown, by far the most beautiful woman there, and as wholesome and sweet and natural as the violets at her belt.

Finally she rose, and we made our adieus. On reaching the State Dining Room again in search of my wrap I found another pretty picture. A flaxen haired child was in possession—little Marian, the President's youngest daughter—standing gravely by her nurse's knee, while slender Mrs. McMillan wearing her bridal robes, and Mrs. Stevenson in red were literally on the floor at her feet.

XXV

UNIMPORTANT FOLK

PEOPLE say that Washington has no great business interests. In answer somebody has pointed out that Uncle Sam does rather a large business, and that the paid employees in his service number many more than those of several large corporations put together. So even in a business way the town can hold its own.

Uncle Sam, the principal employer, is a very real personage, amiable and kindly in his intentions, but absent-minded and inclined to presume a little on his relationship toward obscure nephews. And they on their part sometimes let loyalty and family affection influence their actions in a way that in the long run may not be particularly good for them or for Uncle Sam. They like their employment, like their employer, like their environment, and so labor in government service for a lifetime, though "getting nowhere" in a worldly sense, partly out of inertia, partly out of affection. Such men, to be found in every branch of every bureau, are laughed at and imposed upon by their associates, but always relied on in an emergency, and are ready to give the last drop of their heart's blood to the cause they serve.

Usually their work is of the sort that goes into the files and does not show, being expressed in columns of figures or folios of writing, but occasionally one labors in a medium that leaves a visible record as the work progresses. One such man, the king of all these patient workers, was Constantino Brumidi, who spent the last thirty years of a long life covering the Capitol walls with frescos. The canopy of the dome, the great unfinished frieze of monochrome figures upon which he was at work when he died at the age of eighty, and the rich decorations in the Senate end of the building are all his. Trained in Rome, a young painter entrusted by the Vatican with restoring Raphael's frescos, he threw down his brushes to take up the sword in the cause of liberty and was a revolutionist for twenty years, before fleeing to America in middle life. Taking out his naturalization papers, he spent his old age in this labor of love, covering not only important walls but endless lengths of dim corridors with wreaths and panels and shields enriched with minute painstaking portraits of the birds and animals and flora of America. Whether his work was good art, or the best possible way of decorating such spaces, is beside the mark. He gave the best that was in him, unstintingly; and it is worth a journey from a far city to walk through those corridors and study his devotion.

In this great business in which Uncle Sam is engaged, there are proportionately more "white-collar jobs" than in any other, which is good for the general aspect of the town, though likely to be bad for the individual. From the nature of their calling, clerks, and even the department employees below the grade of clerks, are forced to adopt a standard of dress and behavior which sometimes they can ill afford. It was the same in the old days. "Those who cannot afford it are anxious to make an equal show with those who can; and the one half of the salaries public officials get, would, aside from ostentation, be just as good for them as the whole," was written by an observer of Washington life long ago.

At the time when the prototypes of the two newest additions to the White House stretched away to the east and west, one housing the Presidential cows and the other the Presidential horses, the vacant stalls in the latter, as well as sheds erected near the department buildings, were appropriated by clerks who drove or rode in daily from their homes in the suburbs. How they managed to keep horses on their salaries, let alone pay the high annual tax on calashes and private carriages, is a mystery, but they did it somehow, believing their position required it. It was only a spartan old aristocrat like John Quincy Adams who could afford to walk to his work.

An Englishman touring the United States in Monroe's time wrote, "Aristocrats are breeding fast in America," and pointed in proof to this town where trade was looked down upon, and the government departments harbored distinct strata of officials, each spurning the ones below it.

It is true that society and trade are here divided by a gulf broad as that which separates them on the other side of the water, and that the question asked first of all about a man in Washington is not, "Who is he?" meaning, as it would in Baltimore or Philadelphia, "Who were his grandparents?" or, in the speech of New York, "What is his business and how much is he worth?" but, "What office does he hold?" And the amusing and illogical part of it is that when, as has happened several times during the last twenty-five years, a merchant prince has been induced to come to Washington to assume a cabinet position, it is not his success in trade (which has presumably made him desirable for the office) that avails him and his household socially, but the title he bears for the time being, with the pittance he draws from the United States Treasury. The many millions otherwise at his disposal add to the brilliance of his sojourn, but lurking in the mind of many a spectator is the snobbish desire to excuse the fact of his *merchant* princeliness, the crowning absurdity being that these same people, meeting him in their home towns where standards are different, would deem that his very first claim upon their respectful admiration.

Since we are a commercial nation, this presents one more anomaly of the kind we frequently encounter in Washington, where there is usually a notable calm at the center of the political storm, and the District of Columbia is voteless at the heart of a government dominated by the ballot.

But to return to our unimportant people. In 1920 the population of the city was estimated at 437,571, and rather more than half of them—53⁹⁄₁₀ per cent., to be exact—were listed as "gainfully employed." Of these only about 30,000 were of foreign birth. Doubtless substituting the words "foreign parentage" would greatly have increased the number. There were more married men than married women in town, but far more widows than widowers.

This brings to notice the large number of women in government service. Keeping boarding-houses long ago ceased to be the chief and characteristic gainful occupation of women in Washington. Who was the first woman to break through a tradition that barred the sex from government departments, and how she did it, is a bit of history already lost in the mazes of tradition. One tale not devoid of picturesqueness credits General Spinner with appointing a spinster to a job in his office whose sole requirements were honesty and physical ability to wield a pair of long shears. By the end of her first day in government employ she had demonstrated her ability to do it as well as any man who had ever held the shears. Doubtless the great exodus from the departments at the beginning of the Civil War opened the doors wider, for work increased and empty desks had to be filled. Then the long list of misfortunes brought about by battle and sudden death entrenched the women in places they had temporarily assumed.

There came a time, shortly after the Civil War, when the question of the salaries paid women in the departments was gravely debated. Representative Holman, frequently called the Watchdog of the Treasury because of his aversion to paying anything out of it, argued that for the same work they ought to receive the same pay as men. Mr. Dawes of Massachusetts pointed out what President Cleveland would have called "a condition, not a theory." These were very worthy ladies, he said, doing excellent work; many were widows or daughters of men who had been killed in the war, and it would work great hardship to dismiss them. Yet conditions were such, the women having no vote, that if the positions they occupied carried salaries that men were willing to accept, the result would be the wholesale dismissal of women and the appointment in their places of men who could cast ballots themselves and were very likely in a position to influence the votes of others.

That was when people were beginning to think uneasily about civil service, but had not acted upon it. It has not proved an unqualified success, but it is certainly a step in the right direction, one of the things we forget when we talk glibly about degenerate modern times and lament the passing of old Washington.

Equal pay for equal work is still a dream far short of realization though the Nineteenth Amendment has given women equal voting privileges with men. The women employed by the Government have steadily increased in numbers and decreased in average age, until, as Kenneth Roberts averred not long ago, women "resplendent in very thick fur coats and very thin silk stockings" issue from the departments at the lunch-hour and give the impression "that all the girls' schools in North America have suddenly poured their students into the streets of Washington."

The history of local schools is a phase of the city's life that would yield, were there time to go into it, as much color as any other feature of its happy-go-lucky development. In early days almost every ill-paid minister eked out his salary by teaching, for the stigma of pauper instruction clung to the public schools, which were established rather earlier here than in other regions so far south. And in addition to this the odd places in which such schools were held—a stable deemed no longer good enough for Presidential horses, an abandoned brewery, and a tin-and-paint-shop whose smells and noises punctuated the course of study—were not calculated to make the paths of a common-school education pleasant or easy.

The District's small territory, partly under federal control, made it an ideal spot in which to try experiments. School authorities have kept on trying them from that day to this, often to the advantage but frequently to the bewilderment of teachers and pupils. About the time of our second war with England the "Lancastrian System" was imported from the mother-country and extolled as a great and wonderful reform. This applied factory methods to education, with the commendable purpose of extending its benefits and lessening its costs. Watts's hymn-book and the Bible were adopted as text-books, not alone on account of their solid worth but because every household was supposed to own them, and this reduced the bill for school supplies. Scripture instruction by question and answer prolonged the delights of the Westminster catechism throughout the week. The leaves of a single dismembered spelling-book, pasted upon cards and distributed among the classes, went far; while a teacher's supervision was extended in the same way by the use of military signals, and mentors with a little brief authority recruited from among the older pupils. It was a won-

THE CONNECTICUT AVENUE BRIDGE OVER ROCK CREEK

derful theory, but it worked out in practice much as Polk's administration worked out in politics. The rival "Pestalozzi system," however, that stressed quality at the expense of quantity, died within three years for lack of support.

Among the teachers of private schools there were odd people. One master used to "wind up his school like a clock" and then go out and boast of it to his neighbors, inviting them to drop in and see for themselves how perfectly it worked without supervision. Old John McLeod, who inscribed "Order is Heaven's First Law!" over his portal, disapproved of long vacations as disturbing to that order; required his pupils to be on hand at six o'clock in the morning and to bring their lunches with them so as not to waste time at noon; and lived up to his own requirements by dying, when his time came, in the Christmas holidays, when it would not be upsetting to routine. There was Miss English, who fitted so many girls of fashion for a genteel career; and elegant Mrs. Lee, who advertised, on an engraved card with a chaste border, her desire to "embellish the minds" of her pupils, and her belief that the knowledge of geography should be "properly imbibed" at an early age.

The twentieth-century equivalent of Miss English's School for Girls may be found in half a dozen large, excellently equipped establishments in the suburbs, which fit young women for college, or "finish" them for society, and give them meanwhile a memorable if superficial view of social and official Washington. On any Friday night they may be seen at the theater, occupying expensive seats, properly chaperoned and looking like a gay parterre of flowers, their eyes as keen for celebrities in the audience as for anything that takes place upon the stage.

In the development of the public schools there came innovations one after the other; experiments with a high school for boys, then one for girls which was speedily discontinued for the rather baffling reason that so many girls wished to avail themselves of it; the normal school, the kindergarten, and all the modern frills; high-school cadets, whose annual drill under the inspection of army officers of exalted rank has supplanted as a spectacle the old school processions; manual training, athletics, dramatics, cooking, dressmaking, nature study, atypical schools, classes for tubercular children, and so on—developments that would have scandalized stern Mr. Ironsides, master of one of the Lancastrian schools, and delighted Pestalozzi.

As a unit by which to measure present-day success we have the great Central High School, a building of Tudor design standing on an eminence overlooking the city known to the directory as Clifton Street, between Eleventh and Thirteenth streets, but to readers of history as being near the confines of the old Jockey Club. Its location, coupled with its name, tells the story of the city's growth. One feature of its interior arrangements is an auditorium whose stage is larger than that of any theater in town, while its corridors rise story upon story and lengthen out until the students complain that they can hardly avail themselves of the swimming-pool or the gymnasium in their free time, because it takes so long to get back to the class rooms.

This is only one of four great high schools and many large if lesser buildings, most of which were very good at the time they were built, but which now spell failure, since they are utterly inadequate to hold the numbers of young people who crowd them, even with the addition of temporary "movable" structures to catch the overflow, while the system goes limping along with half-time instruction, poorly paid teachers, and a curriculum altered every few months to try out some new theory.

Yet, in spite of all drawbacks, where else in the country is there a place to equal Washington for a certain class of educational advantages? Where else does embodied history walk the streets as here; and where do the buildings one sees and the people one meets so constantly bring to mind our complicated system of government? Where else, too, if teacher and pupil have the wit to look for them, is there better opportunity to study new marvels of invention and science, than in the growing collections of the Smithsonian and the National Museum?

While the great university of which Washington dreamed, as part of the Federal Capital, has not yet materialized, there are already so many smaller institutions of learning scattered about, that soon there will be a circle of schools and religious institutions around the city, as a circle of forts girdled it during the Civil War.

Of these, Kendall Green is the most unique, being the one college for the deaf in the United States. It is not on the outskirts, but quite in the city now, though it was country for many years after Amos Kendall rescued a little band of deaf and blind waifs from a man seeking to exploit them, sent back to their homes all whose parents he could locate, and with the others began his school, calling to the head of it a young man only twenty years old, son of the Dr. Gallaudet of Hartford whose school for such unfortunates was already famous.

It was the pupils of this elder Dr. Gallaudet who so entranced President John Quincy Adams, when they were brought on to show Congress how such children might be taught, that the conscientious President entirely forgot a cabinet meeting, or else abandoned it to its fate.

"I asked Mr. Gallaudet if he could make them [the pupils] understand the difference between irrefrangible and incontrovertible," he wrote in his diary. Dr. Gallaudet confessed that he could not himself immediately see the distinction. Then the President began interrogating the pupils and had such a wonderful time that one o'clock, the hour for the cabinet meeting, came and went, and so did two o'clock, and it was three before he returned to the White House and found that the cabinet members had wearied of waiting and gone home.

The son of this Dr. Gallaudet who so frankly tried to shield his charges from the onslaught of the Adams intellect, remained for fifty-three years the head of the Washington institution, which grew under his presidency from a school of scarcely a dozen pupils to the well-equipped Columbian Institution for the Deaf, with its collegiate department and preparatory school housed in buildings in the beautiful park that was Amos Kendall's suburban estate. The story of the ups and downs of the institution during his stewardship contains much that is inspiring, much that is humorous, and much also that is pathetic, besides enough dread and uncertainty to bring it well within the fairy-story category. Except for Mr. Kendall's gift of houses and land, the institution was and still is dependent upon annual appropriations from Congress, a heartbreakingly casual manner of providing for needs that are constant and growing. It became as important a part of the young educator's duty to educate successive congresses as it was to see that the students had the best he could give them; and new congresses come and old ones go every two years.

Another important educational institution in its own field is Howard University for colored youth. How large that field is in the District is emphasized by the survey of Washington's population already referred to, which states that for every three white inhabitants the city has one negro. If we should imagine all the white people getting into their cars some fine afternoon and riding away (and there are plenty of automobiles to take them), the human beings left behind would constitute one of the largest negro communities in the world. Let us think of it for a moment: a town of over one hundred thousand black men, women, and children with churches and schools, shops and restaurants of their own, two daily newspapers out of the seven the town supports printed by them for circulation among their own people, who show as many grades of intelligence as the white people. They have their own theater and their own moving-picture houses of varying grades, the higher of which are as clean and well conducted as many frequented by whites and better ventilated, while their audiences, barring their darker tone, are quite as distinguished in appearance. In civic work, like that of the Associated Charities, they more than hold their own with the whites, in proportion to their means; and in places like the crowded internal-revenue office, when citizenship such as we have in the District keeps the two races waiting together on an absolute equality, it is apt to be among the colored schoolteachers, and not among white people, that talk drifts away from their own discomfort to subjects of public interest.

The colored folk are still our very picturesque peasantry, as anybody can prove for himself who is willing to look at them immediately after a return from Europe with exactly the same receptive glance that he bestowed upon Holland fisherfolk and Italian *contadini*. A youth with golden-brown skin, dressed in a torn and faded blue shirt open at the throat, faded plum-colored breeches, and a dull-crimson sweater, one striped sock and one green one, lolling grandly on his high seat as he drives a team of mules in brass-studded harness, makes a satisfying picture, though he may be an unsatisfactory employee.

And outside the markets, particularly Center Market on Saturdays, may be seen family groups to rival any genre picture ever painted. Decrepit "uncles" and fat old "aunties" who have driven before daylight over several miles of Virginia roads, bring in the harvest from their sketchily tilled garden-plot, a stock in trade of a little pile of vegetables, a twist of brown tobacco leaves, a few eggs, a skinny chicken or two, some pokeweed, and half a dozen nosegays tied up with bits of ancient cotton rag. Sometimes they are accompanied by younger members of the family—a dressy, progressive son, intent on getting away from the old folk as soon as possible, to his own job of work or loafing; and two or three small grandchildren, who look on or take their minor part in the day's transactions with round and rolling eyes. "Auntie" keeps hawk-like watch over them, and admonishes or praises while she does business with her customers. For these she has a persuasive tone, and is always ready to indulge in an exchange of friendly repartee. Her garments are both fearful and wonderful, presenting, layer upon layer, as many historic strata as may be seen during a morning's stroll in the Roman Forum.

Her ample skirt may date from Buchanan's administration, when it belonged to a lady of Southern pride and prejudice. On her head in winter she usually wears a shapeless quilted hood whose original hue long since passed from human ken. A checked apron is of more recent vintage, owing to the perishable nature of the material, and her coat, of much harassed plush, has probably been the pride of several successive owners. What lies hidden under this layer, no mortal knows, but we may be sure that underneath all beats the warm, ignorant heart of Afro-America; and the chances are that she considers herself "quality" and is known in her own circle by a name that was famous in colonial or Revolutionary days.

There was a time when an effort was made to enforce the rule that negroes should travel only in street cars provided for their use, but for some reason it did not succeed. That tall black sybil Sojourner Truth, who preached before the Senate itself on women's suffrage, disposed of the matter characteristically by saying grandly:

"Street cars is fo' culled people. White gentlemen an' ladies rides in their own carriages!"

Though in some respects we have grown much more liberal, the sight could scarcely be seen to-day which met the eyes of President John Quincy Adams when he crossed Lafayette Square one Sunday in the year 1827, to attend afternoon service at St. John's. Instead of finding his good friend Pastor Hawley in his accustomed place, he saw a black man ascend the pulpit and listened to a sermon from him on the text "Follow me." He made no reference to slavery and addressed much of his discourse to members of his own race in the gallery, but the truthful Adams, whose interest in the negroes was by no means a matter of the heart, felt constrained to admit that the sermon was "not below mediocrity in composition, and quite upon a level with the average Sunday discourse from white preachers," and that the man's manner combined "both ease and solemnity."

But, on the other hand, we must not forget that at the dedication of the Lincoln Memorial, it was the President of Tuskegee who made the principal address. Taken all in all, there is a distinct if slow improvement, and both races are climbing upward. Fortunately, the beloved old house servant is not yet extinct, though growing rheumatic, and captious with the crankiness of age. Did not President Harding's cook become a national figure through her proficiency in making waffles, and Mrs. Wilson's Susie make her way through the palaces of Europe, leaving a trail of humor and glory behind her? Undoubtedly there are fewer of these delightful creatures than formerly, but to balance the account there are many really competent doctors and preachers and teachers with dark skins. In government positions also there are colored men who do their work with a thoroughness and bear themselves with a courtesy not to be excelled. Richard Green of the Treasury and Arthur Brooks of the White House, to mention only two of recent years, are justly counted among the finest of their race. And if there is a discouraging number of incompetents in domestic service, the same is true among white girls and men. The utterly inefficient young person of color who responded to her mistress's impatient, "Put your mind on it! Don't you ever think about what you are doing?" with the indignant, "No 'm. I does n't think about my work. I thinks noble thoughts," really had rather the best of it, for she was indicting a whole educational system, which appears to be near the breaking point for whites and blacks alike.

An honest desire on the part of the authorities to give every negro child a chance to develop whatever capacity the Lord has given it, has built up, since negro schools were first established in 1862, a whole system within the system, duplicating in every essential that for the whites, so that now the schools of Washington resemble one of those double-faced fabrics woven—only experts know how—to present to the world a surface all white on one side and all black on the other, yet in which the threads are inextricably mingled. The professor of Howard University at one end of the line and the crap-shooting loafer at the other, present a long gamut of mental retrogression, but no longer nor greater than our own race can show.

Ambitious pupils, natural racial indolence, inexperience, the determination of women whose whole lives have been spent over grimy tasks that their children shall not be drudges, the cravings for showy trappings of success, only natural in a people who in point of years are after all not very far removed from savagery compared with the time the white race has taken to cover the same ground—all combine to give the problem many amusing and serious angles.

It was as early as 1867, only five years after the blacks of the city had their first public schools, that a generous donor gave them their higher institution of learning. All sorts and kinds manage to pass the entrance examination for Howard, as is the case at white colleges. In Washington, bell-boys and elevator operators in every large building may be seen casting their eyes, at odd moments, into books that have no connection whatever with their occupation.

One of the riddles of the day was epitomized in a little scene that took place one morning in a crowded street car between two of the students, who were no more intellectual than the average, but at least had an idea of what was expected of them. One leaned forward and asked the other, across the lady who sat between them:

"Say Jim, is yo' done yo' Greek?"

XXVI

"THE FATHER OF ALL THE CHILDREN"

PERSPECTIVE does queer things, in history as well as in art. It works injustice to individuals, while bringing them into truer relations to their surroundings. The Encyclopædia Britannica explains Benjamin Harrison, who occupied the White House between the two terms of President Cleveland, by saying:

His administration was marked by a revival of American industries and a reduction of the public debt; and at its conclusion the country was left in a condition of prosperity and on friendly terms with foreign nations.

This is a record of which any ambitious American might be proud, but for historical effect his four beneficent years count as nothing beside the fact that he had a grandfather and also a grandson. His own name does not induce a single thrill while that of his grandfather is one on which Americans love to dwell, though the most effective use William Henry Harrison made of the Executive Mansion was to die in it. As for Benjamin Harrison's grandson "Baby McKee," he rivaled Mrs. Hayes in ability to "run the White House," if we may trust contemporary news paragraphs. President Harrison was so lacking in salient traits upon which to hang stories, that the press welcomed the perfectly normal pranks and ailments of a petted youngster as manna sent from heaven.

The liveliest bit of administration history that has come down to us from those years concerns itself with a purely domestic episode —Baby McKee in a little cart drawn by a goat, which suddenly bolts and swings out of the White House gate at top pace, with the gray-bearded, short-legged President leaping in hot pursuit. That the baby sat tight and was not spilled, and that his grandfather caught him in the nick of time, complete the tale both for efficiency and lack of excitement.

Perspective is still more unkind in the case of the next Republican occupant of the White House. One of the campaign stories of the year he was elected quotes a grizzled farmer as saying he did n't "know much about McKinley, but that wife Hannah of his was certainly an all-fired smart woman." Franklin K. Lane, McKinley's Secretary of the Navy, wrote that his chief was "at bottom a dear boy of kind heart, who put his hand into the big fist of Mark Hanna and was led to glory." The wistaria-shaded dwelling on Lafayette Square where Senator Hanna lived, next door to Dolly Madison's old home, was known as the "Little White House," and fully as many curious eyes were cast upon it and almost as many people knocked at its door as at the big white mansion half a block away.

Under the "all-fired smart" leader and this President of facile speech and winning personality, the people of the United States experienced many emotions, not only the sequence which began with the wrecking of the *Maine* and ended in Dewey's victory that made us masters, in spite of ourselves, of territory half around the planet, but the feelings induced by the stand the Administration took in the Boxer uprising, when America had the new sensation of leading the world in aggression. In addition there was personal admiration for the President who bore a domestic grief with loving fortitude; and horror when he was stricken down in his prime, by an assassin's bullet. Yet we pass over world events and the private tragedies of his life and of his death, to dwell on the brave, tumultuous personality of the man who succeeded him.

Roosevelt was a constant challenge to the maker of epigrams. Mrs. Anderson quotes a Yale policeman who said, "He's a lovely man, but distressin'," and we all remember that most comprehensive summing up of his character as "a mixture of St. Paul and St. Vitus."

Just before the outbreak of the Spanish-American War this dynamic person was Assistant-Secretary of the Navy, and Secretary Lane was beset with difficulties of his own because of it. His health was poor and it was imperative that he take some rest, yet he dared not leave the department to the superabundant vitality of this young man. He tried the experiment of letting go of affairs for one day, and then wrote in his diary:

> I had a splendid night last night, and return to the office, both because I feel so much better and because I find that Roosevelt in his precipitate way has come very near causing more of an explosion than happened on the *Maine*. His wife is very ill, and his little boy is just recovering from a long and dangerous illness; so his natural nervousness is so much accentuated that I really think he is hardly fit to be entrusted with the responsibility of the Department at this critical time. He is full of suggestions. . . . and his spirited and forceful habit is a good tonic for one who is disposed to be as conservative and careful as I am, . . . but the very devil seemed to pòssess him yesterday afternoon. . . . He immediately began to launch peremptory orders, distributing ships, ordering ammunition, which there was no means to move to places where there is no means to store it, . . . sending messages to Congress for immediate legislation; authorizing the enlistment of an unlimited number of seamen. . . . He has gone at things like a bull in a china shop. . . . It shows how the best fellow in the world, and with splendid capacities, is worse than no use, if he lack a cool head and careful discretion.

Yet when Roosevelt announced his intention of resigning, four days after war was declared, his chief was even more distressed, finding how much he had come to rely upon him:

> He has lost his head to this unutterable folly of deserting the post where he is of most service, and running off to ride a horse and probably brush mosquitos from his neck on the Florida sands. . . . And yet how absurd all this will sound, if by some turn of fortune he should accomplish some great thing and strike a very high mark!

At a later date he added: "P.S. Roosevelt was right and we his friends were all wrong. His going into the army led straight to the Presidency."

The St. Paul side of his nature manifested itself in his earnestness where matters of government were concerned. Fond as he was of jests, he could not bear them at the expense of a man's duty to the State. One diplomat's career was entirely ruined so long as

Roosevelt remained President, because of a dinner-table remark that Holland was the ideal billet for a man below the rank of ambassador. Mr. Roosevelt asked why, expecting some profound reason, and was told, "Because it takes such a short time to get to the opera or a dinner in Paris or Berlin." "Think of it!" he exploded, mentioning the matter years later to a friend. The offender found himself firmly retrograded, until at the end of Roosevelt's term he was "gnashing his teeth in Persia" and begging to be sent back to civilization.

There is no better example of this earnestness than a story told by the President's sister Mrs. Robinson. She had returned from Porto Rico, bringing proof of the iniquity of a certain officer, and telegraphed on landing, asking for an appointment "on Porto Rican business." Quick as the wires could carry it she received the laconic answer, "Come to-morrow." The month was April. Washington was at its loveliest, and as she drove up to the White House her brother was mounting for his afternoon ride. He told her that Mrs. Roosevelt was out of town and that they would have dinner tête-à-tête on the south portico, and rode off. The dinner was a time of magic, with moonlight, scent of flowers in the air, the view toward the monument never more beautiful, and her brother in the best of moods. He recited Kipling and Swinburne, and then in more serious vein gave her a vivid account of his latest disagreement with Congress. The moon had set and the stars had grown bright and deep before they left the portico,—"We never could go to bed when we were together, and I am so glad we never did,"—but not a word had been said about Porto Rico.

Next morning he ran gaily downstairs to the eight-o'clock breakfast with the children with which his day invariably began, stopping on the way, as a telephone bell rang, to pick up the receiver. As he listened, she saw a broad smile overspread his face and he answered the piping voice at the other end:

"No, I am not Archie. I am Archie's father. All right. I will tell him. I won't forget," and rang off, laughing. "How the creatures order you about!" he quoted from "Alice in Wonderland," and sketched for his sister's benefit the disgust of the small boy at the other end of the line when he found he was talking to the President of the United States and not to his chum.

After the merry breakfast, Mrs. Robinson and her brother walked together for a short time in the grounds south of the White House. He talked about birds, but would not listen to business, reminding her, when she tried to bring it up, that her appointment was for nine o'clock. Then he squared his shoulders and marched off to the day's work, and she followed his example by going to her room and dressing for the street as carefully as though a long journey lay ahead of her, though she only passed out of the White-House door and along the few feet of path leading to the new Executive Offices, to present herself there like the other visitors. When she was ushered into the President's private room, she found him seated before a table covered with papers relating to Porto Rico, one of which he was reading. The eyes he lifted to hers gave her a shock, they were so different from the merry, affectionate eyes with which he had looked at her only a few moments before. These seemed almost opaque and a little cold, "the eyes of a just judge . . . turned upon his sister as they would have been upon any other individual who came to him with a question such as she had brought." He waved her to a chair, finished the paper he was reading, and turning to her said formally:

"I believe you have come to see me on business connected with Porto Rico. Kindly be as condensed as possible."

Meeting him on his own ground, she made her eyes as much like his as she could and told her story in the fewest possible words. Listening carefully, he asked sternly, "Have you proof of this?" and she answered, "I should not be here wasting your time and mine, did I not have proof," and handed him notes that she had brought with her, made by the Governor of Porto Rico, and proceeded to explain them. After reading these he became a little less stern, but no less serious, reminding her that he must be absolutely sure of the facts before he acted, since a man's whole future hung upon the decision. She felt for a moment like an executioner, but remembering the offense, backed up all that the governor had written.

I can still hear the sound of the President's pen as he took out the paper on which the man's name was inscribed, and with one strong stroke effaced that name from official connection with Porto Rico forever. That was the way that Theodore Roosevelt did business with his sister.

The room in which this odd interview took place was part of the alteration made in the White House under the supervision of Mr. and Mrs. Roosevelt. Up to that time the President's family had not exactly been required to live over the shop, but the shop had been over the drawing-rooms, the east half of the second story of the mansion being set aside for office use. Mrs. Taft mentions an incident that may have had its part in hastening the alteration. When Prince Henry of Prussia visited Washington, the President invited him to ride, and the prince presented himself at the White House in street clothes, evidently expecting to change there. But there was not a single corner in the Executive Mansion that day which could be used as a princely dressing-room, and he had to be sent back to the German Embassy to prepare for his ride.

As for the offices, as far back as 1889 General Sherman wrote a letter describing a business visit to the White House, when he said he found himself standing in the President's office with half a hundred other men, while twice that number waited their turn in an adjoining room. Mr. Blaine wished to present officially Whitelaw Reid, who was about to depart for Paris; Senator Hawley desired to introduce an English friend. General Banks paced the floor restlessly, looking at his watch, a senator from the Pacific slope was anxious to speak to the President about discrimnations in the Interstate bill in favor of foreign corporations. And while these gentlemen were fuming, the President, across the room, was defending himself as best he could from a delegation of citizens who had brought with them their candidate for a fourth-class postmaster's place and were urging his claim.

"This is, I presume," wrote General Sherman, "a fair sample of what happens every day." He had a little ax of his own to grind that morning, but carried it home as dull as when he took it in.

There were stronger reasons than princely inconvenience, or even official crowding, to warrant rebuilding the White House. A portion of it had become structurally unsafe. The servants' quarters, contrived as an afterthought in the attic, were veritable fire-traps, accessible only by elevator and in case of fire to be escaped from only by way of heaven. Efforts made from time to time to instal the various new inventions that real-estate advertisements describe as "mod. imps." had resulted in such defective electric wiring that beams had become actually charred, while the medley of pipes for water and heating was bewildering in the extreme. In order to give the workmen free rein, the President and his family took their personal belongings to 22 Jackson Place, a house removed from Admiral Decatur's old home only by a vacant lot, and lived there several months.

When they returned, sentiment and the heaviest walls were about all that remained of the mansion they had left; for in addition to making it sanitary and safe and removing the old office quarters, the occasion had been seized to sweep away alleged embellishments added from time to time which were entirely out of harmony with the style of the building, such as "pure Greek" decorations of the period of 1873, done with the aid of embossed paper, and the magic Tiffany worked in Arthur's day with crimson and opalescent glass. The house had been brought back strictly to its own period, with modern necessities like the lift and telephones hidden unobtrusively from view.

The greatest change in its outward appearance resulted from tearing down the conservatory that since Buchanan's time had opened from the western end of the main hall, and building out in its place the long, low terrace-like laundries, store-rooms, etc, and beyond them the Executive Offices, balancing these at the opposite end with another terrace-like structure containing the necessary exits and entrances to handle large crowds at official receptions, thus doing away with the time-honored necessity for escaping through a window. This change stretched a screen of buildings entirely across the little park in which the White House stands, and had the added advantage of making the southern half of it more private for family use.

Evidently the Roosevelts discovered, as many another family has done, that the only way to get workmen out of a house is to move in and crowd them out, so they returned before the alterations were completed. A letter recently found in an old portfolio shows that they did not allow a little thing like builders' confusion to interfere with the family habit of inviting friends to break bread with them. Informal luncheons were a feature of their White-House life, the guests at such meals being recruited very much as Sunday congregations used to be at the Capitol—from the material at hand at the moment. Engagements were made beforehand as well, but at the last moment the President might send word that one or a dozen more had been invited in the course of the morning. This old letter reads:

The luncheon yesterday at the White House was great fun. The party consisted of the President and Mrs. Roosevelt, Mrs. Hay, Mr. Von Briesen, a New York lawyer with a white beard, a strong accent and eyes blue as a baby's, Mr. Wilcox of Buffalo, likewise a lawyer and a good judge of horseflesh, I take it, Theodore Jr. and yours truly.

The whole lower floor of the White House is in a mess, undergoing alterations that will improve it immensely. There was a strong smell of turpentine everywhere, and we were relieved of our wraps while standing in the great vestibule, on one foot, so to speak, clutching our skirts to keep them out of the carpenters' dust on the floor. Then we were ushered into the Red Parlor whose walls have been covered with deep red velvet, with results rather startling. At least to my mind they combine the fascinations of a pall and a sleeping car. The room is at present furnished with a misfit collection of leather chairs and lounges. The real furniture is being made to order we are told. It also is to be covered with leather because the room is to be used for smoking on occasion, and the furniture must not be of a material to hold the smoke. Fancy—with those walls!

In a few minutes Mr. Von Briesen was ushered in. Then Mrs. Roosevelt appeared, dressed in white wool. She has a wonderfully pleasant voice and a sweet face. A few minutes later Mr. Wilcox was announced. After that there was a long wait, during which conversation of a kindly gossipy nature was carried on, chiefly by the two matrons. When a little after two o'clock the door opened and the President came in—teeth and all—no time was lost in making for the diningroom. He took out Mrs. Hay, the rest of us followed in a group. Mrs. Roosevelt stopped a moment at the door of the State diningroom to point out some change, and the President, having seated his lady,

© *Ernest L. Crandall, Washington, D. C.*

THE INTIMATE SIDE OF THE WHITE HOUSE

came bouncing back, like a rubber ball, to see why we did not come on. The poor man was frankly hungry, having been on his feet since 9.20 A. M. seeing people, deciding questions all in a minute, and emphatically leading the strenuous life. He said he felt as though he had been galloping.

He talked most entertainingly throughout the meal, and managed besides to dispose of a goodly amount of food. You will laugh when I give you the *menu*—bouillon, salt fish, chicken with rice, rolls, and baked beans. Of beans and the salt fish the President had a second helping. For dessert there was Bavarian cream, served with preserves and cakes. There was one kind of wine, which most of the party declined, and tea, poured by Mrs. Roosevelt, who made it for all the rest just as her husband liked his, "and no questions asked." Cigars were passed after the meal, and lighted by the two lawyers. Mr. Roosevelt did not smoke.

The china was miscellaneous: nice enough but not extraordinary. I only remember some pretty Haviland, and that the bread and butter plates were in the form of flags of the different nations. The President had the Star Spangled Banner, the rest of us got what was left. The German drew the tricolor, I the Union Jack. The waiters were two spry slim colored youths, not in livery, and they were kept rather busy. My impression is that they were always moving toward the President.

If my life depended on it I could not tell you about the centrepiece. There must have been one: but the truth is that Mr. Roosevelt was so rattlingly lively, yet so earnest and dignified, his wife so kind and unaffected, and the whole meal so informal in character, that what was on the table dwindled to minor importance. Theodore Jr. appeared after we were all seated, shook hands all around, took part in the talk with the aplomb of young America and excused himself before dessert to go riding with his small sister—having meanwhile extracted from his mother permission to use her horse.

It was just a nice lively United States family entertaining with heartiness and pot-luck chance visitors of the hour. The only visible difference was that the President was served first, then Mrs. Roosevelt, and after them the guests. Oh yes. Another detail not customary. U. S. was embroidered on the plate doylies. The President and Mrs. Roosevelt sat opposite each other at the sides, not the ends, of the oval table.

The talk ranged over many subjects—importunate senators; Colonel Hay's Bavarian ancestors; the negro problem; the impossibility of doing more than establish certain fixed principles in his own mind and live up to them regardless, and his feeling of the deep obligation he was under, as President, to do this; anecdotes of pet riding horses and a humorous account of a portrait recently painted of him, which was, he said, the only portrait of himself he had ever liked. He liked it because it did not resemble him in the least, but looked as he would like to look. It was the picture he wished to leave to his grandchildren, if he ever had any.

In spite of his almost incessant talk I was impressed with the care he took—the care of a generous thoughtful host, to bring up topics that would interest and draw out the best from each one of his guests in turn. Von Briesen had worked with him in civic matters in New York, and his praise caused the German to turn shy and rosy as a girl.

References to books and authors showed how much reading the President managed to do, while the rapidity with which his mind worked kept us all on the jump. He seemed to follow the usual processes of reasoning but to do so at twice or thrice the usual rate of speed, with the result of apparently leaping from conclusion to conclusion, while the rest of us hurried breathlessly after him. I was reminded of that rhyme in which strange animals "hilariously hopped from bough to bough."

But the impression above all others is of a man *living* with every fiber of his being, ardently as well as arduously, and having the best time of anybody who ever inhabited the White House.

He felt that way about it himself, for in one of the letters to his children he wrote:

I am having a reasonable amount of work and rather more than a reasonable amount of worry. But, after all, life is lovely here. The country is beautiful, and I do not think that any two people ever got more enjoyment out of the White House than Mother and I. We love the house itself, without and within, for its associations, for its stillness, and its simplicity. We love the garden, and we like Washington. We almost always take our breakfast on the south portico now, Mother looking very pretty and dainty in her summer dresses. Then we stroll about the garden for fifteen or twenty minutes, looking at the flowers and the fountain and admiring the trees. Then I work until between four and five, usually having some official people to lunch.

In another letter we get a confession about the Japanese wrestling:

> I am very glad I have been doing this, . . . but . . . I am not at all sure I shall ever try it again while I am so busy with other work as I am now. Often by the time I get to five o'clock in the afternoon I will be feeling like a stewed owl, after eight hours' grapple with Senators, Congressmen, etc., then I find the wrestling a trifle too vehement for mere rest. My right ankle and my left wrist and one thumb and both great toes are swollen sufficiently to more or less impair their usefulness, and I am well mottled with bruises elsewhere. Still I have made good progress, and since you left they have taught me three new throws that are perfect corkers.

Statecraft and history, lawn-tennis, nature-fakers and other sons of Ananias, jiu-jitsu and Irish sages by no means exhausted his energies or his vocabulary. He once confessed that the only matters on which he did not feel qualified to pass judgment were matters of art—and he had strong preferences there.

As for his impulsiveness, John Hay summed that up one day with a reminiscent smile by saying:

"The President is all right, provided you can restrain him for the first fifteen minutes after he has conceived a new idea." The President used to stop at Secretary Hay's house almost every Sunday, on his way home from church, for a call of just about that length of time, and the sounds that issued from the library, the boom of his voice and the quieter tone of his host, with bursts of hearty laughter indicated that the process of exchanging ideas, and possibly of being restrained, were joyous and agreeable.

According to his favorite aide, Major Butt, he possessed, in addition to St. Paul's earnestness, something of that great man's ability to preach. The President said he knew he was no orator, and admitted that his own style would bore him unutterably if he had to listen to it. In fact, that all public speaking bored him, but that, when it was inevitable, he much preferred to administer the torture than submit to it.

It is said that his favorite scripture passage was from the Prophet Micah:

He hath shewed thee, O man, what is good; and what doth the Lord require of thee, but to do justly, and to love mercy, and to walk humbly with thy God?

He walked humbly with Him, but with no one else. With men he walked fraternally, genially, never humbly, and that was one secret of his power, for people love a born leader. Even fraternally he claimed an elder brother's privilege of being something of a dictator.

A youngster who saw him one day in Rock Creek Park, surrounded by a pack of his sons' friends, plump suddenly into the stream, set up an astonished wail:

"Oh! the father of all the children has fallen into the water!"

He happened to be the father of only about two fifteenths of that flock, but he acted as though they were all his offspring. He had not tumbled, he had deliberately walked into the water, but, having done so, he expected every one of the lads to follow him. This was one of the famous "obstacle walks" imported from Oyster Bay, whose rule was to follow the leader "over or through" but never "around."

On such mad scrambles the strenuous President sometimes led adults as well as children; not only his younger aides, but gentlemen burdened with years and flesh and official titles who had to go to bed for twenty-four hours to recover from such a tramp. He liked it just as well when his companions were boys.

I am really touched at the way in which your children as well as my own treat me as a friend and playmate, [he wrote to a relative after a Christmas party.] It has its comic side. Thus, the last day the boys were here they were all bent upon having me take them for a scramble down Rock Creek. Of course there was absolutely no reason why they could not go alone, but they obviously felt that my presence was needed to give zest to the entertainment. Accordingly, off I went. . . . I do not think that one of them saw anything incongruous in the President's getting as bedaubed with mud as they got, or in my wriggling and clambering around jutting rocks, through cracks, and up what were really small cliff faces just like the rest of them; and whenever any one of them beat me at any point, he felt and expressed simple and whole-hearted delight, exactly as if it had been a triumph over a rival of his own age.

In such adventures he ran risks that no President of the United States has a right to court for pleasure, as in his quieter moods he would have been the first to confess. He wrote to Archie:

The other day while taking a scramble walk in Rock Creek, when I came to that smoothface of rock which we get round by holding on to the little bit of knob that we call the Button, the top of this button came off between my thumb and forefinger. I had n't supposed that I was putting much weight on it, but evidently I was: for I promptly lost my balance, and finding I was falling, I sprang out into the creek. There were big rocks in it, and the water was rather shallow, but I landed all right and did n't hurt myself the least bit in the world.

These were his St. Vitus moments, explainable only as Mr. Lane explained his acts on that afternoon when he was left to run the Navy Department: "The Devil entered into him."

With a parent so forceful to furnish copy, the correspondents had little space to devote to the children of the Roosevelts unless they did something really unusual, as when Quentin, to turn an honest penny, carried "a small squealish pig" under his arm in the street car to sell it to Schmidt the animal man—he was not put off, the conductor being a friend of his—and Schmidt, with a flair for advertising, had it decked with red ribbons and paraded through the streets.

He bought it for a dollar and sold it to Schmidt for a dollar and a quarter, and feels as if he had found a permanent line of business, I gather that Quentin led it around for part of the parade, but he was somewhat vague on this point, evidently being a little uncertain as to our approval of the move.

This same small boy learned early the wisdom of a certain aloofness of manner when talking with reporters. Mr. Roosevelt was greatly amused when Quentin, aged eight, answered some question about his father with a polite:

"Yes, I see him sometimes; but I know nothing about his family life."

The President took his family life joyously, but also seriously, and tried his best to fulfil what he called his "duties as vice-mother" when Mrs. Roosevelt was away. He had misgivings that he did not always succeed. "I think Archie escaped with a minimum of washing for three days," he confessed on one occasion. But, having what Secretary Lane called "a sort of Divine right idea," and feeling like the father of all the children he came in contact with, he did not hesitate to administer discipline where and upon whom he thought it necessary. Once when he discovered the extent of the mischief into which a group of his son's friends had fallen, he routed his own offspring out of bed to repair the damage, and required him next day

> . . . to bring in the three other culprits before me. I explained to them that they had acted like boors: that it would have been a disgrace to have behaved so in any gentleman's house: that Quentin could have no friend to see him, and the other three could not come inside the White House until I felt that a sufficient time had elapsed to serve as punishment. They were four very sheepish small boys when I got through with them.

The reference, in the letter describing a Roosevelt luncheon, to the President's jest about a portrait which did not look in the least like him, brings to mind a phase of White-House life rarely dwelt upon: the preparations that have to be made to leave it as a term nears its end. The more successful a President has been, the more there is to do and the harder it is to do it. No private family can live in an ordinary house four years or more without accumulating a quantity of belongings both useful and sentimental, and a lot of rubbish which is neither. Multiply this by official position and the tendency well-meaning patriots have to send every conceivable sort of gift to the President, and the result begins to dawn upon one. In what Archie Butt called the twilight zone between two administrations, inventories have to be made and personal belongings sorted out from the belongings of Uncle Sam. And sometimes there are knotty questions to be settled in deciding who is the real owner.

Then there is the question what is to be done with worn-out articles that really belong to Uncle Sam. In 1882, after Tiffany had redecorated parts of the White House, twenty-four wagon-loads of discarded articles were sold at public auction, including moth-eaten parlor furniture, hair mattresses, maps, chandeliers, two infants' high-chairs, a plaster model of San Domingo, and the rat-trap that was said to have caught the rat that ate up President Lincoln's suit of clothes. This was the first clearing out of the White House attics since the Buchanan administration, and the sale was attended by five thousand people and much publicity. These words are being written on a desk bought at that very sale, which had been used by President Lincoln and his secretaries, and in this way came legitimately into the possession of the family that would prize it most; yet an auction seems hardly a dignified way of disposing of such articles.

Mrs. Roosevelt worked as diligently as any good housekeeper would, to leave every nook and corner of the White House swept and garnished for her successor; but there were certain things she refused to leave behind or to take with her, or to have fall into the hands of the auctioneer. The nicked and broken White-House china was assumed by precedent to be the property of the President's wife, to dispose of as she chose. Mrs. Roosevelt determined that the best thing to do with this was to have it broken into bits too small to be reassembled and then thrown into the river, which was done, the fragments possibly going to seek those of the pope's memorial stone. There were three portraits of her husband that Mrs. Roosevelt was unwilling to have descend to posterity. Presumably that about which he had jested was one of the trio. Major Butt was commissioned to destroy these, secretly and thoroughly, and performed the task in the seclusion of the White-House furnace room, feeding to the flames the last scrap, even to the beautifully painted hand of one of the portraits that he longed to retain as a souvenir.

With the closing days of February, 1909, the emotional strain grew intense, for all the women who went to the White House for a farewell visit left in tears or on the verge of weeping, and some of the men would have done so had it been seemly. The President divided his foils and spurs and hand sticks among his aides and most intimate friends, and sent the members of the cabinet canes made of wood from historic spots. Mrs. Roosevelt also distributed keepsakes, at interviews that were difficult but in which she retained her poise better than her friends.

Finally there came a moment when both she and the President broke down. It was almost their last evening in the White House, when, on going to dress for dinner, she discovered upon her bureau a strand of diamonds set in platinum that fifty or sixty of the women of Washington had presented as a farewell gift. Her husband and daughter were with her when she found it, with its little note of presentation. They had just been talking about the personal friendship manifested in these last days, and this, coming so unexpectedly, caused her tears to overflow. When she showed it to her daughter and said that one day it should be hers, Miss Ethel began to cry too, and the President, striving to comfort them, found himself engulfed in the same wave of emotion.

But only for a moment. He had a sense of humor and a buoyancy that helped him to carry off such scenes, and as usual, he rose to the occasion.

XXVII

PERIPATETIC MONUMENTS

WE are told that our city has one of the largest statue populations in the world. We know that at the end of almost every tree-shaded vista there seems to be a bit of sculpture, good, bad, or indifferent. And let it be said right here that, peculiar as some of these are, taken all in all they bear comparison well with an equal number elsewhere. Many of them are equestrian, and so many, both horse and foot, have been moved from the sites first selected for them, that it is not a far-stretched fancy to see a procession of these bronze and stone memorials moving silently and secretly through the streets, on some ghostly All Souls' Eve.

For the first half-century Washington had little outdoor sculpture, but it was kept in circulation. The first monument, that to the sailors who fell in the war with Tripoli, remained the pride of the Navy Yard until 1831, when it was moved to stand in the pool on the west front of the Capitol. By 1860 it was no longer desired there, and was sent into dignified banishment at Annapolis, where it stands in the grounds of the academy, in a spot visible to all but where it is really seen by few.

Next in point of date, came the "negro image" of Jefferson, as the bronze standing figure was called that Commodore Levy had made, to offer to Congress. It was modeled by David d'Angers, and Lafayette is said to have been so pleased with the likeness, that he threw his arms about the statue and called it his *cher ami*. But bronze statues were few in the United States, and such merits as it had were entirely obscured by its dark complexion.

It was given a place in the Capitol, but when Greenough's Washington arrived it was pushed into the Library of Congress and allowed to remain for eight years. Then it was sent to the White

House, where it found the door shut, but was tolerated on the lawn in the place now occupied by the north fountain. Here Jefferson remained until the upheavals of Shepherd's time sent him back to the Capitol. Since then he has been hustled about inside the building like a vagrant, made to "move on," now upstairs, now down, at the whim of those in authority.

By far the most famous of these roving pieces of sculpture is Horatio Greenough's Washington, ordered by Congress in the burst of enthusiasm attending the celebration of the centenary of his birth in 1832, about the time Adams lamented that no monument could ever be raised to him. To get at the true genesis of this work of art, we must hark back to the gilded image of George III in his royal robes that stood in New York in colonial times, representing the monarch on a clumsy rearing charger, whose equilibrium was kept as a kangaroo maintains his, by means of a stout and useful tail. For all its gilding, it was only lead, and was hacked to pieces and boiled into bullets for patriot guns, as every student remembers.

The Continental forces having victoriously used the bullets, it was natural to wish to honor the general who had won their fight, and it was equally natural for the patriots to imagine a statue like that of the king, only better. Less than two years after Yorktown, the Continental Congress voted to erect to Washington an equestrian statue with symbolism all complete, "at the place where the residence of Congress shall be established." It was to be of bronze instead of lead; he was to be depicted in Roman dress instead of English royal robes and to wear a wreath of laurel instead of a kingly crown; while the pedestal was to tell in bas-relief the history of his achievements at Trenton, Princeton, Monmouth, and Yorktown. As Congress had no permanent place of residence, little more could be done except to vote that the statue should be executed under the direction of the Minister to France and by the best sculptor in Europe. A tentative engagement was made of Carrachi, who was living in Rome.

Symbolism was a serious matter with educated Americans in those days, though there was an irreverent party that called it absurd in a country where so few people were educated to recognize a classical allusion when they met it. Benjamin Latrobe and good Dr. Thornton once got into a great argument about it at one of the *symposia,* Latrobe maintaining that it was open to misinterpretation, and Thornton waxing eloquent over the kind of statue he wished to see raised to Washington in the rotunda of the Capitol.

"I would place an immense rock of granite in the center of the dome," said Dr. Thornton. "On the top of this rock should stand a beautiful female figure to represent Eternity or Immortality. Around her neck as a necklace, a serpent, the rattlesnake of our country, should be hung with its tail in its mouth—the ancient and beautiful symbol of endless duration. At the foot of the rock, another female figure, stretching her hands upward in the attitude of distressful entreaty, should appear, ready to climb the steep. Around her a group of children, representing Agriculture, the Arts, and Science, should appear to join in the supplication of the female. This female is to personify Time, or our present state of existence. Just ascending the rock, the noble figure of General Washington should appear to move upward, invited by Immortality, but also expressing some reluctance in leaving the children of his care."

The good doctor, beaming with his great idea, defied Latrobe to show how the meaning of such a symbolic group could be misunderstood. He was so happy and so much in earnest that Latrobe sought to evade the issue; but Thornton, riding his hobby, pressed him too far, and Latrobe answered:

"Supposing the name and character of General Washington to be forgotten, antiquarians coming upon the group would probably say, 'There is a beautiful woman on the top of a dangerous precipice to which she invites a man apparently well enough inclined to follow her. Who is this woman? Certainly not a very good sort, . . . for she has a snake about her neck. The snake indicates assuredly her character, cold, cunning and poisonous. She can represent none but some celebrated courtezan of the day. But there is another woman at the foot of the rock, modest and sorrowful and surrounded by a family of small children. She is in the posture of entreaty, and the man appears half inclined to return to her. She can be no other than his wife. What an expressive group! How admirable the art which has thus exposed the dangerous precipice to which the beauty and the cunning of the abandoned would entice the virtuous!"

Laughter cut him short, and Dr. Thornton, who had never forgiven Latrobe for criticizing his plans for the Capitol, was confirmed in his opinion of the architect.

Meantime Washington died and plans were made and abandoned for using the crypt under the center of the Capitol as his burial-place. Then came the celebration of the centenary of his birth, and the order for a statue given to Greenough. As it was destined for the rotunda, the idea of portraying him on horseback was abandoned, but both sculptor and Congress appear to have remained under the thrall of symbolism. Greenough labored at the statue for eight years, in his studio in Florence, and evolved what one kindly critic called "a sort of domestic Jupiter," a majestic seated figure in Roman dress, in one hand holding a truncheon, while the other hand is upraised. The sculptor explained that he sought not so much to make a portrait as "a political abstract of Washington's whole career."

And he appears to have been well satisfied with the result. "I have sacrificed to it the flower of my days and the freshness of my strength," he wrote. "Its every lineament has been moistened with the sweat of my toil and the tears of my exile. I would not barter its association with my name for the proudest fortune that Avarice ever dreamed of." Avarice was probably just as content to let Greenough and his statue alone.

Every mile of its progress from Italy was beset with difficulty. The hatches of the frigate sent to bring it to the United States proved too small to admit its twelve-foot-square, fourteen-ton bulk, and a merchant ship had to be chartered and made over. When the statue reached the city, in 1841, it had to be transferred to a smaller boat for the transit up the Eastern Branch and along the canal to the spot on Maryland Avenue nearest the Capitol. From that point neither horse-power nor congressional brawn sufficed to move it, and the final stage of its journey was made upon a platform drawn by capstans. About one eighth of the total amount paid for the statue was spent on this last mile of its journey.

THE ADAMS MEMORIAL BY ST. GAUDENS

At the Capitol the main door of the rotunda had to be temporarily enlarged to admit it and presumably enlarged again to eject it; for, after all this trouble, it was not satisfactory to the public or the authorities. It was pronounced "out of scale," and although this was fully twenty-five years after the "nudities" on French clocks had so embarrassed United States agents in making their purchases for the White House, American taste was not yet educated to the point of accepting without question an effigy of the Father of his Country so lightly clad. Even in our less exigent day it seems incongruous to find the features of this particular Virginia gentleman rising above shoulders on which a toga is worn with a carelessness he would scarcely have tolerated in his own dressing-room. The edict went forth that the statue must go, the reason assigned being that it was "too heavy" for the rotunda floor, but it is hard to determine whether the weight was entirely that of marble pressing upon the floor at so many pounds per cubic inch, or partly its pressure on the sensibilities of Washington's admirers.

Ejected from the rotunda, it was set up in the center of the eastern plaza, where the rain and sun beat down upon its bare shoulders from April to November, and twice a year children watched for the transit along city streets of the little wooden hut built to protect it from the storms of winter. Sentimentalists by nature, they loved the inscription on the statue's pedestal: "First in War, First in Peace, First in the Hearts of his Countrymen"; and they recognized the calm and the majesty of the seated figure. But why George Washington, who crossed the Delaware and never told a lie, should be represented wearing sandals and holding in his hand something that looked like a wooden sword, was a mystery they could not fathom. In 1908 the compassionate, all-embracing Smithsonian offered the statue asylum, and there it has been sitting ever since, in decent privacy.

In spite of the dissatisfaction felt at Greenough's attempt to make over a perfectly good Washington into an imitation Jupiter, he was given another commission—to make a group to stand at the head of the stately flight of steps leading to the east portico of the Capitol. For this he modeled the pioneer defending his family from Indian attack, a subject into which Roman dress or accoutrements could not enter.

Persico, meanwhile, had carried out under President Adams's close direction the latter's idea for the tympanum over the east portico, "America listening to the inspiration of Hope and indicating her reliance on Justice," and had also modeled huge figures of War and Peace to stand one on each side of the bronze doors leading into the rotunda. He had taken great pains with Hope's anchor, to get it nautically correct, and was accorded credit for it, but critics complained that his War seemed to have fallen asleep at the post of duty, and that Peace, though dressed like a lady, was of forbidding and masculine countenance. They liked better Persico's group modeled to stand at the head of the flight of steps, opposite Greenough's "Pioneer." To represent the "Discovery of America," this shows an Indian maiden crouched at the feet of an energetic, natty Columbus, most adequately clothed in a suit of armor, which was copied faithfully from one the navigator was supposed to have worn.

Columbus holds in one outstretched hand a globe, and when Greenough's Washington sat enthroned in the center of the plaza, with his arm majestically raised, a certain little girl used to weave her own symbolism and imagine that the discoverer was lightly tossing the ball of the world across to the Father of his Country. Boys would have hooted at the idea, knowing that no ball could be thrown or caught with those gestures.

The great statue of "Armed Liberty," by Crawford, on the dome, is of much later date, having been put in place in December, 1863, to the dipping of flags and a salute of a hundred guns. It is said that Jefferson Davis took much interest in the details of its execution and casting at Bladensburg and suggested the feather headdress that the figure wears, to replace the circlet studded with stars in Mr. Crawford's original design. Others advocated giving Liberty the French Cap, and altogether her bonnet appears to have aroused more comment and elicited more advice than any other part of her equipment. There may be a bit of allegory here!

Another famous statue, which, however, has not been moved, is the "Brass Jackson," placed, for some unexplained reason, in the square named for Lafayette. This, like the Capitol and like our beloved Government itself, may be classed as a very clever amateur job, showing the virtues and faults of untrained genius, rather than work by trained professionals. The sculptor, Clark Mills, was a young plasterer of Charleston, South Carolina, whose sole ambitious work, a bust of Calhoun, showed such promise that his fellow townsmen raised a purse to send him abroad for study. He had reached Washington on his way to take ship, when the Jackson Democratic Association invited him to submit a model for this piece of work. He declined at first, on the ground of inexperience, then reconsidered, and finally gave up his trip abroad to undertake the commission.

The compensation agreed upon was twelve thousand dollars, to be raised by popular subscription, the bronze being provided from cannon captured by Jackson at Pensacola. This must have seemed munificent to the young man; but subscriptions lagged, and the expenses of building a foundry at Bladensburg for this first large piece of bronze cast in the United States, with the fact that the work had to be done over several times before perfect results were obtained, took all the money there was, leaving nothing for the sculptor himself. He would have fared badly, had not John W. Maury, leading citizen, banker, mayor, and philanthropist, a combination providentially found more than once in the city's history, advanced the necessary funds to tide him over until another commission set him square with the world.

The Jackson statue was unveiled on the thirty-eighth anniversary of the Battle of New Orleans, with spellbinder oratory by Senator Douglas and a prayer by the Reverend Dr. Butler. When the enveloping flags dropped away, there was a general feeling that prayer might have been more effective if used earlier in the proceedings. The disappointment may have been partly due to the statue's lack of size, for it is scarcely larger than life, and seemed insignificant as the central object of a park filled with forest trees. Those who had known the general, admitted that the likeness was true and spirited; but they objected to the horse, which paws the air, the position being maintained not by the clumsy device of having him sit on his tail, as in the case of King George's horse, but by the amount of metal in his flowing tail being nicely calculated to balance that in the rest of the statue. It is literally a rocking horse, though bolted to the pedestal for safety's sake.

Mills, being a true son of Carolina, resented criticisms of his horse, maintaining that he knew as much about horse anatomy as any man living and had studied this one from life, prance and all. Though it is the fashion to laugh at it, it is not bad as equestrian statues go, and there are some who would not exchange Jackson on his neatly balanced steed for several later and more sophisticated efforts.

But Washingtonians developed excessive sensitiveness on the subject, and many who could view "War" and "Peace" with serenity, winced when they had to exhibit this latest statue to visiting strangers. Senator Sumner, who acted as guide to Thackeray when he visited Washington in 1853, confessed to the qualms he felt when driving the distinguished visitor past Lafayette Square. Thackeray looked straight ahead and feigned not to see it, which woke gratitude in Sumner's heart. "Here," he said to himself, "is a man of rare consideration." But an obtuse member of Congress, one of the earnest hundred-per-cent-Americans of the period, cornered Thackeray at last and wanted to know what he thought of Mills's masterpiece. Thackeray admitted that he had seen better statues, to which the representative answered earnestly:

"But you must remember that Mr. Mills had never seen a statue when he made this one."

In spite of adverse criticism, Congress gave the sculptor another commission, for the statue of the Father of his Country which stands in Washington Circle. This is less happy than his Jackson, Mr. Mills having chosen to portray a moment in Washington's career that offers an excellent subject for a poem or a sermon, but not a sermon in stone or bronze. It represents that instant at the Battle of Princeton when Washington found himself so near the British lines that his mount, with commendable good sense, refused to go farther. The horse stands rooted as if in terror, in an invisible rain of shot and shell, while his rider could not be more placid if sitting in an easy-chair on his veranda at Mount Vernon. The lack of harmony in emotion between the two is distressing, when it was meant to be impressive. Mr. Mills did not design it to be seen on the simple pedestal it occupies, but as the crowning figure of a massive monument in three tiers, each representing an epoch in the country's history, adorned with bas-reliefs and life-sized equestrian groups at the four corners—an ambitious project he had to forego for lack of funds.

By this time he had become a fixed habit with the Government, as Greenough and Persico had been before him. He was called upon as a matter of course after the Civil War to plan an elaborate monument to Lincoln, which, happily, was never erected. Of what we may name the desultory memorials to Lincoln, of which the city has five or six, like Vinnie Ream's statue, Borglum's great head in the rotunda, the Emancipation group by Thomas Ball in Lincoln Park, and the tablet at Fort Stevens, the earliest was modeled by an ex-Confederate soldier, Lott Flannery, to stand before the City Hall. This was an order given by the Lincoln National Monument Association, formed in Washington only two weeks after the President's death. Mr. Flannery conceived of Lincoln as a slender, rather woebegone figure on a pedestal so tall and slight as to recall one of those early mystics who attained sanctity by living at great inconvenience on top of a pillar. Its chief recommendation in this case was that its position rendered the figure virtually invisible.

In 1919, after enlargements and improvements at the City Hall, the Fine Arts Commission decreed that the Lincoln statue must go, since the changes placed it out of alignment, and it was not a thing to be proud of anyway. It was carted off and put in storage, but for once the commission failed to take sentiment into account, and the act raised a storm of protest. Verse-makers burst into rhyme over the enormity of consigning to limbo the first statue raised to Lincoln. Various states expressed their desire to treat it honorably. Howard University, the colored collegiate institution of the District, asked that it might be placed on its campus; the G. A. R. resolved that it ought never to be moved from the Court House, and the Society of Oldest Inhabitants, which had constituted itself the statue's guardian and had already blocked attempts to get rid of it, awoke once more from the drowsiness of old age and made a great fuss. In three years the statue was back, on a pedestal cut down from thirty-six feet to near six, which brings it more into the range of vision than ever before.

Since the Civil War we have been raising statues at an ever-accelerating pace, reservation after reservation receiving its piece of sculpture, which has been orated over and prayed upon and decorated with flags and honored by the presence of high officials and pretty ladies on the day of its unveiling. Such ceremonies have come to take the place of the corner-stone-layings of the city's earlier history. Some are moving statues and some are not. That of Frederick the Great has vanished from the sight of men. A present from the German kaiser when he was accounted a respectable member of society, it was unveiled with much pomp in front of the War College, but ignominiously removed at the beginning of the World War and secreted in some place unknown.

In strict justice, the statue of Garfield standing where Maryland Avenue S.W. enters the Capitol grounds, should not be mentioned here, for it has not been moved, but the temptation is irresistible, because the three reclining bronze figures at its base, representing Law, Justice, and Prosperity, are so lifelike and full of repose that on the first warm nights after the statue was unveiled, over-zealous policemen attempted several times to arrest them for vagrants, in the belief that they were trying to steal a night's lodging under the protection of the President.

Last of all, in point of time, in the list of moving statues would come Admiral Dupont, turned out of his place in the circle that bears his name, at the request of his own family, to permit the erection of what they consider a more worthy memorial. This latter is a white marble fountain of graceful lines, the joint work of the two artists of the Lincoln Memorial, Daniel Chester French and Henry Bacon.

Following at the very end of the procession would be the strangest statue in Washington, if in truth it is worthy of that name at all. From a single block of marble emerge the heads and shoulders of three well-known women, Lucretia Mott in her Quaker cap, Susan B. Anthony's strong features and smooth bands of hair, and Elizabeth Cady Stanton's comfortable round face and white puffs.

Embedded below the shoulders in one glacial block, these suffrage leaders gaze at the beholder in petrified discomfort. It was soon after the success of the suffrage amendment that this work of a woman sculptor was unveiled by the Women's Party, in the rotunda of the Capitol, with a great and triumphant display of white and yellow and violet banners. They expected that it would remain in a place of honor; but very quickly that form of banishment was pronounced against it from which there is no appeal. It was adjudged "too heavy" for any part of the building above the crypt, and there the worthy ladies endure their double imprisonment, down in that part of the Capitol denounced by Ann Royal as a place "where no decent woman ought to be seen."

True to custom the world over, most of the statues and monuments in Washington are raised to military heroes; but we have the dark-hued Jefferson, and a gray Franklin; Martin Luther, a militant figure in doctor's robes, standing near the church of his faith; Chief-Justice Marshall sitting at ease half-way down the west terrace of the Capitol; Columbus welcoming strangers as they approach the Union Station; Longfellow quiescent near the busy stream of motors on Connecticut Avenue; "Boss" Shepherd squaring his shoulders in front of the Municipal Building; Dr. Thomas Gallaudet teaching a slip of a deaf girl on the campus of Columbian College for the Deaf; Dante erect and stern in a park overlooking the city; Burke caught in a moment of impassioned oratory; a monument to Daguerre in close proximity to the statue to Professor Henry, in the old Smithsonian grounds and an anemic Dr. Hahnemann, founder of homeopathy, sitting on a bench under a shallow green niche in a little reservation on one side of Scott Circle, while balancing him on the opposite side is a colossal standing Webster. Between the two, stout old General Scott, on a rather frail horse, looks down Sixteenth Street toward the White House that he would have liked to occupy. The witty John D. Long took one glance at these three figures and remarked:

"I presume they represent the departments of State, War, and the Interior!"

Lafayette Square has become overpopulated with statues, for in addition to Jackson on his horse, in the center, standing figures of foreigners have been placed in the four corners, Lafayette, Rochambeau, Von Steuben, and Kosciuszko. When the last was unveiled, the city's foremost cartoonist, Clifford Berryman, made a drawing of the crowded condition of the park with the legend, "Standing room only."

In passing we may mention one ambitious monument that it is safe to say will never be built. After Roosevelt's death it was proposed to cut a great swath through Rock Creek park and dam the creek to make a reflecting pool in which to mirror a lion thirty feet high as a memorial to him. He would not have approved, nor does his widow. "Mr. Roosevelt and I always thought of Washington as the city of Washington and Lincoln, and that it behooved lesser persons to be modest," she said, when the plan was brought to her notice.

Of more than sixty persons honored in effigy in the parks of the city, about one fifth are of foreign birth, but only two of these, Pulaski and Joan of Arc, are allowed to ride horseback. We Americans prefer to keep in the saddle ourselves. Of the sculptured horses some are in violent action, like that of the Sheridan statue, which, suddenly arrested in its gallop, forms a strange pyramid of legs and arching neck and flying mane. Others are as devoid of motion as a clothes-horse in a hotel lobby. Some of the statues are placed rather oddly. It seems strange, for example, that John Paul Jones, down in Potomac Park, should stand with his back uncompromisingly toward the water. More characteristic, but doubtless wholly without unkind intent, is the position assigned General McClellan, where diverging streets give him what he appeared to desire in war, "four lines of retreat, but only one of advance."

Joan of Arc is, so far as we know, the one woman honored with an outdoor monument in Washington; and that was given us by France! And "Frances Willard in a marble gown," as Susan Hale crisply described her, is the sole representative of her sex in the strange jumble of characters that State pride has brought together in Statuary Hall.

Male and female created they them, of varying degrees of excellence; but in memory most of the statues and monuments of

THE WASHINGTON MONUMENT AND THE CHERRY BLOSSOMS

Washington take their place in the decorative scheme of parks and vistas as more or less attractive bits of bronze and marble. In an entirely different category three stand out, the two great memorials to our greatest Presidents and one private monument, the bronze figure by St. Gaudens on the Adams burial-lot in Rock Creek Cemetery that has been called "The Mystery of the Hereafter." A figure of repose and haunting mystery, neither old nor young, man nor woman, it sits at ease yet upright on its bench of soft-toned pinkish gray marble, shaded by laurels and dark evergreens. Opposite is a long curved bench on which mortals may rest and question, to go away unanswered but comforted.

After General Washington's death, Congressman John Marshall offered a resolution that "a marble monument so designed as to commemorate the great events of his military and political life" be erected in the city, and that the general's family be requested to permit his body to be buried under it. He had in mind as a site for this the open space in front of the Capitol; but thirty years later nothing had been done, except to prepare a crypt under the rotunda, and then to give up the project of removing Washington's remains from Mount Vernon.

To be sure, the Greenough statue had recently been ordered, but this confirmed the Chief Justice and others in the belief expressed by Adams that democracy cares little for the past and raises no worthy monuments. Convinced that Congress alone would never put up an adequate memorial, the Washington National Monument Society was formed at a meeting held in the aldermen's room of the City Hall in September, 1833, with John Marshall as its president, Judge Cranch as first vice-president, and George Watterson, Librarian of Congress, as secretary. Madison succeeded Marshall as its president, and on his death the society's constitution was so amended that the President of the United States became ex-officio president of the organization, Andrew Jackson being the first to assume the office.

The desire of the association being to erect a really national memorial, with the whole people contributing, it was agreed that the amount to be received from any one person in the course of a year should be limited to one dollar. But progress under this rule was disappointingly slow, and the panic of 1837 put an end to such gifts altogether.

An ambitious design had meanwhile been drawn by Robert Mills, the architect of the Treasury, providing for an obelisk shaft rising five hundred feet in the air above a circular colonnade one hundred feet high, which would serve in time as a national pantheon. There was also to be a colossal statue of Washington in a chariot drawn by six horses. The society never adopted the design in its entirety, knowing its funds to be inadequate, but concentrated its efforts upon the shaft.

The dollar limit was removed, and many devices were suggested by many people to rouse enthusiasm. School-children were appealed to, contribution boxes were installed in post-offices, and census-takers were supplied with subscription blanks to present while on their rounds; and "ladies committees," that unfailing source to tap for worthy objects, were besought to raise special funds. Even so, it was not until 1847 that enough money was in sight to warrant the beginning of actual work.

Up to that time no definite spot appears to have been selected, for a resolution was offered in Congress that the corner-stone be laid on the coming twenty-second of February, "provided that a suitable site can be obtained in time." The ceremonies took place, instead, on the Fourth of July, 1848; and an "Address to the Country," printed later, explained that the spot was selected because its elevation would permit the monument to be seen from Mount Vernon as well as from all parts of town, while its nearness to the river made it convenient for landing supplies. No thought appears to have been given to its relation to the Capitol, or that it was within a few rods of the center of the District, the location favored by Washington and marked upon L'Enfant's map for a monument to the Revolution. A test of the ground at that exact spot had led to a slight change of site to secure a better foundation.

A huge block, presented by a citizen of Baltimore from his own quarry to serve as corner-stone, was transported free by the railroad and dragged from the station by workmen from the Navy Yard assisted by enthusiastic volunteers. Ex-President Adams was invited to deliver the address, but reluctantly declined on account of ill health. Webster was then asked, but declined, alleging pressure of business and the short time allowed for preparation. It was still a third son of Massachusetts, Robert C. Winthrop, Speaker of the House of Representatives, who delivered the oration in presence of all the notables the city could get together, including Presidents past present and future, Mrs. Madison, Mrs. Alexander Hamilton, who did not allow her ninety-one years to stand in the way, delegations from all the states and territories, a group of the ever-present Indians, and a live American eagle that had survived the part it unwillingly played in Alexandria's welcome to Lafayette.

The monument had reached about a third of its present height on that hot Independence Day in 1850 which proved too much for the endurance of General Taylor. Four years later it got entangled in local politics and religious quarrels at a time when Know-nothing, Native American, anti-Catholic sentiment was rampant. Representatives of that movement not only broke up the stone sent from Rome by the pope, but they succeeded, by means of a packed election for members of the board of managers of the association, in getting possession of its offices and books and held them several years, until the party disintegrated and they were voluntarily returned.

The practical effect of this episode was to bring work upon the memorial to a standstill and render it more difficult to raise contributions. During the interval two courses were added to the monument as an evidence of good faith, but imperfect blocks were used which had been rejected by those formerly in control and they had to be removed when work was resumed in earnest.

By 1859 doubts had arisen as to the stability of the foundations; then the Civil War intervened, and it was not until several years after its close that work could be continued. Once more the solidity of the foundations was called in question. Examination proved that the monument was already out of the perpendicular and a delicate piece of engineering had to be done in reënforcing and adding to the foundations, and, by digging down a little on this side and a little on that, allowing the mass of stone to settle of its own weight into proper position.

By 1880 this task was accomplished, and on August 7th of that year, after a very private little ceremony on top of the monument in which President and Mrs. Hayes took part, actual building began again "at one minute to eleven." It had been originally hoped that the monument would be ready for dedication in 1876, as a feature of the Centennial year; but it was not until December 6, 1884,—a rainy, blustery day when the wind blew at the rate of sixty miles an hour,—that the capstone slid into place with perfect ease, thanks to the skill with which Bernard Green, the engineer actually in charge, had planned the necessary machinery to move the huge block five hundred and fifty feet up in the air.

Arthur was President when the formal dedication occurred, on February 21, 1885. He spoke his few words in the presence of a multitude of people, while more formal exercises were held in the Hall of Representatives, when an oration prepared by the aged Mr. Winthrop, who had been the speaker thirty-five years earlier at the laying of the corner-stone, was read by John D. Long, and the voice of Virginia was heard in an address by John W. Daniel.

Of the sum of $1,187,710.31 that the monument actually cost, only about $300,000 had been contributed directly by the people, the rest having been appropriated by Congress. Hard times and the Civil War were in part responsible for its delayed completion, but there was also much dissatisfaction with the design. There were people who objected to an obelisk, and more people who thought they were objecting to that form when in truth they had not imagination enough to see it and were actually objecting to the unsightly half-finished structure, like a factory chimney, that had stood so long surrounded by blocks of stone in the unkempt fields of the Mall. One of the many appeals for funds had been a suggestion for a Fourth-of-July offering in 1875, which brought forth this criticism from the New York "Tribune":

> The appeal for a fourth of July contribution to the Washington Monument will not amount to much. Public judgment on that abortion has been made up. The country has failed in many ways to honor the memory of its first President, but the neglect to finish this Monument is not to be reckoned among them. A wretched design, a wretched location, and insecure foundation match well with its empty treasury.

ALONG THE RIVER FRONT IN POTOMAC PARK

Few will now agree with this summary, or regret that Mills's design was thrust upon the country shorn of its surrounding columns, to give us this simple shaft rising straight into the air, devoid of all ornament but played upon by the winds and lights of heaven. Whether flushed with rosy color at sunset, or sharply outlined against the blue, or seen with ragged rain clouds trailing their edges across its cap, it is always beautiful, always inspiring.

The country waited more than a century for this adequate monument to Washington. It waited half a century before building its memorial to Lincoln, erected it in five years instead of thirty-five, and spent upon it more than twice the sum spent on the great shaft. But it had increased enormously in wealth and population meantime, and also in impatience and sophistication. Perhaps if all these factors were considered and weighed at their true worth, the answers to the two sums would be very similar. At any rate, figures alone are the least trustworthy measure of the forces that go into such a work.

A Lincoln Memorial Association was incorporated within two years of the President's death, with the purpose to erect "a monument commemorative of the great charter of emancipation and universal liberty in America." The cost that the incorporators had in mind was $100,000 and the Postmaster-General authorized postmasters throughout the country to act as collectors. When $10,000 had been raised, Clark Mills, the sculptor of the Jackson statue in Lafayette Park, was invited to choose a location for the monument and to make a design. He selected a site in the Capitol grounds, near the Senate end of the building, and made an elaborate design.

The monument was to be seventy feet high, and called for a granite pedestal of triangular form, with truncated angles, and so many bronze figures that somebody called it "not a monument to Lincoln, but a biographical dictionary." A colossal figure of Lincoln signing the Emancipation Proclamation was indeed to crown the structure, but on bastions thrown out from the angles were to stand six generals, Grant, Sherman, Thomas, Sheridan, Howard, and Wadsworth; and elsewhere space was to be found for twenty-one statesmen, philanthropists, and civilians who had been conspicuously helpful and loyal during the war. In addition to these there were to be figures of the Liberated Slave, the Private Soldier, and Woman caring for the Wounded; while those hard-worked allegorical ladies Justice, Liberty, and Equality were to be on duty as usual. In spite of all his former experience, the sculptor estimated the cost of this horror to be only $300,000.

Fortunately the design was lost to posterity, fortunately also a real beginning was not made until 1911, by which time Congress had awakened to the needs and possibilities of the city, had created the Fine Arts Commission to watch over such new enterprises, and in the act providing for a memorial provided also for the commission's coöperation in choosing its site and form. In about a year it was recommended that the memorial be erected in Potomac Park, from designs prepared by Henry Bacon. To some the site selected seemed utterly absurd, remembering the former condition of this park, which is mainly retrieved from the quaking morass of the Potomac Flats. "Uncle Joe" Cannon's comment was that if the memorial were built in that spot it would shake itself down with loneliness and ague.

Here also doubts and criticisms have been silenced by the completed work. In addition to the difficulty of making an adequate foundation on land that had not existed in Lincoln's day, it seemed incongruous to fix upon a Greek temple as a memorial to him of all men.

One year of the five consumed in building was devoted to solving the problems of the foundation. One hundred and twenty-two giant steel cylinders were sunk until they were embedded in the solid rock, and were then filled with concrete. This was the mere beginning. In and between and around them the lower foundation was constructed to a depth varying from forty-four to sixty-five feet. Upon this came an upper foundation of forty-five feet, the height of an ordinary building, both of which are now completely hidden from view. On top of these the memorial itself was erected. What was actually done, therefore, as an enterprising newspaper correspondent pointed out, was to build a tower one hundred and fifty feet high and bury two thirds of it. The upper foundation forms the hillock on which the temple stands, an artificial mound twenty feet higher than the base of the Washington Monument.

After Mr. Taft turned the first spadeful of earth, it took a year to complete this preliminary part of the work; and while the strange sunken tower was rising unclothed, the proportions of the memorial seemed as uncouth as Lincoln himself was popularly supposed to be. When the building was up, there was much yet to be done in terracing and filling in, in completing and placing the statue, in finishing the paintings and making that long reflecting pool which mirrors the Washington Monument at one end and the memorial at the other. An amusing bit of congressional psychology is disclosed in the fact that so long as this sheet of water was called a "lagoon," a term reminiscent in the planners' minds of the beauty of the Chicago exposition, but evidently calling up other images to the average congressman, the appropriation was steadfastly refused; but as soon as somebody had the wit to change the name to "reflecting pool," it was granted without a murmur.

It happened, by coincidence, or as a matter of forethought, that the stone used in the Washington Monument came mostly from Maryland and Massachusetts, two regions very active in furthering the cause of the Revolution; while the stone chosen for the Lincoln Memorial came from Colorado, the marble for the great statue of Lincoln from Georgia, and that for the pedestal from Tennessee. Henry Bacon, the architect, was of Illinois birth, and Jules Guerin, who did the mural paintings that so skilfully unite the bronze and yellow tones of its roof with the cool austerity of the lower walls, was born in Missouri: so that both the builders and the materials came from the West and the South, the sections that gave Lincoln birth and fame.

When the memorial was finally dedicated on May 30, 1922, President Harding and Chief-Justice Taft took part in the exercises, but the principal orator was President Moton of Tuskegee, a member of the race freed by Lincoln's hand.

As one mounts the many steps leading to the memorial, something happens. Perhaps it is the effort of ascent; perhaps it is the ever closer view of the big fluted columns toward which one climbs. Things of the outer world seem to grow less important as one nears the top. But even so, the mind is scarcely prepared for the quiet and the sense of awe that prevail within as one faces the great seated figure with its head bent forward and its hands resting on the arms of its chair, one fist clenched, the fingers of the other hand relaxed but by no means nerveless. For an instant, perhaps, the knees and square-toed boots of the statue seem a little too much in evidence, but only for a moment. After that they merely stand for the homely qualities of speech and idiom that people forgot after they had been with Lincoln for a brief time.

It is a strange figure to enthrone in a temple of Greek outline, a man of rugged features, in the dress of the nineteenth century, but it is a figure absolutely adequate in its simple dignity. Huge as it is, some twenty-one feet in height, the walls and columns with which it is surrounded are on such a scale that it seems merely imposing, not over large. Only when people happen to pass across the open space in front of it does the magic of proportions work to reduce them to mere pygmies, while the statue sets the measure of what human beings ought to be and to do. Men instinctively take off their hats under that roof of thin slabs of marble through which the light falls yellowed and softened. People walk reverently and even children cease their prattle. Egotism alone prevents one's spirit from being blotted out as completely as are the bodies of the other pygmies. There is a sense of being alone there, face to face with a great soul and the principles for which he stood.

Once it was the writer's fortune to enter the place in company with an Indian of our Western country, a man who has the genius of his race in terse speech.

"It is a temple," he said as he bared his head.

Only four short words: but could more be said?

XXVIII

THE HIGH POINT

IT is now almost two centuries since George Gordon built his Rolling House at the confluence of Rock Creek and the Potomac, where Indians had traded long before he came. The original log structure was replaced in time by one of brick which people yet living have seen standing unused. At intervals, when its sagging doors were opened, children darted in to dig in the fragrant tobacco-scented corners for little bells and long Indian beads that it still yielded generously to patient search. All such relics are buried now beyond resurrection under layers of concrete that surround the terminal of the electric railroad.

From the small but surprisingly gay little Georgetown that Braddock found on the edge of the wilderness, "a town of houses without streets," as Washington fifty years later was known as a city of streets without houses, buildings have stretched out beyond the District line toward Cabin John Bridge. In the other direction they cover all the space L'Enfant studied in his surveys, clear to the Eastern Branch and beyond, while northward from the Potomac to the District line and on into Maryland there are houses and houses and houses.

After the vigorous digging up it experienced in 1871–74, Washington blundered along for a quarter of a century, stretching lines of asphalt ever farther into fields that had been lying fallow since tobacco-culture went into a decline. Beyond the asphalt in certain directions lines of newly laid curbstones and primly planted saplings showed where speculators had centered their hopes upon future subdivisions.

With the coming of wealthy winter residents the growth was more rapid, but it remained decidedly haphazard, with little thought for the city's general plan. Flocks of dwellings of varying elegance rose in different sections. On K Street and Massachusetts Avenue, and the newly developed Connecticut Avenue as far as Dupont Circle, some were veritable palaces, others merely handsome homes; but, all told, they were numerous enough to crowd out a large number of the negro cabins that used to lean so confidingly against older buildings. In the northeast section, where Amos Kendall had built his suburban home for his old age, houses were for the most part put up in neat rows of a style suited to the purses of low-salaried clerks—comfortable little places, but as uninteresting in appearance as so many button-boxes. In the new additions beyond the original city limits, architecture ran to shingle and clapboard effects painted in many colors, the "Queen-Anne-Mary-Anne" type that developed coincidently with women's clubs and represented the same ideal, that of opening a vista out of household drudgery to something beyond. Fortunately the type speedily gave way to others equally stimulating to the imagination but on simpler, better lines.

F Street had meantime drawn to itself fashionable shops at the expense of Pennsylvania Avenue, which remained virtually unchanged, but grew shabbier by comparison. The houses of Georgetown and Washington had already met, making the two in effect one city. They became legally one a few years later, though to this day the older place keeps many of its former characteristics. The Island and Capitol Hill, like Pennsylvania Avenue, were little altered, save for better paving and the shade trees that grew and flourished.

Then suddenly, almost overnight it seemed, the trees of the city, and the houses in its better portions, became really impressive. Looking down wide avenues was to see, under arching branches, the Capitol or the White House, or a bit of well-kept park; and walking under those same trees on a June afternoon of sunshine and shower was to move in a light that seemed filtered through emeralds.

It was the celebration of the District's centennial, in 1900, that brought this transformation forcibly home to its residents. Thanks largely to a commissioner then in office, Mr. H. B. F. Macfarland, whose belief in the city's future was inexhaustible, the event was celebrated with due pomp; and everybody was given a chance to ponder on what remained to be done as well as to rejoice over all that had been accomplished. Fortunately, Mr. Mcfarland's early training as a newspaper man fitted him alike for missions of glorification and propaganda.

The study of early plans in arranging for this celebration revealed threatening dangers, and showed how busy the city's guardian angel had been during the past century, lopping off and pruning unwise legislation and periodically dragging lax authorities back to a sense of their duty. A comparison of original plans with the city as it then stood showed how much more might have been done with the same effort had the original ideals been held consistently in mind; and how, despite the best efforts of the guardian angel, serious inroads had been made upon the Mall, the city's one large park. The tracks of the Pennsylvania Railroad ran through its center to a station erected on public land; and private buildings of doubtful character had also been allowed to gain foothold upon it.

The same study showed that the city had already lived through three distinct eras in public building and stood sadly in need of a fourth and better one. First came the freestone period, when the Capitol and the White House and the Court House were begun. This was the season of stately plans, executed not in the best materials but the best the country could afford. The Court House was not even freestone, merely stucco. Next came the era of marble, adopted under Jackson from motives of economy. This had been inaugurated by building the earliest parts of the Patent Office and Post Office on F Street, and had taken in the large new wings of the Capitol, but ended on the downward grade in granite in the State, War, and Navy building, begun soon after the Civil War. After that followed an ugly utilitarian era of brick, of which the Pension Office was the most depressing result and the National Museum, built to house left-over treasures of the Centennial, the largest.

A French resident described the Pension Office with its circling frieze of three-foot-high clay soldiers as resembling, in brick, "Ze

Ufizzi palace, wiz a r-r-rail-r-r-road depot on top o' dat, an' a g-r-ain elevator on top o' dat!" General Sheridan remarked that the worst thing about it was that it was fireproof.

The National Museum was not nearly so bad architecturally, being a frank adaptation of train-shed construction to museum uses, but its brick walls decorated with blue and yellow tiles were not a happy foil for the Smithsonian, and it was placed distressingly near, almost touching it, in fact, for one peculiarity of this period was the seeming desire of Congress to crowd every park in the heart of the city full of discordant buildings.

Votive wreaths should be kept ever green to the memory of the propagandists of the District's centennial. Their work bore its first fruit a year later, when Senator McMillan, Chairman of the Senate Committee on the District of Columbia, a man of force and vision, reported a plan covering the entire District for the development of a park system and for the location of new public buildings. It called for no immediate outlay, but was in effect a reaffirmation of the creed of beauty formulated by L'Enfant, and was submitted as a chart to guide future developments. This well-studied plan, whereby the opening of new streets and the erection of new public buildings should add to and not detract from what had already been done, was the combined work of two architects, Daniel H. Burnham and Charles F. McKim, Augustus St. Gaudens the sculptor, and Frederick Law Olmstead the landscape architect. The first three and the father of the fourth had been active in creating the beauty of the Columbian Exposition at Chicago in 1893.

They made no claim to originality in this plan for Washington, but said they merely carried out the spirit of L'Enfant's conception in the light of new needs and new knowledge. The scheme for an enlarged Washington therefore appears to have its genesis in two glorious ideas, a century apart, L'Enfant's original inspiration and the mirage city that rested for a twelvemonth on the shores of Lake Michigan.

In the presentation of the plan to Congress, the fact that it carried with it no demand for immediate outlay was greatly in its favor; and its sponsors were careful to dwell on the great number of years that must elapse before part of it could be carried out. But

THE TRIPOLI NAVAL MONUMENT

many good people are incapable of visualizing a plan on paper, and, to bring the new Washington actually before the eyes of unimaginative folk, somebody was inspired to have made for exhibition purposes two models of the city, each about ten feet long, one showing the town as it then appeared and the other as it might become. The crowds that pored over these, hunted out their own city blocks, and discussed the proposed changes, gave evidence of the interest aroused.

As might have been expected, President Roosevelt proved an enthusiastic ally and did everything in his power to aid the project. Indeed, he became so interested in the welfare of the city that he did not stop at these large measures, but carried the spirit of reform to equally important but less showy details by appointing a Homes Commission to investigate housing conditions, especially in the alleys. In them, be it admitted to our shame, there are still spots that rival the worst slums of New York, though instead of climbing heavenward as in the larger city, the dwellings crowd close to the ground in the centers of innocent-looking blocks.

L'Enfant's plan contained provision for about three hundred small reservations at the intersection of streets and avenues, but there was no extensive park except the Mall, which had suffered serious inroads and had barely escaped worse ones. Congress had even been petitioned at one time for leave to cut up all of this tract that lay west of Seventh Street into building lots to be sold for the benefit of the old canal project, the bribe offered being substantial sums that the Canal Company was willing to subscribe toward a city high school and Columbian College. Fortunately, at that moment Congress took little interest in higher education!

Fortunately, too, public-spirited citizens, since 1880, had interested themselves to secure additional tracts outside of the city limits for park uses. One of these gentlemen was Mr. Corcoran's successor as president in the bank which holds much the same relation to the city's financial institutions that St. John's Church holds among its places of worship. Most of the great and many of the good keep their consciences in one and their financial credit in the other. It was about the time that the city was beginning to rally from Boss Shepherd's surgery that Mr. C. C. Glover began his agitation for more parks. He wished Washington to profit by the fate of New York and Chicago, and not allow its tree-shaded water-front to degenerate into cinder-covered railway tracks and unsightly ferry-slips.

But, knowing the temper of Congress, he persuaded his friends, as a first step, to introduce a bill for the reclamation of the areas that were subject to floods. In the spring, water backed up in the swampy region south of Center Market, and in exceptional years sometimes covered Pennsylvania Avenue from the market to the Peace Monument at the foot of the Capitol grounds. At such times the railroad station at sixth and B streets was reached by boats; and in the last flood of this character a worthy horse was drowned in the performance of duty on Pennsylvania Avenue and had his obituary printed in the newspapers.

The prevention of such floods was a measure practical enough to appeal to the most utilitarian of congressmen, and the measure received President Arthur's signature shortly after he assumed office. Its ultimate effect was to add about seven hundred acres to the park system, little as that may have been in the minds of those who voted for it. Securing the reclaimed area for park uses was, however, a matter attained only sixteen years later in the face of considerable opposition, the railroads having meantime come to covet it for their own use.

The greater part of Potomac Park, including that portion where the Lincoln Memorial stands, and the long tongue of land with its circling drive that extends down opposite Greenleaf's Point, is the result of laboriously building sea-walls and dredging the river-bottom. Mrs. Taft, with affectionate memories of the Luneta at Manila, helped make it fashionable as an afternoon drive; and she and Eliza Ruhama Scidmore are rivals in claiming credit for the wealth of cherry-blossoms that now glorifies it in springtime.

Mrs. Taft says it was she who suggested planting the trees, an experiment attended with difficulty, first because all the nurseries of the country could muster only about two hundred specimens of the Japanese flowering varieties desired and secondly because a first large consignment, sent over as a gift from Tokio, was found to be afflicted with a contagious disease and had to be summarily destroyed. On her part, Miss Scidmore claims that she began talking as early as 1885 about planting flowering cherries, and that part of the initiation of every commissioner who took office after that date was a visit from her, with this as the object of her call. She admits, however, that nothing came of it until 1909, when the President's wife interested herself. So it is evident that it required the lively tongue of one lady and the high official position of the other to bring about a result in which everybody rejoices.

All Washington turns out now in the early spring to walk or drive through miles of blossoming trees so skilfully planted that as the flowers of one group fade they are succeeded by others even more wonderful. Some are almost white, some deep rose. The most ravishing sight of all is the first grand flowering of an early single variety planted in great profusion around the tidal basin. These make a wonder of bloom, out of which, when seen across the water, the tall shaft of the Washington Monument and the temple-like beauty of the Lincoln Memorial rise as from a cloud of pale color, while in another direction the dome of the Capitol and the lower, gilded dome of the Library are seen above the same fairy bank of color.

After the cherry-trees have put off their blossoms for sober leaves, clumps of peonies and iris, almost by the half-acre, bloom beside the silver stretches of the river. And in addition to all this beauty, the park has very practical advantages. It is easily accessible, and has been laid out for polo and with a public golf-course. It has a popular and populous bathing-beach that has developed from the original private enterprise of a single old man, who lived in a tent and for a small consideration watched over the clothes and interests of swimmers. The park has also, hidden behind a screening hedge, a large camping-ground for migratory automobiles.

Before any of this had developed beyond its chrysalis stage, Mr. Glover and Mr. Bancroft and Mr. Spofford and others who loved the wildness of Rock Creek Valley, and often turned their horses' heads in that direction for their afternoon rides, were laboring to have that region set aside for park uses. But the amount of missionary work needed was prodigious, and here there was no entering wedge of utilitarianism with which to begin. At times Mr. Glover deserted his banking business entirely to join the suspected ranks of the lobbyists, and he and others interested were accused of managing the whole affair for their personal profit. On one day that seemed very like a return to the good old times, this exemplary bank president and a member of Congress came to actual blows.

At last the kiddies cast the deciding vote. Congressmen and senators who were parents and grandparents consented to a zoological garden to be located in the middle of the desired tract. This was accepted as considerably better than nothing at all, and soon other slices were added to the metaphorical half loaf. But the city could easily "do" with more park land than it has been allowed to acquire. In the developments beyond the original boundaries no provision whatever has been made for the small circles and triangles and green breathing-places that are such a feature in older portions of the city. In this we have lived but not learned.

That which most disfigured the original plan and threatened most difficulty in carrying out the new one, was the smudge of railroad track through the center of the Mall. It seemed too much to expect a soulless corporation to give up, without a struggle, such an advantageous position. A lesser obstacle was the unfortunate location of the Botanic Garden, with its high iron fence and its greenhouses at the foot of Capitol Hill, where the new plan called for a plaza to facilitate approach to the Capitol and to balance the open space on its eastern side. But as the removal of the Botanic Garden was a matter entirely within the control of Congress, comparatively little difficulty was anticipated.

The members of the Parks Commission, who had gone abroad in the summer of 1901 to study the treatment of parks in connection with public buildings, before submitting the plan for a new and greater Washington, carried the problem of the railroad tracks with them. Learning that President Cassatt of the Pennsylvania system was also abroad, they arranged a meeting, but with no enthusiasm and anticipating trouble. It was quite in keeping with the unexpected turns in Washington's development, that instead of the mouthpiece of a soulless corporation they found him to be a gentleman actuated by motives very like their own. He was ready to agree to the removal of the tracks under reasonable guarantees, and willing to assume in addition the task of building a station to accommodate all the railways entering Washington.

The lesser problem of moving the Botanic Gardens proved in the long run the greater one, it being harder to overcome the inertia of several hundred members of Congress than to work in harmony with one progressive railroad president.

Before his lamented death, in 1902, Senator McMillan had secured the necessary legislation for the removal of the tracks from the Mall. Mr. Burnham had gone eagerly to work after the interview with Mr. Cassatt upon plans for the new Union Station, and it is to him that Washington owes the white-stone building through which travelers now enter Washington—a building low enough to be subordinate to the group around the Capitol, yet stately enough to be a fitting gateway to the city. Its concourse, which is a little longer than the entire Capitol, is said to be the largest room under a single roof in the world. It was used for the first time in 1905, at the time of Roosevelt's inauguration, and once every four years, at least, is none too large.

President Roosevelt, and President Taft after him, called in, from time to time, eminent architects and specialists in their lines to give advice in carrying out the plans of the Park Commission; but it was found that this gave rise to jealousy and resulted in lack of continuity in executing the measures agreed upon. As a remedy Congress created in 1910 a Commission of Fine Arts of seven members, as the authorized body to which all such matters might be referred, not only by the Government but by individuals who have the city's welfare at heart. Mr. Burnham was its first chairman and served until his death.

Studying the two maps of the city side by side, it is interesting to trace the development of one into the other. In the early one the important buildings are the Capitol and the White House, with Pennsylvania Avenue as a direct street connection between them, and the Mall serving as their common pleasure-ground. The new plan still keeps the Capitol and the White House dominant, but enlarges each to a group of buildings and brings into the orderly scheme the Washington Monument, which, as we have seen, was built a little off the main axis, by making the Lincoln Memorial, with its long reflecting pool, a new point to which the eye is led in line with the monument and the Capitol.

South of the White House, across green parks, space has been set aside for some future memorial. This will bring the Washington Monument, with the tree-covered terraces and the sunken gardens that are planned to surround its base, once more into the middle of the picture. The Mall, restored to its original use, will have a central space of elm-bordered formal alleys leading from the monument to an open plaza embellished by statues at the foot of Capitol Hill, the wide tree-bordered alley being flanked by the museums and art galleries and other public edifices that may be built from time to time, all in the stately style for which precedents were established in L'Enfant's day. The New National Museum, the Freer Art Gallery, the new Department of Agriculture, and several others fall naturally into the scheme; for, thanks to the efficient guardian angel, very little that has already been done will have to be wholly undone.

In addition to this great kite-shaped reservation in the center of the city, which forms the heart of official Washington, there are smaller reservations and subordinate groups of public buildings large and small. The Navy Yard makes one. Recently the old Court House on Judiciary Square was made over and enlarged in a style in keeping with the old plans. The line of stone palaces stretching down from Pennsylvania Avenue toward the river, on Seventeenth Street—the Corcoran Gallery, the Red Cross Building, Continental Hall, and the Pan American Building, all facing the park south of the White House—make in themselves an avenue of public buildings of great beauty. Arlington across the river, with its historic Lee mansion, and its huge new marble amphitheater, is brought into the scheme by the Memorial Bridge yet to be built. In time, encircling boulevards and parks will link it with Mount Vernon; and already the suggestion has been made that a public reservation be established, a National Forest Reserve stretching to Baltimore.

On the high ground northwest of the city, the United States Naval Observatory, the Astro-Physical Laboratory, and the large Bureau of Standards, where almost everything in daily use, from the commonest to the most rare, is measured and weighed and tested, form another center. Directly out Sixteenth Street, which runs due north from the White House to the District line, at a point where the land is high and on clear days there is a view of the Potomac, it is proposed to make a park with terraces and a gateway and an obelisk, to serve as an entrance to the city and also as a memorial to President Roosevelt.

In addition to the streets which stretch out in all directions until, for those that are lettered, the alphabet has been exhausted thrice over, once merely with letters, a second time with names of two syllables, like Adams and Bangor and Clifton, and again with those of three syllables, Buchanan, Crittenden, and so on, other streets are already being planned, to bear the names of trees. In the suburbs are scattered the religious and educational institutions which at the same time add to and gain strength from a city's resources.

The Episcopal Cathedral of St. Peter and St. Paul, now building on the height known as Mount St. Alban's, beyond the Zoölogical Park, already stands silhouetted in Gothic impressiveness against the sky, though only one eighth of its length has yet risen. Sixteenth Street, a mile or more from the White House, which was unimproved hill country only a few short years ago, has become an avenue of "national" churches of varying denominations, alternating with foreign legations that are veritable palaces. Georgetown College, the oldest institution of learning in the District, crowns one of the hills of Georgetown. The newer Catholic University, the Franciscan Monastery, and at least two large Catholic schools for girls, testify that one great branch of the Christian church is not neglecting its opportunities. The American Methodist University, beyond the Naval Observatory, has ambitious plans not yet fully in execution; and, down in the heart of the city, George Washington University has hundreds of students.

Such, in broadest outline, is the town of near half a million souls that has developed on the banks of the Potomac in a century and a quarter. With all its beauty and many faults,—that, happily, may still be cured,—it belongs to the whole people. Cold calculation tells us that Americans pay, for the honor and glory of having such a capital, a tax of about six cents per person per year.

Is it to be lightly prized in future because it costs so little, or, Providence helping as heretofore and Congress coöperating more willingly, is it to be accepted with all its possibilities and responsibilities as a joyous challenge?

It knew itself to be large and believed itself to be cosmopolitan before the World War, but it became a city only when America entered that struggle. At that time it was a rambling, self-satisfied community with some of the characteristics of a watering-place and some of a village, and more still of a thriving county-seat. Precedents and prejudices and conventions hedged it about. Things were "done" or "not done" because of rules that had grown up in the State Department or in committee rooms of Congress or around tea-tables, nobody knew how, imperceptibly, as the dropping of water in a cave creates stalactites and stalagmites—with the same rather fantastic and impeding results. Man's chief business was making laws or applying them; woman's, receiving visits or returning them, according to set rules.

Suddenly, just as the growth of the trees had seemed to change the place overnight, this other change took place. Old prejudices gave way to passionate new beliefs. Old precedents were wrecked in an endeavor to live up to the duty of the hour. The one invariable rule seemed to be that every individual was found doing something he or she had never dreamed of doing before. The rule worked even in those somnolent parts of Georgetown that seem under the spell of a Rip Van Winkle sleep.

Some of us cherish the memory of an incident that took place in a little shop there when a lady entered to make a small purchase, the only kind the shop seemed likely to afford. An old man and an old woman were in attendance, both as shrunken and aged as their stock in trade. The man continued to read his paper, regardless of a mere customer, but after a decent interval the woman came forward and in answer to a question whether she kept the desired article answered with sweet resignation:

"I don't know, dearie; just look on the shelves and see."

This was so like restful, forgotten days that the lady began conversation while they searched the shelves together, dwelling on the

Courtesy of the United States Army Air Service

AN AIR PICTURE OF WASHINGTON

strange vicissitudes of life, and how the war had set people at impossible tasks:

"Yes," agreed the little business woman, with a sigh. "Look at me. I never thought I could stand the turmoil of a shop."

That is the only quiet memory, and almost the only humorous one, remaining from those busy days when energy flowed into the nation's capital in a warm vital flood, bringing with it an undertow of pathos and tragic disillusionment. Some were exalted by it; some were wrecked; but the town was infused with new spirit. Life seemed suddenly to acquire a vivid scarlet lining.

Memories of those days return in pictures of crowds—always crowds. The first of all is a procession of soldiers, different from any procession that ever marched the length of Pennsylvania Avenue, though it has seen soldiers of all our wars, including the Revolution. It was not that these men were old. In such processions age is no novelty. Veterans cling to life and return with their latest breath to this scene of former reunions. Soldiers of 1812 held an encampment here two years after Grant became President; and Grant's men have been returning ever since the Grand Review was held in 1865. By 1917 they had dwindled from numbers that required two days to pass a given point to a comparative handful of bent and limping graybeards, but that year they came with numbers doubled. Each man in blue had beside him as guest a man in gray, as old as himself, and as happy to be walking fraternally up the avenue with the enemies of his youth. The avenue had flung out many banners in their honor, and at the center of almost every group of stars and stripes was the flag the men in gray had followed for four long years, the stars and bars. That was itself a sight some of us thought never to see. It caused a catch in the breath. A sight of the men themselves caused something very like a sob, they were so jauntily youthful, even when their steps were feeble and uncertain.

Grandsons of the veterans of both armies escorted them, wearing one uniform of khaki brown, and marched their very best; partly because they were on parade, partly from respectful emulation. That day they were a guard of honor. Next day or next month they would be taking ship for France. The veterans eyed them with mingled pride and envy. Younger grandsons, mere Boy Scouts, had the welfare of the gray-coated visitors very much at heart. After an inspection of the sleeping-quarters provided for such as had no friends to entertain them and no money to spend on hotel bills, these lads hurried to demand of mothers and aunts all the bedding they could spare, including the best blankets, "Because, honest, those old chaps have n't nearly enough!"

Youths read to their elders well-deserved lessons in courtesy at that time, they were so free from the prejudices with which the intervening generation had been born.

While the war was a cruel devourer of youth on the one hand, it was a renewer of youth on the other. Men who had acquired a middle-aged slouch in civilian dress held themselves erect when buttoned into tunics; tunics are cut that way. Men who were suspected of being too old to enter the service were willing to act a lie, if not to tell one, and moved with accelerated sprightliness. Parks and open spaces were full of lads on their way to training-camps who appeared scarcely older than the children playing on sand-piles. Lonely boys in town on leave, with no place to go, looked idly and longingly at houses with gardens that reminded them perhaps of home. The sight tugged at one's heartstrings. On the first Thanksgiving Day after our entry into the war every household in Washington that could afford to cook a holiday dinner opened its doors and entertained strange boys in khaki that it would probably never see again.

Training-camp boys, off for a few hours' leave, were the only loiterers in Washington. Every one else moved briskly, neither sauntering for pleasure nor plodding dully, but as if hurrying to tasks in which they had vital concern.

One memory that lingers is of the avenue full of eager figures, not in procession but converging on the Treasury, where at high noon ceremonies incident to launching a new war loan were to take place. Clerks in the departments had been dismissed a few minutes ahead of time that they might take part, and all hurried toward the huge brilliant flag that hung between two gray pillars of the Treasury and showed where the speakers were to stand. The women looked as a rule sturdier than the men, for many of the latter were unfit for military service; but the marked thing about men and women alike was their appearance of youth. In their eagerness not one looked over twenty, though there were many in the throng who would never see forty again.

With this new spirit and the rushing to untried tasks, new menaces to safety appeared upon the wide streets. For a time the sight of the elegant uniforms and erratic driving of ladies who steered official motors sent pedestrians scurrying to cover in a manner suggesting panic; but they quickly learned their business and pursued it on one side or the other of the Atlantic with a devotion beyond all praise.

The great Union Station swarmed, day and night. Men who were important personages at home lost their identity when they entered it and emerged dollar-a-year men, to spend months strenuously directing enterprises about which few heard or cared. Young women arrived by every train to do "war work," coming with the magnificent trustfulness of youth without a thought as to where they should lodge or how they were to be fed after they arrived. It was literally true that householders who lived on a car line might answer a ring at the doorbell late at night and find standing on the step an obviously "nice" girl, suit-case in hand, who was at the end of her physical and emotional resources and begged to be taken in for the night.

So many of these young things rushed to Washington with more enthusiasm than discretion, that the term "war worker" came to sound almost like a reproach in the mouths of conservative folk. How unjustly they were regarded, one household discovered only after a dastardly crime came to light. A driver in the employ of a grocery firm entered a house one night to rob it, and killed a woman as she lay sleeping. The next day a mistress was told by her servant that the man had been in the habit of delivering goods in her kitchen, and when the lady expressed her horror at the crime and the criminal, the domestic took her to task:

"'Deed, Mis' Blank, yo' ought not to talk lak dat. Why, de woman he killed was nothin' but a war worker!"

There was endless Red-Cross work. Self-forgetful women rose

at unheard-of hours, night after night, to meet trains and serve food to hungry soldiers. Some attained self-mastery in this, their first real work in a real world; others found in work in hospitals and canteens the only possible anodyne for personal grief. The fireless, lightless, breadless days were grumbled at here as elsewhere, and as loyally kept. Everybody, even dwellers high up in apartment-houses were besought to

JOIN A POTATO CLUB!
Plant vegetables *this* spring.
Do your bit!
Cut the high cost of living by cultivating waste ground!

The recreational work grew to immense proportions. It had been in merest embryo back in the sixties when Horace Greeley sponsored the Hutchinson family, and Lincoln praised it for going into camps and hospitals with its little repertory of cheer. In 1917 women went about eternally knitting up good wool and good intentions into well-meant misshapen garments. Most fantastic spy-stories flew from lip to lip. There were whispers of plots to blow up the public buildings. There were cheers and tears; sudden marriages and sudden farewells. Limping, bandaged soldiers came back, with dazed eyes and lips sealed against the horrors they had seen. And endlessly there was the suspense of waiting for the next war news.

We rose a dozen times a day to the National Anthem, and when foreign visitors of importance were in town, paid similar respect to their national airs. Distinguished generals came, and royalty. When kings and queens arrived, the Government borrowed houses in which to entertain them. The unusual spectacle of our boys in khaki pacing back and forth as guards before the Leiter mansion or the McLean house, made us wonder what the doughboys probably thought of it, and what sensations the owners of the houses experienced when they entered them as guests. All these are woven inextricably into the memory of those gorgeous, wasteful, heartbreaking years of trying to help.

One spot alone seemed free from hurrying footsteps. The gates to the grounds surrounding the White House were closed and locked before our entry into the war, and kept so for three years. At first this was deemed wise as a precaution against possible outrages. Then, an enemy having entered that no bolts could withstand, the same measures were continued to gain quiet for the President who was waging his battle against disease. If more mystery surrounded the patient than was necessary, or than was good for the country, we must remember how hard it is for a strong, self-willed man to admit that Nature has conquered and that his race is run.

In the last weeks of President Wilson's administration the White House was a strange, silent, baffling place. A few officials came and went; many rumors flew about; but of what was really taking place within its walls the public knew no more than if it had been situated in Tibet instead of a stone's throw from Pennsylvania Avenue's hurrying throngs. A reporter who gained permission to enter the East Room, at the very end of Wilson's term, found it dark almost as the tomb, with a moving-picture outfit installed, where the distinguished patient had been allowed to witness on the screen shadows of events to which he had become as a shadow himself—an impotence after great power that must have been more bitter than death.

An odd manifestation of mass psychology occurred when Wilson left the White House and Harding entered it. The grounds were thrown open, and for several days carriages and motors rolled in at one gate, swept up the semicircle of driveway to the north entrance and out by the other, making no effort to stop and for no purpose whatever except to enjoy a privilege long denied. Perhaps this expressed a feeling that throwing open the gates was a forerunner of happier days and of ways of peace.

Washington has never returned to its pre-war habits. It never can, any more than it can shrink again to its pre-war size. For a time we hopefully looked forward to the day when all would be as it had been. But after khaki had become the exception and not the rule upon the streets, and dollar-a-year men and war workers had departed, we realized that the leisurely town we loved had changed to a busy city, with motors enough in its wide streets to contract them, seemingly, to narrow ones.

Old Washington vanished, never to return, when its skyline changed from one of dormer windows and aspiring chimneys to the great impersonal apartment-houses of tile and light-colored brick, with their square outlines, and the private houses of French Renaissance or modified colonial types, also light in color, that have replaced the deep-red brick beloved of Mr. Corcoran and his contemporaries. On the whole, these newer dwellings give a tone of greater gaiety to the streets.

Pessimists bewail the passing of old Washington, but it is not likely they would be overjoyed to see it return. No one would welcome the Potomac water of uncertain color, verging toward dark cloudy amber, with which we were familiar before the deep-sand filtration plant was installed. Nor should we care to return to the horse-drawn street cars crawling along at snail's pace. Their only advantage was that if you entered one, paid your fare, and possessed your soul in patience, you arrived ultimately at the end of the route, the one fixed goal of the cars in those days. Now each one bears a different label, and in some mysterious way branches off from the main line on a tangent of its own.

Nor would we give up our taxis for the jogging old herdic cab, with its two wheels and crimson-lined, smelly interior, in which those not fortunate enough to own carriages went to parties. They were so safe and so slow that we used to call them the "Washington chaperon."

Gone with jingling horse-car bells are many of the old street cries. "Fresh strawberries" are still with us, from January to June, but we no longer hear, "Deviled crabs!" sung in a high, explosive staccato that made it hard to decide whether they were "Democrats" or shell-fish. Nobody died from eating these dainties, sold on the hot streets from push-carts the size of toy express wagons; but in what dark and unhallowed spots they were prepared, was a fathomless secret. This was a cry that began with the blossoming of the first syringa bush and was heard until the exiled oyster returned to its own. The song of the oyster man has also been stilled. It was one of infinite variety. One vender, who had an anthracite complexion and the manner of a jovial opera tenor, used to chant in a sort of recitative:

"Here 's your oysters, fresh and fine
All read-dy for sup-per time;
Little ones for the ladies
Big ones for the babies
An' some for ole men an' young men too!"

The ash-man carried a tin horn of prodigious size, shaped like Gabriel's trumpet in the old paintings, and used to perform marvelous solos upon it in the early morning hours. He too was relegated to the limbo of silence, about the time winter residents began to build their homes in Washington. Now nothing really violent is heard except the tooting of their motors all day long and a large part of the night. Occasionally, through this heavy bombardment of sound, sweet and far off as though heard from a great distance (as indeed it is chronologically) comes the wail of a barrel-organ. There is one whose tunes date back to "Silver threads among the gold."

The shops are not what they used to be. In the old days you did your serious fall shopping in Philadelphia or New York on the way home from your summer vacation, or saved up errands until they warranted the outlay of a railroad journey to Baltimore. Yet when, pressed by necessity, you visited Madame Delarue's tiny place of business on Pennsylvania Avenue in search of party gloves or a bit of "real" lace, she or Miss Elise or Miss Rose, waiting on you with the manners of one gentlewoman aiding another, brought forth from secret boxes really surprising treasures. At Perry's, where you went to buy merino or table linen, the clerk who served you knew your great-aunt personally. Entering a bookshop has become—alas!—a mere business transaction. It is no longer good form to drop in socially and browse along the shelves for a half-hour and come out again without spending a cent; and the stock has become sadly distended and diluted by the addition of expensive knick-knacks and cheap postcards by the acre.

Window-dressing has become a profession. On a discordant day in February, when slush and ice clog the streets and wind and watery sunshine contend in the air, the shop-windows array themselves like wantons to catch the Southern trade. Filigree edges of lace and artificial orchids surround groups of wax figures in sport clothes, holding tennis-rackets at unconvincing angles; and wire frames display bathing-suits that no self-respecting wax figure could wear without melting with shame.

Out on the curb the leavings from yesterday's stock in the florists' shops still make a first-class appearance as they are offered at temptingly reduced rates. A Salvation-Army lassie takes up her stand near them to put silently the question, "Luxury or Giving?" and a street faker strolls by with his satchel full of whistles. Motors roll up in endless succession, and pedestrians, thin and plump, short and tall, pass or enter. Most of the women wear fur coats and the latest cut of shoes, and the latest shade in face-powder. It is a crowd such as could not have been seen in Washington ten years ago, or even five. Like the apartment-houses, it is bigger and gayer-looking and more impersonal.

But sometimes a bit of old Washington shows itself, even on F Street and in business circles. Only three years ago a notice announcing the opening of a new banking house assured the public, "There is nothing stiff and formal about this bank." At our shopping corner Mrs. Secretary Blank has scarcely been helped out of her motor by the carriage-opener (it is not many years that we have had carriage-openers in the business section of Washington) when two little women of middle age, in hats that were never fashionable and coats that may have been made over by superhuman cleverness from army overcoats that took part in the siege against Richmond, come out of the big shop and cling to each other in a way that shows their presence on that busy corner to be in itself an adventure.

Their faces are the only things about them that have not been made over, and for that reason alone they are conspicuous. They bear the lines care cuts into the brows and cheeks of women who get the maximum of hard work and the minimum of fun out of life, but momentarily their expression is one of rapturous wonder. For them frothy laces and shameless bathing-suits do not exist. They do not even see the shop-windows; their gaze is lifted toward the bare treetops, where they search with delight and incredulity for the bird whose trills and warbles assail their ears. The bird is really only a toy whistle in the mouth of the fat grimy little street vender in his ulster, walking near the curb with his stock in trade in a satchel strapped over his shoulder. But for them a miracle has happened. On a February afternoon, with snow on the ground and a wind that is no respecter of persons tugging at their faded coats, they have heard, actually heard, a mocking-bird!

Two crowded days of this last period must not be forgotten. First, the reception given to that false rumor of peace, when people mad with joy, crowded Pennsylvania Avenue from curb to curb, and second, the solemn pageant at Arlington on the anniversary of signing the armistice, when everybody who could do so took his way to the Virginia shore to pay tribute to the Unknown Soldier.

It was an ideal autumn day, with no wind, a cool air, and the sun shining through a thin film of cloud. Potomac Park, lying beside deserted pearly stretches of river, was very beautiful on the way out, and Arlington's many oaks were deep wine red. Against them as a background the sparse leaves on an occasional yellow tree shone like minted gold. The great amphitheater had been hung with garlands of laurel and banners and festoons of flowers.

Most of the great crowd saw it only from the outside, for huge as it is the amphitheater was too small to hold the officials, resident and foreign, who were bidden to the ceremony. It was said that even the Commandant of Fort Meyer, who was in a way the host, was not allowed a ticket of admission. Arlington grounds were open, however, to all who chose to enter, though only the privileged could enter in their motors. The rest parked theirs in a wilderness of cars on the cavalry drill ground.

A space around the amphitheater had been reserved to insure plenty of room for the arrival of the procession and for its component parts after it disbanded. But the roping off had been cleverly done in a wavy line that almost doubled the possibility of securing front places, with their optical and mental advantages. People who had been crossing the bridges since early morning took their stand and waited contentedly for hours, watching and trying to identify the groups that went up the marble steps into the amphitheater.

There were civilian dignitaries of the Disarmament Conference, in high hats and frock coats, and foreign soldiers in strange uniforms—none of them more odd or picturesque than the French with their long capes of horizon blue, and as a token of official mourning, sweeping veils of crape hanging from their red caps. Most impressive of all were our own wounded boys from Walter Reed Hospital; especially the two who had to be carried into the amphitheater face downward on the backs of their comrades. Another group was made up of four Indians in white buckskin and gorgeous war-bonnets, who brought their tribute to lay on the tomb. It was not alone their regal dress and bearing that stirred the imagination, but the dramatic part their race had played as scouts in the war, swimming rivers with mud-concealed faces and in No Man's Land using their inherited skill, to aid the allies who had well nigh exterminated them.

An airplane circled about, photographing; a bird hung almost directly overhead, and far off there was a distant throb of drums, so faint as to resemble at first a feeling rather than a sound. Then it drew nearer and grew louder, and the eye caught the color of crape-enshrouded flags and a glint of bayonets winding among the trees.

Finally the stately procession came into full view, with its groups of officers on beautiful horses, its men in varied uniforms, and true to the spirit of the century, women also, both those who had served overseas and war mothers who had made the richest sacrifice of all. These came wearing their gold stars over their hearts. Strictly according to scripture the last were first. The earliest soldiers to come into view were mere boys in years, though they carried a "Veterans'" banner. The few G.A.R. men in quaint Civil War caps looked incredibly old in comparison. The horses, keeping step to the music, seemed to realize as fully as their riders the solemn stateliness of the occasion. They were halted near the main entrance, while the caisson with its burden rumbled on to the spot where a vested choir waited to lead the way into the amphitheater. A few flowers lay upon the coffin, but not enough to dim the glory of the flag or hide the broad white ribbon Mrs. Harding had placed upon it at the Capitol.

When the services began, the chaplain's voice was plainly heard by all in the vast throng and, thanks to the radio, was followed in distant cities. The people standing among the graves at Arlington joined the President in repeating the Lord's Prayer, their response sounding like the sighing of the wind, for each one spoke low, and the many murmuring together made a noise that was like a summer breeze when it stirs and stops and begins again.

The impressive moment came when the shrill sweet note of the bugle called for the silent tribute, and a stillness settled over the great throng, broken only by soft inarticulate noises made by little children.

After two minutes the crowd stirred and woke to life again, but remained standing quietly as, one after another, the envoys from foreign countries stepped forward to make their citations and speak words of respectful praise. Then gradually the people dispersed and Arlington was left alone with its dead. There are so many more dead than before the last war—graves stretch away in rows where there used to be only grass and trees.

In front of the old Lee mansion is a tomb that was unnoticed on the day when tribute was paid to the Unknown Soldier, but before which it behooves those who visit the capital to stand a moment in silent respect. L'Enfant lies buried there; given his rightful place at last. It was in 1912, on a day when a summer thunder-shower furnished salvos of artillery and a mocking-bird acted as chorister, that his dust was taken from the neglected grave at Green Hill and brought to lie in state in the rotunda of the Capitol. Then a procession wound with it across the river and up the road to this most sacred of America's burial-places, to lay it on a slope overlooking the city he first saw in his dreams and loved so passionately to the end of his disappointed, sordid life. In truth, his spirit has seemed to guide its development through all the hundred years that his body has been dust.

Looking over the plain that was field and woodland when he

knew it, and is now filled with houses and parks, we trace the outlines of his plan, see rising over it the Capitol dome, faintly luminous like a great pearl in the afternoon light, and, turning, follow the same lines upon his tomb, where his old map of the city has been engraved, for epitaph and memorial.

But the plan is engraved deeper still in our hearts.

INDEX

INDEX

Abbott, Mrs., "Mantua Maker from London," 222

Adams, Abigail, 66, 68, 69, 73-75

Adams, Henry, early recollections of Washington, 130, 274; Washington home, 437, 440; memorial in Rock Creek Cemetery, 492

Adams, John, lodges at Tunnicliffs' Hotel, 62; removal to Washington, 65; letters to Mrs. Adams, 65, 66; manner, 68, 69, 75; defeat, 70; last weeks of his presidency, 72, 73

Adams, John Quincy, opinion of Jefferson, 75; records of social life, 82, 91-92, 128-129, 133-135, 189, 301; residence on F street, 126; elected President, 140-145, 436; entertains Lafayette, 153-154; chooses subject for sculpture at Capitol, 165; his human side, 166, 417-419; opinion of Madam Planton, 188; relations with Jackson, 189, 190, 194, 215; last weeks of his administration, 190-193; comment on Harrison inaugural parade, 227; attends funeral of General Brown, 231; advice about funeral in Diplomatic Corps, 235; cousin of James Greenleaf, 275; measurement of skull sent to Edinburgh, 317; in Congress, 305, 417, 419-424; attitude towards science, 320; opinion of the negro, 420; illness and death, 421-422; pedestrianism, 453; interest in exhibition by deaf-mute children, 459; hears negro preacher, 462; thinks no monument will be raised to Washington, 482, 493; unable to deliver address when corner-stone of Washington Monument is laid, 494

Adams, John Quincy, Mrs., campaign, 1824, 141-142; social activities, 150, 189, 301; invited to Mrs. Madison's "christening," 267

Adams, Louisa, 267

Adams, Mary, 267

African Colonization Society, 315, 343-344

Agg, 189

Agriculture, Department of, 323, 325, 510

Alcott, Louisa M., 378

Alexandria, Va., formerly Bell Haven, 20; first boundary stone, District of Columbia set in, 29; occupied by British, 114; ferry landing in Washington, 125; entertains Lafayette, 151; death of Ellsworth, 369

Anacostia River (or Eastern Branch of Potomac), Indian remains upon, 6; original boundary, 28, 31, 37; War of 1812, 107

Anderson, Larz, Mrs., 466

d'Angers, David, 481

Anthony, Susan B., 490

Arc, Joan of, 324, 492

Arlington, Custis estate, 138; Government experimental farm, 325; aspect, 1824, 342; during Civil War, 374-375; in new plan for city, 510; ceremonies November 11, 1919, 521-523; burial of L'Enfant, 523-524

Armstrong, Robert, 107-108

Arthur, Chester A., relations with Blaine, 412-413; his presidency, 413; favored third term for Grant, 413; lacked congressional experience, 417; social leadership, 438; makes formal dedication, Washington Monument, 496; signs bill to reclaim swampy area, 506

Arts Club, 117

Ashburton, Lord, 238, 264

Ashby, General and Mrs., 298, 305

Bacon, Henry, Dupont fountain, 490; Lincoln Memorial, 498-500

Bailey, Dr. and Mrs., 353-355

Baily, Francis, 60

Baird, Spencer F., 322
Balch, Stephen B., 231
Ball, Thomas, 489
Baltimore, Lord, 16, 35
Bancroft, George, 440-441, 507
Bangs, John Kendrick, 439
Banks, Nathaniel P., 470
Banneker, Benjamin, 44
Barbour, 317
Barlow, Joel, Mr. and Mrs., 83, 84, 180, 209
Barney, Joshua, Captain, 107, 110, 114
Barnum, P. T., 310, 312
Barron, James, Commodore, 139
Barton, Clara, 378
Bates, Edward, 362
Bayard, Thomas F., 395
Beall, George, 19-20
Beaujour, Felix de, 100
Bell, Alexander Graham, 184, 401, 428
Benton, Thomas H., Mr. and Mrs., friend of Jackson, 201, Mrs. Benton in social life, 205, 301; injured by explosion on *Princeton*, 241; urges vigor in Mexican War, 250; fire at his home, 271-272; New Year reception, 1846, 301; manner in debate, 426, 430
Bernhardt, Sarah, 408
Berrien, John H., 207
Berryman, Clifford K., 492
Beverley, Robert, 14, 16, 18
Bismarck von, Otto E. L., Prince, 409
Black, Jeremiah S., 356
Blackhawk, 209
Bladensburg, Md., founded, 19; during the Revolution, 22-23; battle of, 109-110, 117; Decatur duel fought on battle site, 139; mentioned, 6, 30, 58, 60
Blaine, James G., at funeral of Charles Sumner, 234; estimate of Mrs. Madison, 262; political prominence, 400, 409; ambitions of, 409-410; personal manner, 409-410, 414; his new home, 410, 437-438; relations with Chester A. Arthur, 412-413; illness, 413-414; manner as Speaker, H. R., 435; at White House, 1889, 470
Blaine, James G., Mrs., letters at time of Garfield's assassination, 410-412
Blaine, Thomas, 411
Blaine, Walker, 411
Blair, Frank P., 198
Bliss, Mrs. (Betty Taylor), 251, 307
Blitz, Signor, 342
Blodgett, Samuel, Jr., 51-53, 57, 116
Boccaccio, 84
Bodisco, Baron, marriage, 221-224; his nephews, 222, 236; funeral of, 235-236; mentioned, 301, 311
Bodisco, Madame (Harriet Beall Williams), marriage to Bodisco, 221-224; to Captain Scott, 224; her beauty and social activities, 245, 301, 304
Bomfort, George, Colonel and Mrs., 83, 210-211
Borglum, Gutzon, 489
Botanic Gardens, 415, 508, 509
Bowen, Sayles J., 391
Braddock, General, 20-21, 64, 69, 501
Bragdon, J. B., 283
Bremer, Frederika, notes about President Taylor, 251-252; description of Washington Hotel, 294; mentions Jenny Lind, 310; on slavery in D. C., 349-350
Brent, Robert, 123
"Brick Capitol," building of, 120-121; occupied by Congress, 131; used as prison during Civil War, 377; gun trained upon, 383
Brooks, Arthur, 462
Brooks, Preston, 425
Brown, Jacob, 148, 231, 418
Bruff, Dr., 83
Brumidi, Constantino, 452-453
Bryan, William Jennings, 221, 434
Bryant, William Cullen, 298
Bryce, James, 34
Buchanan, James, at Mme. Bodisco's first and second weddings, 222-223, 224; elected President, 252; not a musician, 259; kindness to Mrs. Madison, 266; pallbearer for a notorious gambler, 285; at Polk's New Year reception, 1846, 300; grand party at Carusi's, 302-304; hears J. Q. Adams speak in House, 305; career, 326; inauguration, 326, 330-331; orders marines to Northern Liberties Market, 328; his personality, 329; administration's social qual-

ity, 330-337; his indecision, 332, 356; authorizes military precautions for Lincoln's inauguration, 357; letter to ex-President Tyler, 357
Bulfinch, Charles, 165, 167
Burke, Edmund, 491
Burnes, David, 36-37, 59, 123
Burnett, Frances Hodgson, 440
Burnham, Daniel H., 504, 509
Burnside, Ambrose E., 434
Burr, Aaron, elected Vice-President, 71-72; his daughter Theodosia, 73; becomes Vice-President, 73-74; presiding officer of Senate, 87-89, 213; at Jefferson's second inauguration, 89; trial at Richmond, 90; Van Buren's model, 217; mentioned, 73, 156
Burroughs, John, 378
Butler, Benjamin F., 434
Butler, Rev. Dr., 487
Butler, Senator, 251
Butt, Archie, Major, 475, 478, 479

Cabin, John Bridge, 279, 501
Caldwell, Elias B., 116
Calhoun, John C., favors second war with England, 104; Vice-President, 140-141, 193-194; relations with Jackson, 203-204, 208; nullification activity, 213, 215, 420; coffin of, 234-235; civil to Mrs. Tyler, 243; admires Mrs. Porter, 255-256; at White House January 1, 1846, 300; measurement of skull sent to Edinburgh, 317; opposes accepting Smithson legacy, 320; popular enthusiasm for, 417; his ambition and long service, 429; death, 429-430
Calhoun, John C., Mrs., bereavement of, 134, 139; part in campaign of 1824, 141-142; in the Eaton controversy, 207; at Buchanan's party, 303-304; absent when her husband died, 430
Calhoun, Madam, comment on Jackson, 207; character and social prominence, 261
Cameron, Simon, 363
Canal, Potomac Company's plan to unite East and West, 21; laborers, 56; revived as Chesapeake and Ohio Co., rival of B. and O. Railroad, 286-287; asks leave to cut up part of Mall into building lots, 505
Cannon, Joseph, 431, 435-436, 498
Capitol, site and foundations, 16, 21, 35, 38; William Thornton, Architect, 49-50; cornerstones laid, 50, 163, 170; growth of, 55, 58-59, 78, 155-173; destruction and rebuilding, 110, 120, 121; reception to Lafayette in rotunda, 149; materials used in construction, 156-157, 503; crypt designed for Washington's tomb, 163, 484; description of rotunda, 1842, 164-166; visits of ladies to, in early days, 254; rotunda occupied by inventors, 275; modern lighting in, 278, 401; grounds enlarged, 317; volunteers quartered in, 1861, 365; decorated to celebrate fall of Richmond, 382; painting of Electoral Commission in, 400; fence, 415; pervaded by Congress, 415; assaults in, 425-426; religious services in, 426-427; columns for west front, 428; lobbyists, 431-433; restaurants in, 434; Tripoli monument removed from, 481; Jefferson statue in, 481; Washington memorials, 481-485; dominates enlarged plan of city, 509; *Hall of Representatives*—the "Oven," 155-162; scene of Madison's inauguration, 94; Latrobe changes plan for, 156; gorgeousness of, 156-160; new hall occupied, 170; memorial service for Morse, 184; fall of chandelier, 278; seat of J. Q. Adams in, 421; the jar of snuff, 425; fights and religious services, 425-427; dedication exercises for Washington Monument, 496 *Senate Chamber*—restored chamber occupied, 156, 160; new chamber occupied, 171; funeral of Charles Sumner in, 234; volunteers quartered in, 365; jar of snuff in, 425
Carlisle, John G., Mrs., 447
Carnegie Public Library, 328, 397
Carrachi, 482
Carroll, Daniel, 29, 46, 61
Carroll, Daniel of Duddington, 40, 41, 120-121, 275
Carroll, Henry, 119

Carroll, John, Bishop of Maryland, 100
Carrollsburg, Md., 19, 30, 31, 36
Carusi's, 227, 244, 302-304, 314
Cass, Lewis, 247, 334-335
Cassatt, John J., 508-509
Cathedral of St. Peter and St. Paul, 511
Centennial of D. C., 502-504
Chandler, William E., 412
Charls I, grant to Lord Baltimore, 3
Chartres, Duke of, 249
Chase, impeachment trial of, 88-89
Chase, Salmon P., 362, 377
Chipman, Norman B., 394
Choate, Rufus, 371
City Charters, 79, 99, 389, 390
City Government, varied forms of, 389, 390, 391, 394, 416
City Hall, erection of, 112, 276, 503; nucleus of fashion, 124, 276, 377; reception to William Henry Harrison, 226; enlarged, 489, 510
Clark, Champ, 435
Clark, William, 80, 90
Clay, Clement C., Mr. and Mrs., 294-295, 333
Clay, Henry, advocates second war with England, 104; misunderstanding with Senate Committee, 131; presidential candidate, 140-145; president-maker, 1824, 143-144 Adams's Secretary of State, 144-145, 190; welcome to Lafayette, 146; in speaker's chair, 159; Jackson's attitude toward, 190, 195, 208; relations with Van Buren, 221; at Bodisco wedding, 223; estrangement from Harrison, 229; coffin of, 234-235; reference to Tyler's partizans, 237; acquires information about Miss Martineau, 260; at White House fire, 272; likeness on Pennsylvania Avenue omnibus, 285; his passion for cards, 292-293, 429; room at National Hotel, 294; measurements of skull sent to Edinburgh, 317; his Missouri Compromise, 339; member African Colonization Society, 343; popular enthusiasm for, 417; long service in Congress, 429
Clephane, James Ogilvie, 185
Cleveland, Grover, lacked congressional experience, 417; interest in international copyright, 441; before and after marriage, 441-445; partial to children, 442; marriage, 443; host, 444-446
Cleveland, Grover, Mrs. (Frances Folsom), marriage, 437, 443; beauty and charm, 437, 443; a luncheon given by her, 439; manner as hostess, 441-451; her last public reception, 446-451
Cleveland, Rose Elizabeth, 443
Clinton, George, 204, 232-233
Coast Survey, 319-320
Cobb, ——, 433
Cobb, Howell, 143
Cockburn, George, 106-114
Colleges and Universities, American Methodist University, 511; Catholic University, 511; Columbia Institution for the Deaf, 459-460; Columbian College, 505; Georgetown University, 100, 115, 125, 511; George Washington University, 505, 511; Howard University, 460, 463-464, 489
Columbus, Christopher, 486, 491
Congress, Continental, 25, 32-33, 482
Congress, U. S., chooses site of permanent capital, 25-28; dissatisfaction with work upon, 39, 58, 59, 62; disallows bill for transporting officials to, 65; grants city charters, 79, 99, 389, 390; appropriations to refurnish White House, 96, 136-137; declines to move after British fire, 115-116; meets in Patent Office, 116, 120; refuses to finance "Brick Capitol," 120-121; attitude toward street improvements, 128; official honors to Lafayette, 146; buys Jefferson library, 167; adopts Walters plan to enlarge Capitol, 169-170; authorizes building Congressional Library, 172; work of, 174; grants to inventors, 179-183; attitude of members toward art, 186-187; authorizes Jackson to receive gift of lion, 210; funeral customs, 232-234; investigates anti-Tyler demonstration, 238; attitude toward Tyler, 238; battles of Mexican War fought in, 247; politeness to ladies in early years, 254, 427; buys Madi-

son papers, 266; adjourns to attend fire, *272*; buys Force collection of Americana, 280; establishes Bureau of Printing, 281; appropriation for White House library, 308; banquet to Kossuth, 310; grants charter to Columbian Institute, 316; act creating Smithsonian Institution, 321; appears ill-tempered to first Japanese visitors, 335; withdrawals from before Civil War, 356; conflict with President Johnson, 387; authorizes new State, War and Navy building, 390; gives D. C. territorial government, 391; investigates A. R. Shepherd's activities, 395-398; changes D. C. government to commission form, 398; rival of President, 415-417; oratory in, 422-423, 430; beverages consumed by, 425; encounters upon floor of, 425-426; diversions of, 427-429; where its work is done, 430-431; attitude toward Dorothea Dix, 432; changing, yet the same, 432-434, 436; fight for international copyright, 441; Roosevelt sends messages to, as acting Secretary of the Navy, 467; sums appropriated by for Washington Monument, 496; creates Fine Arts Commission, 498; adopts plans for development of park system, 504-506, 508; *House of Representatives* — Elects Jefferson President, 71-72; visit of Sedi Cellanelli, 92; elects J. Q. Adams President, 143-144; occupies the "Oven," 155; meets in new hall, 170; office building of, 173; refuses to hear petitions upon slavery, 420; welcome to J. Q. Adams, 421; dignity in inverse ratio to its size, 422; defense of, 422-423; dull session described by J. Q. Adams, 423-424; armed encounters, 425-426; *Senate*—Burr's farewell to, 89; adjourns to receive Sedi Cellanelli, 92; assists at count of electoral vote, 1825, 143-144; office building, 173; confirms Jackson's nominations, 196; refuses to ratify nomination of A. R. Shepherd, 398; galleries deserted when Adams speaks, 421; more dignified than House, 422; addressed by Sojourner Truth, 462; committee on District of Columbia, 504
Congressional cemetery, 231-233, 415-416
Conkling, Roscoe, 413, 433-434
Constitutional Convention, 25
Cooke, Henry D., 393, 398
Cooke, Jay, 393, 398
Cooper's Bookstore, 106
Cooper, J. Fenimore, 163
Corcoran Gallery of Art, relieves Smithsonian of care of pictures, 323; its beginnings, 402-403; first and second homes, 403, 510
Corcoran, W. W., house selected for a hospital, 1861, 374; builds Louise Home, 396; critic of A. R. Shepherd's, 396; career and public spirit, 402; art gallery, 402-403; house replaced by building for U. S. Chamber of Commerce, 403; as a lobbyist, 432
Corwin, "Tom," retort to Cass, 247
Cox, Samuel Sullivan, 433
Craik, James, Dr., 21
Cranch, William, 137-138, 493
Crandall, Reuben, Dr., 353
Crawford, Thomas, 486
Crawford, William H., Mr. and Mrs., 140-143, 150-152, 436
Crockett, David, 199-200
Culpeper, Lord Thomas, 338
Culum, Mr., 296
Cushman, Charlotte, 362
Custis, George Washington Parke, at Arlington, 138; receives Lafayette at Mount Vernon, 152-153; dramatic writings, 313; his slaves, 342
Cutbush, Edward, Dr., 316
Cutts, J. Madison, 266
Cutts, Richard, Mr. and Mrs., his daily visits to Madison, 97; hosts to the Madisons after British fire, 117; build house on Lafayette Square, 124; death of Mrs. Cutts, 140; he loses office under Jackson, 196; house becomes property of Mrs. Madison, 263-264

Daguerre, 491
Daniel, John W., 496

Dante, 491
Davidson, Major, 127
Davis, Jefferson, interest in enlarged Capitol, 170; residence on G Street, 256; connection with Cabin John Bridge, 279; plan of crazy man to capture, 379; interest in Crawford's statue of "Armed Liberty," 486
Dawes, Henry L., 455
Decatur, Stephen, Commodore and Mrs., their home and social life, 123-124, 139; the Decatur-Barron duel, 139; his naval exploits, 209; her social prominence in later life, 261-262
Depew, Chauncey M., 403
Dewey, George, Admiral, 466
Dexter, Samuel, 65
Dickens, Charles, 288-289
Diggs, Dudley, 42
Diplomats in early Washington, 70
District jail, 122
Dix, Dorothea, 364, 432
Dix, General, 259
Dixon, Mr. and Mrs., 296
Donelson, Andrew Jackson, Mr. and Mrs., 201-202, 206, 209
Dorsey, Lieut., 23, 24
Douglas, Stephen A., Senator and Mrs. (Adele Cutts), builds home, 274-275; deprecates growing lawlessness in city, 327; comment on Lincoln at time of inauguration, 360; orator at unveiling of Jackson statue, 487
Douglass, Frederick, 389
Dow, Reuben, 121-122
Downing, A. J., 279
Duncanson, William M., 275
Dupont, Samuel F., 490
Dupont Circle, 438, 439, 490

Eames, Mr. and Mrs., 361-362
Eaton, John H., General and Mrs., his wife, 62, 138, 203-208; he rides to meet Jackson, 192; his positions, 207, 208
Eccleston, Archbishop, 236
Edmunds, George F., 396
Edward III, 176
Electoral Commission, 400
Ellicott, Andrew, surveys boundaries, District of Columbia, 29; letter to his wife, 30; succeeds L'Enfant and resigns, 44-45; redraws city plan, 45, 177; mentioned, 50
Ellicott, Benjamin and Joseph, 44
Elliott, William, 125
Ellsworth, Annie, 182
Ellsworth, —— (Commissioner of Patents), 182-183
Ellsworth, Ephraim Elmer, Colonel, 360, 369
Emery, Matthew Galt, 170, 391
English, Lydia S., Miss, 222
Engraving and Printing, Bureau of, 281
Eppes, John W., Mrs. (Maria Jefferson), 74
Erskine, M., 82
Ethnology, Bureau of, 325
Evarts, William M., Senator and Mrs., 400, 405, 407, 408
Everett, Edward, 256

Fairfax, Lord, 19
Fane, Georgiana, Lady, 362
Faulkner, Mrs., 446-447
Faux, William, 125, 127
Field, Stephen J., Justice, 408
Fillmore, Millard, lays cornerstone of enlarged Capitol, 170; funerals during his administration, 234-235; fills out President Taylor's term, 252; his wife and daughter, 307, 308; occupies White House, 307; instals bath-tub and range in White House, 308; interest in Washington schools, 309; calls on Jenny Lind, 311; attends Thackeray's reading, 312
Fine Arts Commission, 489-490, 498-499, 509
Fires, destruction of Blodgett's hotel, 177; fire companies, 269-270; inventions to prevent, 270-271; society at, 271-272; at White House and Treasury, 272
Fish, Hamilton, Mr. and Mrs., 400, 401
Flagg, Ernest, 403
Flannery, Lott, 489
Fleete, Henry, 6, 13, 19
Foote, Henry S., 426
Force, Peter, 280
Forts surrounding Washington, 106-107, 116, 373, 378

Foster, Augustus, Sir, 81-82, 86, 130, 427
Foster, Stephen, 308
Foundry Methodist Church, 113
Fowler, O., 235
Fox, Henry, 222-223, 227
Foxhall, Henry, 23, 113
Franciscan Monastery, 511
Franklin, Benjamin, 20, 175, 178, 491
Franzoni Family, 158
Frederick the Great, 490
Freer Art Gallery, 510
Frelinghuysen, ——, 260
Fremont, John C., Mrs. (Jessie Benton), visits Jackson with her father, 201; at Bodisco wedding, 223; elopement, 249; characterization of Washington, 253; social customs in her girlhood, 259; attends her father's New Year reception, 1846, 301
French, Daniel Chester, 490, 499-500
Fulton, Robert, 84, 175, 180
Funeral customs, 139, 230-236

Gales, Joseph, Jr., 84, 118, 280-281, 285
Gallatin, Albert, 63, 200
Gallaudet, Edward Miner, 459-460
Gallaudet, Thomas, 459, 491
Gardiner, Alexis, 246
Gardiner, ——, 241
Garfield, James R., presidency and death, 409-412; his wife and mother, 411-412; statue to, 490
Garrett, John W., 398
Garrison, William Lloyd, 354
Gas works, 163, 278, 327, 401
Geological survey, 320
George III, 482
Georgetown, early history, 19-21; part in the Revolution, 22-23; interest in Federal city, 28; town of "houses without streets," 60; offers hospitality to Congress, 1814, 115; writers seek homes there, 440; growth, 501; World War incident, 512-513
Geroldt, von, 259
Gerry, Elbridge, 233
Gibson, General, 285
Giddings, Joshua R., 420
Gilder, Richard Watson, 442
Gilmer, 241
Gilmore, Lieutenant, 447
Girard, ——, 321
Glover, C. C., 505-508
Godwin, Parke, Mr. and Mrs., 298
Goldsborough, R., 127
Gordon, George, 19-20, 64, 501
Gouverneur, Marian, Mrs., 361
Gouverneur, Mr., 138-139
Grant, Ulysses S., name in decorations of Treasury building after fall of Richmond, 382; his character, 387; the city during his term of office, 387-399; his horses, 393; appoints D. C. territorial officials, 393-394; appoints A. R. Shepherd Governor D. C., 398; nominates him Commissioner D. C., 398; assists at opening of Corcoran Gallery, 403; temperance reforms begun in his administration, 405; his wife, 407, 446; lacked legislative experience, 417
Greeley, Horace, 387, 516
Green, Bernard R., 496
Green, Duff, General, editor Jackson organ, 192, 198; his wife, 301; brick buildings erected by, 377
Green, Richard, 462
Greenleaf, James, 53-54, 58, 275
Greenough, Horatio, 169, 481-482, 484-486
Greenwood, Grace (Mrs. S. J. C. Lippincott), 354, 440
Greuhm, Baron Frederick, 235, 293
Grevelot, bas-relief in rotunda, 164
Grimsley, Mrs., 362
Guerin, Jules, 499
Guiteau, Charles J., 411-413
Gurowski, Count, 233
Gwinn, Mrs., 332-333

Hadfield, George, 122
Hagner, Augustus B., 201-202
Hahnemann, Dr., 491
Hale, Edward Everett, 438
Hale, John P., 385
Hale, Sarah, Mrs., 297
Hale, Susan, Miss, 414, 438-439, 492
Hall, Basil, 159, 350, 430
Hall, Dr., 280
Halleck, Henry Wager, 379
Hallett, Stephen, 49-50
Hamburg, Md. (or Funkstown), 19
Hamilton, Alexander, 27-28, 49, 59

Hamilton, Alexander, Mrs., 261, 301, 304, 495
Hamilton, Gail (Miss Mary Abigail Dodge), 354, 409, 432
Hamilton, John H., Colonel, 195, 197
Hanna, Marcus, 434, 466
Hannegan, Senator, 299-301
Harding, Warren G., Mr. and Mrs., 462, 499, 517, 523
Harmon, Mrs., 447
Haskins, Mrs., 304
Harrison, Benjamin, 465-466
Harrison, William Henry, nomination and election, 224-225; arrival and inauguration, 225-228; character and administration, 228-230; death and funeral of, 230, 465; did not attend theatre in Washington, 312
Hassler, Ferdinand R., 320
Hay, Mrs., 132, 134
Hay, John, extract from letter, 277; installed at White House, 359, 361; before the inauguration, 360; extracts from letters and diary, 364-368; rides to Arlington, 374-375; Washington home, 437, 440; his wife, 472; remark about President Roosevelt, 475
Hayes, Rutherford B., efforts to secure Force collection for Library of Congress, 280; becomes President, 400-401; changes during his term of office, 401; advocates official Board of Charities, 401; deprives Chester A. Arthur of office, 413; at ceremony on top of Washington Monument, 496
Hayes, Rutherford B., Mrs., character and charm, 404-405, 407, 465; afternoon receptions, 407-408; at ceremony on top of Washington Monument, 496
Hawley, Joseph R., 470
Hawley, William, Rev., 230, 231, 267-268, 462
Hayne, Robert Y., 213, 429, 430
Health in D. C., prevalence of malaria, 101-103, 125; yellow fever menace, 1800, 102; sickness in 1822, 139-140; in last weeks of Adams's administration, 190-191; cholera epidemic, 202-203; "National Hotel sickness," 326-327; decrease of malaria, 401
Heister, Daniel, 231
Henry, Joseph, 322-323, 491
Henry, Patrick, 22
Henry of Prussia, Prince, 470
Hickman, "Beau," 393
Hill, Mrs., 429
Hines, Christian, 116
Hoban, James, 48, 121
Hodgson, Allen, 427
Holly, Mrs., 261, 301
Holman, William S., 455
Holmes, William H., 4-6
Holt, Joseph, 356, 386
Hospitals, 102, 114
Hotels, Blodgett's, 51-52, 116, 120, 177, 274; Brown's or Indian Queen, 309; City Hotel, 66; Coleman's National, 293-298, 301-306; Conrad & McMunn's, 71-72; Franklin House, 62, 117, 204; Fuller's Hotel, 288-289; Gadsby's, 192, 295; Long's, 95, 289; McKeowan's, 312; St. Charles, 393; Stelle's, 289; Tunnicliff's, 62; Willard's Hotel, 288-289, 309, 310, 359-360, 364-365, 369, 378, 382; Williamsons, 146
Houston, Sam, 430
Howe, Julia Ward, 431
Hubbard, Mr. and Mrs., 296, 304-305
Humboldt, F. H. A. von, 60
Hunt, Mr. and Mrs., 305
Hunter, David, Major, 364, 365, 382
Hunter, Nainsworthy, 231
Hutchinson family, 516

Indians, original inhabitants D. C., 3-13; capture Henry Fleete, 14; attend Jefferson's New Year reception, 92-93; patrons of theatre, 314-315; at tomb of Unknown Soldier, Arlington, 522
Ingalls, John J., 433
Inventors and inventions, 175-185
Irving, Washington, 104-105
"Island," The, 124

Jackson, Andrew, victory at New Orleans, 118; ovation after accession of Florida, 137; presidential candidate, 140-145; meets Lafayette, 150; per-

sonality and presidency of, 189-215; sentiments toward J. Q. Adams, 190, 192; dislike of Clay, 190, 195, 208; letter to Monroe, 196; perfection of his political machine, 199; champions Mrs. Eaton, 204-208; fight against Nullification, 208, 211-215, 256; farewell address, 215; at Van Buren's inauguration, 216-217; White House expenditures under, 218; makes R. M. Johnson his messenger, 221; chooses site for new Treasury, 273, 503; selects marble for new public buildings, 274; drama by Mr. Custis part of his Washington farewell, 313; popular admiration for, 417; ex-officio president Washington National Monument Society, 493
Jackson, Andrew, Mrs., 142-143, 150, 204, 205-206
Japanese Embassy, 1860, 333-336
Jay, John, 160
Jefferson, Joseph, 314
Jefferson, Thomas, on increase in value of Virginia property, 16; part in locating permanent capital, 27-28; sketch map for capital, 34-35, 38; invites L'Enfant to dinner, 40; attends first sale of lots, 47; elected president, 71-72; lodgings, 72, 440; first inauguration, 73; manners and policy, 74-77, 79-81, 209; second inauguration, 88-90; at Madison's inauguration, 94-95; departs for Monticello, 96; interest in inoculation, 102; offers to sell his library to Congress, 167; inventor, 175-176; attitude toward science, 320; opinion of negroes, 343; unconventional behavior, 415; attends services at Capital, 426; bronze statue of, 481
Jeffreys, Francis, 94
Jennings, Paul, 120, 265
Jockey Club, 78, 85-87, 275
Johnson, Andrew, opposes buying Madison papers, 266; speech after fall of Richmond, 382; rumor of his assassination, 382; distrust of, 384; his presidency, 384-387; vacates J. Q. Adams's seat in Hall of Representatives, 421
Johnson, Cave, 182, 183
Johnson, Reverdy, Mrs. and Daughters, 295
Johnson, Richard M., 207, 221
Johnson, Thomas, 29
Johnson, Thomas, Jr., 57
Johnston, Josiah S., Mrs., 256
Joinville, Prince de, 336
Jones, John Paul, 492
"Juba of Roanoke," 345-346
Jusserand, J. J., 32

Kalorama, bought by Joel Barlow, 83; Latrobe and Paine plan improvements, 84; interment of Decatur, 139; scene of Fulton's experiments, 180; inherited by Colonel Bomfort, 210; becomes hospital for contagious diseases, 374
Kane, Elisha, 308
Kaufman, D., 235
Kendall, Amos, Jackson's friend and adviser, 196; official positions, 198, 274; on Jackson's temper and language, 200; at Patent Office fire, 274; founds school for the deaf, 459
Kendall Green—*see* Columbia Institution for the Deaf
Kennon, Beverly, Captain, U.S.N., 241
Kettles, Willie, 381
Key, Francis Scott, 114, 343
Key, Mrs., 407-408
Kidwell, Dr., 277
Kindener, Baron, 206
King, Cyrus, 167
King, Mr., 296
Kingsley, Mrs., 142
Know-Nothing Party, 328
Kosciuszko, 492
Kossuth, Louis, 309-310
Kuhl, Dr., 283

Labbé, François, 259
Lafayette, visit to United States, 1824-1825, 146-154; member African Colonization Society, 343; likes d'Anger's statue of Jefferson, 481; statue of, 492
Lafayette, George Washington, 151-153
Lafayette Square, originally "President's Square," 78; early a center of

fashion, 123-124, 437; funeral march around, 231; proposal to cover with huge public building, 273; "curbstone parties," 439; statuary in, 486-488, 491-492
Lamon, Ward H., 363
Lamont, Daniel, Mr. and Mrs., 444, 447
Lander, Frederick, Mrs. (Jean M. Davenport), 365
Lane, Franklin K., 466-467, 477, 478
Lane, Harriet, 330-331, 334, 337
Lane, "Jim," Colonel, 364, 366, 368
Lane, Samuel, Colonel, 136-137
Langley, S. P., 184-185
La Rochefoucauld, 58
Latrobe, Benjamin H., plans improvements at Kalorama, 84; architect of Capitol, plans Navy Yard gate, 90, 99; completes Hall of Representatives, 94; helps Mrs. Madison refurnish White House, 96; pessimistic over city's future, 100-101; surveys route for canal, 103; architect of Van Ness mansion, St. John's Church, Brentwood and Decatur house, 123; changes Thornton's plan, 156; resignation and return, 157; brings foreign sculptors to decorate Capitol, 156-157, 164; argument with Dr. Thornton, 483-484
Lavasseur, Colonel, 143-144, 149-150, 151, 342
Law, Thomas, Mr. and Mrs. (Elizabeth Parke Custis), Washington career of, 54-55; marriage, 55; home on Greenleaf's Point, 61; Mrs. Law's hospitality, 69; first Washington home, 71, 449; writings of, 84; divorce, 90; advocates building canal, 102-103; his sons, 105, 112, 140; erects "Brick Capitol," 120-121; "Poem" read at opening of "Brick Capitol," 121; prologue for opening of theatre at Blodgett's Hotel, 312; home across the Eastern Branch, 428-429
Lawrence, Amos, 265
Lawrence, Amos (Revolutionary soldier), 152
Lear, Tobias, 52, 233, 256, 327
Lefferts, Colonel, 367
Leiter, Levi Z., 437, 438, 516
L'Enfant, Pierre Charles, chosen to plan permanent capital, 31; labors and character, 31-41, 504; dismissal, 41, 275; subsequent history, 41-43; plans for public buildings, 48; opinion of Washington's situation for defense, 106; in charge of work at Fort Washington, 116; offer of professional services to Van Ness, 123; growth of city he surveyed, 501; burial at Arlington, 523-524
Lenox, Walter, 309
Leutze, Emanuel, 362
Levy, Commodore, 481
Lewis, Major, 196, 198
Lewis, Mr., 301, 304
Lewis, Meriwether, 80, 90
Library of Congress, rooms and collection in Capitol, 155, 166-168; new building, 172-173, 507; enriched by Force collection, 280; takes over Smithsonian library, 323; anecdote of, 416; Miss Dix as a lobbyist in, 432
Limpert, Caspar, 259
Lincoln, Abraham, capital plaza at dates of his inaugurations, 171; house where he lodged, 172; inventor, 176; visits to hospitals, 209; thought retrocession of land to Virginia a mistake, 246; votes on Wilmot Proviso, 247; lodgings while member of Congress, 248; at theatre, 314; effect of his election on city, 356-358; arrival in Washington, 358; stays at Willard's before inauguration, 359-360; receives delegates to Peace Congress, 360; incidents of his presidency, 360-380; his remark to General Schenck, 380; at City Point, 381; assassination of, 382-383; funeral, 384; appearance, 435; praise of Hutchinson family, 516
Lincoln Memorial, 403, 462
Lincoln, Robert, 360, 374-375
Lincoln, "Tad," 360
Lincoln, William, 360, 384
Lind, Jenny, 310-312
Livingston, Brockholst, 161
Livingston, Edward, Mr. and Mrs. 256

Lobbying, 175, 179-183, 186-187
Lodge, Henry Cabot, 434
Long, John D., 491, 496
Longfellow, Henry W., 491
Lotteries, 51-52, 122
Louis Philippe, 60, 209
Louise Home, 396
Lowden, Mrs., 304
Lowrie, Senator, 142
Lyons, Lord, 377

McClellan, George B., 492
McDowell, Irwin, 372
McKim, Charles F., 504
McKinley, William, 466
McMillan, James, 504, 509
McMillan, Mrs., 451
Macfarland, H. B. F., 502, 503
Macomb, Alexander, General, 313
Madison, James, part in locating permanent capital, 26; offers appointment to L'Enfant, 42; attends first sale of lots, 47; inaugurated President, 94-95; occupies the White House, 96; manner and appearance, 96-97; opposes second war with England, 104; declaration of war, 105; rage against him, 107; during attack upon Washington, 108-109; occupies Octagon House, 117; receives Treaty of Ghent, 119-120; estates involved, 263; opinion of slavery, 343; member African Colonization Society, 343; president Washington Monument Society, 493
Madison, James, Mrs., acts as hostess for Jefferson, 74; attitude toward Mrs. Merry, 80; attentions to Lewis and Clark, 80; on inauguration day, 1809, 95; superintends changes at White House, 96; housekeeping and social duties, 96-98; during attack upon Washington, 109; occupies Octagon House, 117; hostess at peace celebration, 120; crowns Peggy O'Neil, 204; coffin of, 234-235; guest on the *Princeton*, 241; assistance she gave her husband, 254; last years in Washington, 262-267; funeral of, 267-268; her New Year reception, 1846, 301; guest of Mrs. Polk, 303; attends Buchanan's grand party, 304; her use of books, 308; runaway slave, 352; smiles and diplomacy, 415; popularity and charm, 437; attends corner-stone ceremonies for Washington Monument, 495
Magruder, William B., Dr., 328
Maltitz, Baron, 235
Mann, Horace, 339, 352
Marcy, William L., 345
Markets, *Centre Market*, 78, 125, 291, 461; *East Capital Street*, 148; *Northern Liberties*, 328, 353, 397
Markoe, Francis, Jr., 318
Marshall, John, reaches Federal City, 65; administers oath to Jefferson, 73; career and personality, 160-161; administers oath to Jackson, 194; measurement of skull sent to Edinburgh, 317; statue to, 491; resolution in Congress for memorial to Washington, 493; president Washington National Monument Society, 493
Martin, Luther, 88
Martineau, Harriet, 174, 198, 259-260
Martiti, Chevalier de, 223
Maryland, religion in, in Colonial days, 18; part in locating permanent capital, 28; grant to D. C., 46; Maryland slaves in D. C., 340
Mason, James M., 182, 266, 305, 429
Matthews, Father, 202
Maury, John D., 432
Maxey, Virgil, 241
May, Frederick, Dr., 102, 120-121
May, George, Dr., 102
Mercer, ——, 424
Merry, Anthony, Mr. and Mrs., 79-81, 88
Middleton, Mr. ——, 129
Middleton, Wesley, 293
Miller, Joaquin, 440
Mills, Clark, 486-489, 497-498
Mills, Robert, 273, 284, 494, 497
Monroe, James, advocates second war with England, 104; in Madison's Cabinet, 104-105; residence while Secretary of State, 117; refuses City Hall a site on Pennsylvania Avenue, 122; first inauguration, 131; presidency of, 131-145; reception of La-

fayette, 150; lays corner-stone of rotunda, 163; letter of advice from Jackson, 196; member African Colonization Society, 343
Monroe, James, Mrs., 132-138, 304
Monroe, Maria, 132, 138
Monuments and Statues, Adams Memorial, 492-493; Arc, Joan of, 324, 492; Burke, Edmund, 491; Columbus, 486, 491; Daguerre, 491; Dante, 491; Dupont, 490; Franklin, 491; Frederick the Great, 490; Gallaudet, 491; Garfield, 490; George III, 482; Hahnemann, 491; Henry, Joseph, 491; Jackson, 486-488; Jefferson, 481-482, 491; Jones, John Paul, 492; Kosciuszko, 492; Lafayette, 491; Liberty (on Capitol dome), 486; Lincoln: emancipation statue, Lincoln Park, 388; figure at City Hall, 489-490; head by Borglum, 489; memorial, 497-500, 506, 507, 509-510; statue by Vinnie Ream, 489; Longfellow, 491; Luther, 491; Marshall, 491; Peace Monument, 506; pioneer defending his family, 486-488; Pulaski, 492; Rochambeau, 492; Roosevelt lion (rejected), 492; Scott, 491; Shepherd, A. R., 491; Sheridan, 492; Steuben, 492; suffrage leaders, 490-491; Tripoli Monument, 99, 115, 168, 481; War and Peace, 169, 486-488; Washington: at battle of Princeton, 488; equestrian statue voted by Continental Congress, 482; Greenough statue, 169, 481-482, 484-485, 493; Monument, 251, 493-497, 507, 509-510; Dr. Thornton's idea for group in rotunda, 483-484; Webster, 491; Willard, Frances, 492
Moore, Thomas, lampoon on Washington, D. C., 17, 84
Morgan, Comm., 235
Morris, Robert, 26-27, 42, 54, 58
Morse, S. F. B., artist before inventor, 175, 181; lobbyist and inventor, 181-183; memorial service, 184
Morton, Levi P., 434
Moton, Robert R., 462, 499
Mott, Lucretia, 490
Mount Vernon, 37, 152-153, 510
Mullett, A. B., 394
Murray, Charles Augustus, 171
Myre, Mrs., 290

Napoleon Bonaparte, 35
Napoleon, Louis, 409
National Institute, 318
National Museum, exhibits in, 185, 323-325; germ of, 317; growth, 323-324; construction, 503-504; new National Museum, 324, 510
National Theatre, 244, 310
Navy Department, 117
Navy Yard, development under Jefferson, 77; employees take part in Jefferson's second inauguration, 90; destroyed August, 1814, 110; practically a separate community, 124, 275; visit of Japanese to, 1860, 335-336; during Civil War, 376-377; Tripoli monument removed from, 481; part in the new city plan, 510
Negroes, cheer news that J. Q. Adams is elected, 144; Good Samaritans among them, 264-265; President Fillmore's cook, 309; in D. C., 339-355; churches for, 341; Jefferson's opinion of, 343; opinion of Colonization Society, 343; crowd to Washington after emancipation, 377, 388; their shanties display mourning for Lincoln's death, 383; granted the franchise in D. C., 389; J. Q. Adams's opinion of, 420, 462; at the present day, 460-465; educational opportunities for, 460, 463-464; effort to have street cars exclusively for, 461-462; popular opinion regarding, 462; exceptional men and women, 462-463
Neuville, Hyde de, 134
New Assembly Rooms, Louisiana Avenue, 227-228
Newcomb, Simon, 323
Newport, Captain, 13
Newspapers, City Gazette, 125; Evening Star, 3, 357, 381, 382, 393, 395, 406; Globe, 244, 310; Impartial Observer & Washington Advertiser, 57; National Era, 353-355; National Intelligencer, 82, 84, 111, 115, 117-118, 203, 227, 232; Paul Pry, later The Huntress, 188; The Potomac Alma-

nac or Washington Ephemeris, 50; Telegraph, 192; Washington Union, 362
Nicholson, John, 54, 58
Nicholson, Joseph H., 72
Nicolay, John G., extracts from letters of, 358-364, 367-374, 378-380, 383-384; made Lincoln's private secretary, 359; visit to Arlington, 374-375; interview with crazy man, 378; difficulty of his position, 380; impressions of Andrew Johnson, 385
Niemcewicz, Julian Ursin, 60
Nilsson, Christine, 438
Nullification, 211-215

Ochiltree, Tom, 433
Octagon House, 79, 117, 119-120, 402
Ogilvie, James, 82-84
Ogle of Pennsylvania, 219
Olmstead, Frederick Law, 504
Olney, Richard, Mrs., 447
O'Neil, Peggy, *see* Eaton, General and Mrs.
O'Neil, William, 52, 117, 138, 204-205
Osborne, Thomas B., 162, 238-239, 421, 422-423
Otis, Harrison Gray, Mrs., 256
Owen, "of Lanark," 151

Packenham, Sir Edward, 243, 305
Page, Charles, 185
Paine, Thomas, 83, 113
Pan-American Building, 510
Paris, Count of, 249
Parkinson, Richard, 60
Parks (*see also* Lafayette Square), Braddock's Rock in Potomac Park, 21; in L'Enfant's plan, 39, 505; surrounding the Capitol, 168-169, 173; Mr. Downing's labors, 279; reservation of the Columbian Institute, 316; proposed Roosevelt Memorial Park, 492, 511; plan of Parks Commission, 504-505; cherry trees in, 505-507; growth of park area, 505-511
Patent Office, spared by British, 111-112; injured by storm, 115; meeting place of Congress, 116; development of, 175-179; destroyed by fire, 177, 274; exhibition of industrial arts in, 1853, 234; new building for, 274, 287; National Institute assigned rooms in, 318; visit of Japanese to, 335; mass-meeting near, after fall of Richmond, 382; built of marble, 503
Paternotre, Madame, 447
Patterson, Elizabeth, 85, 86
Patti, Adelina, 312
Payne, Anne, 267-268
Pendleton, Mr. and Mrs., his "Palace of Fortune," 284-285; her carriage, 284; his funeral, 285; his paintings and carvings, 402
Penitentiary, 222
Penn, William, 164
Pennsylvania Avenue, opening of, 59; in Jefferson's time, 78; Benjamin Stoddert's stepping stones, 99; business and hotels on, 125; condition of, 128; deflected by new Treasury, 273-274; gas mains laid, 278; paved in Jackson's time, 281-282; stores upon, 282-283; stage-coaches upon, 285; daily parade after office hours, 285-286; state during and after Civil War, 375-376, 388; rejoicing upon after fall of Richmond, 381; carnival to celebrate new paving of, 392-393; removal of grade crossing, 397-398; trees and paving, 502; floods upon, 506; place in enlarged plan, 509; crowds upon during World War, 514
Pension Office, 503-504
Perry, Matthew C., 333
Persico, Luigi, 165, 169, 486, 488
Peter, Mrs. Thomas, 81, 138
Philadelphia, Pa., temporary seat of government, 25, 28; Jefferson's liking for plan of, 35, 38; offers Government its old quarters, 1814, 115
Piccolomini, Maria, 332
Pierce, Franklin, Mr. and Mrs., 252, 261, 312, 329
Pinckney, Charles, 430, 433
Planton, Madame, 187-188
Plitt, Mrs., 304
Plumb, "Professor," 235, 284
Poinsett, Mr., 422
Police, 238, 272, 327-328
Polk, James K., nomination of, 183; guest of President Tyler, 243; personality, 245, 248; administration,

245-250; proclaims retrocession of land to Virginia, 246; on handshaking, etc., 248-249, 284; New Year reception, 300; attends theatre, 312; lays corner-stone of Smithsonian, 321-322
Polk, James K., Mrs., 243-245, 300, 312
Polk, Miss, 422
Pope Pius IX, 328
Pope, Thomas, 17
Porter, Peter B., General and Mrs., in cabinet of J. Q. Adams, 191, 256; her charity and social graces, 191, 255; entertain Ex-President Adams, 194
Porter, Susan, 303
Post Office Department, location of, 116, 274; marble building, 287, 503
Potomac River, importance in primitive life, 5-8, 11, 13; Barons of the Potomac, 17; towns upon, 19; location of capital, 26, 28, 31, 33-34; natural highway of trade, 53; settlers arrive by, 61; flats form and increase, 276-277, 327, 328; color of its water, 388, 518
Powers, Hiram, 402
Powhatan, 4, 9
Preston, Mrs., 271-272
Prout, Mrs., 275
Pulaski, Casimir, 492

Quincy, Josiah, 200

Railroads, rivalry of B. and O. with Chesapeake and Ohio Canal, 286; tracks on public reservations, 286-287; B. and O. stations, 287; track across Pennsylvania Avenue, 388, 397-398; encroachment of, on the Mall, 503, 508; old Pennsylvania station reached by boats in times of flood, 506; new Union Station, 508-509
Raleigh, Walter, Sir, 7
Ralph (Mrs. Madison's servant), 267
Ramsey, Mrs., 407
Randolph, John, of Roanoke, prosecutor in trial of Justice Chase, 88; reference to Congressional Cemetery, 232; admiration for Mrs. Livingston, 256; his servant, Juba, 345-346; his consumption of "toast-water," 425; gesticulation, 430
Randolph, T. M., Mrs. (Martha Jefferson), 74, 80, 91-92
Rantoul, R., 235
Ream, Vinnie, 489
Red Cross Building, 510
Reed, Thomas B., 433, 435
Reid, Whitelaw, 470
Reily, Captain, 210
Renfrew, Baron—Prince of Wales, 336-337
Richardson, Henry Holman, 437
Ricketts, Mrs., 401
Riley, William, 117-118
Ringgold, Tench, official part in ceremonies of Lafayette's visit, 149, 153; in Supreme Courtroom, 163; marshal in Jackson inaugural parade, 193; at funeral of General Brown, 231
Robbins, Elizabeth, 426
Robbins, Jonathan, 161
Roberdeau, Isaac, 40, 44
Roberts, Kenneth, 456
Robinson, Douglas, Mrs., 468-469
Rochambeau, 492
Rock Creek, 276-277, 323, 440
Rockwell, Mr. and Mrs., 296
Rodgers, John, Commodore, 127
Rogers, Commodore, 152
Romero, Senor and Madame, 447
Roosevelt, Archie, 468, 477, 478
Roosevelt, Ethel, 473, 480
Roosevelt, Quentin, 477, 478
Roosevelt, Theodore, restores name of Jefferson Davis to Cabin John Bridge, 279; relics at National Museum, 324; lacked congressional experience, 417; personality and administration, 466-480; portraits of, 479; proposed memorials to, 492, 511; interest in work of Parks Commission, 505, 509
Roosevelt, Theodore, Mrs., illness, 467; absence from White House, 468; her part in restoring the White House, 471-472; manner as hostess, 472-473; affection for White House, 474; makes White House ready for her successor, 479; keepsakes given

and received, 480; disapproved of proposed memorial to, 492
Roosevelt, Theodore, Jr., 472-473
Ross, Alexander, General, 106-114
Royal, Ann, opinion of Capitol crypt, 163, 491; life in Washington, 188; call upon Mr. and Mrs. Hugh White, 304-305; story of persecuting J. Q. Adams, 419
Rumsey, James, 180-181
Rush, Richard, 321

St. Elizabeth, Govt. Hospital for the Insane, 16
St. Gaudens, Augustus, 493, 504
St. John's Episcopal Church, erection of, 123; Scott-Bodisco wedding, 224; attended by Harrison, 229; negro conducts afternoon service, 1827, 462; place in the community, 505
St. Patrick's Catholic Church, 126, 139
Schenck, Robert C., 380
Schoolcraft, Mary Howard, 354, 355
Schools, early public schools, 99-100, 456; lottery to obtain funds for, 122; Miss English's private school, 222, 259, 457; President Fillmore's interest in, 309; forbidden to slaves, 341; dismissed on news of fall of Richmond, 381; experiments in education, 456-458; John McLeod's theory and practice, 457-458; Mrs. Lee's select school, 457; Mr. Ironsides' Lancastrian school, 457-458; the Pestalozzi system dies, 457; modern public and private schools, 458; modern public schools for negroes, 463
Schurz, Carl, 189, 368
Scidmore, Eliza Ruhama, 506, 507
Scott, Captain ——, 224
Scott, Walter, 106
Scott, Winfield, pupil of James Ogilvie, 82; ordered south by Jackson, 214; success in Mexico, 250; plans for defense of Washington, 357; vigilance of, 363; on day of battle of Bull Run, 371-372; statue of, 491
Seaton, William W., Mr. and Mrs., publisher "National Intelligencer," 84; her accomplishments, 84; her description of White House dinner, 97; entertain William Henry Harrison, 225; business partners, 254; her knowledge of Miss Martineau, 265; efforts to aid Mrs. Madison, 265; Whig supper party, 302
Secession sentiment, 356-358, 383
Sedi, Cellanelli, 90-93
Sessford, John, 269, 276, 278, 404
Seward, William H., deprecates lawlessness in city, 327; recommends "Uncle Tom's Cabin" to Southern senators, 354; brings news to White House of defeat at Bull Run, 372; home on Lafayette Square, 380; house decorated after fall of Richmond, 382; rumor of his assassination, 382
Shepherd, Alexander R., 391-399, 491
Sheridan, Phil, General, 409, 492
Sherman, John, Mrs., 407
Sherman, William T., 409, 470
Shidd, Sarah, 317
Shields, James, General, 249
Silkworm culture, 275-276
Sioussat, Jean Pierre, Mrs. Madison's steward, 97; during attack upon Washington, 109; celebrates peace of Ghent, 120; faithfulness to Mrs. Madison, 265
Slavery, relation to Mexican War, 247; "new slave bill," a standing topic, 1850, 310; American Colonization Society, 315; pro-slavery leaders in Buchanan's administration, 329, 336-337; in our national history, 338-339; in local history, 339-355; Madison and Jefferson upon, 343; varied sentiments upon in D. C., 352; labors of J. Q. Adams for emancipation, 420; House of Representatives refuses to hear petitions upon, 420
Slaves, their labor upon government buildings, 56; conduct during attack on Washington, 114; funerals of, 236; domestic service of, 257, 290-291, 339-47; accommodations for, St. Charles Hotel, 293; slave-trade in D. C., 339, 348-352; laws concerning, 340-341; John Randolph's Juba, 345-346; diversions of, 342, 345, 347-348; fugitive slaves, 351-352; old man at Arlington, 375
Smallwood's Daguerrean Gallery, 235

Smallwood, Samuel N., 148
Smith, Ann, 108
Smith, ——, 181
Smith, ——, Gen., 89
Smith, John, Captain, 7, 10
Smith, Samuel Harrison, Mr. and Mrs., hospitality, 69, 82; editor National Intelligencer, 82; her writings, 84, 85; during attack on Washington, 108, 110; her comment on Jackson's inauguration, 195; explains Miss Martineau, 260; he becomes trustee for Mrs. Madison's fund, 266
Smith, Susan Harrison, 82
Smith, Truman, Mr. and Mrs., 296
Smithsonian Institution, S. P. Langley director, 184-185; grounds improved by Downing, 279; origin and growth, 315-325; Astrophysical Observatory, 325, 510; educational value of, 458; Greenough statue in, 485
Snow, Beverly, 353
Soldier's Home, 374, 380
Southard, Samuel, 260
Southworth, Mrs. E. D. E. N., 354
Spinner, General, 455
Spofford, Ainsworth R., 172, 440, 441, 507
Sprigg, Mrs., 248
Sproh, Rev. Mr., 297, 306
Stackelberg, Baron, 235
Staley, —— (North Carolina Representative), 182
Standards, Bureau of, 325, 510
Stanton, Edwin M., in Buchanan's cabinet, 356; address after fall of Richmond, 381; serenaded, 382; exclamation on Lincoln's death, 383; difficult position during reconstruction, 386
Stanton, Elizabeth Cady, 245, 490
State Department, occupies part of Treasury, 53; quarters after British fire, 116-117; decorations of after fall of Richmond, 382; new building authorized, 396; built of granite, 503
Stebbins, ——, Miss, 362
Stephens, Alexander H., 266, 294
Steuben, Baron von, 492
Stevens, Mrs. Commodore and daughters, 295
Stevenson, A., Mrs., 447, 448, 451
Stewart, Senator, 390-391
Stoddert, Benjamin, 67, 99
Story, Joseph, 161-162
Stott, Charles, 276
Stowe, Harriet Beecher, 354, 355
Streets, land occupied by, not paid for, 37; condition of, 128; Massachusetts Avenue in 1850, 274; animals at large in, 276; lighting system, 277; 9th Street N. W., 280-281, 376; 10th Street N. W., 376; 19th Street N. W., 377; Vermont Avenue's "coal-tar concrete," 388; "Star's" description of in 1871, 395; gradual improvement, 399, 437; extension of, 501-502, 511; beauty of trees upon, 502; plan of Parks Commission, 504; modern F Street, 520
Stuart, David, Dr., 29, 41, 47, 59
Stuart, Gilbert, 83, 109
Sumner, Charles, funeral of, 234; not a musician, 259; his dress suit, 331; recommends "Uncle Tom's Cabin" to Southern senators, 354; his paintings and photographs, 402; assault upon by Preston Brooks, 425; manner in debate, 430; appearance, 435; acts as guide to Thackeray, 488
Supreme Court, its meeting-places, 116, 149, 160; growing importance, 160; atmosphere of, 162-163; meeting of Electoral Commission in its room, 400; suite in the Capitol, 415; room deserted during Adams's speech on right of petition, 421; dignity in inverse ratio to its size, 422; jar of snuff in courtroom, 425
Suter's Tavern, Georgetown, 46-47

Taft, William Howard, lacked congressional experience, 417; turns first spadeful of earth for Lincoln Memorial, 499; takes part in dedication, 499; interest in work of Parks Commission, 509
Taft, William Howard, Mrs., 470, 506, 507
Taney, Roger B., 183
Tayloe, John, Mr. and Mrs., 79, 86, 260
Taylor, Zachary, successes in Mexico, 249-250; elected President, 250; in-

auguration, short term, death, 250-252, 261, 495; without legislative experience, 417
Taylor, Zachary, Mrs., 250, 307
Telegraph, invention, 181-183; tablet marking site of first public office in Washington, 184; news of Polk's inauguration by, 183, 246; used by Prof. Henry to make weather map, 323
Templeton, John, 58
Thackeray, William M., 253, 312, 488
Thanksgiving Day, 295, 297
Theatres, earliest in Blodgett's hotel, 116; hard fate of, in Washington, 126, 312-313; attitude of Presidents toward, 312, 314; Mr. Law's prologue, 312; home-grown drama, 313; actors of note, 314; Indian patrons, 314-315; attendance of negroes regulated, 341; Ford's Theatre, 376
Thompson, Adam, 308
Thompson, George, 16, 35
Thornton, William, Dr., draws plan for Capitol, 49-50; befriends Samuel Blodgett, 52; Commissioner D. C., 59; host to John Marshall, 65; his optimism, 66; designs Octagon House, 79; impediment in speech, 84; aids wife of French Minister, 87; aids dying man, 102; saves Patent Office, August, 1814, 111, 112; changes made in his plan for Capitol, 156; Superintendent of Patents, 176; claims Potomac Flats, 277; pass for his slave, 344-345; argument with Latrobe over statue to Washington, 483-484
Thornton, William, Mrs., praises a Washington shop, 63; extract from diary, 68; her hospitality, 69; extract from diary, 102; assistance she gave her husband, 254; attacked by slave, 353
Threlkeld, John, 84
Thumb, Tom, 314
"Tiber" (formerly Goose Creek), mentioned, 17, 31, 33, 36, 51, 63, 84-85, 102, 119, 123, 124, 125, 192, 276
Tilden, Samuel J., 400
Timberlake, Virginia, 241, 245
Tingey, Captain Thomas, 90, 110, 152, 165
Tobacco, traffic in Colonial days, 11-15, 20; site of Capitol paid for in, 16; decline of trade in, 64, 276-277
Todd, Payne (Mrs. Madison's son), 263, 266-268, 276
Toombs, Robert, 293
Towson, Nathan, Colonel, 193
Treasury, building erected near White House, 53; quarters after British fire, 117; destruction by fire, 272; rebuilt, 273-274; decorations after fall of Richmond, 382; War Loan ceremonies, World War, 514-515
Trollope, Mrs., 199
Trumbull, John, 164, 179
Truth, Sojourner, 461-462
Tunnicliffe, William, 62, 65, 121
Turreau de Garambonville, 87
Tuyll, Baron de, 235
Twain, Mark, 185
Tyler, John, installation as Vice-President, 227; succeeds Harrison, 237-238; character and policy, 237-240, 385; institutes band concerts at White House, 240; personal appearance, 240-241; death of his first wife, 241; second marriage to Julia Gardiner, 241-242; entertains his successor, 243; departure from Washington, 243-244; chairman Peace Congress, 357, 360
Tyler, John (son of President), 242

Union Station, 508-509, 515
United States Chamber of Commerce, 403
United States Naval Observatory, 320, 335-336, 510
Upshur, Abel P., 241

Van Buren, John, 220
Van Buren, Martin, favors Crawford, campaign of 1824, 142; inspects Morse's invention, 181; Jackson's Secretary of State, 195; compares Jackson to Duke of Wellington, 200; polite to Mrs. Eaton, 206; toast at Nullification dinner, 213; inauguration, 216-217; character and administration, 216-226, 237; relations with

Clay, 221; Bodisco wedding festivities, 222-224; fails of reelection, 224-225; entertains Harrison, 225; refuses to interfere in erection of new Treasury, 272-273
Van Cortland, Philip, 85, 266
Van Ness, John P., General, builds Van Ness mansion, 123; hospitality of, 138; Mayor, 192; inventory of his slaves, 344; his home a ruin, 388
Van Ness, John P., Mrs., daughter of David Burnes, 123; hospitality of, 138; charitable, 191, 210; death, 210
Van Rensselaer, Stephen, denounced for casting vote to make J. Q. Adams President, 144; not literary, 260-261; his wife, 260-261
Varden, John, 317-318
Vaughan, Charles Richard, 206
Victoria, Queen, 249, 330, 337
Virginia, Indians of, 7-14; early tobacco culture, 12-16; value of land and slaves in, 16; Colonial customs, 14-19; part in the Revolution, 22; location of permanent capital, 26-28; grant to D. C., 46; retrocession of D. C. land to, 246; Lord Culpeper on slavery in, 338; Virginia slaves in D. C., 340; act of 1715 relating to slaves, 341
Volney, Constantin François de Chasseboeuf de, 60
Von Briesen, 472, 474

Waite, Morrison R., 408
Walter, Thomas U., 169
War, Civil, 363-381; peace rejoicings on fall of Richmond, 381-382; opens Departments to women workers, 455; work of Hutchinson family, 516; Mexican, 169, 245-250; of 1812, 104-114, 118, 119, 138; of the Revolution, 20, 22-24, 104; Spanish-American, 466-467; World, 512-517
War Department, 117
Ward, Sam, 431-432
Warder, Mr. and Mrs., 437-439
Washington, Bushrod, 161
Washington, George, joins Braddock's expedition, 21; espouses cause of Colonists, 22; active in locating permanent capital, 28-40; liberal ideas for capital, 31, 34-35, 48; letter about L'Enfant, 31; regard for L'Enfant, 32; meets landowners, 36-38; efforts to reconcile L'Enfant and Commissioners, 40; compares L'Enfant and Ellicott, 44; tries to reconcile Ellicott and Commissioners, 45; recommends resident superintendent in D. C., 45; attends first sale of lots, 47; report to Congress, 47; attends laying corner-stone of Capitol, 50; buys lottery ticket, 52; belief in commercial future of capital, 53; urges importing foreign laborers, 55-56; urges speed in building Capitol, 58-59; believes city well situated for defense, 106; his portrait by Stuart, 109; city property burned by British, 115; his inauguration, 131, 194; social precedent set by, 134; legacy finishes Tudor Place, 138; kindness to George Lafayette, 151; burial place prepared for in Capitol, 163; patron of inventors, 175; number of post offices during his presidency, 199; dream of a university, 320; called "August Presence," 415; centenary of his birth, 482; plans for monuments to, 482; burial in Washington given up, 493
Washington, Lawrence, 19
Washington, Lund, 58
Washington Monument, *see* Monuments and Statues
Washington National Monument Society, 493-497
Water, from springs and pumps, 126-127, 168, 202; Washington Aqueduct begun, 278-279; supply insufficient and unfiltered, 388
Watterson, George, 167, 188, 493
Watterson, Henry, 166, 312
Weather Bureau, 322
Webster, Daniel, announces vote of House for J. Q. Adams, 144; opposes buying Jefferson's library, 167; oration at corner-stone laying at Capitol, 1851, 170; on Jackson's appointments to office, 196; on Jackson's manners, 200; in Nullification debate, 211; revises Harrison inaugural address, 227, 229; coffin of, 234-235; remains in Tyler's cabinet, 238; tells Senate of President Tay-

lor's impending death, 251-252; meets Lord Ashburton at Mrs. Madison's, 264; interest in Mrs. Madison's affairs, 265; note to Dr. Hall, 280; places of residence, 293; Mrs. Hugh White's description of, 298-299; at Jenny Lind concert, 311; measurements of head sent to Edinburgh, 317; occupied Corcoran residence, 403; popular enthusiasm for, 417; judge of spirits, 429; long service in Congress, 429; statue of, 491; declines to make address at laying of corner-stone for Washington Monument, 495

Wellington, Duke of, 200

White, Alexander, 59

White, "Dr. and Lady," 249

White House, site of, 21; Washington helps choose location, 38; James Hoban's plan for, 48; progress in building, 58; condition when first occupied, 66-68; protest of carpenters, 67; condition under Jefferson, 74-77; under Mrs. Madison, 96-98; burned by the British, 110-111; in Monroe's day, 133, 135-139; Lafayette's reception, 150; expenditures under Jackson and Van Buren, 218-220, 224; mob threatens, 238; band concerts in grounds, 240; funeral of *Princeton* victims, 241; festivities in Polk's day, 248-249, 299-303; fire in laundry, 272; "White pest-house," 272; gas introduced, 278; Mrs. Fillmore's library, 307-308; first bathtub and kitchen range, 308-309; in Pierce's administration, 329; in Buchanan's day, 329-335, 337; Easter egg-rolling, 330, 442; in Lincoln's day, 359, 361, 364-369, 378-379; volunteers bivouac on East Room floor, 364; Ellsworth's funeral, 369; deserted after fall of Richmond, 381; after Lincoln's death, 383-384; new china in Hayes administration, 404; innovations of Mrs. Hayes, 404-405, 407; New Year receptions after Civil War, 406; first White House fence, 415; reception in honor of men of letters, 441; functions in Cleveland's day, 443-451; horse and cow sheds, 453; beauty in spring, 468; alterations while Roosevelt was President, 470-472; changes in Arthur's day, 471; sales of discarded furniture, 479; built of freestone, 503; place in enlarged plan of city, 509; during World War, 516-517.

White, Hugh, Mr. and Mrs., Mrs. White's letters describing congressional "mess" life and social functions, 294-306

White, John, 7, 9

White, M. M., 235

Whitman, Walt, 378, 440

Whitney, Eli, 338

Whitney, William C., 438

Whittier, John Greenleaf, 53, 354

Widner, General, 108-110

Wightman, Roger C., 148

Wilcox, ——, 472

Willard, Frances, 492

William (Cleveland's valet), 443

William II of Germany, 409

Williams, Bodisco, Dr., 393

Williams, Miss, 360

Williamsburg, Va., 35

Willis, Nathaniel Parker, 362

Wilson, Henry, 362

Wilson, John M., General, 444-447, 449, 450

Wilson, Woodrow, 314, 517

Wilson, Woodrow, Mrs., 462

Winthrop, Robert C., 265, 495, 496

Wirt, William, Mr. and Mrs., 256

Wise, Henry A., opinion of Jackson, 197; personal description of Tyler, 240-241; advice to Tyler, 242; accuses J. Q. Adams of working to destroy the Union, 421; manner in debate, 430

Wise, Mr. (tavern-keeper), 29

Wolcott, Oliver, 66

Women's Suffrage, 245, 408, 462

Wright, The Misses, 150-151

Wright, Silas, 183

Young, Nicholas, protest against drawing wood, 68

Young, Notley, 16, 22, 28, 68

Young, Notley (descendant of above), builds house in middle of projected street, 40-41; refuses to sign L'Enfant testimonial, 41

Zoological Park, 323, 508, 511